UEL Early Childhood Studies Reader

Selected by
CAROLYN SILBERFELD

SAGE

Los Angeles | London | New Delhi
Singapore | Washington DC

Preface and editorial selection © Carolyn Silberfeld, 2009

Chapter 1 © Thomas Keenan, 2002
Chapter 2 © Thomas Keenan, 2002
Chapter 3 © Thomas Keenan, 2002
Chapter 4 © Liz Brooker and Lynn Broadbent, 2007
Chapter 5 © Vicky Hutchin, 2006
Chapter 6 © Cathy Nutbrown, 2006
Chapter 7 © Tina Bruce, 2004
Chapter 8 © Marian Whitehead, 2007
Chapter 9 © Elizabeth Wood and Jane Attfield, 2005
Chapter 10 © Cathy Nutbrown, 2006
Chapter 11 © Pia Christensen and Alan Prout, 2005
Chapter 12 © Bob Sanders 2004
Chapter 13 © Tim Waller 2005
Chapter 14 © Deborah Albon and Penny Mukherji, 2008

Chapter 15 © Deborah Albon and Penny Mukherji, 2008
Chapter 16 © Glenn Laverack, 2004
Chapter 17 © Lynn Plimley and Maggie Bowen, 2007
Chapter 18 © Kate Wall, 2006
Chapter 19 © Chris Beckett, 2007
Chapter 20 © Peter Baldock, Damien Fitzgerald and Janet Kay, 2005
Chapter 21 © Peter Baldock, Damien Fitzgerald and Janet Kay, 2005
Chapter 22 © Gillie Bolton, 2005
Chapter 23 © Christine Forde, Margery McMahon, Alastair D. McPhee and Fiona Patrick, 2006
Chapter 24 © Kate Wall, 2006
Chapter 25 © Carol Aubrey, 2007

Reprinted 2010

SAGE Publications Ltd
1 Oliver's Yard
55 City Road
London EC1Y 1SP

SAGE Publications Inc.
2455 Teller Road
Thousand Oaks, California 91320

SAGE Publications India Pvt Ltd
B 1/I 1 Mohan Cooperative Industrial Area
Mathura Road
New Delhi 110 044

SAGE Publications Asia-Pacific Pte Ltd
33 Pekin Street #02-01
Far East Square
Singapore 048763

Library of Congress Control Number: 2008941082

British Library Cataloguing in Publication data

A catalogue record for this book is available from the British Library

ISBN 978-1-84860-867-2 (pbk)

Typeset by C&M Digitals (P) Ltd, Chennai, India
Printed and bound by TJI Digital, Padstow, Cornwall
Printed on paper from sustainable resources

FSC
Mixed Sources
Product group from well-managed forests and other controlled sources
Cert no. SGS-COC-2482
www.fsc.org
© 1996 Forest Stewardship Council
Text pages are FSC certified

Contents

Preface

We, the early childhood lecturers at UEL, have put this text together to facilitate the learning opportunities for students who undertake the BA Early Childhood Studies at the University of East London.

The degree programme offers a comprehensive and holistic approach to early childhood studies, not only through the modules we offer, but also through the delivery of the programme by an experienced and cohesive programme team, who come from diverse professional, social, cultural and educational backgrounds. This book is aimed at the students who have chosen to study this popular programme, who also come from very diverse educational and cultural backgrounds and share our enthusiasm and passion for the subject.

The literature we have selected for this book will provide the students with many key concepts and ideas relating to, and underpinning, early childhood studies and the modules within the programme. We have included literature relating to child development, socio-cultural perspectives, health and nutrition, special needs, social policy and professional development. It has been very challenging to put together because we had to make difficult choices not to include some excellent literature.

The chapters in this book have been chosen deliberately for their different styles of writing to encourage students on this course to read widely and more critically. This should facilitate their understanding of the subject as well as developing their analytical skills. We must stress that this text will not provide students with everything they need to know about early childhood studies. What it will provide is a collection of readings which will be useful throughout the course of their studies and will stimulate further reading of the many interesting and varied texts within the field. In essence, this will be a key book on the shelf!

As an academic and researcher who, for the past 15 years, has been wholeheartedly committed to the field of early childhood studies, I have always envisaged a text such as this, which gives the deserved recognition to a growing and strengthening academic discipline. It has been very challenging to put together as we, the early childhood lecturers, had to carefully select reading material which we consider essential for this course.

About the Book

This book is a collection of chapters from a number of SAGE books. At the end of each chapter, there is more information about the book that the chapter appears in. For further information about these books or any of our other publications please visit www.sagepub.co.uk

Students will also find 10% discount vouchers for all the books that make up this Reader, at the back of this book redeemable at the John Smith's bookshop at UEL Stratford. There are additional vouchers for the following three books:

C. Nutbrown, P. Clough and P. Selbie (2008) *Early Childhood Education*, 978-1-4129-4498-4

L. Porter (2003) *Young Children's Behaviour*, Second Edition, 978-0-7619-4324-2

G. Pugh and B. Duffy (2006) *Contemporary Issues in the Early Years*, Fourth Edition, 978-1-4129-2107-7

Theories of Development

THOMAS KEENAN

LEARNING AIMS

At the end of this chapter you should:

- **be able to explain the importance and function of theories**
- **be aware of and able to explain the essence of each of the theoretical positions covered**
- **be able to define and give examples of the key concepts associated with each of the theoretical positions covered**

What is a theory?

A theory is an interconnected, logical system of concepts that provides a framework for organizing and understanding observations. The function of a theory is to allow us to understand and predict the behaviour of some aspect of the world (e.g., the tendency of an object to slide down an inclined plane or the ability to infer the feelings of a friend from their behaviour). Theories can be either **formal** or **informal**; what differentiates formal from informal theories is how explicit the concepts which make up the theory are made. Formal theories take the form of an interconnected set of hypotheses, definitions, axioms, and laws, each of which is an explicit concept which fits with or can be deducted from the overall theory (Miller, 1993). Formal theories can be expressed in a variety of ways: using ordinary language; in mathematical form; or sometimes in the form of logical principles. Ideally, a formal theory should be logically consistent and contain no contradictions, fit well with empirical observations (rather than be contradicted by them), be testable, be as simple as possible, and should cover a reasonable range of phenomena (Miller, 1993). In contrast, informal theories take a less rigorous form than formal theories; they are often little more than organized sets of intuitions or expectations about our world (these informal theories are often referred to as *implicit theories*). In developmental psychology, we have no formal theories of human development (Miller, 1993), although most theories of child development are somewhat more developed than the intuitive expectations about human behaviour that we all hold. However, we can evaluate developmental theories in terms of how likely they are to develop into formal theories using the criteria for a formal theory.

A good theory must state the range of phenomena it is trying to explain. For example, a theory of intellectual development may include hypotheses about the evolution of the brain, or the growth of symbolic abilities, but we would not expect the theory to explain changes in motor ability. Understanding the focus of a theory helps us identify its **range of applicability**, that is, the range of phenomena to which it properly applies. We must also know what **assumptions** a theory is based on. Assumptions are the guiding premises underlying the logic of a theory. For example, evolutionary psychologists take for granted the assumption that natural selection is the only process which can produce changes in physical structures of an organism over time. In order to properly evaluate a theory, you must first understand what its assumptions are. This is because the assumptions of a theory may be questionable or even incorrect. Assumptions may be influenced by cultural contexts and belief systems, by the sample the researcher was observing, or by the current knowledge base of the field.

Now that we know what a theory is, we can ask 'what do theories do?' First, theories are constructed to organize and interpret our observations of the world and to help us identify orderly relationships among many diverse events. They help us to distinguish factors which are central to understanding a behaviour from factors which are only related in a peripheral way. Our theories give meaning to the facts we discover about the world, serving as a framework within which to interpret facts and integrate new information with previously acquired knowledge. Second, theories guide the acquisition of new knowledge. The statement of a theory should make specific predictions which can be tested. Theories can also cause us to reinterpret knowledge which we have previously acquired; that is, the formulation of a theory may require us to look more carefully at factors we had previously taken for granted or ignored. For more on the role of theories in the study of psychology, see Haslam and McGarty (1998).

According to Miller (1993), theories of human development differ from other theories in a particular way. The critical aspect of developmental theories is a focus on change over time in some particular behaviour or domain of functioning. Miller further argues that any developmental theory should manage three tasks. First, it needs to describe change within a given domain or domains. For example, if one is proposing a theory of emotional development, a good theory would describe what the development of emotion looks like: are there particular emotional states which proceed or follow others? Do we come endowed with any emotional expressions and, if so, how do these change or remain stable with development? Second, it needs to describe changes in the relationships between domains. For example, do changes in cognitive functioning give rise to changes in social or emotional functioning? Third, it should explain how the changes in behaviour that have been described take place; that is, what accounts for the transitions between different states of development? Are the observed changes a function of maturation, learning, or an interaction of both? A developmental theory needs a clear description of the mechanisms which guide change.

Now that we have considered what a theory is and what it should provide, let us next examine a selection of theories which are currently used or have previously been important to the study of child development.

Theories of human development

In this section, we review a number of the most important theories of child development. Some theories such as Freud's psychosexual theory of development are discussed not because they are currently important to the field of child development, but for their historical value to the discipline. Other theories are discussed because of their current importance to the field.

While there are a large number of theories of human development, the search for underlying commonalities across these theories has revealed that all developmental theories can be classified as based on at least one of two philosophical models (Dixon & Lerner, 1999): **organicism** and **mechanism**. These models detail the assumptions about the nature of human development that underlie the various theories which we will review here. Models based on organicism stress the qualitative features of developmental change and emphasize the organism's role in bringing about these changes; that is, organicism focuses on developmental change which is a reorganization based on previous forms and is not simply a change in the quantity of a given behaviour. In contrast, mechanistic theories stress quantitative changes in behaviour and emphasize that factors outside the control of the organism play the major role in developmental change. Of course, not all theories of development are based exclusively on one model; some theories have adopted elements of both mechanism and organicism to explain human development. As we review each of the theories, see if you can classify the theories discussed in terms of whether they subscribe to organicism, mechanism, or some combination of the two positions.

Psychodynamic theory
Modern **psychodynamic** theories of human behaviour and development have their roots in the thinking of Sigmund Freud (1856–1939). While there are few psychologists who are strict adherents to Freudian theory (which we discuss later), psychodynamic theories continue to influence many theorists.

At their heart, psychodynamic theories emphasize the belief that forces or dynamics within the individual are responsible for our behaviour. In general, psychodynamic theories (although Erikson's work is an exception) are more influential in therapeutic contexts than they are in developmental theory. However, as Dixon and Lerner (1999) suggest, psychodynamic theories have exerted an influence on developmental theory, thus it would be unwise to ignore them.

In his theory of human personality, Freud stressed the formative nature of early experience and of biologically based drives; his belief was that development is the result of a balance being struck between unconscious drives and a conscious need to adapt one's self to the reality in which we find ourselves. Freud (1917) believed that our personality is made up of three structures: the **id**, the **ego**, and the **superego**. The id is the part of our personality which is made up of instinctual drives. The id operates according to what Freud termed the **pleasure principle**; that is, the id is directed towards maximizing its pleasure in an immediate fashion. Freud believed that the id dominated an infant's behaviour. As we develop and our instincts come into conflict with reality, the ego emerges. The ego works to satisfy our drives but does so in a socially acceptable manner; it attempts to gratify our needs through constructive and socially appropriate methods. For example, the ego redirects aggressive urges such as a desire to lash out physically at another into more socially acceptable forms such as verbal aggression or vigorous physical play. As the ego operates in this fashion, we begin to internalize the values of our parents and the wider society around us, forming the structure that Freud called the superego. During the preschool years, children accept their parents' values and take these on in the form of their conscience as they apply these standards to their own behaviour. The ego now takes on the role of arbitrating between the id and the superego in an attempt to satisfy both sets of demands. According to Freud, the dynamics of this struggle, occurring during early childhood, sets the stage for our adult personality.

In Freud's view, development is a discontinuous process. Freud postulated five stages of development in his theory of psychosexual development: the *oral*, *anal*, *phallic*, *latency*, and *genital* stages. Each stage revolves around the movement of sexual impulses from one **erogenous zone** to the next. In the first year and a half of life, during the oral stage of development, the infant's pleasure is centred around the mouth and involves behaviours such as biting, chewing, and sucking as the sources of pleasure. The behaviours infants engage in change during the second year as they enter the anal stage and their pleasure becomes centred around the eliminative function. A potential source of conflict during this stage is the child's desire to immediately expel faeces coming up against their parents' attempts to train the child into waiting to use the toilet. The phallic stage, which occurs from about the ages of three to six years is centred around the genitals and the discovery that their own genitalia provide them with a sense of pleasure. During the phallic stage, Freud believed that children must cope with a sexual attraction to the opposite sex parent which must eventually be relinquished and replaced by an identification with the same sex parent. This process of identification leads to the latency stage, which lasts until puberty, during which the child suppresses sexual drives and instead focuses on developing social and intellectual skills. Finally, during the genital stage which occurs during puberty, the sexual desires reawaken and the adolescent looks for appropriate peers (instead of family) to which to direct their sexual drives.

Freud's theory was influential in that it focused developmentalists' attention on the role of early experiences in personality formation. It also emphasized a view of development as shaped by the dynamics of the conflict between the individual's biological drives and society's restrictions on the expression of these drives, which many subsequent theorists (such as Erik Erikson) found inspiring. Finally, Freud's theory, notwithstanding the many negative assessments it has faced, has been a rich source of hypotheses about development (Miller, 1993). Despite all of these benefits, Freud's theory has been heavily criticized. Freud focused largely on males (as exemplified by his labelling the second phase of development 'phallic'), and neglected to examine issues which might be important to the development of females. In addition, Freud's theory relied mainly on the use of methods such as free association, and the use of dream analysis, which make scientific tests of his theory difficult, if not impossible. Most tellingly, when Freud's claims have been put to the test, many of the most significant claims have not been supported by empirical tests. Thus, Freud's views do not stand up well to modern psychology's demand for scientific validation.

Psychoanalytic theory has been revised significantly and has spawned many offshoots or schools of thought such as *object relations theory*. Modern psychoanalysts emphasize the role of unconscious processes in our behaviour, but place less emphasis on sexual and aggressive instincts and spend more effort highlighting the importance of experience and an understanding of one's life history.

Psychosocial theory

In contrast to Freud's emphasis on sexual and aggressive drives, Erik Erikson (1902–1990) proposed a theory of development which emphasized the role of social and cultural factors in development. In addition, Erikson's theory did not characterize development as ending with adolescence but proposed a true life-span developmental theory which suggests development continues through to old age.

Erikson (1963) believed that human development is best understood as the interaction of three different systems: the *somatic* system, the **ego** system, and the *societal* system. The somatic system is all of those biological processes necessary for the functioning of the individual. The ego system includes those processes central to thinking and reasoning. Finally, the societal system is those processes by which a person becomes integrated into their society. Thus, Erikson's psychosocial approach focuses the study of development on the interaction between changes in these three systems.

Erikson (1963) took a discontinuous view to development, believing that each of us progresses through eight stages of development. Erikson viewed these stages as occurring in an orderly sequence and he believed that each individual must pass through the stages in this order. At each stage, the individual is confronted with a unique **crisis**, an age-related task, which must be faced and resolved by the individual. How successfully an individual resolves each crisis determines the nature of further development: successful resolutions lead to healthier developmental outcomes while unsuccessful or incomplete resolutions lead to less optimal outcomes. In addition, at each stage of development, the accomplishments from the previous stage serve as resources to be applied towards mastering the present crisis or challenge. Each stage is unique and leads to the acquisition of new skills and capabilities.

As noted, Erikson proposed eight stages of psychosocial development: (1) basic trust versus mistrust (birth to 1 year); (2) autonomy versus shame and doubt (1 to 3 years); (3) initiative versus guilt (3 to 6 years); (4) industry versus inferiority (6 to 11 years); (5) identity versus identity diffusion (adolescence); (6) intimacy versus isolation (young adulthood); (7) generativity versus stagnation (middle adulthood); (8) ego integrity versus despair (old age) (see Table 2.1). In what follows, we briefly consider the task of development at each of the eight stages of life proposed by Erikson.

During infancy (*trust/mistrust*), the infant's first task is to develop a sense of trust and a sense of comfort in their caregivers, and eventually, in their environment and in themselves; infants who fail to resolve this crisis in a positive manner may end up mistrusting both themselves and others. During the second stage (*autonomy/shame and doubt*), the infant develops a sense of their independence and autonomy. However, shame and doubt in one's self may arise if the child is forced into activities which they do not choose. In the third stage (*initiative/guilt*), the young child develops a sense of initiative, a desire to master their environment. However, guilt can arise if the child shows too much aggression or is irresponsible. During middle childhood (*industry/inferiority*), children are keen to master intellectual and social challenges but failures may lead to feelings of inferiority and incompetence. During adolescence (*identity/ identity diffusion*), individuals strive to discover who they are, that is, to develop a self-identity. Adolescents who fail to adequately explore alternative pathways

TABLE 2.1 Erikson's eight stages of development

Stage of development	Age	Crisis
Trust vs. mistrust	Birth to 1 year	Developing a sense of trust in caregivers, the environment, and one's self
Autonomy vs. shame and doubt	1 to 3 years	Developing a sense of one's autonomy and independence from the caregiver
Initiative vs. guilt	3 to 6 years	Developing a sense of mastery over aspects of one's environment, coping with challenges and assumption of increasing responsibility
Industry vs. inferiority	6 years to adolescence	Mastering intellectual and social challenges
Identity vs. identity diffusion	Adolescence (12 to 20 years)	Developing a self-identity, that is, a knowledge of what kind of a person one is
Intimacy vs. isolation	Young adulthood (20 to 40 years)	Developing stable and intimate relationships with another person
Generativity vs. stagnation	Middle adulthood (40 to 60 years)	Creating something so that one can avoid feelings of stagnation
Integrity vs. despair	Old age (60 years +)	Evaluating one's life by looking back; developing a sense of integrity through this evaluative process

for themselves or who allow their identity to be determined by parents and others may experience confusion about who they are. During young adulthood (*intimacy/isolation*), the task is to achieve a stable and intimate sexual relationship with another person. How well the individual has resolved previous crises (e.g., learning to trust others; making friends and developing social skills) will determine how successful the individual is in achieving intimacy with others; individuals who cannot achieve intimacy are vulnerable to isolation. In middle adulthood (*generativity/stagnation*), the creation of something, whether it is children or something more abstract like ideas or art becomes the central task. The failure to express one's self in this way can lead to feelings of stagnation and the feeling that one has no meaningful accomplishments. Finally, in old age (*ego integrity/despair*) we look back and assess our lives. The individual who has resolved previous stages in a negative fashion will tend to look back on their lives with a feeling of despair and gloom while the individual who has been successful will look back on a life well spent and can derive a sense of integrity.

Erikson's theory of development has been criticized as taking the form of a loosely connected set of ideas which lacks a systematic quality, rather than as a coherent theory of development (Miller, 1993). Concepts such as *generativity* are used in a way that is different from their normal meaning and thus they are somewhat difficult to understand. More problematic is the fact that his theory is difficult to test empirically. Finally, Erikson's theory proposes no specific mechanisms for how development occurs, that is, how a person moves from one stage to the next. It *describes* the roles of factors such as maturation and social forces but fails to clearly state *how* these factors create movement between stages. Despite its weaknesses, Erikson's theory has a number of strengths. One of these was Erikson's push to widen the scope of psychoanalytic theory through the integration of social and cultural factors in development. Erikson also stimulated a renewed interest in topics such as the development of a sense of identity in adolescence (e.g., Waterman, 1985) and generativity in adulthood (Hawkins & Dollahite, 1997).

Behaviourism and social learning theory

Modern behaviourist theory began with the work of John B. Watson (1878–1958). Watson wanted to create an objective science of psychology and he believed that directly observable events should be the focus of the study, not hypothetical internal constructs like Freud's *id*, and *ego* or the cognitive psychologist's appeal to constructs such as *mind*. Watson (Watson & Raynor, 1920) applied Pavlov's principles of classical conditioning to children's behaviour. In one of his most famous research programmes Watson trained Albert, a 9-month-old baby, to fear a neutral stimulus (a white rat) after presenting it several times in the company of a loud sound (clanging an iron bar behind the infant's head). While initially Albert reached out to touch the rat, he soon learned to fear the rat, crying and turning his head away from the sight of the animal. On the basis of findings like these, Watson concluded that the environment was the most important factor in child development. Watson believed that children could be moulded in any direction adults desired if they carefully controlled stimulus–response associations. Watson and his fellow behaviourists eschewed all notions that cognitive processes intervened in the shaping of the individual. In Watson's behaviourism, learning became the key element in explaining development, whereas biological factors were relegated to the sidelines and believed to be important only in providing a basic foundation for learned responses.

Another variant of behaviourism was B.F. Skinner's **operant conditioning** theory. According to this theory, the likelihood of a child's behaviour reoccurring can be increased by following it with a wide variety of rewards or **reinforcers**, things such as praise or a friendly smile. Furthermore, Skinner believed that the likelihood of behaviour can be decreased with the use of **punishments** such as the withdrawal of privileges, parental disapproval, or being sent alone to one's room. In other words, reward increases the likelihood of a behaviour reoccurring while punishment decreases the likelihood of its reoccurring. The result of Skinner's work was that operant conditioning became broadly applied to the study of child development.

A variant of traditional behaviourist views on development comes from the work of Albert Bandura (1977, 1989) on **social learning theory**. Bandura believed that the principles of conditioning and reinforcement elaborated by Skinner and others were important mechanisms of development, but he expanded on how children and adults acquired new responses. Bandura is responsible for an extensive line of laboratory research demonstrating that **observational learning** (often referred to as **modelling**), is the basis of the development of a wide variety of behaviours, such as *aggression, helping, sharing,* and even *sex-typed responses*. Bandura recognized that, from an early age, children acquire many skills in the absence of rewards and punishments, simply by watching and listening to others around them. However, children do not imitate everyone around them; children are more selective, being drawn towards models who are warm and powerful and who possess desirable objects and characteristics.

Bandura continues to influence much of the work in the area of children's and adult's social development (Rubin, Coplan, Nelson, Cheah & Lagace-Seguin, 1999). Over time, Bandura's theory has become increasingly cognitive (e.g., Bandura, 1989, 1992), acknowledging that children's ability to listen, remember, and abstract general rules from complex sets of observed behaviour affects their imitation and their learning. In Bandura's more recent work, his emphasis has been on the development of a sense of **self-efficacy**, beliefs about one's own effectiveness and competence that guide one's ability to cope with particular situations such as difficult academic problems at school. According to Bandura, children develop a sense of self-efficacy through observation, watching others comment on their own behaviour and developing standards based on these experiences. Thus, children who are exposed to positive models who demonstrate qualities such as persistence are likely to develop a stronger sense of self-efficacy than children exposed to models that demonstrate less positive qualities such as giving up in response to frustration.

A strength of Bandura's social learning theory is its emphasis on particular aspects of the environment, such as the nature of the role models available to children, which can impact on their development. In addition, social learning theory is easily testable (Miller, 1993): the variables of interest are clearly defined and its hypotheses are stated in a precise fashion. The resultant testing of the theory has led to substantial revisions such as its increased emphasis on cognitive factors. At the same time, the cognitive model which underlies the theory has been criticized for being poorly worked out in comparison to information processing theories which present detailed models of cognitive processes. Finally, social learning theory has been criticized for not paying enough attention to a wide range of contextual variables which may impact on children's observational learning. While the theory has addressed some contextual variables like the characteristics of models which effect development, other context effects such as socioeconomic factors, race, sex and education remain relatively unexplored (Miller, 1993).

The ethological perspective

Ethology is a perspective on the study of animal behaviour which began to be applied to research on children during the 1960s and continues to be influential today. Ethology is concerned with understanding the adaptive value of behaviour and its evolutionary history. The origins of ethology can be traced to Charles Darwin and his work on evolution, however, the modern theory owes its origins to the work of two European zoologists, Konrad Lorenz, and Niko Tinbergen. In his theory of evolution, Darwin proposed that we evolved from more simple forms of life through a process called **natural selection**. Natural selection works through the effects of a trait on survival; if a change to our physical structure or behaviour leads to a survival advantage, the change is more likely to be passed on through the genes to the organism's offspring during mating. If the change leads to no advantages, it is less likely to be passed on, and the trait will tend to disappear. Thus, only traits which lead to a survival advantage for the organism are passed on. Natural selection is so called because nature weeds out those individuals who are unfit; in other words, natural selection is the 'survival of the fittest'.

Based on the careful observation of animals in their natural habitats, researchers like Lorenz and Tinbergen noted that many animal species come equipped with a number of behaviour patterns that promote their survival. One of these behaviour patterns studied by Lorenz is known as **imprinting**. Imprinting refers to the 'following behaviour' of many species of birds. Imprinting is a behaviour which is acquired extremely rapidly and serves to ensure that the offspring will stay close to the mother so as to be fed and protected from predators. While nothing like imprinting seems to occur in human beings, a related concept from ethology has been very usefully applied to the study of child development. In birds such as geese, imprinting occurs during a restricted time period of development known as a **critical period**. A critical period is a time when an organism is biologically prepared to acquire a particular behaviour. For example, using geese, Lorenz found that if the mother goose was not present during the critical period, her goslings would imprint on a moving object which resembled her important features, such as Lorenz himself. Lorenz (1963) showed that the gosling's instinct to follow its mother was not preprogrammed. Instead, the *tendency* to acquire a particular behaviour is programmed but the support of the environment is critical to the acquisition of this behaviour.

Ethologists' observations of a wide variety of animal behaviours have sparked investigations with humans regarding the development of such social behaviours as attachment, dominance hierarchies, aggression, and cooperation. For example, Strayer and Strayer (1976) recorded naturally occurring conflicts among preschoolers and found evidence of a stable dominance hierarchy (see Chapter 9), with some children being more dominant and less likely to be aggressed against by other children. John Bowlby's work on the attachment bond between caregivers and their children was also inspired by attachment theory (see Chapter 8). Bowlby argued that infants have a built-in signalling system to which mothers are geared to respond, a system which is designed to promote nurturance and protective behaviours by the parent.

Are there critical periods in human development? Bornstein (1989) suggested that the term **sensitive period** is a better descriptor of human development than the term critical period. According to Bornstein, a sensitive period is a window of time in a child's development during which they are particularly responsive to environmental influences. For example, there is a sensitive period for the acquisition of human language which lasts from shortly after birth to early adolescence (see Chapter 7). Learning language is particularly easy for children during this period, but extremely difficult after it. Given the length of time involved for language acquisition, it seems that the notion of a critical period is an inaccurate descriptor of how language learning takes place. Clearly, the notion of a sensitive period for language provides a more accurate picture of language acquisition.

Ethological theory has been extremely important to the study of child development in regard to its methodological contributions to the field (Rubin et al., 1999). Behavioural observations using techniques developed by ethologists are widely employed by researchers studying children. In addition, the emphasis on the evolutionary roots of behaviours has proven to be an important theoretical development within the study of child development. Asking how environmental pressures may have operated to select for a particular behaviour such that, over time, it becomes widely distributed in the species helps us to understand the cause of many important behaviours such as attachment behaviour. In addition, concepts such as sensitive periods have been criticized in that they only put off the question of an ultimate explanation for a particular behaviour; more work needs to go into discovering how sensitive periods operate. Finally, looking for the causes of a particular behaviour in our evolutionary history is difficult because we cannot go back in time. The sources of information that are available are not always reliable and are often extremely ambiguous.

Evolutionary developmental theory

According to a recent review of the history of developmental psychology (Dixon & Lerner, 1999), Charles Darwin's theory of evolution has had a profound influence on theories of human development. As we have just seen, evolutionary theory influenced the development of ethological theories of human development. Evolutionary theory has also influenced theories of development as diverse as Freud's psychosexual theory, to information processing theories of cognitive development (Siegler, 1996). Perhaps not surprisingly, evolutionary theory has come into its own as a theory of human behaviour (e.g., Barkow, Cosmides, & Tooby, 1992). As David Buss argues: 'Any reasonably comprehensive theory of human development must include an account of where people come from, where they are going, and how long they live' (1995: 24). In Buss' view, an evolutionary psychological approach to human development has much to offer in the attempt to address these issues.

Geary and Bjorkland (2000) have recently applied the evolutionary psychology framework to generating an increased understanding of human development. In their view, **evolutionary developmental psychology** is the 'study of the genetic and ecological mechanisms that govern the development of social and cognitive competencies common to all human beings and the epigenetic processes that adapt these competencies to local conditions' (Geary & Bjorkland, 2000: 57). Let's examine this definition more closely.

Perhaps the first point of interest is that the consideration of development from an evolutionary framework involves the study of *both* biological factors such as the hereditary transmission of traits from parents to their children, *and* the ecology in which development occurs (i.e., environmental effects on behaviour). The second point is that Geary and Bjorkland do not advocate a simplistic division between biological and environmental factors (or nature versus nurture); rather, they suggest that development is governed by **epigenetic** processes, that is to say, *interactions* of genes and environments. In their view, genes provide the instructions for guiding the development of observable traits such as height or personality, but that these genetic blueprints are highly sensitive to 'local conditions' – that is, aspects of the environment that may require changes to the genetic blueprints in order for a trait to lead to optimal outcomes.

What has an evolutionary developmental psychology contributed to our understanding? To date, relatively little research has been conducted from this perspective, in large part, because the theory is a relatively recent arrival on the scene. Buss (1995) cites a number of instances where an evolutionary developmental framework has contributed to a greater understanding of developmental phenomena. For example, research on children's relationships with their parents and the warmth of the parent–child bond has been viewed as an evolved system which facilitates parental investment in the child, promoting their survival and ensuring cohesive family relations. The timing of puberty and the effects of early environments on physical maturation is another area which Buss suggests has been aided by an evolutionary analysis. As we discuss in Chapter 4, recent research (Moffit, Caspi, Belsky, and Silva, 1992) demonstrated that ecological factors such as family conflict and the absence of fathers in the household predicted the earlier onset of menstruation in females. Belsky, Steinberg, and Draper (1991) explained these findings by suggesting that particular events during childhood predispose the child towards different developmental pathways. The presence of the father during childhood may push the child towards a later mating strategy which will be characterized by long-term relationships and high levels of parental investment. In contrast, early father absence may push the child towards an earlier mating strategy marked by early sexual maturation and more short-term relationships. These are just a few examples of the sort of contributions that evolutionary developmental psychology has made to the study of child development. However, much more work remains to be done in elaborating the theory and assessing how useful it will be to generating a better understanding of child development.

The bioecological model of development

A view which has received an increasing amount of attention from developmental psychologists is Urie Bronfenbrenner's **bioecological model** of human development (Bronfenbrenner & Morris, 1998) (see Figure 2.1). Bronfenbrenner (1974) is famous for his suggestion that an overemphasis on lab research had caused developmental psychology to become 'the study of the strange behaviour of children in strange situations for the briefest possible period of time'. In contrast to the bulk of developmental research which is conducted in laboratory settings, Bronfenbrenner argued that the proper study of development required one to observe children and adults in their actual environment; most laboratory research misses out on critical information which can only be gained by studying children in natural contexts. In addition, a great deal of laboratory-based research is not generalizable to the everyday contexts in which humans live and grow (Bronfenbrenner, 1979).

When psychologists examine the effects of the environment on children, the environment is typically construed in a very static and narrow fashion – often as the child's immediate surroundings. In contrast, Bronfenbrenner (1989) views the environment as a dynamic entity which is constantly changing. In addition, in Bronfenbrenner's (1979) bioecological model of human development, the environment is conceived of in a very wide sense, as a series of nested structures that extends beyond the child's immediate

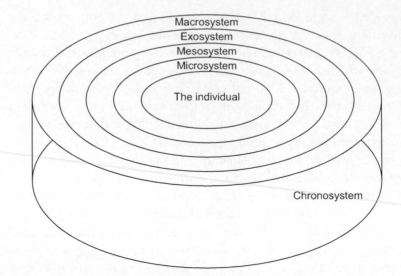

FIGURE 2.1 Bronfenbrenner's bioecological model of development

environment (e.g., their home or neighbourhood) to include their school, community, and the social and cultural institutions that impact on their lives. In Bronfenbrenner's model, the individual is the centre of a system which includes four layers, each representing different aspects of the environment. Each of the four layers is regarded as having a powerful impact on the child's development.

The innermost level is called the **microsystem**. The microsystem is the immediate setting in which a child lives; it refers to family, peers, school as well as the activities, roles, and relationships in their immediate surroundings. In Bronfenbrenner's view, the individual is viewed as an active force, exerting an influence on the people around her and on the relationships she has with others. The child is not a passive recipient of others' attention and actions. Thus, within the microsystem, development is often understood in terms of complex, interacting relationships.

The second level of Bronfenbrenner's model is called the **mesosystem**. It refers to relationships among microsystems, such as home, school, neighbourhood, and childcare centre. One could think about the mesosystem as the connections which bring together the different contexts in which a child develops. For example, a child's ability to learn to read may depend not just on learning activities that take place in school, but also on the extent to which those activities carry over to the home environment, such as the presence of books in the home or how much time parents spend reading with their children. The view that 'it takes a village to raise a child' is a recognition of the importance of the mesosystem in development. Bronfenbrenner and

Morris (1998) suggested that the best and most complete picture of a child's development will be obtained when they are examined in multiple contexts rather than just in the home or the school.

Exosystems are broad social settings that provide support for the development of children and adults. These are social settings and institutions that do not directly involve children yet which can have a profound impact on their development. Exosystems include formal settings such as community health services, parks, recreation centres, city government, and informal groups such as one's extended family, social support networks, and the workplace. These groups can provide important support for the family – such as flexible work schedules, paid maternity and paternity leave, or low-cost childcare – support that can enhance the development of children. Negative impacts on development can also result when the exosystem breaks down. For example, families who are affected by unemployment show an increased incidence of child abuse and neglect.

At the outermost level of Bronfenbrenner's model is the **macrosystem**. The macrosystem is not a specific environmental context but, rather, the overarching ideology, values, laws, regulations, and customs of a given culture. Cultural influences can have a powerful effect on children's development. Comparisons made across cultures have the potential to provide very important information about the effects of culture on development.

Bronfenbrenner also included in his model the notion that development occurs in historical time within his model. He called this temporal aspect the **chronosystem**. The chronosystem involves all aspects of time, and how they impact on development. For example, research on the timing of puberty has shown that the age at which puberty begins can have a profound impact on later development (Jones & Bayley, 1950). Historical events which occur in time also have important effects on development. For example, the work of Elder (1974) showed that the economic depression of the 1930s had significant impact on the lives of children growing up during that period. In these ways and many others, the chronosystem has a powerful influence on development.

Life-course theory

In a recent review of his bioecological theory of development, Bronfenbrenner (Bronfenbrenner & Morris, 1998) emphasized the importance of time as a variable which demands the attention of developmental psychologists. Another theoretical orientation which emphasizes the role of time in human development is **life-course theory** (Elder, 1995, 1998). The **life course**, refers to a 'sequence of socially defined, age-graded events and roles that the individual enacts over time' (Elder, 1998: 941). According to Elder, our lives are defined in large part by the social context in which we develop. For example, in many Western societies, parents' conceptions of when it is appropriate for their children to begin dating are changing, partly as our societal expectations for what constitutes normal, age-appropriate experiences evolves.

Life-course theory emphasizes the view that human development must be understood in terms of four interdependent principles. First, human lives are situated in historical time and place. The timing of an individual's birth is an important determinant of the development trajectories they will likely follow. Historical influences can impact on us in different ways. One way in which historical forces impact on us is through **cohort effects**. A cohort is a group of people born at a particular point in time (e.g., 'baby boomers' or 'generation X'). A cohort effect occurs when people from different birth cohorts are differentially impacted upon by some historical event. For example, in his work on the effects of the US economic depression in the 1930s, Elder (1974) showed that younger children were more adversely effected by the impact of the depression than were older children. Another type of historical effect is called a **period effect**. This occurs when a historical event exerts a relatively uniform influence across different birth cohorts. For example, Elder notes that whatever cause is responsible for the increase in divorce rates over the past four decades, it has affected most birth cohorts in a similar fashion. Finally, in regard to historical time and place, Elder notes that geographical settings are often an extremely important factor neglected in developmental studies, and furthermore, that time and place are often inextricably linked.

A second key element of life-course theory is the idea that developmental studies must pay attention to the timing of lives. Our lives are socially timed in that the way social roles and events are organized has much to do with what is considered normative for a particular age group by the society in which an individual develops. We often ask of ourselves or others, whether we are 'on course' or 'on time' in regard to specific aspects of our development. For example, it is highly likely that our parents worried about whether our academic performance as adolescents was 'normal' relative to other adolescents. The social timing of lives can have profound effects on development: consider the woman who puts off having a child until her career is established versus the teenage girl who becomes pregnant. Clearly, this choice entails different developmental pathways for the two women, with each pathway offering opportunities for personal growth, albeit of different kinds.

Third, life-course theory emphasizes that human lives are interdependent or linked with each other. Our lives are embedded in family relationships, peer relationships, romantic relationships and in various other relationships such as those we have with our coworkers or classmates. Attachment theory suggests that the quality of the relationship that we form with our primary caregiver in infancy has an impact on later relationships we form with friends and, eventually, with our romantic partners. In turn, our attachment relationship with our own children is affected by the relationship we had with our caregivers. Attachment theory is built on the premise that human lives are linked with each other. Throughout this text we will continue to examine how relationships affect children's development.

Finally, the fourth principle of life-course theory is that within certain social constraints, human beings have *agency*, that is, the power to make decisions and change our lives. The social environment places constraints on the kinds of actions that people can take to change their lives. For example, one cannot pursue a career in engineering without the appropriate education, thus, a person's choice of career is necessarily limited by the education they have chosen to pursue. However, although there are constraints, our choices have a high degree of impact on our lives. For example, Rutter and Rutter (1993) note that how we choose to behave with and relate to other people serves to shape and select the environment that we actually experience. In addition, Rutter and Rutter note that planning one's decisions proves to be a protective process in the long term whereas the lack of planning is considered to be a risk factor for poor outcomes. Going back to an earlier example, the adolescent who anticipates engaging in sexual activity, and takes steps to obtain contraception reduces not only the risk of an unwanted pregnancy or sexually transmitted disease, but also the risk of embarking on a developmental pathway which may lead to unhappiness.

In summary, life-course theory has much in common with theories such as Bronfenbrenner's bioecological theory with its emphasis on the importance of the various types of environments which impact on development and with the principles of Baltes' (1987) life-span developmental psychology which emphasizes the importance of contexts and timing. However, in Elder's view, social environments should be the major emphasis of developmental studies. This differs from the views of Bronfenbrenner and Baltes, who both place the individual at the centre of their models of development.

Dynamic systems theory

Dynamic system theories of development emerge out of a growing disenchantment with the traditional theories' focus on environmental causes, biological causes, and interactions of biology and environment as explanations of development. A growing number of researchers have put forward theories which emphasize systems thinking (e.g., Bertalanffy, 1968; Sameroff, 1983; Thelen & Smith, 1994). These researchers have suggested that human beings and their environments can be thought of as a collection of systems, where a system is defined as being composed of a number of elements which are organized in some fashion. A family is a good example of a system. Families consist of a number of elements such as father, mother, children. Moreover, the relations of the elements to one another can be described; for example, children normally obey mother's and father's rules. However, the behaviour of the family can only be truly understood in systems terms, that is, by considering the interrelations among all the parts, the family's history, and external influences which may operate to stabilize or destabilize its functioning. In other words, the family's behaviour is more than just the sum of its individual parts.

So then, what is dynamic systems theory? According to a review by Thelen and Smith (1998), dynamic systems theory is a *metatheory*; that is, it is an approach to studying development that can be widely applied to many domains, for example, from areas as diverse as **embryology** (the study of how a fertilized egg becomes an infant), family functioning, and the development of motor skills (Thelen & Ulrich, 1991). However, Thelen and Smith also argue that dynamic systems theory can be employed as a specific theory of how humans gain knowledge via action, perhaps best exemplified in Thelen's work on the development of motor skills.

Thelen and Smith (1998) suggest a metaphor which is useful in understanding the way in which dynamic systems theorists view development. They ask us to consider a fast-moving mountain stream. The stream shows stable patterns in its flow, for example, whirlpools, eddies, and ripples which occur because of rocks in the stream bed, or waves and spray where the stream bed is shallow and steep. Thelen and Smith argue that no one would explain the regularities in the flow of the stream by invoking a 'grand plan'. Instead, we recognize that the stream shows the patterns it does because of the constraints under which it operates. The regularities in the patterns we observe occur because of multiple factors operating simultaneously: the configuration of the stream bed and the placement of rocks; the rate of flow of water; the erosion of the stream bed. Thelen and Smith suggest that this metaphor of a mountain stream depicts development as truly epigenetic, that is, as constructed by the system's own history, by its current activity, and by the constraints under which the system operates.

How can a dynamic systems perspective be applied to the study of child development? Thelen has led the way in her own research, illustrating how a dynamic systems approach can help us to better understand behaviour. For example, it is well known that newborns, when held upright in a standing position, show a stepping reflex. After some time, this reflex disappears and later re-emerges. In contrast to theories which postulated that this process was under the control of genetic factors, Thelen and Fisher (1982) showed that the reflex 'disappears' because of changes in other aspects of the infant's physiology. In the case of the stepping reflex, body fat begins to accumulate on the infant's leg, making the leg heavier. However, muscle mass is not added at the same rate, meaning the infant is no longer able to physically lift their leg, thus the stepping reflex 'disappears'. However, the stepping reflex can be made to reappear by immersing the infant in water from the waist down. The effects of buoyancy act to reduce the weight of the infant's legs and the stepping reflex reappears. In Thelen's view, the best way in which to understand this finding is from a dynamic systems perspective: as changes are made to the system, behaviours are reorganized in a dynamic fashion. The stable patterns previously observed can be brought back by changing the effects of the constraints which altered the behaviour.

Consider another example from the study of infant motor development. Previous theories of motor development have suggested that behaviours such as the development of 'creeping' or 'crawling' are programmed to emerge prior to walking. Thelen and Smith (1998) suggest it is unnecessary to invoke a genetic programme to explain this fact, rather, they suggest that we can think of the development of crawling as a behaviour which is **softly assembled** from previously existing competencies. In other words, a genetic blueprint for crawling does not suddenly emerge and guide the baby towards this behaviour; instead, the infant creates the behaviour based on the constraints under which they operate, plus their goals and desires. The infant may desire a toy which is across the room and intends to move towards it. The state of their neuromuscular system is such that they cannot yet maintain enough balance to walk upright so the infant employs another solution, crawling, which allows them to make use of the skills they have already acquired. The development of crawling behaviour is a predictable outcome of the infant's desires and its current range of abilities. However, it is not an inevitable solution: some infants develop alternative methods such as crawling on their bellies or scooting along on their bottoms by using their arms. The development of such alternative strategies depends on the infant's previous history of motor skills and the current state of maturation of their musculature and suggests that crawling is not simply the outcome of a genetic blueprint which dictates development.

Cognitive developmental theories

In regard to the study of cognitive development, there are three theories which have had a dramatic impact on the field. These are Piaget's **cognitive-developmental** theory (e.g., Piaget, 1983), Vygotsky's **sociocultural theory** development (Vygotsky, 1978, 1986), and the **information processing approach** to cognitive development (Klahr & MacWhinney, 1998; Siegler, 1996). Given that these three theories are primarily to do with cognitive development, we will cover them in more detail in Chapter 6. What follows here is a brief summary of each one.

Jean Piaget's theory of cognitive development

Jean Piaget (1896–1980) is widely acknowledged as the theorist who has had the greatest impact on research and theory in the field of child development (e.g., Siegler, 1998). Piaget began working in developmental psychology in the 1920s but it was not until the 1960s that his work garnered much attention as it became increasingly available. Piaget's work was largely at odds with the behaviourist tradition which was dominant in North America until the 1960s. Unlike the behaviourists of the day, Piaget did not view the child as a passive recipient of knowledge whose development is the product of reinforcement or punishment, but, rather, as an active participant in the creation of their own understanding.

Piaget's (1971) theory of development borrowed heavily from the field of evolutionary biology. A central concept in Piagetian theory is the idea that our cognitive structures (i.e., our minds) are *adaptations* which help ensure that our knowledge provides a good 'fit' to the world. Piaget viewed human intelligence as an adaptation which ultimately enhanced our chances of survival. Of course, we know from experience (often, painfully so) that our knowledge does not always match reality perfectly. For example, we often act on the basis of false assumptions, incorrect knowledge or a partial under-standing. Young children's thinking is also rife with misunderstandings about the nature of the world. For example, Piaget noted that preschool children's thinking is often strongly tied to the child's own point of view and fails to consider the fact that another person might have a very different perspective on a situation. According to Piaget, cognitive development is a process of revision: children revise their knowledge to provide an increasingly better fit to reality. Piaget referred to this process as the establishment of *equilibrium* between the child's cognitive structures and the nature of the physical and social world.

Piaget viewed children's cognitive development as progressing through four stages. By *stage*, Piaget meant a period of development which is characterized by knowledge structures which are *qualitatively* similar and lead to distinctive modes of thought. In the *sensorimotor stage* of development, lasting from birth to about 2 years of age, the infant thinks about the world through their actions on it. Piaget believed that the basis of our ability to think abstractly is rooted in our ability to act on the world. Eventually, the infant's actions become increasingly organized, leading to the next stage of development which Piaget termed the *preoperational stage*. The major feature of this stage (which char-acterizes development from the ages of 2 to 7) is the ability to think using symbolic representations, that is, the child no longer has to act on the world to think but can use symbols and carry out operations mentally. The third stage of development, lasting from 7 to 12 years of age, is the *concrete operational stage*, characterized by the increasingly logical character of a child's thinking.

Finally, at the *formal operational stage*, the adolescent gains the ability to think abstractly. Unlike the concrete operational child, the adolescent's thinking is no longer tied to concrete reality but can move into the possible or hypothetical.

As mentioned earlier, Piaget's theory has proven extremely influential to the study of children's cognitive development; however, in recent years, the theory has come under an increasing level of criticism. For example, many developmental psychologists are dissatisfied with Piaget's portrayal of the child as a solitary learner and feel that he did not give enough attention to the role of social and cultural factors in children's cognitive development (e.g., Rogoff, 1998). In Chapter 6, we examine Piaget's theory in detail, and consider both the strengths and weaknesses of the theory.

Vygotsky's sociocultural theory of development

Like Piaget, Lev Vygotsky (1896–1934) was a firm believer that children actively explored their environment and were influential in shaping their own knowledge. Unlike Piaget, however, Vygotsky emphasized that the child's social environment was an extremely important force in their development. Vygotsky (1935/1978) believed that it was through social interactions with more experienced and more knowledgeable members of their society – parents, relatives, teachers, peers – that children are able to acquire the knowledge and skills that a culture deems to be important. Thus, according to Vygotsky, development is a social process: social interactions are a necessary aspect of cognitive development.

Vygotsky also believed that children's development follows a particular pattern. Any development occurs at two different levels: children first evidence development in *interpersonal* interactions which occur between themselves and other people. Only later do children show evidence of development on an individual or *intrapersonal* level. Vygotsky labelled this shift from development being evidenced on the interpersonal to an intrapersonal level as *internalization*. An example of internalization can be seen in children's self-talk while problem solving. Children take the kinds of dialogues they engage in with parents or teachers (e.g., '*take your time*' or '*be careful*') while solving problems and talk to themselves while working on problems alone. Eventually, this self-talk is internalized and the child no longer needs to talk out loud.

Finally, Vygotsky noted that parents and teachers tend to interact with children in the context of a teaching task in a particular fashion. Parents tend to adjust their level of interaction dynamically, responding to the child's level of ability, and trying to pitch their teaching at a level which is just outside what the child can do on their own but at a level which is within the child's ability to do with help. Vygotsky believed that parents and teachers worked at a level that is optimal for stimulating children's development. This example highlights Vygotsky's belief that social interactions are critical to children's cognitive development.

Information processing accounts of development

In recent years, an account of cognitive development has emerged which is founded on the analogy between the digital computer and the human mind. Computers are rule-based systems which process information according to a limited and concretely specified set of rules. Information is input into the system and is encoded into a form that the computer can manipulate. This information is then transformed via a series of operations into useful output, for example, the solution to an equation. Similarly, the human mind is believed to operate in the same fashion, by encoding information input via our senses and transforming it into useful output. For example, we take in sound waves from the environment and transform this information via a specified set of operations into meaningful sentences. Human beings and computers share other similar features which enhance the strength of this analogy, such as the ability to manipulate symbols or the constraints on information processing caused by memory limitations. According to information processing theorists, the digital computer provides a useful tool for testing theories of cognitive development via the modelling of cognitive processes (Klahr & MacWhinney, 1998).

Information processing theories are useful to the study of cognitive development in that they require the researcher to map out the series of steps which they believe best describes the flow of information through the human mind. This process of mapping information flow adds a degree of precision to these accounts of cognitive development which is generally open to empirical tests. Thus, information processing models are often readily tested and updated on the basis of experimentation. Information processing theories also stress the importance of identifying the mechanisms which underlie developmental change; they do not simply provide a description of change but also model how change occurs. Finally, information processing theories often force us to address factors that affect development but which previously may not have been considered.

There are a wide variety of information processing models of children's cognition, ranging from models of children's developing ability to perform addition problems to models of children's learning of the rule for making verbs indicate the past tense in English (Klahr & MacWhinney, 1998). Whereas in the past, information processing theories have been criticized for their lack of attention to cognition in real world tasks, this trend is changing as newer information processing models begin to address this issue via the

TABLE 2.2 Theories of human development

Theory	Organicism vs. mechanism	Discontinuity vs. continuity	Nature vs. nurture
Psychoanalytic theory	Organismic	Discontinuous: Emphasizes stages of development that are qualitatively different	Nature (biological drives) and nurture (role of early experience) both play a role
Psychosocial theory	Organismic	Discontinuous: Emphasizes stages of development that are qualitatively different	Nurture: Age-related social demands are the primary determinants of development
Behaviourism and social learning theory	Mechanistic	Continuous: Increase in learned behaviours is continuous	Nurture: Principles of learning are based on environmental contingencies
Ethological theory	Organismic	Continuous and discontinuous elements: Learned behaviours increase continuously but critical/ sensitive periods may lead to qualitative changes	Nature (biologically based, instinctive behaviours, genetic factors) and nurture (experience plays an important role in learning) interact
Evolutionary developmental theory	Organismic	Not clearly specified	Nature (genetic factors canalize behaviour) and nurture (experiences play an important role in shaping behaviour)
Bioecological theory	Organismic	Not clearly specified	Nature (individual characteristics) and nurture (a variety of environmental influences act on the individual)
Life course theory	Organismic	Discontinuous: Age-related demands lead to qualitative developmental change	Nurture: Social demands and environmental influences play an important role in determining development
Dynamic systems theory	Mechanistic	Continuous and discontinuous elements: Learned behaviours increase continuously with the possibility for qualitative reorganizations	Nature (biological constraints) interacts with nurture (experience in context) to produce developmental change
Cognitive developmental theories			
Piagetian theory	Organismic	Discontinuous: Emphasizes emergence of stages of development that are qualitatively distinct	Nature (reflexive behaviours and drive for organization) and nurture (experience with the environment) interacts to produce development
Vygotsky's sociocultural theory	Organismic	Continuous: Interactions with more competent members of one's culture leads to developmental change in a continuous fashion	Nurture: Social interactions with others are the primary influence on development
Information processing theory	Mechanistic and organismic elements	Continuous: The development of skills and strategies increases in a continuous fashion	Not clearly specified

modelling of performance on everyday tasks such as reading comprehension. A more recent trend in the study of information processing is the use of *connectionist* models, which are models of information processing based on the structure of the human brain and its ability to carry out processing in parallel (that is, to perform multiple operations simultaneously). (See Table 2.2 for an overview of the theories of human development.)

SUMMARY

It should be apparent from our brief survey in Chapter 2 that there are a rather large number of theories of human development. Importantly, the theories we cover here are not mutually exclusive: quite often, the theories focus on distinct parts of the life span (e.g., infancy or adolescence) or different domains of development (e.g., emotion or cognition). Our coverage of theories was not exhaustive but is, in fact, representative of the types of theories which are currently invoked to understand children's development. Developing a knowledge of the different theoretical positions is an important task, as it will help you to better understand the research literature which we will cover throughout this text.

Glossary

Assumptions are the guiding premises underlying the logic of a theory.

Bioecological model is a model in which development is viewed as the product of interactions between an individual's capabilities and a dynamic environment.

Chronosystem In Bronfenbrenner's theory, the notion that development occurs in historical time.

Classical conditioning is a form of learning in which the pairing of a response with a stimulus leads to the ability of the stimulus to evoke the response.

Cognitive developmental theory refers to theories regarding the development of cognition, the most famous of which is Piaget's theory of cognitive development.

Cohort effects A cohort is a group of people born at a particular point in time. Cohort effect events have differential impacts on different birth cohorts.

Crisis refers to Erikson's belief that individuals must resolve a series of age-related tasks. How successfully an individual resolves each crisis determines the course of later development.

Critical period is a time when an organism is biologically prepared to acquire a particular behaviour.

Dynamic system theory is a theory of development which suggests that individuals develop within systems. The proper study of development includes a focus on these systems.

Ego In Freud's theory, the part of the personality that works to satisfy instinctive drives in a socially acceptable manner.

Embryology is the study of how a fertilized egg becomes an infant.

Epigenetic processes refer to the interactions of genes and environments.

Erogenous zones Parts of the body which afford pleasure through their stimulation. In Freud's theory, the erogenous zones change with development.

Ethology is a theory of behaviour concerned with understanding the adaptive value of behaviour and its evolutionary history.

Evolutionary developmental psychology is the study of the genetic and environmental mechanisms that govern the development of competencies common to all human beings and the epigenetic processes that adapt these competencies to local conditions.

Exosystems In Bronfenbrenner's theory, the broad social settings that provide support for the development of children and adults but which do not directly involve children (e.g., community health services, parks, recreation centres).

Id The part of our personality which, according to Freud, is made up of instinctual drives.

Imprinting refers to the extremely rapid acquisition of 'following behaviour' in geese.

Information processing theories Theories of development which focus on documenting how information flows through the cognitive system and the cognitive operations which transform that information.

Life course refers to a sequence of socially defined and age-graded events and roles that the individual enacts over time.

Macrosystem In Bronfenbrenner's theory, the overarching ideology, values, laws, regulations, and customs of a given culture.

Mechanism refers to a class of developmental theories that stress quantitative changes in behaviour and emphasize that factors outside the control of the organism play the major role in developmental change.

Mesosystem In Bronfenbrenner's theory, the relationships among microsystems.

Microsystem In Bronfenbrenner's theory, the immediate setting in which a child lives (e.g., neighbourhood, school, family).

Natural selection works through the effects of a trait on survival; if a change to our physical structure or behaviour leads to a survival advantage, the change will be passed on through the genes to the organism's offspring during mating. If the change leads to no advantages, it will not be passed on and the trait will disappear. Thus, only traits which lead to a survival advantage for the organism are passed on.

Observational learning (often referred to as **modelling**) is the acquisition of a behaviour through the observation or imitation of others around one.

Operant conditioning refers to a type of learning where the likelihood of a behaviour reoccurring can be increased by reinforcements and decreased by punishments.

Organicism refers to a class of developmental theories that stress the qualitative features of developmental change and which emphasize the organism's role in bringing about these changes.

Period effects occur when a historical event exerts a relatively uniform influence across different birth cohorts.

Pleasure principle Freud's belief that the id attempts to maximize its pleasure in an immediate fashion.

Psychodynamic theories emphasize the belief that forces or dynamics within the individual are responsible for our behaviour.

Punishments are the consequences of a behaviour that decrease the likelihood of the behaviour reoccurring.

Range of applicability is the range of phenomena to which a theory properly applies.

Reinforcers are the consequences of a behaviour that increase the likelihood of the behaviour reoccurring.

Self-efficacy refers to beliefs about one's own effectiveness and competence to cope with a situation.

Sensitive period is a window of time in development during which an organism is particularly responsive to environmental influences.

Social learning theory Bandura's theory that the principles of operant conditioning and observational learning are important mechanisms of development.

Sociocultural theory refers to Vygotsky's theory which views development as dependent on the child's interactions with other, more skilled members of the culture.

Softly-assembled the idea, from dynamic systems theory, that a given behaviour does not depend on a genetic blueprint but occurs as a result of changing constraints and supports from the context in which the behaviour occurs.

Superego In Freud's theory, the part of the personality which is the internalized values and standards of the child's parents and culture.

Theories take the form of an interconnected set of concepts used to integrate and to interpret empirical observations. **Formal theories** should be logically consistent and contain no contradictions, fit well with empirical observations, be testable, remain as simple as possible, and cover a defined range of phenomena. **Informal theories** are organized sets of intuitions or expectations about the world, often referred to as *implicit theories*.

This chapter is taken from:
Keenan, T. (2002) *An Introduction to Child Development*
978-0-7619-6220-5

2 The Biological Foundations of Development

THOMAS KEENAN

LEARNING AIMS

At the end of this chapter you should:

- be able to describe the developmental course of physical growth and articulate the principles which growth follows
- be familiar with the factors which can influence physical growth and sexual maturation
- be able to describe the course of motor development and recognize the difference between *gross* and *fine motor* development
- be able to recognize and label the major parts of the human brain and understand the neuron
- be familiar with concepts such as *hemispheric specialization* and *experience-expectant* and *experience-dependent* development
- be able to explain the logic of behaviour genetics, twin designs, and associated concepts such as *heritability*, *niche picking*, and *range of reaction*

The course of physical growth

In comparison to other species, the course of physical growth in human beings is a long drawn-out process. Evolutionary theorists have suggested that our lengthy period of physical immaturity provides us with added time to acquire the skills and the knowledge which are required in a complex social world. This suggestion emphasizes the fact that physical growth is not simply a set of maturational processes that operate independently of input from the environment: rather, physical growth occurs within an environmental context. Environments, including factors such as cultural practices, nutrition and opportunities for experience play an important role in physical development.

The patterns of growth

Physical growth does not proceed randomly; instead, it follows orderly patterns known as **cephalocaudal** and **proximodistal** development. The cephalocaudal pattern of development refers to the fact that growth occurs in a head to toe direction. For example, two months after conception, the human infant's head is very large in contrast to its total height and by birth, this ratio is much smaller as the rate of growth in the rest of the body begins to catch-up. Within the head itself the eyes and the brain grow faster than the jaw. These examples illustrate the head to toe direction of physical growth. The proximodistal pattern of development refers to the fact that development occurs outwards from the centre of the body. For example, a baby will acquire control over the muscles of the neck and trunk before it acquires control over the fingers and the toes.

Body size

Changes in body size are the most obvious manifestation of physical growth. During infancy, changes in growth are extremely rapid. An example which readily comes to mind is the dramatic changes in height. By 1 year of age, infants average a growth of approximately 11 inches (approximately 32.5 cm) over their size at birth (Malina, 1975). Similarly impressive gains are noted in weight. At 2 years of age, an infant's weight will have quadrupled since birth. In general, physical developments in height and weight tend to occur very rapidly in infancy, continue at a relatively steady pace throughout childhood, and then slow down towards puberty.

At puberty, there is a marked *growth spurt*, that is, a very rapid increase in size and weight. The pubertal growth spurt varies from person to person in terms of its intensity, its duration, and its age of onset. The pubertal growth spurt tends to last around 4½ years, girls usually showing their pubertal growth spurt around age 11, whereas in boys the same process begins at approximately age 13. According to Tanner (1990), girls finish pubertal growth by about age 16 whereas boys continue to grow until approximately 18 years of age; however, in both sexes growth may still take place after the completion of the pubertal growth spurt.

A number of studies have provided evidence that hereditary factors play a strong role in physical growth. Work by Wilson (1986) examining correlations in a variety of physical indices showed that the correlation in height between identical twins was approximately 0.94 at 4 years of age, and this correlation remained stable after this time. For fraternal twins, the correlation for height was relatively high at birth but became increasingly smaller over time, moving from 0.77 at birth to 0.49 at 9 years of age (at which point it became stable). The large and stable correlations observed in identical twins and the smaller correlations observed for fraternal twins suggests that genetic factors play an important role in determining height. Similar patterns are observed for weight as well as for the timing of growth spurts (Wilson, 1986).

Environmental factors in physical growth: nutrition
Of course, genetic factors are unlikely to tell the entire story of physical growth. Not surprisingly, growth is highly dependent on our nutritional intake, that is, what kinds of food we eat, and how much of them we eat. Height and weight are clearly affected by nutritional intake. Studies during World War II showed that the restrictive diets imposed by wartime conditions in Europe led to a general decline in average height, reversing a trend towards increasing height which had been apparent since the end of World War I (Tanner, 1990). However, more than just our height and weight can be affected by nutritional intake: research has indicated that dietary restrictions during the war also had an effect on puberty. Studies of French women showed that **menarche**, the onset of menstruation, was delayed by up to 3 years (Tanner, 1990).

Cognitive development has also been related to nutrition. For example, *anaemia*, the condition where a person suffers from low levels of iron in the bloodstream, has been associated with a slowing of intellectual development (Pollitt, 1994). A striking example of nutritional effects on cognitive development comes to us from the examination of intestinal worms. Intestinal worms sit in our digestive tract and rob us of valuable nutrients which fuel our growth. Watkins and Pollitt (1997) showed that children who have high levels of intestinal worms show reduced performance on psychometric tests of cognitive ability. In some cases, studies have shown that these effects can be quite severe.

Hormonal influences
In large part, the physical changes observed at puberty are controlled by **hormones**. The hormones are a set of chemical substances manufactured by glands and are received by various cells throughout the body to trigger other chemical changes. The most important of these glands is the **pituitary gland** located near the base of the brain. The pituitary gland triggers changes both directly, via the hormones it secretes into the bloodstream, which act on various tissues to produce growth and indirectly by triggering other glands to release different hormones.

The physical changes associated with puberty, specifically **primary sexual characteristics** (growth involving the reproductive organs: the penis, scrotum and testes in males and the vagina, uterus and ovaries in females) and the **secondary sexual characteristics** (visible changes which are associated with sexual maturation such as the development of breasts in females, facial hair in males and pubic hair for both males and females) are also controlled through the pituitary gland which stimulates the release of the sex hormones. In boys, **testosterone** is released in large quantities, leading to the growth of male sexual characteristics, while in females **oestrogens** are associated with female sexual maturation. Both types of hormones are actually present in both sexes although in quite different amounts.

Sexual maturation

In terms of sexual maturity, the most important changes to result are **menarche** and **spermarche**, that is, the first menstruation in females and the first ejaculation in males. These two milestones are commonly believed to indicate a readiness to reproduce although in actuality, there is often a short period of sterility which can last about one year in both females and males in which menstruation and ejaculations occur but no eggs or sperm are released (Tanner, 1990).

The factors which determine the timing of puberty are multiple and complex, ranging from genetic determination to the nature and quality of family relationships. Genetic factors are certainly involved in determining when the pituitary gland begins releasing the hormonal signals which begin the physical transformations, but interestingly, they are not the sole cause of when pubertal timing occurs for an individual. In young women, physical exercise can delay the onset of the physical changes associated with puberty. For example, Brooks-Gunn (1988b) found that very few ballet dancers actually had their first menstruation at the 'normal' time. Family factors can also play an important role in pubertal timing. Moffitt et al. (1992) found that family conflict and the absence of fathers predicted an earlier onset of menarche. Steinberg (1987) found that an increased psychological distancing between girls and their fathers also predicted an earlier menarche. A more recent study by Ellis et al. (1999) showed that the quality of fathers' investment in their daughters was positively associated with the timing of puberty; when fathers had good quality relationships with their daughters, the onset of pubertal maturation in their daughters came later. Together, these studies highlight the importance of environmental factors in sexual maturation, demonstrating the necessity of examining interactions between genetic and environmental causes in studying development.

Besides examining the questions of when and why adolescents enter puberty earlier or later than their peers, we can ask what effects early or late maturation has on individuals. A classic study by Jones and Bayley (1950; see also Jones, 1965) suggested that early maturation carries distinct advantages for boys but not for females. Jones and Bayley tracked 16 early-maturing and 16 late-maturing boys for a six-year period. Late-maturing boys were characterized as lower in physical attractiveness, masculinity, and were rated as more childish, eager and attention seeking than early-maturing boys. In contrast, early-maturing boys were characterized as independent, self-confident, and as making better leaders and athletes. Jones showed that for women, the reverse effects obtained (Jones & Mussen, 1958): early-maturing girls were more likely to show social difficulties than late-maturing girls. They were also less popular, less self-confident, held fewer leadership positions and were more withdrawn than late-maturing girls. More recent research has confirmed and extended these findings. Early-maturing girls tend to have a poorer body image than normally maturing or late-maturing girls (Brooks-Gunn, 1988a), at least in part because the normal weight gains which accompany pubertal maturation violate the cultural ideal for thinness. This trend is exactly the reverse for males: early-maturing boys tend to have a much more positive body image, in large part because many cultures seem to value traits like height and muscularity.

Behavioural problems have also been associated with early versus late maturation, particularly in girls. The explanations for these problems seem to reduce to two types. Caspi and Moffit (1991) argue for a dispositional account, believing that it is not early maturation *per se* that creates problems for girls, but rather, early maturation on top of a previous history of behaviour problems. Their argument is that when stressful events such as early maturation occur, they may highlight dispositional factors (tendencies to behave in a particular fashion, possibly due to genetic factors or previously acquired habits). It is these dispositions which Caspi and Moffit believe are ultimately responsible for the behaviour problems. In contrast, Graber, Brooks-Gunn and Warren (1995) believe that *psychosocial factors* – factors such as parental warmth, parental approval, and the level of family conflict – play an important role in how girls react to early maturation. Research from Sweden has tended to support the view that psychosocial factors play an important role in the effects of early maturation on girls (Stattin & Magnusson, 1990). These researchers found that early-maturing girls tended to have smaller networks of friends, to associate with older friends who often engaged in deviant behaviours, and were more likely to engage in risky behaviours such as smoking, drinking alcohol, and sexual inter-course. While the findings to date do suggest a risk to early-maturing girls, it is clear that contextual and psychosocial factors play an important role: not all early-maturing girls will experience problems and some early-maturing girls may show very positive developmental outcomes (Brooks-Gunn, 1988a).

TABLE 4.1 Selected milestones in motor development

Age	Milestone
6 weeks	Hold head upright while in a prone position
2 months	Roll from back onto side
3 months	Directed reaching for objects
5 to 7 months	Sit without support
9 to 14 months	Stand without support
8 to 12 months	Walk with support
12 months	Use of pincer grasp when reaching
12 to 14 months	Walk alone

Motor development

Human infants start life with very limited motor skills, yet by about 1 year of age, they are walking independently. In between birth and learning to walk a great many skills are acquired. What does the course of motor development in infancy look like? Nancy Bayley (1969) provides us with a description of the average age at which infants and toddlers acquire many of the most common motor skills. According to Bayley, infants can hold their heads upright by 6 weeks of age; by 2 months they can roll from their sides onto their back; by 3 months of age they can grasp an object; by 7 months infants can sit alone and begin to crawl; by 12 months they walk on their own (see Table 4.1).

Also included in Bayley's work is a description of the age range at which 90 percent of children achieve a particular skill. For example, while the average infant sits upright alone by 7 months of age, 90 percent of infants will acquire this skill somewhere between 5 and 9 months of age. Bayley's data highlight an important fact regarding the variability of motor development: while the sequence of motor development is relatively uniform, progress in the acquisition of motor skills is highly variable. For example, some infants will learn to walk as early as 9 months while others will not take their first steps until 17 months. It is important to remember that individual children will not conform exactly to any description of the average age at which developmental milestones are achieved; some variability is normal and early progress or lack of the same is not a good predictor of the final level of development.

A principle known as **differentiation** comes into play when we try to describe the acquisition of motor skill (Bühler, 1930). Differentiation refers to the fact that, initially, motor skills are rather global reactions to a particular stimulus; only with time and practise do motor behaviours become more precise and adapted to particular ends. Consider the reaction of an infant to having an unwanted blanket placed on top of her. A very young infant might twist and writhe in a random fashion which may or may not achieve the desired effect. Older infants will grasp the blanket and pull it away; they use a more specific, more precise behaviour to accomplish their goals. The principles of cephalocaudal and proximodistal development also apply to the acquisition of motor skills. For example, infants learn to hold their head upright before they learn to sit upright or to pull themselves to a standing position.

Maturation vs. experience

The maturation of the neural and muscular systems determines, to a large extent, when children will acquire a particular skill. Early research on motor skill highlighted a maturationist viewpoint, that is, that development is under the control of inherited programmes that are genetic in origin (Gesell & Thompson, 1929; McGraw, 1935). These researchers were reacting against behaviourists like John B. Watson (see Chapter 2) who believed that motor skills like walking were simply conditioned reflexes. In contrast, maturationists like Gesell and McGraw believed that motor behaviours like walking emerged according to a preprogrammed genetic timetable.

Gesell devised a simple design to demonstrate the effects of maturation. Using identical twins allowed Gesell to control for biological factors since identical twins share 100 percent of their genes. One twin would be given extra practise at a particular motor task while the control twin received no extra training. When tested after a period of training, *both* twins showed significant evidence of acquiring the motor skill, not simply the twin who had been given extra practise as might be predicted (Gesell & Thompson, 1929). Such findings led Gesell to the conclusion that maturation and not experience is the prime factor in determining when children acquire skills.

However, as Thelen (1995) notes, the development of motor skill is not simply the outcome of genetic programming: transactions with the environment must play a crucial role in the timing of motor skill acquisition. Thus, an important aspect of when children acquire a particular motor skill is experience. In contrast to the work of Gesell, opportunities to practise particular motor skills have been shown to promote their earlier appearance (Zelazo, Zelazo, & Kolb, 1972). The acquisition of motor skills also varies across cultures in ways which are not consistent with genetic factors. Some cultures emphasize practices which encourage the earlier or later appearance of a skill. For example, Hopkins and Westra (1988) found that mothers in the West Indies have babies which walk considerably earlier than the average North American infant. West Indian mothers use a particular routine, passed down to them by other members of their culture, which encourages the early development of walking and other motor skills. As this example shows, environments can have important effects on when skills are acquired.

Gross and fine motor development

Bertenthal and Clifton (1998) note that control over one's motor behaviour ranks among the infant's greatest achievements. Psychologists who study the acquisition of motor skills find it useful to distinguish between **gross motor development**, that is, motor skills which help children to get around in their environment such as crawling and walking, and **fine motor development**, which refers to smaller movement sequences like reaching and grasping. The development of motor skill has implications beyond simply learning how to perform new actions: motor skills can have profound effects on development. For example, researchers have shown that infants with locomotor experience were less likely to make errors while searching for hidden objects (Campos & Bertenthal, 1989; Horobin & Acredolo, 1986). The ability to initiate movement about one's environment stimulates the development of spatial encoding abilities, making hidden object tasks easier to solve. Rovee-Collier (1997) has made a similar point in regard to memory development. She argues that the onset of independent locomotion around 9 months of age marks an important transition in memory development. Children who can move about the environment develop an understanding of locations such as 'here' and 'there'. Because infant memory is initially highly dependent on context – that is, the similarity between the situation where information is encoded and where it is recalled – infants who have experience moving about the environment and who learn to spatially encode information become less dependent on context for successful recall. These examples show that motor development has implications beyond the immediately apparent benefits of crawling or walking.

Piaget (1952) argued that the development of reaching and grasping was a key aspect of cognitive development because it forms an important link between biological adaptation and intellectual adaptation. Reaching and grasping are voluntary actions under the infant's control, and as such, they open up exciting new possibilities in the infant's ability to explore their environment. The infant who reaches for and grasps an object so as to explore it pushes his development forwards as he engages in processes such as adapting his grip to the size and shape of the object. Piaget argued that these early processes of assimilation and accommodation to objects drive cognitive development in the sensory motor period.

The development of reaching begins early in life. Newborn infants seated in an upright position will swipe and reach towards an object placed in front of them, a behaviour labelled **prereaching**. These poorly coordinated behaviours start to decline around 2 months of age (Bower, 1982) and are replaced by **directed reaching**, which begins at about 3 months of age (Thelen, Corbetta, Kamm, Spencer, Schneider, & Zernicke, 1993). At this time reaching becomes more coordinated, efficient, and improves in accuracy

(Bushnell, 1985). According to research conducted by Clifton, Rochat, Robin, and Berthier (1994) the infant's reaching does not depend simply on the guidance of the hand and arm by the visual system but is controlled by **proprioception**, the sensation of movement and location based on stimulation arising from bodily sources such as muscle contractions. By about 9 months of age, infants can adjust their reaching to take into account a moving object. However, 9-month-olds are far from expert reachers and a good deal of skill remains to develop.

Once infants begin reaching they also begin to grasp the objects that are the target of their reaches. The **ulnar** grasp is seen when infants first engage in directed reaching. The ulnar grasp is a primitive form of grasping in which the infant's fingers close against their palm. The fingers seem to act as a whole, requiring the use of the palm in order to hold an object. Shortly after this accomplishment, when infants can sit upright on their own, infants acquire the ability to transfer objects from hand to hand. By around the end of the first year, infants have graduated to using the **pincer** grasp (Halverson, 1931) wherein they use their index finger and their thumb in an opposable manner, resulting in a more coordinated and finely tuned grip. This allows for the exploration of very small objects or objects which demand specific actions for their operation, such as the knobs on a stereo system which require turning to the left or right to adjust volume.

The development of motor skill beyond infancy

Beyond infancy, not a great deal is known about the development of motor skill. Gallahue (1989) suggests that, beyond infancy, three fundamental sets of motor skills emerge in the child's repertoire. These are *locomotor movements*, which include walking, running, jumping, hopping, skipping and climbing; *manipulative movements* including throwing, catching and kicking; and *stability movements* (centered around controlling one's body) including bending, stretching, rolling, balancing, and walking on one's hands.

The development of motor skill progresses through three stages (Gallahue, 1989). Consider an example such as learning to swing a tennis racquet. Initially, a child tries to execute the motor skill, however, they fail to follow through with the movement. They also fail to engage in any sort of anticipatory movements which prepare them to execute the action. Young children's stroke often looks more like a swipe, barely resembling the straight-armed, locked-wrist style that mature players use. By the second stage, what we might think of as a transitional stage in the development of the skill, children can execute the individual components of the swing more competently, however, they fail to organize the components into a smoothly sequenced whole. At this stage, children may adopt a straight arm, start with their racquet well behind their body and follow through, but on any given swing they are unlikely to execute all three of these aspects of an accomplished stroke together. Finally, by the third stage all components of the behaviour are integrated into a coordinated whole. Motor skills continue to improve as related developments in the sensory and perceptual skills, as well as the maturation of the nervous system, take place. However, increased practise will speed children's acquisition of a skilled behaviour.

Brain development

Perhaps the most obvious change in the developing brain is its size. At birth, an infant's brain is approximately 400 grams or 25 percent of the weight of an average adult brain, which weighs in at about 1,400 grams (Segalowitz, 1995). By the time the infant is 6 months old the brain weighs about half as much as an adult brain, and by age 2 it is 75 percent of the weight of an adult brain (Restak, 1984). Like many other aspects of development, brain growth is not smooth and continuous, but rather, occurs in spurts (Segalowitz, 1995).

The structure of the brain

The brain is made up of two **hemispheres**, together known as the **cerebrum** (see Figure 4.1). These hemispheres are connected by a set of nerve fibres known as the **corpus callosum**. The left and right hemispheres of the brain are anatomically distinct and control different functions (Segalowitz, 1983b; Springer & Deutsch, 1993). For example, the temporal lobe, an area associated with language, seems to be larger on the left side of the brain than on the right. However, whether these anatomical differences are related to functional differences remains a question which is open for further research.

The cerebrum is covered by a layer known as the **cerebral cortex**. This layer of cells is extremely convoluted giving rise to the distinctive look of brain tissue. The cerebral cortex accounts for approximately 90 percent of the brain's total number of cells. It is also the most advanced part of the brain, supporting complex functions such as language, vision and motor skills. The cerebral cortex is divided into four main areas called **lobes**, and two other areas known as the **association areas**. The four lobes of the brain are known as the **frontal lobe** (which supports planning, organization, and other higher mental functions), the **temporal lobe** (involved in language, hearing, and smell), the **parietal lobe** (involved in the processing of bodily sensations) and the **occipital lobe** (which is involved in visual processing). The **anterior association** area (located at the front of the brain) and **posterior association area** (located near the rear of the brain) are involved in linking up information from various parts of the brain.

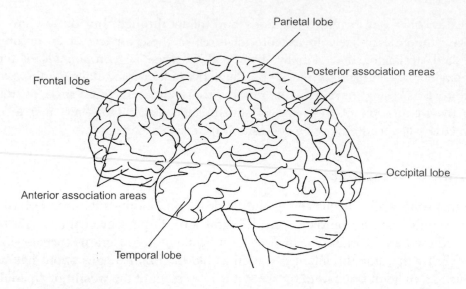

Parietal lobe

Posterior association areas

Frontal lobe

Occipital lobe

Anterior association areas

Temporal lobe

FIGURE 4.1 The human brain

Neuronal development

So far we have described the structure of the brain at a macro level. Let us now consider the micro level structure of the brain. The brain is made up of a number of different types of cells. **Neurons** are the name given to the nerve cells which send and receive neural impulses (electrical signals) throughout the brain and the nervous system. The average human brain is made up of some 100 billion neurons, each with as many as 15,000 connections to other cells. The second type of cell which make up the brain are **glial cells**. These are the cells which provide structural support to the neurons, regulate the nutrient concentrations delivered to neurons, and are important to the task of **myelination**, in which neurons are covered with an insulating layer of *myelin* (a fatty substance) which makes the neuron a more effective transmitter of electrical information (Johnson, 1998).

The neuron itself is made up of **dendrites**, a **cell body**, an **axon**, and **terminal buttons** (see Figure 4.2). The dendrite is the part of the cell which receives signals from other neurons and which transmits this information to the cell body. The information collected is than transmitted along the axon to the terminal buttons which send information across the **synapse** (the gap between the terminal buttons of one neuron and the dendrites of another neuron) to other neurons. This transmission across the synapse is carried out by means of special chemical signals known as **neurotransmitters**.

The development of neurons begins the embryonic period, with most neurons present by the 7th month after conception (Rakic, 1995). Recall that an average human brain is made up of about 100 billion neurons. This

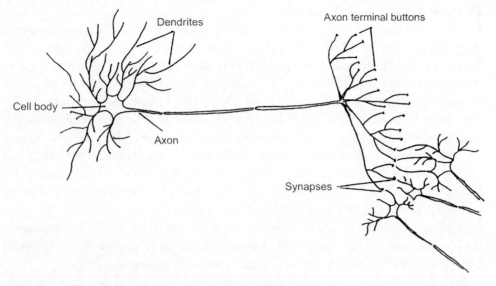

Dendrites

Axon terminal buttons

Cell body

Axon

Synapses

FIGURE 4.2 The neuron

means that neurons are being generated in the brain at the rate of about 250,000 per minute in a process known as *neuron proliferation*. Neurons which are generated often travel to other locations in the brain, guided by a set of complex neurochemical processes.

The brain has a peculiar property of overproducing both neurons and synaptic connections between neurons. Segalowitz (1995) argues that while the purpose of this overproduction is not completely known, two functions are presumed to result from this process. First, it allows experience to dictate which connections between neurons are kept and which connections are lost, thereby ensuring that the child acquires all of the skills and information required to enable development to take place. Second, the overproduction of neurons and synapses ensures *plasticity*. By plasticity, it is meant that the brain can compensate for early damage by either replacing connections which have been lost or transferring functions to other areas of the brain. The available evidence suggests that, if brain injury occurs reasonably early in life, the likelihood of recovering the function is good (Fox, Calkins, & Bell, 1994). However, while the brain is genetically programmed to overproduce synapses and neurons in the early years, this overproduction is soon curtailed. This **thinning** of neurons and synapses (Huttenlocher, 1990; 1994a, b; Segalowitz, 1995) is accomplished through two processes: **neuronal death**, in which some neurons are programmed to die, apparently to provide more space for crucial cell clusters, and **synaptic pruning**, in which the brain disposes of a neuron's connections to other neurons. According to Huttenlocher (1994a, b), the goal of both processes is to increase the efficiency of transmission between neurons.

Hemispheric specialization

One of the most important aspects, and often one of the most misunderstood (Segalowitz, 1983b), is the left–right organization of the brain across its two hemispheres. **Hemispheric specialization** refers to the differential functions carried out by the two cerebral hemispheres. Hemispheric specialization begins at birth and the differences between the two hemispheres remain largely the same into adulthood. This belief, that there is a lack of change in the organization of function across the two hemispheres, has come to be known as the **invariance hypothesis**. However, as Segalowitz (1995) notes, what *will* change is what the child is able to do with the information that is processed by the two halves of the brain. Also of note is the fact that the two hemispheres of the brain mature at different rates, with the evidence suggesting that the right hemisphere of the brain matures earlier than the left (Best, 1988). Interestingly, this earlier maturation of the right hemisphere mirrors the growth of functional differences carried out by the two hemispheres (Segalowitz, 1995).

So, what are these functional differences attributed to the left and the right hemispheres? Movement and sensation are each controlled by a single hemisphere. The left side of the brain controls movement and sensation of the right side of the body while the right side of the brain controls movement and sensation for the left side of the body. The only exception to this pattern is the eyes which send input to both sides of the brain. The left side of the brain is specialized for language processing. In contrast, the right side of the brain is specialized for processing spatial information, music and the perception of faces. The two hemispheres are also believed to be differentially involved in the processing of emotion. According to Davidson (1994b) the left hemisphere of the brain is responsible for the expression of emotions associated with approach to the external environment, emotions such as *interest, anger* and *joy*. In contrast, the right side of the brain is responsible for processing emotions associated with withdrawal from the environment such as *fear, distress* and *disgust*. While the evidence is clear that some functions are associated with a particular hemisphere, it is important to note that the separation of function across the hemispheres is not absolute. For example, a number of studies conducted with individuals who have right brain damage have demonstrated that these people have difficulty processing nonliteral forms of language such as sarcastic speech (Kaplan, Brownell, Jacobs, & Gardner, 1990), suggesting that the right hemisphere may be associated with particular aspects of language processing such as *pragmatics* (Siegal, Carrington, & Radel, 1996). **Lateralization** is the term used to describe the processes by which the two halves of the brain become specialized to carry out specific functions. Research in developmental neuropsychology suggests that the lateralization of brain function across the left and right hemispheres is a very complex process which is not yet well understood.

Brain maturation and developmental change

As discussed earlier, the brain undergoes several growth spurts over the course of its development. Recordings of brain electrical activity as reflected in the electroencephalogram (EEG) appear to show correlations between growth spurts and major periods of cognitive development (Fischer & Rose, 1994; 1995). Indeed, many developmental psychologists and neuropsychologists have drawn connections between developments within the brain itself (changes due to the growth of synapses, synaptic pruning, the development of the frontal lobes and the myelinization of neurons) and cognitive development (Case, 1992c; Thatcher, 1994). For example, Case (1992c) argued that major stage changes in children's developing cognitive ability mapped onto changes in brain development. While it is tempting to make such leaps, Segalowitz (1995) provides a caution in doing so, arguing that studying global changes in brain structure is less informative than examining how regional developments in the brain develop to support specific functions.

A related point comes from neuropsychological work on the distinction between **experience-expectant** development and **experience-dependent** development made by Greenough, Black and Wallace (1987). These authors have shown how neural circuitry is related to environmental events. Some neural circuits require input from the environment in order to begin growing, a process which Greenough et al. refer to as experience-expectant development. In contrast, other types of neural circuits are strongly influenced by the types of environmental input they receive, what Greenough et al. term experience-dependent development. The development of the brain is critically dependent on environmental experience. Brain structures in and of themselves do not cause development. (Similarly, experience with the environment will not produce developmental changes if the brain structures which underlie those changes have not yet matured.) Thus, a theory of cognitive development which attempts to relate changes in brain structure to other developmental changes must also factor in the role of experience in this association. Given that experience is involved, the correlation between brain maturation and developmental change will never be perfect.

Genes and behaviour

Heredity: the process of genetic transmission

The processes underlying the hereditary transmission of parental characteristics to their offspring are remarkably complex. Consider your own siblings or a friend you know who has brothers or sisters: are you or your friend exactly the same as your or his/her bother or sister? The answer (even if you have an identical twin) is probably 'no'. Siblings share half their genes with each other; that is, half of your genetic material is the same as your brother or sister, but these shared genes are not enough to ensure a high degree of similarity. This is because genes interact with the environment to produce observable characteristics such as eye colour, and height or behaviours such as personality and intelligence. When we speak of an individual's **genotype**, we refer to their genetic makeup, that is, the particular set of genes which they have inherited from their parents. As a result of development, environments act on individuals to produce their **phenotype**, that is, their observable characteristics.

In our discussion of genetics and human development, we will take for granted that by this point in your career you have acquired an understanding of sexual reproduction and instead will focus on the key genetic aspects of the process. At conception, a single **sperm** from males unites with the **ovum** or egg from the female to create a fertilized egg called a **zygote**. Sperm and egg are unique cells in that they are the only cells in the human body to carry 23 chromosomes (all other cells carry 46 chromosomes). These special cells are known as **gametes**. **Chromosomes** are a very special chemical structure made up of a series of proteins known as deoxyribonucleic acid or DNA. They have a thread-like appearance and are found in the nucleus of a cell. Chromosomes come in 23 pairs; half of these come from the mother and half from the father. The chromosomes carry the **genes** which are the units of hereditary transmission. Genes are sequences of proteins, a part of the DNA molecule. They work by triggering the production of proteins when instructed to do so by environmental signals or by other genes.

Remember that chromosomes come in pairs, one from the father and one from the mother. Thus, a gene on one chromosome has a partner or an alternate form on the other chromosome. This alternate form of the gene is called an **allele**. To further complicate matters, the alleles of a gene from both parents can be similar or dissimilar in their genotype. If the alleles are alike, the child is said to be **homozygous** for the trait coded for by the gene; if the genes are dissimilar the child is **heterozygous**. Homozygous children will display the trait which is coded for by the genes whereas the relationships between the two alleles will determine how the trait is expressed for heterozygous children. Consider eye colour as an example. The genes which code for eye colour can have different forms, an allele which specifies blue eyes and an allele which specifies brown eyes. If the child's parents both carry the brown-eyed allele, the child will have brown eyes.

The relationships between alleles are described in terms of **dominant** and **recessive** alleles. In some cases, one allele is more powerful or dominant than another and will always express its effects over those of another allele. This is the case for hair colour. The brown hair allele is dominant over the red hair allele. Thus a child who inherits a red hair allele from one parent and a brown hair allele from the other will always develop brown hair. If we represent a dominant allele by **A** and a recessive allele by **a** than you should recognize that a person could have the following combinations of alleles: **AA**, **Aa**, **aA**, and **aa**. These reduce to three patterns. **AA** is homozygous and represents two dominant genes. **Aa** and **aA** are heterozygous and represent combinations where the dominant gene will be expressed. The combination **aa** is again homozygous and represents a person with two recessive genes. In our example of hair colour, this is the *only* combination of genes which would result in a red-haired child. There is yet another possibility which can occur, called **codominance**. Codominance occurs when heterozygous alleles both express their traits with equal force. For example, the blood types A and B are codominant alleles such that a person who inherits the A allele from one parent and the B allele from the other will have blood type AB.

Many harmful traits coded for by genes are recessive, a fact which has the happy effect of greatly reducing their occurrence in the population. An example of this is the allele for **phenylketonuria** or **PKU**. PKU is a genetic disorder in which the child is unable to metabolize a protein called phenylalanine, a problem which can lead to brain damage and to profound mental retardation. The allele which codes for the normal metabolizing of phenylalanine is dominant while the gene which leads to PKU is recessive. When both parents carry the recessive allele for PKU there is a one in four chance that their offspring will have the disorder (as we described earlier).

Genes and environments

In contemporary developmental psychology, rarely will one find a psychologist taking up a position that emphasizes either genes or environments as the sole cause of behaviour. Instead, modern psychologists recognize that genes and environments *interact* to shape the course of development. Research has shown clearly how genetic factors serve to restrict the range of possible courses that development can take, while at the same time we have gained an ever more sophisticated understanding of how environments exert a tremendous influence on development, both supporting and restricting it.

We also know that genes can shape environments. This may strike you as an odd idea, one which violates your intuitive notions of the direction in which biological effects should go. According to the work of Sandra Scarr (1992, 1996; Scarr & McCartney, 1983), genes can have effects on the environment in at least three ways. First, genes can have what Scarr referred to as **passive** effects. Children's environments are most often dictated by parents. Because parents and children share some of their genes, it is not surprising that parents will create a home environment which is supportive of the child's genotype. Consider musical talent. Musical parents will likely have musical children. As a result of their own predisposition, musical parents will create a musical environment for their children. Thus, the parent's efforts provide an ideal environment for the child's genes which code for musical talent to be expressed. Second, genes may have an **evocative** relationship with the environment. This occurs when some trait in the child causes others to react in a certain way which has the effect of strengthening the trait. For example, temperamentally 'easy' babies who smile and act sociably will elicit positive social reactions from others which reinforces the baby's behaviours and ultimately strengthens their genetic predisposition. Finally, genes can effect the environment in an **active** way. This occurs when children seek out environments which are compatible with their genetic makeup. For example, athletically talented children will eventually move towards participation in school sports while musically talented children will join the band. This process, which Scarr (1996) calls **niche picking**, is an active process based on one's genetic predisposition. As Scarr notes, niche picking increases in importance as people move towards adulthood and begin to take increasing control over their own environments. This process may also play a role in explaining why correlations for traits such as cognitive ability show increasing concordance over time.

As suggested earlier, environments also have profound effects on genetic factors. One way in which this relationship has been conceptualized is through the concept of **range of reaction** (Gottesman, 1963). According to range of reaction concept, genes do not fix behaviour in a rigid fashion but establish a range of possibilities which depend heavily on environmental circumstances. In a sense, you can think of a person's genotype as placing boundaries on their ability which differ depending on environmental circumstances. For example, if a child is born into an impoverished environment, their genotype may place specific limits on how far their cognitive abilities may develop. This child may show very low ability under impoverished environments, and only slightly higher levels of achievement under more enriched environments. In this case, we would say the child has a small range of reaction. In contrast, another child with a different genotype may perform slightly better in impoverished environments but extremely well under an enriched environment. This child would show a much larger range of reaction.

The reaction range concept has been criticized by Gilbert Gottlieb (1991; Gottlieb, Wahlsten & Lickliter, 1998). Gottlieb suggests that genes play a much less deterministic role than is suggested by the range of reaction concept which emphasizes the limit-setting effect of genes. He suggests that genes and environments engage in a process of *coaction* wherein the relationships between genes, environments, and other levels of behaviour such as neural activity all mutually influence one another. The influences between any levels are bidirectional, that is, they go both ways. Thus, genes are simply part of a system which are affected by events at other levels of the system.

Behaviour genetics

So far we have covered cases of genetic transmission that conform to a simple model where a gene is causally related to a particular trait such as eye colour. However, most behaviours that are inherited are multifactorial, that is, they have more than one cause. When some trait is affected by more than one gene, geneticists speak of **polygenetic inheritance**. Given the state of genetic research, it is very difficult at this point in time to specify exactly which genes contribute to some trait, but researchers are beginning to make some progress in this regard. A recent report (Chorney et al., 1998) identified a particular gene which is associated with cognitive ability. However, more often than not, researchers are only able to specify how important genetic factors are relative to environmental factors in the cause of some particular trait, that is, how much of the variance in a given trait is caused by genetic factors and how much is caused by environmental factors. This area of inquiry, examining the relationship between genetic and environmental factors is known as **behaviour genetics**.

We know genetic factors play a critical role in human development. For example, researchers have identified a form of a gene which, if present in an individual, increases the risk of developing Alzheimer's disease by a factor of four over the normal population (Plomin, DeFries, McClearn & Rutter, 1997). Beyond such high profile cases as a genetic cause for Alzheimer's disease, behaviour geneticists have shown that genetics play important roles in the development of psychological traits such cognitive abilities, school achievement, personality, self-esteem, and drug use. In the following section we will examine some of the findings of behaviour genetic research.

Heritability

Behaviour geneticists employ a concept known as **heritability** to measure the effects of genetic factors on a trait. Essentially, heritability is an estimate of the relative influence of genetic versus environmental factors. According to Plomin et al. (1997: 79), heritability can be defined as 'the proportion of phenotypic variance that can be accounted for by genetic differences among individuals'. It is estimated by examining the correlations for some trait among relatives and is generally expressed as an *intraclass correlation*, that is a correlation which can be straightforwardly interpreted as a percentage. In other words, an intraclass correlation of 0.80 between identical twins for IQ would suggest that 80 percent of the variance in IQ scores between the twins was due to genetic factors.

Heritability has been criticized as a concept by many authors. Bronfenbrenner (1972) demonstrated that heritability cannot be straightfor-wardly interpreted as simply an index of genetic causation. In his analyses, Bronfenbrenner shows how environmental factors have a clear impact on the calculation of heritability. While not at all refuting the importance of genetic factors in development, Bronfenbrenner's argument is that heritability should be interpreted as reflecting the capacity of the environment to invoke and nurture the development of a trait. In his critique of research on racial differences in intelligence, Block (1995) questions the common assumption that heritability is simply an index of genetic causation. Block points out that heritability is calculated as a ratio of *genetically caused* variation to *total variation* in some trait. Again, while not refuting the importance of genetic factors in human development, Block's argument is that a characteristic can be highly heritable even if it is not caused by genetic factors. Take a trait such as long hair. Block would argue that in 1950, long hair was caused genetically. That is, in Western cultures, only women wore long hair and since women are genetically different than men, the cause of wearing long hair could be construed as genetic. The ratio of genetic variation (sex: men or women) to total variation (women: only women wore long hair) was close to one, indicating high heritability. However, now that variability in who wears their hair long (as both men and women commonly do these days) has increased, the heritability of long hair has decreased. However, neither in 1950 nor today is wearing long hair genetically determined in the normal sense. Men did not usually wear long hair in the 1950 due to strong social pressures to conform (i.e., environmental reasons); when the environmental reasons change, so too does the heritability of the trait. While this example may seem frivolous, the point it makes is very important to how we interpret heritability. The student of developmental psychology needs to remember that heritability does not necessarily imply genetic causation.

Research designs in behaviour genetics
Most commonly, heritability is estimated using **twin studies**. In one common twin study design, the correlation on some trait (for example, intel-ligence) is measured between pairs of **monozygotic twins** and **dizygotic twins**. Monozygotic twins are born of the same fertilized egg, a zygote which has split in half, and thus they share 100 percent of their genes. Dizygotic, or fraternal twins, develop in the womb at the same time but are of two different fertilized eggs, and, as a consequence, they share only 50 percent of their genes. If one makes the assumption that the environments of identical twins

are no different than the environments of fraternal twins, then higher correlations for the trait between identical twins is thought to be the result of their genetic similarity. It is important to note that this conclusion is based on an assumption of *equal environments* between identical and fraternal twins. Bronfenbrenner (1972) highlighted the reasons why this assumption is problematic. Think for yourself about this issue. Do you think identical twins might be treated differently from fraternal twins in some way? If you bring to mind issues such as parents dressing twins exactly alike or friends and relatives confusing identical twins then you have identified some of the factors that Bronfenbrenner felt might be problematic for the twin design, and which violate the equal environments assumption. Again, while such problems pose issues for how exactly we interpret the findings of behaviour genetic research, they by no means suggest that genetic factors are unimportant determinants of human development.

A large number of behaviour genetic studies have been conducted to examine the heritability of intelligence. A review of many of these studies by Bouchard and McGue (1981) showed that the average correlation between same sex pairs of monozygotic twins measured for general intelligence was 0.86. A correlation of 0.62 was obtained for fraternal twins. Both of these results indicate a substantial effect for genetic factors (although keep in mind the potential interpretative problems discussed earlier). When Bouchard and McGue examined the findings for twins reared apart, the correlation dropped to 0.72, again, indicating a substantial role for genetic factors. Further work on the importance of genetic factors across the life span has come to the intriguing conclusion that genetic factors become more salient to explaining the correlations between the IQ scores of twins as time goes on. In other words, as age increases so does the correlation for general intelligence between twins (DeFries, Plomin & Fulker, 1994; Plomin, Pedersen, Lichtenstein, & McClearn, 1994; Plomin et al., 1997). As many of these researchers would note, the findings described, while indicating a substantial role for genetic factors in the development of general intelligence, also indicate the importance of environmental factors in determining intelligence.

Finally, we briefly consider genetic effects on personality. Behaviour genetic research in the area of personality has suggested that as much as 50 percent of the personality differences between people are due to genetic factors (Bouchard, 1994). Loehlin (1992) reported evidence of significant genetic effects on two commonly measured aspects of personality: *neuroticism* (emotional instability) and *extraversion* (sociability). Intraclass correlations for identical twins reared together were around 0.50 for both traits, suggesting a strong link between genetics and personality. Another trait known as *sensation seeking*, which is comprised of behaviours such as thrill seeking, searching out novel experiences, and susceptibility to boredom, showed a correlation of 0.54

in a sample of identical twins reared apart. Plomin et al. (1997) suggest that there is also strong evidence that a variety of personality disorders such as schizotypal, obsessive-compulsive, and borderline personality disorder are all at least partially heritable.

SUMMARY

Acquiring an understanding of the maturation of our bodies, our brain and central nervous system, and the importance of genetic factors to our development is the foundation for understanding other key areas of child development such as perception, cognition, and emotion. While the study of our biology is important in its own right, it is also tied to development in these other domains, and it is necessary to examine this at an early point in our study of children.

Glossary

Active effects are genetic effects which occur when children begin to seek out environments compatible with their genetic makeup. For example, athletically gifted children may seek out athletic environments.

Allele refers to the alternate form of a gene.

Association areas refers to two parts of the brain, the **anterior association** area (located at the front of the brain) and **posterior association area** (located near the rear of the brain) that are involved in linking up information from various parts of the brain.

Axon refers to the part of the neuron which ends in the terminal buttons.

Behaviour genetics is the area of inquiry examining the relationship between genetic and environmental factors in development.

Cell body is the body of the neuron which contains the nucleus and other structures.

Cephalocaudal development refers to the idea that physical growth occurs in a head to toe direction.

Cerebral cortex is the outer layer of cells which covers the cerebrum. It is also the most advanced part of the brain, supporting complex functions such as language, vision, and motor skills.

Cerebrum refers to the two interconnected hemispheres, or halves of the brain.

Chromosomes are a very special chemical structure, found in the nucleus of a cell, which is made up of a series of proteins known as deoxyribonucleic acid or DNA.

Codominance occurs when heterozygous alleles both express their traits with equal force.

Corpus callosum is the bundle of fibres which connects the two hemispheres, or halves of the brain.

Dendrites are the part of the neuron which receives signals from other neurons, and which transmits this information to the cell body.

Differentiation refers to the fact that, initially, motor skills are rather global reactions to a particular stimulus, and only become more precise and adapted to particular ends with time.

Directed reaching describes reaching which has become more coordinated, efficient, and has improved in accuracy.

Dizygotic twins are twins which are born at the same time but which develop from separate fertilized ova.

Dominance refers to the fact that one allele for a trait is more powerful or dominant than another and will always express its effects over those of another allele.

Evocative effects occur when children's traits cause others in their environment to behave towards them in a particular way. For example, temperamentally easy babies may elicit higher levels of social interactions from others which strengthens their disposition to engage in and enjoy social interaction.

Experience-dependent development is a process which describes how the growth of some types of neural circuits are strongly influenced by the types of environmental input they receive.

Experience-expectant development is a process which describes how some neural circuits require input from the environment in order to begin growing.

Fine motor development refers to small movement sequences like reaching and grasping.

Gametes are the specialized sex cells from males and females (sperm and ovum) which combine to form a new life. Each gamete contains only 23 chromosomes, half the number of a regular cell.

Genes are the units of hereditary transmission. A gene refers to a portion of DNA located at a particular site on the chromosome.

Genotype is our genetic makeup, that is, the particular set of genes which we have inherited from our parents.

Glial cells are the cells which provide structural support to the neurons.

Gross motor development refers to the various motor skills such as crawling and walking which help children to move around in their environment.

Hemispheric specialization refers to the differential functions carried out by the two cerebral hemispheres. Hemispheric specialization begins at birth and the differences between the two hemispheres remain largely the same into adulthood.

Heritability is an estimated measure of the effects of the relative effect of genetic factors on a trait.

Heterozygous a child is said to be heterozygous for a trait coded for by the gene if both forms of the gene are different.

Homozygous a child is said to be homozygous for a trait coded for by the gene if both forms of the gene are alike.

Hormones are a set of chemical substances manufactured by glands, which, received by specialized receptor cells throughout the body, can trigger other chemical changes.

Invariance hypothesis the hypothesis which proposes that the functions attributed to the two hemispheres of the brain remain constant, or invariant, across the lifespan.

Lateralization is the term used to describe the processes by which the two halves of the brain become specialized to carry out specific functions.

Lobes the cerebral cortex is divided into four main areas called **lobes** and two other areas known as the **association areas**. The four lobes of the brains are called the **frontal lobe**, **temporal lobe**, **parietal lobe**, and the **occipital lobe**.

Menarche refers to the onset of menstruation.

Monozygotic twins are often called 'identical twins'. Refers to twins who are born of the same fertilized egg. This occurs when a zygote splits into two clusters of cells which develop into two genetically identical individuals.

Myelination is a process in which neurons are covered with an insulating layer of *myelin*, a fatty substance which makes the neuron a more effective transmitter of electrical information.

Neuronal death is a process in which some neurons are programmed to die, apparently to provide more space for crucial cell clusters.

Neurons are the name given to the nerve cells which send and receive neural impulses (electrical signals) throughout the brain and the nervous system.

Neurotransmitters are a special class of chemicals which are released across the synapse by the terminal buttons.

Niche picking is an active process whereby one's genetic predisposition leads one to arrange the environment to suit one's dispositions.

Oestrogens are hormones that are associated with female sexual maturation.

Ovum is the female germ cell which unites with a male's sperm at conception.

Passive effects occur when parents structure the child's environment in ways which are consistent with genetic traits shared by parents and child. For example, musical parents may provide a musical environment for their children which may lead to the expression of genes which code for musical talent.

Phenotype refers to the observable characteristics of an organism, created by the interaction of the genotype with the environment.

Phenylketonuria (**PKU**) is a genetic disorder in which the child is unable to metabolize a protein called phenylalanine which can lead to brain damage and mental retardation.

Pincer grasp refers to a grasp where infants use their index finger and their thumb in an opposable manner, resulting in a more coordinated, and finely tuned grip.

Pituitary gland is a gland located near the base of the brain which (1) triggers physical growth by releasing hormones, and (2) controls other hormone-releasing glands via its chemical secretions.

Polygenetic inheritance is said to occur when some trait is affected by more than one gene.

Prereaching is a behaviour wherein newborn infants seated in an upright position will swipe and reach towards an object placed in front of them.

Primary sexual characteristics refer to the reproductive organs: the penis, scrotum, and testes in males, and the vagina, uterus, and ovaries in females.

Proprioception is the sensation of movement and location based on stimulation arising from bodily sources such as muscle contractions.

Proximodistal development refers to the idea that physical growth occurs outwards from the centre of the body towards the hands and feet.

Range of reaction refers to the fact that genes do not fix behaviour in a rigid fashion, but establish a range of possibilities which depend heavily on the environment.

Recessive refers to the weaker of the two alleles.

Secondary sexual characteristics refer to the visible changes which are associated with sexual maturation such as the development of breasts in females, facial hair in males, and pubic hair for both sexes.

Sperm is the male germ cell which unites with a female's ovum at conception.

Spermarche refers to the first ejaculation in males.

Synapse is the gap between the terminal buttons of one neuron and the dendrites of another neuron.

Synaptic pruning is a process in which the brain disposes of a neuron's connections to other neurons.

Terminal buttons are the ends of a neuron which release neurotransmitters across the synapse to be received by other neurons.

Testosterone is a male hormone which is responsible for the production of sperm and for the development of primary and secondary sexual characteristics.

Thinning is the process by which the brain reduces the number of neurons and synaptic connections between neurons in early development including neuronal death and synaptic pruning.

Twin studies refers to a class of research designs that employ twins as research subjects. These designs are often used to tease apart the genetic and environmental effects on a particular trait.

Ulnar grasp is a primitive form of grasping in which the infant's fingers close against their palm.

Zygote is a fertilized egg, created by the union of a sperm and an ovum. Refers to the first two weeks of life.

This chapter is taken from:
Keenan, T. (2002) *An Introduction to Child Development*
978-0-7619-6220-5

3 Emotional Development

THOMAS KEENAN

LEARNING AIMS

At the end of this chapter you should:

- be able to describe the developmental course of emotion expression, emotion understanding, and emotion regulation
- be able to explain key concepts such as *social referencing*, *basic emotions*, and *emotional display rules*
- be able to describe the important aspects of attachment theory, know the four phases of attachment, and be able to describe the differences between securely and insecurely attached children
- understand and be able to define the concept of temperament and key concepts such as *goodness of fit*
- be able to comment on evidence for and against the stability of temperament

Introduction

Emotions are one of the most salient aspects of our experiences and it is not surprising that the study of emotion has captured the attention of developmental researchers of nearly all theoretical persuasions. Emotions play an extremely important role in our behaviour, a role of which psychologists have only recently become aware. The study of emotion has recently been undergoing a series of dramatic changes (Saarni, Mumme, & Campos, 1998). While there are a variety of theoretical perspectives that guide the study of emotion, the most important theory to emerge is the **functionalist** approach. Functionalist theories stress that emotions are adaptive processes which organize functioning in a variety of domains of human development including the social, cognitive, and perceptual (Barrett & Campos, 1987; Campos, Barrett, Lamb, Goldsmith & Stenberg, 1983). While emotions may interfere with or undermine an individual's functioning, emotion can also guide and motivate adaptive processes (Thompson, 1991). In most current work on emotional development, emotion is viewed as a regulator of both social and cognitive behaviour.

Taking a functionalist approach in their review of the study of emotional development, Saarni et al. (1998: 238) defined emotion as: 'the person's readiness to establish, maintain, or change the relation between the person and the environment on matters of significance to that person'. The authors note that this definition may strike the reader as odd because of its lack of emphasis on what are seen as the traditional components of emotion such as internal states, feelings, and facial expressions. Instead of focusing on these aspects of emotion, functionalist theories emphasize the relevance of emotions to a person's goals, the close ties between emotion and actions, and the consequences of emotional states. In the following review of emotional development, functionalist views on emotion dominate much of the research.

The development of emotional expressions

Early emotions

A number of researchers have argued through the years that infants are born with a set of readily observable and discrete emotions. The belief that infants enter into the world with the ability to experience and communicate a set of emotions within the first few weeks of life is a belief in the presence of a set of **basic emotions**. The basic emotions which most psychologists seem to agree on are *disgust, happiness, fear, anger, sadness, interest*, and *surprise* (Campos et al., 1983). The evidence for basic emotions is the presence of facial expressions corresponding to the hypothesized emotional states, and, somewhat later, the correspondence between facial expressions, gaze, tone of voice, and the relation between emotions and situations. The argument for the presence of basic emotions is controversial, but most psychologists would agree that by 6 months of age, most of these emotions have made their appearance (e.g., Izard, 1994; Sroufe, 1996). According to Izard (1994; Izard & Malatesta, 1987), the first emotional expressions to appear in the infant's repertoire are *startled, disgust*, and *distress*. Around the third month, infants begin to display facial expressions of *anger, interest, surprise*, and *sadness. Fear* develops at around 7 months of age (Camras, Malatesta, & Izard, 1991). Sroufe (1996) has described a developmental progression of emotional expression which is very similar to that proposed by Izard and his colleagues. Let us briefly consider the development of some emotions appearing early in infancy.

Expressions of happiness are often observed when infants master a new problem or develop a new skill. They also have the positive effect of creating stronger ties between the infant and other people. *Smiles* and *laughter* generate similar responses in the caregiver, creating feelings of warmth and increasing the strength of the bond between parent and infant. Initially, an infant's smiles do not occur in reaction to external stimulation. In fact, very young infants will often smile mysteriously in their sleep. However, by 6 to 10 weeks of age, infants smile in response to social exchanges, such as smiling human faces, and to interesting events that capture their attention. By 3 months of age, an infant's smiles are elicited most often by a responsive person who interacts contingently with the infant (Ellsworth, Muir & Hains, 1993). In the first 6 months of infancy, repeated exposure to a stimulus may be required to generate a smile or other positive response, but after 6 months, emotional reactions are more immediate (Camras, Oster, Campos, Miyake, & Bradshaw, 1992; Sroufe, 1996). Laughter appears first around 3 to 4 months of age and reflects the infant's increased cognitive ability to perceive discrepancies, such as changes from their normal experience, for example, daddy talking in a funny voice or making a face (Sroufe & Wunsch, 1972). By the beginning of their first year and throughout their second year, infants laugh increasingly in response to their own activities and actions; by the preschool years, laughter becomes more and more of a social event, occurring in the presence of others.

Of course, the infant's emotional expressions are not all positive. In the first 6 months expressions of *anger* and *fear* are evident in the infant's emotional repertoire. Perhaps the most salient of these expressions (much to the chagrin of many parents) is the fear aroused in an infant by strangers. Through their interactions with the world, infants naturally start to differentiate the familiar from the unfamiliar and as a result, infants' reactions to unfamiliar people change over time. Whereas a 3-month-old will smile indiscriminately at strangers and parents alike, by 4 months of age infants begin to smile preferentially at caregivers and show some *wariness* to unfamiliar people (Sroufe, 1996). However, somewhere in between the age of 7 to 9 months, infants begin to show a genuine fear of strangers, what has been termed **stranger distress** (Sroufe, 1996). Typically, stranger distress lasts for 2 to 3 months and may continue into their second year (Emde, Gaensbauer, & Harmon, 1976; Waters, Matas, & Sroufe, 1975). Stranger distress has all the aspects of a true fear reaction including crying and whimpering, avoidance reactions such as pulling away from the stranger, and a general wariness of the stranger. As Sroufe et al. (1974) point out, it is not simply *novelty* which engenders stranger distress from an infant, as mothers can perform novel actions (such as approaching the infant while wearing a mask) which do not upset them. Contextual factors such as whether the infant meets the stranger in their own home or in unfamiliar surroundings make an important difference to whether or not distress is elicited (Sroufe et al., 1974). The characteristics of the stranger also play an important role in eliciting distress: infants are less afraid of young children than they are of adults (Lewis & Brooks, 1974) and infants react poorly to strangers who are sober and quiet as opposed to strangers who smile, gesture, and interact in an active, friendly manner. Importantly, each of these points shows that infants react not simply to the occurrence of an event but, rather, on the basis of its meaning; that is, they evaluate situations and appraise the threats they pose.

Emotional development beyond infancy

The development of emotional expression clearly extends beyond infancy and in fact, continues well into adolescence. Emotions such as shame, guilt, pride, and envy are first seen in toddlers (Campos et al., 1983). These developments seem to go hand in hand with developments in their cognitive abilities. Of course, many changes in emotional expression have little to do with cognitive changes but instead, reflect the **socialization** attempts of people in the child's life such as parents, siblings, peers, and others. Work on mother–infant interactions has shown that mothers selectively reinforce their infant's emotional expressions, rewarding expressions of positive affect and not responding to negative expressions (Malatesta & Haviland, 1982). They also shape emotional expressions differently for boys and girls. Mothers tend to reinforce a wider range of emotional expression in female infants than they do in male infants (Malatesta & Haviland, 1985). Socialization is also carried out by the wider culture in which the child is raised. Different cultures have varying standards for the appropriate expression of emotion and thus, we find large differences in emotion socialization across cultures (Gordon, 1989). Emotion socialization is a powerful means of shaping the growing child's emotional expressions and adults use a wide variety of means to accomplish this.

As we will discuss later in this chapter, one of the child's major challenges with respect to emotional development is the process of learning how to control their emotional expression and experience (Saarni, 1990). Much of the early development in the control of emotion is due to adults' attempts at emotion socialization in children. During the preschool years, children begin to learn to control their emotional expressions, adopting these to fit with what is expected of them. In essence, children learn a series of 'rules' about emotional expression, what we call **emotional display rules**. Simply put, these are rules which dictate which emotions are appropriate to express in a given circumstance (Saarni et al., 1998). For example, toddlers learn to substitute one emotional expression (e.g., pouting) for another more appropriate expression (e.g., crying). Later on, children gain a deeper understanding of display rules as they come to learn the social norms of their culture. They come to understand situations where it is inappropriate to laugh or to cry. Moreover, they learn to feign a variety of emotional expressions to accomplish certain ends, such as deceiving a sibling. In summary, learning to follow display rules is an important accomplishment for the developing child.

As we have seen, early on children put display rules into use but they have little understanding of the gap between what they feel and what they actually express (Harris, 1989). Somewhat later, children learn to separate their true feelings from the emotions they express. In one study, Gross and Harris (1988) showed that 6-year-olds were able to distinguish between how a story character would look and how that same character would really feel. In contrast, 4-year-olds were unable to make this distinction, conflating how the character would really feel with how they looked. In other words, the children failed to distinguish between real and apparent emotions. These data support Harris's conclusion that preschool children can employ display rules but have little understanding of them.

The development of emotional understanding

Using emotional information: social referencing

It is not only the range of emotional expressions that infants are capable of expressing which develops throughout infancy and early childhood, but also their *understanding* of emotion. One of the first examples of a developing understanding of emotion is a phenomenon which has been labelled **social referencing** (see Table 8.1). Social referencing, simply put, is the use of another's emotional expressions as a source of information, allowing a person to interpret events or situations that are either ambiguous or too difficult to grasp (Sorce, Emde, Campos, & Klinnert, 1985). Before we explore this phenomenon in infants and young children, think about your own experience with respect to social referencing. Many people have found themselves in a situation where, for example, someone makes what appears to be a joke, and you are not sure whether laughter is appropriate. What do you do? One common strategy is to look to other people's behaviour. Are they laughing or smiling? Other people's emotional expressions can provide us with a valuable source of information for making sense of such situations, and deciding on the appropriate course of behaviour. Recall our discussion of functionalism for a moment; one of the important functions of emotion is their ability to serve as a signalling system about our own and other peoples' internal states. Social referencing exploits this fact about emotion.

Social referencing is first observed at about 12 months of age. One tool used to study how infants employ social referencing is the experimental paradigm known as the visual cliff (see Chapter 5). In this work by Sorce et al. (1985), 12-month-old infants were placed at the top of the visual cliff, on the shallow side of the apparatus. Infants' mothers stood on the opposite side of the cliff and were asked to pose either *happy* or *frightened* emotional expressions at the time when their infants approached the edge of the cliff (remember, the

TABLE 8.1 Milestones in the development of emotional expression and understanding

Age	Emotional expressions	Emotional understanding
0 to 3 months	Startle, disgust, distress, the social smile	
3 to 6 months	Laughter, anger, interest, surprise, sadness	
7 months	Fear	
7 to 9 months	Stranger distress	
12 months		Social referencing
18 to 24 months	Shame, pride	
2 to 3 years	Envy, guilt, embarrassment	
3 to 5 years		Emotional display rules
6 to 8 years		Awareness that two emotions can occur in sequence
9 years and beyond		Awareness that emotions of the same valence can occur simultaneously
11 years		Awareness that one event can elicit a range of feelings

cliff is covered by plexiglass so infants are in no actual danger). The results of the study showed an effect of the emotional expression: when mothers posed happy expressions, most of the infants crossed the cliff. In contrast, when mothers posed frightened expressions, most infants refused to cross. Other studies have shown that mothers' facial expressions can affect how their infants react to new toys or to new people (Klinnert, Emde, Butterfield, & Campos, 1986). Recent research by Ruffman (2000) has demonstrated that young children continue to use emotional information in their understanding of social situations.

The development of complex emotions

Of course, emotions continue to develop after infancy. Another development in the nature of the emotions that we experience is the appearance of what are sometimes called the **self-conscious** emotions (Barrett, 1997; Campos et al., 1983; Lewis, Sullivan, Stanger, & Weiss, 1989). This term is used to describe emotions such as *guilt, shame, envy, embarrassment*, and *pride*, emotions which typically emerge in the second half of the second year. What makes these emotions different from others such as anger or happiness is that they emerge out of the child's developing sense of self-awareness, that is, their sense of having a unique self which is different from the world around them. Moreover, they require the child to consider multiple factors which may influence a given situation, for example, integrating or differentiating more than one perspective. This can be made clear by considering a specific example of a self-conscious emotion – embarrassment. Think of what goes on when you are embarrassed: typically you feel embarrassed when you have done something which you think others may judge to be silly, wrong, or at a level which does not suit you. You evaluate your behaviour against a social standard or a perceived point of view and find your behaviour wanting in some way. Other self-conscious emotions such as envy occur when the child evaluates themselves against particular others. Pride occurs when children feel good about their accomplishments, comparing their performance to specific others or to perceived standards. The developing understanding of emotions such as pride also goes hand in hand with cognitive development in other areas. Children's conceptions of pride, for example, are closely tied to their ability to evaluate the difficulty of an activity. By 3 years of age, children know that they are more likely to feel pride if they solve a difficult task as opposed to an easy task (Lewis, Alessandri & Sullivan, 1992).

Understanding multiple emotions

Throughout childhood and into early adolescence, children gradually become aware that people can experience multiple emotions at the same time (Harter & Buddin, 1987; Wintre & Vallance, 1994). Whereas toddlers and young children clearly *experience* conflicting emotions or blends of emotions, the ability to *understand* these multiple emotions in one's self and others lags well behind. According to Harter and Buddin (1987), there are five stages in the development of multiple emotions. Between 4 to 6 years of age, children can conceive of a person holding only one emotion at a time. They can imagine situations that will arouse one emotion but see it as impossible to provoke two simultaneous emotions. From about 6 to 8 years of age, children begin to grasp that people can hold two emotions, but see these as occurring in sequence rather than simultaneously. Around 8 to 9 years of age, children can describe another as holding two different emotions simultaneously as long as they are of the same valence (e.g., 'If she hit me I'd be *angry* and *upset*') or if they arise in response to two different situations (e.g., 'I would be happy if I did well but proud if I won'). At age 10, children start describing opposing feelings in response to different aspects of a single situation and finally, by age 11, children are able to understand that a single event can cause very different sets of feelings. Harter and Buddin's work shows a clear developmental progression in the complexity of children's emotional understanding, the development of which is not complete until early adolescence.

Emotion scripts

As we have seen, children's understanding of emotional experience undergoes significant developments between infancy and adolescence. Similar developments are observed in the meaning of emotion-specific words and the typical situations that evoke these emotions. This development can be viewed as the child's acquisition of emotion-specific knowledge which takes the form of **scripts** (Lewis, 1989), that is, knowledge of what kinds of emotions a particular event or situation might arouse. Research by Borke (1971) showed that even 3- to 4-year-old children were able to match possible emotional reactions (using depictions of facial expressions printed on cards) to particular stories about events such as a birthday party or an argument. Children can also work backwards, specifying the types of situations that might arouse particular emotions such as *happiness, surprise,* or *anger* (Trabasso, Stein & Johnson, 1981). Of course, as they mature, children's emotional scripts increase in complexity (Harris, 1989) to the point where eventually adolescents are able to attribute emotions to others even when there are no obvious behavioural manifestations such as facial expressions.

Children also learn that emotions are intimately tied to a person's *desires, intentions,* and *beliefs* (Harris, 1989). For example, in a study by Harris and his colleagues (Harris, Johnson, Hutton, Andrews & Cook, 1989) 4- and 6-year-old children watched as the investigator acted out a story with two puppets. For example, in one story, they are shown a puppet called Ellie the Elephant with a carton of milk and are told that Ellie only likes to drink milk. While Ellie is temporarily absent, another puppet, Mickey the Monkey comes along and pours Ellie's milk out and fills the carton with a orange juice. Children at both ages were accurate at predicting how Ellie would feel when she took a drink and found juice. However, when children were asked to state how Ellie would feel *before* she took a drink, 4-year-olds failed to take Ellie's mistaken belief into account and predicted she would be sad on being presented with the deceptive milk carton. Only by age 6 were children able to take Ellie's mistaken belief into account, recognizing that she would feel happy on seeing the milk carton because she was unaware of the true contents. Harris (1989) argues that understanding and predicting another's emotions requires the child to do more than simply acquire script-like knowledge; they must also view emotions as psychological states which depend on a consideration of their desires and beliefs. More recent work by Ruffman and Keenan (1996) has examined children's understanding of *surprise* and has confirmed that the ability to predict and understand the conditions under which another will be surprised follows a similar developmental course to that described by Harris.

Emotion regulation

Recall that, in functionalist accounts of emotional development, emotions have the potential to organize or to disrupt functioning. The extent to which emotions can organize or interfere with functioning on a given task is, to a large extent, governed by the individual's capacity to *regulate* their emotions. The disruptive effects of a negative affect such as *anxiety* on cognitive perform- ance has been well documented. You can probably recall a time when anxiety has interfered with your ability to think clearly about a problem, for example, during an exam. However, positive emotions can have similar effects. Try and recall a time when excitement has led to someone you know behaving in unacceptable ways, for example, the child who gets too excited on Christmas morning and cannot sleep. Clearly, emotions, both positive and negative, need to be maintained within certain limits. **Emotion regulation**, the processes by which an individual's emotional arousal is maintained within their capacity to cope is defined by Thompson (1991: 271) as 'the extrinsic and intrinsic processes responsible for monitoring, evaluating, and modifying emotional reactions, especially their intensive and temporal features'. Thompson argues that the study of emotion regulation is critical to an understanding of emo- tional development in that it provides a window into the growth of personality and social functioning. Let's examine Thompson's definition of emotion regulation as well as its development throughout childhood.

One key aspect of this definition is the inclusion of a role for both **extrinsic** and **intrinsic** processes of emotion regulation. By intrinsic pro- cesses, Thompson refers to the developments within the individual which allow for the regulation of emotion. Developments in the nervous system and brain, changes in cognitive abilities, and the growth of linguistic skill are all examples of intrinsic processes which promote emotion regulation. In con- trast, extrinsic processes refer to those processes which stem from outside the individual and which serve the goal of regulating emotion. The soothing and comforting provided to an infant in distress by its parents, the chance to talk about one's feelings to a close friend, or the cultural prescriptions for how one should feel in a given situation are examples of extrinsic processes by which emotion is regulated. As Thompson (1991) notes, the extrinsic regulation of emotion continues throughout the life span, but is most prevalent during infancy. Infants are initially highly dependent on their caregivers to regulate their emotions but become increasingly able to take over the regulation of their affect.

At birth, the nervous system is far from mature. Therefore, the ability to exert control over the emotional processes is still immature. Two processes are particularly important in developing emotional control. The ability to regulate emotion via the parasympathetic nervous system (Porges, 1991) is one such process. These changes, which occur primarily in the first year of life, allow the infant to gain some control over its feelings, responding in degrees rather than in an 'all or none' fashion (Thompson, 1991). The second change occurs in inhibitory controls over emotional responding. Inhibitory development allows for the suppression or modulation of an emotional response. These developments rely on maturational changes in the cortex and the frontal lobes of the brain. Both developments allow for the infant to tolerate a greater degree of stimulation and to regulate their degree of responding to a particular event or interaction, for example, suppressing a desire to cry or changing the tone of a cry to attract the caregiver's attention.

Changes in the child's cognitive functioning also lead to new developments in the ability to modulate emotional processes. The development of the child's representational abilities, occurring during the preschool years, allows them to evoke memories in order to alter emotional responses. For example, the child experiencing separation anxiety when briefly removed from their caregiver can think about the caregiver in order to soothe themselves and reduce their anxiety (Miller & Green, 1985; Thompson, 1990). Older children can use their cognitive processes in even more sophisticated ways. Whereas preschool children understand that their emotions can be altered by simply avoiding thinking about something, by redirecting their thought processes, or by refocusing their attention, older children understand that a situation or event which makes them feel a particular way can be reframed and thought about in an entirely different way (Band & Weisz, 1988). Thus, older children learn that they can choose to reinterpret a situation as a method to alter their feelings.

Changes in language ability also play an important role in emotion regulation. Language allows us to conceptualize and convey our emotional experiences to others. As a consequence of this, we can encourage extrinsic forms of regulation by discussing our feelings with others. Verbal interactions around emotion can effect changes in emotion regulation in several ways (Thompson, 1991). First, parents can direct their children's regulatory processes through commands (e.g., 'don't get so excited', or 'please stop crying'). Second, parent–child talk about emotion can also suggest to the child new ways of thinking about their feelings allowing them to better manage them. Finally, parents can suggest emotion regulation strategies directly to the child, such as getting them to think about a comfortable image, to rethink their goals, or to engage in some sort of self-soothing behaviour.

By adolescence, the developments in self-understanding which have occurred lay the groundwork for the development of what Thompson (1991) referred to as a **theory of personal emotion**. A theory of personal emotion is essentially a coherent network of beliefs about one's own emotional processes. For example, an adolescent may recognize that they naturally shy away from social interaction and realize that in order to be accepted by their peers, they need to find ways in which to overcome this tendency, such as expressing more positive affect to others, and making a conscious effort to smile and make eye contact. In middle childhood, children begin to appreciate the fact that their emotional experiences may differ from those of others, they start to acquire general knowledge about their own emotional processes, such as the particular idiosyncrasies that may characterize their own emotional experiences. In addition, as they grow children acquire more refined knowledge about coping strategies, and, more specifically, which coping strategies work best for them depending on the situation. However, it is during adolescence that the theory of personal emotion acquires its coherence. As adolescents develop a progressively more complex network of self-referential beliefs, their theory of personal emotion is incorporated into their conception of themselves.

The development of attachment

Bowlby's theory of attachment
Like the young of many species, human infants are relatively helpless at birth, and for the first few months thereafter. We are born with very limited sensory abilities, little in the way of physical motor skills, and few cognitive abilities. This fact means that human infants are vulnerable at birth, and for sometime thereafter. While it is unlikely that in these modern times an infant is likely to be carried off by a predator, our situation was not always so secure. During one point in our evolutionary history, conditions were such that this threat was a very real one. Thus, it is not surprising that we have developed behaviours which help us to adapt to such conditions.

The study of bonding between parents and infants owes much to the pioneering work of John Bowlby (1958, 1960). Bowlby formulated a theory of the relationship between the caregiver and the infant – what he called an **attachment relationship** – drawing largely from work in psychoanalytic theory, ethological theory, and work in cognitive and developmental psychology (Ainsworth et al., 1978). Attachment theory focuses on both the processes which lead to the bonding of parents and children, and the impact of this relationship on psychological development. Furthermore, attachment theory focuses our attention on the development of affectional ties between the caregiver and infant, and on the behaviours and cognitive structures by which these ties are maintained over time.

In contrast to Sigmund Freud who believed that an infant's affectional tie to his caregiver was developed on the basis of being fed by the caregiver, Bowlby believed that selection pressures acting over the course of human evolution led to infants having an innate set of behaviours which caused them to seek an appropriate level of *proximity* to the caregiver. Proximity refers to the physical distance between the infant and the caregiver. By staying close to a caregiver who can protect them against dangers such as predators, an infant has a better chance of survival. Thus, these behaviours are passed on from generation to generation. Human infants also come equipped with a communicative system of cries and facial expressions which allows them to signal for the caregiver to increase their proximity. In other words, we can initiate proximity through means such as crying or smiling. Bowlby argued that both affectional ties and the behaviours that promote proximity to one's caregiver have an evolutionary basis (Campos et al., 1983) in that they are unlearned and instinctive, that is, part of our biological heritage.

Of course, the effectiveness of the infant's communicative signals depends on the ability of the adult to receive and interpret them, thus, human adults must also have a complementary system by which to interpret these signals (e.g., Frodi & Lamb, 1978). Attachment is a two-way process, a relationship between two people; it is *not* simply a set of learned behaviours emitted by infants or adults (Ainsworth et al., 1978; Sroufe, 1996). The effectiveness of the infant's signals depends on the ability to the caregiver to understand and react appropriately to them. In an important way, attachment theory extends the study of emotional development into the social realm, breaking down traditional barriers that focus solely on the individual as opposed to the individual as situated in relationships with other people.

Bowlby's attachment theory was also influenced by work in control systems theory (Ainsworth et al., 1978). According to control systems theory, behaviours which serve a common function are grouped together with the purpose of achieving a particular goal. The behaviours are activated to achieve the goal of the system; if the goal changes, the behaviours are altered to achieve the new goal. Consider the example of an infant that is placed in an unfamiliar room. Given the unfamiliar surroundings, the initial goal of the control system will be to maintain proximity to the caregiver. After some time, as the infant begins to feel comfortable, the goal of the system is altered and the need to maintain proximity is relaxed, freeing the infant to move about and explore. This move away from the mother may be interrupted by the entrance of a stranger. If the infant interprets the stranger as threatening, the need for proximity will be reasserted and the infant will seek out the caregiver. If the infant feels secure with the stranger, exploration will continue and no increase in proximity will be called for.

Another major contributor to attachment theory, Mary Ainsworth (1973), noted that infants use adults both as a **safe haven** and as a **secure base**; that is, infants organize their attachment behaviours so that they use the adult as a refuge and source of comfort when they are distressed but also as a safe vantage point from which to explore their environment. One of Ainsworth's major contributions to attachment theory was the study of how infants' secure base behaviour can be used to inform us about the quality of an infant's attachment relationship with its caregiver, a topic explored in the next section.

Much of the research in attachment focuses on the attachment between mothers and infants. However, Bowlby recognized that infants form attachments to other people as well. Infants form attachment relationships with fathers, grandparents, siblings, and peers, among others (Lamb, 1981; Lewis, 1987; Schaffer, 1996). These attachments differ in important ways across individuals, yet at the same time, Bowlby argued that the nature of the infant's attachment to its primary caregiver has a profound effect on its other relationships. Bowlby claimed that this influence is exerted by the development of what has been called an **internal working model** (Bowlby, 1973). An internal working model is a mental representation or 'mental model' of the infant's experiences with their primary attachment figure. Internal working models are relatively stable over time, however, Bowlby chose the term *working model* to highlight that they are updated on the basis of experience. Importantly, internal working models serve to combine cognitive representations of the infant's relationship with their caregiver with an affective component, that is, how the infant *feels* about the attachment relationship. Bowlby believed that the child's attachment relationship with their primary caregiver influenced all of the child's subsequent relationships. A child who is not securely attached to their primary caregiver is more likely to have difficulty in forming and maintaining other relationships.

The development of the attachment relationship

Attachment relationships do not occur suddenly but, instead, emerge gradually throughout the first 2 years of life. There are four phases in the development of attachment (Ainsworth et al., 1978; Schaffer, 1996). Initially, infants show little preference for particular others; their social behaviours are indiscriminately directed towards others. This phase, called *preattachment*, encompasses the first two months of the life span. In the second phase, *attachment-in-the-making*, which runs from 2 to 7 months of age, infants begin to discriminate familiar from unfamiliar people and show a distinct preference for the attachment figure. At about 7 months of age, the third phase, *clear-cut attachment*, begins. At this time, infants develop marked attachments to particular people with whom they have regular contact, such as their mother and father, grandparents, and daycare workers. Infants actively seek out these people and often protest or are upset when they leave. The final phase of attachment, which begins at 2 years of age, is called a *goal-corrected partnership*. In this phase, the child begins to take into account the feelings and plans of the attachment figure when planning their own actions. The responsibility for the attachment relationship begins to shift from the mother to the child as the child develops the ability to communicate their thoughts and feelings through language. The child has truly become a partner in maintaining the relationship between themselves and their caregiver. At this final phase, the attachment relationship between caregiver and child has reached a new level of sophistication (Ainsworth et al., 1978).

Quality of attachment and the strange situation

Ideally, the attachment relationship serves as a source of affection and nurturance. The attachment relationship allows the infant to feel confident and secure while exploring and learning about the world. Ainsworth was among the first to highlight the importance of parenting in fostering the development of a secure attachment in children (Ainsworth, Bell and Stayton, 1974). The caregivers of securely attached infants usually show a high degree of **sensitivity**. That is, these parents are generally responsive to their infant's needs and engage in consistent patterns of behaviour (Cassidy & Berlin, 1994). Their caregiving allows the infant to play a role in these daily inter-actions. Ainsworth et al. (1978) argued that when mothers are *insensitive* to their infant's needs, either by being overly *intrusive* or by *neglecting* them, the infant can develop an **insecure attachment**. Insecure attachments are attachment relationships that fail to provide the infant with a sense of confidence and security. Interestingly, the suggestion has been made that the various forms of insecure attachment may actually be *adaptive* solutions for these infants, in that they allow the infant to make sense of a difficult relationship (e.g., Cassidy, 1994; Main & Solomon, 1990). For example, an avoidant attachment relationship helps to minimize the importance of the caregiver for the infant and allows the infant to avoid the negative affect associated with being rejected or neglected by their caregiver.

The quality of an infant's attachment to its caregiver can be measured using a testing paradigm known as the **strange situation** (Ainsworth et al., 1978; Waters, Vaughn, Posada, & Kondo-Ikemura, 1995). Briefly, in the strange situation, the infant is separated from its mother, exposed to a stranger, and then reunited with the mother. The use of the strange situation allows the experimenter to examine differences in attachment behaviour which differ as a function of the infant's quality of attachment to the caregiver. Using a classification system designed by Ainsworth and her colleagues (Ainsworth et al., 1978), infants' attachment relationships with the caregiver can be described as falling into one of three categories. Most commonly observed in a sample of normal children is a **secure attachment**. Securely attached infants are only minimally disturbed by separations from the caregiver, continue to explore the environment while the caregiver is present, and show positive affect on the caregiver's return after separation. In contrast, infants classified as showing an **insecure-avoidant** attachment tended to show little distress on separation from the caregiver. However, they are clearly upset by her departure as a study by Spangler and Grossman (1993), which measured the infant's heart rate, revealed. In addition, when the caregiver returns, insecure-avoidant infants typically pay no attention to her and actively *avoid* contact with her. A third type of insecure attachment is the **insecure-resistant** type (this type is sometimes labelled **insecure ambivalent**). These infants are most often extremely distressed by separation from the caregiver, showing high levels of crying and upset. However, when the caregiver returns insecure-resistant children show a pattern of alternately seeking contact with her and then resisting contact or pushing away from the caregiver. Ainsworth's research with the strange situation showed that for American samples, some 60 to 65 percent of infants were classified as secure, 20 percent as insecure avoidant, and some 10 to 15 percent as insecure resistant. Work by Main and Solomon (1990) revealed a fourth type of insecure attachment which they called **insecure-disorganized**. Insecure-disorganized infants display extremely peculiar behaviours in the strange situation: they often engage in repetitive movements such as rocking, show a tendency to freeze (i.e., remain extremely immobile) in the middle of a movement, and in general, seem confused or disoriented during the reunion with the mother. Sadly, researchers have found that insecure-disorganized attachments often co-occur with child mistreatment (Carlson et al., 1989; Lyons-Ruth et al., 1990) and maternal depression (Field, 1990). In the study by Carlson et al., 82 percent of a sample of mistreated infants developed insecure-disorganized attachments whereas only 19 percent of children who were not mistreated showed this pattern. Unfortunately for these infants, insecure-disorganized attachment has been associated with negative developmental outcomes (Main & Solomon, 1990).

The stability of attachment

An aspect of attachment theory suggested by Bowlby, and confirmed by many researchers, is the assertion that the quality of attachment relationships is stable over time. Waters (1978) studied the stability of attachment classifications in children from 12 to 18 months of age. He found a near-perfect consistency in the classifications across this time span. Similarly, Main and Cassidy (1988) studied a sample of infants who were seen in the strange situation at 12 months of age and were then observed again at 6 years of age. At 6 years the children were given a measure of attachment security used with older children. Main and Cassidy found a high level of consistency for attachment classifications from infancy to 6 years. These and other findings suggest that attachment is highly stable across time (Sroufe, 1979; Vaughn et al., 1979).

These early studies have been criticized on a number of grounds, one of these being that early research on the stability of attachment tended to use largely middle-class samples in the hopes of reducing factors such as stressful life events which might impact on the consistency of attachment classifications. What happens when researchers take into account the effects of stressful life events such as changes in employment (e.g., becoming unemployed or being forced into a lower paying job) or changes in marital status (e.g., divorce or separation)? When such factors are examined, the results provide less evidence for stability in attachment classifications over time. Studies have found that stressful life events as reported by parents were associated with changes in attachment classifications in their children (Thompson et al., 1982; Vaughn et al., 1979). Interestingly, changes in attachment classifications were bidirectional, that is, they could move from secure to insecure or vice versa. Thus, improvements in family life can lead to the development of secure attachments. More recently, Thompson (1998) and Sroufe (1996) have suggested that attachment relationships continue to develop over time and that changes in the stability of a child's attachment relationship is a function of their environment. Stable environments will tend to lead to stable attachment relationships.

The consequences of attachment relationships

Many attachment theorists including Bowlby argued that the quality of an infant's attachment to their caregiver has important consequences for development. One such theory is that the quality of the attachment relationship will act as an organizer for further development (Erikson, 1963). That is, attachment security is associated with different developmental pathways: securely attached children will tend to follow certain pathways through life whereas insecurely attached infants will follow different paths. According to Sroufe (1979), secure attachments are the foundation of healthy psychological development. Infants who form secure attachments should develop into competent, healthy children who are able to form satisfying relationships with others, whereas infants with insecure attachments will have a basic distrust of themselves and their social world, feelings of anxiety and guilt, and difficulties in forming relationships (Bowlby, 1969). A fundamental prediction of attachment theory is that our early social experience has a profound effect on later development in the social, emotional and cognitive domains.

One of the first studies to demonstrate the effects of secure attachments on later outcomes was carried out by Matas, Arend, and Sroufe (1978). In this study, a sample of toddlers were seen at 18 months of age and their attachment quality to their mother was assessed. These same children were then observed at 24 months of age and were asked to engage in a series of problem-solving tasks and a play task. In general, securely attached children were less negative, cried and whined less often, and showed less aggression during the tasks than did insecurely attached children. Securely attached children were more enthusiastic on the problem solving tasks, were frustrated less easily, and were more persistent in trying to find a solution than insecurely attached infants. Securely attached infants also tended to engage in more symbolic play than did insecurely attached children. Finally, securely attached children were more compliant: when their mother made suggestions for solving the tasks, securely attached children were more likely to make use of these suggestions than were insecure children.

Further research showed that these same benefits associated with a secure attachment relationship held into the preschool years, with preschool teachers rating securely attached children as less aggressive toward their peers, less dependent on help from the teacher, and more competent than insecurely attached children (Lafreniere & Sroufe, 1985; Waters, Wippman, & Sroufe, 1979). Recent work by Elizabeth Meins (Meins, Russell, Fernyhough & Clark-Carter, 1998) showed that securely attached children did better on theory of mind tasks at age 4; these children were more likely to pass the false belief task (see Chapter 9) than insecurely attached children. Finally, Lyons-Ruth et al. (1997) found that infants who were judged to be securely attached at 18 months of age were highly likely to be functioning well in interpersonal contexts at school when measured at age 7. In contrast, children assessed as showing disorganized attachments at 18 months were likely to develop *externalizing behaviours* such as hostility towards their peers, and acting up in class. Children whose attachment relationships were classified as avoidant were likely to show *internalizing behaviours* at age 7, such as depression, anxiety and self-criticism. (Internalizing and externalizing behaviours are discussed in greater detail in Chapter 10.) In general, the research by Matas and her colleagues, as well as a host of studies by other researchers, has demonstrated several important benefits to emotional, cognitive, and social development following the formation of a secure attachment relationship.

Temperament

Defining temperament

Early studies of children (e.g., Gesell, 1928) noted that there were striking individual differences between children in terms of their 'core of personality' (Shirley, 1933). Importantly, these researchers recognized that these differences in infants' traits were not fixed and often showed considerable change over time, yet they seemed to be constant enough in most cases that one could plausibly argue that these traits were constitutionally based, that is, rooted in the child's biological makeup. Another aspect of this early research was the examination of how these differences across children led to a variety of possible developmental outcomes. For example, Gesell described how particular traits such as sociability might predispose one towards generally positive outcomes later in life. Much of this early work on what we now call **temperament** has been confirmed by current research. These early observations of individual differences in infants and children highlight three issues central to the study of temperament today: temperamental traits are inherent, constitutionally based characteristics that make up the core of personality; although stability is a feature of many temperamental traits, it is widely recognized that stability greatly depends on the social context in which the child grows; temperament is related to a variety of possible long-term outcomes such as the quality of relationships with peers, psychological adjustment, and psychopathology.

So what is temperament? Temperament involves the study of individual differences in the basic psychological processes that constitute 'the affective, activational, and attentional core of personality and its development' (Rothbart & Bates, 1998: 108). Temperament is strongly tied to emotion, hence its inclusion in this chapter. For example, Allport (1937: 54) described temperament as the characteristics of an individual's emotional nature, such as his susceptibility to emotional stimulation, the nature of his typical emotional responses, and the quality of his prevailing mood. Most recently, temperament has been defined as 'constitutionally based individual differences in emotional, motor, and attentional reactivity and self-regulation' (Rothbart & Bates, 1998: 109). Note that the most recent definition of temperament stresses the inclusion of *attention* and *self-regulation* as critical to the construct of temperament, since these two characteristics of an individual's behaviour have strong implications for one's emotional life. Self-regulatory processes are those processes such as attention which serve to modulate reactivity to a stimulus. For example, when distressed by a particular thought, you can consciously distract yourself by thinking about other more pleasant thoughts. As research has shown, differences in self-regulatory behaviour seem to have a constitutional basis and show a degree of stability which has led many researchers to view them as fundamental aspects of temperament.

Temperament is considered central to an individual's emerging personality and indeed, there is a great deal of overlap between the characteristics identified as being related to temperament and those related to personality. However, it is important to note that temperament and personality are not identical. Although researchers have identified links between early temperament and later personality (e.g., Caspi & Silva, 1995), much work remains to establish exactly how these are linked (Rothbart & Bates, 1998).

Most, if not all, theories of temperament argue that the individual differences which are central to the study of temperament are genetically or biologically rooted (see Chapter 5 for further discussion on the genetic and

TABLE 8.2 Temperamental dimensions and types

Dimension	Description
Activity level	The frequency and tempo of an infant's motor activity
Rhythmicity	The extent to which activities (like sleeping) are regular
Approach/withdrawal	How the infants reacts to novel situations
Adaptability	How easily a response is modified to fit a new situation
Intensity	How energetic the infant's usual reactions are
Threshold	How intense stimulation needs to be before the infant reacts
Mood	The general quality of the infant's mood (e.g., friendly and cheerful vs. unfriendly behaviour)
Distractibility	How easily the infant's activities can be interrupted
Attention span/persistence	How long the infant remains engaged in an activity
Typology	
Easy	Cheerful, rhythmic, and adaptable
Difficult	Low on rhythmicity, easily upset by novelty, cries often
Slow to warm	Adjusts slowly to new experiences, negative mood, and inactive

biological basis of behaviour), attested to by the focus on 'constitutionally based' in our two definitions (Kagan, 1998). Of course, genetic and biological predispositions are strongly influenced by maturation and experience (Bates, 1989; Goldsmith et al., 1987). Thus, all temperamental effects on behaviour represent a combination of biological and environmental effects and are best characterized as *interactions* of the two factors. It is important to keep this fact in mind as we discuss research on temperament and its role in emotional and social development.

Initial work on temperament in infancy by Thomas and Chess (1977) identified nine dimensions of temperament. These are: *activity level* (the frequency and tempo of an infant's motor activity); *rhythmicity* (the extent to which activities such as sleeping and eating are regular or predictable); *approach/withdrawal* (how the infant reacts to new situations); *adaptability* (how easily a response is modified to fit a new situation); *intensity* (how energetic the infant's typical reactions are); *threshold* (how strong a response needs to be before the infant reacts); *mood* (the general quality of the infant's mood); *distractibility* (ease with which the infant's activities can be interrupted); *attention span/persistence* (the extent to which an infant remains engaged in activity) (see Table 8.2). Recent research has gone beyond these descriptive categories of behaviour to focus on additional qualities such as the ability to regulate one's own behaviour (Rothbart, 1989) and makes finer subdivisions between the variability within the broad dimensions identified by Thomas and Chess (1977) and other researchers (Rothbart & Bates, 1988).

Based on their analysis of these dimensions, Thomas and Chess (1986) proposed a typology of temperament that has gained wide acceptance, perhaps largely due to its intuitive appeal. Under their scheme, infants can be classified as **easy**, **difficult**, or **slow-to-warm**. *Easy* infants are sociable, happy, rhythmic, and adaptable. In contrast, *difficult* infants are easily upset by novelty, tend to fuss and cry often, and are low on rhythmicity, having difficulty sleeping and eating regularly. *Slow-to-warm* infants fall in between easy and difficult. These infants tend to initially respond to novel experiences poorly but over time or repeated contact show a pattern of gradually warming to and accepting the experience. Thomas and Chess found that easy children constituted approximately 40 percent of their sample while difficult and slow-to-warm infants made up 10 and 50 percent of the remainder.

The measurement of temperament

A wide variety of methods have been developed to measure temperament. These include: caregiver reports for infants and young children; teacher reports for the preschool and school-aged child; self-reports for older children and adolescents; naturalistic or observational assessments; and laboratory procedures. Not surprisingly, each methodology has its own benefits and its own limitations. For example, parent reports of temperament provide a unique insight from the people who spend the most time with the child, yet they are also open to bias as the parents' report is a function of their own characteristics. Laboratory assessments get around this issue of bias by subjecting children to standard procedures, however, they suffer from particular limitations such as carryover effects from repeated testing, and the constraints placed on the type of responses children can give. Accordingly in their review of research on temperament, Rothbart and Bates (1998) suggest that all measures of temperament require further refinements.

The continuity of temperament

Research evaluating the continuity of temperament over time has produced mixed assessments. While most early research in the field emphasized the stability of temperament across assessments (e.g., Buss & Plomin 1975), more recent work has suggested that temperament develops throughout childhood and is thus modified over time (Goldsmith, 1996). The course of this development reveals that initial individual differences in motor activity and emotionality are modified as developing self-regulatory systems 'come online' (Rothbart & Bates, 1998). The stability of temperamental classifications also varies depending on the temperamental dimension being measured, and the time periods across which it is measured. For example, research with a sample of New Zealand children (Caspi & Silva, 1995) reported that 3-year-olds rated as shy and subdued tended to describe themselves at age 18 (using a personality inventory) as shy or reserved. In contrast, work on the temperamental dimension of *distress proneness* showed little stability for distress measured over the first 3 months of life (Worobey & Lewis, 1989). Rothbart (1986) showed that positive and negative affects measured at 3 months of age were not correlated with the same measures at 9 months of age. However, distress measured later in infancy tended to show stability well into the school years, at 6 to 7 years of age (Rothbart, Derryberry, & Hershey, 1995). In a sample of 5- and 6-year-old Australian children (Pedlow, Sanson, Prior, & Oberklaid, 1993), those who were difficult to soothe showed the same characteristics later in childhood. Clearly, research on this question has produced mixed results.

The attempt to show stability in temperament is hampered in at least two ways. First, measures of temperament appropriate for one age group (e.g., infants) are not necessarily appropriate for another (e.g., school-aged children). For example, infants show their distress by crying while school-aged children are much more likely to demonstrate distress in a wide variety of ways. This means the temperament researcher needs to develop different measures for different age groups. Using different measures for different age groups means there is a possibility that somewhat different things are being measured and thus, it remains uncertain how much change is a function of development and how much is associated with measurement error. Second, a variety of developmental phenomena may interfere with attempts to show stability. For example, during the period between 1 and 3 months of age, infants find it extremely difficult to disengage their attention from a location and, as a consequence, tend to show a high degree of irritability. Measures of temperamental dimensions (such as *mood*) given during this time when infants are naturally irritable may not present an accurate picture of their core temperament, but rather, reflect a perfectly natural state in the infant's development (Johnson, Posner, & Rothbart, 1991). For these and other reasons, further research remains to be done on the question of whether temperament remains stable over time.

Genetic influences on temperament

As we have seen, most theories of temperament assume a biological basis. What evidence is there that this is indeed the case? Behaviour genetic research (see Chapter 4 for a discussion of behaviour genetics) has established reasonable evidence that many aspects of our temperament have a genetic basis. For example, Plomin (1987) has shown that in the first year, monozygotic (i.e., identical) twins show significantly greater similarity in their activity levels, their sociability, and their proneness to fear than do dizygotic (i.e., fraternal) twins. Monozygotic twins also show higher correlations for traits such as shyness, behavioural inhibition, and irritability (Emde et al., 1992; Goldsmith & Gottesman, 1981; Plomin, 1987). Studies in which children are adopted out to foster families show that by 2 years of age, there are significant correlations between adopted children and their biological mothers. In short, a wide variety of evidence points to a genetic basis to many temperamental traits.

However, it is not simply the case that a child's temperament is fixed and unchangeable. Behaviour genetic studies strongly suggest a biological basis to temperament, but these studies should not be taken as suggesting temperament is fully determined by our genetic inheritance. In fact, behaviour genetic research suggests that there are important environmental effects on temperament. Rothbart and Bates (1998) summarize a variety of studies that highlight aspects of temperament which show that a child's environment plays an important role in determining the nature of her temperament. As they suggest, the time is past when we can think of temperament as genetically determined. Instead, we need to recognize that both biological and environmental processes contribute to shaping behaviour.

Goodness of fit

An important aspect of theories of temperament is the idea that temperament is rooted in our biology. As we have discussed in this chapter, behaviour genetic research suggests that temperament is not fixed but, rather, is modified by experience. Therefore, it is not the case that a difficult infant will necessarily remain a difficult infant, although temperament is often stable and resistant to change. A difficult temperament can be modified over time with the provision of appropriate caregiving. Thomas and Chess (1986) introduced the concept **goodness of fit** to the study of temperament in order to explain how temperament can change. By goodness of fit, Thomas and Chess referred to the fit between a child's temperament and their parents' expectations and behaviours towards the child. For example, parents who had strong expectations for a quiet, sociable, and happy child may have difficulty adapting to their difficult infant. They may lack the resources (e.g., coping skills, social support) to deal with a difficult infant and may behave towards the infant in ways that do little to promote change in the infant's behaviours. As a consequence, their behaviours may reinforce the undesirable aspects of that infant's temperament. In contrast, the same infant, when born into a family where the parents are able to respond calmly, positively, and warmly to their child's temperamental traits have a much greater chance of altering the infant's behaviour. As Thomas and Chess point out, with patience and caring, parents help the child to make the most out of their traits.

To date, research on the goodness of fit hypothesis has been mixed. The idea itself seems intuitively appealing and provides a useful explanatory tool for developmentalists interested in temperament and behaviour but researchers have found it a difficult hypothesis to confirm (e.g., Crockenberg, 1986). Further work remains to be done in this area.

Temperament and adjustment

As we noted earlier, since the earliest research on temperament, psychologists have attempted to examine exactly how early temperament leads to later behavioural outcomes. That is, are the observed individual differences in adjustment among children predictable as a function of their temperamental classification? Studies of the developmental outcomes associated with temperamental classifications vary in their assessments of whether there are demonstrable relationships between early measures of temperament and later measures of children's level of adjustment. For example, in work based on the Dunedin Longitudinal Study in New Zealand, Caspi and Silva (1995) showed that children who were rated as inhibited at 3 years of age were more likely to score low on *aggression* and low on *social potency* (a measure of how effective one is in social situations) at 18 years of age. In a study of temperament and social behaviour in 6- and 7-year-olds, Rothbart, Ahadi, & Hershey (1994) found that negative affectivity measured using parent reports was associated with particular social traits such as aggressiveness. They also found that a small subsample of the children in this study who had been through a laboratory assessment of temperament as infants showed a similar pattern: infant measures of negative affectivity were associated with higher levels of aggressiveness and help seeking at 6 to 7 years of age. Eisenberg at al. (1996) showed that school children identified by teachers' reports as showing low self-regulation were more likely to show behaviour problems such as acting out in class. In regard to the relationship between temperament and positive behaviours, Kochanska (1995) provided evidence that temperament was also related to children's moral development. In summary, there is some evidence that specific temperamental dimensions are related to internalizing behaviours (e.g., shyness, depression and anxiety) and externalizing behaviours (acting up, aggressiveness) in childhood as well as to some positive behaviours (Rothbart & Bates, 1998).

It should be clear to you that the study of emotional development takes in a wide variety of topics, from the study of changes in emotional expressions and understanding to how we learn to control our emotions. Also current in the study of emotional development are the topics of attachment and temperament, constructs which emphasize the importance of our emotional nature to growth in other areas. You should recognize that the study of emotional development is intimately tied to developments in cognition and social understanding. In many ways, these overlaps between areas such as cognition and emotion are among the most interesting areas of study in child development.

SUMMARY

Glossary

Attachment relationship is the emotional bond which is formed between an infant and a caregiver.

Basic emotions refers to the set of emotions which most psychologists would agree are innate and develop within the first few weeks of life. This list normally includes disgust, happiness, fear, anger, sadness, interest and surprise.

Difficult according to Thomas and Chess, a temperamental style where infants are easily upset, react poorly to novelty and are not rhythmic. Difficult babies can be challenging children to parent. Difficult infants can become easy infants given an environment which allows them to express themselves and is supportive of their behaviours.

Easy according to Thomas and Chess, a temperamental style where infants are sociable, happy, rhythmic and adaptable. Easy babies are so-called because they tend to be easy children to parent.

Emotion regulation refers to the processes by which an individual's emotional arousal is maintained within their capacity to cope.

Emotional display rules are the rules which dictate which emotions are appropriate to express in a given circumstance.

Extrinsic regulation processes are ways of regulating emotion that depend on factors outside of or external to the individual, such as soothing and comforting interventions given by a caregiver.

Functionalist theory of emotion functionalist theories stress that emotions are adaptive processes which organize functioning in a variety of domains of human development.

Goodness of fit refers to the fit between a child's temperament and their parents' expectations and behaviours towards the child.

Insecure attachments are attachment relationships which fail to provide the infant with a sense of confidence and security and comprise three subtypes: infants who show an **insecure-avoidant** attachment typically avoid contact with the mother during reunion; infants who show an **insecure-resistant** attachment show a pattern of alternately seeking and resisting contact with the caregiver; infants who show an **insecure-disorganized** attachment seem confused or disoriented during the reunion with the mother.

Internal working model is a mental representation of the infant's relationship with their primary caregiver.

Intrinsic regulation processes are ways of regulating emotions that depend on processes internal to the individual. Developments in language abilities, the brain and cognitive abilities are all examples of intrinsic processes.

Scripts are a form of mental representation which includes a knowledge of what kinds of behaviours and emotions are appropriate to a particular event or situation.

Secure attachment securely attached infants show only minimal disruption during separations from the caregiver and positive affect on reunion with the caregiver.

Secure base/Safe haven refers to the function of the caregiver as a refuge and source of comfort from which to explore their environment.

Self-conscious emotion is the term given to emotions such as guilt, shame, envy, embarrassment, and pride.

Sensitivity refers to the parental behaviour that is consistent and responsive to the infant's needs.

Social referencing is the use of another's emotional expressions as a source of information, allowing the child to interpret the meaning of events and situations.

Socialization refers to the processes by which parents, siblings, peers, and others work to shape children's behaviour.

Strange situation is a situation for testing attachment wherein the infant is separated from the caregiver, its mother, exposed to a stranger, and then reunited with the mother in order to assess the quality of the attachment relationship.

Stranger distress is a fear of strangers shown by infants that first emerges around 7 to 9 months of age.

Temperament refers to constitutionally based, individual differences in emotional, motor, and attentional reactivity and self-regulation.

Theory of personal emotion is a coherent network of beliefs about one's own emotional processes.

This chapter is taken from:
Keenan, T. (2002) *An Introduction to Child Development*
978-0-7619-6220-5

4 Personal, Social and Emotional Development: Learning to be strong in a world of change

LIZ BROOKER AND LYNNE BROADBENT

> *It is now very clear that unless a child achieves at least a minimal level of social competence by about the age of six, he or she is at risk for the rest of his or her life. The risks are not only in subsequent social functioning – many aspects of mental health, the ability to form stable relationships, to maintain employment, and to function well in marital and parental roles; the current evidence indicates that insufficient social competence leads to premature dropping out of school.*
>
> (Katz, in Dowling, 2000: vii)

This chapter considers spiritual and moral development as integral with personal, social and emotional growth, and includes:

- Personal, social and emotional development and the idea of 'well-being'
- Learning about myself: constructing an identity in early environments
- Learning about relationships: family, friends and others
- Learning dispositions: becoming a lifelong learner.

Personal, social and emotional development and the idea of 'well-being'

Introduction

This chapter, like all the others in this book, is about the child as a *learner*. But perhaps even more than other chapters it is conscious of the child as a learner from *birth*, in every moment of his or her experiences – learning in infancy while being bathed, soothed and rocked; learning as a toddler from visiting grandparents or watching older children in a playground. Personal, social and emotional development (PSE) is a life-long process. Our discussion in this section of children's learning in this area from 3 to 7, and in educational settings, focuses on a quite small, though very significant, part of a complex process which takes place in many settings.

This emphasis on 'learning' is also a reminder that personal, social and emotional development in children occurs *through* learning and is not something that 'just happens' in the early years. Although research suggests that babies are endowed with some personality traits and tendencies from birth, it shows too that a very large part of the person they become results from learning through social interaction in an ever-widening set of contexts. A small child's first move out of the family and community into an institutional setting such as a school or pre-school brings with it huge new opportunities for learning.

In the short span of years since the first edition of this book appeared, personal, social and emotional development has been increasingly acknowledged as the foundation for all learning. As the Foundation Stage curriculum for 3–5-year-olds (DfEE/QCA, 2000) is replaced by *The Statutory Framework for the Early Years Foundation Stage* (DfES, 2007), for 0–5 years, it is clear that the more holistic notion of 'well-being' which underpins recent government thinking has placed PSE at the forefront of all services for young children, including the work of teachers in schools, and of multi-agency staff in settings.

The integration of all previous guidelines into a single framework for children under 5 has facilitated an unprecedented focus on the 'whole child', rather than on the compartmentalized aspects of the child's curriculum learning. This broad focus changes, as practitioners as well as policy-makers are aware, when children move into Key Stage 1, where the curriculum requirements become more subject-specific (DfEE/QCA, 1999). Teachers working with this age group know, however, that children do not suddenly complete their personal, social and emotional development at the age of 5, and that support in this area is still needed in Year 1 and beyond.

This chapter shows how the important themes from a child's earliest home experiences, and her pre-school learning, can be carried through into the National Curriculum years. It also explores the links between these areas and the moral and spiritual development of children, showing how closely the ideas from each perspective interweave and overlap in children's daily lives at home and school. Through examples from our own experience we try to show that opportunities for promoting children's personal, social and emotional development can occur spontaneously, as well as through planned activities, and that the role of the skilled practitioner is to be alert to the multiple meanings of children's everyday experiences in and out of the classroom.

By the age of 3 a child has taken many giant strides: towards constructing a complex and durable personal identity, or sense of self; towards learning about relationships with others; and towards discovering the intrinsic pleasure of learning itself. Most 3-year-olds can tell you who they are and who they belong to, their preferences (what they like and dislike) and their accomplishments (what they are good at and not so good at). Most of them, once they have settled into a new setting, are 'ready, willing and able' to go on learning. Our aim in exploring the opportunities offered by the PSE 'curriculum' is to ensure that all children not only reach this point of readiness but also maintain it, with sufficient reserves and resilience to see them through the later school years when learning will not always be 'fun' or self-initiated.

How this chapter is organized:

This chapter has four sections. The present section offers a brief introduction to the area, directing the reader to the statutory guidelines and curriculum frameworks which necessarily underpin both policies and planning in schools and settings. The second, third and fourth sections explore three major strands of learning in the area from 3 to 7: we have called these 'learning about myself', 'learning about relationships' and 'learning dispositions'. Within each strand we have tried to address the curriculum contexts for the under-5s and over-5s, and the continuities and discontinuities which may become apparent as children make the transition between phases.

Three aspects of the learning process are also exemplified throughout:

- learning through the child's own exploration of the environment;
- learning through interaction with peers and siblings; and
- learning with adult support and guidance.

Adults are key to children's continued healthy development, and we will try to touch on all aspects of professional practice, from assessment and evaluation to working with parents and families.

We begin by looking at the documents which guide this area of learning.

Starting points in planning for PSE: working towards well-being

An enormous shift in emphasis has occurred in provision for children and families since the previous edition of this book, with the development of a new children's agenda which encompasses all services for children from birth to 14, and a set of 'outcomes' which all educators and other professionals must work towards. The *Every Child Matters* framework (set out in the 2003 Green Paper) and the subsequent 2004 Children Act, have drawn together all our society's aspirations for children under the key concept of 'well-being' (DfES, 2003).

This capacious term, though not synonymous with PSE, encompasses all the areas of learning we associate with the personal, social, emotional and health curriculum. It addresses, not only the well-being of the *individual* child in the *present*, but the well-being of families and communities, in the near and long-term future. These future-oriented goals describe a society in which poverty, injustice and social exclusion have been drastically reduced, and social cohesion and commitment have been greatly enhanced; in which individual life-chances are supported by healthy social networks. In the immediate term, educators and other professionals working with children and families must plan for five outcomes. Children should:

- be healthy;
- stay safe;
- enjoy and achieve;
- make a positive contribution; and
- achieve economic well-being.

While the third outcome, 'enjoy and achieve' has the most explicitly 'educational' goals, it is clearly inseparable from the other four. Children who are, in the words of this outcome, 'getting the most out of life and developing broad skills for adulthood', are at the same time being helped to 'make a contribution to society', and being safe-guarded against the poverty which may prevent them from 'achieving their full potential'. These we hope would be the *consequences* of 'enjoying and achieving'. But the *precursors* of this goal are in the first two outcomes: 'enjoying good physical and mental health' and 'growing up able to look after themselves', and these are the foundations of the PSE curriculum, as it is currently evolving.

The Statutory Framework for the Early Years Foundation Stage (EYFS)

Whereas the *Curriculum Guidance for the Foundation Stage* had goals for six strands of PSE (dispositions and attitudes; self-confidence and self-esteem; making relationships; behaviour and self-control; self-care; and sense of community) the new EYFS framework develops three broad areas.

- *dispositions and attitudes*, including themes on learning dispositions and on self-care;
- *social development*, with themes on making relationships, and sense of community;
- *emotional development*, encompassing self-confidence and self-esteem, and behaviour and self-control.

The content is similar in many ways to the earlier document, but the foregrounding of emotional development as a main strand marks a significant shift of emphasis, which can be traced to the research undertaken for an intervening document, the *Birth to Three Matters* framework (Sure Start, 2002). The four strands of this framework included that of 'A Strong Child', with sub-themes of 'being acknowledged and affirmed; me, myself and I; developing self-assurance; and a sense of belonging'. This 'strong child' reflects the image of the learner which underpins both the new EYFS and the evolving National Curriculum; and her characteristics are strongly underpinned in turn by the guidance on moral and spiritual development. These important themes will be woven through the next three sections, including their application in the Key Stage 1 curriculum.

The Key Stage 1 curriculum

The revised National Curriculum (DfEE/QCA, 1999) is framed by statements of value and purpose which indicate a powerful underlying concern for the development of the whole child – personal and social, moral and spiritual. Its statement of aims makes reference to identity construction, to emotional security, and to relationships and respect. While PSE and Citizenship remain non-statutory as curriculum areas in Key Stage 1, primary schools as well as pre-schools are entrusted with working towards the five outcomes of *Every Child Matters*, and some schools have already made this a priority in their development plans. The non-statutory guidance for PSHE, for children in Years 1 and 2, develops the themes established for work with under-5s, through a curriculum based on four areas:

- developing confidence and responsibility and making the most of their abilities;
- preparing to take an active role as citizens;
- developing a healthy, safer lifestyle; and
- developing good relationships and respecting the differences between people.

It is to be hoped that the requirement to work towards the *Every Child Matters* outcomes will encourage schools to take these non-statutory areas very seriously, as a means towards this end.

Concerns over the difficulties experienced by many children at the point of transition from Foundation Stage to Key Stage 1 (Cassidy, 2005) have encouraged a slow but steady process of blurring the boundaries between the two phases, and in particular of applying some key principles from provision for under-5s to the learning of children of statutory school age. This book, of course, both reflects and supports this intention.

The contribution of spiritual and moral development

Spiritual and moral development are distinctive yet interrelated aspects of personal, social and emotional development. In recent years, education documents have linked spiritual and moral development with specific, but different, areas of personal development; for example, the Practical Guidance for the Early Years Foundation Stage (DfES, 2007) refers to 'emotional, moral, spiritual and social development alongside intellectual development', while the National Curriculum Handbook (DfEE/QCA, 2000) cites, as the second of its two aims, that the curriculum should 'promote pupils' spiritual, moral, social and cultural development'.

The relationship between moral development and personal, social and emotional development will be clearly evident, for without a developing awareness of the need to share both toys and teacher time, a willingness to reflect on a repertoire of behavioural choices and an ability to modify emotional responses, a child will not thrive in the social setting of the nursery or classroom. The relationship between spiritual development and personal, social and emotional development is, perhaps, immediately less clear. The key to understanding the concept of 'the spiritual' is to recognize that in an educational context, the term 'spiritual' is not synonymous with the term 'religion' or 'religious' (OFSTED, 1994), it is understood as being much broader than this, something fundamental to all human beings, religious or not. Although difficult to define, the spiritual can usually be recognized in the classroom, in those moments of awe, wonder and mystery when children spot the first fall of snow or experience the delight of newborn chicks; or, in contrast, in the sadness and questioning which follows the death of a pet or family member; or in those moments of total concentration when the child is engrossed in a story or creative task, be it painting or building a tower from bricks. In moments such as these there is often a sense of timelessness, of seeing the world – or even oneself – in a new way. Eaude (2006: 17) suggests that by enhancing spiritual development, we are enabling children to 'create increasingly coherent personal narratives about themselves' by addressing questions of meaning and purpose, questions such as Who am I? Where do I fit in? Why am I here? – questions which in personal, moral, social and emotional contexts have a range of answers.

So how does the 'spiritual' relate to the 'moral'? And if the 'spiritual' relates to the child's responses to the natural world, to encounters of birth and death, to joy and sadness, to intense involvement in creative activity, then how does this relate to the role of the teacher, and furthermore, how can we speak of 'the spiritual' in terms of development? The 'spiritual' is indeed personal as illustrated above, but it can also be interpersonal, the intense involvement in a group play and role play, sharing spontaneous laughter or valuing a friend's help or being part of a group, for while the spiritual may involve a sense of timelessness, a sense of extraordinary moments, it may also relate to a sense of 'depth' in everyday experiences. And this may be the meeting point with the 'moral', for if spiritual development is to do with developing an understanding and valuing of one's self in the universe, then from this comes an understanding of how one relates to and should act towards others in that same universe. Eaude's matrix (Eaude, 2006: 11) is helpful here, suggesting that the spiritual relates to meaning, moral to action, social to interaction and cultural to belonging. Spiritual and moral development, the Office for Standards in Education (OFSTED) acknowledges (OFSTED, 1994: 6), it may not necessarily be 'a smooth, continuous process' and may be dependent on opportunities for the child to value, explore and reflect upon experiences and questions of meaning and purpose. And this is where the teacher's awareness, sensitivity and skills come in!

Spiritual and moral development are significant aspects of personal, social and emotional development. Both aspects may flourish spontaneously in a learning environment in which space and time for questioning, reflection, imagination and creativity are protected. There remains however a requirement to plan activities and, at Key Stage 1, to track provision for these aspects of development through all subjects in the taught curriculum, including Religious Education which identifies (NSFRE, QCA/DfES, 2004) for Key Stage 1 children the themes of 'Myself and my uniqueness' and 'Belonging', two of the themes developed through this chapter.

Summary

This section has briefly presented the context within which our exploration of personal, social, emotional *and* moral and spiritual education is situated. These aspects of well-being are addressed in the sections which follow, beginning with the development and maintenance of a positive sense of identity.

Learning about myself: constructing an identity in early environments

Where are we at 3?

Developing a sense of self is often seen in Western cultures as the long process of becoming a self-aware individual – becoming aware, for example, of what you look like, your gender, what makes you happy and sad, what roles you play ... All the things which delineate you as an individual. (Miell, 1995: 190)

How does this process come about? Research shows us that it begins very early, and proceeds very rapidly, in an infant's life. Babies soon learn about themselves from seeing themselves mirrored in the attentions of others, especially their 'significant others' such as early caregivers. Early interactions with caregivers are bi-directional – babies socialize adults as much as adults socialize babies (Gopnik et al, 1999; Murray and Andrews, 2000). Their spontaneous sounds and movements are mimicked by loving adults and become a part of the infant's unique and expanding repertoire. Their accidental effects on their environment (knocking a mobile with a flailing arm, dislodging a soft toy with an energetic leg movement) teach them that they have agency of their own and encourage them to repeat each movement over and over to confirm that they themselves are the cause. From 15 months babies begin to demonstrate awareness of their own appearance and, by 24 months, many can identify themselves by name and by gender – most babies' early experience of adult talk, after all, consists of being told they are a 'good boy' or a 'clever girl'.

At the same time another important aspect of the child's identity is emerging, of great concern to early educators: the child's self-esteem. Self-esteem has been described as the *value* a child assigns him or herself: attempts to describe it have focused on the disparity between what a child would *like* to be like and that child's view of how he or she actually is. But in early childhood it principally reflects the value the child perceives he or she has in the eyes of others, particularly those 'significant others' whose opinions count the most for the child. And although children in the later pre-school years can separate and evaluate different aspects of themselves (being good at football, drawing or making up stories), young children have a simpler, 'global' self-concept. For this reason, 'Self-esteem is only likely to be fostered in situations where all aspects of all children are esteemed' (Dowling, 2005: 10) and is very vulnerable to the views of important people in children's lives.

Recent research reminds us that children's unequal life chances in this area of development begin before they are even born. Poor nutrition, environmental toxins, substance abuse and parental stress, which impair brain development in the womb, may continue to shape the environment in infancy, while maternal depression and other stress factors can deny children the experiences they need to grow healthy attitudes in their early months (Shonkoff and Phillips, 2001). Practitioners working with pre-school children know that they have a vital role to play in compensating for some children's early experiences, and supporting them and their families into a greater state of well-being.

Learning about myself from 3 to 5

For all children, even the most confident, entering their first group care setting is more than a step into a new world, full of promise; it is a step away from the familiar world of home and carries with it innumerable anxieties which may revive memories of the child's earliest experiences. Literally from birth, children have undergone the pain of separation and loss. Most will have come to terms with temporary absences and feelings of grief and learnt that their important people do, usually, come back to them. Nevertheless, the dawning understanding that this new stage in their lives means something different – means saying goodbye, regularly and for long periods, to their familiar caregivers and acquiring new caregivers to take their place – is something that many children understandably resist.

Although young children are increasingly placed in group care from their early months of life, the third birthday remains the time when almost all our children are enrolled in educational settings, five days a week. From this moment the 'self' which until now has developed gradually, separating itself in tiny steps from the others who surround and enfold it, takes on an independent identity, mirrored in the eyes and actions of a whole new company of 'significant others'.

Transitions and separations

Dealing with separation may dominate the child's early pre-school sessions, but most parents and practitioners have strategies for supporting children at this time. Close links between home and 'school' adults are usually established through home visits to the child and parental presence in the setting; children's own important objects – teddy bears, books or special blankets – are usually accommodated until the child no longer needs them; children may be encouraged to bring photographs of their family to be displayed in the setting; and daily exchanges between key workers and parents can help to ensure continuity between the two parts of the child's daily experience (Dalli, 2000).

Gottman (1997) argues that children's feelings of sadness should be confronted directly, rather than disguised or suppressed. Well-meaning adults may wish to prevent children from experiencing unhappiness, and seek to repair such unhappiness when it occurs, but to do so is to deny children their right to learn about emotions. As Dowling points out, learning about sadness is an important part of emotional development, and acknowledging a child's sadness 'will at least show the child that she is being taken seriously' (2005: 74).

Self-concept and self-esteem

Separation brings with it a very positive step in any child's learning: acquiring a sense of themselves as 'being a person' in more than one setting. As life at school, playgroup or the childminder's becomes an integral part of the child's experience, it contributes to the expansion of identity: the child can now see herself as someone who drinks from the family's mugs at home, but from a plastic beaker at nursery or a Disneyland mug at the minder's; who throws her cardigan over a chair at home but hangs it on her peg at pre-school; who tips her toys into a toybox at home but tidies things into separate crates in daycare; who *belongs* in more than one place. This awareness of one's different roles enables the child to reflect more consciously on her own identity: on occasion she may have to introduce herself to new adults in the setting, and explain about her life outside the setting – 'I get picked up by Kelly's mum because my mum has to get my big brother first'. Through these experiences the child's own self-concept and self-awareness expand dramatically.

One important aspect of children's self-concept is their self-esteem, and it is important to remember that this may fluctuate at different times and in different contexts. Schaffer (1996: 164) emphasizes that 'self-esteem is at its most volatile during its initial formation in childhood, and remains easily influenced by experience right through adolescence'. It is particularly vulnerable at times of transition, when children are moving into new environments and relationships. Early childhood practitioners have rightly prioritized this area, but sometimes with a limited understanding of the sources of self-esteem, which may lead them to offer children affirmation for their identity through a rather thoughtless use of praise. Starting from children's earliest days in a setting, they may seek to encourage them by constant approval and admiration – *Well done! Good girl! Lovely! You're a star!* Such enthusiasm is well meant (and may make all the difference while a child is feeling especially vulnerable), but will lose all meaning or value for the child if it is habitual. It may even do harm in two ways: first, because it makes the child dependent on adult approval, showing her that her efforts are not of value unless an adult says so; and, secondly, because it gives the child no information on which to base her *own* independent assessments of her efforts and discourages her from evaluating her own learning in a realistic way. As Roberts argues: 'the use of strategies such as habitual empty praise, gold stars, smiley stickers and meaningless statements, are more likely to feed children's self-preoccupation and narcissism than to help them form a genuine sense of their own worth' (2002: 106). Genuine self-esteem comes from a realistic assessment of one's efforts and outcomes, and when children are praised for efforts of which they are not particularly proud, they will understandably question the trustworthiness of the adults (Gura, 1996).

The honest alternative to praising is to give the child both *attention* and *information*. A careful look at a painting, followed by a question or comment ('Is this anybody I know? This red bit's all dribbly, we must have made the paint too runny') invites the child to enter into a meaningful dialogue which will be far more rewarding than a glib cry of *Lovely!*

Belonging

The sense of belonging – in different settings, with different people and possibly among different sets of cultural values – is one of the most important aspects of identity development. In the early years curriculum in New Zealand (Carr, 2001), 'belonging' is one of five key strands in children's experience. *The Practice Guidance for the Early Years Foundation Stage*, drawing on earlier curriculum models, indicates that, as they grow in their early childhood setting, children should acquire 'a sense of self as a member of different communities' (DfES, 2007: 38)

Many features of the traditional nursery environment contribute to this sense – the name on the coat peg, the picture on the mug, the photo above the snack table, the key worker group and the 'home base'. It is reinforced when practitioners draw children's attention to the different aspects of their lives, talking with them about their homes and families, their journey to and from the setting and their activities in the community. As the Practice Guidance suggests, children should talk freely about their home and community (DfES 2007: 38), and this is particularly vital when practitioners do not share the background of children in their setting. Knowing that you 'belong' to your own group in pre-school *and* to your own family and community helps the child to become aware of the multi-faceted nature of her identity. As Learning story 2.1 shows, practitioners have an important role to play in this process.

Learning story 2.1　Preethi's trousers

Preethi settled into nursery without difficulty, and formed good friendships. Her family were well educated and articulate, so her nursery workers had no reason to suspect that she would be vulnerable on account of her bilingualism or her family culture. In her early months in the nursery she seemed to have a very positive sense of self.

Around Easter Preethi's demeanour began to change: she became reserved and diffident, and often declined an adult's invitation to join a group activity. At outside time, she drifted against the fence and watched from a distance while other girls played. A key worker investigated, and gradually discovered what had gone wrong. Preethi's playmates had been showing off their summer skirts and dresses, and had challenged her statement that 'you got to always have trousers on your legs' by saying that only boys had to wear trousers. Preethi was desolate and very confused. A practitioner with some picture books of children from different cultures was able to help all the children understand that in fact, 'everyone was right, no one had got it wrong'.

Celebrating together is a powerful means of expressing belonging. Engaging in the celebration of the key religious and cultural festivals marked by the children provides a link between home and school experiences, and acknowledges the rich cultural diversity represented in the nursery or Foundation Stage class. It also validates, and shares, each child's home experience thereby contributing to a positive self image and enhanced self-esteem, an aspect of spiritual development (SCAA, 1995). Family members can be encouraged into the school community to introduce artefacts used during home rituals and celebrations, to bring special foods to share and to tell or read the stories told at the festival, while children can search the dressing-up box and experiment with clothes for a special occasion, make cards, act out stories, sing songs and make traditional sweets. Such activities foster cultural and social awareness, developing knowledge about the different communities within the locality, but also they contribute to spiritual and moral development as the children expand their experience of, and respect for, difference, in forms of dress, languages and expressions of greeting, rituals, stories and artefacts. A growing familiarity with the differences within their own community transforms 'strangeness' into 'the norm' and provides the child with a broader experience of social and cultural discourse.

Making a contribution

Closely linked with small children's sense of their worth is their acquisition of a sense of responsibility, the sense of *making a contribution* to the group or setting. Too often, when children are much older, both parents and teachers lament their *lack* of such a sense. Do they ever think back to when those children were small and anxious to be involved in everything their caregivers and older siblings did?

The *Every Child Matters* framework (like the Te Whaariki curriculum) makes a deliberate focus on children's ability to 'make a contribution' to the social group they inhabit. Early years settings often attempt to inculcate this sense of contribution with their routines, involving children in 'helping' with wiping the tables, handing out the snacks or putting the dolls to bed. These tasks are often quite limited and undemanding – 'pretend' responsibilities which socialize children into conformity. When children volunteer to help with a real task, such as lifting equipment, switching on a plug at a socket or fetching a sharp knife, they are likely to be shooed away and told that only grown-ups do that. Yet these same children may be used to making a contribution at home: caring for a younger sibling or handling tools alongside responsible adults. Researchers in cross-cultural settings (Rogoff, 1990) have shown just how widespread this 'apprenticeship' to adult life is, outside the English-speaking world. Even within the UK, many of our children, including those from traveller families and from the Asian community (Brooker, 2002; Cousins, 1990), experience such 'guided participation' in adult life in their homes and communities.

Children can only learn to be responsible by being given responsibility, and the present 'health and safety' mentality drilled into practitioners may discourage risk-taking of any kind. In consequence, some children may neither achieve a realistic assessment of dangers, such as fire and electricity, nor acquire the skills to use tools safely and circumspectly. In settings as in homes, children's physical safety must never be compromised. But there are many ways in which they can learn about responsibility and come to view themselves as competent, without putting themselves at risk. Talking about responsibility is one valuable means to achieving this particular 'goal', as Darren's story shows (Learning story 2.2).

Learning story 2.2 Darren: thinking about responsibility

Darren had a new baby brother. He had announced the news as soon as he had entered the reception class that morning. Sitting on the carpet the teacher encouraged other children to talk about their siblings. She introduced language such as 'a new brother or sister becoming part of your family'. The conversation continued with discussion about what babies did, the clothes they wore and the care they needed and, at this point, the teacher asked Darren what he could do for his new brother. Through question and answer it was established that Darren would be able to tell mum when the baby was crying; he would be able to distract the baby's tears at times by talking to him, touching his hand or playing with his soft toys; he would be able to assist at nappy-changing time and could help mum gain greater access to the supermarket shelves while pushing the baby by fetching shopping items for her. Some of the children then moved to the home corner and practised bath and nappy-changing time and experienced pushing a baby around in a buggy. By the end of the morning, and through the teacher's skilful questioning and improvised plans, Darren and the other children had developed an understanding of what it meant to belong to the social group of the family and a sense of joint responsibility for different members of that group and, most importantly, a whole repertoire of skills which they could put to immediate use in the care of a brother and thus be able to experience being an accepted and responsible member of a social group.

Learning about myself from 5 to 7

Getting started in Year 1 is not always viewed as one of life's major landmarks; by now most children have made at least two big transitions – from home to pre-school and from pre-school to the 'real school' in which their reception class is housed. Ideally, their reception year should have acclimatized them, from within the secure framework of the Foundation Stage, to the world of statutory schooling. Ideally, too, they should be ready for the next step: a more formal learning environment in which large chunks of the day's activities are predetermined – not by the teacher but by the statutory requirement to introduce the *Primary National Strategy Framework for Literacy and Mathematics* (DfES, 2006) by the end of reception.

The Early Learning Goals suggest what children may have achieved by now in constructing a positive identity. The framework for PSE at Key Stage 1 is intended to build on these goals so that pupils 'learn to recognise their own worth, work well with others and become increasingly responsible for their own learning'. If we look again at the aspects of a sense of self which dominated the pre-school years, we may identify some of the opportunities (and difficulties) of securing their continued development in Year 1.

Transitions

Separation from familiar adults and environments is given little consideration at this stage but may well prove significant for children (Cassidy, 2005). Earlier transitions in their lives were managed with supportive strategies and thoughtful planning: continuity between homes and schools, parents and professionals, is highlighted in the pre-school years; routines such as group times are carefully designed to make room for children's emotional needs; informal instructional sessions allow for continuous social talk between children and adults; and a play-based curriculum enables children to learn in their own way and at their own pace, as well as by following their own interests. Few of these conditions are found in Key Stage 1. Too often the drive to complete statutory requirements by lunchtime forces teachers to ignore parents who are waiting to chat, and to rush through the morning group time without offering children opportunities to express their concerns and needs. A child who is distressed or a parent with a problem to communicate may be seen as obstacles in the path of teachers with a crowded timetable to manage.

Although most children adapt well to a more formal environment, practitioners need to be alert to their feelings and remember that home influences on the child's learning are still extremely important, and that links between families and schools are vital. Parents' interest and involvement in their children's school learning may *appear* to dwindle once the children leave the Foundation Stage but, research tells us this is not the case (Hughes, 1996). The increasing separateness of the settings in which the children pass their lives, as Bronfenbrenner (1979) has shown, is not beneficial for their social, emotional or cognitive learning.

Self-concept and self-esteem

Children's self-concept and self-esteem, which may have been securely achieved in their early settings, again becomes vulnerable and subject to rapid transformations as the child enters a more formal regime. The process of 'becoming a pupil', which begins in the Foundation Stage, now assumes major significance (Boyle and Woods, 1998; Brooker, 2002), as pupils are socialized into the discourse of the school and adapt their behaviour to a new set of expectations. Some pupils are less successful than others in making this adjustment: as Schaffer reminds us, self-concept 'is affected by experience, especially of success and failure and the feelings of competence or incompetence derived therefrom' (1996: 159). The child who discovers that he or she is viewed as less competent by a new teacher or new classmates risks becoming less competent in his or her own self-evaluation.

Parents are well aware of the effects on children's self-esteem of new, more formal methods of instruction and, possibly, more explicit and critical forms of assessment; and they too may feel somewhat bewildered by the different institutional style of Key Stage 1 (Hughes et al., 1994). Both the ethos of the school and the ethos of the individual classroom are crucial in providing a framework in which children and parents can feel secure and supported as they nervously embark on a new stage in their educational career.

Certain aspects of children's identity are particularly vulnerable in this process. Research findings (Connolly, 1998; 2003; Connolly et al., 2002) reveal the strongly sexualized and racialized discourse used by children aged 5–7 in constructing their own and other children's identities in the classroom and playground. Transitions into new environments create challenges to settled identities, and children may well retreat into stereotypical behaviour and attitudes as a result of their own insecurity (Brooker, 2006; Lloyd and Duveen, 1992). In Key Stage 1, and particularly during unsupervised playtimes, quite hurtful attacks on children's identity and sense of self may occur, as their peers seek to safeguard and maintain their own identity categories. Such issues are often addressed in circle time; but an additional brief group time may be necessary at the start of every session, to discuss and defuse fears, anxieties and hostilities that have arisen in the playground. Despite the pressures of the timetable this space for discussion may be vital for children's well-being, and their learning.

Belonging

On the positive side are the new opportunities for belonging afforded by the new role of pupil. Classroom rituals and routines, as long as they are fair and inclusive, can bind children together into a supportive subculture: most practitioners spend important sessions with their new class deciding on the 'golden rules' for their group – rules which should acknowledge the importance of the learning process as well as the rights of the individual child and the fostering of social relationships. Another perspective on the self is now available to the child as she reflects on herself, not only as a member of her continuing family and new class but as someone with a history in different settings – someone who *used* to attend a particular pre-school or reception class and is now a member of a new social group. Both the continuity of self and the changing nature of self become part of the child's reality as she formulates this new view of herself as a person with many guises.

A theme of 'belonging' and its potential contribution to spiritual, social, cultural and moral development

The Key Stage 1 curriculum can present opportunities for the theme of 'belonging' to become an explicit focus for learning both within and beyond the classroom. Such a theme can draw upon parental interest and involvement and build bridges between the child, her parents and the wider local community. The non-statutory framework for religious education (QCA/DfES, 2004) identifies this theme for Key Stage 1, suggesting that children should consider 'where and how people belong and why belonging is important'. The recommended learning experiences include visiting places of worship, listening and responding to visitors from local faith communities, using their senses and having times of quiet reflection. A case study may serve to illustrate the potential of such a visit, designed by one school to dovetail into local initiatives for personal, social and health education, spiritual, moral, social and cultural education and citizenship education.

The inner-city primary school, in an attempt to forge positive links between the school and local faith communities, took 22 Year 1 children, accompanied by teachers, teaching assistants and several parents, on a visit to a local mosque during the autumn term. The secretary of the mosque gave the traditional greeting of 'As Salamu Alaykum' and pointed to the different designs and colours of the wall tiles which complemented each other and made a beautiful pattern. This, he said, was like the people and religions in the local community. Then, one of the children, Ahmed, quite spontaneously, wanted to show how he prayed when he came to the mosque. He took his place confidently before the mihrab, facing towards Mecca, and began to demonstrate the prayer positions. His father, one of the parent helpers, called to him to recite, as well as demonstrate, the prayers. His father was proud that he and his son had been able to participate in the educational process and Ahmed's classmates and teachers were mesmerized that this quiet and shy boy could be so confident in a different environment. As the children designed tiles, drew clock faces and copied Arabic writing, parents questioned members of the community, one asking, 'When you pray to Allah, is it the same God that we pray to?' The visit to the mosque provided a rich learning experience which fostered the spiritual, moral, social and cultural development not only of the children but of the teachers and parents alike.

Responsibility

We conclude this section with another example of the way that responsibility in the classroom can contribute to a child's sense of self – see Learning story 2.3.

Learning story 2.3 Omar: taking responsibility in Year 1

Omar had learning difficulties: a physical speech impediment combined with language delay in his first language and limited proficiency in English made communication in class a great struggle for him. Although his teacher had established ground rules for supporting Omar with the class, she was not able to ensure that he was always included in children's self-directed activities.

The class operated a 'helper' system whereby a new child each day – the next child in an alphabetical list of first names – took responsibility for collecting the register, bringing children to the carpet for group times, instigating clearing up, leading the children to lunch and so on. The first time the list reached 'O', Omar was absent, somewhat to his teacher's relief but, as his turn approached again, Omar was visibly excited, waving his arms at the list and stammering desperately in his efforts to communicate his awareness of his impending role. When the day arrived, Omar pulled his mother into the classroom, marched over to the name chart and moved the marker to his name, then set about arranging the small chairs and cushions for group time, blurted out his intention of fetching the register and sat quietly waiting to hand it to his teacher with the appropriate pens. The children responded patiently and respectfully all day to his instructions and management: Omar signalled tidy-up time by walking around the room banging a drum, and the children quickly reminded each other to pack away; Omar tried to tell them to wash their hands before lunch and they went more quickly than usual; Omar chose a picture book for story-time and several children said 'Oh, thanks, Omar, I like that one'. Not only was this, in his teacher's view, the happiest day in school ever for Omar, but its effects persisted in improved confidence for Omar and improved relationships with his classmates.

Summary

This section has discussed the development of young children's sense of self, from its small beginnings as a reflection of the child's place in an intimate caregiver relationship, to a more varied and complex and volatile construct, revealed in different ways in different contexts. Throughout, the emphasis has been on the adult's role and responsibility for responding sensitively to children's varied needs: for protection and affection, for reassurance and responsibility, and for modelling ways of being in the world.

Further reading

Dowling, M. (2005) *Young Children's Personal, Social and Emotional Development*. 2nd edition. London: Paul Chapman Publishing.

Schaffer, H.R. (1996) *Social Development*. Oxford: Blackwell.

Learning about relationships: families, friends and others

Early relationships

All personal and social learning, as we have seen, begins in interactions so that 'learning about myself', the child's first concern, is achieved *through* relationships. Between the ages of 3 and 7, however, relationships with others, both adults and children, become increasingly important in their own right as the child's focus of attention moves outwards. Children's play behaviour provides clear evidence of this shift. Studies of children's self-directed play (Broadhead, 1997) confirm that from around the age of 3, children in group settings spend much of their time playing sociably with others, and by 4 or 5, peer friendships have assumed great importance for many children (Dunn, 2004). At the same time, adults continue to play a vital role in supporting and extending children's social and emotional learning. Early years settings often plan their provision around this 'relationships' agenda, but relationships with peers and teachers continue to dominate children's experience of the learning environment throughout childhood. As Dowling (2005: 30) points out: 'We all need other people to help us learn and young children need adults and other children. Thus, a child's ability to form good relationships not only enhances her personal development but helps her progress intellectually.'

Learning about relationships from 3 to 5

The Early Years Foundation Stage includes in its objectives the statements 'Form friendships with other children' and 'Form good relationships with adults and peers' (DfES, 2007: 30 and 32), and sets goals like these within an overarching commitment to play as 'a key way in which young children learn with enjoyment and challenge'. Learning about relationships through play begins with the earliest peek-a-boo games played by infants and their caregivers and continues throughout their early years. We identify here some important aspects of this learning.

Social competence

A three-year-old is a socially aware person who is capable of making and keeping friends and of negotiating interesting co-operations and tests of understandings with a wide range of acquaintances. (Trevarthen, 1998: 97)

In order to make and sustain relationships, we need to acquire a range of related social 'skills'. These include learning about turn-taking, sharing, negotiating, co-operating and empathizing. All these skills may be learnt from the modelling behaviour of adults towards children, but all spring too from an important underlying ability which is achieved during the early years – the ability to take the perspective of others, to understand and appreciate their point of view. In identifying and fostering this ability in children, we are recognizing them as contributors to their own social development and learning; as individuals who are developing appropriate social strategies because they are able to construct an authentic reason for them, based on their recognition that others have similar needs to themselves.

Despite evidence to the contrary, there is still a 'folk belief' – which early childhood practitioners are in a position to counter – that children are self-centred and egocentric in their pre-school years. We know from research that children who hear feelings discussed are able to empathize and take on the perspectives of others from an early age – possibly as young as 2 – and that in most families girls are far more likely to be offered this opportunity than boys (Dunn et al., 1991). Part of the challenge for practitioners concerned to reduce gender stereotyping is to create an environment in which everyone's feelings count and the discussion of feelings is for everyone to share. Stories are an excellent starting point for such discussions

Realistically, we can expect young children to be motivated (as adults are) by a mixture of self-interest and altruism. Adults supporting children in their play disputes intuitively offer both perspectives to children, pointing out that sharing a toy enables both children to enjoy it, that taking turns allows more children to participate, that relinquishing a desired object to a playmate leaves the child free to take up another offered activity. When these cause-and-effect relationships are made explicit to children, they can include them in their own repertoire of strategies for resolving conflicts *and* in their own social-justice vocabulary of what is 'fair' and 'not fair'.

Social play

Almost every aspect of play in a social group involves negotiation and conversation: over the ownership of bikes and blocks, or the right to play the role of superhero or princess. Good relationships with peers and adults make such negotiations worthwhile for children, ensuring both the emotional satisfaction of developing friendships and the pleasure of prolonged and successful play bouts in which the negotiated 'rules' enable both exciting improvisations, and familiar repetitions, to occur.

Play theorists have traditionally focused on socio-dramatic, or 'pretend', play as the pre-eminent vehicle for such learning. The theories of Piaget, who saw *symbolic play* as the characteristic activity for 3–6-year-olds, and Vygotsky, who taught us to look at the value of peer interactions for learning language and culture, are cited in support of this view, and research has shown strong associations between children's engagement in pretend play and their learning in several dimensions (Smilansky, 1990). There can be no doubt that perspective-taking is a pre-requisite for successful pretend play: most children will concede that if someone else is the mummy, she must be allowed to get on with the cooking, however much the child with the role of baby or dog would like a turn with the pots and pans.

Recent studies show that there is far more to social play than socio-dramatic play. Faulkner (1995) argues that all forms of play and games can contribute to children's development of social competence. Vygotsky, she points out, 'saw play between children as creating a zone in which their performance is in advance of their actual developmental level'. This zone (the ZPD) can be seen as 'a sort of inter-psychological, social space in which children can explore new knowledge and ideas through conversation and other forms of interaction' (Faulkner, 1995: 241). Not only pretend play but social play of all kinds – with sand and water, with blocks and bricks, with small-world toys and malleable materials – lends itself to such explorations.

More radically, studies by Broadhead (1997; 2001) and Holland (2003) have convincingly demonstrated that the kinds of play which have not traditionally been approved in pre-schools – rough and tumble, aggressive play and even gun play – can have hugely positive outcomes for children's social and emotional development. Broadhead's development of a 'Social Play Continuum' allows practitioners to identify the development of children's social skills through entering and participating in play bouts, while Holland's work in nursery settings gives powerful evidence of the depth of emotional understanding, and social bonding, that can develop among boys especially while they are 'play-fighting'. Evidence from such studies reminds us of the need to reflect on and challenge our professional assumptions about what is 'good for children' and what is not.

Early years settings are full of opportunities to explore feelings. Experienced practitioners know what happens when they quietly sit alongside children who are playing with malleable materials or making patterns with pegs and cubes. These are often the occasions when children, in a relaxed and unhurried manner, confide their stories about happy and unhappy events and their worries about changes in their lives. They may also be occasions when adults should suppress the impulses of their professional training (to verbalize, elaborate and extend children's thoughts and words) and simply listen!

Friendship

Children's friendships develop, in the pre-school years, from associations based on convenience and contingency (mixing with the children of neighbours; playing with the other children in the child's key worker group or home room) to relationships based on shared identities and individual preferences. By the time they are 4 it is commonly observed that many boys play almost entirely with boys, and that minority ethnic children in a setting are frequently found together. Studies of children in reception and kindergarten classes (Brooker, 2006) have shown that children work hard at maintaining their gender and ethnic identities, and the choice of playmates from their own 'group' provides both a scaffold and a safety net in avoiding risky mistakes about appropriate attitudes and behaviour.

When children meet new challenges, such as transition to a new class or a new school, these friendships support and sustain them, providing 'the emotional and cognitive resources necessary for successful adaptation to their social world' (Faulkner and Miell, 1993: 25). The EYFS framework includes countless contexts for making friends – including, to some people's surprise – learning at the computer (see Learning story 2.4).

Learning story 2.4 Georgia: playing together at the computer

The nursery class at Barrack Road Primary is a microcosm of the local neighbourhood: its intake includes children whose parents are from Bangladesh and Pakistan, Somalia, Sierra Leone, Turkey and Kosovo. Despite the staff's efforts to encourage children from different linguistic backgrounds to mix, most interact almost exclusively with others from their own group.

Georgia (age 4, white UK), who is quite a skilful computer user, joins a small group of less experienced children who are attempting to find their way though an open-ended software program called Henry's Party. These four – Kol, a boy from Kosovo; Hafsa, a girl of Bangladeshi background; Alican, a boy from Turkey; and Ali, a boy from Somalia – crowd round her enthusiastically as she starts to play. She clicks on a 'birthday party' where farmyard animals are singing 'Happy Birthday' and all five children sway and sing along with the music. But when she starts to select other options, by clicking on different parts of the picture, Georgia rapidly becomes annoyed: all three boys are standing with their hands or fingers on the screen to request an item, and she is unable to see to make her own choice. She complains loudly and brushes their hands aside while they protest verbally in the limited English they can command ('it my turn', 'no, him one').

When Georgia selects a sorting game she demonstrates both her physical skill and control (dragging and dropping items on screen) and her lack of cognitive sophistication (she sorts almost every item incorrectly). The other children seem to believe that she is making deliberate mistakes: they all happily join in saying 'uh-oh' with the computer, as each incorrect choice is made. Ali roars with laughter and Kol turns to the nearby researcher to make sure she has understood the joke. All five children are engrossed in their shared experience of the activity, although they are otherwise unable to communicate with each other at all.

Not all children find it easy to make friends, and practitioners may need to devise specific strategies to support children who, for any reason, are not accepted within the group culture of the setting. Fortunately most practitioners are very alert to such exclusions and have strategies for promoting the self-esteem of 'outsiders'.

Learning values: a case study in promoting moral and spiritual development

The EYFS framework, and the environment it promotes, offer many opportunities for children to learn values through their daily activities and relationships in the setting. Children are expected to 'work as part of a group or class' and to understand the need for 'agreed values and codes of behaviour for groups of people'. A case study may illustrate how, even in a reception class, if given the opportunity, children can be capable of quite sophisticated levels of negotiation in order to achieve a common goal.

The class was embarking on a topic of 'Special Places' which began with the children discussing their own special places and describing why they were special to them. For many, their special place was their bedroom, or a house created underneath a large table or even a garden shed and they talked about the presence of favourite colours, treasured stories, toys and even pets. These were places where the children felt safe but able to be alone, places where they obviously had a measure of control over their environment. Sullivan (Erricker et al., 1997: 173) in his research with young children noted their need to 'escape from the hurly-burly of day-to-day living' and their sense of 'sacred space', while Nye (Hay with Nye, 1998: 99) reminds us of the need to be alert to individual children expressing their spirituality in distinct ways. The next stage was for the children to recreate the Home Corner as a 'special place' and this involved negotiating what would or would not be included and valuing the contributions and wishes of others. The 'Special Place' was established and to the teacher's astonishment, the children themselves requested that there should be rules on how to behave in this special place. The children, with support from the teacher, negotiated once more and a list of rules was duly posted outside the Home Corner.

Concrete learning of abstract concepts, such as appropriate and inappropriate behaviour, occurs when adults take time to discuss with children the fairness of decisions, the consequences of actions, intentional and unintentional, and the kinds of behaviour which have positive outcomes for the 'common good' of the whole group, rather than benefiting one child.

When they are 4 or 5, many children, perhaps stimulated by finding a dead bird or animal or by the death of a family pet, begin to take an interest in the 'big' questions of life and death. Those working with the children may feel uncomfortable and ill-equipped to discuss such issues, but children are puzzled by and have a need to talk about what makes something alive and what makes it dead and discuss the matter with a natural fascination and unselfconscious ease not experienced by adults. Beginning to get to grips with these life-cycle events is an important aspect of personal and spiritual development. Usually there is no need for the adult to offer viewpoints or explanations about life and death: listening to children, accepting their feelings and supporting their efforts to make sense of the world is the most important contribution a practitioner can make. The children in Learning story 2.5 are responding, without prompting, to a story they have just heard.

Learning story 2.5 Talking about feelings: the grasshopper and the butterfly

The reception class had shared a story about a grasshopper and a butterfly. In circle time, the children began to talk:

Amy   I'm playing sad music for the grasshopper (strumming the sole of her shoe) 'cos he's died.

Ashley   I think God will make the grasshopper alive again. Once there was a snail outside getting near the water, by the pond. I moved it in case it fell in and it can't swim.

Rachel   If you see a little bird and it can't fly, put a plaster on it and put some flowers if it's died. And water. That's to say we loved the thing that died, and the water's for the bird and the flowers …

Navdeep When my grandma died I put lots of flowers on my grandma, on the body, I've got a picture of her in my house and, in my garden in India, I did hold a bird. (Bennett, 1997: 10–11)

Circle time provided these children with a space and a time to reflect on the story, to make links with their own experiences and to share these within the social context of the group. In terms of 'spiritual' development, they were enabled to explore their experiences of awe and wonder at the natural world, their feelings of sadness and love and their attempts to make sense of patterns of life and death, while the process of sharing with their peers, listening and being listened to fostered their feelings of self-esteem and confidence.

Learning about relationships from 5 to 7

'Becoming a pupil' in Key Stage 1 requires a child to enter into quite new relationships in which there may be fewer opportunities for considering personal feelings and emotions. The non-statutory guidance, however, recommends that pupils *should be taught*:

- to recognize how their behaviour affects other people;
- to listen to other people, and play and work co-operatively;
- to identify and respect the differences; and similarities between people;
- that family and friends should care for each other; and
- that there are different types of teasing and bullying, that bullying is wrong, and how to get help to stop bullying.

These aspects of learning should provide children with strong foundations, both for their relationships with peers and adults, and for their future role as citizens.

Social competence

In the Key Stage 1 classroom, the social competencies children have acquired through informal interactions and play experiences become essential prerequisites for interactions around 'work' of an increasingly formal kind. In a more structured environment, which includes whole-class tasks as well as individual or group activities, sharing resources and taking turns, and respecting the space and needs of others are priorities for harmonious working. The group culture of the classroom can support children who struggle with this aspect of group membership: discussing 'classroom rules' or 'golden rules' is usually part of the settling-in period in a new class, and skilful practitioners work with children to construct rules which are positive rather than prohibitive. Children of this age generally find it easy to generate a long list of don'ts, and the activity of transforming these into positive statements can be an important learning experience. Positive rules almost always involve *thinking about the effect on others* of one's own actions: if children are encouraged to ask themselves about this in all their daily decision-making, they will learn not only to be an effective pupil but to be an effective member of society.

Play with peers

Practitioners as well as parents observe with pleasure children's growing ability in these years to participate in 'games with rules', described by Piaget as the characteristic form of play as children approach middle childhood. The need for rules such as turn-taking and fairness is evident to children once they are old enough to organize their own game-playing; many are passionate about ensuring fair play.

Children's enthusiasm for games, and genuine involvement in them, is a context for both social and cognitive learning. Games such as board and card games, quizzes and puzzles, and computer games are an appropriate vehicle for much of the teaching and learning in the Key Stage 1 curriculum, including the reinforcement of components of the *PNS Framework for Literacy and Mathematics*. Even if few of the pre-school play opportunities remain, games and puzzles, as well as construction toys, allow children to continue to construct their own learning through interactions in an environment where teaching otherwise tends to be more directive. The view of play as a zone of proximal development, a social space in which peer interactions among a group with different levels of knowledge and skill provide support for less experienced participants, applies to board games and computer games, as well as to role play.

Games can also be a staple ingredient of life in playgrounds, although research has shown that playtime is not always a time for fun and amusement, and that some children experience considerable unkindness and aggression from their peers in this child-ordered environment. Sluckin (1987) and Connolly (1998) both demonstrated that hierarchies constructed by children to include and exclude particular individuals and groups mirrored those of the adult world and were often rooted in gendered and racial prejudice and discrimination. Children's social interactions in the playground, sometimes viewed as a 'preparation for life', can be very damaging for some children.

Most practitioners recognize the valuable space that outdoor play offers for privacy and friendships as children grow into middle childhood, and the importance of children developing strong peer cultures. But it is vital to ensure that the key messages in the non-statutory guidance (about friendship, teasing and bullying) are taught in thoughtful and effective ways from the start of primary school.

Friendship and citizenship

By the time they are 5 or 6, most children will have acquired the cultural rules both for initiating new friendships and repairing damaged ones (Dunn, 2004). As children's experience of school learning and classroom organization becomes more formal, their friendship groups become part of the group dynamic of the setting, a force to be reckoned with by a teacher in her planning for social learning and in her everyday management of the class. Friendship groups support children in their continuing identity formation and in their negotiations with school adults: any particular group will identify itself against other groups (starting with girls' and boys' frequent rejection of each other's tastes and preferences) and in relation to perceived authority, such as the teacher in the classroom. Wise practitioners will build on their knowledge of children's friendship groups when planning for group work and active learning, and will use circle times to support children's positive attitudes towards each other's differences – both individual and group differences.

In Key Stage 1, schools will seek to make explicit links between the subjects in the taught curriculum and the guidelines for personal, social and health education and citizenship education. The guidelines indicate that pupils should be taught 'that they belong to various groups and communities, such as family and school' and 'to identify and respect the differences and similarities between people'. Learning story 2.6 shows how closely these goals link to moral and spiritual development through a programme of learning in religious education (RE).

Learning story 2.6 Celebrating diversity in Year 1

The classroom assistant was getting married and had invited the Year 1 children to attend the wedding service! The class teacher decided that the RE programme for that term should focus on weddings, which would include learning about the ceremony, the symbols used to show that the couple were joined together and the promises made to each other. The children learnt about and constructed replicas of the church building, they focused on the symbolism of the wedding ring and discussed why promises are made and what those promises should be. As the school was in a multi-faith area, the class then visited the local gurdwara to learn about Sikh weddings and, on their return to school, created a role play of a Sikh wedding with the couple walking around the holy book and symbolizing their union through the draping of a scarf, or chunni, around the shoulders of the couple.

These planned experiences fostered children's learning by introducing them to diverse communities and religious practices present in their local community, by providing opportunities to meet and talk with members of faith communities, and by providing opportunities to consider a social and moral dilemma, such as the making, and keeping, of promises which they were able to relate to their own experience.

Learning values

Theories of moral development, and research into children's cultures, demonstrate the active role of children in constructing beliefs about right and wrong, but it is clear that children's moral development cannot be left to occur unsupported. Adults need to ensure that every child has the opportunity to reflect on values and is supported in reflecting on the outcomes of his or her actions. As in the pre-school years, adults play a crucial role, not only in modelling 'moral' behaviour but in modelling the process of thinking about cause and effect. This includes thinking through the consequences of actions for other people (both altruistic acts such as making a card for a classroom assistant who is unwell, and selfish ones such as using equipment that another class planned to use), and making time to unravel the rights and wrongs of playground disputes, which in turn will enable children to develop their skills of negotiation and conflict resolution. Taking bullying, name-calling and racism seriously may be the most important lesson in values a practitioner can offer. Once again, the skill of perspective-taking is essential to this process, as Vincent's story shows (Learning story 2.7). Over the year, Vincent's class learnt to discuss issues of prejudice knowledgeably and openly, and when the local mosque was despoiled many of the children spontaneously sympathized with, and supported, the Muslim children in the school.

Learning story 2.7 Vincent: thinking about right and wrong

In Year 2, the curriculum required children to develop understanding and empathy for those remote from them in time and space – historical people and those in the 'distant places' of the geography curriculum. One class worked on these skills through the practice of 'talking to the child in the picture', which their teacher had introduced. A large photograph – of small children in a public playground in Delhi, for instance – would be discussed by the class, and individual children would then role play the children in the picture by answering questions put to them by their classmates: 'Is it hot where you are?' 'Um, yeah, it's really, really hot, I need a drink!'

The same practice lent itself to discussions of difference (of age or appearance, gender or ethnicity) and to discussion of feelings. One such discussion revolved around a close-up photograph of a black child sobbing miserably. The children questioned 'the child in the photo' sympathetically: 'Did your mum say you can't play out?' 'Did your mate say he won't play?' and debated the appropriateness of such questions ('He wouldn't be that upset'). They gave lengthier consideration to a suggestion that the child's mother had gone to work without saying goodbye but were still unconvinced. The matter was apparently resolved for them by Vincent, a white child from a family rumoured to be both 'rough' and racist, who asked: 'Did they call you black bastard?' Some children gasped and many looked at their teacher for her reaction, but no one spoke; it seemed as if everyone thought Vincent had found the most likely answer.

Summary

This chapter has discussed the growing importance of relationships with adults outside the home, and with peers, as children move from infancy through the pre-school years and into school. Increasingly, friendships can provide the strongest motivation for children to join in group activities and pursue their own learning interests, but in recognizing their importance, practitioners must be proactive in ensuring that they are contributing to children's well-being, rather than undermining it.

Further reading

Dunn, J. (2004) *Children's Friendships: The Beginnings of Intimacy*. Oxford: Blackwell.
Dunn, J., Brown, J.R. and Beardsall, L. (1991), 'Family talk about feeling states and children's later understanding of others' emotions', *Developmental Psychology*, 27: 448–55.

Learning dispositions: becoming a lifelong learner

What do we mean by dispositions?

Recent research on learning dispositions has confirmed something that experienced practitioners have known intuitively – that children's academic progress and their ultimate achievements depend in large part on their attitude to learning: their initial enthusiasm and openness and their longer-term persistence in problem-solving. Practitioners, like parents, have sighed over children who 'could do it if they wanted to', could 'get there if they tried a bit harder' or who 'have the ability, if only they didn't give up so easily'. Research has given us some insights into the reasons for children's different levels of motivation and persistence and, in doing so, gives some clues as to how we can foster these important dispositions in the early years.

Lillian Katz (1995) argues that, although babies are born with some innate *predispositions* – personality traits which are genetically acquired – these are not the most important influences on the *dispositions* they display in their pre-school and school settings. *Dispositions*, like the young child's other personal and social behaviours, are *learnt*, through early experience, and can be un-learnt through subsequent experiences. This may be one of the most important challenges for practitioners but it is one that pays off handsomely. The effort put into fostering positive dispositions is rewarded by children who are more purposeful and successful and less likely to become disaffected. As Anning and Edwards claim:

> Those of us who are involved in the education of young children ... need to focus on helping children to become learners, to enjoy learning and to feel that they are people who are able to learn. This is no small challenge but it is a safe bet that investment in children's dispositions to learn will pay dividends. (1999: 59)

Developmental psychologists have demonstrated that children's own theories about learning, often acquired from their parents, produce specific and predictable patterns of behaviour when they are confronted with new learning tasks. These patterns were given the shorthand tags of 'helpless' and 'mastery' orientations towards learning and were seen in children who, respectively, gave up easily and relied on others to coach them through tasks, or took on new tasks with an enthusiasm and determination to succeed with them. The underlying theories children held (about intelligence and achievement) interacted with their experiences in educational settings so that their theories were, on the whole, confirmed by their real-life successes and failures (Dweck and Leggett, 1988; Smiley and Dweck, 1984).

Over the past decade, early years educators have translated this research evidence into recommendations for practice. Before turning to their suggestions, let us look at 4-year-old Kelly's dispositions in her second week at school (Learning story 2.8). Kelly's teacher, clearly, needs to foster her fearless disposition and help Kelly to use it in a wide range of activities.

Learning story 2.8 Kelly – creating challenges

Kelly, along with her classmates, was being assessed on a baseline measure of completing simple jigsaw puzzles. She was experienced with puzzles after spending a year in nursery and progressed rapidly through the array of increasingly difficult puzzles the staff had set out, seizing a new puzzle with one hand as she fitted the last piece to the previous one and pushed it away from her. Having exhausted them she quickly improvised her own challenge, turning a 12-piece puzzle upside down (so that the picture was hidden) and announcing 'Now I'm going to do it the hard way'. She completed the puzzle by trial and error, with considerable effort and concentration, and instructed the researcher, 'Now you mix some of them up for me while I shut my eyes, to make it harder this time'. Eventually she tried putting some puzzles together, by feel with her eyes still closed; after several failed attempts, when she remarked 'I've done it wrong, I'll have to have another go', she gave up and pranced away without further concern. At no time did she seem interested in the adult's view of her performance.

Learning dispositions from 3 to 7: theory into practice

The Practice Guidance for the Early Years Foundation Stage prioritizes learning dispositions, because the first 'goals' in the framework are that children should 'Continue to be interested, excited and motivated to learn' (DfES, 2007: 25). The Stepping Stones towards this goal specify that children should 'Have a strong exploratory impulse', 'develop self-confidence and a belief in themselves' and 'persist for extended periods of time'. All these attributes are associated with the 'mastery' dispositions which enable children to carry on learning throughout their school career, and in the face of difficulties and frustrations.

Dispositions have been defined by Katz as 'relatively enduring habits of mind or characteristic ways of responding to experience across types of situations' (1995: 62). She goes on to stress that 'not all dispositions are desirable, and curriculum and teaching practices must address not only how to strengthen desirable dispositions but how to address an undesirable one' (Katz, 1995: 63). Katz outlines some reasons why this should be a goal of early childhood education:

- Without appropriate dispositions, children in educational settings will acquire knowledge and skills which they do not then use: all children, for instance, know how to listen, but some children are not inclined to do so! Katz argues that, since skills improve with use, it is important to strengthen the disposition to use them.
- The process of acquiring knowledge and skills may actually decrease children's motivation to use them. Katz's example here is early formal instruction in reading, which may not only teach children to read but also teach them there is no fun in reading. In such a case it can be argued that the disposition to have a go at reading is more important than the skill of reading.
- Some dispositions to learn (such as exploration) are inborn – wired into the child's brain – but these dispositions can be damaged or extinguished for good by inappropriate learning experiences.
- Close observation of children at this age can show what kind of feedback from adults works for each child: some children for instance will be motivated by praise for their performance, while others will become dependent and unable to self-motivate if praised too highly. Striking the balance for each child is of paramount importance.
- Dispositions are most likely to be acquired through adult modelling of behaviours rather than through direct teaching. Early educators can model exploratory and curious behaviour and demonstrate that feeling uncertain and making mistakes are part of the learning process.

High-quality early education has consistently demonstrated the importance of efforts to strengthen learning dispositions. Systematic reviews of the long-term outcomes of well-planned programmes such as High/Scope (Schweinhart et al., 1993) show that a change in children's attitudes towards themselves and their learning, rather than a change in their measurable IQ (intelligence quotient), is the most important factor in transforming the life chances of children from disadvantaged communities. Reviewing the effectiveness of early education, Sylva (1994: 94) concluded that 'The most important learning in pre-school concerns aspiration, task commitment, social skills and feelings of efficacy'. This is the mechanism which enables early education to 'make a difference' in children's lives which stays with them into adulthood, so it is important to get it right.

The Te Whaariki curriculum in New Zealand (Carr and May, 2000) identifies five domains of children's well-being and enthusiasm for learning: taking an interest; being involved; persisting with difficulty or uncertainty; communicating with others; and taking responsibility. Carr (2001) further demonstrates the dynamic way that these domains can be put into practice when planning for children's learning and assessing the learning behaviours of individuals. She collapses the five domains into a deceptively simple formula of being *ready, willing and able* to learn within the setting. For any individual child, these conditions can only be fulfilled when he or she has a sense of his or her own efficacy (good self-esteem, based on realistic evaluations) *and* is presented with interesting and relevant opportunities, *and* feels safe and secure in his or her settings and his or her relationships. If these conditions are met, most children will be in a position to 'take an interest, get involved, persist with difficulties, communicate with others, and take responsibility' for their own learning.

All these themes are elaborated in a paper (Claxton and Carr, 2004) which argues that the responsibility for educators trying to prepare children for an uncertain future is that of 'developing young people's ability to be skilful and confident when facing complex predicaments of all kinds' (2004: 87) – in other words, to give children the skills and habits of mind to cope in changing circumstances. These authors present the view that a 'learning curriculum' focused on developing dispositions is at least as important as a 'content curriculum' focused on the transmission of existing knowledge and skills, and they suggest ways that practitioners can get to grips with these very implicit processes. One way of approaching this is to advocate that children's learning dispositions are made more *robust*, *broad* and *rich*, so that they are strengthened and deepened as they are applied in different contexts. Another is to describe the environments offered to young children as *prohibiting, affording, inviting* or *potentiating* – where the latter enhances children's dispositions by offering 'frequent participation in shared activity' (2004: 92).

Much of the responsibility for children's learning dispositions lies with adults, who themselves need to be *ready, willing and able* to perform a supportive role as children acquire the learning dispositions that will see them through the lifelong learning ahead of them. Tyler's story (see Learning story 2.9) shows how a skilled practitioner can intervene to transform a child's 'feelings of efficacy'.

Learning story 2.9 Tyler – fear of failure in reception class

Tyler started school with great promise. He had attended an excellent nursery and his mother had bought him as she said 'hundreds of books' as well as educational tapes and videos for early literacy learning. Tyler was a cheerful, sociable and articulate boy who enjoyed conversations with adults and quickly established good relationships. So it was surprising to discover that he wanted nothing at all to do with reading or writing: if an adult approached while he was drawing he would put his pencil down, push his paper away and say: 'I can't write, you know – I'm not gonna write.' If an adult sat close by while he was looking in a book, he would sometimes shut the book and say: 'I'm not reading, I can't read!'

Tyler's teacher realized that he had probably absorbed a certain amount of anxiety and unconscious pressure from his mother, who was desperately keen for him to learn to read. She adopted an entirely carefree and casual tone in her reading sessions with Tyler, sharing small jokes with him, drawing his attention to humorous illustrations, chatting about non-sense rhymes, but never focusing his attention on decoding the actual text in the early reading books. In her written messages to the family, in Tyler's home reading bag, she rec-ommended the same practices, suggesting that his parents read to him, or invite him to 'read' the pictures rather than the words or make up nonsense rhymes. After a few months, to his great relief (and his mother's), Tyler began to notice that he could read – that he knew what the words said! Armed with this confidence he was able to get involved in all the learning activities of his literacy-rich classroom.

How does this supportive work continue into Key Stage 1? The National Curriculum guidance (DfEE/QCA, 1999) is not very specific, although its first aim clearly refers to learning dispositions: 'The school curriculum should develop enjoyment of, and com-mitment to, learning … It should build on pupils' strengths, interests and experiences and develop their confidence in their capacity to learn and work independently and collaboratively.' Transition and continuity are again of the utmost importance: a sudden jump from the informality and play-based learning of the EYFS to the formal curriculum of Year 1 may undermine children's confidence in themselves as learners and undo many of the important lessons they have learnt. Practitioners need to allow for a period of adjustment and help children to become proud of their new, more grown-up ways of learning. The progress and behaviour of individuals must be care-fully monitored in the early weeks of the new key stage: children who are feeling insecure about their competence and status may find different ways of showing it, and both the shy withdrawn child and the boastful bullying one need sensitive support.

Strategies for fostering children's personal and social identity, discussed earlier in this chapter, are an essential foundation for the maintenance of good learning disposi-tions. Children who are secure in their relationships with adults and peers will be more willing to take risks, ask questions and admit difficulties. The outcome of 'Enjoying and Achieving' is crucially dependent on this sense of self-belief as a learner, and prac-titioners must work hard to prioritize it. In Key Stage 1 circle times may be held less frequently because of timetable pressures, but once a week at least the class should have the chance to review what has been new, what has been difficult, what has been fun and what has been surprising for them, collectively and individually. Teachers play a crucial role in creating the ethos that informs these sessions so that children's contri-butions are both positive and realistic. As in the pre-school setting, adults' modelling of dispositions and behaviours – of feeling curious, feeling fed up, deciding to have another try, admiring the success of others – helps children to identify these feelings in themselves and to recognize that they are all part of the learning process.

Learning dispositions and spiritual and moral development

> Unless children's emotional needs are met, all learning is impaired. (Eaude, 2006: 63)

As indicated in the paragraphs above, children's emotional needs are complex, and they require a supportive environment which acknowledges the religious, spiritual, moral and cultural contexts in which children's learning takes place. Without explicitly acknowledging these areas of the child's experience, a significant aspect of her identity or personality may be 'disengaged' from the nursery or classroom and impede the child from fully accessing the learning opportunities provided. Many children come from homes where religious beliefs influence their daily experience, for example, the food they eat, their out-of-school friendships and celebrations, their experience of belonging and community and their sense of place, both emotionally and geographically. The spiritual context relates to the child's need to create, in Eaude's words, 'an increasingly coherent narrative about themselves' (Eaude, 2006: 63). The child then needs an environment which fosters their sense of awe in the natural world, a safe environment where she can explore those 'big' questions of meaning, an environment which accepts and supports feelings of joy and of sadness in the face of birth, loss and death. Opportunities are needed to develop skills and confidence to deal with interpersonal dilemmas and conflicts, and exposure to a wealth of cultural images and stories through which a child might find herself reflected in the life of the classroom.

Stories, accompanied by opportunities for reflection, are two powerful means of fostering children's spiritual and moral, and social and cultural, development. 'Good' stories, that is, stories with many layers of meaning, can provide a source through which children can explore questions of identity and belonging, relationships with others and with the natural world. Stories provide characters through whom children can explore different identities, they can feel what it's like to be a 'goody' or a 'baddy' and can 'play with' different behaviours, ways of resolving conflicts and different outcomes. Stories provide a landscape in which children can confront and reflect on emotions and experiences too frightening to confront in daily life, feelings of anger, jealousy and confusion. And good stories are not over in an instant but continue to speak to the child and 'interact' with her developing experience. As Bausch says, the story 'has a life of its own (even when you're done with it, it is not done with you) and it kind of rinses through you. You can't quite put into words what the effect is, but there is a resonance' (Bausch, 1984: 39). Emotional development, for both children and adults, hinges on the ability to make meaning of one's experience in an often bewildering world and it is often stories which capture the imagination and provide the vehicle for that process of meaning-making.

A learning environment which addresses children's spiritual and moral development and provides strategies and resources which in some respect mirror the child's experiences and enables them to reflect on and begin to make sense of their world, has a significant impact on learning potential. By taking seriously the diverse and bewildering experiences which impinge on the child's world, a practitioner fosters the development of an inner self-esteem, a sense of real belonging, a sense of resilience in the face of difficulties and a confidence to fully engage with the learning process.

Assessment for learning

Realistic evaluation and self-evaluation become even more important as children encounter the more difficult tasks, and more challenging curriculum, of Key Stage 1. The traditional types of teacher 'marking' of work can rapidly undo all the progress children have made in forming an appropriate sense of their own achievements, even for pupils who do well. If you hand your 'work' to a teacher and it comes back covered in ticks and stars, you may come to depend on the teacher's view of your work to validate your efforts: in future, your motivation may be satisfying the teacher rather than satisfying yourself. If it comes back covered in crosses and underlinings it is hard to feel motivated at all. As Barrett (1989) warned, children's disaffection begins at an early age and is hard to overcome.

One way to avert disaffection is to enable children to develop self-assessment skills – a continuation of the kind of 'reviewing' of one's own activities that is emphasized in the High/Scope pedagogy. Discussions with individual children about the activities they have completed are time-consuming but can be recognized as an integral part of the child's learning and an invaluable aspect of the teacher's teaching. Once children become skilled at evaluating their own and others' work, they slip into a routine where it is second nature and becomes an ongoing aspect of their work rather than an add-on at the end. Roisin's story (see Learning story 2.10) describes the value of the practice.

Learning story 2.10 Roisin: learning about self-assessment

Roisin was an expert on school: she had been instructed in the rules and routines of the classroom by an older sister and already knew about school practices before she began. In consequence she found it hard to assimilate messages which conflicted with these expectations. When her Year 1 teacher gradually introduced the practice of self-assessment, withholding her own comments on children's processes and products and inviting children to give their opinion of any project they had undertaken, Roisin was uncomfortable. Outwardly she appeared to accept the new routine but, in practice, she continued with her existing habits under a new guise: when invited to comment on a drawing, model or piece of writing, she would instruct her teacher to write 'Lovely', 'Good girl' or 'Well done', and would add her own large ticks or a star before returning her book to her tray or her drawing to its pile. After a time her teacher noticed that Roisin was simply side-stepping the whole process of evaluation by adding the ticks and stars herself, at the same time as putting in a final full stop and disposing of her work without showing it to anyone. Once alerted, she made a point of spending time with Roisin as she completed tasks, discussing 'what you would like me to write about how you have worked' and gently probing the evaluative judgements ('Lovely work!'), encouraging her to replace them with informative ones ('I didn't know how to do "daddy" but Catriona showed me and now I know', 'I remembered about the spaces between the words but not all of them'). Roisin was helped in this process by peer modelling as she observed less self-conscious children discussing what 'comment' they would ask for, and comparing their writing and drawing with earlier examples and with each other's work.

Summary

Children's personal, social and emotional development – and their moral and spiritual development – is intertwined with every aspect of their experience in early childhood settings: with their play, their friendships and their conversations, as well as with the curriculum and the culture of the school. Careful planning is essential for these aspects of learning as it is for their academic learning. But just as essential is the practitioner's own sensitivity – her own ability to tune in to the ways that children's experiences, at home and at school, are shaping their emerging identity.

We might summarize by suggesting that practitioners should be:

- *ready* – to take children's emotional lives seriously and to prioritize these aspects of children's learning in their planning;
- *willing* – to listen and learn, from children, parents and colleagues, about their own concerns and priorities and the ways they think about them; and
- *able* – to exercise their skills confidently and flexibly, responding to children's personal, social and emotional needs as they present themselves.

Further reading

Claxton, G. and Carr, M. (2004) 'A framework for teaching learning: the dynamics of dispositions', *Early Years*, 24(1): 87–97.
Katz, L. (1995) *Talks with Teachers of Young Children*. Norwood, NJ: Ablex.

References

Anning, A. and Edwards, A. (1999) *Promoting Children's Learning from Birth to Five: Developing the New Early Years Professional*. Buckingham: Open University Press.
Barrett, G. (ed.) (1989) *Disaffection from School? The Early Years*. London: Falmer.
Bausch, William J. (1984) *Storytelling: Imagination and Faith*. Connecticut: Twenty-Third Publications.
Bennett, J. (1997) 'Can I tell that story something in a circle?', *Resource*, 19(3): 10–11.

Boyle, M. and Woods, P. (1998) 'Becoming a proper pupil: bilingual children's experience of starting school', *Studies in Educational Ethnography*, 1: 93–113.

Broadhead, P. (1997) 'Promoting sociability and cooperation in nursery settings', *British Educational Research Journal*, 23(4): 513–31.

Broadhead, P. (2001) 'Investigating sociability and cooperation in four and five year olds in reception class settings', *International Journal of Early Years Education*, 9(1) 23–35.

Bronfenbrenner, U. (1979) *The Ecology of Human Development*. Cambridge, MA: Harvard University Press.

Brooker, L. (2002) *Starting School: Young Children Learning Cultures*. Buckingham: Open University Press.

Brooker, L. (2006) 'From home to the home corner: observing children's identity-maintenance in early childhood settings', *Children & Society*, 20: 116–27.

Carr, M. (2001) *Assessment in Early Childhood Settings: Learning Stories*. London: Paul Chapman Publishing.

Carr, M. and May, H. (2000) 'Te Whaariki', in H. Penn (ed.), *Early Childhood Services*. Buckingham: Open University Press.

Cassidy, M. (2005) '"They do it anyway": a study of primary 1 teachers' perceptions of children's transition into primary education', *Early Years*, 25(2) 143–53.

Claxton, G. and Carr, M. (2004) 'A framework for teaching learning: the dynamics of dispositions', *Early Years*, 24(1): 87–97.

Connolly, P. (1998) *Racism, Gender Identities and Young Children: Social Relations in a Multi-Ethnic Inner-City Primary School*. London: Routledge.

Connolly, P., Smith, A. and Kelly, B. (2002) *Too Young to Notice? The Cultural and Political Awareness of 3–6 Year Olds in Northern Ireland*. Belfast: Community Relations Council.

Cousins, J. (1990) 'Are your little Humpty Dumpties floating or sinking? What sense do children of 4 make of the reception class at school?', *Early Years*, 10(2) 28–38.

Dalli, C. (2000) 'Starting child care: what young children learn about relating to adults in the first weeks of starting child care', *Early Childhood Research and Practice*, 2(2): 1–31.

Department for Education and Employment/Qualifications and Curriculum Authority (DfEE/QCA) (1999) *The National Curriculum. Handbook for Primary Teachers in England*. London: DfEE.

Department for Education and Employment/Qualifications and Curriculum Authority (DfEE/QCA) (2000) *Curriculum Guidance for the Foundation Stage*. London: QCA.

Department for Education and Skills (DfES) (2003) *Every Child Matters* (Green Paper). London: HMSO

Department for Education and Skills (DfES) (2007) *The Statutory Framework for the Early Years Foundation Stage*. London: HMSO.

Department for Education and Skills (DfES) (2007) *The Practice Guidance for the Early Years Foundation Stage*. London: DfES Publications.

Dowling, M. (2000) *Young Children's Personal, Social and Emotional Development*. London: Paul Chapman Publishing.

Dowling, M. (2005) *Young Children's Personal, Social and Emotional Development*. 2nd edition. London: Paul Chapman Publishing.

Dunn, J. (2004) *Children's Friendships: The Beginnings of Intimacy*. Oxford: Blackwell.

Dunn, J. Brown, J.R. and Beardsall, L. (1991), 'Family talk about feeling states and children's later understanding of others' emotions', *Developmental Psychology*, 27: 448–55.

Dweck, C. and Leggett, E. (1988) 'A social-cognitive approach to motivation and personality', *Psychological Review*, 95(2): 256–73.

Eaude, T. (2006) *Children's Spiritual, Moral, Social and Cultural Development: Primary and Early Years*. Learning Matters: Exeter.

Eaude, T. (2006) 'Strangely familiar? – teachers making sense of young children's spiritual development', *Early Years*, Vol 25, 3.

Erricker C., Erricker, J., Ots C, Sullivan D. and Fletcher M. (1997) *The Education of the Whole Child*. London: Cassell.

Faulkner, D. (1995) 'Play, self and the social world', in P. Barnes (ed.), *Personal, Social and Emotional Development of Children*. Oxford: Blackwell/Open University.

Faulkner, D. and Miell, D. (1993) 'Settling into school: the importance of early friendships for the development of children's social understanding and communicative competence', *International Journal of Early Years Education*, 1(1): 23–45.

Gopnik, A., Meltzoff, A. and Kuhl, P. (1999) *The Scientist in the Crib: Minds, Brains and How Children Learn*. New York: HarperCollins.

Gottman, J. (1997) *The Heart of Parenting: How to Raise an Emotionally Intelligent child*. London: Bloomsbury.

Gura, P. (1996) 'What I want for Cinderella: self-esteem and self-assessment', *Early Education*, 19: 3–5.

Hay, D. with Nye, R. (1998): *The Spirit of the Child*. London: Fount.

Holland, P. (2003) *We Don't Play with Guns Here: War, Weapon and Superhero Play in the Early Years*. Milton Keynes: Open University Press.

Hughes, M. (1996) 'Parents, teachers and schools', in B. Bernstein and J. Brannen (eds), *Children, Research and Policy*. London: Taylor & Francis.

Hughes, M., Wikely, F. and Nash, T. (1994) *Parents and their Children's Schools*. Oxford: Blackwell.

Katz, L. (1995) *Talks with Teachers of Young Children*. Norwood, NJ: Ablex.

Lloyd, B and Duveen, G. (1992) *Gender Identities and Education: The Impact of Starting School*. New York: St Martin's Press.

Miell, D. (1995) 'Developing a sense of self', in P. Barnes (ed.), *Personal, Social and Emotional Development of Children*. Oxford: Blackwell/Open University.

Murray, L. and Andrews, L. (2000) *The Social Baby*. Richmond, VA: CP Publishing.

National Curriculum Council (1993) *Spiritual and Moral Development: A Discussion Paper*. York: National Curriculum Council.

OFSTED (1994) *Spiritual, Moral, Social and Cultural Development: An Ofsted Discussion Paper*. London: OFSTED.

Qualifications Curriculum Authority/Department for Education and Skills (QCA/DfES) (2004): *Religious education: The non-statutory national framework*.

Roberts, R. (2002) *Self-esteem and Early Learning*. London: Paul Chapman Publishing.

Rogoff, B. (1990) *Apprenticeship in thinking: Cognitive development in Social Context*. New York: Oxford University Press.

SCAA (1995): Spiritual and Moral Development: SCAA Discussion Papers No.3.

Schaffer, H.R. (1996) *Social Development*. Oxford: Blackwell.

Schweinhart, L.J., Barnes, H.V. and Weikart, D.P. (1993) *Significant Benefits: The High/Scope Perry Preschool Study through Age 27*. Ypsilanti, MI: High/Scope Education Research Foundation.

Shonkoff, J. and Phillips, D. (eds) (2001) *From Neurons to Neighbourhoods: The Science of Early Childhood Development*. Washington: Board on Children, Youth and families; Committee on Integrating the Science of Early Childhood Development.

Sluckin, A. (1987) 'The culture of the primary school playground', in A. Pollard (ed.), *Children and their Primary Schools*. Lewes: Falmer.

Smilansky, S. (1990) 'Socio-dramatic play: its relevance to behaviour and achievement in school', in E. Klugman and S. Smilansky (eds), *Children's Play and Learning: Perspectives and Policy Implications*. New York: Teachers College Press.

Smiley, P. and Dweck, C. (1984) 'Individual differences in achievement goals among young children', *Child Development*, 65: 1723–43.

Sure Start Unit (2002) *Birth to Three Matters: A Framework to Support Children in their Earliest Years*. London: DfES.

Sylva, K. (1994) 'The impact of early learning on children's later development', in C. Ball (ed.), *Start Right: The Importance of Early Learning*. London: Royal Society of Arts.

Trevarthen, C. (1998) 'A child's need to learn a culture', in M. Woodhead, D. Faulker and K. Littleton (eds), *Cultural Worlds of Early Childhood*. London: Routledge.

This chapter is taken from:
Riley, J. (ed.) (2007) *Learning in the Early Years 3–7,* Second Edition
978-1-4129-2995-0

Working with Children: Meeting individual needs

VICKY HUTCHIN

Vicky Hutchin, Regional Adviser for the Foundation Stage in the DfES National Strategies, has worked first in playgroups and then as an early years teacher and advisory teacher. She has written three books, published by Hodder & Stoughton, on effective early years practice, especially observation and assessment.

Aims

To develop understanding of:

☐ and consider why it is important to meet children's individual needs
☐ and consider the essential role of observation in working with young children, 0–6 yrs
☐ and consider the special significance of observing play, with reference to some theories about the role of play in child development
☐ and examine some of the practical skills necessary for an effective observation/assessment/ planning cycle.

To ensure children are confident, happy and engaged in learning, their individual needs must be met. This may sound simple, but it is a highly complex task, requiring practitioners to be constantly alert and responsive. As one experienced nursery teacher put it: 'It's about seeing something happen with a child. You need to think about what is happening then suddenly you start to understand what is going on and you begin to work out how you can intervene appropriately to support the child.'

The importance of meeting individual needs is well established in recent guidelines for early childhood practitioners. The English *Curriculum Guidance for the Foundation Stage* (CGFS) states that we should 'ensure that all children feel included, secure and valued' and 'treat children as individuals' (CGFS, 2000: 11); the underpinning principles of *Birth to Three Matters* (Sure Start, 2002: 4) assert that: 'schedules and routines must flow with the child's needs'. These principles are incorporated into the framework for services for children birth to five, Early Years Foundation Stage, 2006. Similar points are reiterated, for example, in the Scottish document *Birth to Three: Supporting our Youngest Children* (LT Scotland, 2005). But none of this is possible unless practitioners tune into children through observing them, interacting with them and listening to what their parents/carers have to say about them. Key questions need to be answered:

- How does this child respond in different situations?
- What sort of things interest and absorb her/him?
- In what situations does she/he show most confidence?
- What does she/he appear to find challenging and/or frustrating?

And most important of all, in the light of what we know about this child:

- What can we do to further her/his development and learning?

In very broad terms children develop along a similar path as they mature. But the order and time span in which 'developmental milestones' are achieved may differ considerably from child to child. As noted in *Birth to Three Matters* 'growth and development are less predictable for some children than for others' (DfES, 2002: 14).

Tuning into children

Each child responds differently to events, the environment and situations. A few close observations of children will reveal this. Joshua is now 4 years and 9 months old. Observations in his record folder have been collected since he first began nursery school five terms ago and judging by the number which involve play with cars or trucks, this type of play has been a major interest for him for some considerable time. Many of these observations show how cars and trucks have led him to experiment and solve problems. Here are two observations from his record:

> Joshua and friends were in the sandpit. They were calling out 'HELP! HELP!' Their trucks were stuck in a big hole they had dug, just like in 'The Big Red Bus' story.

> A car was caught in a tree. Joshua had told me about it and then went to try and rescue it. He tried throwing things at it; he tried a stick to poke. Nothing worked. Then he thought how to get higher and went and got a big heavy metal A frame (climbing frame) and pulled it under the tree. He climbed up so that he could reach the high branches and rescued the little car.

Observations of Hettie, who is of a similar age to Joshua, show her involvement in quite different sorts of play from Joshua, especially fantasy play.

> Hettie sets up homes and encampments at every opportunity. Even when we go out to the adventure playground, Hettie is to be found sometimes alone, sometimes with others, arranging her homes and camps. Today she had a picnic in the garden. She explained that she keeps all her food in the house. 'My mum and dad have died so I do all the work.' She was busy with her domestic chores and told me that she had to look after her five brothers all by herself. 'Mud in the house!' she cried and she set about sweeping vigorously.

What interests a child at any particular time can be deeply significant to her/him, a burning concern or passion. It cannot be ignored: it is the starting point for supporting a child's learning and development. 'Whenever I think about children's differences, my sense of the excitement of teaching mounts. Without the uniqueness of each child, teaching would be a dull repetitive exercise' (Paley, 1990: 47). Vivian Gussin Paley, who wrote this statement, has written extensively about young children's learning. Her books are built on real examples taken from tape transcripts she made daily of the children with whom she worked in Chicago, USA. The books are full of deep insights into how children develop their ideas, concepts and competence in very individual ways, through imagination and relationships.

The role of observation in Early Years practice

One of the underpinning principles of the English CGFS states that 'practitioners must be able to observe and respond appropriately to children' (CGFS, 2000: 11). The importance of observation across the age range is strengthened in the Early Years Foundation Stage (2006).

Observing is also seen as a key aspect of the practitioner's role working with children up to 3 in *Birth to Three: Supporting Our Youngest Children* in Scotland: 'Being tuned in to the child means … being closely observant, attentive and responsive' (LT Scotland, 2005: 27).

Margaret Edgington points out that 'Observation has traditionally been a feature of effective early years practice' (Edgington, 2004: 148), but she is concerned that all too often assumptions are made about children, rather than using observation, resulting in inappropriate learning experiences being presented, thus running 'the risk of switching children off from learning' (ibid.: 147). There is ample backing from recent research about the importance of observation. The REPEY research project (Siraj-Blatchford et al., 2002) examined the small group of early years settings, highlighted through the EPPE project 1997–2003 (Sylva et al., 2004) in which children made the greatest progress. One of the key findings of the REPEY research (Siraj-Blatchford et al., 2002) states that: 'The more knowledge the adult has of the child, the better matched their support and the more effective the subsequent learning.' Two other sources of information are vital in order to tune in to children. These are talking with parents/carers and communicating with the children themselves.

Talking with parents/carers

Parents/carers know their children intimately. For practitioners, therefore, building a close, trusting and reciprocal relationship with parents needs to begin before a child starts in a setting. This ongoing relationship can be started in many ways, such as home visits, parents' meetings and visits to the setting. These events are invaluable in helping staff to get to know the children. There are several sources of useful questions to ask parents about their child (see, for example, Hutchin, 1999: 66, or Edgington, 2004: 160). There are also some excellent projects aimed at building closer partnerships with parents to promote a deeper understanding by both practitioners and parents of children's development (see, for example, 'Involving Parents in Their Children's Learning', Research, Development and Training Base, Pen Green Centre, 2000, and DfES, 2005).

The role of parents in the process of assessment and planning has been strengthened in England through the introduction of the Foundation Stage Profile in 2003. This is the first statutory assessment of children's learning which takes place when a child reaches the end of the Foundation Stage. There is *an expectation* that parents will be involved in a continuing dialogue about their child's development: 'practitioners should involve parents from the time when the children arrive in the setting … working with them to gain a shared picture of their children' (QCA, 2003: 102).

Development and learning is bound to be hindered for the child if the care and support a child receives in the setting is inconsistent with what happens at home. Scepticism from practitioners about the information they gather from parents sometimes occurs because parents may see their child very differently from how she/he is perceived in the setting. As Hutchin (2003: 66) suggests 'this is precisely the point: to build a full picture of the child, an idea of what the child is doing at home is invaluable. Parents and principal carers do know their child better than anyone else ever could.'

Finding out from the children themselves

'Tuning in' must involve communicating directly with the child. Often the child's interpretation of an event may be quite different from that of the adults involved. Reading the wonderful books by Vivian Gussin Paley will help students to see how wrong our interpretations can sometimes be (see, for example, Paley, 1988: 36–7).

Gathering information from the children about themselves requires careful thought and planning. Young children will have varying degrees of competence in language and communication skills. Many children will be learning English as an additional language, some will already have competence in more than one other language and some will have specific language difficulties. *Listening to Young Children: The Mosaic Approach* by Clark and Moss (2001) describes a research project on collecting children's views about their settings, from age 2 upwards. The project used many different techniques to elicit their views, such as getting them to take photographs of the people, spaces and things which were important to them. The research showed that, as well as talking with children in their preferred medium, such as English, home language, signing or picture exchange, for example, using several techniques (a 'mosaic') is the best way to achieve an in-depth understanding of the child's perspective. However, asking children about themselves in a group may result in the children giving answers similar to each other. It is best to talk to them individually or in very small groups where they feel most at home and comfortable.

The what and how of observing

The purpose of observing is to assess children's achievements and needs, in order to ensure that planning and provision is appropriate. To be effective it requires practitioners to develop skills in:

- observing
- writing observations
- analysing what they have observed and making assessments
- deciding what to do next as a result of what was seen.

The skill of observing

An observation needs to describe as accurately as possible what was seen and/or heard. Knowledge of child development is important: what are you likely to see? The following aspects of development may be of greatest importance:

- emotional and social
- dispositions and attitudes (for example curiosity, confidence, independence, enthusiasm and persistence)

- physical skills
- communication skills
- cognitive development – how the child is making connections, demonstrating creativity, exploring and investigating.

However, keeping an open mind to other possibilities which might be evident is important. For example, observing a 3- or 4-year-old child in a small group of children in the home corner, the practitioner might intend to observe how the child relates to others. In the course of the observation she/he may also notice how the child:

- makes connections between real-life experiences and fantasy play – often in unexpected ways (cognitive and creative)
- shows confidence, enthusiasm and independence (dispositions)
- sequences an event such as cooking (cognitive)
- dresses and undresses with dressing up clothes (physical)
- writes a message on the telephone pad in own emergent writing (communication skills and cognitive)
- explains how something worked to another child (communication and cognitive)
- develops the storyline for the play in collaboration with another child (creative and social).

In the space of a 3-minute observation, a great deal of information about the child's all – round development can be gathered.

Different types of observations

Children need to be observed in different situations and contexts to arrive at a holistic picture of their development. Some observations need to be planned and others are just collected in the course of a normal day. The method of observation will depend on what else the practitioner is actually doing at the time, and different situations require different observation techniques. For example, there are:

- *Participant observations* – when practitioners are involved in play or an activity with the child
- *'Catch as you can' notes/observations* – something the practitioner noticed but was not involved in
- *Planned, focused observations* – when practitioner stands back to observe, tracking a child in an independently chosen activity or play, for a few minutes. These are *narrative* observations, recounting of what happens.

The planned, 'focused' observation needs to be planned into the daily timetable, so that the observer is not interrupted while observing. It requires the practictioner to observe closely over several minutes, writing or videoing what the child is doing. Usually 4–5 minutes of observation time is quite enough, but time is needed to analyse the observation as well. It is essential that the child is observed in a play situation, or at least involved in independent self-chosen activities. Why?

Play gives opportunities for self-expression and creativity, opportunities to collaborate and negotiate with others, to practise newly acquired skills as well as to try out some not yet fully acquired. Vygotsky (1978: 102) believed that in play children operate at their highest level, 'beyond his average age, above his daily behaviour; in play it is as though he were a head taller than himself'.

As Susan Isaacs puts it: 'The most fertile means of education is the child's spontaneous play … It provides the normal means of growth in manipulative skill and imaginative expression, in discovery, thought and reasoning' (Isaacs, 1935: 40). And as Vivian Gussin Paley has stated more recently: 'fantasy play is the glue that binds together all other pursuits', it 'provides the nourishing habitat for the growth of cognitive, narrative and social connectivity in young children' (Paley, 2004: 8).

A breadth of evidence is likely to come from a planned, focused observation of play, which is not easily gathered in other ways. Narrative observations of this type should take place on each child at regular intervals, at least once every two to three months, depending on the age of the child and speed at which changes are developing.

What to write in an observation

The amount and type of detail needed during an observation depends on how well the child is already known to the observer. Generally, unless carrying out a narrative observation, the practitioner should look out for things which seem significant: something new or different. Below is a typical example of a 'catch as you can' observation. Through this snippet on 2-year-old Matilda, written as the practitioner played with her, we get a real insight into her curiosity about herself and life in general.

> Matilda is standing next to me in the home corner. She suddenly informs me: I'm growing bigger … I'm growing bigger and bigger but I can't feel myself growing.

Suzzanne, the practitioner, analysed her observation, noting how Matilda is puzzled by her growth and she added a point for planning: 'Revisit "self" books with her in book corner and add some of these to home corner.'

Knowing what to look for

Although it is easiest to notice visible skills, if these are over emphasised, evidence of the child's developing dispositions, attitudes and emotional development which can be of greatest significance may be missed. In her book *Learning Stories: Assessment in Early Childhood*

Settings (2001), Margaret Carr, working in New Zealand, discusses a new approach to assessing children's learning, based on observations. The assessment of children's *dispositions* is central to this approach. Carr calls these observations 'Learning Stories'. They are narrative observations which document the child's learning in greater depth than one-off observations. 'Learning Stories can capture the complexity of the child's learning and development ... integrate the social with the cognitive and the affective ... and incorporate the child's voice' (ibid.: 95). They may be built up from a sequence of observations which show how a child is solving problems and grappling with new skills and ideas, and often include photographic evidence. Many early childhood centres and nursery schools and classes in Britain now use this approach to recording observation.

Here is Matilda again, still aged 2. This observation is like a Learning Story and consists of photographs as well as the written observation:

Matilda tells me she'd like to make a flag. I tell her I don't know how to do it – does she?

Matilda: 'I think we need a stick.'
Me: 'We don't have any sticks.'
Matilda: 'Maybe we could use a brush.' She fetches one from the sink. 'We could put this paper on here.'
Me: 'How shall we stick it?'
Matilda: 'Maybe with a little bit of glue. We could then stick it together.'

The practitioner, Suzzanne then adds her analysis and assessment:

Matilda shows she is able to make suggestions for how to make things and then design independently with little help from an adult.

Analysing observations and making assessments

Analysing an observation means questioning the evidence.

- What does this tell us about this child's learning and development?
- What areas or aspects of learning and development are evident?
- What can we do next to support this child's development? (That is, what are the implications for planning?)

Sometimes the analysis may require a few moments' thinking time or a quick discussion with other team members at the end of the session. With experience, the process becomes easier to do immediately after the observation. When observing play, it can be helpful to have some assessment questions to hand. The questions below are linked to specific Foundation Stage areas of learning but could be adapted for younger children. Similar questions for each area or aspect of learning could be devised.

Assessing a Child In Play or Child-Initiated Activities: Some Useful Assessment Questions

Personal, social and emotional development

Dispositions and attitudes: who initiated the play/activity? Did the child introduce new ideas – if so, what? Did the child select or create any 'props' to use – if so, how? How involved was the child – did she/he show persistence/determination? How confident did the child seem?

Social development: was there any new evidence of building relationships, negotiating skills, sharing and co-operating with others? Was there evidence of respect for others and growing cultural awareness?

Emotional development: how did the child express feelings and/or respond to the feelings of others? Was there evidence of growing control over own behaviour – if so, how was this shown?

Communication, language and literacy

What type of language was in evidence? For example: talking about present, past or future events; sustaining a conversation with adult or child; using language to express imaginary or real ideas; using language to create or add to a storyline; using language to question or clarify thoughts. Note which language or form of communication was used.

(*Source:* Hutchin, 2003)

How observation informs assessment *for* learning

Every observation is likely to have some implications for planning: first, with regard to the individual child and, secondly, for the staff and setting – perhaps changing a routine or introducing something new. A set of questions to consider when asking 'what next for this child?' might be:

- What can we do to extend this child's skills or understanding in relation to what has been observed?
- What activities, learning opportunities or resources should we provide?
- How will staff be involved?

For the setting and staff possible questions might be:

- What do we need to change or develop to build on this child's interests?
- Can all children access the full range of learning opportunities we provide?

The processes described so far in this chapter have been those of formative assessment, *informing* future planning for the children concerned. A term which has become increasingly prevalent in primary and secondary education for a certain type of formative assessment is 'assessment *for* learning'. It is formative assessment which fully involves children and practitioners together in deciding 'where the learners are in their learning, where they need to go and how best to get there' (DfES, 2004b: 10). For primary school children (Year 1 upwards) it means sharing learning goals with the children, helping children to recognise what they are aiming for, involving children in assessing themselves as well as group assessment with their peers, giving the children feedback on their learning and helping them to identify their own next steps.

However, for younger children (up to the age of 6 years) assessment *for* learning needs to be quite different from the processes used with older children. As stated in the Foundation Stage Profile training guide: 'Given the open ended and play based nature of many of the learning experiences that children encounter within the foundation stage, it may not always be appropriate to share learning objectives with children before they begin activities' (QCA, 2003: 22).

Below is a good example of analysing observations to make assessments and then devising plans to support the child's future development. The nursery teacher, Glynis, in a nursery school had been concerned about how best to help Hannan, 3 years 8 months for a few weeks. The observations show the difficulties Hannan was having in building relationships with her peers. Hannan was new to learning English when she had first started at nursery a few months earlier.

> *Observation:* Hannan hurt her friend but agreed to bring her inside and see that she was looked after. She bought her some ice to hold on her hurt hand. She then agreed to get a story and tell it to her friend.

> *Analysis:* Hannan is beginning to understand that there are consequences to her actions. She is becoming aware that she needs to make her friends feel better if she has caused their hurt. (PSED: managing conflict, feelings and emotions)

A month later a second observation shows how an event resulted in Glynis feeling more confident in developing an approach which would really help support Hannan deal with conflict and develop her ability to form relationships.

> Hannan really wanted to ride the red bike this morning but another child got it first. She shouted, stamped and cried, then came to me the nearest adult for support. I tried a comforting approach rather than a stern 'matter of fact' one and it worked well. It let her get to grips emotionally with what had happened.

The teacher, Glynis, then went on to describe the approach:

1. Comfort her – open arms to cuddle, concerned expression, bring onto lap.
2. Explore her concerns – what is wrong?

3. Give her the words for her feelings – 'you are disappointed, you are sad and cross because … '
4. Involve others to consolidate the words used – 'Hey look come and see, Hannan is really disappointed/sad/cross. Do you know what happened? … '
5. Sometimes this will be enough, but we may need to help her get involved in something else afterwards.

A great deal of thought, teasing out the best responses, went into this example of planning to meet individual needs. Such depth of thinking is not always needed as much learning is more straightforward. For example, the following two examples are of the same child.

16 September: Hannan brought a photo from home to nursery today and proudly showed it to staff. She talked about who was in the photo but did not describe the event (Hannan is at an early stage of learning English).

Next steps: make a photobook about her and her family with agreed sentences she can tell everyone.

22 September: Hannan was being shopkeeper in the nursery shop today. She told me what was for sale: 'Tomato, banana, orange' but did not offer words for melon, apple, lemon or pear.

Next steps: build up her food vocabulary – invite her to name items on food posters and lunch choices.

Sharing observations and giving children feedback

Wherever possible all practitioners should discuss the learning with the children, giving them feedback and identifying next steps, when appropriate, without interrupting their play. This is part of the 'assessment *for* learning' process. The children's records used in the examples in this chapter were presented so that they can be shared at any time with children. They are in the rooms, accessible to children, parents and staff. The observations are kept together with photographs of the children *in action* and samples such as drawings or other art work.

A key finding in the REPEY research (Siraj-Blatchford et al., 2002) was that settings where children made most progress tended to give children feedback on their learning during the learning activity or event. The research calls this process 'focused, formative feedback' to children. It takes place moment by moment as practitioners and children interact together but it is not usually recorded in written observations.

How observation informs assessment *of* learning

Although the most important type of assessment is assessment for learning, from time to time *summative assessment* is useful. The reviews most settings and schools do for parents on a regular basis and at transition times are summative assessments. They enable staff and parents to discuss the child's progress and development together. The Foundation Stage Profile is the statutory summative assessment for children at the end of the Foundation Stage (QCA, 2003).

Summative assessment in the early years must be based on the observations which practitioners and parents have made over time. This means reviewing records, noting any gaps (for example an area or aspect of learning) and making a more general assessment on the child's progress and development, then deciding, with parents and the child, what might be the next steps to support further learning and development. If every observation has been analysed already and points for planning have been suggested, then the summative assessment will be easy to collate. The process ensures that the planning points from each observation, not already addressed, are brought together, ready to feed into what is planned. This is an early years 'target setting' process, more accurately called in the early years context 'learning priorities'. They need to be:

- individual, geared to the child's specific needs
- achievable
- relevant to the child's interests and learning styles
- as far as possible, set with parent and child involvement.

Joycie is in her second term at nursery school. Reviews (summative assessments) are carried out termly. This school has a form with two simple headings:

1. Summary of observations.
2. Next steps.

Here is her review.

Summary of observations

- Accesses collage and workshop well.
- Beginning to mark make and write her name.
- Skilful and creative communicator, able to tell others clearly how to do things.
- Often complains of being tired, especially when asked to tidy up or try a new activity – may mean she is unsure of what to do or how to approach it.

Next steps

- Make an 'I can' book to give her confidence in herself as a learner and ideas as to what things she can do next.
- Structure tidy up tasks for her to ensure success – short goals, obvious tasks, perhaps place her in charge of a younger helper.

These points do not rest in the review section of a child's folder – they are shared with all staff, discussed at a staff planning meeting and built into the normal planning for the children. The school that Joycie attends takes this part of their work very seriously, organising regular reviews of every child's records as well as evaluating how the day went for the children and the staff at the end of every day.

The following term Joycie's review includes these comments:

Summary of observations

- Often helpful to adults and children.
- Much busier now – gets lots done.

In conclusion

Meeting children's individual needs is a complex process, but it is at the heart of the role of the early years practitioner. It must be based on observing children in action and teasing out evidence about the child's development, learning and overall dispositions. For many early years practitioners it is the joy of observing children and the challenge this presents as they try to understand the child and figure out what to do next to support the child which is the most exciting part of the work. It is not the assessment itself which is important, but what we do with what we know. As Pascal and Bertram (in Fisher, 1999: 92) tell us: 'We live in an audited society where what is measurable is seen as significant. We need to ensure that what we are measuring truly matters and that we are not simply focusing on those things that are easily measured.'

EXERCISE 4.1

Carry out a planned, focused observation on a child in your setting in play or a self chosen activity. Use the assessment questions on (page 37 in this chapter) to help you analyse the observation, then make some suggestions for future planning based on what you have seen. The learning priorities bullet points on page 40 may help you with the planning. If possible, ask a colleague to observe the same child with you, then analyse together what you have written.

EXERCISE 4.2

Group activity: ask participants to take part in a turn-taking board game together. After 5–7 minutes of the game ask them to decide what types of skills, dispositions and attitudes as well as knowledge could have been observed by someone watching the game. What would they prioritise in importance? Compare this with the list of possible aspects of development to look for on pages 33–4.

EXERCISE 4.3

Discuss with colleagues in your workplace the arrangements you have for sharing records with parents and children, as well as regularly reviewing records. How does it compare with the points raised in this chapter – are there any points for development agreed by the group?

With thanks to the children, staff and parents at Maxilla Nursery School and Maxilla Nursery Centre.

Further reading

Bartholomew, L. and Bruce, T. (1993), *Getting to Know You*. London: Hodder & Stoughton Educational.
Chapter 2 has a very useful account of the importance of observation in the study of child development as well as for educational purposes.

QCA (2003), *Building the Foundation Stage Profile: Training Materials.*

QCA (2005) *Observing Children – Building the Profile: Training Materials.* Ref. QCA/05/1569
A CD-ROM of the above title is also available, ref. QCA/04/1304 as is a video, *Building Foundation Stage Profile.*

Seeing Steps in Children's Learning (2005) QCA/05/1546.
This is a booklet and DVD illustrating the learning journeys of five children in early years settings, with commentaries which make links to the CGFS stepping stones and early learning goals.

QCA materials are available from QCA Orderline 08700 60 60 15.
The following publications, published by the DfES in conjunction with the Primary National Strategy are available free of charge. They are available from Prolog, tel: 0845 60 222 60:

Foundation Stage Parents: Partners in Learning (2005) (folder) DfES 1210-2005G.

Celebrating Young Children and those who live and work with them (2005) DfES 1211-2005.
This DVD contains very useful footage about 12 children in the Foundation Stage in different early years settings. It includes interviews with their parents and the practitioners who work with them and provides ideal material on the topic of 'meeting individual needs'.

Excellence & Enjoyment in Primary Years Containing Learning and Teaching – Professional Development Materials (2004) DfES 0519-2004 CDI.

EPPE and REPEY: Summary reports of these two research papers are available as downloadable PDF files from various sources, for example: www.ioe.ac.uk/cdl/eppe/pdfs/eppe_brief 2503.pdf and www. surestart. gov.uk/_doc/0-B51527.pdf

This chapter is taken from:
Bruce, T. (ed.) (2006) *Early Childhood*
978-1-4129-2076-6

Thinking about Young Children Learning

CATHY NUTBROWN

> A 3-year-old sits on the edge of a river bank, her toes just touching the gently flowing water. She watches the insects skimming the surface, stares intently at a tiny fish which swims near to her feet. For some twenty minutes this little girl watches patiently. No one knows what she is thinking, but there is no doubt that her diligent study of the environment around her is something which takes up the whole of her being. No one tells her to study the water and the wildlife around her, no one asks her to sit still, to be quiet and to watch. Her interest is fuelled by a natural and instinctive curiosity about the world around her.

Adults who teach young children must remain constantly aware that young children are capable of being patient observers, especially when given space and time to do so. Young children cannot be taught effectively if planned learning is always artificially divided into man-made compartments called subjects. Just as the child on the river bank studied intently the experiences around her, children will explore scientific ideas, learn about mathematics and develop their language while engaged in many different experiences in home and community situations as well as through experiences specifically planned for such learning in early education settings.

In the following examples children are learning through real and immediate experiences. They are all playing or working with water, and these observations show the immediate and engaging experience of water in providing playful learning opportunities. Three observations follow: Zoe (aged 4), Ashaq (aged 6) and Karmen and John (aged 8 and 7).

Zoe aged 4

Zoe was playing in the water trough at the nursery. She was experimenting with a jug and water wheel, spending a considerable time filling the jug, pouring the water over the wheel and watching it turn. She poured water at different speeds and from different heights. Her teacher watched and eventually asked: 'Can you tell me what is happening?' Zoe looked at her and began her explanation: 'The wheel doesn't like to get wet, so it runs fast to get away from the water. When all the water is gone, it stays still again!' Zoe knew that the water made the wheel turn but ascribed attributes of thought and feeling to the wheel. Early experiences of the scientific principles of force, gravity and power are present in this example, as well as the beginnings of reasoned thought. Zoe was beginning to grapple with ideas of speed and of cause, function and effect.

Ashaq aged 6

Ashaq was watching his mother using a jet spray at the garage to wash her car. He observed intently for some time and then asked if he could have a turn. After concentrating the jet of water on one muddy wheel and watching the dirt wash away he said: 'If I put it nearer the dirt goes away faster. That's because the water hits it harder if it doesn't spray so far. If I spray a long way away then not all the dirt goes.'

This 6-year-old told his teacher about the car washing. She used jets, sprays and the advantage of a hot summer day to work with him to develop further this understanding and to extend his interest. Water flowed from the hosepipe in the yard outside the classroom as did questions of 'How?', 'Why?' and 'What if?' Ashaq made reasoned answers to all the questions the teacher raised. He also asked questions of his own. The principles of syphoning were mastered and the appropriate terminology was introduced by the teacher. A small group of children worked purposefully to create and solve their own water-oriented problems.

Learning does not begin and end in school. The visit to the garage with his mother opened up the child's thinking which Ashaq, with the help of his teacher, was able to build on with his peers in school.

Karmen and John aged 8 and 7

Karmen and John were at home in their garden bathing dolls and washing all their clothes. The dolls and clothes were covered in an ever-increasing amount of soap suds. The children had rather overestimated the quantity of washing powder they needed, reasoning that the dolls were extremely dirty and so must need a lot of soap to get them clean. John decided to change the water and wash everything again, this time not putting in any more soap. The following conversation gives an interesting insight into the children's reasoning and understanding:

Karmen:	Make the water cooler this time, it disperses the bubbles.
John:	How?
Karmen:	Not sure, but it does, mum does that with the jumpers in the sink. It sort of pops them.
John:	Is it that cold water is too cold for them and it makes them pop?
Karmen:	Maybe, it's thinner and gets through the membranes.
John:	Brains! Do bubbles have brains?

Karmen:	No! Membranes! It's like an invisible sort of film, like a sort of skin thing to keep the air trapped, they have them on *Tomorrow's World* on telly sometimes.
John:	How does the air get in there?
Karmen:	Well, it's the soap. Get the cold water now.
John:	How cold?
Karmen:	Cold! Don't put any warm in, though you could put a bit, tepid water, 'hand-hot' my mum calls it I think.
John:	Does that mean as hot as my hand?
Karmen:	It means you can put your hand in and it doesn't make it red hot or freezing cold so it hurts your fingers.
John:	I bet we could do it quicker than changing all this water.
Karmen:	How?
John:	Stick them all under the tap till all the bubbles run off then squeeze them!
Karmen:	Or! We could use the shower thing in the bathroom and give them a shower. That would work.
John:	I saw that on telly.
Karmen:	What, doing the washing?
John:	No, spraying the oil.
Karmen:	What?
John:	If you spray oil it breaks up, pollutes the environment and the sea, oil does.
Karmen:	Like if you get soap on your hair and use the shower to rinse it off. We'll do the dolls first, their hair is all bubbles.
John:	The particles bombard the oil and hit it to break it up. Dad said.
Karmen:	Does oil have membranes?
John:	Don't know. Give me that jacket. Oil's not as heavy as water though. It floats on top. I saw that on telly too!
Karmen:	We've got brains!
John:	If it works we have. But I bet it does. My mum puts me in the shower on holiday!

Karmen and John were transferring elements of their knowledge gleaned from different sources, including their parents and the television, and using what they knew to try to solve their present difficulty. They were exploring, discovering, checking out each other's meanings, predicting results, forming hypotheses and drawing conclusions. They played cooperatively and with intensity of purpose.

As children get older and more experienced, if adults have spent time with them, extending their interests and explaining things about the world, stimulating their actions and thoughts into new areas and talking with them, children come to use different language and terminology to explain their reasoning. It is their language which indicates to us their grasp of meaning and their understanding. If children articulate their thinking, their parents, teachers and other educators are in a better position to help them to refine and further develop their ideas.

If we reflect on the use of language in the three examples of children using water we see different thoughts and understandings. Four-year-old Zoe explained: 'It runs away from the water.' Six-year-old Ashaq observed: 'If I put it nearer the dirt goes away faster.' Seven-year-old John said: 'The particles bombard the oil and hit it to break it up.' Eight-year-old Karmen said: 'Membranes, it's like an invisible sort of film; like a sort of skin thing, to keep the air trapped.' If children have played in their earlier years with the stuff of the world (water, sand, mud and clay), they are in a better position to develop further concepts through these media. Children who have had few encounters with these natural materials will need time to explore their properties and attributes so that they can then tackle other challenges and questions when they work with such materials.

Worries about children's safety and urban living now inhibit the freedom of children to explore their world. Concerns for children's well-being include fear of illness from polluted rivers, beaches, and food, and of abduction or abuse. Other threats to children's heath and well-being centre around poor diet (Oliver, 2005) and the over-use of technology by children which in turn inhibits their outdoor and creative play (Miller and Almon, 2004; Palmer, 2006). Adults who wish to support children's learning now often bring the stuff of the world into safe, defined but falsely created boundaries. The vastness of the seashore and the expanse of the riverbank are reduced to small quantities of sand and water in specially designed plastic containers, and children often wear aprons to protect their clothing from wet and dirt. But an essential part of the learning experience is the process of getting sandy, dirty and wet! Instead of making mud pies in the outdoors, children use small quantities of clay in a confined space at an allotted time. The role of the adult in protecting the opportunities for learning and enabling children's own ways of thinking and exploring is crucial. Children need the freedom to play and learn, and educators need to create opportunities which provide this freedom to learn in safe environments which, as far as possible, removes the inhibiting restriction which arises from exaggerated fear for children's safety. The restrictions which are placed on children and the consequences of this in terms of their subsequent development were considered some 30 years ago by Tinbergen (1976), who discussed the ways in which young children learn through play in their natural environments. Tinbergen suggested even then, that society had inhibited children's freedom to play and, just as young animals find their own way of learning, young children could do the same if they were in an appropriate environment. The concerns expressed by Tinbergen three decades ago have now multiplied to the point where children's freedom to learn is restricted and limited (often in the interests of keeping them safe) and their opportunties to play outdoors are, in many cases, being seriously threatened.

John Brierley's contribution to our understanding of children's brain growth and development provided insights for all who have responsibility and concerns for young children. Brierley asserted that the years from 0 to 5 are crucial for brain development and that the first ten years are the years during which the brain reaches 95% of its adult weight. He wrote:

During these years of swift brain growth a child's eyes, ears and touch sense in particular are absorbing experiences of all kinds through imitation and exploration. It is obvious that the quality of experience is vital for sound development. In addition to sensory experience, talk is as vital to human life as pure air.

(Brierley, 1987, p. 28)

Recent scientific research suggests that babies and young children are born with the capacity to understand a lot more than was previously thought to be the case (Gopnik, Meltzoff and Kuhl, 1999). Such studies have challenged long-held views of babies' 'ignorance' suggesting that babies, indeed, have an innate capacity from the moment they are born (Gopnik, Meltzoff and Kuhl, 1999, p. 27; Brierley, 1994, p. 81) and confirms the importance of providing babies with novelty and stimulation in their environments. Bruner's 1960 theory of 'cognitive growth' suggested that environmental and experiential factors were influences on a child's development (Smith, 2002). Trevarthen's (1977) focus on the communication of babies during their first six months of life concluded that a pattern of development in social behaviour was forming in all five infants in the study. While interesting and affirming of practices based on belief and observation, the results of the studies of neuroscience may be of limited use to early childhood educators. Hannon (2003) argues that such studies are unlikely to change current practice and Wilson (2002) also suggests that brain science has little to offer parents who struggle in circumstances of poverty and other social difficulty.

Gopnik, Meltzoff and Kuhl (1999) suggest that despite extensive studies, it is at times difficult to grasp the amazing phenomenon of how young children think. They summarise this notion in terms of three elements: *Foundation* where babies are able to translate information and interpret their experiences in particular ways predicting new events; *Learning* when babies use their experiences to modify and reshape their initial representation thus achieving more complex and abstract representations; and *Other People* who care for the children actively yet, unconsciously promote, encourage and influence children's representations.

In his work Brierley identified 21 principles for teaching and learning based upon knowledge of brain development. He made it clear that the more children learn, the more their brains have the capacity to learn. The following two principles help to focus on implications for young children's learning:

All forms of play appear to be essential for the intellectual, imaginative and emotional development of the child and may well be necessary steps to a further stage of development. The brain thrives on variety and stimulation. Monotony of surroundings, toys that only do one thing, a classroom display kept up for too long are soon disregarded by the brain.

(Brierley, 1994, p. 111)

It was variety, stimulation and the important experiences of talking with adults which prompted the questioning and thinking from the children in the following two examples. Young thinkers construct some wonderful and apparently bizarre reasons for why things happen, drawing on their present knowledge to create explanations which are logical to them at that time (Paley, 1981). The following examples illustrate children's skills as thinkers as they struggle to explain and reason things which puzzle them about their world.

A 5-year-old boy asked his parents, 'Why are there trees?' A satisfactory answer took his parents into many reasons and a long discussion which justified the existence of trees: shady places to sit on a hot day; for making wooden furniture; equatorial rain forests; conservation; food and habitats for wildlife; and finally 'somewhere for Robin Hood to hide'. This last reason followed a visit to Sherwood Forest and the Major Oak. One part of the answer led to another question or a further reason and so dialogue between parents and child continued with an interested and lively 5-year-old applying his mind and pursuing this line of thought, continuing to think, assimilate and understand, acquiring more information along the way which extended and further stimulated his thinking. The questioning stopped when, for the moment, he was satisfied with the explanation which had been generated.

A 4-year-old girl asked her father, 'Why does the sea go in and out?' Her father gave the most reasonable explanation he could, mentioning the Moon and the spinning of the earth and the need for the sea to come into the harbours of other parts of the world. She thought that the sea came into the harbour of the small town where she lived to let the boats float so that the fisherman could go fishing, and that it went out to stop children swimming in the sea all day so that their skin did not get wrinkled! She thought that this going in and coming out of the sea was all 'a waste of time' and that the sea should stay in the harbour all the time so that the boats could always float, people could go fishing whenever they wished and the children could swim whenever they wanted to. Her search for reason and justification led her to create an explanation and some logical reasoning from what she presently knew and how she wanted things to be.

Piaget's insights into children's thought and language contribute to our understanding of young children's minds. Piaget (1953) gave some fascinating lists of 'why' questions which were asked by children, providing illustration of children's thinking and their search for reason. The children about whom Piaget wrote asked questions of causality and questions of justification. Those who spend time with young children will find a familiar tone in questions like 'Why does the sea go in and out?' and 'Why are there trees?' Young children ask questions which Piaget would categorise as 'Whys of logical justification' when they look for logical and sensible reasons for the things they see and are told. While Piaget thought young children 'egocentric', this term need not be considered in a selfish sense, nor should children's egocentricity be thought of as a deficit (Piaget, 1972). Young children work hard to make sense of the things they encounter and use all that they know to try to understand. To reply to a child's why question with an answer such as 'because it is' or even 'because I say so!' will not suffice because such responses are neither logical nor satisfactory in terms of their thinking, and do not do justice to children's capacity to think through what they encounter as they try to make sense of what they find.

Children's questions, puzzles, problems, solutions and fascinations have formed the substance of this chapter demonstrating the active and creative ways in which children learn, how they think about the world and make sense of their experiences of it. The view of children as capable and serious learners and thinkers is a recurring theme throughout this book.

This chapter is taken from:
Nutbrown, C. (2006) *Threads of Thinking*, Third Edition
978-1-4129-1084-2

Why is Play Important?

TINA BRUCE

Key themes

Play is an umbrella word (Bruce, 1991) which is impossible to pin down. It has fascinated thinkers since ancient times, as they observed young children at play. It was Froebel who first embraced the learning that children engage in through their play and made it part of a child's education.

Some theories emphasize the ideas and thoughts children have as they develop their learning through play. Others focus on the way that play helps children to experiment and cope with their feelings, and to deal with them through its self-healing powers. These theories also give us insights into the way play helps children to understand other people and to relate to others. We should not underestimate the way that play also helps children to be physically co-ordinated, which links with the development of their self-esteem and well-being. Free-flow play applies throughout life.

Practitioners are finding practical ways of supporting and extending children's development and learning through play. Different theories offer support in different ways.

A great deal of lip-service is paid to the importance of play in developing the learning of young children. There is widespread confusion about what it is. We need to try to clarify the concept of play, so that we can work effectively with children and their families.

> *In everyday conversation, it is generally unfair and provoking to ask for precise definitions of familiar words. But when a familiar concept like aggression, intelligence, or personality becomes an object of study, then it must be defined or delineated, at least clearly enough so that those who contribute to the study and those who may benefit from it know they are talking about the same thing. Play has been a particularly recalcitrant notion.* (Garvey, 1977: 10)

Play is probably one of the least understood aspects of an early-childhood practitioner's work. In this chapter we will explore the key issues of this complex and sophisticated concept, and look at the contribution play makes in developing learning, in which play is a central mechanism and needs to be nurtured during childhood. This is a challenge for practitioners of all kinds, and for parents too.

Research (Siraj-Blatchford et al., 2002: 115) shows that the richest play is found especially in nursery schools and early-excellence centres, many of which were originally nursery schools, where heads and teachers have trained to a high level in the early years and have a deep understanding of child development and how learning develops in young children. The studies found that play is often thought by practitioners only to involve 'imaginative play'. 'This narrow conceptualisation of play is shared by many other early childhood practitioners for whom play is considered essential, as an activity promoting learning and yet only relevant to some areas of the curriculum. According to Wood and Attfield (1996), despite constant validation from academics (Bruce, 1991; Moyles, 1989) play continues to have an insecure place in delivering the curriculum.' (Siraj-Blatchford et al., 2002: 115)

Pioneers of play

Plato, c. 428–347 BCE

Plato wanted to help children participate in what he called high culture as a means of protecting them from the advance of 'uncivilised influences' (Egan, 1997: 12).

Ideas important to the culture: the forms of knowledge

Plato believed that the human mind has in it an intuitive understanding of the important ideas of the culture. He called these the highest 'forms of knowledge'. He suggested that the important ideas of the culture (the forms of knowledge) are unchanging in an ever-changing world. Education is about the pursuit of these highest forms of knowledge, which are central to the culture.

Play as making the forms of knowledge accessible to young children

Some educators still adhere to the Platonic pursuit of high culture which makes schools separate places of learning from real life. However, most educators of young children, supported by research evidence (Siraj-Blatchford et al., 2002,) now think that play is an important means by which children are helped to connect with high culture.

For example, by creating play scenarios with 'goodies' and 'baddies' (Holland, 2003) children are led to the fundamental aspects of Greek or Shakespearean literature and drama, with time-honoured battles between good and evil. This play benefits from being supported and extended by sensitive adults.

Immanuel Kant, 1724–1804

Immanuel Kant probably has the most holistic approach since Plato (Magee, 1987: 187).

Concepts, our windows on the world

Kant believed that we have windows on the world which are our concepts. Each individual has different experiences, using the senses and feedback from movement, and this has a deep effect on the way we look through the windows which are our concepts. Kant believed that these shared concepts (ideas) lead us to share, dialogue and exchange thoughts, feelings and relationships with each other. They have a unifying effect. According to Collinson (1988: 90), Kant argued 'that knowledge is founded on subjective experiences which are produced by external entities that affect our senses ... In this way a subjective sensory experience may be transformed into objective conceptual knowledge.'

Kant's influence on Froebel

Although Kant does not write about play, his thinking influenced the pioneer educator Friedrich Froebel, whose view was that play was an important way in which children organize their learning into a whole.

Friedrich Froebel, 1782–1852

Before theories about play were established (when the discipline of psychology emerged), support for the importance of play came from philosophy for practitioners. Froebel's ideas about play in his schools and learning communities were greatly influenced by Kant, whom he studied while reading mathematics at university.

Play as developing learning

Throughout the history of early childhood practice during the last 100 years, a concept has been handed down from generation to generation of practitioners which presents play as central in the learning of young children.

Friedrich Froebel pioneered the view that play acts as an organizing function which integrates learning and helps children to apply their knowledge and understanding in relation to their developing ideas, feelings, physical bodies and relationships. He was working before there were any theories about play in the modern sense.

Learning developing into a co-ordinated whole through play

Froebel developed a theory drawing on the philosophy of his day. He proposed that play is the way children integrate and bring together what they know, understand and feel into a whole. Play, he believed, shows children applying what they can do and understand at the highest levels of which they are capable. Play makes it possible for very young children to think flexibly, to adapt what they know, try out different possibilities and reach abstract levels of functioning in a way that is appropriate.

Froebel and Vygotsky

The work of Vygotsky resonates with some aspects of Froebel's earlier claims, although he did not know about his work. Froebel argued that play is the highest level of learning and that it is therefore the most spiritual activity of the child. By this he meant that children begin to understand themselves, others and the universe, and play is the organizing mechanism through which this occurs.

Theories such as these outlining the importance of play have only emerged in the last 100 years. But theories do not give us evidence; they give us frameworks through which we can make sense of human behaviour and development and be enabled to make predictions.

Theories help us to explore and gather evidence about the value of play in developing learning.

Theories about play

In this section we look at some of the theories which emerged after Froebel's death, each of which suggests why play is central to the learning of young children.

Work and play have been separated and placed in opposition in several influential early theories of play. The damaging impact of this polarization still lurks today, although in the 1930s Susan Isaacs made an attempt to rescue the situation by suggesting that play is in fact a child's work, which has an air of damage limitation about it. The following two theories divide work from play.

Play as recreation

Play takes huge energy and concentration. It is anything but recreation or relaxation. When the children have wallowed in rich free-flow play, they are exhausted once it fades, and they may then need recreation and the opportunity to relax. This view of play gives it a low status.

Play as the means by which children burn off excess energy

This is another damaging theory about play, one that was influenced by the particular events of its historic and cultural context. This was Herbert Spencer's (1882–1903) theory, which came into being during the industrial revolution at around the time when compulsory schooling was introduced by the Education Act (1872).

The theory is that children are like industrial machines and need to release excess energy and let off steam in the playground between lessons. Children were regarded as cogs in the machinery, like those who worked in the factories. Rough-and-tumble play and play involving lively chasing, were viewed as low-level releases of unwanted energy. Play was necessary to avoid explosions of bottled-up energy.

School playgrounds are still too often influenced by this theory. However, nursery schools never subscribed to it, and the outdoor area was and is regarded as an important half of the learning area. Nursery schools drew on theories about play developing learning at home and in group settings (Brehony, 2000), and did not divide work from play but integrated the two.

Other theories

During the 1920s the new discipline of psychology emerged, and new unpublished theories of play were formed. Stanley Hall (1884–1924) suggested that during play children work through the history of humanity. They are hunters and gatherers, warriors, builders of settlements, farmers, tool-makers, carers of their young, crafts-makers, nomads, law-makers, punishers, justice-makers. They show the development of the species in the correct order. Egan (1997: 27) suggests that he was influenced by Spencer, whom he quotes. 'If there be an order in which the human race has mastered its various kinds of knowledge, there will arise in every child an aptitude to acquire these minds of the same order.' (Spencer, 1861: 76)

By the 1930s more sophisticated theories of play had emerged. This had a huge impact on the way practitioners worked with children in group settings.

Play as preparation for and rehearsal of the future

Karl Groos

In the 1920s Groos developed his theory that children quite naturally prepare for their adult lives by rehearsing adult events and ways of doing things in their play both physically and socially.

Johan Huizinga

Huizinga (1949) went further than this. He argued that civilizations are marked by the phenomenon that adults continue their play into adulthood, the theory of *homo ludens*. This keeps their wits sharpened and their bodies fully functioning, and enables them to be flexible and forward-looking adaptive people.

Jerome Bruner

Bruner (1983: 43) sees play as 'preparation for the technical and social life that constitutes human culture'. During the 1960s Bruner's theory exerted a wide influence. He suggested that mammals have long childhoods because there is so much for them to learn in preparation for adult life. He was uneasy about free-flow play, emphasizing instead games with rules, such as songs, rhymes and peekaboo.

This approach has led to adults dominating the play of children, with methods variously called guided play, structured play, play tutoring or learning the play way. The emphasis is on what Egan (1997: 11) calls the 'homogenisation' of children. The way that play is encouraged in early childhood settings is inevitably affected by the fact that at the heart of schooling is the desire to socialize by homogenizing and inducing conformity. Egan (1997: 12) points out that when pushed to extremes, this can become totalitarian in its demands for conformity.

Adult-dominated tasks are not play

Unfortunately play in group settings, especially in primary schools, too often results in desultory sessions in which children are guided in their play into pre-structured adult-led outcomes. This is not play. It is children being initiated into adult-led tasks, which certainly have their place, and are an important part of direct teaching. However, teaching children to use the tools of a woodwork bench, to cook, to mix paint, showing them how to study beetles without squashing them, reading to them or scribing for them are not play. But all of these things are important for children to learn about.

Play as a process with no product

Play 'free flows' (Bruce, 1991) along, bringing clarification and illumination of ideas, feelings, relationships and understandings of the human body in an entirely different way.

There is a real difference between inculcating children into the culture of adults and encouraging them through their play culture to make sense of the adult world. Kalliala (2002: 32) gives the example of Tommi, who is required to write a composition, but is regularly disappointed because his teacher is not pleased with his efforts at writing. Because he always writes about rally racing, the teacher bans the topic for him. But Mika makes play scenarios about world championship ice-hockey. He makes a rink out of a mat, and has a torch for the spotlight, sings the music and announces the players (ice-hockey cards) as they enter.

In these examples, Tommi is being inculcated into the adult culture, whereas Mika, through his play, is making sense of adult culture.

Pleasure play

This theory of play saw the joy of physical movement as the heart of play. It was pioneered by Charlotte Buhler in the 1930s. It resonates with the health and beauty movement and the outdoor camps for children in woodlands during the summer months in Europe and the US. It emphasizes the pleasure in movement which activates unconscious physical and mental learning. Play is seen as a process with no purpose on the part of the child. This is play aiding natural learning.

Theories about feelings and play

Another unfortunate divide developed with the emergence of psychological theories about human development, which stressed the importance of feelings. Piaget's work was mainly concerned with thoughts and ideas children have, and he had (Piaget, 1952) great respect for the pioneering work of Sigmund Freud on the emotions. His own work did not make a separation of emotion and intellect, which he thought gave different emphases to the various aspects of human development.

> There is never a purely intellectual action, and numerous emotions, interests, values, impressions of harmony, etc., intervene for example, in the solving of a mathematical problem. Likewise, there is never a purely affective act, e.g., love presupposes comprehension. Always and everywhere, in object-related behaviour as well as in interpersonal behaviour, both elements are involved because the one presupposes the other. There are those who are more interested in people than things or abstractions and vice versa, which makes the former appear more sentimental and the latter more arid, but it is merely a question of different behaviour and different emotions. Each necessarily employs both intelligence and affectivity. (Piaget, 1964: 34)

Both the psychodynamic theories arising from Freud's work and Piagetian theory made the concept of balance central. Freud saw this as a fixed state (homeostasis), whereas for Piaget balancing (equilibration) was more like riding a bicycle. The importance of play is that it keeps children well balanced in both theories.

Anna Freud, 1895–1982

Interestingly, Anna Freud, who was an outstanding teacher as well as an analyst (Coles, 1992), was criticized by her colleague Melanie Klein (Kohan, 1986: 38–40; Bell, 1999: 11) because Freud saw that children are whole people first, and that even children who have experienced trauma benefit from as natural a childhood as possible, surrounded by love, nurtured, encouraged and helped to play.

> *Anna Freud's preference for respectful observation rather than intrusive assault in clinical exploration as well as selection of candidates is reflected in her well known struggles with Melanie Klein ... who was very much a follower of the early [Sigmund] Freud who explored the unconscious with daring and courageous conjecture. She believed the child analyst can know a lot about the preverbal child, and can work with conviction and dispatch to obtain an analytic intimacy with young children not unlike the kind that develops between analysts and their grown-up patients ... Miss Freud was inclined to be wary of what she regarded at best as the surmises and guesses of those who followed Mrs. Klein.* (Coles, 1992: 121)

Play as healing emotional pain and helping children to be forward-looking

Anna Freud believed that play was a cathartic experience for children. In their play children can move in and out of reality. As they play they can exert some control over their lives. They can experiment with how to deal with their feelings so that they can better manage their emotions. As well as the conflicts and sadnesses of life, play also helps children to experience joy and be forward-looking. Play helps children to interpret experiences and makes them become whole people.

Vivian Gussin Paley, whose work resonates in a modern way with the approach of Anna Freud, shows how children play out what frightens them in order to control their fears:

> *'Help, help!' Barney screams. 'I'm destroying! The king! The invisible bad king! He told me to get you. Now I'm all chained up. I'm the glue person!'*
>
> *'Don't worry, Barney bat. I'll save you. Here, I'm melting you with my face. There! Now break yourself out.'*
>
> *'Whew! Thanks, Fredrick. You saved me. I was starting to die. Now I can live for the whole forever.'* (Gussin Paley, 1986: 118)

Melanie Klein, 1882–1960

Melanie Klein, as we saw above, took a different view. She believed that children could be helped through analysis at a very young age. She did not consider it necessary to wait until the oedipal stage (between four and six years of age), which followed the oral (birth to two years) and anal stages (between two and four years). She disagreed with Anna Freud's caution, instead making 'confident and suggestive inquiry' (Coles, 1992: 121), a concept which influenced British psychoanalysis at the time. She dismissed Anna Freud's questions.

- *How is one to do psychoanalytic work with children scarcely able to speak?*
- *How can re-enactment of childhood attitudes toward parents get going in children who are only now beginning to develop their initial, sustained attitudes toward their parents?*
- *How exact is the analogy between children's play with toys, or their drawings, on the one hand, and the 'free associations' that adult analysands [those analysed] are asked to produce, on the other?* (Coles, 1992: 121–2)

Erik Erikson, 1902–1994

Erik Erikson was a student of Anna Freud. He believed that through their play children become partners with their futures. He invited children to construct scenes based on imaginary films, and was interested in the way that the play scenarios they invented seemed to serve as metaphors for their future lives and 'intimately related to the dynamics of the person's life history' (Erikson, 1963: 95). The scenes reflected their interests and fears, their strengths and challenges. He visited the children as adults later and found that their lifestyles held resonances of their childhood play (Erikson, 1963).

Erikson established eight stages of development, each of which involved a dilemma (Maier, 1978: 132; Bruce and Meggitt, 2002). In the first stage, the dilemma is between trust and mistrust. The second stage is that of the play stage, when autonomy emerges (or not). Through play children develop initiative and are strengthened to face disappointments and failures and to approach life with involvement and purpose.

Erikson's view was that children in their free-flow play (Bruce, 1991) deal with their experiences by creating a model situation which they can master, plan and experiment with. He says the child 'relives their past and thus relives left-over affects. He anticipates the future from the point of view of a corrected and shared past' (Erikson, 1963: 222)

Donald Winnicott, 1896–1971

Winnicott developed his understanding of play through what he called the transitional object. This can be a substitute for people who are important for the child emotionally, when they are not present. A transitional object can also help the child to enjoy the presence of those they love. In short, a transitional object links the child to loved people. 'In order to give a space to playing I postulated a *potential space* between the mother (carer) and the baby. This potential space varies a very great deal according to the life experiences of the baby in relation to the mother or mother-figure, and I contrast this potential space (a) with the inner world ... and (b) with actual, or external reality.' (Winnicott, 1971: 47–8)

Transitional objects and play

Transitional objects work in two ways. As well as being a natural and healthy link with those they love, they also support the child in early imaginative play. The teddy stands for the absent father who will return after work, but also has a life of imaginative play with the child, taking meals together, sleeping together and having adventures together.

> Jason, a summer-born child, started school in a very formal reception class in which the teacher introduced the formal group teaching of literacy and number work for two hours a day from the autumn entry term. After a week he began to cry and say he did not want to go to school. He said he found the work too hard. His mother spoke to the classteacher, who unwillingly agreed that he could bring his teddy to school with him. After the first day when teddy joined him, his mother asked him if he had found school better. He said he did, because when he had tears in his eyes he could wipe them with teddy's ears, and teddy would whisper, 'Never mind, you will soon be at home.'
>
> He had found comfort from his transitional object when separated from his home, linking him to the comfort of his mother. He had also taken teddy into imaginative play which eased his unhappiness. Play is about dealing with difficulties and sadness as much as with happiness. He was being asked to behave in ways which were too formal too soon, and without the teddy might have coped less well in a far from ideal situation.

These are different from transitional objects; they do not take on an imaginative life, or stand for someone in their absence, or increase enjoyment in someone they love's company. Not all children have transitional objects, or imaginative friends. Objects of transition (Bruce, 2001b: 77) are different because they simply ease the transition from home to the group or childminder and then back to the home.

Winnicott, like Erikson, was more inclined to the views of Anna Freud than of Melanie Klein.

Cognitive theories of play

The theories that deal with feelings are different from the other theories in this chapter, because they make strong links between childhood play and adult creativity, that is, how childhood's imaginative, pretend play develops into drama, dance or music improvisations, artistic happenings or scientific problem-solving and hypothesizing.

These theories, which focus on how children develop their ideas and thoughts, see play as part of childhood only, possibly implying that play turns into the ability to take part in games with rules during middle childhood.

Jean Piaget, 1896–1980

Play as unifying learning

Although Piaget (1951) stresses the way early childhood play turns into games with rules, he agrees with Anna Freud, Klein, Erikson and Winnicott that childhood play unifies ideas, feelings and relationships and the physical body movements.

Play as giving balance to learning

Piaget agreed that the psycho-dynamic theories of play that balance (equilibrium) is of central importance, and that play contributes to children being well-balanced. According to him, we can never reach a constant state of balance. It is a state of becoming rather than being. Free-flow play is a process, and not a steady state. He called the process of balancing equilibration, which has two aspects, accommodation and assimilation. Accommodation is about adapting to situations, and assimilation is about adding the familiar to what is known already. Play is mainly to do with assimilation. It is about applying what has already been learnt.

Three kinds of play

Piaget thought there were three kinds of play, which developed in order.

- First there was sensory-motor play, which involved the senses and movement. This is the play of babies and toddlers.
- Then there was pretend, imaginative play during early childhood.
- Finally, there were games with rules, which led into sports and rule-bound games in middle childhood. This kind of play was with objects and also with people.

From early childhood play to games with rules

Piaget saw a linear development from play to games with rules, rather than understanding free-flow play as something that develops into drama, literature, dance choreography, musical composition, creative writing, painting, research in science or experimentation with mathematically elegant answers during middle childhood, adolescence and adult life. He did think of games and play as two different aspects of a network of learning which feed off and into each other.

The high status of play in developing learning in young children

Piaget's theories have had a major impact on early childhood education since the 1960s, because they stress the central importance of play as a learning mechanism during early childhood (although he thought it faded by the end of middle childhood).

Lev Vygotsky, 1896–1934

Learning through social relationships

Since the 1990s Vygotsky's theory of play has not been explored as much as his view that children participate in their culture and learn what is important for them to know through social relationships with others, especially adults.

Play as creating a zone of potential learning

Vygotsky sees play as creating a zone of potential development, in which children operate at their highest level of functioning, beyond their present-day possibilities, so that they become ahead of themselves. Both adults or more skilled children can be catalysts in this process. Vygotsky (1978: 101) considers play to be 'a leading factor in development'. This makes it 'the highest level of preschool development. The child moves forward essentially through play activity.' (Vygotsky, 1978: 102–3)

Emphasis on imaginative play

In Vygotsky's theory play is conceived of as imaginative play. 'Thus, in establishing criteria for distinguishing a child's play from other forms of activity, we conclude that in play a child creates an imaginary situation.' (Vygotsky, 1978: 95)

Because he has a narrow view of what play is, he states: 'Play in an imaginary situation is essentially impossible for a child under three in that it is a novel form of behaviour liberating the child from constraints.' (Vygotsky, 1978: 96)

Play for Vygotsky is the way that children free themselves from the constraints of reality. 'The child sees one thing but acts differently in relation to what he sees. Thus, a condition is reached in which the child begins to act independently of what he sees.' He adds, that 'it is terribly difficult for a child to sever thought (the meaning of a word) from object.' (Vygotsky, 1978: 97)

Emphasis on language in play

Because young children do not find it easy to separate the meanings of words from what they represent, the development of imaginative play is linked with language development.

Play becoming games with rules

Vygotsky agrees with Piaget that imaginative play leads into games with rules. 'Just as the imaginary situation has to contain rules of behaviour, so every game with rules contains an imaginary situation.' (Vygotsky, 1978: 95) He also agrees that childhood play turns into sports and games with rules in middle childhood. However, Piaget has a broader view of play, more in tune with modern research on the early development of the brain, which suggests that play involves the senses and movement as well as developing the imagination and rule behaviour.

Other theorists of play we have looked at in this chapter believe that play is possible from birth to death, and not, as Vygotsky suggests, mainly from three years old until middle childhood. This is because play is not just imaginative, although that is an important feature (Moyles, 1989; Bruce, 1991, 2001a; Wood and Attfield, 1996; Siraj-Blatchford et al, 2002).

Vygotsky stresses the social side of play more than Piaget. They both see people and objects as important in play. Unlike Piaget's or Froebel's theories, or the affective theories of play, Vygotsky puts the emphasis on social relationships, imaginative play and language. This is a narrow view of play compared with other theories, which means that it is of limited use when working with babies and toddlers, children with disabilities and children who have suffered trauma.

Attempting to define play and pin it down

It is clear from the literature that although play has been discussed for centuries, there is no clear definition of it. It is still an umbrella word (Garvey, 1977; Bruce, 1991). This has made it a very hazy concept.

A trawl through the research literature on play (in the English language) reveals some recurring themes which build a picture for us of the contribution play makes to developing learning. Translations from other languages, especially those from the Nordic languages, suggest that whereas in the US and UK adults are seen to have a leading role in playing with children, in other parts of the world, including mainland Europe, children's play culture is respected and adults do not dominate so much (Kalliala, 2004, in press). Lofdahl's study of hegemonies (power relationships) in children's play culture shows how children are active agents in their own learning.

As children play, resistance to power relationships appears, and children use their agency and become powerful meaning makers as they develop their knowledge. Together, children show their knowledge of daily life with its winners and losers, decision makers, norms and rules to be followed. Play gives opportunities to try out what is not allowed, to test boundaries and be aware of what can happen if they are broken. Rather than seeing, in children's actions and play, fear of authority, children show what they know about, how to deal with authorities, and how to gain authority. (Lofdahl, 2002: 45)

Play – does it develop outside in or inside out?

In Chapter 1 we looked at the way brain development is triggered by the environment as children learn through and from other people. We saw how these social experiences quite literally sculpt the brain (Meade, 2003). We are individuals. Froebel in the nineteenth century believed that it is the role of the educator to make the inner outer and the outer inner (Liebschner, 1991, 1992). But which comes first?

On the one hand, no one can play unless the mechanisms for play are formed in the human brain (the inner). On the other, play will not develop unless the external environment triggers the mechanisms causing play to develop (the outer). Teasing out which comes first is at the centre of all the theories of play we have looked at in this chapter. Both the development of the inner life (through the brain) and the outer life (through the people we meet and the experiences we have) influence the way play is supported and extended by adults. This in turn has an impact on the way the brain develops (Brown, 1998).

Looking for clues in the natural play of children at home

Dunn (1995) looks at natural play in the family setting at home. She found that toddlers engaged in pretend play with their older brothers and sisters as part of everyday life. The older children would give specific instructions on how to role-play, and guide them into the narrative of the play. This helped the toddlers to participate appropriately.

Dunn's belief in the importance of studying children's play in natural everyday settings at home makes a stark contrast with the kind of play found in many group early-childhood settings. This may be because in these situations adults feel the need to teach play, but they tend to do so in a very different way from the way older siblings teach their younger brothers and sisters to play.

Play in early childhood groups: Vivian Gussin Paley

Gussin Paley writes about children playing in early years settings or schools. One of the problems practitioners face in emphasizing the importance of play in these group settings is that they may feel pressured to teach play directly rather than causing it to arise through indirect teaching.

Gussin Paley avoids over-teaching. Her strength lies in the way she describes play in fine detail as it unfurls, so that we share the atmosphere she creates in which play can thrive. This is planning an environment conducive for play, complementary in spirit to the documents guiding the play curricula of the four UK countries, the Steinerian approach articulated by Jenkinson (2002), the theories of Anna Freud or the focus on children's play culture prevalent in the literature of other Euopean countries (Kalliala, 2003). It is planned play because the adults set up atmospheres and provide time, spaces and their informed support in encouraging children to play (Singer and Singer, 1990).

In her books, (1984, 1986, 1990) Gussin Paley like Jerome and Dorothy Singer (1990) emphasizes the importance of providing children with places to play, play materials and adult support, but not adult domination of the play. She extends play by offering to scribe stories children want to tell her, which have arisen as they play. She helps them to realize implicitly that these play scenarios can be written down as literature.

Gussin Paley extends children's play into the canon of drama and literature of their culture, with some dance and music here and there. She does not write about the way she extends play into two- or three-dimensional art, or into mathematical explorations or scientific hypothesizing and experimentation. Her work has a fine focus within the range she has chosen. She leads children from the inner to the outer, linking them with their culture, with literature and drama in particular.

Janet Moyles

Moyles (1989) has developed a play spiral in which the inner and the outer are addressed in succession. After a period of free exploration of materials, the practitioner directs the play. 'Appropriately directed play will ensure the child learns from his or her current state of knowledge and skill' (Moyles, 1989: 17). She then, after the period of directed play, encourages children to initiate their own free play using what they have been taught in the directed and guided play. Adults withdraw and encourage children to develop their own play. The adult does not participate in the children's free play, but rather observes it and then teaches, acting on the observations.

Where does this lead us?

Neither Gussin Paley nor Moyles participates and joins in with the children's free play. Both, from their different perspectives, see free play as independent of adults. Moyles sees free play as the part of her spiral where children need to be left alone to try out what they have learnt through the adult directed play. Gussin Paley believes that she does not know the rhythms and cadences of the play sufficiently to be able to do this.

> *Christopher does not try to enter the ongoing play, now that he realises it is play, but his syncopation is off. I would gladly teach him the method, if I could, but my rhythms don't work either. He must watch the children, find his own style, and practice a great deal. One thing I can do for Christopher is to stop jumping in so quickly. By substituting my own cadence too often, I may be delaying his adaptation to the rhythm of the group.* (Gussin Paley, 1986: 84)

Her way of taking the inner play of children and connecting it with curriculum content is to have discussions around but not during the play, especially when scribing the stories of children, or at group time.

It is somewhat of a chicken-and-egg situation to determine whether the outer should come before the inner in developing children's play, but we can see that the starting-point will make a big difference to the way adults develop learning through play.

Wood (1990) unlike Moyles and Gussin Paley, focuses on the outer aspects of play. She gives a major role to the adult and emphasizes the importance of developing links to official curriculum documents. Gussin Paley works with the inner aspects of play, giving backstage and follow-up support. Moyles alternates free play and direct teaching through tutoring. Wood and Moyles write about children from 3 years, and it is only recently that Gussin Paley has begun to write books about younger children (2001).

In practice

- Do you feel that children are learning more when they are doing something tangible? Doing a drawing or painting? Making a wooden block-play construction? Sitting in a group doing something an adult leads?
- If so, perhaps your home corner, workshop area, garden, are not cultivating children's possibilities for free-flow play. Children can only play richly and deeply if they have a conducive environment. They need time to play, places to set up their play and people who help them to play.
- Do you observe children enough to be able to realize when they need help with discussing what to do when two people want to be in the same role?
- Do you observe with enough understanding to work out how to extend the provision to cultivate children developing through their play a storyline, or hopping, skipping and jumping, or playing with patterns of pebbles?
- Do you remind yourself that play helps flexible thinking, that is, different ways of doing the same thing? Supposing, as if, pretending, or three thousand ways to tie a knot?

Further reading

Bruce, T. (1991) *Time to Play in Early Childhood Education*. London: Hodder and Stoughton.

Gussin Paley, V. (1984) *Boys and Girls: Superheroes in the Doll Corner*. Chicago, IL: University of Chicago Press.

Gussin Paley, V. (1986) *Mollie is Three*. Chicago, IL: University of Chicago Press.

Gussin Paley, V. (1990) *The Boy Who Would Be a Helicopter*. Cambridge, MA: University of Harvard Press.

Holland, P. (2003) *We Don't Play with Guns Here: War, Weapon and Superhero Play in the Early Years*. Maidenhead: Open University Press.

Jennings, J. (2002) 'A Broad Vision and a Narrow Focus', *Early Childhood Practice: The Journal for Multi-Professional Partnerships* 4(1): 50–60.

Moyles, J. (1989) *Just Playing? The Role and Status of Play in Early Childhood*. Buckingham: Open University Press.

This chapter is taken from:
Bruce, T. (2004) *Developing Learning in Early Childhood*
978-0-7619-4176-7

Stories, Narrative and Play with Language

MARIAN R. WHITEHEAD

The previous chapters have been concerned with communication and spoken language development in early childhood and this chapter will focus on the links between oral language and emerging literacy. The child's growing understanding of these links will not be fostered by ever-earlier phonics training and writing lessons, despite the current pressures that suggest otherwise, but by participating in the creation and exchange of stories and playfully exploring the nature of language. The discussion which follows tries to build a bridge from spoken language to literacy, a bridge which takes us from the study of stories and narrative, by way of play with language, to choosing and using literature in early years settings.

Stories

Wherever there are people there are stories. Stories were drawn on cave walls by prehistoric human groups and stories have continued to be sculpted, danced, acted, sung and recited. But most commonly stories are told, so commonly in fact, that we may take them for granted and not appreciate their significance. Yet at all stages in our lives we create and share stories, whatever the occasion.

Stories are basically about the 'what' of human experience and thinking: what I believe, what happens to me, what I know, what I feel. Indeed, any enquiry, whether it be a major research survey (Whitehead, 1994), or just asking after someone's health, is likely to elicit a story. Similar stories, or fragments of stories, created by young children appear frequently in the observations recorded by early years practitioners:

> *I sorted out some more paint – some of the jars were empty so I mixed up some*
> *more with the children – lots of conversation –*
> *A: 'Is it hot?' (because the powder paint when poured gave out clouds of dust).*

A's question is an analogy drawn from the scientific story she must have been told, probably at home, when she noticed that the process of heating water and food created steam.

A reception class in the same school had listened to an information story about black bears and built a model of a black bear habitat. Their teacher had also provided models of bears for the habitat and observed the children's play with these resources. It is clear that the 'facts' about black bears were remembered and understood by the children because of their experiences of story extended by imaginative play:

> *C (five years): Yum, flowers.*
> *J (five years): No, they don't eat flowers. They're very good climbers and swim-*
> *mers and jumpers, 'cause they're black bears.*

Published research is another rich source of early years stories in which the young tellers are apparently pinning down what they know about people, moral values and society:

> *Lisa: (Pouring [pretend] tea.) My daddy says black people come from Africa.*
> *Wally: I come from Chicago.*
> *Lisa: White people are born in America.*
> *Wally: I'm black and I was born in Chicago.*
> (Paley, 1981, p. 47)

Even at the end of our lives we are still telling stories about what has happened to us, or our families, as many age reminiscence projects have demonstrated:

> *Well, my mother saw Queen Victoria when she was a child ... Anyway, she went*
> *in this crowd and my grandfather put her on his shoulders, 'cos she couldn't see*
> *very much, and she said: 'All I saw was a very grumpy old lady sitting in a car-*
> *riage.' She was quite disgusted about the whole thing.*
> (Jones and Medlicott, 1989, p. 23)

So what is going on here? What are they all doing, these children and adults from diverse cultures? The short answer must be that they are making sense of their experiences. Not only of things that happen to them, but also of experiences they have encountered in the stories of other people. The stories seem to be hooks on which they can hang a significant event, incident or feeling, and hold on to it and revisit it. We do go over our stories again and again; this is very noticeable in gossip, reminiscences, jokes and folk tales. This would suggest that repeating and re-assembling the events of a story is a significant way of thinking about things and sorting them out. So stories are about understanding, a view supported by observations of young children playing. They frequently re-enact and retell stories about puzzling and alarming incidents, as the following observation from a nursery teacher shows:

> R (Four years ten months) had a nasty cut to the head while outside and had to be taken from the nursery to the hospital. The children were all concerned, there was a lot of blood on the floor. Two members of staff were involved in administering first aid and R was carried to the ambulance. One child asked if R was dead.
>
> A (Four years three months) was particularly disturbed by the accident and clung to his parents after school ... the next afternoon A constructed himself a white bandeau out of three pieces of paper and wore it round his head. When asked about what he had made he simply replied, 'R's bandage, of course'.

Play is not the only medium through which children rework a challenging story; they frequently use drawing, painting and the manipulation of materials and objects as ways of representing their thinking about experiences. Whatever the medium, the representation is often accompanied by a verbalised story commentary:

> I'll have to put you in the yard soon – with the horses and chickens and cows. Special department for you – you'll be the only goat. Oh no you won't – 'cos I bought the whole family – I think.
>
> (Britton, 1992, p. 74)

In this brief excerpt from a much longer sequence, Clare, at four years eight months, uses a story-like commentary to organise her own drawing and also to manage, with some humour, the boisterous interruptions from her two-and-a-half-year-old sister who is 'acting the goat'.

At this point we can put down a marker for later literacy:

Very young children are soon at ease with story forms and use orally the language structures and ways of thinking about experience which occur in the written system.

It is also clear that in stories children and adults have a very special tool for thinking about what they encounter. We now need to know more about how this tool works.

Narrative

We have seen that stories fasten on the 'what' of experiences and events, real and imaginary. Narrative, however, is the spoken, written or visual representation that relates a story's events. Narrative is the 'how' of story and is always focused on a telling of some kind. It is an ancient and basic language activity. 'Someone telling someone else that something happened' (Smith, 1980; 1981, p. 228) is at the root of all legends, histories, folk tales, biographies and novels.

Yet narrative is not just random 'telling', it is concerned with time: it sequences events in time in order to tell about them. In this respect it appears to be closely linked with the organisation and functioning of memory. We have already seen, above, how memories are recalled and told as if they were a story.

Narrative is not simply limited to endless lists of events to be told about in temporal order. In fact, we would soon tire of 'and then ... and then ... ' in any account; it is as if we require something more 'meaty' in our narratives. The meat we look for is some hint of the narrator's attitudes, judgements and values, even if we disagree strongly with them. Narrative is concerned with values and choices and most typically speculates on the human condition, whether the narrative is found in high culture, casual gossip or children's play.

Narrative is the backbone of all the stories we hear and tell. Narrative is a telling which selects and orders events in time and speculates on life and human behaviour. This selecting, ordering and evaluating gives meaning and a pattern to the random sensations and happenings of daily existence.

The evidence to support such a strong claim is found in the narratives created by whole communities, as well as by individuals, and the development of narrative competence can be studied in young children.

Narrative and communities

The explanatory narratives of communities and cultural groups are more famil-iar to us as myths, legends, folk tales, rhymes, sayings, beliefs and proverbs. These originated in the pre-literate oral traditions of societies, although we now meet most of them fixed in print. They were constantly modified and changed as they travelled down the centuries by word of mouth. Oral narratives held the shared history of a group and constantly reminded both tellers and listeners of enemies, battles, defeats, victories and family loyalties. They were also the hold-ers of a group's beliefs about human origins, values and moral behaviour as well as handy little rules of thumb about anything, from child-rearing to weather forecasts:

Spare the rod and spoil the child.

Red sky at night, shepherd's delight.
Red sky in the morning, shepherd's warning.

The antiquity of such material can tend to obscure the undoubted fact that cul-tures and groups still go on making sense of shared experiences and forging group assumptions. This ongoing account lists group successes and disasters and is the central feature of any culture. The dynamic struggle to shape the stories and, therefore, the meanings of a culture, is found in contemporary media, politics and popular entertainment. As societies become more complex and pluralist they generate many apparently conflicting stories. Some mis-matches may arise when narrowly specific stories are forced on a complex society, but broader and more universal narratives about human relationships, our links with the wider society and our aspirations for our children, do still evolve and bind communities together.

The significance of these community narratives for young children lies in their function as useful ways into the shared beliefs and meaning-making strategies of the culture. We all know 'the big bad wolf' as a kind of shorthand for danger and threat in the wider world. Similarly, Anansi can represent human cunning and ingenuity, while Cinderella is an almost universal symbol of the triumphant maturity of the poorest and most undervalued child. Com-munity narratives are ready-made resources which children shape to their own needs as they parade through playrooms and gardens being 'the queen', 'the police' or 'Superman'.

Community narratives help to build the literacy bridge because they are often the first and most familiar written materials introduced to young children, in the form of traditional rhyme and story books, religious texts and folk tales.

Personal narratives

The need to record our own existence and make some mark in the world is at the heart of our personal memories and daydreams, as the stories at the start of the chapter indicated. The community, or cultural group, provides some helpful blueprints (Hughes, 1995) but individual narratives are about personal identity and the pleasures and difficulties of particular relationships.

Researchers and scholars have built a very strong case for the claim that narrative is a primary function of the mind and the organising principle of memory (Hardy, 1977). Our constant storytelling about almost everything is now seen as a kind of 'brain fiction' (Gregory, 1977) which creates and then mulls over a whole range of possibilities. It is as if we plan lots of possible strategies and scenarios in story form before taking action. This brings us very close to behaving like scientists who always have a possible story-like explanation for any event, only they call their brain fictions 'hypotheses'. We are all, young children and adults alike, creators of imaginary worlds and stories which enable us to try out alternatives, predict possibilities and make sense of experience.

Very young children are often in the same position as the research scientist: they are constantly meeting new events and situations and must create some kind of predictive and explanatory story which will help them to cope successfully. This is shown in their extraordinary skill in making up story-hypotheses about what they observe, whether it be the 'steam' from the powder paints (above), or the problems of age and growth as experienced by Mollie at two years eleven months:

> *'I'm not too big to reach that,' she says, trying to hang up her jacket. 'But my already birthday is going to come now. Then I can be big to reach it.'*
>
> (Paley, 1986, p. 4)

Mollie reminds us that personal narratives create ways of thinking about abstract and difficult ideas and formulating hypotheses which can be modified in the light of further experience and information. These processes are more usually described as learning.

The personal narratives of young children are exciting glimpses of learning as it occurs. They are also acts of self-assertion and identity. Once again these narratives can be linked with early language and mark-making because they assert 'I am here, I exist, look at me'. There is some evidence of a developmental pattern in the growth of children's narrative competence. For example, carers make up little stories about their infants' appearance and personalities, literally from birth, and repeat these tales to their infants again and again. Two-year-olds alone in bed are able to tell themselves the story of their day: not only do they talk about events and interactions with important people, they also try out and practise new words and invent nonsense rhymes (Nelson, 1989). From two years children take over and use the narratives and literary conventions of their immediate culture. Here is Lem, a black two-year-old in the USA, explaining to himself the unexpected sound of a bell:

Way
Far
Now
It a church bell
Ringin'
Dey singin'
Ringin'
You hear it?
I hear it
Far
Now.

(Heath, 1983, p. 170)

The style and influence of memorable and highly participatory visits to a gospel church are clear in this little song – as clear as the traditional story-book language in three-and-a-half-year-old Adam's opening lines:

Hey listen to me
I'm going to tell a story
Once upon a time there were three little crocodiles
named Flopsy, Mopsy and Cotton Tail …

(Sheridan, 1979, p. 12)

This narrative continues as a tale of wish-fulfilment and narrowly averted disasters which have more to do with Adam's desires than the adventures of his famously named characters! It is clear that Lem and Adam are mulling over their experiences and thinking about 'me' in the world.

Personal narratives are bridges to literacy because they involve young children in thinking and using language like real writers. They formulate story-like hypotheses and scenarios about their lives and experiences and 'tell it like' the oral and literary traditions of their cultures.

The roots of literature

The strong impulse to narrate everything enables children to learn about the world by selecting, ordering, evaluating and predicting. This narrative drive also prepares children for the literary forms of their culture by accustoming them to being in the roles of storytellers about their own lives. More than that, they also learn to tell stories about themselves and their families, as if they were characters in books:

> [Wally:] Once there was a boy hunter. His little sister didn't like him so he ran away. So he found a baby girl lion.

> (Paley, 1981, p. 29)

Early years professionals are so familiar with this kind of spoken narrative that they may fail to be impressed by it, yet what is happening is at the heart of literature and literacy. Five-year-old Wally is an expert at talking like a book and fictionalising himself and his concerns. He has been supported in this by the traditional stories and rhymes he has heard in kindergarten, and the gossip and narratives he has participated in at home.

Literature reflects our human narrative competence; it selects and orders events in order to tell about them, it makes meaningful patterns out of random occurrences and it speculates on the chances of life. Literature also introduces us to more people and experiences than we can ever encounter in reality in one lifetime; it enriches our lives immeasurably and extends the possible range of our attitudes, values and responses. Literature does all this for very young children, as any adult who has shared *Noisy Nora* (Wells, 1973), *The Bear Under the Stairs* (Cooper, 1993) or *Six Dinner Sid* (Moore, 1990) with a young child will know.

Literature is also special in its treatment of language. Such things as selection, pattern and order are very obvious in the language of story and poetry and the effects of sounds, rhymes and repetition are carefully orchestrated. This special language arrests our attention, demands repetition and lodges in the mind.

Along with our children we know 'Humpty Dumpty' and 'Hickory Dickory Dock' off by heart. We are also aware that these rhyming mini-narratives have a strange and disturbing playfulness.

Play with language

Sounds

Linguists have often noted that very young children enjoy playing about with the sound possibilities of the languages they are in the process of learning, even if there is no one around to hear them. The following example from the pre-sleep monologues of two-and-a-half-year-old Anthony explores the alliteration and the rhyming possibilities of English:

> *bink*
> *let bobo bink*
> *bink ben bink*
> *blue kink*

> (Weir, 1962, p. 105)

This delightful example comes from a famous study that inspired many later researchers, but the 'father' of this tradition of listening to young children's play with language was Kornei Chukovsky.

Nonsense and reality

Chukovsky's study of Russian two- to five-year-olds was written in the 1920s and demonstrated that children do not simply muck about with the sounds of a language, they also play with ideas and turn reality on its head. The explanation for this 'topsy turvy' play with ideas is that it is a confirmation of children's grasp of reality. Jokes and nonsense depend on knowing the right way to do things. This certainly explains the appeal of nonsense verse and nursery rhymes, as well as the determination with which little children take imaginative liberties with words, objects and information:

> *Adult: 'Isn't there something to eat in the cupboard?'*
> *Child: 'There's only a small piece of cake, but it's middle-aged.'*

> (Chukovsky, 1963, p. 3)

A British study of the spoken vocabulary of five-year-olds (Raban, 1988) revealed that there was a surprising amount of language used by them which can only be described as poetic, or nonsensical. At the time little was made of the fact that the children were frequently saying such things as 'oops-a-daisy', 'rock-a-bye', 'ding-a-dong' and 'rat-a-tat-tat', although nursery rhymes and games with carers are clearly the source of this material.

Early phonological awareness

It is now increasingly clear, and well documented, that very young children's later success in reading is partly related to their early knowledge of nursery rhymes and their sensitivity to rhyme and poetically repetitive sounds in their languages (Bryant and Bradley, 1985; Goswami and Bryant, 1990). This knowledge is now called early phonological awareness. Regular phonological patterns can be heard in the beginning sounds of words and when these are the same we call them alliteration. Repeated and similar-sounding endings are called rhyme. Many poor readers in primary schools are remarkably insensitive to rhymes and to the beginning sounds of words, but very young children with an interest in the sounds and poetry of language may well be on the road to reading, writing and spelling successfully.

Implications for literacy

We need to be aware of these findings and supportive of young children's interest in language, sounds, nonsense and play with words. This suggests a curriculum rich in many kinds of music, songs, poetry, chants, riddles, tongue-twisters and jokes, as well as all kinds of verbal nonsense, from 'knock, knock' jokes and 'raps' to Spoonerisms, traditional and contemporary nonsense verse and Dr Seuss.

The significance of the poetic, playful and subversive elements in language should be celebrated in early years settings and classes. Children can be helped to make up and record – on tape, computer disk and in handmade books – their own rhymes, songs, alliterative chants, nonsense and mini-stories. They can also build up alphabets of their names, or likes and dislikes, or collect sets of names or foods that begin with the same sounds. All this is so much more exciting and intellectually stimulating than introducing commercially produced phonics wall charts or the totally arbitrary choice of a different 'sound' to concentrate on each week. Play with language should pervade everything we do in the early years and there is no need for children under eight to be locked into a daily literacy experience of highly contrived phonics that undermines their own sensitivity to the sounds of language.

Parents, carers and early years professionals can take heart from the support which modern research gives to young children's experiments with early writing and inventive spelling. This will be developed in the next chapter but we can note here the important insights that children gain into the relationship between the sounds and the symbols of a written language, if they are allowed to try out their own theories about writing.

A prerequisite of literacy is some level of awareness on the part of the learner that speaking and writing are different, and that writing is a system for representing most of the sounds of the spoken language, as well as aspects of its rhythms, intonation patterns and ways of expressing ideas and feelings. These complex insights are not beyond young children who have already acquired a language or two, without direct teaching. Such insights can be nurtured and extended by 'collecting' and talking about language – our differing languages, accents, dialects and varieties like rhyming slang and Caribbean Creoles. These are the things that professional linguists do and they call this kind of 'language about language' *metalinguistics*. In England the study of language is a strand running through National Curriculum English, the National Literacy Strategy and the Early Years Foundation Stage. The communication, language and literacy 'goals' for the end of the Early Years Foundation Stage (DfES, 2006) include enjoyment of narrative, story, poetry and music, and active experimentation with sounds, words and texts. These activities might also be called playing with sounds and sense and learning to love language.

This discussion has highlighted the great importance of literature in the early years, particularly that literature which is rooted in the old oral traditions (Figure 3). We need to tell this material to young children, as well as introducing them to the written versions. This means lots of exposure to folk tales, fairy tales, myths, legends, nursery rhymes and ballads, as well as modern reworkings of traditional themes and a wide range of contemporary literature.

Observations and records

We can create our own guidelines for what we need to note about children's early language and literary development using such headings as:

Figure 3   A picture of Robin Hood (Daniel, five years and one month), reception class, South Wales

- languages spoken;
- story and narrative responses;
- evidence of play with language;
- familiarity with stories, poetry and rhymes;
- sensitivity to music, rhythm and repetition;
- awareness of alliteration and rhymes in language;
- general interest in how languages work and are different at the levels of words and sounds (as in dialects, accents and pronunciation);
- willingness to draw and write messages and stories and invent spelling patterns;
- knowledge of alphabet letter names and their common sound equivalents;
- knowledge of other writing systems and literacy traditions;
- interest in books and written material of all kinds.

These aspects of development can be written out as lists or observation guidelines, but whatever types of records are kept, they must show: the date; preferably the time; the child's name; age in years and months; and the setting or context in which the child's behaviour or response occurred. Some kind of space should also be left for the practitioner's reflections on the significance of the recorded event, behaviour or response, and her plans for following it up with new provision and/or other strategies.

Choosing and using literature

This section offers some advice on the important art of storytelling, as distinct from story-reading, in early years settings. It also suggests a few priorities to consider when choosing books for young children and has some comments about the environment in which children are encouraged to enjoy literature. Finally, a list of books to start a collection, or enrich an existing one, is offered – very tentatively.

Storytelling

Much as I love books, I have to admit that good storytelling sessions are magical because no books or pictures come between the listeners and the tale. In early years settings the lifeline between the imaginations of young listeners and the tale is the teller, but good telling is an art which can be perfected. The following hints may help.

A sense of story

The teller must enjoy the story and find it worth telling; a sense of story means understanding the plot, its repeated patterns and its climaxes, its final outcome as well as the nature of the characters. Language is the heart of any telling and must be enjoyed for its sounds, rhythms and repetitions.

The telling

The voice of the teller must convey the plot, the characters and the moral and emotional propositions of the story by many subtle changes of pitch, volume and pauses. A range of language registers, styles and accents will often be needed to differentiate characters. Eye-contact with the listeners, facial expressions, gestures, body posture and an element of mime are essential to support the teller's words and help the listeners' understanding.

The listeners

Closeness to the teller and reasonable comfort are essential, and the traditional storytelling circle, or semi-circle, is probably the best way to achieve them. Participation in the telling should come from joining in with the repeated questions, answers, choruses and refrains found in traditional and modern tales; sometimes questions and requests for advice, in role, should be directly addressed to the audience, although excessive interruptions from young listeners can be gently postponed until the end of the story (but never forgotten!). Showing objects that relate to the story helps listeners to concentrate (a magic stone, a character's hat). Some traditional storytellers always sit in a special chair, or wear a special hat or shawl, or play a simple musical instrument at the start and the conclusion of a tale.

We can learn from all these techniques, but the secret is to enjoy ourselves. We do not have to be word perfect and learn stories off by heart: the bare bones are all that is needed because the flesh is put on in the telling. We also need to remember that other storytellers can be recruited from the children themselves, their parents, the wider community, especially the elderly, and from older children.

Choosing books

Choosing books for young children is a great responsibility because we are directly influencing the views they will develop about literature, books and reading. The unspoken question is always, what is in it for them? With this in mind I shall merely pick out some priorities that can guide adults who choose books for young children. Detailed reviews of the full range of books published for children are available in specialist journals, for example, *Books For Keeps*, 1 Effingham Road, Lee, London, SE12 8NZ (www.booksforkeeps.co.uk), and should be consulted by early years practitioners. Publishers of children's books sometimes produce free annotated book lists designed specifically for the 'early years', as do libraries and national newspapers.

Quality literature

Ensuring that children encounter quality literature will involve us in looking at the language of books, their illustrations and the range of challenges they offer. Quality language includes interesting and unusual words, realistic conversations, humour and ambiguous meanings and a variety of styles.

Illustrations are no longer extra accompaniments to the text in children's books: they may even tell a different story! They usually extend the meanings of the text and, such is the prestige of the picture book, many are works of art in their own right. The significance of the images in a book is now much greater: we live in a world of television, film and computers where children develop sophisticated abilities to read pictures, symbols and icons at an early age.

Quality literature always offers a range of social, emotional and moral challenges and young readers will need to explore, sometimes with an interested adult and sometimes alone, their own thoughts on the new issues they meet in books. They will also need the support and reassurance of familiar well-loved texts which they have made their own.

Equal opportunities

The range of books that we provide for our children should enable all of them to feel at home in the world of literature. Powerful signals about who is 'invisible', who is not competent or who is not valued can be given by the themes, characters, language and illustrations of books. Books are immensely prestigious in a literate culture and particular groups of children, or whole communities, whose existence is not reflected accurately in books may be humiliated and rendered powerless. There is still a long way to go in the provision of quality literature which values all our children, but we can find some books which celebrate the lives of children from many ethnic groups. There are also a number of books with determined and strong females and thoughtful and caring males in them, but only a few quality books for younger children have central characters with physical and mental disabilities, or working-class backgrounds.

Choice and quality

Children's books are not usually associated with trash, but there are plenty of poorly produced, cheaply illustrated books with predictable and boring plots aimed at children. They are found in the corner shops, petrol stations, chain stores and supermarkets where we all shop, sometimes displayed next to books of acknowledged quality. These poor-quality books often claim to be educational and include very predictable 'A for apple' alphabets, 'counting' and 'colours' books. I would not rush to condemn them, particularly if parents and carers can afford to buy them to read with their children and teach them about letters and numbers. Furthermore, children's own book choices should be respected and acknowledged, even if they are not always what we would choose. Literary discrimination and a passion for reading are based on a very wide experience of books and other written materials, and we all need a bit of undemanding reading at times. What do you read in trains and waiting rooms, or on holiday? And who can ever know what deep psychological needs of a young child are met and comforted by some cute fluffy bunny story?

Non-fiction in picture books

Many quality picture books for young children have a strong non-fiction or information content which can extend children's current interests and introduce new ones. Early years professionals have always used excellent picture-story books like *The Lighthouse Keeper's Lunch* (Armitage and Armitage, 1977), or the series of *Katie Morag* stories by Mairi Hedderwick, as starting points for scientific and geographical projects. At home many parents and carers find themselves borrowing and buying books about dinosaurs, robots or trains in order to keep up with the enthusiasms their very young children develop, as well as having to visit museums and aquaria or go for trips on real steam engines (Figure 4). Good-quality picture books can develop young children's expert knowledge and start a lifetime's habit of using books as one important source of information. The fact that picture books do this while telling a good story is developmentally appropriate because young children do not make narrow watertight distinctions between 'facts' and 'fictions' and their encounters with information in books should be pleasurable from the earliest years (Mallett, 1999).

The setting

It is not enough to provide the books, read them to the children and have frequent storytelling sessions. Careful thought and organisation must go into the environment in which children hear stories and investigate books.

The right physical environment can help young children to feel good about sitting alone with a book, sharing books with their friends, or settling down in a big group to listen to book-reading and storytelling by an adult. Priority should be given to creating an area which is screened off from potentially messy and boisterous activities; ideally it should be carpeted, have cushions, one or two tables and room for a few pictures, plants and soft toys. Displays of natural objects like stones, shells, seeds and spices or collections of buttons, keys, marbles and even attractive bottles will add to the appeal of the area.

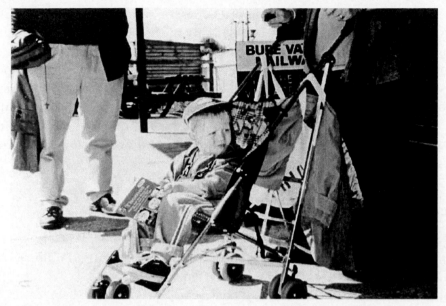

Figure 4 Waiting for the steam train – Dylan (20 months) with his 'Thomas' book

The books should be displayed on tables and low shelves with their attractive covers showing, or open at interesting illustrations. A large, unsorted collection of books can be overwhelming and very unappealing, especially if it is jammed tightly in wire racks and heavy boxes. An early years collection should be small and changed frequently, although especially popular books may never be rested and eventually fall apart with loving use. A good end for any book!

Books should certainly migrate to other parts of the room and the outside area when they are required to extend a display, provide information about an activity, encourage a new interest or just accompany a young reader on a little walk. There should also be a special place where the children know they can find the books that the adults are currently reading to them. Access to a well-known text helps children retell for themselves a very familiar sequence of pictures, events or words: this activity is another crucial factor in early reading success.

Starting a collection

The following lists are no more than personal choices from a huge range of literature and your own special favourites may well be missing. If my list disappoints, then you are probably a true book-lover and will already be giving the children in your care a literary education.

The selection is grouped into broad categories, or genres, and includes well-known favourites and some newer books. Many of the books would be equally at home in several of the lists: stories written in rhyme, for example, and picture books of traditional material. Picture books appear in all the categories and, along with traditional literature, dominate this selection. The appeal of these kinds of books for the early years should not blind us, however, to their significance for much older readers. I have included a few modern retellings of traditional material which subvert the old themes and even meddle with the conventions of book design.

Traditional literature

Alderson, Brian and Wegner, Fritz (1999) *The Tale of the Turnip*, Walker.

Briggs, Raymond (1970) *Jim and the Beanstalk*, Hamish Hamilton, Puffin.

Brown, Ruth (1981) *A Dark, Dark Tale*, Andersen.

Browne, Anthony (1989) *The Tunnel*, Julia Macrae, Walker.

Carter, Angela and Foreman, Michael (1982) *Sleeping Beauty and Other Favourite Fairy Tales*, Gollancz.

Causley, Charles and Foreman, Michael (1999) *The Merrymaid of Zennor*, Orchard Books.

Child, Lauren and Borland, Polly (2005) *The Princess and the Pea*, Puffin.

Foreman, Michael (1999) *The Little Red Hen*, Andersen.

Jaffrey, Madhur (1985) *Seasons of Splendour*, Pavilion, Puffin.

McKissak, Patricia C. and Isadora, Rachel (1986) *Flossie and the Fox*, Kestrel, Puffin.

Ormerod, Jan (1985) *The Story of Chicken Licken*, Walker.

Patterson, Geoffrey (1986) *The Goose that Laid the Golden Egg*, Deutsch, Picture Piper.

Poole, Josephine (1993) *Snow-White*, Red Fox.

Ross, Tony (1976) *Goldilocks and the Three Bears*, Andersen, Sparrow.

Scieszka, Jon (1989) *The True Story of the 3 Little Pigs*, Puffin.

Scieszka, Jon (1992) *The Stinky Cheese Man and Other Fairly Stupid Tales*, Puffin.

Steptoe, John (1987) *Mufaro's Beautiful Daughters*, Hamish Hamilton, Hodder and Stoughton.

Trivizas, Eugene (1993) *The Three little Wolves and the Big Bad Pig*, Heinemann.

Picture books

Ahlberg, Janet and Allan (1986) *The Jolly Postman*, Heinemann.

Bang, Molly (1983) *Ten, Nine, Eight*, Puffin.

Blake, Quentin (1989) *Quentin Blake's ABC*, Cape.

Blake, Quentin (1993) *Cockatoos*, Cape.

Burningham, John (1977) *Come Away from the Water, Shirley*, Cape, Picture Lions.

Butterworth, Nick (1992) *Jasper's Beanstalk*, Hodder and Stoughton.

Carle, Eric (1999) *Dream Snow*, Hamish Hamilton.

Castle, Caroline and Childs, Sam (1999) *Gorgeous!* Random House.

Cooper, Helen (1993) *The Bear Under the Stairs*, Doubleday.

Cooper, Helen (1996) *The Baby Who Wouldn't Go To Bed*, Doubleday.

Graham, Bob (2001) *Max*, Walker.

Hughes, Shirley (1981) *Alfie Gets in First*, Bodley Head, Picture Lions.

Kelly, Mij and Russell, Ayto (2004) *One More Sheep*, Hodder.

Kerr, Judith (1968) *The Tiger Who Came to Tea*, Collins.

Kitamura, Satoshi (1986) *When Sheep cannot Sleep*, A. and C. Black, Beaver.

Lord, John Vernon (1972) *The Giant Jam Sandwich*, Cape.

McKee, David (1980) *Not Now, Bernard*, Andersen, Arrow.

Ormerod, Jan (1981) *Sunshine*, Kestrel, Puffin.

Sendak, Maurice (1967) *Where the Wild Things Are*, Bodley Head, Puffin.

Simmons, Jane (2000) *Daisy and the Beastie*, Orchard.

Vipont, Elfrida and Briggs, Raymond (1969) *The Elephant and the Bad Baby*, Hamish Hamilton, Puffin.

Waddell, Martin and Firth, Barbara (1988) *Can't You Sleep, Little Bear?*, Walker.

Walsh, Jill Payton and Northway, Jennifer (1981) *Babylon*, Deutsch.

Wormell, Chris (1999) *Blue Rabbit and Friends*, Cape.

Wormell, Chris (1999) *Blue Rabbit and the Runaway Wheel*, Cape.

Poetry and rhyme

Aardema, Verna and Vidal, Beatriz (1981) *Bringing the Rain to Kapiti Plain*, Macmillan.

Agard, John and Gretz, Susanna (1983) *I Din Do Nuttin*, Bodley Head.

Agard, John and Nichols, Grace (eds) (1994) *A Caribbean Dozen*, Walker.

Ahlberg, Allan (1983) *Please, Mrs. Butler*, Kestrel, Puffin.

Ahlberg, Janet and Allan (1978) *Each Peach Pear Plum*, Kestrel, Picture Lions.

Blake, Quentin (1995) *Quentin Blake's Nursery Rhyme Book*, Cape.

Burningham, John (2000) *Husherbye*, Cape.

Cope, Wendy (ed.) (1993) *The Orchard Book of Funny Poems*, Orchard.

Matterson, Elizabeth (ed.) (1969) *This Little Puffin*, Puffin.

Opie, Iona (ed.) (1996) *My Very First Mother Goose*, Walker.

Opie, Iona and Peter (eds) (1992) *I Saw Esau. The Schoolchild's Pocket Book*, Walker.

Rosen, Michael (1983) *Quick, Let's Get Out of Here*, Deutsch, Puffin.

Rosen, Michael and Oxenbury, Helen (1989) *We're Going on a Bear Hunt*, Walker.

Stevenson, Robert Louis and Foreman, Michael (1998) *A Child's Garden of Verses*, Gollancz.

Families

Breinburg, Petronella and Lloyd, Errol (1973) *My Brother Sean*, Bodley Head, Puffin.

Browne, Anthony (1983) *Gorilla*, Julia Macrae, Little Mammoth.

Browne, Anthony (1986) *Piggybook*, Julia Macrae, Magnet.

Burningham, John (1982) *Avocado Baby*, Cape, Picture Lions.

Edwards, Hazel (1980) *There's a Hippopotamus on our Roof Eating Cake*, Picture Knight.

Foreman, Michael (1993) *Grandfather's Pencil and the Room of Stories*, Andersen.

Gray, Nigel and Foreman, Michael (1985) *I'll Take You to Mrs. Cole*, Picturemac.

Hayes, Sarah and Ormerod, Jan (1988) *Eat Up, Gemma*, Walker.

Heap, Sue (1998) *Cowboy Baby*, Walker.

Hoban, Russell and Lillian (1964) *Bread and Jam for Frances*, Penguin.

Hoffman, Mary and Binch, Caroline (1991) *Amazing Grace*, Frances Lincoln.

Hughes, Shirley (1977) *Dogger*, Bodley Head.

Hughes, Shirley (1999) *Abel's Moon*, Bodley Head.

Hutchins, Pat (1971) *Titch*, Puffin.

Murphy, Jill (1986) *Five Minutes' Peace*, Walker.

Ormerod, Jan (1998) *Who's Who In Our Street?* Bodley Head.

Wells, Rosemary (1973) *Noisy Nora*, Collins, Picture Lions.

Animals

Barber, Antonia and Bayley, Nicola (1990) *The Mousehole Cat*, Walker.

Burningham, John (1994) *Courtney*, Cape, Puffin.

Cooper, Helen (1998) *Pumpkin Soup*, Doubleday.

Deacon, Alexis (2002) *Slow Loris*, Hutchinson.

Felix, Monique (1981) *Another Story of … the Little Mouse Trapped in a Book*, Methuen.

Geraghty, Paul (1991) *Slobcat*, Hutchinson.
Graham, Amanda (1984) *Arthur*, Puffin.
Hutchins, Pat (1968) *Rosie's Walk*, Bodley Head, Puffin.
King-Smith, Dick (1983) *The Sheep-Pig*, Gollancz, Puffin.
Kitamura, Satoshi (1999) *Me and My Cat*, Andersen.
McKee, David (1989) *Elmer*, Random House.
Moore, Inga (1990) *Six Dinner Sid*, Simon and Schuster Young Books.
Simmonds, Posy (1987) *Fred*, Cape, Puffin.
Simmonds, Posy (1995) *F-Freezing ABC*, Cape.
Waddell, Martin and Oxenbury, Helen (1991) *Farmer Duck*, Walker.

Issues

Ahlberg, Janet and Allan (1988) *Starting School*, Viking Kestrel.
Allan, Nicholas (2000) *You're All Animals*, Hutchinson.
Baker, Jeannie (1988) *Window*, Walker.
Browne, Anthony (1992) *Zoo*, Julia Macrae, Red Fox.
Burningham, John (1984) *Granpa*, Cape, Puffin.
Burningham, John (1991) *Aldo*, Cape, Puffin.
Burningham, John (2006) *Edwardo: The Horriblest Boy in the Whole Wide World*, Jonathan Cape.
Foreman, Michael (1996) *Seal Surfer*, Andersen.
Keats, Ezra Jack (1969) *Goggles*, Bodley Head, Puffin.
Patten, Brian (1999) *The Blue and Green Ark*, Scholastic.
Seuss, Dr (1961) *The Sneetches and Other Stories*, Collins.
Stewart, Pauline and Maland, Nick (2000) *Sunshine, Showers and Four O'Clock Flowers*, Bodley Head.
Varley, Susan (1984) *Badger's Parting Gifts*, Andersen, Picture Lions.
Wagner, Jenny and Brooks, Ron (1977) *John Brown, Rose and the Midnight Cat*, Kestrel, Puffin.
Wells, Rosemary (1973) *Benjamin and Tulip*, Kestrel, Puffin.

Longer 'reads', collections and series

Boston, Lucy (1965) *The Castle of Yew*, Bodley Head.
Brown, Jeff (1968) *Flat Stanley*, Methuen, Mammoth.
Dahl, Roald (1961) *James and the Giant Peach*, Puffin.
Dahl, Roald (1970) *Fantastic Mr. Fox*, Viking, Puffin.

Dahl, Roald (1982) *The B.F.G.*, Puffin.
Edwards, Dorothy (1952) *My Naughty Little Sister*, Methuen, Puffin.
Gavin, Jamila (1994) *Grandpa Chatterji*, Mammoth.
Hughes, Ted (1968) *The Iron Man*, Faber.
Jarman, Julia (1994) *The Jessame Stories*, Heinemann.
Leaf, Munro (1937) *The Story of Ferdinand*, Hamish Hamilton, Puffin.
Mark, Jan (1977; 1980) *Nothing To Be Afraid Of*, Kestrel, Puffin.
Norton, Mary (1952) *The Borrowers*, Dent, Puffin.
Storr, Catherine (1955) *Clever Polly and the Stupid Wolf*, Faber, Puffin.
Tomlinson, Jill (1968) *The Owl who was Afraid of the Dark*, Methuen, Puffin.
Williams, Ursula Moray (1994) *Adventures of the Little Wooden Horse*, Penguin.
Willis, Jeanne (1988) *Dr Xargle's Book of Earthlets*; (1993) *Dr Xargle's Book of Earth Relations*, etc., Andersen, Red Fox.

Non-fiction content in picture books

Awdry, W. (1997) *Meet Thomas and His Friends*, Reed International.
Blathwayt, Benedict (1999) *Blue Tractor*, Julia Macrae.
Campbell, Rod (1982) *Dear Zoo*, Macmillan.
Carmine, Mary and Baynton, Martin (1990) *Daniel's Dinosaur*, Scholastic.
Davies, Nicola and Maland, Nick (1977) *Big Blue Whale*, Walker.
Davies, Nicola and Blythe, Gary (2005) *Ice Bear*, Walker.
French, Vivian and Voake, Charlotte (1993) *Caterpillar, Caterpillar*, Walker.
Gravett, Emily (2005) *Wolves*, Macmillan.
Grey, Mini (2002) *Egg Drop*, Jonathan Cape.
Griffin, Andrew (1999) *Shark-Mad Stanley*, Ticktock Publishing.
Hooper, Meredith and Coady, Chris (1996) *The Pebble in my Pocket*, Frances Lincoln.
Lia, Simone (2000) *Billy Bean's Dream*, David and Charles.
Sheldon, Dyan and Blyth, Gary (1993) *The Garden*, Red Fox.
Whybrow, Ian and Reynolds, Adrian (1999) *Harry and the Bucketful of Dinosaurs*, David and Charles.
Whybrow, Ian and Reynolds, Adrian (2000) *Harry and the Robots*, David and Charles.

This chapter is taken from:
Whitehead, M. (2007) *Developing Language and Literacy with Young Children*, Third Edition
978-1-4129-3424-4

Developing a Pedagogy of Play

ELIZABETH WOOD AND JANE ATTFIELD

Mari, age three and a half, has been watching a group of children playing together, but does not have the skills or confidence to join in. She asks the teacher to join in her play:

> Mari: You come on my bus. I'm the driver, you're the Mummy. (*Sits in driver's seat and pretends to drive the bus. Holds imaginary steering wheel and makes engine noises.*)
> Teacher: Where shall we go?
> Mari: Shall we go to Portland?
> Teacher: Is that a long way?
> Mari: Not very far, it's not very far. I've been there, we go to the zoo.
> Teacher: That would be good. I'd love to go to the zoo. How long will it take to get there?
> Mari: I don't know, it's not very far.
> Teacher: Will it take a few minutes or half an hour?
> Mari: What time is it? You look at your watch.
> Teacher: Ten o' clock.
> Mari: It's not very far. We go to see pandas. Oh we're there, it didn't take very long. You can come in as well.
> Teacher: Do I have to pay any money to get in?
> Mari: Yes.
> Teacher: How much does it cost?
> Mari: (*crossly*) I don't know, you've got the watch. (*Mari then turned away and lost interest in the play.*)

We have opened this chapter on the adult's role in play with an example of what not to do and when not to do it. Mari had the confidence to approach the teacher as a play partner: she was able to assign roles, communicate the pretence and define the action, showing abstract and symbolic thinking. Unfortunately the teacher was more concerned with eliciting Mari's concepts of space, time, distance and money. The barrage of questions eventually left Mari cross and frustrated: the teacher was not a good player and failed to enter into the role, the flow or the spirit of the play.

This vignette illustrates some of the dilemmas that practitioners face when considering their role in play. Ideologically, practitioners often consider that children should have ownership and control of their play, and that play is their private world. Intervention may be seen as intrusive, particularly in role play where adults may limit or change the direction of the play in ways not intended by the children. In contrast, highly structured play, where resources and tools are used for specific purposes, may allow little space for the child's creative thought and self-initiated activity. Adult-initiated activities are often perceived as having different (usually higher) status, intentions and outcomes to child-initiated activities. Practitioners are more likely to be involved in the former than the latter, with the result that learning opportunities are missed. In the study by Bennett *et al.* (1997) the participating teachers identified many episodes of play where children would have benefited from adult involvement, because they did not always know how to enter a play situation or to solve problems as they arose. Activities sometimes broke down because children lacked the skills of negotiation, cooperation or conflict resolution. The teachers realized that they made assumptions about children's abilities to share resources, include their peers, sustain friendships and share their expertise. As a result of participating in the study, the teachers changed their beliefs: they acknowledged that if play provides valuable contexts for learning, then it also provides valuable opportunities for teaching. Therefore a key challenge is to create unity between playing, learning and teaching so that the flow and spirit of play are enhanced rather than disrupted. So what support can practitioners draw on in order to develop a pedagogy of play?

There is substantial evidence to support the view that a socio-cultural model of teaching and learning can help practitioners to improve their practice (Anning *et al*, 2004; Sayeed and Guerin, 2000). These theories are equally applicable to developing a *pedagogy of play*, which is defined as:

- the ways in which practitioners make provision for playful and play-based activities

- how they plan play/learning environments

- all the pedagogical techniques and strategies they use to support or enhance learning through play (Wood, 2004).

Practitioners have an important role in supporting children's learning and development through play, particularly where play is likely to be a leading form of activity (as recommended in Birth to Three Matters, and the Curriculum Guidance for the Foundation Stage). In Key Stages 1 and 2, teachers should build on early play experiences to support progression and continuity; more challenging play is as important as more challenging work. Becoming a master player is the height of developmental achievement for young children: skilful practitioners make such play possible, and continue to nurture 'can-do' orientations to learning across the play–work continuum (Jones and Reynolds, 1992). In Chapter 5 we outlined the importance of *pedagogical framing* in building a co-constructive curriculum which integrates child- and adult-initiated play activities. This chapter focuses on *pedagogical interactions, techniques and strategies*, and examines key characteristics of the practitioner's role. Practical examples are given in order to relate principles of effective pedagogy to contemporary theories of learning. We are not making the assumption that play is only valuable when it pays into the curriculum, or when practitioners are directly involved. The pedagogical techniques discussed in this chapter outline different levels of involvement and interaction, and are intended to inform practitioners' decisions and actions.

1. BE A FLEXIBLE PLANNER

One of the main challenges in developing a pedagogy of play is planning for child- and adult-initiated activities. But which comes first? There is no right answer to this question, because it depends on the flow of activities in the setting, the age of the children and the range of abilities in the class or group. Younger children may typically need a period of exploration of materials (what does this do?) before they can develop their own flow of activity (what can I do with this?). Older children tend to become absorbed more quickly into play but need time for challenge and extension. As the examples in the previous chapter demonstrated, practitioners can pick up on an idea or area of interest from the children, or they can introduce their own ideas and suggestions. Either way, they can infect children with enthusiasm (Boyce, 1946) for learning and playing by *sharing intentions*. Planning for a rolling programme of topics or themes is not best suited to young children because their agendas may not fit in with the set topics: their interests may change, some play themes last just a few days, while others may span several weeks. The play spiral (Moyles, 1989) provides a useful framework for creating unity between adult- and child-initiated activities, which combines free and directed play (Figure 6.1). In this framework, Moyles reinforces the notion that learning is recursive (children engage in a wide variety of activities, using many

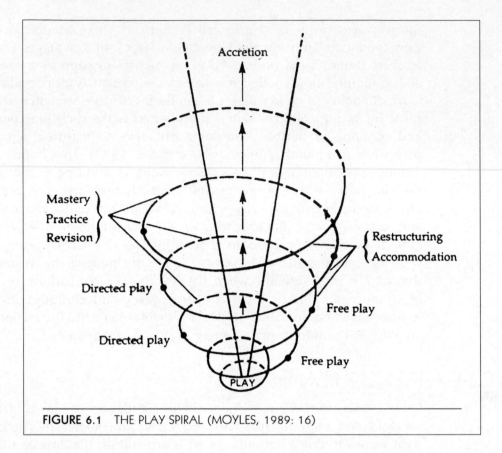

FIGURE 6.1 THE PLAY SPIRAL (MOYLES, 1989: 16)

learning processes) and incremental (learners become more skilled, knowledgeable, competent and confident). Different play activities provide opportunities for revision, practice and mastery, leading to further challenge and extension.

Practitioners plan for *intended learning outcomes* and allow for *possible learning outcomes* because in play activities, the two are not necessarily the same. In Chapter 5 we saw how pedagogical framing can enable practitioners to set up play–learning opportunities which make learning inevitable. At the same time, good assessment strategies (see Chapter 7) will ensure that practitioners are aware of the *actual learning outcomes* achieved by the children. By adopting a co-constructive approach to planning the curriculum, practitioners can ensure that learning experiences relate to, and go beyond, the policy frameworks (teaching, learning and playing can occur 'outside the boxes').

2. BE A SKILLED OBSERVER

Observation is an essential skill which is validated in all curriculum models. Being a skilled observer enables practitioners to tune in to children's play activities, understand the meaning of play in their terms, and identify learning processes and outcomes. However, observing play raises questions about the rights of children to play without undue interference – play often becomes more interesting when it takes place outside the controlling gaze of adults. Being a sensitive observer is an integral part of being an effective practitioner; knowing when to stand back and allow the play to flow can be a conscious pedagogical decision. So what are the benefits of being a skilled observer of play?

Observation enables practitioners to

- identify possible dangers and ensure safety

- ensure that all children receive attention

- be alert to new patterns and themes in play (for groups and individuals)

- be alert to problems (children being excluded or bullied)

- identify ways to support and extend play

- identify opportunities for challenge

- learn about individual children: their patterns of action and interaction, interests, agendas, dispositions

- learn about children's meanings and intentions

- show interest in, and value, children's play

- inform planning for individuals and for groups

- provide evidence to inform discussions about children's learning and share with others in the setting

- share experiences and inform discussions with parents, carers and other professionals

- provide evidence that stimulates reflection and evaluation of the quality of the curriculum offered, and what use children are making of the environment and resources (human and material)

- make links between theory and practice, raise questions and propose solutions

- support professional development.

Observation serves different purposes, and can be carried out in several ways. There is a difference between the spontaneous, ongoing observations that practitioners engage in on a day to day basis, and more planned, systematic observations. In the latter, practitioners need to decide:

- **Who** to observe: individual child, group, adult–child or peer interactions

- **When** to observe: beginning, middle, end or whole play session

- **What** to observe: whether to follow a child through one/many activities or follow different children at one/many activities

- **How long** to observe: a general 'sweep' of the area or classroom is always useful to check on what is happening in a group or in the room. Time sampling is useful for focusing on a child/activity/routine at specific times and intervals.

- **Where** to observe: indoors or outdoors, in a specific area such as role play, construction, sand, water

- **How** to observe: participant or non-participant

- **How** to record observations: written notes, digital photographs or video, checklist.

Fitness for purpose is a central concern. Observation techniques and strategies vary according to whether practitioners want to learn more about:

- a particular child or group of children (for example, boys/girls, friendships, ability groups)

- the effectiveness of the curriculum

- the effectiveness of specific activities

- the effectiveness of routines

- the actions and interactions of staff in the setting

■ the value of doing observations as a research or professional development activity.

Becoming a skilled observer takes time and practice. However, time is often a major difficulty for busy practitioners. Therefore, play-based observations should be planned as an ongoing part of the daily or weekly routine. The aim is to capture the child as player/learner in the playing/learning context. *Participant observations* can be carried out as part of everyday interactions with children in play activities. A notepad or checklist can be used to record information: for example, how a child enters a role-play area; what skills, knowledge and competences children are using in large construction; use of language and other forms of representation. Digital cameras are also helpful for recording critical or significant incidents. In participant observations, practitioners can maintain an active and interactive role with the children, which is useful for tracking the effects of an intervention (for example, introducing new ideas or resources into the play). In *non-participant observations*, the practitioner is not involved in the activity, but will be placed nearby in order to record information. Using a digital camera, a video with a good microphone, or placing a tape recorder nearby, captures information that can be used at a later date for reflection and discussion.

Although being a skilled observer is an essential characteristic of effective practitioners, there are *ethical issues* involved in such activities. All observations should be sensitive to the children: having an adult present, or nearby, can influence the flow and spirit of play. Children may play differently (in a more restrained or self-conscious way) or may not play at all. Observation can impose an unequal power relationship in that adults may intrude on aspects of play that children would prefer to remain private. Practitioners should also be mindful of how they use recorded information, particularly video and still images, and with whom the information is shared. On the positive side, children often enjoy looking at the photos and video recordings, and may offer additional information about their actions and meanings. Video recordings are useful for tracking learning and development for children with special educational needs, especially where information has to be shared with other professionals. Regular, systematic observations can sensitize practitioners to the ways in which children master the cultural tools of school, home and society and how these are integrated in their play. These insights can inform documenting and discussing play with parents, and provide evidence that play is a valuable tool for learning.

3. BE A GOOD LISTENER

Play activities provide flexible, open-ended opportunities for children to create their own sense and meaning. Play is multi-faceted and multi-layered, and the meanings that children construct are not always immediately visible to adults. Being a good listener enables practitioners to respect and engage with children on their own terms, within their own frames of meaning as they negotiate the real–not real boundaries in play activities. Respectful listening also implies emotional engagement, thus enabling practitioners to take an interest in every child. Being a respectful listener involves being alert to the different ways in which children communicate, and their definitions of reality within the play context.

Children use meta-communication – talking about their talk, their symbolization, and their actions. They speak and act 'as if' they are a different character, but at the same time communicate the action in order to manage themselves and others. They step in and out of the shared fantasy in order to structure, define, negotiate and direct the play sequence. This involves different modes of communication and perspective-taking as they separate the management of the play from the pretence. It is often the case that children who are perceived as having poor listening skills in adult-directed activities may have significantly better listening skills in play because they are more motivated and engaged. Children have to be good listeners in order to filter the complex flow of information that helps to sustain the sequence of the play activity. For example, actions, gestures, language and symbols may be combined rapidly in a play sequence, with children clarifying the meaning of tools and symbols as the play progresses. Practitioners can learn a great deal about the child's playful state of mind, and the ways in which children communicate 'what is happening inside their heads' and transform this into 'what is happening in the play'. Many forms of play involve sophisticated levels of abstraction and symbolism which practitioners need to understand in order to inform their interactions and subsequent planning.

4. BE A GOOD COMMUNICATOR

Being a skilful co-player involves communicating with children in many different ways. In play (especially role play), children often use exaggerated gestures, body language and facial expressions, all of which help to signal 'this is play'. They clarify the meaning of tools and symbols both verbally and physically. Adults need to pick up on and use these signals to indicate that they are also in playing mode. For children with special educational needs, visual and tactile modes of communication, including British Sign Language, Makaton or Braille, promote inclusion and stimulate playfulness. Being a good communicator involves shared conversations, rather than question-and-answer routines (what might be termed typical 'teacherly' behaviours). Commenting on action, using out-loud thinking, questioning and reasoning, pretending not to know, conveying emotions, are effective pedagogical strategies, especially where practitioners go with the flow and spirit of the play. Communicating approval, validation and enthusiasm are also important strategies: practitioners can give powerful messages that what children are learning and doing in their play is as valuable as their 'work'. Being a playful communicator involves responding to children's ideas, language and actions, for example, by taking on a role, by showing interest and becoming involved as a co-player.

5. INFECT CHILDREN WITH ENTHUSIASM

Many play scholars provide examples of practitioners inspiring and supporting children's play. Hall (2000) describes a curriculum development project in a Year 1 classroom, which focused on children's literacy development. The role play began with a visit to a garage, followed by the children making the garage area (a workshop and office), and providing props and resources. Hall goes on to describe a wide variety of literacy activities that reflected authentic practices, and inspired play, including:

- writing to the Town Hall planning department for planning permission to build the garage

- receiving objections to the planning application

- writing advertisements for jobs and job applications

- writing estimates for repairs and bills

- writing safety rules

- writing notices, using clipboards to make notes about the jobs.

Because these activities were open-ended, children across the ability range were able to engage at different levels. As a result of the teacher's involvement in the play (pedagogical framing), all children engaged in reading and writing with intensity and purpose, because their activities were situated in authentic contexts:

> The constant association with the socio-dramatic play meant that the writing experiences were meaningful, were used to make things happen, were means-ended, were linked to a past and future that had real significance, involved a wide range of audiences and purposes, was highly social, and reflected the children's beliefs and values about how to use literacy appropriately – in short, all the things characteristic of literacy use. (Hall, 2000: 204)

BOX OF DELIGHTS Inspired by Hall's research, Jacqui Bamford, a Year 1 classroom assistant, worked with the class teacher to develop playful approaches to teaching literacy. They were concerned to address the teaching objectives in the National Literacy Framework for Teaching, but in a more child-centred way. The objectives focused on fiction and poetry: stories with familiar settings, stories and rhymes with predictable and repeating patterns. They wanted to transform the teaching objectives into worthwhile learning experiences which would

- engage children's interest in reading and writing through play-based and teacher-directed activities

- empower them to make choices and decisions

- encourage them to be creative and imaginative

- enable them to use a wide variety of skills (physical, cognitive, emotional and social)

- make connections across a range of curriculum subjects.

Over a period of several weeks, the children were told traditional tales. They discussed the plot, characters, sequence and setting for each tale. The children were organized into ability groups and each group was given three boxes to transform into miniature puppet theatres to represent the beginning, middle and end of the tale. The practitioners provided assistance for the different stages of the task. The children planned and made the backdrops and scenery. Some characters were attached to the backdrop, and some were made as puppets on sticks so that they that could be moved across the stage. The scenes were set for dramas to unfold.

The children were encouraged to retell the stories and make up their own versions. The adults suggested writing frames, such as retelling the story with changes to the plot and ending; writing letters (for example, from the wolf to the three little pigs); and writing scripts (for example, what Red Riding Hood said to her Mum when she got home). The boxes also provided a setting for the children to develop role play around the characters in the stories, making up dialogue, developing and changing the stories. The involvement of practitioners as co-players was integral to this project: they modelled taking on the role of a character, retelling the story, and inviting questions from the children. In the role-play area in the classroom, links were made between adult-initiated activities and children's playful exploration of literacy and language. Gradually they developed their stories, using literacy and language for many different purposes:

- taking telephone messages from Red Riding Hood to her mother

- Goldilocks writing a letter of apology to the three bears

- writing a recipe for the Little Pink Pig to bake a peach tart

- directing their own play scripts and writing their own stories.

This example of a child's story, based on Little Red Riding Hood, shows detailed understanding of plot, sequence, script, and structure:

> First little red riding hode [hood] was plaing [playing] in her garden. Later on her mum calld [called] her can you take some flowers and some wine to your grandma yes she side [said]. So she got her basket and then she put her red coat on and out she went. Hello side [said] her grandma wut [what] is in ther [there] side [said] gran some wine and some flowers. Then she herd [heard] a noys [noise] saying let me out. Then she pulld [pulled] the cuther [cover] off grandma and then the big bad wolf gobard [gobbled] her up after that her dad heard a noys [noise] like a big fat wolf coming from grans house so he cwikly [quickly] ran ther and slamd [slammed] the door. Then her dad ran home and tolld [told] mum. Then mum ran to grandmas house and then thay [they] cried ther [their] eyes out. The end.

As a result of this integrated approach, the literacy teaching objectives were met in a more holistic way. The Box of Delights project was particularly motivating for children who were struggling with literacy because they could participate successfully in different ways and at different levels. The children read their own versions of the stories, and performed some of their plays for the whole school. The success of this playful approach was evident in the learning outcomes, which included:

- improvements in children's text and word-level work (children using phonic knowledge, and beginning to use punctuation correctly)

- willingness to have a go and take risks

- creativity, imagination and empathy

- improved motivation and participation across the whole class, but particularly for the lower-ability children

- higher levels of confidence in developing plot and sequencing

- using a more adventurous vocabulary (oral and written)

- collaborative peer-tutoring, and enhanced social skills

- creating and solving problems

- enhanced self-esteem.

The project also infected the children with enthusiasm across the curriculum:

- Design and technology: designing the boxes and puppets, physical and manipulative skills such as painting, joining, fixing, cutting out.

- Maths: scale and size of boxes and puppets; area; measurement; using mathematical language and concepts in storytelling.

- Personal, social and emotional education: collaboration, turn-taking, making group decisions; peer-group modelling and interaction; peer affiliation; empathy with characters in the stories; exploring moral issues through the stories; self-esteem.

6. SUPERVISE FOR SAFETY, ACCESS AND EQUAL OPPORTUNITIES

Effective practitioners are always alert to the safety and well-being of the children in terms of the physical, social and emotional environment. All educational settings should reflect the pluralist society in which we live, and should enable children to function effectively as active citizens in their present and future lives (Siraj-Blatchford and Siraj-Blatchford, 1995). Brooker (2002) emphasizes the importance of understanding and valuing children's home and community cultures, and ensuring that these are reflected in the resources of the school. The curriculum should not just reflect home and community cultures (for example, food, festivals, clothing and rituals), but should enable children to co-construct learning through activities that integrate all aspects of their lives.

Although we have taken a positive view of the benefits of play, it is important to remember that children demonstrate anti-social behaviours, especially where they play beyond the adult gaze, and engage in covert or subversive activities. Play provides a means by which children come to understand and master the plural cultures of home, school and society. At the same time, they may convey negative or stereotypical attitudes. Children play with powerful concepts such as strength and weakness, good and evil, justice and injustice, belonging and rejecting. Play enables them to feel powerful in an adult-dominated world, which has both positive and negative connotations. They may include and exclude others on the grounds of ethnicity, gender, physical appearance and capabilities, and can behave in quite cruel ways – teasing, bullying, name-calling and other forms of social aggression. Discriminatory or abusive comments can occur beyond the adult gaze. For example, Cook (2003) identified instances of individual children being excluded from play, and of boys excluding girls or disrupting their play. For older children, school playgrounds can provide ideal opportunities for bullying and aggression, especially where they begin to challenge all forms of authority and establish their place in the peer-group pecking order (Bishop and Curtis, 2001).

Practitioners need to intervene to resolve disputes and challenge anti-social behaviours and, where possible, encourage the play to continue with minimal disruption. At the same time, it is important to reflect on the reasons for 'managerial' interventions in play. In Cook's study, the play transcripts revealed some gender discrimination in such interventions. The boys' play was often energetic and boisterous, and sometimes strayed beyond the boundaries of the role-play area. Play themes included chasing, dying or being killed, rescuing and being rescued, naughty dogs, sharks and crocodiles. The teacher and classroom assistant were more likely to intervene in the noisy play of boys than in the quiet, domestic play of the girls, even where the latter was stereotypical and repetitive (cleaning, tidying and looking after the baby). As a result of reflecting on her observations, Cook realized that the boys' play was often rich in terms of their play scripts and dialogue, and deeply absorbing. As a result, she became more accepting of the noise levels and more tuned in to the dramatic quality and educational potential of their play.

Ensuring access to play is particularly important for children with special educational needs. For example, when Lina started in a nursery class, she was unwilling to speak; she had few social skills and did not know how to play. She had been neglected by inadequate parents who left her alone for long periods of time, with little stimulation. She was passive and spent a long time sitting and watching the other children. The teacher and nursery nurse embarked on a long programme to encourage Lina to participate in play and other activities. This involved some play-tutoring, first in a one-to-one context and then gradually involving other children. After a shaky start Lina gradually learned to communicate and began to interact on her own initiative. It took about a year for her to learn the social skills for being a co-player, such as joining a game, taking on and staying in a role, and being able to pretend. Children with special educational needs often take small steps in their learning and playing, and take more time to build their skills and confidence. Therefore practitioners need to ensure that play activities are appropriate and accessible across all levels of ability.

Practitioners also need to ensure that children feel emotionally safe. In Chapter 2 we discussed the benefits and challenges of superhero and rough-and-tumble play. Not all children engage in these forms of play, and practitioners struggle with the moral and ethical issues involved in play-fighting, especially where they strive to create a democratic, caring ethos in the setting. There are a variety of strategies to deal with these issues:

- Set up discussions in which the children can state how they feel about superhero play and listen to each other's points of view.

- Explain the realities of weapons, aggression and violence in society. Even pre-school children are aware of conflict, violence and war from the media.

- Establish what the problems are and where they are occurring – indoors and/or outdoors – and what behaviours are impacting on other children.

- Encourage the children to explore solutions to the problems.

- Encourage the children to share in the process of making decisions about what happens in the classroom and playground. This can be done as a part of circle time; if the problem is more serious, dedicated time may need to he allocated.

- Implement the agreed solutions and monitor their effectiveness. Be prepared to support the children by teaching conflict-resolution strategies, and developing awareness of their behaviour, and sensitivity to how it affects others.

7. BE A SENSITIVE CO-PLAYER

Jones and Reynolds (1992) argue that practitioners can help children to become master players. Therefore they need to consider appropriate pedagogical strategies that support learning and development but are not overly intrusive or domineering. Again this is a question of balance. In a predominantly *laissez-faire* environment children may miss out on adult support and guidance. In an over-structured environment, children will not learn to be resourceful or creative in their play. Figure 6.2 lists some pedagogical skills and strategies that can be used in children's play, with the guiding principle that all interactions should be sensitive to the child and to the play context. (It is also interesting to note that children use these skills and strategies in their play.)

---

observing, listening, being playful, using humour, questioning, responding to children's initiatives and directions, communicating, demonstrating, modelling, encouraging, praising, advising, guiding, suggesting, challenging, adopting a role, staying in role, playing on the children's terms, instructing, imparting new knowledge, prompting, reminding, extending, structuring, re-structuring, transforming, directing, re-directing, managing, monitoring, assessing, diagnosing,

---

FIGURE 6.2 PEDAGOGICAL SKILLS AND STRATEGIES

It takes time for practitioners to learn when to intervene in children's play, how to adapt to the play context and what strategies to use in different situations. Adult involvement in play is complex because the same activity can serve a variety of different purposes according to the age, skills and prior experiences of the children, and the nature of the activity. Therefore the critical questions are:

- When to be involved?

- How to be involved?

- With what intentions?

WHEN TO BE INVOLVED

Practitioners can be involved in planning and facilitating play, as discussed in Chapter 5. Sometimes the initiative or idea may come from the adult, sometimes from the child. We have already given several examples to show that children who are used to playful adults will readily ask them for support with a self-identified problem. With experience, children learn to identify the support they need, which shapes the nature of the interaction. Skilled practitioners carry a memory bank of children's patterns of learning and previous experience: they can remind children of previous themes and activities, and help them to extend their skills. They can also help children make connections between areas of learning and experience, thus facilitating episodes of sustained shared thinking (Siraj-Blatchford and Sylva, 2004). Because practitioners need to be alert to safety, it may be necessary to intervene directly to resolve a dispute, particularly if the child does not have the skills or confidence. The intervention may provide opportunities to help children to recognize the problem and learn conflict resolution strategies which they can use in other situations.

HOW TO BE INVOLVED

Practitioners adopt a variety of roles as co-players and, at the same time, can use pedagogical skills and strategies to enhance children's play and learning. Episodes of sustained shared thinking often arise through sustained shared playing. Modelling is an important pedagogical strategy because imitation is a powerful spur to learning in early childhood. Bruner (1991) calls this 'observational learning' and argues that it is much more complex than the term 'imitation' implies. The practitioner can actively model skills, strategies, attitudes, behaviours and learning processes by using out-loud thinking, questioning, reflection on action and feelings. This assists the process of guided reinvention in which children internalize or actively construct knowledge and acquire tools for thinking and learning.

Direct instruction is often skills-based, and can be appropriate as long as practitioners tune their interactions with the child's observed needs and interests. Direct instruction may also involve out-loud thinking, talking through the task, modelling skills for the child, then checking whether the child has internalized the new skills or processes. These strategies are relevant in constructive play, sand, water, art and technology where children may need support with using tools and materials, and creating new uses and combinations. Different types of play require different roles. For example, in constructive play many of the kits available today are quite sophisticated and need specialized manipulative skills, technical language and understanding of concepts related to design and technology. By teaching relevant skills, concepts and knowledge, practitioners can enable children to develop their skills and play with their own ideas. With experience, children can extend their skills in planning, designing and building which reflect many of the processes adults use in authentic contexts. They also become more confident in problem creating and problem solving as the following example shows.

Joe, Helen, Katy and Martin are discussing their ideas for renovating an area used previously as a bank. They have decided to change it to an art gallery and want to put up black wallpaper to show up the paintings. They have already stripped the walls, removed the staples, cleaned it out and are now talking about the door that is old and has several holes in it:

> Joe: We could take the old door off and make a new one.
> Martin: We can't do that Joe cos if we cut the old door off we won't be able to get a new one back on.
> Joe: We'll put some cardboard down cos there's holes in it.
> Katy: Mmm, yes, it would be stronger then.
> Helen: Yes, you can put string through the holes so it will open.
> Katy: There's too many holes to do that. You'll get tangled.
> Joe: There's a big hole in the actual door bit. You could put a door handle there.
> Martin: I know how to make a door handle. You could get those screws like you use on a bath. You could get a screw and screw it on through the other side then you'd have a handle.
> Katy: There's a lot of little holes. We could cover those up with cardboard and paint over them and the big hole could be where the handle is.

Helen: Yes, and you could use string to put round the handle and it would hold the door back like the hall door.

(*After this task was completed successfully, the children moved on to papering the walls.*)

Joe: We'll have to cut the shape there (*where the paper overlaps the door*), it's too big.

Teacher: Don't cut it. Instead of cutting it fold the paper under and staple it there. That will make the edges stronger than a cut edge and the edges will be smoother. If it's too big you can always fold it, if it's too small you can't make it fit.

Katy goes to stick the wallpaper up in the middle of the wall. The teacher shows her how to place it up against the corner and outside edge. Joe starts to measure the size of the paper needed by placing the metre rule down the centre of the paper. The teacher shows them how to measure the outside edge. The children have measured to find the size of the wallpaper they have to cut from a roll. They measure and cut one piece and stick it on. They need three whole pieces the same size for each wall.

Martin: Start at the next bit now. It's 1 metre 55 centimetres isn't it?

Teacher: That's right. How many pieces do you think we'll need for this wall?

Helen: Two.

Joe: Um, three.

Teacher: Yes, three I think, you'll need the same piece of paper how many times?

Joe and Helen: Three.

Teacher: How about this time then we cut the next piece, then roll out the wallpaper again and lay this piece on the top, mark it and cut it to the right size?

Martin: That'll be quicker.

The children are measuring another piece of wallpaper that has to be 1 m 20 cm long. They lay down a one-metre ruler and get another one to continue measuring. The end of the second ruler gets caught on a nearby cupboard.

Teacher: Do you think we need to measure the next bit with the metre ruler? We've got 1 metre, we need our paper to be how much longer?

Katy: 1 metre 20 centimetres we said –

Joe: Twenty more.

Teacher: Yes we only need twenty centimetres more. Would it be easier to use a smaller ruler? It has centimetres the same as the metre ruler.

Helen: They'd be the same wouldn't they? (doubtfully)

Teacher: Let's try.

Helen picks up the metre ruler and checks to see if her measuring is the same as the teacher's and then uses the smaller ruler.

Joe: It will be the same, Helen.
Teacher: It's always a good idea to check if you're not sure.

The involvement of the teacher as mediator promotes the development of new skills, thinking and understanding using the children's existing knowledge. This activity also demonstrates the continuum between play and work: it was child-initiated and enabled the children to follow their intentions. The children were pretending to renovate the bank and create an art gallery but at the same time needed real-world skills and competences to sustain the pretence. They were transforming ideas, materials and their environment. The teacher acted as a more knowledgeable other by demonstrating skills, using out-loud thinking, and prompting the children's metacognitive activity. She was responsive but not intrusive and the children accepted her presence on this basis. The children also assisted each other in order to sustain the activity. They brought energy and motivation to this task because they knew that their peers were creating their own works of art to hang in the gallery. Play provided an integrating mechanism for their knowledge, experience and social skills and prompted further learning.

It is perhaps easier for practitioners to respond to children's activities in similar play contexts where there are visible, ongoing opportunities for interaction with a co-constructed agenda. Role play poses different problems because it is a qualitatively different form of play. The main motives for role play are the development of relationships and moral consciousness, and the exercise of will. Practitioners are often reluctant to intervene in role play because of its free-flow nature. Many report that they see good opportunities for adult involvement but are constrained by their beliefs that they should respect children's privacy and ownership. Or they have forgotten how to play and feel that they need to rediscover these skills in order to play on the children's terms. In order to be a successful co-player, practitioners need to observe the play and understand what the children are playing with and playing at. They need to be sensitive to children's ongoing themes, rules, conventions, groupings, play partners, preferences and their use of space and resources.

Reflecting on the socio-cultural theories outlined in Chapters 3 and 4, practitioners do have an important function in role play, even where the motives arise from the children and they carry out most of the negotiation and management. The adult should respond to the children's initiatives, largely on their terms, and not take over, direct or control the play to the extent that it loses its spontaneity and becomes teacher- rather than child-centred. This can be problematic for adults who are uncomfortable with a shift in power relationships, particularly where children subvert or challenge classroom rules. In the study by Bennett *et al* (1997), one Reception teacher (Gina) set up a role-play area as a shop: the children made and priced the goods, and she anticipated that they would use their mathematical knowledge in buying and selling. However, the children were more interested in playing cops, robbers and guard dogs, and their play was often boisterous, noisy and disruptive. Gina believed that children should have opportunities for free play, without adult intervention. However, she acknowledged that some intervention was necessary in order to understand and nurture this play. Rather than banning the cops, robbers and dogs play, she actively nurtured the children's interests during teacher-initiated activities. Gina encouraged the children to write story boards and cartoons of play scenarios which they subsequently developed in the role-play area. On reflection, it is hardly surprising that the children wanted to enliven their shop play with cops, robbers and guard dogs: their play was much more dramatic and emotionally engaging than merely buying and selling goods, and they drew on television programmes, cartoons and characters in developing their play scripts and scenarios.

OW, OW, MY POOR ANKLE The following example shows how a teacher entered successfully into role play (Attfield, 1992). Jenny (age seven years two months) is playing as a nurse in the role-play area which was a health centre. The teacher registered as a patient with an injured ankle:

> Adult: Ow, ow, my poor ankle, what shall I do nurse?
> Jenny: I think that you should stay in for two days and calm yourself down and stop rubbing it.
> Adult: Is it broken nurse? Can I sit down? Ow, ow.
> Jenny: Yes, you'd better sit here. I'll go and get the X-ray . . . no you have sprained it. I'm going to bandage it before I water it.
> Adult: You're going to water my ankle? Why are you going to water my ankle, nurse, it's not a flower?
> Jenny: No I'm going to dab it and then I'll put this bandage on.
> *(Begins to put the bandage on over the adult's shoe)*
> Adult: Ow, ow. Do you think I should take my shoe off?
> Jenny: Oh yes. Nurse come and help me *(to another child)* . . . you hold the safety pin and give it to me when I've done this.
> Adult: Can I walk on my ankle or should I rest it?
> Jenny: I'll give you some crutches and when you get home you've got to put it on a stool or table or something soft.
> Adult: Do I have to take any tablets for the pain?
> Jenny: I'll give you a 'scription *(asks for help with writing here)*.
> *(Later – to another child who has had a car crash)*

Jenny: I'll put the bandage on your arm and you must never put it on the table like that or it'll get even more bad and you can still play football but try not to hit anyone with your hand and be careful you don't cut it when you're washing up. There now, come back in two weeks.

The adult's questioning prompts Jenny's wide understanding of a nurse's role and related activities. The role play continued for some time and enabled the teacher to make some detailed assessments of Jenny's skills, knowledge and understanding as the record sheet shows:

Emotional: Jenny is quietly confident and able to organize other children in role play. She showed perception of the caring role of a nurse and sustained this attitude throughout the play.

Social: Takes an organizing role, involves others in the play. Takes turns with equipment and demonstrates skills to others.

Attitudes: Motivated to write and continued in role for an hour. Much enjoyment evident. Sustained concentration throughout the play and was fully absorbed in her role.

Language: Used language for directing, explaining, talking on the telephone, questioning her patients in her role as a nurse. She listened to others before making decisions. Used writing for different purposes – making appointments and writing prescriptions.

Mathematical: Experience of writing appointment times with the help of an adult.

Scientific: Naming parts of the human body (pelvis, hinge joint), knowledge of X-rays and what they are used for.

Physical: Used props for bathing wounds (tweezers and cotton wool), fastening bandages, tying slings. Organized layout of health centre, set up equipment, led patients around.

Problem-solving: Organizing one or more play partners, involving other children to help, thinking about caring for the patients and seeing to their injuries.

The teacher noted that Jenny wanted to know more about X-rays and bones and how plaster is used to set broken bones. She needed to develop more confidence in writing for different reasons and in different contexts. This information provided vital feedback into the curriculum to support further learning.

JACK AND THE BEANSTALK Practitioners often find it quite challenging to go with the flow of children's ideas and interests and follow unplanned developments. However, this strategy can be informed by observation of the children's activities, and joint creativity. A Reception class teacher noticed that the home corner was used in a repetitive, stereotypical way, mostly by girls. She used the story of Jack and the Beanstalk to extend and enrich the children's play. They were involved in planning the new setting, designing and making some of the resources, making suggestions for representing ideas in the story. The giant's treasure chest was filled with milk-bottle tops and a variety of resources that the children brought from home. A three-dimensional beanstalk was made which wandered up the walls and across the ceiling. The teacher added many other resources such as different sizes of clothes and cooking equipment to contrast Jack's home with the giant's home. Because the children were involved in planning and decision-making, interpersonal skills were developed such as negotiation, cooperation, establishing rules, and taking responsibility for looking after the props and resources. Time and opportunities were made for adult involvement, though not as much as the teacher would have liked, and the children were encouraged to talk about their play, add further resources and develop the theme as they wished. This model was both enabling and empowering. It allowed children to have ownership of their play but at the same time the teacher felt that they were enjoying higher-quality play with many opportunities for learning that were embedded in a meaningful context.

8. BE A RESEARCHER

Effective practitioners are good researchers: they are alert to the complexities of children's learning, and have an enquiry-based approach to improving the quality of their provision and engaging in professional development. Children are complex, fascinating and often enigmatic. Working and playing with children raises many questions, problems and challenges which are not always solved in the everyday flow of activities. Being a researcher helps practitioners to become reflective, thoughtful and analytical. Many of the examples in this book are drawn from small-scale research studies carried out by teachers and other practitioners on advanced study modules. They often set out with burning questions, issues they felt strongly about, tensions between their beliefs and the demands of policy frameworks, and a genuine desire to better understand playing, learning and teaching. Studies that have engaged practitioners as researchers in their own settings have reported positive benefits:

■ Taking time to stand back and look more critically at what is happening in their setting.

■ Learning skills and strategies for observing, recording and analyzing their practice.

■ Learning collaboratively in a community of practice.

■ Reflecting on their evidence, and generating strategies for improvement (sometimes at whole-school level).

■ Feeling empowered by developing their skills and knowledge.

■ Being able to challenge taken-for-granted assumptions.

■ Changing their theories and/or practices (Bennett *et al.*, 1997; MacNaughton, 2000; Broadhead, 2004).

These processes are exemplified in the following observations that were carried out by Charlotte Rowland in her Reception/Year 1 class. The research activity was planned in a module on Teaching and Learning Through Play. The participants were asked to carry out ten-minute observations on two children, a girl and a boy, and bring their evidence for shared discussion and analysis. Charlotte's first observation enabled her to understand the meaning of Paul's play in the context of his activity, and his explanation:

Observation one, child two

Name: Paul   Age: 5
Date: Wednesday 5th February 2003   Time: 2 p.m.

Context: Outside area, during free play. Four/five other children present but not playing with Paul.

Observation: Paul was sitting on top of the caterpillar (play tunnel) and watching children playing in the home corner. The children left the home corner area after two or three minutes and Paul immediately went over to this area. He picked up the play dustbin and started to fill it up with play food and plates that had been left on the floor. Paul carried the bin over to the caterpillar and leaned over the top of it to empty the contents of the bin on the floor behind the caterpillar. He went back to the home corner and filled the bin up, and emptied it, in the same way. Paul did this three more times until there was nothing left in the home corner.

He then walked away from the area with a smile on his face.

He came over to me so I asked him why he had done that: he replied 'It's bin day. I'm the bin man. It's all gone to the dump.'

This observation shows how the meaning and purpose of a child's activity (especially in solitary play) is better understood within the context of play over a sustained period of time. On reflection, Charlotte considered that if she had only seen Paul filling and emptying the bin, she might have thought he was being naughty. His activity made more sense in relation to his imaginary context, and to his real-world knowledge. The next observation exemplifies the significance of observational learning (discussed above). The paradoxical nature of this episode is fascinating: the children are real pupils in a real classroom, but are playing at being pupils, and playing with typical teacher–pupil interactions, rules and routines. In this case, it is the teacher's behaviours that have been carefully observed, and reproduced by the children:

Observation two, child one

Name: Helen   Age: 5.4 (Year 1)
Date: Friday 14th February 2003   Time: 2.05 p.m.

Context: In classroom during activity time. Helen is playing 'schools' with two other children. Using teacher's easel, pens, etc.

Observation: Helen has previously been observed playing schools on her own, with imaginary pupils. Helen asked the teacher if she could play schools. She then collected the items she needed and asked two children to play with her – Khalid and Ella. Abi joined in briefly towards the end.

He: Do you wanna play schools?
El: Okay can I be Mrs F?
Kh: I wanna be Miss R
He: No I'm Miss R!
Kh: Ohhh! But . . .
He: We could take turns.
Kh: Okay. (*Helen sits on chair and picks up pen and paper*)
He: It's register time so you need to use your ears to listen.
El: I'm Mrs F.
Kh: When's it my turn?
He: Be quiet and listen!
Kh: Yes Miss R.
He: Now we will start 'Good Morning Khalid'.
Kh: Good morning, Miss R.

He: Now we will do an activity together on the carpet. I want you to listen
   very, very carefully.
Kh: But who's going to be special helper?
He: Oh you can be!
El: I'm still Mrs F.
He: Yes I know.
Kh: Can I have my turn soon?
He: Mrs F please would you sit with Khalid because he keeps talking and
   he should be listening.
El: (*moves next to Khalid*) Yes, be quiet Khalid and listen to Miss R!
He: Now let's start. We are going to do some counting this morning. (*Abi
   comes to join play.*)
Ab: Can I play? I wanna be Miss R.
Kh: It's my turn next.
He: You be you, Abi.
Ab: No I'll play later.
He: Let's get on now shall we, listen Khalid! We'll count to twenty.
All: Count to twenty together. (*Wind chimes – tidy up time*)
Kh: I didn't get a turn!
He: You can next time.

In this episode, the children have astute understanding of pedagogical
routines, power relationships between teachers and pupils, and the rules
of classroom discourse. These short observations reveal the child as
player/learner, and the child in the playing/learning context. They also
provide valuable evidence for discussion and reflection regarding the
nature and purposes of play, and the ways in which children co-construct
their play themes. In addition to having practical value, such observations
also have theoretical value, in that they can enable the practitioner-as-
researcher to understand the culture of play and the systems of shared
meanings that children construct in socio-cultural contexts (as discussed
in Chapters 3 and 4). Being a researcher can also inform the processes of
assessment and evaluation, which will be explored in more detail in
Chapter 7.

SO CAN WE DEFINE A PEDAGOGY OF PLAY?

In summary, this chapter has shown that the practitioner's role in play
can be multi-faceted and multi-layered. The guiding principle is that adult
interactions and interventions should be tuned in to what is happening

in the play, and should respect the flow and spirit of the play. Both adult- and child-initiated play can provide ideas and interests that can be developed and extended. Practitioners can infect children with enthusiasm for playing, which can have positive effects on their learning. This is not to claim that play is only valuable when it pays into learning outcomes, or that play always has to be structured and organized by adults. Spontaneous, playful interactions can occur in adult-directed activities, just as children can be deeply engrossed and 'workful' in their play. The concepts of pedagogical framing and pedagogical interactions, techniques and strategies provide some guidance on how practitioners can think creatively about their roles in play, and help to create unity between playing, learning and teaching.

This chapter is taken from:
Wood, E. and Attfield, J. (2005) *Play, Learning and the Early Childhood Curriculum,* Second Edition
978-0-7619-4174-3

10 Nourishing Children's Thinking Through Stories

CATHY NUTBROWN

Stories are fundamental to human experience, and stories experienced in early childhood can extend children's thinking, foster new knowledge and validate their emotions. Given the fundamental importance of stories to all aspects of children's learning and development it is perhaps surprising that the Foundation Stage guidance (QCA, 2000) stated that effective development and learning in communication, language and literacy needs particular attention in the following:

- providing opportunities for children to communicate thoughts, ideas and feelings and build up relationships with adults and each other;
- incorporating communication, language and literacy development in planned activities in each area of learning;
- giving opportunities to share and enjoy a wide range of rhymes, music, songs, poetry, stories and non-fiction books;
- giving opportunities for linking language with physical movement in action songs and rhymes, role-play and practical experiences such as cookery and gardening;
- planning an environment that reflects the importance of language through signs, notices and books;
- providing opportunities for children to see adults writing and for children to experiment with writing for themselves through making marks, personal writing symbols and conventional script;
- providing time and opportunities to develop spoken language through conversations between children and adults, both one-to-one and in small groups, with particular awareness of, and sensitivity to, the needs of children for whom English is an additional language, using their home language when appropriate;
- planning opportunities for children to become aware of languages and writing systems other than English, and communication systems such as signing and Braille;
- early identification of and response to any particular difficulties in children's language development;

- close teamwork between, where appropriate, bilingual workers, speech therapists and practitioners;
- opportunities for children who use alternative communication systems to develop ways of recording and accessing texts to develop their skills in these methods.

(QCA, 2000, p. 44)

Though stories are mentioned in the exemplars, they are given only minor mention in the opening definition of this area of learning. But stories are essential and this chapter illuminates the importance of fiction in early education and demonstrates the potential of story in fostering children's development and learning. Many examples of early fiction illustrate their important role in developing children's thinking, behaviour, attitudes and beliefs.

Two aspects of narrative in early education will be considered:

1. *Quality in children's literature*, because it is important to ensure that the best of literature is available to children.
2. *Stories as teachers*, because stories contain a wealth of information and stimulus from which children can learn much more than the mechanics of learning to read.

The chapter concludes with a list of stories which can be used as 'nourishment for thinking' to support the ideas developed throughout this chapter.

Quality in children's literature

It is difficult to talk about 'quality' books for children without taking some time to define, however inadequately, what might be meant by this term. One possible interpretation of the term 'quality' in this context could be that books should be neither racist or sexist and should be well illustrated and well written. Directly the problem of defining quality is compounded. Who decides what is 'well illustrated'? Who decides what is 'good writing' for children? To some extent, these are matters of personal opinion. Some books preferred by children and considered to be 'good' may well represent 'bad taste' for their parents or teachers! Because of this dilemma of quality, and because books should maximise opportunities for children, the choices teachers make when they select books for their classrooms and when they read stories to children are crucially important. Children's literature now offers more choice than ever before, and teachers need to ensure breadth of choice and range of books in their classrooms so that children are not restricted to a narrow view of literature, written language and ideas. Those educators who work with children under 5 in a wide variety of settings have a responsibility to provide a wide range of literature for children to share, learn from and enjoy. To do otherwise would be to deny children opportunities in their early encounters with the written word. It is not acceptable only to provide books purchased from jumble sales or car boot sales. Books are a fundamental tool for learning in early education and as such should not be selected from a limited range of 'cast-offs' but from the widest range of currently published titles.

Quality in children's books is more than promoting equal opportunities and positive images of people from ethnic minorities, of male and female and of different abilities. Quality is much more than skilful and compelling illustrations. It is more than poetic and memorable turns of phrase and a story line which absorbs young readers. Children's books need to include all of these things and more. Children need books which nourish their minds and their emotions, because quality is about feelings as well as thought and knowledge. Many books can help to support as well as challenge children's emotional development, reflecting and affirming their feelings, challenging their thinking and presenting characters who experience different emotions of fear, sadness, excitement, love and disappointment.

Victor Watson (1992, p. 1) challenges readers to define what we mean by children's literature, arguing that the very idea of a category of literature called 'children's' is an 'uncertain concept'. It is important that educators reflect on what they mean by a 'good book' and children also need the freedom and the opportunities to decide what makes a 'good book' for them. For children to begin to develop their own views of quality in the literature they read, they need to experience the most wonderful, the most magical and the most entrancing literature available. Books can illuminate for children parts of life which are difficult, sad, lonely, exciting, strange, challenging and frightening. Books can show the importance of being fair, stimulate thinking about equality and immerse children in different worlds – both connected and unassociated with their own. Stories can be shared between children and professional educators in group settings and between children and their families at home. Books are not just an instrument for learning about words and happenings but can be an essential part of a loving and intimate experience shared by children and adults.

Children can develop discerning qualities and the ability to decide and articulate what they feel is 'a good book' if given the opportunity to share stories, to hold on to books and to lose themselves in the pages of a mystery, a fantasy, a thriller, which they feel is just for them.

Practitioners have a responsibility to ensure that literature used by children in school (books which they read for themselves and those which are read to them) is wide-ranging, of high quality and helps to make readers and thinkers flourish.

The books which children encounter in Early Years settings and at home, the books which adults share with children at special times, must be books which light in children that flame of the love of literature which will burn and burn throughout the whole of their lives. Books can spark that passion in children, and adults responsible for children's learning need to find ways to make this possible – their agenda must include not only the development of children as readers, but as lovers of stories and active participants in the most human of experiences. Sharing stories in the early years of childhood is not just about learning to read, it is about relationships: both between adults and children as they read together, and between children and those characters they meet in the text. Children's literature can support the development of children's language, help them to listen attentively, to talk about interesting things and meaningful content. Experience of sharing stories can stimulate children to create their own versions of the familiar and favourite stories they read and hear.

What are the best books for children?

We say that early education should provide the best of literature for children, but it is not so easy to define what is the 'best'. Quality can be very much a question of personal preference. It could even be said that quality, like beauty, is in the eye of the beholder. Reading a book, or sharing a story, is often a personal encounter – a book which one child loves and enjoys over and over again will be firmly rejected by another. Those who work with young children do not simply need a list of good books to use with children. They need to be able to decide *why* they select certain books for children to explore, *why* they read particular stories, *why* they tend to shun others. For example, the classic, *Where the Wild Things Are* (Sendak, 1967) is a humorous and exciting fantasy for some children while others find it a terrifying horror story they wish to avoid; the monster's terrible eyes and gnashing teeth are just too much for some young hearts! Such books are still important to children's experiences, because children bring their own experiences, ideas, thoughts and feelings to the books they read, and books too bring ideas, experiences, information and emotions to the children who read them. When children's own experiences connect in some way to those contained within a story, a match of meaning can occur. Such a match between that which children find important and the stories they read and hear makes the crucial difference between simply hearing a story and really listening with absorbed intent and making it part of their thinking.

Some characteristics of 'good books' can be considered fundamental to children's early literacy experiences. Meek (1988) writes of the 'intertextuality' and the 'multiconsciousness' of books which contain much more than words. There may be two or more stories, different layers of meaning, illustration, timing, one story being conveyed through the text and another, or an embellishment of this story, continuing in the illustrations. Early childhood educators need to develop their own criteria for choosing books for children which maximise opportunities for children to develop their language, literacy and understanding of the world. Criteria will include: the quality of production, illustration, style of language, opportunities for developing particular understandings of text (such as phonological awareness, punctuation, genre), content and (it must be said) the pleasure they offer the reader.

Books can convey powerful images and messages to young children, so the books they are offered need to be chosen carefully. The following books have been examined to see what they might offer in terms of a literacy experience which holds the potential to develop children's knowledge, ideas, thoughts and emotions.

The Tooth Ball (Pearce, 1987) tells the story of Timmy, a young boy who is sad, shy and without friends. His wobbly tooth falls out. He wraps it first in some gold foil which comes from his grandmother's birthday chocolates. Gradually further layers are added, silver foil, a leaf, Christmas paper, writing paper, brown paper, computer paper. The ball gets bigger as layers of wrapping are added, but it also gets lighter. As the tale progresses, Timmy meets another boy who helps him to put more layers of wrapping on the 'tooth ball', an old sock, kitchen paper, newspaper, wallpaper, a duster, cotton wool, a tea towel, an old woolly hat, a tablecloth, a pillow case, a sack, and finally: 'It got bigger and bigger – and lighter and lighter, too, in a most surprising way. They had to wrap it in garden-netting so that Timmy could wind his fingers in it firmly, to stop the tooth ball from bouncing away.' The two boys take the tooth ball to the park and meet several children who become new friends.

This is a book about relationships, burning heartfelt desire for friends and a grandmother's love. It is (perhaps) a fantasy with a happy ending, but with another ingredient. A central theme is the 'covering' which is described in detail and with imagination. This story can stimulate further learning experiences and act as a starting point for work on coverings and wrappings as well as discussions about friends and loneliness. After telling this story to her class of 5-year-olds, a teacher introduced some work on wrapping and packaging. Using different types of wrapping material, including paper, fabrics and plastics, children began to create their own multilayered balls. Children learned that each time a layer goes on, the size of their ball increased, but also recorded that the weight increased too. Children recorded the type and size of the layering material, and the increasing weight of their layered balls. Working in small groups they discussed, experimented, hypothesised and tried out different ideas. Later they tested their products for durability, seeing how long they would stay intact when used outdoors for throwing, rolling and bouncing. These absorbing and worthwhile activities arose from a single story experience, the creative thinking of their teacher and the collaborative involvement of the children. The work contained several links to subject areas in the National Curriculum including English, mathematics, science and technology as well as the collaborative work and recording processes which were transferable: attitudes, aptitudes and skills, important in all areas of learning.

A Book of Boxes (Mason, 1989) demonstrates a perfection in the craft of colour and imagination of children's publishing, concealing surprises in the 'boxes' contained on each page. It is a book full of surprise. A nursery nurse was sharing this book with two 4-year-olds. It was the first time they had seen *A Book of Boxes* and the children explored each page with the adult, talking about experiences of which the boxes and their contents reminded them. The two children were keen to see what was inside the different boxes as they turned each page. Later that day one of the children brought a box to the nursery nurse. She offered it to her and said, with a broad smile, 'What's inside this one?' The adult knelt down to open the box. Inside she found six books. The little girl laughed and said 'It's a box of bookses!' She understood that things the wrong way around might be funny, combined it with her experience of the book and made her own joke, reversing the book title to name the object she had created. Both the book and the child's subsequent 'box of bookses' relate to ideas of 'insideness'.

A Dark, Dark Tale (Brown, 1983) is a long-standing testimony to the power of illustration and the economy of words; the cat receives no mention in the text, but is a main character and features frequently in the illustrations. The enchantment of repetition and the expectation in this book is known and enjoyed by everyone who turns the pages:

Once upon a time there was a dark, dark moor.
On the moor there was a dark, dark wood.

> In the wood there was a dark, dark house.
> At the front of the house there was a dark, dark door.
> Behind the door there was a dark, dark hall.
> In the hall there were some dark, dark stairs.
> Up the stairs there was a dark, dark passage.
> Across the passage was a dark, dark curtain.
> Behind the curtain was a dark, dark room.
> In the room was a dark, dark cupboard.
> In the cupboard was a dark, dark box.
> And in the box there was . . . A MOUSE!

After hearing this story many, many times both at home and at nursery, Annie (3:7) wrote her own version of the book. She used four sheets of paper fixed together with staples. On each page she drew an oval. She brought the book to her teacher who wrote Annie's words on each page:

Front cover	'Dark Book' by Annie
Page 1	'Dark house'
Page 2	'Dark mouse'
Page 3	'Dark cat'
Back cover	'finished!'

This example of a young child's book-making shows how children who are absorbed by certain stories and ideas can extend these ideas further when there is a match between their ideas and new ones. Resources and information need to be offered to them, and adults need to be 'tuned in' to extend and support children's efforts and interests.

These books (and many hundreds more) all have their own distinct qualities. They each offer something particularly special to younger and older readers. They are 'multilayered' (Waterland, 1992). Children benefit from seeing, handling and owning books like these. They need to talk about such books and hear the stories read by their adults at home and in group provision. They need the experience of sharing stories and books with people who share a passion for story and of literature. Books and stories have a prime place in any effective early education curriculum, and can provide and complement lasting experiences for children.

As well as the written story, the tradition of oral storytelling where tales contain compelling and memorable themes and motifs which sustain both younger and older listeners are important experiences for developing children's sense of 'story'. Listeners bring their own experiences to the story just as the storyteller brings experiences of the story to them.

The 'Story of the Tailor'[1] tells of a tailor who acquired a large length of cloth of a quality he had never worked with before. The tailor proudly made a fine long overcoat which he wore until it was all worn through. Unable to bring himself to throw the cloth away he remade the overcoat into a jacket ('for there was still some good cloth in the overcoat'). Over time the jacket wore out and so the tailor made a waistcoat out of the good cloth which was not so worn and still had some quality left in it. The waistcoat in its time was made into a cap, the cap into a tie. Finally, when the large piece of cloth had been made into garments reducing in size each time, the tailor realised that his tie of the fine cloth was truly worn out. But there was one tiny piece of the tie which was not so worn and the tailor made the smallest thing he could, a button 'the finest he ever had'.

Alongside the compelling style of the storyteller (lost here in the condensed, written version) are two main themes: the first of decreasing size, and the second of the pride and pleasure of the craftsman. The first theme supports mathematical ideas of size and sequence, and the second bears a message about feelings of pride and pleasure in creating and owning something beautiful, and never really wanting to part with it. Such themes recur in many stories and can provide a link with children's schematic interests in 'something inside something inside something'. Storytelling is an important part of many cultures and a way of passing on the history, laws and traditions of a people. The storytelling tradition is important to Native Americans who, in parts of Utah, Arizona, Colorado and New Mexico, produce the 'storytellers' – clay models of storytelling dolls – figures with mouths open (telling a story) and many children sitting on their knees, at their feet, leaning over their shoulders. Traditional tales of the tribe are passed on through stories to the youngest children and stories of traditions and history are told and retold through generations.[2] Traditional tales are often full of pattern, repetition, information and experience which are intended to equip the listener with guidance for living.

Picture books and pop-up books

Many books include attractive features of illustration and movable parts. A number of stories where illustration is strongly schematic and the text tells a different story are of interest to children. For example, some books attract children because of their compelling mastery of paper technology, as in *The Wheels on the Bus* (Zelinsky, 2002) and *The Magic Window* (Nister, 1981). These can stimulate dynamic exchanges between children and adults, and adults need to develop finely tuned skills of observation so that they can be alert to those things which children find important in the books they read.

Picture books and books which contain examples of skilful paper engineering can prompt children to design and create their own books, including features such as illustrations and flaps which lift, as in books like *Where's Spot?* (Hill, 2003), *Jasper's Beanstalk* (Butterworth, 1997) and *The Blue Balloon* (Inkpen, 2000) and surprises in pockets such as the letters in *The Jolly Postman* (Ahlberg and Ahlberg, 1999) and the variety of unexpected delights in *A Book of Boxes* (Mason, 1989). Six-year-old Josie created her own version of *The Jolly Postman*. She stapled sheets of paper together and stuck an envelope on each facing page. Over a week, she wrote various letters to the characters in her book, illustrated the pages and made up rhymes to link the letters together as the pages were turned.

Teaching through stories

Children can learn many things through stories. Parents, teachers and other early-childhood educators often seek out a book which they hope will help a child through difficult or challenging times in their lives. *I'll Always Love You* (Wilhelm, 1999) is the story of a small boy and his dog, whom he loves very much. When the dog grows old and dies, the boy's sadness is experienced by all who read this story. *Ben's Baby* (Foreman, 1989) tells of the events and experiences of changes in the life of a little boy whose mother is expecting a second child. Some books convey images and messages about feelings, about the world, about social etiquette and about relationships. Many books written for children portray powerful messages through graphic as well as textual images. In *Rosie's Walk* (Hutchins, 1969) – perhaps an antique in many early years settings but nevertheless a loved classic where the pictures say much more than the words – the main characters are Rosie, the hen and the fox. There are 32 words of text in which there is no mention of the fox, but without the fox in the illustrations, *Rosie's Walk* would have been a quite different story. The important interplay between text and illustration is described by Meek (1988) who relates her interaction with a child reading *Rosie's Walk* and the duality of meaning conveyed through words and pictures.

Earlier chapters have discussed aspects of the form and content of children's thinking. Here stories are considered as a source of rich nourishment for children's developing and lively minds and as such an indispensible resource for teaching. Children's patterns of learning can be enriched by many of the themes which run through stories. Many stories have a number of different themes in common. 'Structures' or 'sub-themes' which lie beneath the content of stories can be identified. Ideas of 'space and place' are important in children's stories (Watson, 1992, p. 11). Watson draws attention to the substructures in *Tom's Midnight Garden* (Pearce, 1958), which is 'full of openings – doors, windows, gaps in hedges' (p. 23). Similarly, *Alice's Adventures in Wonderland* (Carroll, 1865) and *Through the Looking Glass and What Alice Found There* (Carroll, 1871) is a labyrinth of changing size, topsy-turvy, back-to-front and upside-down experiences.

Such underlying structures, themes such as 'insideness', 'up and down', 'rotation and roundness' and 'journeys', are prevalent in children's literature and the examples below illustrate how some children might respond to such story experiences.

'Insideness' in stories

Young children, at different times in their lives, seem to be interested in ideas and experiences of being inside or putting things inside. Being inside, hiding, wrapping things, hiding objects are all part of this apparently compulsive behaviour of young children. Many stories in different ways nourish the theme of insideness. While the form of thinking – 'insideness' – is common in all of the following stories, the variety of content is wide and such stories can therefore be used to stimulate and extend children's ideas and knowledge. As such they are an important teaching resource.

Inside – inside – inside

The development of mathematical concepts of decreasing size can be fostered with stories which tell of an object or objects inside other objects which are themselves inside something else. This idea is the literary equivalent of the Russian Doll which opens to reveal a smaller doll, which also opens to reveal another doll and so on until finally a wee small doll is found inside the penultimate tiny doll. Stories like Ruth Brown's *A Dark, Dark Tale* (see earlier), *Funny Bones* (Ahlberg and Ahlberg, 1982) and Vyanne Samuels's *Boxed In* (1991) fit into this category.

This pattern of thinking is part of the same interest which prompts older children, at the point where they become aware of a larger world and their place in it, to augment their home address by adding, for example: 'London, England, Great Britain, Europe, The World, The Solar System, The Milky Way, The Universe, Infinity'. Even Professors of Education admit to inscribing their school books in this way. Carr tells of his discovery of a school book written when he was 13:

A few years ago while clearing out some books from my mother's attic, I came across an old school history textbook. I turned the flyleaf and read what I had written there.

> Wilfred Carr
> 97 Beresford Street
> Moss Side
> Manchester
> Lancashire
> England
> Great Britain
> United Kingdom
> Europe
> The World
> Solar System
> The Universe

This kind of primitive cosmology was not uncommon in 1957 and it is probably still a popular means for children to secure themselves against their initial lack of placement by locating themselves in a reality that is familiar and knowable.

(Carr, 1995, p. 18)

And the idea of 'one's place' is attractive to novelists too, for the address of Abhijit Das in the novel *A Strange and Sublime Address* is:

> 17 Vivekananda Road
> Calcutta (South)
> West Bengal
> India
> Asia
> Earth
> The Solar System
> The Universe

(Chauduri, 1998)

One enclosure – many things inside

Other ideas of insideness which attract children to the concept of 'fitting in' are the ideas of a single enclosure, for example a house, a bag, a box, which contains an increasing number of things. This is like the carpet bag carried by Mary Poppins, out of which come all manner of objects, large and small, which in reality are far too large to fit inside the bag. Similarly, *A Witch Got on at Paddington Station* (Sheldon and Smith, 1998) tells of a happy witch who gets on a crowded bus on a rainy day. In a tussle with the grumpy conductor her bag breaks and, to the delight of the passengers, out pour its fantastic contents, filling the bus:

> There was a blue moon. There were pink stars.
> There was one fountain. There were two toucans.
> There were three parrots. There were four kittens.
> There were five garden gnomes.

One Snowy Night (Butterworth, 2003) tells the story of a park keeper who is snug and warm in his house on a cold, snowy, winter night. One by one the animals living in the park arrive and ask to be let in to stay the night away from the winter elements. Percy eventually ends up with a squirrel, two rabbits, a fox, a badger, a hedgehog and some mice in his bed. Eventually the animals find other places to snuggle inside: a dressing-gown pocket, a coat pocket, a drawer, a woolly hat and some slippers.

Three-year-old Shelley, having been told this story at home, represented the story in two ways. First, she hid her toy mouse in her father's slipper. When the mouse was discovered she said, 'He was hiding because it was snowy.' Secondly, she drew a rectangle with several ovals inside it and one outside it. She said, 'It's the house and the animals inside but the mole is outside.' She had selected from the story some parts which had meaning for her, and later represented them, first through action, and second through drawing. Her language also matched what she did when she used words like *hiding* and *inside*.

Four-year-old Alistair was retelling his favourite story, *Dinner Time* (Pienkowski, 2000) in which various animals swallow another in turn: a fly, frog, vulture, gorilla, tiger, crocodile and a shark. Alistair mimicked the voices of each animal as he repeated the words in the story, 'I'm going to eat you for my dinner.' Later, playing with a set of zoo animals Alistair re-enacted the story. 'Speaking' for each animal in turn he selected a set of animals ranging from a tiny rabbit to a large elephant. He told the teacher, 'They have to eat the one smaller than them because otherwise it won't fit inside.'

Stories which repeat an idea or a phrase help children in their striving to place some 'order' on their thoughts and on their world. Repetition and patterned texts help children to predict what might come next and to actively engage in storymaking.

Traditional stories based on the theme of insideness include the song of the old woman who swallowed a fly, illustrated in *Fancy That!* (Pienkowski, 1991), 'The House that Jack Built', 'Peter and the Wolf' and 'The Old Woman who Lived in a Shoe'.

Types of enclosure

Stories like *My Presents* (Campbell, 1988), *Dear Zoo* (Campbell, 1997) and *The Jolly Postman* (Ahlberg and Ahlberg, 1999) and traditional tales such as 'The Three Little Pigs' also contain themes about different types of enclosure. Many stories include ideas of 'gobbling up', for example: 'Little Red Riding Hood', 'The Three Billy Goats Gruff' and Aesop's fable of 'The Wolf and his Shadow'. Others tell of deep enclosing forests as in 'The Sleeping Beauty'. Similarly the Bible story of 'Jonah and the Whale' tells of Jonah who is swallowed by a large whale and spends three days and nights inside the whale and is eventually spat out onto land. Another Old Testament story of Joseph, made popular through the musical show *Joseph and the Amazing Technicolor Dreamcoat*, contains several enclosures. Williams retells this tale in *Joseph and His Magnificent Coat of Many Colours* (Williams, 1990) where Joseph experiences many types of enclosure: his magnificent coat, a deep pit and a prison cell.

One enclosure – many uses

Jack's Basket (Catley, 1989), written in rhyme, tells of different uses, over the passage of time, for Jack's baby basket: his bed for the first few months, a wool basket, a pretend car or boat, a picnic basket, a laundry basket, something to gather apples in from the tree in the garden and, finally, battered and worn, it becomes a home for mice in the garden shed. In *Fur* (Mark and Voake, 1996) a cat makes a series of nests ready to give birth to her kittens; she uses a hat, a basket in a cupboard and a skirt, but finally the hat is filled with 'fur' and the kittens have arrived. Maya (4:6), familiar with this story, made 'a hat' from clay, explaining to her mother: 'I did this hat, and tomorrow there will be kittens but they haven't been born from the mummy cat yet.' As children develop some understanding of time, they realise that there are times when there is a need to wait before things happen. Maya knew that there was some waiting involved when a cat has kittens, and here the making of the hat portrayed her understanding.

Coverings

The theme of 'coverings' includes many avenues for exploration and representation: several covers on top of one another, making coverings, disguise and dressing up. Several stories already mentioned enrich these ideas. Many stories have several interrelated ideas which will connect in different ways with children's interests and imaginations.

The Hans Anderson tale of 'The Emperor's New Clothes' is a story which can appeal to children who understand about clothing and covering (and of being tricked) (Anderson, 1992). Children who can imagine the scene may find it funny that so many people were too stupid to admit that the Emperor was not wearing any clothes. A more contemporary story, *Mr Nick's Knitting* (Wild and Huxley, 1999) has as a central theme the making of a blanket from knitted squares. This story describes the deep feelings of real and loving friendship and the need to give something truly unique to a person who is a very special friend.

Children love to dress up and pretend to be a different person. They delight in adopting and creating roles in which they are different from their daily lives – more powerful, more exotic, perhaps more feeble than they see themselves to be. Stories of dressing up or changing appearances through disguise can be used to nourish and extend children's ideas of coverings and of being wrapped inside as well as the fear and excitement of being different and exploring new identities. Two animal stories describe the potential of looking different by taking on a different covering. *Elmer* (McKee, 1990) tells of a multicoloured elephant who covers himself with grey mud so that he looks the same as, and is therefore acceptable to, the rest of the herd. It is a story of difference and of the need to be accepted by one's peers. It shows how effective (and ultimately ineffective) some disguises can be. Accidental disguise, as in *Harry the Dirty Dog* (Zion and Bloy Graham, 1992), also shows reactions to those who look different.

For children, the idea of disguise is quite intriguing. After telling both *Elmer* and *Harry the Dirty Dog* to a group of 4-year-olds, their teacher noted how a small group continued the theme of coverings from the stories into their play that afternoon. The children draped themselves with fabric lengths from the dressing-up wardrobe, approached other children, disguised their voices and asked children to guess who they were or declared that they were a different character. The teacher suggested to the children that they might improve their disguise by making masks. Materials were assembled and the interested children worked with their teachers to make masks of different characters. They later enjoyed the whole idea of surprising and creating puzzlement among their friends and parents who saw them wearing their masks and disguises.

Up and down

Many stories include ideas of vertical movement with concepts of increasing height and of problem-solving related to height. The following examples of stories and children's responses to them show the variety of ideas which can be introduced through this theme. Many traditional stories include ideas of height and of conquering height. Jack climbs the beanstalk to encounter the Giant and achieve wealth and happiness. Rapunzel lets down her long hair for her suitor to climb to meet her.

Illustrators represent variations in height in many different ways. Shirley Hughes's wordless picture book *Up and Up* (1991) tells, in detailed illustrations, the story of a little girl so enthralled with the flight of a bird that she tries to fly. First she makes some wings and launches herself (into an abrupt landing) from the top of a step ladder; then she inflates some balloons and, holding tight onto the strings, she lifts off, only to fall to ground again when the balloons burst. An enormous chocolate egg is delivered to her house, and after eating the contents she seems able to fly; the story proceeds from here with her flight (and the pursuit of many).

This story allows children to tell their own version of events. They can speculate on why she wanted to fly, how else she might have tried, and be asked: 'Can chocolate really make you fly?' They might, as the following example shows, begin to tell their own story in their own way, incorporating their own excitement, fears and anticipations. The following transcript contains the story which one little girl had to tell, starting from her interest in a particular illustration in the book, and building on her ideas about life and that which was important to her. Throughout this exchange the adult tried to reflect the child's own language and ideas back to her without asking new questions that impose an 'adult' agenda on Lucy's story:

Lucy:	She's going up, right up to the roof.
Teacher:	She's up on top of the roof, she's getting higher.
Lucy:	I think she might be in heaven soon.
Teacher:	You think she might be in heaven?
Lucy:	Well, she's nearly high enough to be in heaven, that's why the people are chasing her.
Teacher:	The people are chasing her because they think she's getting as high as heaven?
Lucy:	Yes, as high as heaven, they don't want her to go as high as that!
Teacher:	They don't want her to go as high as heaven?
Lucy:	If you go as high as heaven you get stuck and can't get down. You can get up there but you can't get back. My rabbit did that. Aeroplanes go high but not as high as heaven, so they're OK. I went to my holiday in an aeroplane, but it wasn't in heaven, I went for a long time though.

The picture book *Up and Up* was the trigger for this little girl to tell her own story. Both the book and the reflective language of the teacher enabled the child to tell the story she had formed within her. She had, in her young mind, begun to understand about death and parting and used the explanation that her rabbit has 'gone to heaven', attaching to it her own meaning. To her, going to heaven is not about death, but it is about parting because that loved rabbit was stuck in a place and unable to get back to her. The teacher's important interaction here was to enable Lucy to tell her story, not by asking 'why' or 'how' by adding in ideas of her own or by asking new questions, but by creating a space in which the child could tell her story in her own words, with her own ideas.

Many stories include the idea of increasing size, woven into the text along with other concepts. *Titch* (Hutchins, 2001) conveys the feelings and experiences of many children who are always the little one of the family and this is perhaps why they have survived the test of time. After seeming always to play a less significant role to everyone else in the story, Titch eventually planted a tiny seed which '. . . grew and grew and grew'. *Jasper's Beanstalk* (Butterworth, 1997) follows the same theme of waiting and growing, and links at the end to the story of Jack and the Beanstalk, enforcing the theme of height and growing. *Alfie Gets in First* (Hughes, 1982) is another story of a little child who needs to solve the problem of his lack of height, featuring the trauma of childhood mishaps, the anxiety of adults and eventual resolution. *Jolly Snow* (Hissey, 1998) includes ideas of height and problem-solving; some toy animals who want to play in snow try several ways of making pretend snow indoors. Using a sheet they create a toboggan run:

'Now if we had a slope,' said Rabbit, 'we could whizz down it on the sledge.' . . . Bramwell Brown disappeared into the bedroom and came back pulling a large white sheet. He gave a corner to Jolly. 'Now,' said Bramwell, 'when the others climb on, lift up your end and they should slide all the way down.'

The animals try this but have rather a dubious landing:

'I think we need a softer landing,' said Rabbit, fluffing up his flattened fur and helping Little Bear to his feet. He piled up a heap of cushions against the wall and then all three toys bravely climbed back onto the sheet. 'Ready, steady, go!' they called to Jolly. Up went the sheet. Down went the toys – straight into the heap of cushions . . .

This short extract illustrates ways in which ideas of height, and problem-solving in relation to height, can be introduced or expanded in children's literature, a further resource for teaching.

In *The Teddy Bear Robber* (Beck, 1989) Tom pursues the giant who steals his teddy: 'He slipped down a massive arm, swung on a big iron key and slithered down a mighty leg . . . They came to the Giant's castle. Tom clambered up the steep steps after the Giant . . . higher, and higher, and higher, and higher . . . until they came to a giant door . . .' The words 'higher, and higher, and higher, and higher' interwoven with illustration, illuminate the scene for young readers and listeners.

Some stories which convey ideas of 'up and down' and of increasing or decreasing height contain plots which require certain knowledge to be fully appreciated. Children who understand the prickliness of a hedgehog can appreciate the humour of being catapulted high into the air after sitting on a hedgehog's sharp spines, as is the fate of *Willoughby Wallaby* (Alborough, 1991). Similarly, children need to understand the concept of displacement to grasp a fuller meaning of the story of 'The Fox and the Grapes' (Aesop).

Rotation and roundness

Many traditional rhymes and jingles include ideas of roundness and rotation, which adults can share with children and which can be sung, changed and acted out, for example 'Here We Go Round the Mulberry Bush', 'Sally Go Round the Sun', 'Round and Round the Garden'. Stories too can nurture the ideas of movement and action linked to concepts of rotation and roundness, such as *Cupboard Bear* (Alborough, 1990) which includes the idea of rolling and rotation as Bear dreams of a huge ice-cream ball.

Books with moving parts can also contribute to children's developing ideas about rotation. *The Wheels on the Bus* (Zelinsky, 2002) is a feast of movement and colour based on the rhyme and finger song. It includes wheels, and text, which rotate.

Journeys and journeying

Ideas of journeys and journeying in children's stories often begin with children travelling between different connecting points, for example their house and their friend's house. Stories about journeying, whether around the house, in a local area or across continents, are of relevance to children who are interested in trajectories (that is, ideas of movement from point 'A' to point 'B' and so on). A theme of journeys and journeying will nourish elements of back-and-forth schema, fuelling children's ideas through fantasy and reality of going and coming. Children's literature contains a wealth of material to support this theme.

In *On the Way Home* (Murphy, 1982), Claire meets various friends who ask how she hurt her knee. This gives her the opportunity to tell a number of quite fantastic stories. Eventually when she gets home she tells her mum what really happened. The characters Claire brings into the story through her own interwoven stories make a simple journey home and a grazed knee into quite an adventure. *Hold Tight Bear!* (Maris, 1990) describes the walk of some toys into the forest where they have a picnic: 'Over the hills, across the stream, to a meadow near the woods . . . Bear walks under the tall trees, through the cool quiet woods . . .' The passages of text which describe the journey provide for children some of the language of mapping and mapwork. The story also includes the concepts of direction, position, space and place. Such ideas are also found in *The Ball* (Lloyd and Rees, 1991), where the text describes the path of the moving red ball and the illustrations show the bouncing movement, indicating where the ball has been as well as its present position. Some journeying stories have become well-known classics. *Where the Wild Things Are* (Sendak, 1967) and *The Snowman* (Briggs, 1980) tell of two boys who experience fantastic journeys. Are they dreams or are they fantasy? The reader must decide. Maurice Sendak (1967) describes journeying through time and place to take Max to his adventure with the wild things. Max travels in a private boat:

> . . . he sailed off through night and day
> and in and out of weeks
> and almost over a year
> to where the wild things are.

Oi! Get Off Our Train (Burningham, 1991) tells of another bedtime journey where a little boy and his pyjama-case dog travel on their train through fog, heat, wind, marshland, rain, forest and snow rescuing endangered species as they go. *We're Going on a Bear Hunt* (Rosen and Oxenbury, 2005) tells of a journey and an eventful return home revisiting all the landmarks of the outward trip.

Young children who are interested in places and journeying often create their own maps, diagrams and recreations of spaces and places they know. Kirstie was absorbed with ideas of space and place and, in particular, with the idea of getting from one place to another. She used wooden bricks to recreate her own local community environment, labelling various blocks, 'my house', 'Auntie June's house', 'nursery', 'Adam's house'. She used small people to represent different characters and moved them from one place to another. Her words provided a running commentary of her thinking and the action:

Kirstie doll: I'm going to Auntie June's house.
Mummy doll: (*Protests*) You can't go on your own.

Kirstie doll:	Yes I can – I won't talk to the wolf.
Mummy doll:	Oh all right – but don't pick flowers in the forest. (*Kirstie walks the doll around her brick world to Adam's house*)
Kirstie doll:	Knock knock – is Adam coming with me? (*Adam doll is brought into the game and Kirstie with Adam doll in one hand and the doll representing herself in the other continues her tale as she moves both dolls around the brick village she has created*)
Kirstie doll:	Shall we go to Auntie June's?
Adam doll:	Oh all right.
Kirstie doll:	We're there now – knock knock (*nothing happens*)
Adam doll:	She's not in.
Kirstie doll:	Well, we can't go in the woods – 'cos the wolf might get us. (*Kirstie walks the dolls around again, humming to herself. She takes them in and out of brick enclosures, through tiny gaps in the bricks and eventually back to her house*)

Kirstie later drew what she called 'my house'. It consisted of four square enclosures and connecting dotted lines. Pointing to appropriate parts of her drawing, Kirstie told her teacher, 'My house, Auntie June's house, Adam's house, nursery,' then tracing her finger along the dotted line she said, 'That's the way we go to nursery. We get Adam first, then go through there and along there and down there, past the phone box and to nursery in there.' Kirstie's map showing the way to nursery was created from her knowledge of her local environment, her life experiences, her understanding and experience of stories and her understanding and skill in using symbols to represent things. Her journey may not have been quite as fantastic as those of Max or the boy who flew with the Snowman, but it was founded in her own experiences and perhaps validated by many of the stories she had heard.

Stories and curriculum

The tremendous potential of stories as a resource for teaching has been demonstrated. As well as nourishing more 'traditional' areas of learning as defined in terms of subjects, such as mathematics, science, history, geography and others, stories can nurture other important elements in children's learning and development often overlooked by those who determine and prescribe the National Curriculum. For example, *The Stop Watch* (Lloyd and Dale, 1986) is a story which focuses on timing events; it supports concepts of time and timing but is also about competition and the relationship between a brother and sister. Similarly, stories such as *Oi! Get Off Our Train* (Burningham, 1991) can be used to highlight and reinforce effects of environmental damage with human and emotional content as well. Stories are an important resource for helping children to affirm and recognise their emotions.

Children's ways of learning do not change because national policies or the prescribed curriculum change. The successful understanding of curriculum content depends upon classroom practice, on teachers' interactions with children, on stimulating and challenging resources and experiences and on pedagogy which holds learners and learning as central. Stories, fully and skilfully explored, are a rich source of curriculum content, which can find a 'match' with young children's minds.

The practice of planning curriculum around stories has been developed by several over the years resulting in publications which promote, for example, science, design and technology (Creary et al., 1991; Williams, 1991; Design Council, 1992; Nutbrown and Hirst, 1993); history (Cox and Hughes, 1990); and cross-curricular themes and issues (Development Education Centre, 1991; Emblen and Schmitz, 1991).

Those who work with children under the age of statutory schooling have a curriculum freedom which, whatever form of setting they work in, allows them to draw on the richness of the world to provide nourishment for the minds of young children. Teachers working with children in the early stages of Key Stage 1 can take those ideas from the prescribed curriculum which provides for meaningful curriculum content for children, and add to and enrich them according to the various interests and concerns of the children. Despite prescribed criteria for curriculum inspection, there remains a curriculum freedom in teaching children under 5 which means that they can still experience the more 'natural curriculum' mediated through responsive and respectful pedagogy which nourishes young minds.

Young children need a responsibly crafted curriculum attuned to them which includes the richness of stories and storying experiences. A 'natural' early-education curriculum must contain a wealth of stories: myths, legends, traditional stories from many different cultures, stories from children's own local histories and localities, and Greek myths, Aesop's fables, Bible stories and the Anansi stories. Stories told, read, retold and re-enacted, as is common practice in Steiner Waldorf education, become the hidden teachers of young children, open the doors of their minds to the wider world and validate their own inner worlds of storymaking.

Stories as nourishment for thinking

In the following pages books are listed under broad themes which can be related to the different concepts, topics and schemas which have been discussed in this chapter and throughout this book. Such themes can provide profitable curriculum content and stimulate children's interests and imaginations. This illustrates the wide range of content to be drawn from stories to nourish specific threads of children's thinking. The stories are presented here under the themes already discussed in this chapter: insideness, coverings, up and down, rotation and roundness, and journeys and journeying. These lists are by no means comprehensive and are included to exemplify the range and depth of material which stories can offer.

'Insideness'

Inside – inside – inside

Ahlberg, J. and Ahlberg, A. (1980) *Funny Bones*. London: Picture Lions.
Andreae, G. and Caggan, V. (2002) *There's a House Inside My Mummy*. London: Orchard.

Brown, R. (1983) *A Dark, Dark Tale*. London: Scholastic Publications.
Pienkowski, J. (1991) *Fancy That!* London: Orchard Books.
Pienkowski, J. (2000) *Dinner Time*. London: Gallery Five.
Samuels, V. (1991) *Boxed In*. London: Red Fox.
Traditional tale: 'Peter and the Wolf'.

One enclosure – increasing amount inside

Allan, P. (1990) *Who Sank the Boat?* Harmondsworth: Picture Puffin.
Burninghan, J. (1992) *The Shopping Basket*. London: Jonathan Cape.
Burningham, J. (2001) *Mr Gumpy's Outing*. Harmondsworth: Puffin.
Butterworth, N. (2003) *One Snowy Night*. London: Picture Lions.
Cousins, L. (2003) *Noah's Ark Play Set*. London: Walker Books.
Inkpen, M. (1993) *Kipper's Toybox*. London: Hodder.
Pienkowski, J. (2003) *The Animals Went in Two by Two*. London: Walker Books.
Roffey, M. and Wyllie, S. (1989) *There Was an Old Woman . . .* London: Harper Collins.
Sheldon, D. and Smith, W. (1998) *A Witch Got on at Paddington Station*. London: Red Fox.
Traditional tale: 'The Old Woman Who Lived in a Shoe'.

Types of enclosures

Ahlberg, J. and Ahlberg, A. (1999) *The Jolly Postman or Other People's Letters*. London: Heinemann.
Campbell, R. (1988) *My Presents*. London: Campbell Blackie Books.
Campbell, R. (1997) *Dear Zoe*. Harmondsworth: Puffin.
Hill, E. (2003) *Where's Spot?* London: Heinemann.
Mark, J. and Voake, C. (1996) *Fur*. London: Walker Books.
Mason, L. (1989) *A Book of Boxes*. London: Orchard Books.
Roffey, M. (1985) *Home Sweet Home*. London: Piper.
Satoshi, K. (2000) *What's Inside: The Alphabet Book*. London: Anderson Press.
Sieveking, A. and Lincoln, F. (1989) *What's Inside?* London: Frances Lincoln.
Aesop's fable: 'The Fox and the Grapes', in Clarke, M. and Voake, C. (1990) *The Best of Aesop's Fables*. London: Walker Books.
Traditional tale: 'The Three Little Pigs'.

One enclosure, different uses

Catley, A. (1987) *Jack's Basket*. London: Beaver Books.
Prater, J. (1987) *The Gift*. Harmondsworth: Puffin.

Coverings

Anderson, H.-C., 'The Emperor's New Clothes', in Ash, N. and Higton, B. (eds) (1992) *Fairy Tales from Hans Anderson – A Classic Illustrated Edition*. London: Pavilion Books.
Inkpen, M. (2002) *Kipper's Treehouse*. London: Hodder.
McKee, D. (1990) *Elmer*. London: Andersen Press.
Pearce, P. (1987) *The Tooth Ball*. Harmondsworth: Picture Puffins.
Wild, M. and Huxley, D. (1990) *Mr Nick's Knitting*. London: Picture Knight.
Zion, G. and Bloy Graham, M. (1992) *Harry the Dirty Dog*. London: Red Fox.

Up and down

Alborough, J. (1991) *Willoughby Wallaby*. London: Walker Books.
Alborough, J. (1996) *Can You Jump Like a Kangaroo?* London: Walker Books.
Butterworth, N. (1997) *Jasper's Beanstalk*. London: Picture Lions.
Dale, P. (1991) *The Elephant Tree*. London: Walker Books.
Edwards, H. and Niland, D. (2006) *There's a Hippopotamus on Our Roof Eating Cake!* London: Happy Cat Books.
Hissey, J. (1998) *Jolly Snow*. London: Random Century.
Hughes, S. (1991) *Up and Up*. London: Red Fox.
Hutchins, P. (2001) *Titch*. London: Bodley Head.
Inkpen, M. (2001) *The Blue Balloon*. London: Hodder.
Miko, Y. (1994) *Little Lumpty*. London: Walker Books.
Aesop's fable: 'The Fox and the Grapes', in Clarke, M. and Voake, C. (1990) *The Best of Aesop's Fables*, Walker Books, London.
Traditional tales: 'Jack and the Beanstalk' and 'Rapunzel'.

Rotation and roundness

Alborough, J. (1990) *Cupboard Bear*. London: Walker Books.
Price, M. and Kemp, M. (2003) *Round and Round the Garden*. London: Walker Books.

Books with rotating parts

Nister, E. (1981) *The Magic Window*. Glasgow: HarperCollins.
Zelinsky, P. (2002) *The Wheels on the Bus*. London: Orchard Books.

Journeys and journeying

Bayley, N. and Mayne, W. (1993) *The Patchwork Cat*. London: Red Fox.
Beck, I. (1989) *The Teddy Bear Robber*. Toronto: Doubleday.
Briggs, R. (1980) *The Snowman*. Harmondsworth: Puffin.
Burningham, J. (1963) *Borka – The Adventures of a Goose with no Feathers*. London: Jonathan Cape.
Burningham, J. (1991) *Oi! Get Off Our Train*. London: Red Fox.
Cartwright, R. and Kinmonth, P. (1979) *Mr Potter's Pigeon*. London: Hutchinson Junior Books.
Dale, P. (1991) *The Elephant Tree*. London: Walker Books.
Fair, S. (1989) *Barney's Beanstalk*. London: Macdonald.
Flack, M. and Weise, K. (1991) *The Story about Ping*. London: Random Century.
French, V. and Prater, J. (2000) *The Gingerbread Boy*. London: Walker.
Hughes, S. (1991) *Up and Up*. London: Red Fox.
Hutchins, P. (1969) *Rosie's Walk*. London: Bodley Head.
Lear, E. and Knight, H. (2001) *The Owl and the Pussycat*. London: Simon & Schuster.
Maris, R. (2001) *Hold Tight Bear!* London: Walker Books.
Murphy, J. (1982) *On the Way Home*. London: Pan Macmillan Children's Books.
Pearce, P. (1987) *The Tooth Ball*. Harmondsworth: Picture Puffins.
Prater, J. (1987) *The Gift*. Harmondsworth: Puffin.
Rosen, M. and Oxenbury, H. (2005) *We're Going on a Bear Hunt*. London: Walker Books.
Sendak, M. (1967) *Where the Wild Things Are*. London: Bodley Head.

Shapur, F. (1991) *The Rainbow Balloon*. London: Simon & Schuster.

Wild, M. and Huxley, D. (1990) *Mr Nick's Knitting*. London: Picture Knight.

Zion, G. and Bloy Graham, M. (1960) *Harry the Dirty Dog*. London: Bodley Head.

Aesop's fable: 'The Hare and the Tortoise', in Clarke, M. and Voake, C. (1990) *The Best of Aesop's Fables*. London: Walker Books.

Notes

1. I heard Pat Ryan tell the story of the tailor at the Sheffield Early Years Literacy Association Conference, June 1991.
2. More information on this topic can be found in M. Bahti (1988) *Pueblo Stories and Storytellers*, Treasure Chest Publications, Tucson, AZ.

This chapter is taken from:
Nutbrown, C. (2006) *Threads of Thinking*, Third Edition
978-1-4129-1084-2

Anthropological and Sociological Perspectives on the Study of Children

PIA CHRISTENSEN and ALAN PROUT

During the last fifteen years the social study of children has undergone a fundamental change of perspective. Sometimes called the 'new sociology' or 'new social studies' of childhood, this new perspective accords children conceptual autonomy, looking at them as the direct and primary unit of study. It focuses on children as social actors in their present lives and it examines the ways in which they influence their social circumstances as well as the ways in which they are influenced by them. It sees children as making meaning in social life through their interactions with other children as well as with adults. Finally, childhood is seen as part of society not prior to it and it is subject to the same type of influences that shape other social phenomena. In this chapter we explore this perspective, examining why it came about, how social scientific ideas about children are embedded in wider social and cultural ideas about childhood and outlining the main features of the new approaches. Finally we point to some of the debates and issues that are arising in the field, especially the concept of generational order.

The Paradox of Sameness and Difference

Writing almost thirty years ago Hardman (1973) identified two general problems about children in social and cultural studies: their lack of visibility and their muteness. The situation she described can be seen as similar in some respects to that of women in society and their representation in earlier social science (see for example, Ardener, 1975a, 1975b; Moore, 1988). The critique of this, pioneered by feminists, brought the particular perspectives of women, their social position and everyday experiences to the attention of social scientists (Alanen, 1988) and led to changes in their representation. In contrast, the similar need to make children 'visible' in the social sciences may seem superfluous in view of children's apparent centrality in western cultures, exhibited, for example, in the highly staged material and symbolic worlds of modern childhood. However, what may be challenged are those traditional perspectives that neglect the fact that children have little or no influence over their own social representation. The importance of this is highlighted by Dyer's statement that 'how we are seen determines in part how we are treated, how we treat others is based on how we see them; such seeing comes from representation' (1993: 1). If the child can now be thought of as a subject who is both acted upon and acts in the world, then most earlier anthropological and sociological studies emphasized the former. Their focus left the child as a social person in his or her own right and his or her perceptions and actions in the social and cultural world more or less unaddressed.

Changing the position of children in the social and cultural sciences, then, requires a re-examination of the conceptual frameworks that influence children's representation. A starting point for this is to explore the ways that children are constituted in social and cultural theory. For Jenks (1982) an examination of how children are dealt with in social theory reveals a cease-less paradox. Jenks writes:

> The child is familiar to us and yet strange, she/he inhabits our world and yet seems to answer to another, she/he is essentially of ourselves and yet appears to display a different order of being. (p. 9)

The child cannot be imagined in the absence of an idea about what an adult is, just as it is impossible to picture the adult and his or her society without positing the child. The ambiguity in the relationship between the child and the adult is encapsulated in the notion of 'difference'. This perception of difference, Jenks suggests, may be attributed to a conventional theoretical focus on the social processes of overcoming it – that is, socialization. It is an under-lying western cultural premise that people are made, not born (Riesman, 1990). In this view people are made what they become through the influence of their parents and through education, with both being seen as essential for their successful development and future life. The emphasis is therefore put on understanding children in terms of 'becoming' rather than as 'being' a social person (Qvortrup, 1991; Qvortrup, Bardy, Sgritta, & Wintersberger, 1994).

At the same time as child and adult are seen to form a continuum, there is an implication of a socially and culturally constituted opposition. This mark-ing of boundaries between the categorical positions of child and adult forms a part of cultural ideas about their fundamental separateness. This point is well evidenced in popular culture that addresses generational and familial problems. Films such as *Look Who's Talking Too* and TV soap operas such as *Cosby* all employ a central plot device that works by making a constant con-trast between the world of children (and young people) and the adult world. Traditional (op)positions and commonly perceived conflicts of everyday family life are highlighted by inverting 'child' and 'adult' power, control, competence and responsibility and by exaggerating elements of these dichotomous relationships. Such depictions often portray the embarrassing, weak and preposterous adult in relation to the lively, clever and smart child or demonstrate the adults' shortcomings when confronted with children's manipulative powers and alternative worldviews. Eventually, however, the storyline finds its equilibrium when children and adults are again reinstated into their 'usual' and 'proper' roles and positions.

These examples demonstrate how 'child' and 'adult' are seen as culturally and socially inseparable but at the same time as equally constituted in terms of 'difference'. Crawford's (1994) suggestion that stigmatizing images of the 'other' are founded in a social self that needs this other may, with regard to children, suggest that establishing the norm of the 'adult' in terms of an independent, responsible and active person necessarily constitutes its opposite, which at the same time is its complement. This can be seen through dominant notions of children as essentially dependent, incompetent and vulnerable (Christensen, 2000a; Hutchby & Moran-Ellis, 1998).

Fabian's (1983) notion of coevality serves to summarize these points. Adults are coeval with children; that is, they live and share with them the same historical moment. However, at the same time, emphasis is given to childhood as a phase of development and preparation for future adult life that establishes an 'other-time-worldliness' in which the child's present tends to disappear. This implies that the *present* value of childhood is to be read off (in relation to) a *future* in terms of a *past*. This particular temporal constitution of childhood is, Jenks (1996a: 15) proposes, connected to the core features of modernity. The modern family, he suggests, enabled the state to invest in children, constituting them not as beings but as 'promising' material for the future.

The Development of Western Ideas of Childhood

The propensity to contextualize children through the past or future rather than the present can, however, be understood as consistent with the historical and ideological development of the idea of childhood first noticed by Aries (1962). The child in the Middle Ages, he argues, did not occupy a particular social status and the idea of childhood did not exist. Archard (1993) criticizes this conclusion, suggesting one cannot infer that European medieval societies had no notion of childhood from the premise that they did not share the modern concept of it. Rather they must be seen as having a different idea of childhood. Children formed a part of society and participated in work and other social activities as soon as they did not need constant maternal care and attention. The word 'child' implied a structured lineage, that is, a relationship and position in the family, and did not refer to a hierarchy of age. Children from the age of 6- or 7-years-old were regarded as adults – little adults or deficient ones – with relevant rights and responsibilities. During the seventeenth and eighteenth centuries, there was a shift in values and childhood became constituted through a notion of the intimate and private family and the value placed on learning. These ideas developed into a number of practices and schedules of child care and training. Childhood became a 'quarantine' period where particular protective care was necessary. The child prepared and learned for a future adult life and developed to become a full and accepted member of society. Aries concludes that the care and control thus enacted by family, church, moralists and trustees deprived children of the freedom that they had previously enjoyed among adults.

This constitution of modern childhood was associated with the formation of other features of contemporary European society: motherhood, the early mother–infant relationship and the separation of play, school and work (Alanen, 1988). This furthered the development of professional expertise in relation to children that was based on observing this new social world and viewed children as different from adults. Two sets of ideas may thus be suggested as forming the basis of the general European and North American cultural view of children and the structuration of childhood (Ennew, 1986: 20). One set of ideas separates children from adults and defines the ideal family as a nuclear unit that is seen as the appropriate setting for children's socialization. The family as social institution became the locus for undertaking the proper development and sustenance of both child and parental health (Crawford, 1994). Within the family these perceptions implied the positioning of adults as responsible providers and carers of the child, while the child, as 'not as yet part of society', received care, protection and training. The other set of ideas separated children from adults in production processes, that is, work. Perceptions of children meant that they were formally protected from work. The child had the status of a 'non-worker', was not expected to work and in fact, children (depending on their age) were gradually becoming legally excluded from it. Contemporaneously the child must not and is not expected to work, but has instead the right to play, learning and knowledge.

Dominant perceptions of childhood in European and North American cultures can then be summarized as follows: childhood is ascribed special meaning as a phase in human life; the child is surrounded with care and concern which endeavour to prepare and protect the child; at the same time these perceptions attribute value to childhood and the child mostly in relation to a future adult life through the status of 'non-adult'; the child is more valued as a being in process, that is, being socialized towards a goal through which to take his or her place in society, than in his or her present state.

These views form a remarkable contrast to the position of the child in cultures that are dependent on, and emphasize, children's contributions to family economy in the form of work, support of the elderly or care-taking for younger siblings (see for example, Rodgers & Standing, 1981; Qvortrup et al., 1994). However, even in industrial societies these understandings of modern childhood actually underestimate and render children's contributions to the economy invisible (Morrow, 1996). They deprive children's actions and contributions of any genuine and 'serious' impact or importance for societal life. That the contribution children make may be considerable but still not be properly valued, was demonstrated by a British study which showed that about 10,000 children under the age of 16 were carers of an adult family member (Fallon, 1990). The invisibility of this work carried out by children was underlined by the fact that, unlike adults doing the same work, persons of this age cannot claim a care allowance from the state. Consequently, the exact figure of children involved could only be estimated. The social nonrecognition of their work was accompanied by a frustration on their part because, as children, they were frequently excluded from having any part in negotiations and decisions. The professionals believed that they were too young to be involved.

Socialization: The Mechanical Reproduction of Society and Culture

Despite such examples, the value of children in contemporary society remains largely invested in their future, a view emphasized in the concept of 'socialization'. This designates the social processes by which the child internalizes cultural values and, through learning and development, prepares for adult life. However, within sociology the concept of socialization originally referred to the social forces that drew people together in a society (Durkheim, 1950 [1903]). Socialization was perceived as a primarily collective process, which had as secondary the individual psychological process of internalization. By shifting its meaning towards internalization, socialization has now come to imply a fundamental polarity between an uncivilized and asocial 'human nature' and a civilized and 'social being', a distinction that places the child at the uncivilized pole.

This reinterpretation of socialization as a psychological process has proven to have particular conceptual power. In psychology, socialization is redefined as an individual process of internalization reducing social reality to externally given conditions or milieu. In contrast to earlier understandings of the term, socialization became understood as involving a passive recipient (almost always a child) instead of an active social person in their relations and interactions with others. The child was more or less seen as an empty vessel with 'potential sociality' that would develop through the influences and guidance of significant others (such as the parents and the school). Even though later theories incorporated ideas of socialization as an interactional process, the main concern for socialization research remained to determine the processes by which the social and material environment and the cultural system that the child grows up with (and which are treated as an external given) are internalized by the child and thus reproduced (Denzin, 1977; MacKay, 1973). Socialization processes are thus held to provide a seemingly convincing, but in fact, misleadingly partial framework for understanding children in the social world (Alanen, 1988).

Within anthropology, the interest in children has, until recently, often merely served as 'part of the decoration' in ethnography. The life of children and children's play are used more or less only to colour the background or sketch the atmosphere for what the anthropologist sees as of main concern – namely the adults, their relations and the culture at large. Insofar as children have been present in ethnographies, it has also largely been through an interest in socialization, in anthropology most notably through the work of the Culture and Personality School during the period 1930–60 (see for example, Benedict, 1946; Mead, 1968 [1930], 1955; Whiting & Child, 1953). This school of thought was influenced by Freudian psychoanalysis and focused on cultural child-rearing practices as the basis for the formation of the adult personality and the nature of adult social life. The emphasis was also on children as those who would ensure the continuity of the community, and thus the Culture and Personality School was concerned predominantly with how children were enculturated or socialized and how cultural values, traditions and social organization were maintained. The prevalent idea of children was thus as persons who were molded and shaped into social beings. In this perspective anthropologists observed adults, and especially mothers, caring for and training children as part of society. Adults were interviewed about their perceptions and ideas and, eventually, the anthropologist supplemented his or her interpretations by observing children's behaviour in play and other social activities. It should be noted, however, that in Mead's work children were recognized as informants and child thinking is seen as interesting in its own right.

By the late 1970s, however, Culture and Personality studies began to be criticized for their mechanistic and deterministic model which assumed that events at one point would produce a given result at a later time. In an important review paper, Shweder (1979) concluded that a clear and consistent relation could not be found between child rearing practices in the first years of the child's life, and the adult personality prevalent in a certain culture. Nevertheless, studies still continued to inscribe themselves in this tradition, suggesting the persuasive power of the idea of a cultural connection between the socialization of the small child and adult life (see for example, Levine, Levine and Leiderman, 1994).

Reconstructing the Social Study of Children

So far we have argued that ideas about the determinant character of socialization processes, especially of early childhood in relation to adult life and the constitutive effect for social relations among adults in a society, tend to obscure important aspects of children's lives. In relieving childhood from these presumptions, we are able to ascribe to the idea of childhood and of children's relationships a sense of present value. We wish to argue against seeing childhood only as related to a future goal, as part of a relationship of cause and outcome, but rather to take a perspective that emphasizes the current value for children of their lives and relationships. Related to this is Thorne's (1987) argument that the sociological study of children requires their 'conceptual autonomy'. Through this, children become the direct focus of the analysis rather than necessarily being seen through their link to other social institutions such as family and schooling. This both reconceptualizes childhood and broadens the range of its referents, contexts and meanings.

Recent theoretical advances, especially those derived from ethnographic and qualitative studies that view children as actively participating in the interpretation and reproduction of cultural knowledge, form an essential background to the task of focusing on children's lives in the present. In order to explain this current thinking it is necessary to sketch the argument made by contemporary sociologists of childhood. They have suggested that the notion of 'development' is a dominant discourse of children within European and North American thought (Jenks, 1982; James, Jenks, & Prout, 1998; Prout & James, 1997 [1990]). Although fostered within psychology, the developmental approach has until recently formed an implicit basis for most sociological and anthropological work on childhood (James et al., 1998). Central to this mode of thought are three elements: 'naturalness', 'universality', and 'rationality'. This trio has until recently been thought to tie the biological facts of infancy and growth with the social aspects of childhood. As a consequence, Jenks (1982, 1996b) suggests, the child is seen as progressing from simplicity to complexity, from irrational to rational behaviour, from a stage of biological immaturity, passing through a developmental process and moving into a fully developed human status as adult. Although a harsh judgement on developmental psychology, one that does not adequately acknowledge its diversity and more positive contributions (see Woodhead & Faulkner, 2000), the new sociology of childhood mounted a challenge to it on every point (for a programmatic statement of the new paradigm of the sociology of childhood see Prout & James, 1997 [1990]). The key theoretical move was that of social constructionism. Rather than seeing childhood as a natural or biological phenomenon, it was understood as a product of history, society and culture. This was a highly productive development (albeit one that contains its own dangers, see Prout, 2000) that allowed children to be seen as active, competent beings dealing with complex social worlds.

In the sociology of the 1950s, however, current ideas about child development were directly transferred into theories of socialization. At a time when the social sciences were greatly influenced by positivist and functionalist thinking 'socialization' offered a convincing account of how children 'become social' (Prout & James, 1997 [1990]). The theoretical preoccupation of sociology with the reproduction of the social order replicated the individual–society dualism presupposed by the psychological view of children. The individual was seen as a pre-existing 'cogito' outside of society (Ingleby, 1986); children were seen as immature, irrational, incompetent, asocial, and acultural while adults were regarded as 'mature, rational, competent, social and autonomous' (MacKay, 1973: 27–28). As suggested above, children and adults were thus made to appear as two different instances of the same species. Socialization was seen as the process that transformed the one into the other (for an excellent account and critique see Frønes, 1995).

In this model, children were the passive representatives of the future generation and, in the social processes involved in socialization, adults were, as Elkin (1960: 101) critically describes it, the active and constituent end. In such traditional views the notion of children as 'outcomes' became the principal concern at the expense of attending to the socialization process in itself or even of exploring the possible contradictions and conflicts involved in such processes. In the 1970s, however, the work of socialization theorists was undergoing critical appraisal. Shildkrout, for example, argued that:

> Child culture is seen as a rehearsal for adult life and socialization consists of the processes through which, by one method or another, children are made to conform in cases of 'successful' socialization or become deviants in cases of failed socialization. (1978: 109–110)

These critiques pointed to the overarching determinism characteristic of socialization studies, a point echoed by Shildkrout's contemporaries and challenged in much of the newer work on socialization that employed an interactional perspective and aimed to investigate children's own part in the processes (see for example, Denzin, 1977; MacKay, 1973). Contemporary research has also recognized the increasing complexity of socialization processes, talking for example of the 'double socialization' that occurs when young children begin to spend a large part of their daily life at school, in after-school clubs or in day-care institutions. The German educationalist Giesecke (1985) goes further, arguing that we also have to acknowledge that children, like adults, live in a pluralist society and thus are confronted by a range of competing, complementary and divergent values and perspectives from the media, the consumer society and their peer relations. He suggests parents, teachers and other people with responsibility for the care of children have less power to control and steer these different factors as a whole. It becomes important, therefore, to understand how children make coherence and sense of the world they live in. The new sociology of childhood has offered a solution in this respect. It has moved the perspective away from seeing the child–adult relationship as necessarily the most important factor to seeing children's interrelationships and interactions with others – children as well as adults – as equally important. In doing so, it has allowed a focus on the work that children themselves do to socialize each other (including the way they socialize adults) and how these activities contribute to, and produce, change.

On the basis of these critiques, children came to be seen as much more active in the process of cultural learning as interpreters and creators of meaning rather than simply absorbing the meanings of adults. Contemporary approaches in the ethnography of children depart from this point by seeing socialization as a collective rather than an individual process, by emphasizing the importance of children's peer relations, and by placing socialization in the public rather than the private domain. Corsaro (1992, 1997) has theorized this approach as 'interpretive reproduction'. He emphasizes children's active participation in both interpreting and reproducing culture through three particularly important elements: (1) language and language use; (2) cultural routines that provide actors with a shared understanding of belonging to a social group and supply the frames within which a wide range of sociocultural knowledge can be produced, displayed and interpreted; and (3) by seeing development as reproductive rather than linear.

Taken together these dispense with the idea of seeing the child as outside of society and societal institutions (Cook-Cumperz, Corsaro, & Streek, 1986). As Corsaro puts it:

> children do not simply imitate or internalize the world around them. They strive to interpret or make sense of their culture and to participate in it. In attempting to make sense of the adult world, children come to collectively produce their own peer worlds and cultures. (1997: 24)

Here, then, both children and adults are seen as part of culture and both make contributions to its reproduction and (re)interpretation. This happens both through children's negotiations with adults and through the creative production of a series of peer cultures with other children. Individual development thus becomes embedded in children's collective weaving of their places in the webs of significance that constitute their culture. The social study of children and childhood must, therefore, acknowledge the interplay between adults' and children's perspectives on social relations and culture.

Based on these perspectives, often arrived at separately by researchers working in different contexts, the last two decades have seen an upsurge in such ethnographic and qualitative sociological investigations of children's lives in many different settings. These include children in hospital (Alderson, 1993; Bluebond-Langner, 1978); children's self care at school and after-school clubs (Christensen, 1993, 1999); school sickness absence (Prout, 1986, 1989); identity and chronic illness (James, 1993); ethnicity and gender identity (Connolly, 1998); children's daily life in school (Mayall, 1996); school career and learning identity (Pollard, 1985; Pollard & Filer, 1996); paid work (Nieuwenhys, 1994; Reynolds, 1996; Solberg, 1994) and play (Thorne, 1993). Special mention must also be made here of the ESRC Children 5–16 Research Programme in the UK in which twenty-two linked projects focused on children as social actors in many different contexts of their lives (for an overview see Prout, 2001).

Looking at children as social actors in this way, they are far from being seen as passive subjects in social structures and processes. Instead they are seen as active in the construction and determination of their social lives, active in the lives that other people lead around them and the societies in which they live. Rather than looking only at how children are formed by social life, children are seen as social actors whose actions can both shape and change social life. Giddens (1979: 69) argues that an action that serves to reproduce structure is a productive action, and, as such, it may initiate social change by transforming structure at the same time as it reproduces it. Thus, to acknowledge the simultaneous reproductive and transformative relations between human conduct and culture, one must perceive the person as not only a 'product' of his or her own culture, but also as a co-writer of reality (Hastrup, 1988: 137) and the interpreter as well as mechanical reproducer of society and culture (Cosaro, 1992, 1997). It is important to recognize children as *both* restricted or encapsulated by social structures and as persons acting within or towards the structure (Prout & James, 1997 [1990]).

Childhood as Social Structure

The idea of children as co-constructors of society links studies of children, their peer cultures and their interactions with adults to another important strand in the sociological rediscovery of childhood. This work focuses less on *children* and more on understanding *childhood* as a feature of the social structure. The argument here is that, although its membership may be constantly changing, childhood forms a permanent part of the social structure. The key sociological question in this perspective becomes relating 'the childhood' of a society to the wider social forces operating in and on society. From this perspective Qvortrup has argued that the sociologist can subject childhood to the same sort of analysis as any other social phenomenon, placing it alongside longstanding topics of social analysis such as class and gender (Qvortrup et al., 1994: 5).

Such a perspective encourages the comparative analysis of childhood along a number of dimensions. First, it allows comparison of children with other population groups such as youth, adults and the elderly. For example, it suggests a need to understand the distribution of resources such as income and welfare spending among these different groups. The importance of this is clear when one remembers that trends in the industrialized countries mean both that children are a declining proportion of the population and that the proportion of households including children is also declining (Clarke, 1996; European Commission, 1996; Office for National Statistics, 1991). This, combined with the emergence of political lobbies for the older generation, must provoke questions about who is to speak for children in decisions about resource allocation and how inter-generational distributive justice is to be achieved and maintained (Sgritta, 1994: 361). It is well known, for example, that child poverty in the UK rose sharply during the 1980s and 1990s. Children as a group, however, saw a disproportionate rise in poverty compared to the rest of the population; in effect, as a group, they moved down the income distribution (Adelman & Bradshaw, 1998). This example also illustrates a second type of comparative analysis, that between countries. This shows that poverty among children in the UK rose sharply at a time when it remained more or less stable in most other similar countries. This suggests that, unlike these other countries, the UK did not protect children against worsening economic conditions through welfare and social policy measures (Adelman & Bradshaw, 1998). This type of international comparative approach is also implicit in the reports produced by UNICEF that compare how children in different countries fare according to a series of indicators.

Finally, considering childhood as a structural form has led sociologists to examine how it changes over time, and especially its contemporary trends. On this front, sociologists in the industrialized world have suggested three somewhat contradictory processes that may be going on alongside each other. These have been referred to as: 'institutionalization'; 'familialization' and 'individualization' (Brannen & O'Brien, 1995; Nasman, 1994). These are thought to operate in tension with each other, pushing and pulling childhood in rather different directions. The first of these, institutionalization, reflects that in the Nordic countries especially, but increasingly elsewhere too, children's everyday lives are spent more and more within day-care institutions (such as nurseries and playgroups), school and after-school clubs. Even leisure time is framed in this way for many children because participation in activities, such as sport or music, takes place within some kind of institutional setting. Public debates express the views of professionals, parents and politicians about the possible effects of this increasing institutionalization and fragmentation on children and the potentially undesirable outcomes of growing up in such diverse social environments. Fears are expressed that it may hinder children in forming and developing stable and coherent worldviews and relationships. The highly institutionalized schooling and professional day-care system for children is suspected of creating and sustaining generational divisions in society and, in particular, of creating a gap between children and their parents (who spend most of their everyday lives apart).

Clearly, the trend towards institutionalization is related to wider social changes, especially the increased participation of women in the labour market, of which it is both a consequence and an enabling mechanism. This in turn can be located as part of the breakdown of what has been called the 'male breadwinner model' of society (Creighton, 1999). Although the implications for children of these changes are under-researched, and in many discussions displaced by adult concerns, it remains important for the new social studies of childhood to address them. One way of approaching this is from the institutional perspective as exemplified by researchers such as Smith (2000) who have investigated what children in the UK like and dislike about after-school clubs, leading to a number of suggestions for their improvement. Christensen (2000b), however, has approached it from the family side of the institutionalization process by examining children's views about, and experience of, 'quality time', a frequently promoted solution to the problem of the time squeeze brought about by conflicting parental and employment obligations. She notes that quality time is simply assumed to be a solution from children's point of view without there being any evidence for it. In fact, her ethnography suggests that time in the family is understood by children in much more complex ways than allowed for by the notion of quality time.

The trend towards 'familialization' refers to the tendency for children to be increasingly seen as dependent on, and contained within, their families (Brannen & O'Brien, 1995) and can be seen to be in partial conflict with institutionalization. It is evident, for example, in the international trend towards parental involvement in schools (Edwards, 2002), which, in the UK at least, was accompanied by a parallel decline in the participation of children in school governance (Wyness, 1999). Familialization has corollaries across the range of services directed towards children and young people. In the UK policy environment of the 1980s, the family increasingly replaced the identification of young people as a group. The family became the government's preferred route to policy interventions and recent policy statements confirm this trend (Home Office, 1998).

It also seems that the trend begun in the 1970s (Hillman, Adams, & Whitelegg, 1990) towards the sequestration of children in the family and the decline of children's autonomous movement around their neighbourhood may have continued into the 1990s (O'Brien, 1999). This suggests a double effect: the first is an incipient exclusion of children from public space, where they are seen increasingly as causing problems, as 'out of place' and therefore becoming more subject to regulation and control (see Matthews & Limb, 2000; Valentine, 1996). The second is a simultaneous proliferation of special locations that concentrate groups of children together for activities taking place under more or less adult surveillance and supervision (Furedi, 1997). The effect would seem to be the construction of a way of life for many children that consists of moving from one 'island' of childhood to another. In this sense, the space of childhood, literally as well as metaphorically, may be becoming more specialized and more localized. From this point of view, the institutionalization of childhood is in some senses quite compatible with familialization. Indeed, it is well caught in the contemporary image of the middle-class parent as chauffeur to children whose week is packed with different activities, to and from which they are ferried by car.

Finally, the notion of individualization refers to the tendency for contemporary children to be seen as having a voice in determining their lives and shaping their identity. It is immediately apparent that this resonates with ideas associated with the new social studies of childhood. It is arguable, for example, that sociology's discovery of children as actors and agents is caught up in the individualization of childhood, parallel with, for example, the participation rights promulgated by the United Nations Convention on the Rights of the Child. Beck (1992, 1998) argues that such developments are part of a 'second modernization', central to which is a recent societal propensity towards people – adults and children alike – coming to think of themselves as unique individuals with chosen rather than prescribed or standard identities. A concatenation of factors, rather than a single cause, is said to be responsible for this shift. The emergence of consumption (especially leisure) as a source of identity, the pluralization of family forms, the decline in the authority of expert knowledges, the distribution of norms about the value of democracy and so on, all contribute to a process that has become self-propelling.

Problems and Perspectives

The above discussion has shown how successful the new social studies has been, and we trust will continue to be, in producing new insights about both children as social actors and childhood as a component of social systems. However, it is also evident that the division of the field into these two parts, roughly the division between a focus on children or one on childhood, is not really satisfactory. This is an ongoing debate within the sociology of childhood (see James, Jenks, & Prout, 1998) that has yet to be resolved. It is important not to over-emphasize this problem because by focusing on a particular empirical area, researchers often manage to move productively between these two modes of analysis. Christensen (1993, 1999), for example, in her study of children's self-care around illness and accidents at home, school and at the after-school club, linked large-scale trends in the constitution of Danish childhood, the local interactions of children and adults in these settings and the personal experiences of particular children. She accomplished this by applying Nader's (1981) notion of the 'horizontal' and 'vertical' slices (or perspectives) in social analysis. The former is the processual or interactional level, while the latter refers to the relation between the person and society. Nader argues that ethnographic studies tend to focus on a horizontal level, leaving out of the analysis the vertical perspective. In relation to studies of children, this has resulted in a lack of attention to the complex relation between children and institutions and the formal and informal hierarchies that influence children's lives. Christensen argues that it is important to substantiate both the nature of the relationships between persons and social institutions *and* to understand the structure and meaning of these relationships in the lives of children and their families. Starting at the interactional level, but with a theoretically informed understanding of contemporary childhood as a social phenomenon, she traces through the ideological and material connections to these societal and institutional phenomena.

Nevertheless, there are conceptual inconsistencies between thinking of childhood as a socially constructed phenomenon that varies in time and space and the attempt to characterize childhood as a social structure or form. The former tends towards seeing many different 'childhoods' within a given society, while the latter tends to put different children together into a more unitary entity. Clearly there is a danger of disaggregating children to the extent that every child represents only their own childhood (Qvortrup, 2000). This, however, is paralleled by the danger that in unifying children into a notional 'childhood', significant differences (of gender, class, ethnicity, disability, and so on) between children are underplayed. Frønes for example argues: 'There is not one childhood, but many, formed at the intersection of different cultural, social and economic systems, natural and man-made physical environments. Different positions in society produce different experiences' (1993: 1). A good example of this is found in O'Brien's (1999) study of children's autonomous mobility in cities. While they found an overall decline in this over time, it was also the case that it varied widely according to social class, gender, ethnicity and neighbourhood. There was a differentiation between children that should not be ignored. Nor is this simply a problem of differentiation within a given society. Frønes (1997) has argued that one effect of globalization is that childhoods similar to those of the Euro-American middle classes are being produced and distributed around the world. These often appear within the protected enclaves of elites in developing countries such that the childhoods of privileged children in New York and Delhi may have more in common with each other than with the majority in either location. The nation state may be becoming less salient as a point of comparison. Research on 'transnational childhoods' raises similar questions about the complexity of childhood in a rapidly changing world that in certain respects may be dissolving national boundaries (Orelleana, Thorne, Chee, & Lam, 2001).

Finally, it is important to ask, as Christensen (1999: 30) does, whether the concept of childhood is really an analytical category. She argues that it is better thought of as a focus for empirical enquiry, a field of study to which the analytical and explanatory resources of the social sciences should be brought. Childhood, she suggests, can only be understood in relation to adulthood because both are constituted in the same set of social and cultural practices. Such a relational idea of childhood has been systematically expounded by Alanen (2001), who argues that the central organizing concept of the sociology of childhood should be that of the 'generational order': that is, the systematic pattern of social relationships in which children are located as a social group. Its parallel is with other key dimensions of social differentiation such as class and gender order. It is suggested that theorizing children through generational relationships would enable the sociological analysis of children to find a place alongside such key sociological concepts.

There are real advantages in this: the notion of generational order constitutes childhood not as an essential entity but as one produced within a set of relations. Within these, childhood and adulthood are simultaneously produced in relation to each other. How adulthood is constructed thus always has implications for childhood and vice versa. This also reminds us that adulthood itself is not the finished product towards which children are headed, but a phenomenon constantly in process, review and change (Lee, 1998). The distinction between adulthood as 'being' and childhood as 'becoming' is therefore questioned and destabilized.

However, there are also some dangers and much depends, we would suggest, on how the idea of generational order is developed. In the first place, we suggest that generation should be though of as a verb not a noun (Curt, 1994: 15). In other words, we need to look at generational order*ing* as an active, open-ended and unfinished process. The central analytical task would then be not only to describe relationships between children and adults but to discover how (and when) they are given a generational aspect or meaning. Second, the process of generationing should be seen as plural. Building on the discussion above about whether there can be a single childhood of a society, it seems unlikely to us that there could be a single practice of making or maintaining a generational order. Rather, at any one time there may be several competing, cross-cutting ways of ordering that jostle uneasily alongside each other. Perhaps, too, these are distributed unevenly between contexts such that the generational orderings of school, state, family, and so on, are different and vary through time and space. Nor should it be assumed that adults are the active pole of this process, whereas children are always passive in the face of a power hierarchy that always subordinates them.

Third, there should be a constant guard against re-rendering children invisible in generational orders. As we suggested above, there is a kind of generational politics around and about societal resources in which the presence, rights and needs of children may be overshadowed as their demographic weight declines. This could be reflected easily in the human sciences as ageing becomes a more readily funded and more popular topic of investigation.

Lastly, there is a danger of counterposing the generational perspective to that of life-course. Rather, we suggest that a better analytical purchase could be achieved by combining them and looking for points of intersection. There is still much to be learnt by asking what it means to be, for example, a 5-, 8-, 10-, or 12-year-old child and how these points on a trajectory of growing up are similar yet different. The notion of generational ordering could complement this by highlighting how growing up is constructed within sets of shifting generational relations. Nevertheless, growing up remains crucially important not just for future adulthood outcomes, but also for the experience of childhood itself. As we have argued above, significant relationships in children's life projects include not only those with parents and other adults, but also those with other children, including but not confined to their age peers. Overcoming children's invisibility and muteness in sociology and anthropology, with which we began this chapter, has involved attempting to construct a more detailed and complex account of the social life of children and adults. It has required suspending taken-for-granted notions about the differences and similarities between children and adults and the adoption of more open-minded questioning about how these are constructed in different contexts. This, in turn, has produced an appreciation of the importance of relationships between children and a greater sensitivity to the differences and similarities between them. A sociology that replaced this complex web of shifting relationships with a sole, or even a primary, focus on the generational relationships between adults and children would not necessarily be a step forward.

References

Alderson, P. (1993). *Children's consent to surgery*. Milton Keynes: Open University Press.

Adelman, L. & Bradshaw, J. (1998). *Children in poverty in Britain: An analysis of the family resources survey 1994/5*. York: Social Policy Research Unit, University of York.

Alanen, L. (1988). Rethinking childhood. *Acta Sociologica, 31*(1), 53–67.

Alanen, L. (2001). Childhood as a generational condition. In L. Alanen & B. Mayall (Eds.), *Conceptualising child–adult relationships* (pp. 129–43). London: Falmer Press.

Archard, D. (1993). *Children: Rights and childhood*. London: Routledge.

Ardener, E. (1975a). Belief and the problem of women. In S. Ardener (Ed.), *Perceiving Women* (pp. 1–17). London: J.M. Dent.

Ardener, E. (1975b). The 'problem' revisited. In S. Ardener (Ed.), *Perceiving women* (pp. 19–27). London: J.M. Dent.

Aries, P. (1962). *Centuries of childhood: A social history of family life*. London: Jonathan Cape.

Beck, U. (1992). *Risk society: Towards a new modernity*. London: Sage.

Beck, U. (1998). *Democracy without enemies*. Cambridge: Polity Press.

Benedict, R. (1946). *The chrysanthemum and the sword: Patterns of Japanese culture*. Boston, MA: Houghton Mifflin.

Bluebond-Langner, M. (1978). *The private worlds of dying children*. Princeton, NJ: Princeton University Press.

Bluebond-Langner, M., Perkel, D., & Goertzel, T. (1991). Paediatric cancer patients' peer relationships: The impact of an oncology camp experience. *Journal of Psychosocial Oncology, 19*(2), 67–80.

Brannen, J. & O'Brien, M. (1995). Childhood and the sociological gaze: Paradigms and paradoxes. *Sociology, 29*(4), 729–738.

Christensen, P. (1993). The social construction of help among Danish children: The intentional act and the actual content. *Sociology of Health and Illness. A Journal of Medical Sociology, 15*(4), 488–502.

Christensen, P. (1999). *Towards an anthropology of childhood sickness: An ethnographic study of Danish school children.* Unpublished doctoral dissertation, University of Hull.

Christensen, P. (2000a). Childhood and the cultural constitution of vulnerable bodies. In A. Prout (Ed.), *The body, childhood and society* (pp. 38–59). Basingstoke: Macmillan Press/New York: St Martin's Press.

Christensen, P. (2000b). *Why more quality time is not on the top of children's lists: The qualities of time, content and context.* Paper presented at a meeting at the National Family and Parenting Institute, London, October.

Clarke, L. (1996). Demographic change and the family situation of children. In J. Brannen & M. O'Brien (Eds.), *Children in families: Research and policy* (pp. 66–83). London: Falmer Press.

Connolly, P. (1998). *Racism, gender identities and young children.* London: Routledge.

Cook-Cumperz, J., Corsaro, W., & Streek, J. (Eds.) (1986). *Children's worlds and children's languages.* Berlin: Mouton de Gruyter.

Corsaro, W. (1992). Interpretive reproduction in children's peer cultures. *Social Psychology Quarterly, 55,* 160–177.

Corsaro, W. (1997). *The sociology of childhood.* Thousand Oaks, CA: Pine Forge Press.

Crawford, R. (1994). The boundaries of the self and the unhealthy other: Reflections on health, culture and AIDS. *Social Science and Medicine, 38*(10), 1347–1365.

Creighton, C. (1999). The rise and decline of the male breadwinner family in Britain. *Cambridge Journal of Economics, 23,* 519–542.

Curt, B. (1994). *Textuality and tectonics: Troubling social and psychological science.* Buckingham: Open University Press.

Denzin, N. (1977). *Childhood socialization.* San Francisco, CA: Jossey-Bass.

Durkheim, E. (1950[1903]). *The rules of sociological method.* Chicago: Free Press.

Dyer, R. (1993). *The matter of images: Essays on representations.* London: Routledge.

Edwards, R. (2002). *Children, home and school: Regulation, autonomy or connection?* London: RoutledgeFalmer.

Elkin, F. (1960). *The child and society.* New York: Random House.

Ennew, J. (1986). *The sexual exploitation of children.* Cambridge: Polity.

Ennew, J. (1994). *The environmental health of working children.* Paper presented at the Sociology of Childhood Seminar, Brunel, University of West London.

European Commission. (1996). *The Demographic situation in the European Union – 1995.* European Commission: Brussels.

Fabian, J. (1983). *Time and the other: How anthropology makes its object.* New York: Columbia University Press.

Fallon, K. (1990). An involuntary workforce. *Community Care, 4*(January), 12–13.

Frønes, I. (1993). Changing childhoods. *Childhood, 1,* 1.

Frønes, I. (1995). *Among peers: On the meaning of peers in the process of socialization.* Oslo: Scandanavian University Press.

Frønes, I. (1997). *Children of the post-industrial family* (mimeo). Oslo: Department of Sociology and Human Geography, University of Oslo.

Furedi, F. (1997). *The culture of fear: Risk taking and the morality of low expectations*. London: Cassell.

Giddens, A. (1979). *The central problems of social theory*. London: Macmillan.

Giesecke, H. (1985). *Das Ende der Erziehung (The End of Education)*. Stuttgart: Kiett-Cotta-Verlag.

Hardman, C. (1973). Can there be an anthropology of children? *Journal of the Anthropology Society Oxford*, 4(1), 85–99.

Hastrup, K. (1988). Kultur som analytisk begreb (culture as an analytical concept). In H. Hauge & H. Horstbøll (Eds.), *Kulturbegrebets kulturhistorie* (The cultural history of the concept of culture) (Kulturstudier 1), (pp. 120–139). Aarhus: Aarhus Universitetsforlag.

Hillman, M., Adams, J., & Whitelegg, J. (1990). *One false move: A study of children's independent mobility*. London: Policy Studies Institute.

Home Office. (1998). *Supporting parents: A consultation document*. London.

Hutchby, I. & Moran-Ellis, J. (Eds.) (1998). *Children and social competence: Arenas of action*. London: Falmer Press.

Ingelby, D. (1986). Development in a social context. In M. Richards & P. Light (Eds.), *Children of social worlds* (pp. 297–317). Cambridge: Polity Press.

James, A. (1993). *Childhood identities: Self and social relationships in the experience of the child*. Edinburgh: Edinburgh University Press.

James, A. & Prout, A. (1990/97). *Constructing and reconstructing childhood: Contemporary issues in the sociological study of childhood*. London: Falmer Press.

James, A., Jenks, C., & Prout, A. (1998). *Theorizing childhood*. Cambridge: Polity Press.

Jenks, C. (1982). *The sociology of childhood. Essential reading*. London: Batsford.

Jenks, C. (1996a). The postmodern child. In J. Brannen, & M. O'Brien (Eds.), *Children in families: Research and policy* (pp. 13–25). London: Falmer Press.

Jenks, C. (1996b). *Childhood*. London: Routledge.

Lee, N. (1998). Towards an immature sociology. *Sociological Review*, 46(2), 459–482.

Levine, R., Levine, S., & Leiderman, P.H. (1994). *Child care and culture: Lessons from Africa*. Cambridge: Cambridge University Press.

Mackay, R. (1973). Conceptions of children and models of socialization. In H.P. Dreitzel (Ed.), *Childhood and socialization* (pp. 27–43). London: Macmillan.

Matthews, H. & Limb, M. (2000). *Children and the street*. (ESRC Children 5–16 Research Programme Briefing). Retrieved 29 June 2001 from: http://www.esrc.ac.uk/curprog.html.

Mayall, B. (1996). *Children, health and the social order*. Buckingham: Open University Press.

Mead, M. (1968[1930]). *Growing up in New Guinea*. Harmondsworth: Penguin.

Mead, M. (1955). Theoretical setting. In M. Mead & M. Wolfstein (Eds.), *Childhood in contemporary culture* (pp. 3–20). Chicago: University of Chicago Press.

Moore, H. (1988). *Feminism and anthropology*. Cambridge: Polity Press.

Morrow, V. (1996). Rethinking childhood dependency: Children's contributions to the domestic economy. *Sociological Review*, 44(1), 58–77.

Nader, L. (1981). The vertical slice: Hierarchies and children. In G.M. Britain & R. Cohen (Eds.), *Hierarchy and society: Anthropological perspectives on bureaucracy* (pp. 31–44). Philadelphia, PA: Ishi.

Nasman, E. (1994). Individualization and institutionalization of children. In J. Qvortrup, M. Bardy, G. Sgritta, & H. Wintersberger (Eds.), *Childhood matters: Social theory, practice and politic* (pp. 165–188). Aldershot: Avebury.

Nieuwenhuys, O. (1994). *Children's life worlds: Gender, welfare and labor in the developing world*. London: Routledge.

O'Brien, M. (1999). *Chaperoned and autonomous childhoods: Difference and diversity in children's families*. Paper presented to the ESRC Seminar on Postmodern Kinship, Leeds University, December.

Office for National Statistics (1991). *Social Trends 29*. London: The Stationery Office.

Orellana, M.F., Thorne, B., Chee, A., & Lam, W.S.E. (2001). Transnational childhoods: The participation of children in processes of family migration. *Social Problems, 48*(4), 572–91.

Pollard, A. (1985). *The social world of the primary school*. London: Holt, Rhinehart and Winston.

Pollard, A. & Filer, A. (1996). *The social world of children's learning*. London: Cassell.

Prout, A. (1986). 'Wet children' and 'little actresses': Going sick in primary school. *Sociology of Health and Illness, 8*(2), 111–136.

Prout, A. (1989). Sickness as a dominant symbol in life course transitions: An illustrated theoretical framework. *Sociology of Health and Illness, 11*(4), 336–359.

Prout, A. (2000). Childhood bodies: Construction, agency and hybridity. In A. Prout (Ed.), *The body, childhood and society* (pp. 1–18). Basingstoke: Macmillan Press/ New York: St Martin's Press.

Prout, A. (2001). Representing children: reflections on the Children 5–16 Programme, *Children and Society, 15*, 193–201.

Prout, A. & James, A. (1997 [1990]). A new paradigm for the sociology of childhood? Provenance, promise and problems. In A. James & A. Prout (Eds.), *Constructing and reconstructing childhood* (pp. 7–33). London: Falmer Press.

Qvortrup, J. (1991). *Childhood as a social phenomenon: An Introduction to a series of national reports* (Eurosocial Reports, Vol. 36). Vienna: European Centre.

Qvortrup, J. (2000). Macroanalysis of childhood. In P. Christensen & A. James (Eds.), *Research with children: Perspectives and practice* (pp. 77–97). London: Falmer Press.

Qvortrup, J., Bardy, M., Sgritta, G., & Wintersberger, H. (1994). (Eds.). *Childhood matters: Social theory, practice and politics*. Aldershot: Avebury.

Reynolds, P. (1996). *Traditional healers and children in Zimbabwe*. Athens, Ohio: Ohio University Press.

Rodgers, G. & Standing, G. (Eds.). (1981). *Child work, poverty and underdevelopment*. Geneva: International Labor Organization.

Sgritta, G. (1994). The generational division of welfare: Equity and conflict. In J. Qvortrup, M. Bardy, G. Sgritta, & H. Wintersberger (Eds.), *Childhood matters: social theory, practice and politics* (pp. 335–362). Aldershot: Avebury.

Shildkrout, E. (1978). Roles of children in urban Kano. In J.S. La Fontaine (Ed.), *Sex and age as principles of social differentiation* (pp. 109–39). London: Academic Press.

Shweder, R.A. (1979). Rethinking culture and personality theory. Part 1: A critical examination of two classical postulates. *Ethos, 7*(3), 255–278.

Smith, F. (2000). *Out of school care* (ESRC Children 5–16 Research Programme Briefing). Retrieved 29 June 2001 from: http://www.esrc.ac.uk/curprog.html.

Solberg, A. (1994). *Negotiating age: Empirical investigations and textual representations of children's everyday lives*. Stockholm: Nordic Institute for Studies in Urban and Regional Planning.

Thorne, B. (1987). Re-visioning women and social change: Where are the children? *Gender and Society, 1*, 85–109.

Thorne, B. (1993). *Gender play: Girls and boys in school*. Piscataway, NJ: Rutgers University Press.

Valentine, G. (1996). Children should be seen and not heard? The role of children in public space. *Urban Geography, 17*(3), 205–220.

Whiting, J.W.M. & Child, I. (1953). *Child training and personality: A cross-cultural study.* New Haven, CT: Yale University Press.

Woodhead, M. & Faulkner, D. (2000). Subjects, objects or participants: Dilemmas of psychological research with children. In P. Christensen & A. James (Eds.), *Research with children: Perspectives and practice* (pp. 9–35). London: Falmer Press.

Wyness, M.G. (1999). Childhood, agency and educational reform. *Childhood, 6*(3), 353–368.

This chapter is taken from:
Green, S. and Hogan, D. (eds) (2005) *Researching Children's Experiences*
978-0-7619-7103-0

Childhood in Different Cultures

BOB SANDERS

Contents

- Why study the development of children in a cross-cultural context?
- Culture, ethnocentrism and cultural relativism
- Globalisation
- International conventions
- Conclusion

This chapter asks why it is important to understand how different the experience of being a child can be, depending upon where in the world a child is growing up. It begins by considering why we should study childhood in different cultures – not only because it helps us provide better care for children, but also because we need to understand the power issues that lead to the definition of childrearing patterns in some parts of the world as 'proper' whilst those in other parts are seen as failing to live up to Western notions of what all children should aspire to. The chapter goes on to discuss the concept of culture in more depth, and introduces an issue which has long provided a challenge for anthropologists, that of finding the right balance between *ethnocentrism* and *cultural relativism*.

Why study the development of children in a cross-cultural context?

There are many reasons for studying the cross-cultural context of children's development. First, there are practical reasons. Trawick-Smith (1997) gives an illuminating example, of a relatively experienced care provider who encounters difficulties in her new post in a large urban child care centre, when trying to soothe a young child from a different cultural background. The usual things that she has tried in the past do not seem to work with this child. He asks the question: 'How is it that this lesson had escaped her until now?' (p. 577). The answer he suggests is:

Children in her previous family child care home were of very similar cultural and socio-economic backgrounds. They were primarily sons and daughters of white middle-class professionals. Their family lives were very much like her own. Her new child care setting includes children of many different cultural and social economic backgrounds.

(Trawick-Smith, 1997: 577–8)

To operate effectively with young children, the worker needs not only to learn 'what works' but 'what works for this particular child, from this particular socio-economic and cultural background'.

Another reason for studying children's development across cultures is to appreciate the value of, and the necessity for, diversity in adaptation to different environments. Darwinian principles apply not only to the physical adaptation of living organisms to their environment, but also to their social adaptation. Harkness and Super (1994) have suggested the concept of 'developmental niche', which is conceived in terms of three basic components: the physical and social settings of the child's everyday life, the culturally regulated customs of child care and child rearing, and the psychology of the care takers. It is important to remember that child-rearing patterns vary from culture to culture and represent an adaptation to different environments (physical and social). Given the dynamic nature of the adaptation, they may represent the optimal survival patterns within that particular environment. This also emphasises child development as a continuing dynamic of an individual interacting with, and adapting to, his/her environment – an 'ecological' model of child development that has gained considerable attention in recent years (Barrett, 1998; Bronfenbrenner, 1979).

A third reason is to remind us that the process of attaching values to different cultural practices, whether in relation to child rearing or in relation to other customs and practices, contains a *power* component. In this sense there is a postmodern construction of cultural differences. The 'discourse' within cross-cultural child rearing can be construed as a set of events and circumstances defined and evaluated by those with power, in relation to those without (or with less). Sanders (1999) for example looks at child abuse in a cross-cultural context, and argues that it is essential to understand the power to make definitions about *how* 'abuse' is defined. There is a danger that Westernised concepts of child abuse are taken on board in other cultures and societies where there may be far more urgent threats to children's well-being and survival, certainly dangers that are at least as pressing as the risks posed by intra-familial abuse. Related to this is the importance of beginning to understand the concepts of 'ethnocentrism' and 'cultural relativism', both of which contain inherent difficulties when taken to extremes.

A fourth reason for studying culture in relation to children is to gain a new perspective on our own society. As Rogoff and Morelli put it:

An important function of cross-cultural research has been to allow investigators to look closely at the impact of their own belief systems ... Working with people from a quite different background can make one aware of aspects of human activity that are not noticeable until they are missing or differently arranged, as with the fish who reputedly is unaware of water until removed from it.

(1993: 18)

It is helpful to experience just how different child upbringing can be, so that one's own cultural approach can be set in the context of a range of different approaches. It provides a kind of 'You are here' marker in relation to a world map of diverse cultural child rearing.

Related to this is a fifth and final reason – the value of a 'decentring' exercise, so that one's own experience of being on the receiving end of child rearing does not become the yardstick against which other methods of child rearing are compared. There are other yardsticks for looking at differing child-rearing approaches, which will be discussed below, but using one's own upbringing is a potential pitfall to be avoided. It should be remembered that differences are just that – differences. They should not be seen or interpreted as deficits.

This chapter does not describe the different patterns of child rearing throughout the world; there is simply not enough space to address in a chapter what many books have addressed. Instead, it considers some of the issues around looking at child-rearing patterns across cultures. The chapter considers the issues of culture, ethnocentrism and cultural relativism, globalisation, and the development of international conventions to promote the welfare of children. There is, however, a wealth of information available for students to consider in depth the experiences of growing up in particular societies and cultures.

Not all of this is in the form of textual material, and students are also advised to look at the portrayals of children and childhood in film. Childhood has long been a favourite theme of film makers, and they will often use children as the protagonist in films to highlight issues such as the impact of large-scale adversity (for example, war and political turbulence) on children, or use the 'uncontaminated' eyes of the child to present to the audience a particular view of society. Such films can be seen to contain profound themes in relation to the social construction of childhood, a theme of this book, but on a more immediate level, they contain depictions of everyday life involving children in other societies and cultures.

The following are all highly worthwhile films:

The Blue Kite (China)
My Life as a Dog (Sweden)
Kolya (Czech Republic)
The Bicycle Thieves (Italy)
The 400 Blows (France)
The Boy Who Stopped Talking (Netherlands and Kurdistan)
Ma Vie en Rose (France)
The Spirit of the Beehive (Spain)
Pather Pachali (India)
Whistle Down the Wind (Yorkshire, Britain)
Hope and Glory (Britain)
The Gods Must Be Crazy II (Kalahari, Africa)
Yaaba (Africa)
Los Olvidados (Mexico)

For some of these films the societal context is peripheral to the theme of the film, and we see an unselfconscious depiction of a child in a particular culture at a particular time as conveyed through the eyes of the director. In others – for example, *The Boy Who Stopped Talking, The Blue Kite, Kolya, Ma Vie en Rose, Pather Pachali, Los Olvidados* – the focus is on the interaction between a young child and some powerful influence of the society within which he or she is growing – for instance, war, political ideology, sexist ideology or Third World poverty.

Culture, ethnocentrism and cultural relativism

So how are we to understand culture? At its most basic, culture can be understood as the 'rules and tools' of a society, a definition which has the advantage of being memorable and at the same time encompassing both the tangible and non-tangible aspects of a society. An early definition of culture is in Tylor (1958): 'that complex whole which includes knowledge, belief, arts, morals, law, custom and any other capabilities and habits acquired by man as a member of society'. White (1959: 3) defines culture as comprising 'tools, implements, utensils, clothing, ornaments, customs, institutions, beliefs, rituals, games, works of art, language, etc.' (cited in Kottak, 1994: 36).

Kottak also describes a number of aspects of culture which provide us with a clearer understanding. Culture is *learned* and relies on symbols to convey meaning. Culture is imposed upon nature ('Natural lakes don't close at five, but cultural lakes do'). It is both general and specific: all people have culture, but individuals have different cultures. It is all-encompassing, in the sense that it includes everything that people do, not just the more 'aesthetic' activities. Culture is *shared*; it is learned through interaction with others in the society. Consider for example children who have not had that experience – so-called 'feral' children brought up by animals away from human society (Newton, 2002). Not only do they miss out on learning human language, and that part of thinking that is dependent upon language, but they have also not been *encultured*; they have not engaged in that process through which babies and young children acquire culture. Culture is *patterned* in the sense that aspects of it are linked, so that if one cultural institution changes, for example employment practices, other connected institutions, such as domestic roles within families, may change as a result.

On the other hand, Kottak reminds us that although people may be clear about the requirement to live within a particular culture, people don't always follow the rules, reflecting the tension between the individual and society identified by child development theorists. Likewise, the cultural practices themselves may not be conducive to the well-being, and indeed the long-term survival, of the culture; consider the heavy use of fossil fuels and other environment-threatening practices within the developed nations of the world.

Another aspect of culture described by Kottak (1994) is that it has universality, particularity and generality at the same time. By *universality* is meant those cultural aspects that distinguish human beings from other species and which are present in all people. *Particularity* refers to the uniqueness of every culture; it is like no other. *Generality*, on the other hand, refers to aspects of culture that may link some cultures together into groupings, but not all. In relation to people, there is an expression:

'Every person is, at any one time, like all other people, like some other people and like no other people.' The same could be said to apply to cultures.

Cultures do not exist in a vacuum. They live in a social world within which there is increasing contact at all different levels (see discussion of globalisation below). The early anthropologists were aware of the dangers of imposing external cultural values on the societies they were studying. They began to articulate such notions in the concepts of ethnocentrism and cultural relativism, which may be seen as opposite ends of a continuum. These are difficult concepts to fully understand, and indeed because one (ethnocentrism) has tended to become value-laden as a 'bad thing', and the other (cultural relativism) as a 'good thing', it is sometimes difficult to appreciate that extremes at either end can be unhelpful. After defining the concepts, some examples will be considered.

What is ethnocentrism?

Schultz and Lavenda (1990: 32) offer the view that ethnocentrism is 'the opinion that one's own way of life is natural or correct, indeed the only true way of being fully human'. Seymour-Smith (1986: 97) offers as a definition 'the habit or tendency to judge or interpret other cultures according to the criteria of one's own culture', and considers it to be a universal tendency. Applebaum (1996) considers that one of the greatest achievements of multiculturalism has been a better understanding of the 'indignity' of ethnocentrism, arguing that appreciating diversity and finding value in other cultures do not imply belittling one's own culture. Kottak (1994: 48) describes it as 'the tendency to view one's own culture as best and to judge the behaviour and beliefs of culturally different people by one's own standards'. In connection specifically with child-rearing practices, Barnes (1995: 102) refers to the 'ethnocentric fallacy', which holds that 'what any one culture considers to be optimal child-rearing practices (for example, firm control with clearly explained reasons embedded in a climate of warmth: the authoritarian style ...) will also be optimal for every other culture'. In the same vein Sprott (1994) observes, 'Polarized ideas about parental control dominate the Anglo Dominant Culture's value orientations, reflected in both popular and scientific literature. Parental permissiveness is cast into an opposing category of "noncontrol", imbuing it with negativism.' Prejudice against Eskimo child rearing as being over-indulgent is examined in that context and a method is offered to 'loosen' the grip of Anglo beliefs about parenting.

Kincheloe and Steinberg (1997: 3) write of 'conservative multiculturalism/ monoculturalism', which for our purposes is similar to ethnocentrism. 'Everyone ... would be better off if they could be exposed to the glories of Western Civilization ... From this colonial mind-set Africans and indigenous peoples have been categorized as lower types of human beings devoid of the rights and privileges of the higher (European) types.' However, it is not as simple as it might seem to avoid some degree of ethnocentrism. It can be tantamount to trying to achieve a completely value-free perspective, or a viewpoint that is not based on the history of one's own experiences. Barrett (1996: 20), for example, writes with reference to anthropologists:

Yet the very fact that they have been socialized into a particular culture, a culture which encompasses specific values and institutions and occupies a particular moral and political niche in the world order, inevitably suggests, without even considering the individual anthropologist's personality, that some amount of ethnocentrism must always creep in.

A particular dilemma posed by Seymour-Smith (1986) is how anthropologists should deal with ethnocentrism encountered in the populations they study. He asks: 'should "native ethnocentrism" be respected as part of the indigenous world view, or should the anthropologist combat prejudice and misinterpretation in the community by providing more information about the values and customs of other people?' (p. 97).

What is cultural relativism?

If ethnocentrism is an evil to be avoided, what then is cultural relativism? 'Cultural relativism involves understanding another culture in its own terms sympathetically enough so that the culture appears to be a coherent and meaningful design for living' (Greenwood and Stini, 1977: 182; cited in Schultz and Lavenda, 1990: 32). Kottak (1994: 48) defines it as 'the position that the values and standards of cultures differ and deserve respect. Extreme relativism argues that cultures should be judged solely by their own standards.' Seymour-Smith (1986: 63) defines it as 'An approach or theory in anthropology [in which] each culture or each society possessed its own rationality and coherence in terms of which its customs and beliefs were interpreted'. In all three of these definitions we see a pattern of internal consistency emerging as a defining characteristic. If then, indeed, a culture was to be understood in its own terms, and not according the standards and dictates of other cultures, 'what business did members of one culture have telling those of another what to do?' (Gardner and Lewis, 1996: 28).

But as with ethnocentrism, there are dilemmas. Seymour-Smith (1986: 64) notes, 'One of the major problems in the concept of cultural relativism when held dogmatically is that it leaves the anthropologist without a theoretical basis for comparative generalizations regarding human societies or cultures.' Korbin (1981), in her anthropological examination of child abuse, notes that 'a stance of extreme cultural relativism, in which all judgments of humane treatment of children are suspended in the name of cultural rights, may be used to justify a lesser standard of care for some children'. Barrett (1996: 21) also addresses the issue of abusive cultural practices:

The time-honoured way in which anthropologists have attempted to avoid ethnocentrism is relativism. It has generally been assumed that there are no good or bad cultures or cultural practices. This approach carries with it the danger of slipping into the more radical position of amoral relativism, in which there are no standards whatever. In other words, under the guise of culture, anything goes, because moral judgment is ruled out. This seems to be one of those problems incapable of rational solution. If we criticize someone else's cultural practice, such as clitoridectomy (female circumcision), we would seem to be guilty of ethnocentrism; but if we fail to do so, where do we draw the line? The obvious way around this dilemma is to articulate a set of universal values, but that is easier said than done.

How then is one to approach the issue of cultural practices, particularly as they apply to children, which might be acceptable within the context of one culture but unacceptable when judged by another? At a time when there was much less contact between different cultures, when that contact was limited to anthropologists from Westernised developed nations visiting so-called 'primitive' societies, the issue might have been less significant than it perhaps is today when most nations now have majority and minority ethnic groups, and many countries have a significant number of different cultural groups establishing communities within national borders. These globalising trends place different cultures in contact with each other much more than previously, and this trend is likely to continue. As I have noted elsewhere:

> it would be an oversimplification to say that ethnocentrism is an unmitigated evil, and that cultural relativism is an unequivocal good. One simply has to look at the extremes of both positions to realise that a balance needs to be struck; one which does not go too far towards one or other end of the spectrum. The dangers of an ethnocentric perspective are relatively clear. It is a manifestation of the exercise of power imbalances between different cultures and societies. With ethnocentrism one has cultural hegemony; however, with cultural relativism one lacks a foundation from which to censure female circumcision, the internment of Jewish children (and adults) in concentration camps, the historical practice of foot-binding in China, and ultimately, the practice of child sacrifice as practised in some societies in former times. At its most extreme, cultural relativism would imply the acceptance of such practices on the basis of being only comprehensible within the culture in which they are/were practised, and not susceptible to external judgement.

> (Sanders, 1999: 27–8)

Are there, as suggested by Barrett (1996), universal standards which one can apply? One may perhaps consider the UN Convention on the Rights of the Child as such a set of universal standards. However, as noted by Hodgkin (1994), implementation of the convention can produce difficulties when violations of the rights of children are justified on the basis of cultural practice.

Globalisation

What is globalisation? According to Tomlinson (1999: 2) it is 'the rapidly developing and ever-densening network of interconnections and interdependencies that characterize modern social life'. McGrew (in Hall, 1992) describes it as 'those processes, operating on a global scale, which cut across national boundaries, integrating and connecting communities and organizations in new space–time combinations, making the world in reality and in experience more interconnected'. In both of these cases, it could be argued that the writers, by emphasising the intercommunication aspect, are describing the causes of globalisation rather than the consequences, and as such only focusing on a part of the definition. Pugh (1997) describes it as a 'process in a world in which time and space have become compressed because of the operation of modern transport, communications and the increasing internationalisation of economic activity. Thus, actions in one part of the globe have consequences elsewhere' (p. 101, cited in Pugh and Gould, 1999).

Among these other usages, the concept reflects the increasing trend of cross-influence between different cultures on a world level. It also reflects power differentials within that process of reciprocal influence, which mean that the traffic is predominantly one-way. Despite the proliferation of exotic restaurants within Western societies (very frequently beginning with previously colonised nations – for example British-Indian, French-Vietnamese, Dutch-Indonesian), there is arguably more influence of Westernised, developed and industrialised countries on non-Westernised, non-developed and non-industrialised countries than the other way round. In large part this is because of the desire for overseas markets on the part of multinational companies. Hirst and Thompson (1996: 1) observe:

> It is widely asserted that we live in an era in which the greater part of social life is determined by global processes, in which national cultures, national economies and national borders are dissolving. Central to this perception is the notion of a rapid and recent process of economic globalisation.

With others being more influenced by us and vice versa, one aspect of concern about globalisation is the trend from a planet of diverse societies and cultures towards a planetary cultural homogeneity. It is possible, however, to overstate this. For example, Hall (1992) provides a number of reasons why the concept of cultural homogeneity is 'too simplistic, exaggerated and one-sided' (p. 304). Reasons include the continuing fascination with difference, and the fact that this kind of globalisation is 'unevenly distributed around the world', affecting more so countries in the Western world (in contrast perhaps to what I have argued above). Further, although there is a fascination with difference, our current fascination may be rooted not only in the exotic, but also in the disappearing. In like manner, one might be interested in a Komodo dragon (or indeed any endangered species) not only because one has never encountered it before, but also equally because if the environment continues to change in the way it has, we may be faced with never seeing one in the future.

A perhaps more powerful argument against the ultimate threat of cultural homogeneity emerges when we consider the reasons why we have different cultures. From a Darwinian perspective, it could be argued that one reason human societies differ from each other in the first place is that the world consists of tropical rain forests, vast plains, mountainous areas, deserts, areas of permafrost, and so forth. Culture is perhaps largely a reflection that human species have been compelled to adapt to different environments, thereby reflecting a diversity at least as wide-ranging as the ecological niches within which people are born, grow, live and die. The argument against the threat of eventual cultural homogeneity therefore would be that as long as the world has a variety of different environments within which people can and do survive, and as long as people continue to derive an advantage from living in social groupings rather than in isolation, there will continue to be a wide range of variations in cultures. However, whilst this may reassure us about the threat of the eventual demise of all cultures but one, it does not necessarily reassure us about variations in the levels of cultural diversity around the world.

Let us now consider some further aspects of this concept. It would not be possible to have such a worldwide trade in culture without the incredibly rapid technological advances of the twentieth century. Transport and communication developments in particular have effectively made a reality of the phrase 'It's a small world' – and becoming smaller all the time. Whereas at the beginning of the century it would have taken a month to cross the Atlantic, now one can do it in a matter of hours. Communication technology over the last two centuries has gone from telegraph systems (1837) to transatlantic cables (1858) to the invention (1876) and subsequent development of the telephone, the development of wireless radio (1895), and the subsequent development of public broadcast radio, the development and marketing (1936–8) of televisions, the large-scale distribution of personal computers and the development of the internet during the 1990s. During the same time cars have revolutionised the ability of people to move around within and between countries, and air travel, once the prerogative of the affluent elite, has developed into a widespread necessity of life, enabling people to live and work farther and farther afield from the place where they may have originated.

These technological advances have also contributed to another facet of globalisation, which has been highlighted through 'McDonaldization' and 'Coca Cola-ization' metaphors: 'Wherever you go in the world you will find a McDonald's.' Apart from wonder at the successful marketing of a product that is less than forty years old, and aside from the astounding economic success of the product, there are other cultural implications. First, it is not only bringing an American product, but an American ideology (entrepreneurial enterprise) to many other countries. As noted by Fukuyama (1991, cited in Pugh and Gould, 1999), 'For some writers, globalisation marks the triumphal spread of the capitalist free market influence over the world's economic and political systems.' Nothing exports capitalism nearly so effectively as the fast-food delivery of a Big Mac. The product is both standardised and adapted to the local customs: in Spain one can get shrimp meals at McDonald's. However, with the dominance of McDonald's in the ecosystem of localised fast-food markets, one is tempted to speculate on the disappearance (or non-appearance), through competition, of more locally and culturally derived forms of food that might have been able to fill the particular niche for fast foods. The success of McDonald's draws on the love-hate relationship with the United States throughout the world. Whilst people may have deplored the engineered involvement of the United States in numerous overseas conflicts, protested outside American embassies over a range of political activities, etc., there has ever been a deep fascination with American cultural symbols, and companies in the United States have been quick to exploit these. Levi and Wrangler Jeans, Hollywood icons such as James Dean, Marilyn Monroe, Humphrey Bogart, entertainers such as Elvis Presley, Chuck Berry, Buddy Holly are all 'products' that have been deliberately marketed overseas and have been voraciously devoured by consumers of various nationalities, eager to import American culture, if not American imperialism, into their part of the world.

Let us now briefly consider the role of language in globalisation. The biblical story of the Tower of Babel tells of the origin of different languages; it was God's punishment for the arrogance of mankind, that they should contemplate building a tower that would reach to heaven. To punish them he made them all speak in different tongues, and with that, the ability, and necessity, to collaborate in the building of the tower was lost and the tower was abandoned. The tale highlights the necessity to be able to communicate, and the ability to sell products and services overseas has historically required the ability to communicate in local languages. However, English had become the 'lingua franca' of the world by the end of the twentieth century. In Wales a Welsh-language social work training pack was given the title *They All Speak English Anyway* (Davies, 1994), a sentiment that can be said to apply more and more to the rest of the world. Europe provides a very interesting illustration of the ethnocentric orientation of the English language. In virtually every Western European country except the United Kingdom, children are taught a second and sometimes a third language at an age when they are most receptive – in primary school, usually starting around age seven. By the time European children are eight or nine they are frequently proficient in English. In the United Kingdom other European languages are not taught until children enter secondary school (although in Wales children learn Welsh in primary school). In effect, children of other countries are expected to learn English, but English-speaking countries make little effort to teach their children European languages. Nor is there a likelihood of change; rather it is likely that British participation in European affairs will continue to rest on the assumption that others will learn English.

Elsewhere (Sanders, 1999) I have given examples of models of child protection being influenced across national boundaries, in ways that reflect linguistic similarities (United States and United Kingdom; Belgium, Netherlands and France). If the models adopted to address social problems are indeed, as suggested, derived predominantly from interaction with countries speaking the same language, and if English appears to be headed towards being the Esperanto dream of a language spoken around the world, regardless of what other language is spoken, then it would seem to follow that there is a likelihood, and I would argue a danger, that the future holds the prospect of more and more solutions to social problems being derived from the English-speaking nations.

International conventions

International conventions such as the UN Convention on the Rights of the Child also have implications for the consideration of childhood in different cultures. The UN convention, now ratified by all countries in the world except Somalia and the United States, sets minimum standards against which the treatment of children in different countries can be judged. Provisions such as the right to life, to a name and a nationality, the prevention of kidnapping and abduction, the right to free primary education, the prohibition of torture, cruelty, capital punishment or life imprisonment for children, and protection from the effects of war, appear to relate to issues that are not of pressing concern within the United Kingdom. However, it would be a mistake to be complacent or regard the convention simply as a tool to promote minimum standards in non-Western countries. The United Kingdom is a long way from adequately addressing children's right to express views on matters concerning them. It has a very poor track record when it comes to providing protection for refugee children; the United Kingdom was singled out in a European report as providing poor services in this respect (The *Guardian*, 3 April 2001). Even the articles requiring countries to provide support to both parents to bring up a child, and to promote a child's right to an adequate standard of living, could be said to have been dramatically undermined during the last twenty years in the United Kingdom as more and more British children found themselves growing up in impoverished households.

Likewise, if we look at the European Convention of Human Rights, we see that there are significant differences within Europe in the extent to which children are treated as citizens in their own right (for instance, by countries banning corporal punishment), or the extent to which the state is seen as having a role in the care of children (for instance, by countries providing pre-school programmes for young children). In these ways the interpretation of international standards is coloured by each country's own cultural values.

The final point to be mindful of when looking at provision across countries is whether rich and powerful countries are using their power and economic influence to coerce others to adopt their standards. In other words, the process of implementing international conventions also brings us back to the tension we identified earlier, between ethnocentrism and cultural relativism.

Conclusion

This chapter has focused on themes arising from a better understanding of children's development that students will derive from considering it in a cross-cultural context. It has not attempted to describe the range of different child-rearing approaches in different cultures, as that would be too extensive to be covered in a single chapter, but the student is referred to other sources that can begin to help the student appreciate how different the experience of rearing children can be in a global context.

Rather, the focus in this chapter has been to provide a rationale for studying child rearing in different cultures, an examination of issues of power in defining 'normality' in child development (with particular reference to discourses concerning ethnocentrism and cultural relativism), a discussion of globalisation, and a brief reference to international conventions affecting the welfare of children.

Questions and exercises

1 What are the most important reasons for studying the cross-cultural context of children's development?
2 How can we find out about cultural differences in child rearing?
3 What do we mean when we talk about culture?
4 What is 'ethnocentrism' and what is wrong with it?
5 What is 'cultural relativism' and what are the problems with it?
6 What is 'globalisation' and what are its implications for child rearing and child development?
7 What is the impact of international conventions on the upbringing of children? Can such conventions help us to overcome the problems we have identified with 'ethnocentrism' and 'cultural relativism'?

Reading

Bronfenbrenner, *The Ecology of Human Development* (1979), is indispensable as an introduction to thinking about global differences in children's upbringing. Trawick-Smith, *Early Childhood Development* (1997), is a useful starting point for understanding what sort of differences there are, and provides a particularly good critique of traditional child development theories, when examined from a multicultural perspective. Konner, *Childhood: a Multicultural View* (1991), is an excellent source (with a range of interesting illustrations), highlighting cross-cultural variations in specific aspects of child rearing. Likewise, Keats, *Culture and the Child* (1997), focuses on specific aspects of different societies. Tomlinson, *Globalization and Culture* (1999), is helpful on the issue of globalisation and its implications for culture. Harwood, Miller and Lucca Irizarry, *Culture and Attachment* (1995), and Kağitçibaşi, *Family and Human Development across Cultures* (1996), both reflect powerfully on precisely what difference culture makes in the way children develop, and finally Valsiner, *Culture and Human Development* (2000), describes the relatively new field of cultural developmental psychology and provides interesting cultural contexts of various aspects of children's lives and development.

This chapter is taken from:
Maynard, T. and Thomas, N. (eds) (2004) *An Introduction to Early Childhood Studies*
978-0-7619-7074-3

International Perspectives

TIM WALLER

This chapter discusses a range of findings from recent international comparisons of early childhood education and care. A number of significant similarities and trends are identified, however, it is recognized that wider evidence is needed to represent a world view of early childhood education and care. The chapter provides an overview of early years policy and provision, commenting in more detail on diverse curricula and notions of 'quality'. Two examples of internationally renowned approaches to early years provision (Reggio Emilia in Italy and Te Whāriki from New Zealand) are briefly summarized to introduce students to the critical insights that can be developed through comparison. The chapter concludes with a consideration of the notion that 'children's services' should be replaced by 'children's spaces' (Moss and Petrie, 2002).

This chapter develops an overview of recent international comparisons of early years provision. Current issues and significant trends in early years care and education are identified and discussed. It is not the intention to provide detailed statistics, although some are given, rather to enable students of early childhood to engage in critical reflection on the benefit of cross-national studies.

Increasingly the UK is taking note of early years care and education policy and practice in other countries – notably those within Europe and the OECD (Organisation for Economic Co-operation and Development). This chapter explores the principles and practices adopted by a selected group of countries using the OECD thematic review as a framework. It aims to give students the opportunity to compare a variety of practices and consider possible outcomes and implications for children related to a holistic perspective. The chapter discusses both curricular and policy issues and encourages readers to critically analyse current policy and practice in early years care and education in the UK.

Recently the range of information and knowledge about international aspects of early years has increased due to the availability of online data and publications (see, for example, online early years journals such as *Contemporary Issues in Early Childhood* [*www.wwwords.co.uk/ciec*] and the *Journal of Early Childhood Research* [*ecr.sagepub.com*]). However, it should be acknowledged that most of the online material is available in English and to a large extent concerns English-speaking countries and Europe, so it does not represent a world view and a complete picture of early childhood education and care (see Waller et al., 2004). As Moss et al. (2003) point out, one of the problems of limiting our attention to those countries with which we are similar is that we risk missing some of the most important reasons for doing cross-national study. There is a need for wider comparison through further data from a greater number of countries around the world.

CONTEXT

A number of recent reports concerning early childhood education and care (ECEC) have identified some similarities and trends that allow broad international comparison. They also identify a diverse range of views of children, concepts of childhood and traditions and policies for ECEC adopted by the countries involved.

First the OECD provides a Thematic Review of Early Childhood Education and Care Policy [see *www.oecd.org*]. To date 18 countries have been reviewed: Australia, Belgium (two communities), Canada, Czech Republic, Denmark, Finland, France, Hungary, Ireland, Italy, Korea, Mexico, the Netherlands, Norway, Portugal, Sweden, United Kingdom, United States. Two countries remain to be reviewed in 2004: Austria and Germany. Bennett (2001) reported the following demographic, economic and social trends relevant to early childhood:

● Ageing populations, declining fertility rates, a greater proportion of children living in lone parent families

● A sharp rise in dual earner households, increased female employment rates

- Paid and job protected maternity and family leave seen as essential for parental support and equity but the level of payment and take-up varies across countries
- A significant increase in the number of refugee children and families from areas of conflict around the world – policy and attitude varies across countries.

Also, Moss et al. (2003) reported for the DFES on evidence from 15 countries, which were grouped according to differences in welfare regime. These included four 'English-language' countries (Australia, New Zealand, United Kingdom (UK) and the United States (USA)); four 'Nordic' countries (Denmark, Finland, Norway and Sweden) and seven 'Other European' countries (Belgium, France, Germany, Italy, the Netherlands, Portugal and Spain). The 15 countries were compared in terms of a number of demographic, employment, economic and policy dimensions, in relation to the welfare regime. Generally, there are strong similarities among the Nordic countries and among the English-language countries, with more variation among other European countries (paras. 5.1–5.7). The key findings of this study, which generally concur with Bennett (2001), include:

- Fertility rates are generally low (below replacement level except in the USA)
- The ageing of the European population
- English-language countries have high child poverty rates (defined as the proportion of children living in low income households) and the Nordic countries have low rates
- The US has the highest per capita national income, the highest child poverty and the lowest social expenditure and tax rates.

Moss et al. (2003: para. 5.5) also found that while women's employment is highest in the Nordic countries, part-time employment varies considerably. Employed women are most likely to work part-time in the Netherlands, Australia and the UK, and least likely to do so in Finland and Southern European countries. There are considerable variations in leave entitlements between different countries within the three groupings, in terms of length and payment. Including paid maternity and parental leave entitlements, Nordic countries offer the most generous leave arrangements to employed parents. While taken overall (and including levels of payment), the English-language countries offer the lowest levels of paid leave. The UK provides a longer period of paid leave than some countries in the 'other European' grouping – but most of the UK period of paid maternity leave is at a low flat-rate level, while Netherlands, Portugal and Spain pay an earnings-related benefit for their full maternity leave period.

The OECD report *Starting Strong* (Bennett, 2001) shows that the countries involved have adopted diverse strategies to ECEC policy and provision. These strategies are deeply embedded in particular contexts values, and beliefs. 'Early childhood policy and provision are strongly linked to cultural and social beliefs about young children, the role of the families and government and the purposes of ECEC' (OECD 2001: 38). For example, according to Anning and Edwards (1999: 13) the 'concepts of social responsibility and democratic decision making are high priorities in Danish cultural life'. In Denmark there is a tradition of providing funding for the integrated care of children, managed by local communities. Ofsted (2003) compared the education of six-year-olds in England, Denmark and Finland. They found that the curriculum is more centralized and prescribed in England and more importance is attached in Denmark and Finland to the way children develop as people. More is expected of English six-year-olds in terms of achievement in literacy and numeracy. In England children were also grouped according to 'ability'. These factors and differences relate to cultural values and the way each country views children.

POLICY AND PROVISION

Bennett (2003) argues that ECEC is increasingly viewed as a key component of national policy and that due to changes in economic conditions and child rearing patterns most countries were prepared to invest in ECEC to facilitate employment, promote children's cognitive, social and emotional development and life chances. The OECD (2001) report identifies the main focus of policy developments as:

● expanding provision to universal access
● raising the quality of provision

- promoting coherence and co-ordination of policy and services
- exploring strategies to ensure adequate investment in the system
- improving training and working conditions
- developing pedagogical frameworks for young children
- engaging parents, families and communities.

Within the OECD countries Bennett (2003) identified the following similarities and trends:

- most countries provide nursery education/kindergarten from three years
- considerable variation in provision for 0–3
- a persistent division between education and care.

Curtis and O'Hagan (2003: 201) point out that in Europe there is a general agreement on the division between policy and provision for children aged 0–3 and 3 to school age. However, the responsibility for the provision and the age of starting school varies (see Table 9.1). Curtis and O'Hagan also argue that Europe is 'united' in making inadequate provision for children from birth to three (e.g. poor training, poor salary levels, poor career structure, etc.), with the exception of Finland and Sweden. The UK National Childcare Strategy (2003) identifies three key problems with provision for children under three: the variable quality of provision; the high cost of childcare; the lack of provision in some areas. As Curtis and O'Hagan (2003) point out, legal entitlement to a place in childcare provision for children under three exists only in Sweden and Finland. In Sweden, from 18 months, and in Finland from birth. Both countries have excellent training provision for early childhood workers. Pascal and Bertram (2002) reported that few countries in the INCA survey had national curriculum guidelines for children under the age of three years. However, Pascal and Bertram argued that there was evidence of a general agreement that emphasis on individual children's developing interests and needs, dispositions and social and emotional well-being should be the focus of the curriculum for children under three years.

Table 9.1 Aspects of early years curricula across the study countries

Country	Organising body	Ages	Type of curricula
Nordic Countries			
Denmark	Municipal	0–6	No formal curriculum
Finland	National	0–6	All providers framework curriculum
Norway	National	0–6	All providers framework curriculum – children's culture, activities worked out by environment committee of parents/staff
Sweden	National	0–6	Publicly provided framework curriculum with democracy, citizenship, provision local interpretation environment, creativity (over 90 per cent of total). Welfare and education linked
English-speaking countries			
Australia	Territory	4–7	Public, private and expert driven (variation from territory to territory)
New Zealand	National	0–5	All licensed providers; Guidelines, local bicultural, bilingual not compulsory, i.e. in receipt of public interpretation broad inclusive of different funds principles and goals philosophies
UK (England)	National	3–6	Settings in receipt of expert, outcome-driven equal opportunities and government funding respect for diversity to provide early education
US	State	4–7	Variation from state range – from expert-driven; conflict between state to state to local interpretation curriculum and some national programmes

Table 9.1 *Continued*

Other countries

Belgium	Umbrella	3–6	All providers, expert-driven programme, Flanders and Walloon – each community has own programme
France	National	3–6	Public provision and expert-driven through 'livret scolaire'
Germany	Land	3–6	Public and voluntary basic principles only; local interpretation
Italy	Regional	3–6	Public provision; guidelines, 'oriamenti' citizenship, creativity only at national level
Netherlands	Municipal	4–6	Programme even; kindergarten not school, some private
Portugal	National	3–6	All jardins d'infancia; guidelines, not a programme; many Ministry of Education pedagogical models
Spain	National	0–6	All providers broad general framework; allowance made for initiatives at language and culture regional, local and e.g. Catalan. Pedagogical setting level principles for each curricular block

Source: Adapted from Moss et al., 2003: 8

Most European countries have both private and state provision for 0–3 and 3–5-year-olds. Curtis and O'Hagan argue that this diversity sometimes leads to a lack of co-ordination in services provided. In the UK, for example, despite the very welcomed adoption of the National Childcare Strategy in 1998, Moss and Petrie (2002: 172) suggest that policy and provision for young children has been characterized by a 'contract model' which has led to short-term funding requiring competitive bidding. The effect of this policy is to ensure central control through a standard approach (Gewirtz, 2000). Moss and Petrie discuss data from the Daycare Trust (2001) estimating that there were 45 different sources of funding for 'childcare services' in the UK. Scrivens (2002) distinguishes a tension between market driven policies and a new culture of professional inquiry; an inclusive view of education and care and a tighter outcomes-focused view of policy and practice.

Penn (1999) and Bennett (2003) identify the major policy challenges as: (i) the need to ensure sufficient public funding and adequate co-ordination of the agencies involved, and (ii) to improve the supply of services for children under three to meet the demand and to improve the recruitment training and remuneration of early years professionals (particularly for children under three).

Bennett (2001) and Penn (2003) acknowledge a range of common problems for the ECEC of children under three:

- local inequalities
- cash and funding
- fragmented and incoherent services
- responding to ethnic diversity.

CURRICULUM

Bennett (2003) shows that most OECD countries provide a curriculum framework for young children aged 3–6, but the frameworks differ greatly in terms of length, detail, prescription and pedagogical practice. Bertram and Pascal (2002) and Moss et al. (2003) also identify wide variations in how prescriptive the curricula are. Moss et al. found that leeway for local interpretation is common in the Nordic countries, and central specification strongest in England and France (paras 3.5–3.8). All curricula include general goals of personal development, language and communication. Bertram and Pascal (2002) found that there was some variation in how the ECEC curriculum for children over three was defined: most countries used areas of learning, few used activities, and no country used disciplines or subjects. Many countries emphasized cultural traditions and aimed to enhance social cohesiveness through the ECEC curriculum. Only three countries emphasized early literacy and numeracy within the ECEC curriculum. Moss et al. (2003) also found wide variation in terms of detail and benchmarking on specific subjects, skills and competencies (paras 3.5–3.8). They argued that each country in their report attempted to link curricula for early childhood services with entry to school in different ways. Only Sweden has a curriculum for out-of-school provision, though Finland, Spain, Sweden and France are developing curricula in this area (para. 3.12) (see Table 9.1).

The Qualifications and Curriculum Authority (QCA) in England commissioned an international review of the early years curriculum in 20 countries (Bertram and Pascal, 2002). The countries involved were Australia, Canada, France, Germany, Hong Kong, Hungary, Ireland, Italy, Japan, Korea, Netherlands New Zealand, Singapore, Spain, Sweden, Switzerland, UK England, UK N Ireland, UK Wales and the USA. Bertram and Pascal (2002: 7) identified the following five key areas of early childhood education and care as central to the debate:

1 The early years curriculum, viewed in its widest sense.
2 The issue of pedagogy (including staffing levels and the qualifications of staff).
3 The continuity of a child's experiences (within the setting, before arriving and after leaving the setting).
4 Definitions and measures of quality in early childhood settings.
5 Questions and key issues in the future development of early childhood education.

In their study Bertram and Pascal (2002: 8) argued that there was 'almost universal promotion of an active, play-based pedagogy within the participating countries, where self-management and independence were encouraged. Delegates generally agreed that the role of the adult was to support, scaffold and facilitate rather than to overly direct. Some countries, such as Sweden, specifically discouraged a formal approach.'

Bennett (2004), however, identified two different approaches to the curriculum for ECEC, for children over three years. First the 'social pedagogy' approach adopted by the Nordic countries and Central Europe. According to Bennett, the principle of this approach is a focus on the whole child involving a play-based, active and experiential pedagogy with an emphasis on the outdoors. A strong intergenerational and community outreach ethos is fostered. There is a short core curriculum to guide early education practice and local interpretation is encouraged. There is little systematic monitoring of child outcomes or measures, it is the centre's responsibility. Second the 'infant school' approach adopted by Australia, Belgium, France, Ireland, Korea, Mexico, Netherlands, UK (reception classes) and the USA. The focus of this approach is on 'readiness for school'. For Bennett, this approach is characterized by a restrained, teacher-directed play-based pedagogy where attention is given to achieving curricular aims and to measuring individual performance. There is central specification of a detailed curriculum and parental and community involvement is underplayed except in 'at risk' situations.

Despite the recent welcomed increased attention given to the ECEC of young children throughout many of the wealthier countries of the world, Bertram and Pascal (2002), Bennett (2003) and Moss et al. (2003) identify a number of barriers to development. Continuity in children's early experiences from home to setting and between settings is seen as a key to effective ECEC. The separation of education and care and early years and primary education, with different zones of ministerial responsibility, separate budgets and professional cultures is one of the most significant barriers. Further aspects of ECEC which need urgent attention are the status, training and career progression of staff and the gendered workforce.

The OECD (2001) report has signposted the way forward with the following 'Eight Key Policy Elements for Early Childhood Education and Care':

- a systemic and integrated approach to policy development and implementation
- a strong and equal partnership with the education system
- universal access and SEN
- substantial public investment
- a participatory approach to quality improvement and assurance
- appropriate training and working conditions
- systematic attention to data monitoring and collection
- a stable framework and long-term agenda for research and evaluation.

However, as Penn (2005) argues, while the OECD report provides useful comparative statistics and makes general recommendations, discussion is focused at the level of policy rather than practice. He makes the point that as with the EU, the OECD:

argues that equality of access and quality of practice are important goals for services, but that they can only be achieved by adequate public funding and by a good infrastructure of planning, evaluation and training. By these criteria the USA performs very poorly, almost bottom of the class. Nordic countries do very well. It is ironic that the US model, which stresses individual improvement at programme level, is so enthusiastically adopted by the World Bank and other international donors.

(Penn, 2005: 181)

QUALITY

While many countries have recently focused on expanding provision for young children, there has been at the same time a significant international trend to define and measure the effectiveness and 'quality' of that provision. The EU for example, developed 'A Framework for Quality for Early Childhood Services' (see Penn, 1999) stating that:

> Equal access to good quality early years services is a goal of the European Union. Good quality services are a necessary part of the economic and social infrastructure. Equal access to these services is essential for equality of opportunity between men and women; for the well-being of children, families and communities; and for productive economies. It is a goal to be espoused at all levels – local, regional, national and European – and a goal for which all of these levels can and should work together.
>
> (European Commission Network on Childcare and Other Measures to Reconcile Employment and Family Responsibilities, 1996)

First it is important to recognize that the need for definitions of quality come from a context of greater public accountability and expectations that services will provide 'value for money' (Elfer and Wedge, 1996) and the marketization of public services (Hill, 2003). Moss and Petrie (2002: 69) also discuss how the concept of 'quality' has been incorporated into ECEC from the commercial world. Second as (Pascal and Bertram, 1994: 3) point out, 'quality is value laden, subjective and dynamic'. 'Quality' is not universal but is a relative concept, depending on cultural values and beliefs about the nature of the children and childhood. Moss and Petrie recognize that in the field of early childhood 'quality' is increasingly discussed as a relative term with the possibility of multiple understandings and Raban et al. (2003) argue that acknowledging the complexity of measuring quality is actually desirable. (For a review of the debate about 'universal' or 'culturally specific' definitions of quality see Raban et al., 2003; and Dahlberg et al., 1999 for a more detailed discussion of quality).

As Penn (1999) points out, the notion of quality is meaningless unless there is clarity about values and beliefs that underpin a service. Elfer and Wedge (1996: 66) argue that 'quality is a misleading concept if it encourages the idea that we are all agreed on what we want for children before we have gone through a process to ensure that'. The difficulty is as Pence (1992) put it, who defines what is to be measured? Katz (1992) recognized three dimensions of quality: indicators, stakeholders, beneficiaries, and four perspectives: top-down, outside-inside, inside-out and bottom-up. Pascal and Bertram (1994) developed 10 dimensions of quality as part of their Effective Early Learning (EEL Project).

While there is recognition that a range of different interest groups such as children, parents, practitioners and stakeholders may all have different views of what quality means in terms of early childhood provision, there is an argument for developing common indicators of quality (Raban et al., 2003). Curtis and O'Hagan (2003: 169) discuss the guidelines for 'quality' early years provision that were developed by two international organizations, OMEP (the World Organisation for Early Childhood Education) and ACEI (American Childhood Education International) in 1999 [see *www.ecec21.org*]. These organizations agreed that effective early years provision involves 'a comprehensive network of services that provide:

● environment and physical space settings for children
● curriculum content and pedagogy
● early childhood educators and caregivers
● partnership with families and communities
● services for young children with special needs
● accountability, supervision and management of programmes for young children.

Within each area, special attention must be directed towards:

- services with equal attention to all children
- links between programmes and services
- recognition of the value of those who care for and teach young children including appropriate working conditions and remuneration
- intergenerational approaches whenever feasible
- empowerment of communities, families and children
- a mechanism for adequate and uninterrupted funding
- cost analysis, monitoring and evaluation of programme quality (Curtis and O'Hagan, 2003: 169–70).

Different ways of describing quality are defined as 'quality frameworks' such as the Early Childhood Environment Rating Scale [ECERS] (Harms et al., 1998). This framework has been used in the USA and the UK to evaluate the day-to-day functioning within settings (e.g. social interaction, children's activities, and physical facilities). These aspects are rated on a seven-point scale which is used as a diagnostic and longer-term monitoring tool. However, ECERS are generally used to provide a staff perspective and not that of children or parents. ECERS have also been used in research on early childhood (for example, Phillips et al., 1987; Sylva and Siraj-Blatchford, 2001). In particular, ECERS have provided data for the 'Effective Provision of Pre-school Education' (EPPE) project funded by the UK Department for Education and Skills on the developmental progress of more than 2,800 pre-school children in England [see *www.ioe.ac.uk/cdl/eppe/*].

'Quality' is a problematic concept and there is a real danger of focusing on a framework and on easily measurable standards such as space/size and not on qualitative aspects such as relationships and dispositions and the meanings constructed by those who use the setting. As Dahlberg et al. (1999) and Moss (2001d: 130) argue 'quality is not neutral it is socially constructed'. The concept of quality has created its own discourse ('Centres of Excellence', etc.) and evaluating the effectiveness of early years provision through predetermined, standardized criteria, according to Moss (2001d: 131), leads to 'a pedagogy of uniformity and normalisation ... and a definitive conclusion'. Dahlberg et al. (1999) and Moss (2001d) compare the 'discourse of quality' with an alternative 'discourse of meaning making' which 'recognises the negotiated and provisional nature of understanding and assessment' (Moss, 2001d:

132). The approach of the 'discourse of meaning making' therefore allows for judgements about the effectiveness of early years settings to be constructed, debated and disputed within a particular context based on data meaningful to the setting (for example, the use of pedagogical documentation in Reggio Emilia).

Two examples of internationally renowned early years provision are now discussed to encourage reflection and debate on international aspects of ECEC. For further details of the Reggio Emilia approach and Te Whãriki see *Five Curriculum Outlines*, OECD, 2004.

TE WHÃRIKI

Te Whãriki, the early childhood curriculum framework developed in New Zealand in 1996, has received a great deal of world-wide interest due to its innovative holistic and emergent approach to the curriculum. Whãriki (or mat) is used as a metaphor to signify the weaving together of the principles and strands as well as the diverse peoples, philosophies and services that participate in early education (Anning et al., 2004: 12). The view of the child is as 'a competent learner and communicator' and the approach fosters a holistic approach to curriculum planning and learning: 'The curriculum is founded on the following aspirations for children: to grow up as competent and confident learners and communicators, healthy in mind, body and spirit, secure in their sense of belonging and in the knowledge that they make a valued contribution to society' (MoE, 1996: 9).

According to Podmore (2004: 152), widespread consultation culminated in an innovative bicultural framework, with the document partly written in Maori. Te Whãriki received strong support from practitioners. The framework identifies learning outcomes for children as: working theories about the people, places and things in learner's lives and as learning dispositions (MoE, 1996). Te Whãriki invites practitioners to weave their own curriculum drawing on the framework of Principles, Strands and Goals. The focus is also on children's perspectives to define and evaluate (quality) practices in early childhood centres.

Te Whãriki has four central principles:

1 Empowerment.
2 Holistic development.
3 Family and community.
4 Relationships.

and five strands:

1 Well-being.
2 Belonging.
3 Contribution.
4 Communication.
5 Exploration.

The goals within each strand highlight ways in which practitioners support children, rather than skills or content, promoting a project-based approach drawing from the children's interests. Thus, the content emerges from children's interests which are tracked through the four principles. The guidelines apply to all children in all settings, including those with special educational needs who may be given an Individual Development Plan (IDP).

Local flexibility in content is seen as important to meet the needs of culturally diverse groups, including the Maori, within New Zealand. However, Anning et al. (2004: 12) argue that the strong free play tradition within ECEC in New Zealand has meant that practice has been slow to move away from individual self-selection of activities to collaborative learning through projects. Also, as with many other ECEC programmes across the world, despite the principles of Te Whãriki, Anning et al. identify a problem with top-down pressure from the government for more literacy and numeracy content within the curriculum. Cullen (1996) also argues that the flexibility of Te Whãriki can lead to early childhood programmes of variable quality.

Anning et al. (2004: 11) describe early childhood services in New Zealand 'primarily community based' with little shared history and few links between early childhood and primary education. However, since 2002 the New Zealand government has developed a 10-year strategic plan for early childhood (*Pathways to the Future: Nga Huarahi Aratiki*, MoE, 2002) with the aim to increase participation and quality of ECEC services and to promote collaborative relationships.

REGGIO EMILIA

Reggio Emilia has been internationally renowned for its early childhood programmes for over 40 years. Reggio Emilia is a city in the Emilia Romagna region of northern Italy with approximately 150,000 inhabitants. The region is one of the wealthiest parts of Europe. Since 1963, the municipality of Reggio Emilia has developed its own services for children from birth to six years of age, which have grown to include a network of 33 centres for young children. These are organized into *Asili Nido* (for children from three months to three years) and *Scuole del Infanzia* (3–6 years). The early childhood centres were established in close liaison with parents and the local community and children's rights are seen as paramount.

Loris Malaguzzi (1920–94) was the first head of municipal early childhood centres and significant influence on development of the Reggio approach. He advocated 'a pedagogy of relationships'. He held a positive and participatory view of early education and promoted a generous, optimistic view of human nature. For Moss (2001d), the significance of this positive approach is that it rejects the construction of the 'child at risk' or 'in need' not only because it produces a 'poor child', but also because it has chosen to move from the child as a subject of needs to a subject of rights.

Curtis and O'Hagan (2003: 217) summarise six principles of the Reggio Emilia approach as follows:

1 The study of child development as central to practice.
2 The importance of the teacher–child relationship.
3 The need for children's experiences to be taken into account when building the curriculum.
4 The importance of a rich environment in developing children's learning.
5 The importance of ongoing professional development for teachers.
6 The importance of the role of parents in the life of the school.

The main feature of the Reggio approach is that it advocates communication between adults and children and promotes collegiality and ethos of co-participation with families in the educational project (Nutbrown and Abbott, 2001: 1). Malaguzzi sees children as autonomously capable of making meaning from experience. 'Children's self-learning and co-learning are supported by interactive experiences constructed with the help of adults, who determine the selection and organisation of processes and strategies that are part of and coherent with the goals of early childhood education' (Malaguzzi, 1993: 78). As Rinaldi and Moss (2004: 2) point out in this approach 'learning is a process of constantly constructing, testing and reconstructing theories. Learning is a subject for constant research and must be made visible'. Knowledge is the product of a process of construction, involving interpretation and meaning making. It is co-constructed. Moss (2001d: 128) cites Rinaldi (a former pedagogical director of early years centres in Reggio) 'what children learn emerges from the process of self and social construction'. For Rinaldi 'learning is the subjective process of constructing reality with others'. The practitioner is therefore not a transmitter of knowledge and culture but facilitator in children's co-construction of their own knowledge and culture. The task of the practitioner is to offer a context in which the child can themselves explore and go deeper into a problem (Moss, 2001d: 129). Not only is the child viewed as a strong, powerful and competent learner, the child also has the right to an environment that is integral to the learning experience. Great value is placed on the whole environment as a motivating force:

> It is indisputable that schools should have the right to their own environment, their architecture, their own conceptualization and utilization of spaces, forms and functions. We place enormous value on the role of the environment as a motivating and animating force in creating spaces for relations, options and emotional and cognitive situations that produce a sense of well being and security.
>
> (Malaguzzi, 1996: 40)

As well as its commitment to developing 'deep, deep insight of children by listening to them', Nutbrown and Abbott (2001: 4) identify two further significant features of the Reggio approach. These are *time* (to discuss children and their projects) and *co-operative working* (teachers always work in pairs, each pair being responsible in the pre-schools for a group of children).

The Reggio approach is also characterized by a variety of pedagogical tools for developing early years practice in a rigorous, open and dynamic way. For example, pedagogical documentation, where learning processes are documented in various ways so that they can be shared, discussed, reflected upon and interpreted. Hoyuelos (2004: 7) suggests that this documentation represents an extraordinary tool for dialogue, exchange and sharing. It supports the ideological concept of the transparent school. For Vecchi (1993: 96), the procedure of documentation is a 'democratic possibility to inform the public of the contents of the school' and Rinaldi and Moss (2004: 3) argue that it is 'a unique source of information – precious for teachers, children, the family and anyone who wants to get closer to the strategies in children's ways of thinking'. For a more detailed discussion of pedagogical documentation see Dahlberg et al. (1999).

Reggio Emilia has become one of the best known early education systems in the world. Every year many early years specialists visit Reggio to study the approach and it has become so popular that since 1981 a Reggio exhibition 'The Hundred Languages of Children' has toured the world and there are 'Reggio networks' in 13 countries around the world (see Sightlines for details of the UK network). Reggio has been particularly influential in the USA and Sweden (see Dahlberg et al., 1999). Johnson (1999), however, argues that the widespread acclaim of Reggio Emilia has led to a 'cargo cultism' in early childhood education. He suggests that the Reggio Emilia approach has been 'Disneyfied', and colonized by the USA-dominated institutions and knowledge structures which have promoted it.

While there are clearly difficulties in attempting to replicate a system that developed in a particular (Italian) context and culture, the real significance of Reggio is that following visits to the region or the exhibition, many early years practitioners have been encouraged to critically reflect on and question their own practice (Moss, 2001b). As Curtis and O'Hagan (2003: 218) point out, 'adopting the approach means accepting and understanding the underlying principles and philosophy in the light of one's own culture'. Reggio has a lasting influence because, as Rinaldi and Moss (2004: 2) argue, 'Reggio is not a stable model producing predetermined and predictable outcomes, but a place where questions and uncertainty, change and innovation are welcome'. Moss (2001b: 125) reminds us that 'Reggio asks and expects us to ask many critical questions about ECEC. Reggio is so important because it reminds us that it is possible to think differently'. For Nutbrown and Abbott (2001) 'that capacity to provoke is perhaps one of the greatest and lasting legacies of any personal encounter with the Reggio Emilia experience'. As Gardner (2004: 16) asserts early childhood centres in Reggio 'stand as a shining testament to human possibilities'.

SUMMARY

This chapter has discussed a range of findings from recent international studies of early childhood education and care. A number of significant trends have been identified. Over the last 20 years or so, demographic, political and economic changes have led to significant interest and investment in ECEC. Bertram and Pascal (2002) argue that this 'new ECEC policy dynamic' is starting to make an impact throughout the world, which in some countries is 'revolutionary and unprecedented'. At the same time there is a tension between market driven policies and a new culture of professional inquiry. An inclusive view of education and care and a tighter outcomes-focused view of policy and practice (Scrivens, 2002). This is evident in approaches to the evaluation of ECEC and identification and measurement of 'quality'. The chapter discusses 'quality' as a problematic and culturally relative concept.

Two examples of internationally renowned approaches to early years provision (Reggio Emilia in Italy and Te Whāriki from New Zealand) are briefly summarized to introduce students to the critical insights that can be developed through comparison. As Bertram and Pascal (2002) and Moss et al. (2003) point out there are several benefits to cross-national studies. First by comparing provision in our own region or country with another we may question previously taken for granted traditional assumptions and practices. This process helps to make domestic practice visible and reveals the particular understandings of childhood, etc. that influence policy. It promotes critical thinking. For example, as Moss et al. (2003) point out, why is it that children in the UK start school earlier than almost everywhere else in Europe, and with what consequences? Why is education organized differently in different parts of the UK? There are, of course, limitations to the use of cross-national data and evidence. As Bertram and Pascal (2002) argue, policy and practice in ECEC is deeply located in national understandings of the place of family and childhood in society. The local context therefore needs to be taken into account and cross-national work needs to be interpreted. Given cultural norms, what is appropriate for one nation may be totally unsuitable for another. Differences in language and meaning can be problematic. For example, in the UK the term pre-school is taken to mean provision for children under five years, but in Sweden it is often used to describe the year before the start of formal schooling at seven years of age. The use of international statistics can also be problematic and is open to interpretation.

Moss (2001b) makes several important points regarding provision for young children. He argues that in a consideration of provision we should seek the views of the child. He argues that there are two possible constructions of early childhood institutions: as a place for the efficient production of predetermined outcomes, or as 'children's spaces' which provide opportunities for children and adults, the consequences of which may be unknown. The implication is that the term education and care is too restricting – care is not just about arrangements for working parents. He also suggests that a broader view of childhood is needed to take into account the relationships between the early childhood system and the education system. Further, Moss and Petrie (2002: 40) develop the model of seeking the views of children. They see children 'as young citizens and equal stakeholders with adults'. Moss and Petrie challenge early years practitioners and policy makers to reconceive provision for young children. They argue that as children have equal status and ownership of their environment the notion of 'children's services' should be replaced by 'children's spaces'. Dahlberg and Moss (2005) continue the debate by providing a strong argument for 'a narrative of possibilities' where early years practitioners are encouraged to be open to new thought and possibilities for ECEC (as in Reggio) and not tied down by 'a narrative of outcomes' which restricts early years practice to that which is measurable and predetermined.

QUESTIONS FOR REFLECTION AND DISCUSSION

1. What is the benefit of cross-national study?
2. What critical insights have you gained about ECEC provision in the UK as a result?
3. Do you have to visit a country to gain an understanding of ECEC in that country?
4. Why is measuring the 'quality' of ECEC always subjective?
5. What are the implications of early years practice in Reggio and New Zealand for early years settings in the UK?

Recommended reading

Anning et al. (2004) discuss early years provision and research in three different contexts: Australia, New Zealand and the UK.

Boushel (2000) reviews childrearing across a number of different cultures.

MacNaughton (2003) provides information on approaches to the early years curriculum from a range of countries across the world.

Moss and Petrie (2002) dedicate a whole chapter to ECEC in Sweden.

Penn (1997) compares nursery education and policy in Italy, Spain and the UK.

Penn (2000) presents an overview of global early childhood services.

Penn (2005) includes a chapter with a comparative overview of early years practice in China, North America, Europe and a number transitional countries such as Russia. She also briefly discusses practice and children's lives in a number of Asian and African countries and draws attention to studies such as Tobin (1995) who videoed life in nurseries in China, Japan and the USA.

The website *www.childcareincanada.org* is also a very useful source of international information about ECEC.

This chapter is taken from:
Waller, T. (ed) (2005) *An Introduction to Early Childhood*
978-1-4129-1036-1

Health Inequalities

14

DEBORAH ALBON and PENNY MUKHERJI

> In this chapter, we look at how the health and well-being of individuals is influenced by socio-economic factors, with particular reference to nutritional status. We investigate which parts of the world are most likely to experience food poverty and how globalization affects nutrition in countries in transition. We explore how health inequalities persist in the minority world and how factors such as geography, class, race, gender and disability can all have an impact on health and nutritional status.

In Chapter 2 we noted that 30 per cent of children born into the world today will suffer from malnutrition. Sadly we are familiar with media images of children from the majority world suffering from lack of food. There are many millions of families who do not have sufficient resources to meet even the most basic of their needs; these families are living in **absolute poverty**. In the UK the state benefit system ensures that almost no one lives in absolute poverty and yet there are still differences in the nutritional status of children in families living in **relative poverty** (Townsend, 1979). Economic status has, perhaps, the most pervasive influence on children's nutrition and health; however, other factors such as social class, education, race, gender and ability can all contribute to health inequalities

The following key areas are explored:

▸ Global poverty and health inequalities

▸ Countries in transition and the effect of globalization

▸ Health inequalities in Europe and the UK

▸ Health inequalities and children's nutrition

▸ Nutritional inequalities within families.

Global poverty and health inequalities

The majority of people in the world live in conditions of poverty; an often quoted statistic is that half the population live on less than US$ 2 a day (World

Bank, 2001). There are huge differences in the **gross domestic product** (GDP) per person between different countries, from US$68,800 in Luxembourg to US$600 in Malawi (CIA, 2007). There are also large inequalities within countries between the very rich and the very poor. In 2006 Denmark was calculated as being the most economically equal society, with Namibia having the largest gap between the richest and the poorest inhabitants (UN, 2006).

One of the consequences of poverty is poor health, as measured by life expectancy, childhood mortality, hunger and malnutrition, with the result that in the poorest 50 countries life expectancy at birth is 48.7 years compared with 74.8 years in the 50 richest countries (ESRC, 2006).

The World Health Organization is a multinational organization, representing 193 states, set up by the United Nations (UN) with the objective of helping people attain the highest possible level of health. In September 2000, the WHO adopted the UN Millennium Declaration, setting out goals to be reached by 2015. 'The Millennium Goals include challenges for rich and poor countries alike. They set targets for developing countries to reduce poverty and hunger, and to tackle ill-health, gender inequality, lack of education, lack of access to clean water and environmental degradation' (WHO, 2005a: 1). Three of these goals relate specifically to health:

▸ To reduce child mortality.

▸ To improve maternal health.

▸ To combat diseases such as HIV and malaria.

Every year the WHO publishes a global report. In 2005 the report focused on child, infant and maternal health and commented upon the progress made towards the achievement of the Millennium Goals. The report noted that even now,

> Each year 3.3 million babies – or maybe even more – are stillborn, more than 4 million die within 28 days of coming into the world, and a further 6.6 million young children die before their fifth birthday. Maternal deaths also continue unabated – the annual total now stands at 529 000 often sudden, unpredicted deaths which occur during pregnancy itself (some 68 000 as a consequence of unsafe abortion), during childbirth, or after the baby has been born. (WHO, 2005b)

The report noted that although some progress had been made, the countries with the worst health records were making the least progress, with the situation actually worsening in some countries. Health inequalities between poor and rich countries and between the poor and rich within countries have continued to increase. The reasons for a worsening situation in some countries were put down to:

▸ persistent poverty

▸ lack of money to invest in child and maternal health programmes

▸ difficulties in managing programmes effectively

▸ humanitarian crises resulting from war, natural disasters and climate change

▸ HIV epidemics

▸ all of the above contributing to economic downturn and a health workforce crisis.

Activity

www.povertymap.net/mapsgraphics/graphics/Undernutrition_en.jpg (accessed 28 July 2007).

This gives a good overview of the parts of the world where children are suffering the effects of under-nutrition.

In Chapter 2 we looked in some detail at the effects of under-nutrition on children. Poor nutrition not only has consequences for individual children, but has consequences for the countries they live in:

▸ The increased levels of infant and childhood mortality due to malnutrition means that there will be fewer economically active adults in the future.

▸ Malnourished children are less able to contribute to the economy in the future owing to poor health, time off school (even if schooling is available) and learning difficulties due to lack of nutrition.

There is a complex relationship between malnutrition and HIV/Aids. In some parts of the world, there are no longer sufficient people to farm the land, and there are large numbers of orphan children being cared for by grandparents. This has led to malnutrition in the surviving population, who are then more susceptible to infections and the effects of HIV/Aids (Oxfam, 2002).

Poor countries find themselves in the grip of a vicious cycle where poverty fuels malnutrition, which has a negative effect on the economic viability of the community, resulting in increased levels of poverty.

Activity

There is much debate about the role richer countries have played in the cause and perpetuation of global poverty. It is important that we all are aware of the wider issues and the part that we may be able to play as individuals. The following web sites will give you information.

UNICEF UK, www.unicef.org.uk/aboutus/index.asp

Make Poverty History, www.makepovertyhistory.org/

Globalization and Global Poverty Challenge, www.globalpovertychallenge.com/

Global Poverty Research Group, www.gprg.org/

Global Call to Action Against Poverty, www.whiteband.org/

(All accessed on 28 July 2007.)

Countries in transition and the effect of globalization

In the UK, since the middle of the twentieth century, there has been a remarkable change in the way that we shop, cook and eat. We have made a transition from:

▸ fresh food brought daily, to the increasing use of chilled/frozen foods and foods with a long shelf life

▸ meals produced from basic ingredients, to pre-prepared products (often high in fats, sugars and additives)

▸ food produced locally, to food being imported from all over the world

▸ foods being eaten in season, to foods being available all the year round

▸ small producers, to large, international, industrial-sized producers

▸ meals being eaten in the home, to meals being eaten outside

▸ foods being chosen for taste, freshness, and so on, to foods being chosen by brand name and lifestyle image.

There are real concerns about the environmental impact of transporting food all over the world and the danger of eating pre-prepared foods that are high in fats, sugar and additives, but many of us welcome the choice that is available in our supermarkets. The impact on small shops in the high street may worry us, but the convenience of being able to shop once a week, or online, is valued by many. We may feel uneasy about the impact of advertising on the food choices made by and for children but, for many people, a trip to a popular fast-food outlet is a normal part of life (Martens and Warde, 1997).

These changes have been fuelled, in part, by the process of **globalization**, resulting in many of the foods and food products that we have become familiar with being available throughout the world. The process of globalization is not just a phenomenon of richer countries such as the UK, the USA and Japan; the process can be seen in poorer countries as well. These countries, like the UK before them, are undergoing a process of **nutrition transition**. In the majority world, despite many of the population being malnourished, the consumption of foods high in fats and sugars is increasing amongst those who can afford it. There is a corresponding decrease in the amount of cereals in the diet and a decrease in the amount of fruit and vegetables consumed. This **obesogenic** diet has caused an epidemic of obesity-related diseases worldwide. Although we consider obesity and all the health-related conditions that go with it to be a problem for the richer countries of the minority world, there are now more people dying of heart disease in poorer countries of the majority world. Within different countries there are great health inequalities, with the problem being more serious among the poor (Hawks, 2006). In addition, the obesogenic diet is associated with micronutrient deficiencies that lower immunity to infectious diseases, which has a much greater impact on the health of populations in poorer countries than wealthier ones.

Case study: Kolkata, a city in transition

Penny started visiting Kolkata (formerly known as Calcutta) in West Bengal, India, over 30 years ago. At that time, Kolkata, once the capital of British India, was a bustling, chaotic and noisy city. Being near the border with Bangladesh, Kolkata had absorbed wave after wave of refugees, as well as receiving many thousands of rural Indians from the hinterlands, all hoping to make a living in the city. There was dire poverty, with thousands who only had the pavement as their home, and millions living in slum areas. Even for the emerging middle classes, life was not easy, with food shortages and power cuts being a regular feature of life.

There were no supermarkets, fresh produce being purchased daily as few households had the luxury of a refrigerator. Most people ate only in their own homes, with a diet consisting mainly of rice, lentils and

(Continued)

(Continued)

vegetables. Those who could afford it would try to have fish most days, but meat was for special occasions; many families were vegetarian. Outside the home only the very wealthy could afford to eat in a restaurant, with office workers eating simple snacks prepared by wayside venders if they could afford it. Thirty years on, the situation has radically changed. Although there is still a distressingly high 70 per cent rate of malnutrition among the children of pavement and slum dwellers (Ray et al., 1999), amongst better-off families the rate of obesity is rising. In 2005 it was estimated that between 30 and 40 per cent of children in the 3 to 11 age group in Kolkata were obese (Majumdar, 2005). One contributing factor is a change in food habits. Hundreds of fast-food outlets have sprung up around the city, selling 'Western style' burgers and pizzas to an increasingly affluent middle class. Ice cream and fizzy drinks are available on every street corner and the shops are full of pre-prepared meals, crisps, biscuits and sugary drinks. Within the home, increasing affluence has meant that foods normally reserved for 'treats' are eaten more often and many more children can afford the tempting snacks that are sold in the street. As in the UK, advertisements on the television are targeted at children, to the extent that children are influencing the choice of foods purchased from the increasing number of supermarkets that have been built.

Recently, the more educated sector of the population is becoming aware of the health effects of the obesogenic lifestyle and individuals are choosing to eat healthily and to exercise. Concern is being expressed in the media about the numbers of adults suffering from diabetes and heart disease, but the message has yet to filter down to the majority of the population.

‣   What are the advantages and disadvantages of the opening up of Kolkata to global influences?

‣   In what way was a typical diet of 30 years ago healthier than now?

‣   What strategies could be employed to reduce the level of childhood obesity?

‣   What about the street children and the children of the slum dwellers; what initiatives could be taken to help them?

Health inequalities in Europe and the UK

There have been dramatic changes in the health of people living in Europe over the past 150 years. One measure of health is life expectancy. In 1851, life expectancy at birth in England and Wales was 40 years for males and 44 years for females (Newton, 2006). Now, babies born in England in 2004 can expect to live until they are 76 if they are male and 80 if they are female. There are a variety of reasons behind this dramatic improvement in health in the UK:

▸ The huge investment in public health started by the Victorians means that we now have clean water to drink, effective sewerage and rubbish disposal.

▸ Investment in housing, with inner-city slum areas being regenerated.

▸ Medical advances including prevention of disease by vaccination and the treatment of infectious diseases by antibiotics.

▸ The reduction of absolute poverty by the introduction of Social Security benefits for those in need.

▸ The advent of the National Health Service in 1948.

Health inequalities in the UK

However, although the general health of the nation was improving, some sectors of the population were doing less well than others. In 1980 the Conservative government asked Douglas Black to investigate the difference in health between social classes in Britain. The result of the investigation was disappointing. In the Foreword to the report (Black et al., 1980) Patrick Jenkin, the Secretary for State for Social Services, said:

> It will come as a disappointment to many that over long periods since the inception of the NHS there is generally little sign of health inequalities in Britain actually diminishing and in some cases, they may be increasing. It will be seen that the Group has reached the view that the causes of health inequalities are so deep rooted that only a major and wide-ranging programme of public expenditure is capable of altering the pattern.

The report noted that social class differences in health, as measured by mortality, started at birth. In 1971, deaths within the first month of life were twice as high for children born of fathers in the lowest social class than for children born of fathers in the highest social class. This differential remained throughout life, so that the death rate for adult males from the lowest social class was twice as high as those from the highest social class.

The Black report was published over a bank holiday weekend and it was widely thought that the Conservative government wanted to suppress the findings because of ideological and resource implications.

In 1997, the newly elected Labour government asked Sir Donald Acheson to update the report. His findings, based on statistics for England and Wales, were similar to those of Douglas Black and his team:

▸ Average mortality has fallen over the last 50 years.

▸ Health inequalities have remained the same or, for some sectors of society, have increased (Acheson, 1998).

Acheson found significant inequalities:

▸ across classes, with people in the lower socio-economic groups having poorer health than those in the highest groups

▸ between different racial, cultural and religious groups, with black and South Asian groups having more ill health than the white population, whereas people of Chinese origin appear to have better health than the white population

▸ between the sexes, with women having better health than men

▸ across the age range, with younger people having better health than the elderly.

Why do these inequalities persist, given the improvements in public health and medical interventions? Black et al. (1980) outline four possible explanations:

▸ *Artefact explanations*. Both 'health' and 'social class' are artificial categories constructed to reflect social organization and are so difficult to define that any 'measurment' is fraught with difficulties and may not represent an underlying 'truth'. The way that social class is categorized has changed over the years.

▸ *Natural and social selection*. This explanation derives from the idea that individuals are in the lowest social class because they have worse ill health than others. Those individuals who have good health will obtain education and occupations higher up the social classification. So one would expect the strongest and fittest individuals to be in the higher social classes. In other words, illness itself is a factor in confining an individual to the lower social class.

▸ *Poverty leads to ill health*, through nutrition, housing and environment. Thus, people in the lowest social class have fewer material resources, which has a direct effect on health.

▸ *Cultural and behavioural explanations*. In this explanation the people in the lowest social class are responsible for their own ill health because of poor health behaviours. The reason, for instance, that levels of obesity are highest in the lowest social class, is that they have not changed to a healthy diet.

A close examination of these explanations will show that none fully accounts for the health inequalities seen in society today.

As a result of the Acheson report the government made tackling health inequalities a priority and in 2002 a **cross-cutting review** was published outlining progress made. At that time it was confirmed that wide-ranging inequalities were still exerting a powerful influence on the nation's health (Hyder and Mukherji, 2004).

In July 2003 the government launched 'Tackling Health Inequalities, a Programme for Action'. The main aim of the programme is to reduce inequalities in health outcomes by 10 per cent as measured by infant mortality and life expectancy at birth by 2010. These aims were designated as **public service agreement** targets (PSAs). The Health Inequalities Unit was set up to oversee the cross-governmental programme. One of the aims is to support families, mothers and children. Key initiatives under this aim are the Sure Start initiative and the introduction of Child Tax Credit. This approach to tackling health inequalities is common across the whole of the UK, with similar initiatives being taken in Scotland, Northern Ireland and Wales.

Within each country in the UK, there is a commitment to regular monitoring of the progress of the various health initiatives. In October 2006 the *Health Profile of England* (DoH, 2006b) was published, which provided a picture of the health of people living in England in 2004. The findings showed that, although there was an overall improvement in determinants of health in some areas such as the reduction of smoking, improved housing stock and a reduction in child poverty, there were still areas of concern, such as levels of obesity and high levels of teenage pregnancy. Health inequalities were still pervasive and, although the gap between disadvantaged areas and the national average for cancer and circulatory disease had improved, the figures relating to the two targets had increased:

▸ Infant **mortality rates** had declined in lower socio-economic groups, but the rate of decline was faster in other groups, so the gap continued to widen.

▸ The relative gap in life expectancy between areas in England with the worst health deprivation and figures for England as a whole had widened (DoH, 2006a).

Health inequalities within European countries

Within individual European countries health inequalities, as described for the UK, exist. Bartley (2004) investigated the extent of health inequalities in several European countries. She explains how differences in the way that health and social stratification are measured between different countries makes comparisons difficult, but she concluded that, as in the UK, health inequalities were increasing in all the countries she investigated. In Nordic countries the rise in health difference between different social economic groups was less than in other European countries.

When the UK took over the European Union (EU) presidency in 2005, health inequalities across Europe became a key health theme and reports to look at health challenges facing Europe were commissioned. In one report, Mackenbach (2006) confirms that widespread health inequalities within the different countries of the EU continue to exist. In tandem with this report, a paper by Judd et al. (2006) explored the different approaches made by various EU countries to tackle the problem. The main conclusions are that, although attempts were being made to focus initiatives towards the most disadvantaged sections of communities, the underlying cause of health inequality, the social gradient, was not being tackled directly by any country.

Health inequalities and children's nutrition

In 1999, the British Medical Association (BMA) stressed that one of the most important factors in children's nutritional status is adequate income and it is now universally accepted that the nutritional status of children is one aspect of health that is directly linked to **indices of poverty and disadvantage**. Indeed the adverse effects of poor nutrition in childhood may be the main reason that we see health inequalities persist from one generation to another (Nelson, 2000). But how do poverty and disadvantage affect the nutritional status of children living in the UK?

▸ The 2005 Infant Feeding Survey continues to show, as it has done since it was first initiated, that the numbers of mothers breastfeeding their children is related to indices of disadvantage, such as social class and level of education (Information Centre for Health and Social Care, 2007).

▸ Children living in poverty often have diets that lack fruit and vegetables, and contain levels of fat and sugar that are too high. Graham and Power (2004) link this to negative effects on children's ability to learn, and a risk of infection and cardiovascular disease in adulthood. Poverty can also lead to children being overweight or underweight for their height. The National Children's Homes (NCH) undertook a study of 55 families on a low income and found that 28 per cent never ate green vegetables or salad and 10 per cent of children never ate fruit. The study concluded that it cost more to eat healthily than unhealthily (NCH, 2004).

▸ Children from impoverished families are more likely to have diets lacking in the nutrients required to maintain an effective immune system and are more prone to infections (Nelson, 2000).

▸ There are well documented links between poverty, disadvantage and dental disease. Young children living in the poorest, non-fluoridated communities were six times more likely to suffer from dental disease than children from more advantaged, fluoridated communities (National Alliance for Equity in Dental Health (NAEDH), 2000).

Reducing nutritional inequalities

There are three main approaches to reducing nutritional inequalities in children:

▸ measures aimed at reducing child poverty

▸ measures aimed at improving access and availability of healthy food in disadvantaged areas

▸ measures aimed at supporting individuals in making healthy choices.

Reducing child poverty

The government has made a commitment to reduce child poverty in the UK and has set itself the target of eradicating child poverty by 2020, with a reduction of a quarter by 2005. In March 2006, the Department of Work and Pensions published figures that indicated that the 2005 target had been narrowly missed, with a 23 per cent reduction; however, 5.8 million children are still defined as living in poverty (DWP, 2006). That we still have a long way to go in reducing child poverty has been recognized in the government document *Working for Children* (DWP, 2007), which outlines a variety of initiatives aimed at helping parents into work, with the expectation that this will increase income in vulnerable families.

Activity

Investigate the Child Poverty Action Group web site, www.cpag.org.uk/

What proportion of children that you care for could be classified as living in poverty? Do you think that it is part of your professional role to support organisations such as this?

Investigate the document *Working for Children*. Make a list of the initiatives set in place with the aim of reducing child poverty.

www.dwp.gov.uk/publications/dwp/2007/childpoverty/childpoverty.pdf

(Both web sites accessed 28 July 2007.)

Improving access and availability of healthy foods

One of the difficulties facing families in poverty is that sometimes it is difficult for them to access healthy foods. This inability to find healthy and affordable food is sometimes known as **Food poverty**. According to Tim Lang (Sustain, 2007) 'Food poverty is worse diet, worse access, worse health, higher percentage of income on food and less choice from a restricted range of foods. Above all food poverty is about less or almost no consumption of fruit & vegetables'.

There are a variety of factors that can lead to food poverty including:

▸ *lack of shops in the area*. Some areas of social housing are out of town and it is difficult for those on a low income to afford the cost of transport to shops or supermarkets

▸ *limited range of healthy food in local shops*. Some areas of the UK have been described as 'food deserts' where it is impossible to buy healthy food at affordable prices

▸ *lack of income* can lead to parents having to buy cheaper, less nutritious food

▸ *Fear of crime* can deter individuals from travelling to shops where healthy food is available.

Tackling food poverty requires co-ordinated action between central and local government working in conjunction with local community organizations, and includes initiatives such as:

▸ The UK Healthy Start Scheme, outlined in Chapter 1. This is designed to improve nutrition for pregnant women, mothers and young children by making healthy foods such as fruit and vegetables more easily available.

▸ The Sure Start initiative that was designed to give children in deprived areas the best start in life.

▸ The Free School Meal Scheme.

Chapter 8 looks in more detail at multidisciplinary approaches to improving children's diets.

Supporting individuals in making healthy choices

There is a persistent view that dietary health inequalities in lower socio-economic groups are perpetuated because of lack of knowledge about what constitutes a healthy diet, or a lack of will to implement this knowledge. This belief that individual attitudes and behaviours are amenable to change under-pins a variety of health promotion initiatives, some of which are investigated in Chapter 7. Thus, the onus for tackling dietary health inequalities is seen to rest with the individual, and where the health of children is concerned the focus is primarily on the parents. However, there is a wealth of evidence (Atree, 2006) that suggests that most mothers are well aware of what constitutes a healthy diet for their children, but are constrained by lack of money and all the other factors mentioned previously that contribute to food poverty. One woman summed up the dilemma of how to feed her family on a reduced budget as follows:

> We try to eat proper meals like meat and veg. and that but there just isn't the money to do it all the time. So we eat properly maybe once or twice a week depending on the money and the rest of the time we make do with things like sausages, pies, potatoes and things like beans. The meals aren't as good but they do the job, they'll fill them (children) up and stop them from being hungry. It's the best I can do. (Atree, 2006: 72)

It is unlikely that health promotion campaigns on their own will have much of an effect on the nutritional status of children from disadvantaged families unless there is a co-ordinated approach that aims to alleviate poverty and increase access to healthy food.

Reflection point 〰️

In Chapter 7 you will be looking at how to promote healthy eating in early years settings. How could you use the research findings on the effects of health promotion on lower-income groups to help plan your initiative?

Nutritional inequalities within families

So far, this chapter has looked primarily at the impact of social class and poverty on nutrition and people's health. We need to be careful, when thinking about inequality, that we do not assume that individuals *within* a family have the same access to a nutritious diet. Women, in particular, have a different experience of food and eating within families, on the whole, than men.

Fischler's (1988) work in relation to food and eating notes that within some families there are different entitlements to the types and quantities of food men and women eat. DeVault's (1997) work demonstrates that there is an expectation that men will receive 'man-sized' portions of food and 'decent food', often viewed as food that a woman has taken trouble to prepare. Fitchen's (1997) American study showed that, when feeding a family is difficult owing to poverty, some individuals within the family go underfed. Whilst she did not gather any quantitative data around this, her observations show that children often have a different experience of going hungry than adult males. An example might be through denial of some foods and smaller sized portions, with children with disabilities or who are vulnerable in other ways – such as being children from a previous marriage – being disproportionately affected. Women, in particular, take less of the meat and vegetables they give to the rest of their family and in very poor households, were found to live primarily on starchy foods such as pasta, tortillas and potatoes. This impacts negatively on their health in terms of obesity, poor dental health and, generally, a low nutritional status, factors noted by professionals who work with low-income women in the USA. If pregnant or breastfeeding their children, this might also have a negative impact on the health of the child.

Many people in Fitchen's (1997) study had experienced poverty and hunger as children and suffered food anxiety as adults. Fitchen suggests that this anxiety carries over to subsequent generations. In low-income families, her study found that food was the source of considerable tension, with many family arguments centred round the lack of food or having to make do with food of poorer quality. Ellis (1983) argues that domestic violence incidents, for instance, are often triggered by men complaining about how food is prepared and served in the home. This is not necessarily linked to income. Given that domestic violence often begins during pregnancy and impacts in a range of ways that adversely affect children's emotional health (Humphreys, 2001), we need to take very seriously the way power is exercised around food within families.

Reflection point

Reflect upon your own experience of meal-times. In your experience, do men have differing amounts of certain foods when compared with women? An example might be giving an adult male a greater quantity of meat or the best cut of meat when compared with women.

Summary □

▶ There are great inequalities in wealth across the world with the majority of the world's population living in poverty.

▶ Under-nutrition is both an effect and a cause of poverty.

▶ Increasing globalization has led to a change in dietary habits in both the minority and the majority world, resulting in a global rise in childhood obesity.

▶ Despite the eradication of absolute poverty in the UK and Europe there are still deep and pervasive inequalities in health across socio-economic groups.

▶ There has been a reduction in child poverty in the UK yet there are still profound differences in the nutritional status of children across socio-economic groups. These nutritional inequalities are, perhaps, the reason for persistent health inequalities across the age range.

▶ It is important to remember that inequalities exist within families. Access to food may be differently experienced by men, women and children.

Discussion points

▶ Do early years settings have a moral responsibility to consider global ethical issues such as the promotion of 'Fair Trade' and using locally sourced produce when planning for the children's nutrition?

▶ To what extent should your setting become involved in local community initiatives to increase food accessibility?

Further reading 📖

Atree, P. (2006) 'A critical analysis of UK public health policies in relation to diet and nutrition in low income families', *Maternal and Child Nutrition*, 2: 67–78.

Graham, H. (2007) *Unequal Lives: Health and Socio-Economic Inequalities*. Maidenhead: Open University Press.

Nelson, M. (2000) 'Childhood nutrition and poverty', *Proceedings of the Nutrition Society*, 59: 307–15.

Useful web sites

www.sochealth.co.uk/history/black.htm This web site gives the whole of the Black report with some interesting commentaries that give the historical context.

www.archive.official-documents.co.uk/document/doh/ih/ih.htm This site gives the whole of the Acheson report.

(Both accessed 28 July 2007.)

This chapter is taken from:
Albon, D. and Mukherji, P. (2008) *Food and Health in Early Childhood*
978-1-4129-4722-0

Nutrition, Health and Development

DEBORAH ALBON and PENNY MUKHERJI

In this chapter the fundamental role that nutrition plays in the health, growth and development of young children is explored. The chapter will investigate evidence that suggests that early nutritional experiences have long-term consequences for individuals throughout their lives. The links between a child's nutritional status and learning is emphasized. In order to understand the concepts investigated within this chapter, a brief introduction to nutrition is included, together with a discussion as to how growth and development can be monitored and assessed. The particular challenges of childhood obesity and food allergies will be investigated.

All of us involved in the professional care of children and young people have a responsibility to promote their health and well-being, as was emphasized in the government Green Paper *Every Child Matters* where one of the outcomes for children is: 'Being healthy, enjoying good physical and mental health and living a healthy lifestyle' (DfES, 2003: 6). This outcome was later enshrined in the 2004 Children Act.

This chapter takes a bio-medical look at food and introduces you to some of the key topics in the subject of dietetics, the study of the health-related aspects of nutrition. This is an **empirical** approach to the subject; other chapters will be looking at food and eating from a variety of different perspectives. Nutrition plays a vital role in children's health, growth and development. A sound knowledge of nutrition and the principles that underpin planning for children's nutritional needs is essential for early years practitioners because for many children in our care the nutrition they receive from us comprises the majority of their food intake. Good nutrition in the early years not only promotes healthy growth and development, but also prevents ill health in adulthood and contributes to effective learning and academic achievement.

The following key areas are explored in this chapter:

▸   An introduction to nutrients and food groups

▸   The role of nutrition in the holistic development of adults and children

▸   Food sensitivity

▸   Food additives

▸   Obesity.

An introduction to nutrients and food groups

Hardly a day goes by without an aspect of nutrition being given coverage in the media, be it on the television news or in the newspaper. Words such as 'calorie', 'saturated fat', 'protein' and 'vitamin' are all part of our everyday vocabulary. Although healthy eating is a common topic of conversation today, the science of nutrition is relatively new. From the Middle Ages, there was a recognition that one's diet played a role in one's health, but it was not until the seventeenth to eighteenth centuries that there began to be an understanding of the role of individual **nutrients** within the body. For example, it was Lind in 1747 who is credited with running one of the first ever clinical trials when he demonstrated that citrus fruits could mitigate against the effects of scurvy (Hackett, 2006). It was in the late nineteenth/early twentieth centuries that the concept of essential nutrients was developed and the identification of vitamins and minerals important for health was established.

In attempting to outline the essential components that are needed to keep us healthy, two main approaches have been used. One approach, the nutrient approach, aims to identify and quantify the nutrients we need for healthy growth and development and to suggest foods that contain these nutrients. The other approach places less emphasis on individual nutrients, but looks at the different types of foods we need to include in our diet to ensure a ready supply of important nutrients. This is the **food group** approach.

Activity

In a book such as this it is only possible to give the barest of outlines to these two approaches; fortunately there are very good resources to be found on the Internet.

The British Nutrition Foundation www.nutrition.org.uk/ has a good section on the important nutrients in our diet.

The BBC www.bbc.co.uk/health/healthy_living/nutrition has a good section on food groups.

The nutrient approach

The main nutrients needed for healthy growth and development are divided into two main groups. The **macronutrients** (fats, proteins and carbohydrates) are substances needed in significant quantities in our diets and supply energy. **Micronutrients** (vitamins and minerals) are substances that are only needed in minuscule quantities in our diet to keep us healthy. In addition water and fibre are also essential.

The British Nutrition Foundation (2004) gives the following information about nutrients.

Carbohydrate

Carbohydrate is a macronutrient, providing energy in our diet. There are two main types of carbohydrates: sugars and complex carbohydrates. Sugars that occur naturally, within the cells of foods, are known as intrinsic sugars. Foods containing intrinsic sugars include whole fruits and some vegetables. Extrinsic sugars are those that are not incorporated into the cell structure of foods. These include lactose or milk sugar and sugar found in fruit juice, honey and refined sugar used in cooking and in confectionery.

Complex carbohydrates are of two main types. The first is starch which is found in starchy vegetables, such as potatoes, and foods derived from cereals, such as bread and pasta. The second type of complex carbohydrate is fibre. Fibre is derived from plants (fruits, vegetables, nuts, grains, and so on) and is primarily formed from cellulose cell walls. Fibre is not digested in the small intestine of the body.

The carbohydrate that we consume is ultimately broken down into glucose which is used as energy/fuel by the body's tissues. One gram of carbohydrate will produce approximately 4 kcal of energy. Energy comes from a variety of foods that contain the macronutrients carbohydrate, fat and protein. Alcohol also supplies energy. Energy is stored in the body as fat, so if too much carbohydrate is consumed, it will be converted into fat and we will gain weight. Too little carbohydrate in the diet will mean that the body will use the fat and protein in the diet as fuel, together with the fat reserves.

Protein

Protein is needed for growth and repair in the body and also supplies energy (1 gram of protein will supply 4 kcal of energy). Protein is found in foods derived from animals, such as meat, milk, fish and eggs. It can also be found in foods from plants, such as cereals, pulses, nuts and seeds.

All our body tissues, organs and muscles contain protein which is made from building blocks called amino acids. When we eat foods containing protein, the amino acids are released and are used, in different combinations, to build the proteins that the body needs. The body can make some amino acids for itself, without having to have obtained them from the diet; however, there are a small number of amino acids that the body cannot synthesize. These amino acids are known as indispensable or essential amino acids. The British Nutrition Foundation (BNF) identifies the following as essential: leucine, isoleucine, valine, threonine, methionine, phenylalanine, tryptophan and lysine. For children, histidine is also considered to be an essential amino acid (BNF, 2004).

Foods that contain protein from animal sources are more likely to contain all the essential amino acids that the body needs than foods from plant sources. However, it is perfectly possible for vegetarians to eat only non-animal sources of protein and remain healthy. This is because by eating protein from two different plant sources at the same time, all the essential amino acids may be supplied. For example, eating a cereal such as rice, together with a pulse such as lentils will provide all the essential amino acids.

Fats

Although we only need a little fat in our diet, it is an important nutrient. It is a concentrated source of energy, 1 gram of fat giving approximately 9 kal. Fat is, therefore, a valuable source of energy for babies and infants who have small stomachs and need proportionally more energy-rich foods than older children and adults. Brain tissue comprises 60 per cent fat (Brooks et al., 2000), where the essential fatty acids linoleic acid and alpha linolenic acid are involved in nerve formation. Fat is also essential as a carrier for the fat soluble vitamins A, D, E and K.

There are several different types of fat:

▶ *Saturated fatty acids*, found in milk, meat, dairy products and eggs. Saturated fats are solid at room temperature and are known to raise the level of cholesterol in the blood.

▶ *Monounsaturated fatty acids*, fluid at room temperature, are found in meat, cereals, avocados, olive oil, sunflower oil and nuts. They are considered to be beneficial to health.

▶ *Polyunsaturated fatty acids*, also oils at room temperature, include omega 3 and omega 6. They are known to have a positive effect on cardiovascular health. Foods containing polyunsaturated fatty acids include grain products, fish and sea food (herring, salmon, mackerel and halibut), soybeans, fish oil and soft margarines.

▸ *Trans fatty acids*, are rarely found naturally in the food we eat. These fats are manufactured by adding hydrogen to oils, often in an effort to increase shelf life or raise the temperature at which the fat can be used for cooking. There is mounting evidence that trans fats are harmful and there are moves for manufacturers to disclose the presence of trans fats in their products.

The body can make all the fatty acids it needs except two, known as the essential fatty acids, linoleic acid and alpha linolenic acid. These two nutrients must be supplied by the diet and the best sources are oily fish and fish oil supplements. The meat or eggs of animals fed a diet high in fish oils will also contain significant amounts of the essential fatty acids.

The consumption of too much fat will lead to it being laid down as **adipose tissue**, ultimately leading to overweight and obesity.

Vitamins

These are micronutrients that are only needed in minute quantities in our diet to promote health and without which we will begin to show signs of illness. The knowledge of these complex substances is developing all the time and the number of vitamins identified is steadily increasing. Traditionally the vitamins have been divided into two: the fat soluble vitamins and the water soluble vitamins.

▸ Fat soluble vitamins include vitamins A, D, E and K.

▸ Water soluble vitamins include vitamins C, B1, B2, B6, B12, niacin and folate.

Activity

Look up the vitamins mentioned above. Devise a chart that gives information about the role of each vitamin in the body, the best food sources and the possible consequences of not getting enough of the particular vitamin in the diet.

If one eats a healthy well-balanced diet one should be able to get all the vitamins needed to maintain health without resorting to supplements. The exceptions to this are pregnant women, who are advised to take folate supplements, and infants, who are recommended to be given vitamin drops.

Minerals

Minerals are chemical elements required by the body in small amounts for a variety of functions. Minerals form the structural basis of the bones, are essential components of body fluids and are vital for the normal functioning of enzymes and nerves. The minerals required by the body can be divided into two groups: minerals needed in measurable amounts, and trace elements, needed only in minute quantities.

▶ Minerals needed in measurable amounts include calcium, magnesium, phosphorous, sodium, potassium and iron. Of these, only iron is likely to be deficient in children in the UK.

▶ Trace elements include zinc, iodine, fluoride, selenium, copper, chromium, manganese, molybdenum and boron. Of these, only fluoride is likely to be deficient in children in the UK.

Activity

Look up calcium, iron and fluoride on the Internet. Devise a chart that gives information about the role of each mineral in the body, the best food sources and the possible consequences of not getting enough of the particular mineral in the diet.

Dietary fibre

Dietary fibre, sometimes known as non-starch polysaccarides, is a complex substance, mainly consisting of plant cell walls. It can, therefore, be found in fruit, vegetables, pulses, grains, nuts, and so on. Fibre cannot be digested by the small intestine but it can be digested by micro organisms that live in the large intestine. Although much of the fibre we consume passes through the body undigested, it has a valuable role to play in our health.

▶ Fibre helps prevent constipation.

▶ Fibre helps lower blood cholesterol and glucose level.

A diet low in fibre has been implicated in the onset of bowel cancer and diverticulitis. Small children, however, should not be given too much fibre in their diet as their stomachs are small and they need concentrated forms of energy. Foods containing too much fibre fill them up without supplying the nutrients they need. Guidelines for children are discussed in the next chapter.

Water

Our bodies are made of between 60 and 70 per cent water, and regular fluid intake is vital for health. The various functions of water include:

▶ lubricating eyes and joints

▶ helping us swallow

▸ acting as a medium for biological processes and chemical reactions

▸ helping get rid of waste products

▸ forming the basis of body fluids such as blood and **lymph**

▸ helping regulate body temperature.

The amount of water we need varies according to the weather, the amount of physical activity we undertake, what we are eating and our age. Most of us probably do not drink enough water (or drinks containing water); feelings of thirst arise only after we have become dehydrated.

The food group approach

Although nutritionists are able to tell us exactly how much of each nutrient we need in our diets, this approach is not easy to apply in everyday life. When advising us on healthy eating the experts divide foods into groups that supply similar nutrients.

In the UK the government organization, the Food Standards Agency 2007 (www. food.gov.uk) recommends a set of dietary guidelines called 'The Eatwell Plate'. The guidelines divide foods into five main groups:

▸ bread, Rice, pasta and others starchy foods

▸ fruit and vegetables

▸ milk and dairy foods

▸ meat, fish, eggs, beans and other non-dairy sources of protein

▸ foods and drinks high in fat and/or sugar.

These guidelines are explained further in Chapter 3.

Activity

Using the information about nutrients in the preceding section, identify the main nutrients in each of the food groups outlined above. Then check your understanding by looking at the information on the Food Standards Agency web site. www.food.gov.uk/multimedia/pdfs/bghbooklet.pdf

The role of nutrition in the holistic development of adults and children

'Out of 100 children born today 30 will suffer from malnutrition' (UNICEF, 2006). At the time of writing there are crises in East Africa, especially Kenya, where over 8 million people are on the brink of starvation owing to severe drought, crop failure and loss of livestock. Of those affected, 1.6 million are children under the age of 5. In West Africa the United Nations Children's Fund is appealing for £16 million to reach children affected by the nutrition crisis in Burkina Faso, Mali, Mauritania and Niger. The nutrition crisis primarily affects children under the age of 2, who suffer from low birth weight, poor breastfeeding practices and inadequate access to basic services. In addition, a recent health survey showed that 48 per cent of children in Malawi show signs of malnutrition; 5 per cent of these are severely malnourished. In Darfur, Sudan, lack of food and water affects 1.4 million children under the age of 18 (from the UNICEF web site, www.unicef.org.uk).

In the **majority world**, many families struggle to find the resources to feed children adequately, and the most prevalent form of **malnutrition** is due to insufficient food being available. In the UK some children are also malnourished, but the cause is more likely to be the excessive consumption of food (for the child's energy requirements) or an unbalanced diet, lacking in essential nutrients.

Increasingly in the UK, we are becoming concerned about the adverse health effects of poor diet. In a study by Rayner and Scarborough (2005: 1054) it was estimated that 'food related ill health is responsible for about 10 percent of **morbidity** and **mortality** in the UK and costs the NHS about £6 billion annually'. They conclude that:

> The burden of food related ill health measured in terms of mortality and morbidity is similar to that attributable to smoking. The cost to the NHS is twice the amount attributable to car, train, and other accidents, and more than twice that attributable to smoking. The vast majority of the burden is attributable to unhealthy diets rather than to food borne diseases. (Ibid.)

The effect on health of lack of food has, of course, been understood from prehistoric times, but it took the development of nutrition as a science before a fuller understanding of the role that food plays in maintaining health was achieved. As was noted in the previous section, it was not until the early 1900s that vitamins were discovered. The consequences of poor nutrition were brought home to the UK government in 1917 when it was discovered that

41 per cent of men called up for military service were unfit, with poor nutrition being a huge factor (Chamberlain, 2004). The science of nutrition was further promoted at the time of the Second World War when food was rationed and the government needed advice on how best to keep the population healthy on limited food supplies (see Chapter 1).

Since the end of the Second World War there have been significant changes in the food we eat. From eating fresh food in season that had to be prepared at home, we now have a wide variety of foods available all year from around the world. There is a greater consumption of prepared food and an increase in the amount of fat and sugar in our diet. Affluence has given us the opportunity to indulge in 'fast food', and sugar-rich 'fizzy' drinks are now a regular part of our diet. This, together with a lack of exercise, has led to a rise in the number of adults and children who are overweight and obese.

Reflection point 〰️

How have your diet and lifestyle changed since you were a child? Those of you who are relatively young may not think that your diet has changed that much, but some of you may have seen great changes. If you can, ask someone who lived through the Second World War in the UK and experienced rationing. What are their memories? Some of you may have spent your early years in another country. In what ways have your diet changed?

There is much research evidence about the effect that a poor diet has on health. As well as the health risks associated with obesity, discussed later on in this chapter, there are other common health conditions that are related to poor diet. These include:

▶ *Oral diseases*. Under-nutrition is associated with an increase in gum disease and developmental defects of the enamel. Excess sugar in the diet is implicated in the formation of **dental caries** and the acid in soft drinks is implicated in the erosion of tooth enamel (Moynihan, 2005).

▶ *Iron deficiency anaemia*. This is a disease caused by a deficiency of iron in the diet, which is needed to form red blood cells. Iron is found in red meat, pulses and leafy green vegetables. Iron deficiency anaemia can make people feel tired, irritable and less able to concentrate. In children, it can affect behaviour, development and school achievement. Iron deficiency anaemia is probably the most common nutritional deficiency in the world – in the UK 3 per cent of boys and 8 per cent of girls aged 4–6 years, 1 per cent of boys and 4 per cent of girls aged 7–10 years, and

1 per cent of boys and 9 per cent of girls aged 15–18 years are anaemic (Ruston et al., 2004).

▸ *Vitamin D deficiency*. Vitamin D is a fat-soluble vitamin found primarily in dairy products and oily fish such as salmon, herring and cod liver oil. The action of sunlight on the skin is also a useful source of vitamin D. Children need vitamin D for the formation of healthy bones and teeth and children who are deficient in the vitamin are at risk of developing rickets. There has been a recent re-emergence of rickets amongst certain populations of children with darker skin, especially South Asian and African Caribbean children. Children with fair skin are likely to synthesize adequate levels of vitamin D through their skin, although in areas such as northern Scotland, where daylight hours are low in winter, fair-skinned children may also be at risk. For this reason the Chief Medical Officer for Health recommends that children under 5 years of age are given supplements of vitamin D (CMO, 2005).

Adequate levels of nutrition are also needed to optimize children's ability to learn. Research studies such as Glewwe et al. (2001) have demonstrated that better nourished children in the majority world perform better at school, partly due to children being well enough to start school at the usual age for school entry and partly due to improved health outcomes during their years at school, resulting in less 'lost' time.

The importance of children having an adequate breakfast before school is well documented. In a review of the literature, Papamandjaris (2000) concludes that eating an adequate breakfast before school has beneficial effects for children who are well nourished as well as those who are inadequately nourished. Previously well-nourished children who missed breakfast showed decreases in memory and problem-solving ability. Malnourished children who come to school hungry, show deficits in cognitive tests such as verbal fluency and arithmetic. In schools that operate a breakfast club, children are reported to concentrate better and academic performance is improved.

There have been many studies looking at the effects of **micronutrients** on children's behaviour and learning, with conclusions which give conflicting messages (Dani et al., 2005). Commercial interests have been quick to exploit parental insecurities about their children's diet and there are now a variety of products on the market designed to boost children's intelligence quotient (IQ) and school performance. The value of eating breakfast is even being used to promote the consumption of sugary breakfast cereals.

Dani et al. (2005: 258) have undertaken a literature review of available research in this area and conclude that nutrition has 'potent effects on brain function'. The authors consider that the consumption of breakfast, protein, iodine and iron all have an effect on children's behaviour and learning. In addition they conclude that, in certain behavioural disorders, such as **attention deficit hyperactivity disorder (ADHD)**, micronutrients such as essential fatty acids, minerals and vitamins have an important role. The authors caution that we need to await the results of large-scale trials before we reach conclusions as to the benefits of routinely using supplements for children. However, it is clear that early years practitioners have a responsibility to take the nutrition of the children they care for very seriously.

In July 2006 the Food Standards Agency published the result of a study conducted by Ellis et al., on the effects of diet on children's learning, education and school performance. The study, undertaken by the University of Teesside, looked at a variety of research projects which had published results on the effects of eating breakfast, short-term sugar intake on children with ADHD, fish oil supplements for children with symptoms of learning and behaviour disorder, and studies on vitamin and mineral supplementation. The researchers concluded that there are insufficient good quality research studies to come to any firm conclusions about the role of diet on children's learning for children in general. As in the Dani et al. (2005) review, it was recommended that there should be more studies in this area, using participants that are representative of the whole population, using universal, standardized measures and being of a longer duration. However, the research team did conclude that there was overwhelming evidence to suggest that physical activity, a diet low in fat and sugar, but high in fruits, vegetables and complex carbohydrates should be promoted for all children (Ellis et al., 2006).

Reflection point

If you are involved in an early years setting, examine the policies and procedures that set out the way your setting makes provision for children's food and eating. Do you think that provision reflects the prime importance of this area of care? What provision do you have for children who may not have had breakfast?

Food sensitivity

There is increasing concern about the numbers of children who demonstrate a degree of food sensitivity. Food sensitivity includes two different conditions, food allergy and food intolerance. Food allergy involves the immune system. If children eat something they are allergic to they may have a severe reaction which can be life-threatening. A food intolerance does not involve the immune system and generally symptoms are milder, but can still have adverse effects on a child's health and development (Food Standards Agency, 2006a; 2006b).

Food allergy

Most food allergy is acquired in the first two years of life, with 6 to 8 per cent of infants aged 1 year demonstrating a food allergy, falling until late childhood when a prevalence of 1 to 2 per cent is reported (Wood, 2003). The most commonly reported allergies are to milk, eggs, peanut butter, soy, wheat, shellfish and some fruits and vegetables. As can be seen from the prevalence rates, some of these allergies are relatively short-lived, although some persist throughout adulthood. Symptoms of allergy include coughing, dry, itchy mouth and tongue, itchy rash, nausea, vomiting, diarrhoea, wheezing, shortness of breath, swelling of the lips and throat, runny or blocked nose, sore, red itchy eyes, faintness and collapse (Food Standards Agency, 2006a).

In 2001 a 5-month-old baby died whilst in the care of a private day nursery. The child's parents had informed the nursery that the baby was allergic to cow's milk, but, whilst in nursery, the child was given a breakfast cereal containing a cow's milk product (BBC, 2003).

Case study

Fiona has chosen Morning Star day nursery to care for her 2-year-old toddler when she returns to work full time. She is naturally anxious about leaving Chloe, especially as Chloe has been diagnosed with having a severe nut allergy. Chloe's mother has been given an **EpiPen** to use if Chloe begins to have an allergic reaction. Fiona can still remember the tragic case of the baby who died of an allergic reaction at nursery.

What measures should the staff at the Morning Star nursery take to ensure Chloe's safety in their care and to reassure Fiona that she can confidently leave her daughter with them?

The 'Allergy in schools' web site gives helpful information to help you with your planning: www.allergyinschools.org.uk/

Food allergies appear to be on the rise. This may be because we are more aware of the problem than before and previous figures may reflect a degree of under-diagnosis. However, there are studies that have shown that there is an underlying change. In particular, there appears to be a real increase in the number of cases of peanut allergy (Sicherer et al., 2003). In the following chapter we will be looking at guidelines aimed at reducing the incidence of food allergy in children.

Food intolerance

Food intolerance does not involve the immune system and generally symptoms do not occur as rapidly as with a food allergy and are not life-threatening. The most common foods that children are intolerant to are milk, lactose (milk sugar), gluten, wheat, food preservatives, red wine, cheese, chocolate and caffeine. Symptoms of food intolerance include: diarrhoea, weight loss, bloating, anaemia, flushing and migraine. (Food Standards Agency, 2006b).

Some children are intolerant to the gluten in wheat (Coeliac disease). These children may have symptoms of nausea, wind, tiredness, constipation, reduced growth and skin problems (Food Standards Agency, 2006b). It has been found that avoiding gluten during the weaning process reduces the incidence of Coeliac disease. This is discussed in the next chapter.

Food additives

When we prepare food at home we generally plan to eat the food in the next couple of days. We can extend the life of some foods by freezing or preserving (by using sugar to turn fruit into jam, or by using vinegar to pickle vegetables). Preprepared food that is sold in supermarkets often has to be stored and transported, so manufacturers use a number of substances to maintain the quality of the food and keep it safe to eat. Without many of these additives food would start to 'go off' due to microbial action. Additives include preservatives, colours and flavours.

Activity

Investigate the following web site. It will give you an excellent understanding of what is meant by a food additive.

www.understandingfoodadditives.org/index.htm (accessed 6 September 2007)

There has been growing concern that some of these additives could affect the health and behaviour of children. Van Bever et al. (1986) found that various additives including tartrazine, sodium benzoate, sodium glutamate and sodium metabisulphite had an adverse effect on children's eczema and, as early as 1975, Feingold proposed that food additives may influence the rate of hyperactivity in children (Stevenson, 2006). Following public concern, the Food Standards Agency (FSA) commissioned research by Stevenson to investigate further the effect of additives on children. The results of the study suggested that consumption of certain mixtures of artificial food colours and sodium benzoate preservative are associated with increases in hyperactive behaviour in children (FSA, 2007a). The Food Standards Agency, whilst recognizing that hyperactive behaviour in children can be influenced by factors such as genetics, prematurity, the child's environment and upbringing, advise parents of children who show signs of hyperactivity, or attention deficit hyperactivity disorder, to eliminate the colours used in the Stevenson study from the children's diet. These colours are:

▸ sunset yellow (E110)

▸ quinoline yellow (E104)

▸ carmoisine (E122)

▸ allura red (E129).

It seems sensible, therefore, for practitioners in early years settings to avoid giving children food that contains these colours. By law, any additives in food must be clearly displayed on the label, so it is a straightforward task to monitor this. However, particular care may need to be taken if food is brought into the setting by outside caterers.

Obesity

Incidence of childhood obesity

As a nation, **obesity** rates both for adults and for children are steadily rising, with the proportion who were categorized as obese (**body mass index** [BMI] over 30) increasing from 13.2 per cent of men in 1993 to 23.6 per cent in 2004 and from 16.4 per cent of women in 1993 to 23.8 per cent in 2004 (DoH, 2005). Among boys aged 2–10, between 1995 and 2004, there was an increase in the proportion that were obese, from 10 per cent to 16 per cent. There was a different pattern for girls aged 2–10, with no statistically significant increase in the rate of obesity, which remained at 12 per cent in 2004 (DoH, 2006a). The Millennium Cohort study that has followed a group of children since their birth at the start of the new millennium has found that at 3 years of age 18 per cent of children are already overweight and that 5 per cent are obese (Elliott, 2007).

Although, in adults, it is relatively straightforward to calculate an individual's body mass index, it is less straightforward for children. The adult calculation of weight divided by height squared, is inaccurate because children are still growing. Therefore, to measure obesity in children, special calculations are used which take account of the child's sex and age. The Health Survey of England uses the UK National BMI percentile classification (Jotangia et al., 2006).

Causes of childhood obesity

Previously in the chapter we looked at the three main macronutrients in our diet: fat, sugar and protein. We learned that these three substances supply the energy we need to grow and keep active. It was noted that if our diet supplies more energy than we need for growth and daily activity, the energy is stored as fat deposits in the body. Thus, the cause of childhood obesity is self-evident; these children are consuming diets that contain more energy than they need. However, this explanation does not explain why there has been such a rise in levels of adult and child obesity. Why is it that children are consuming more energy than they need? There is no simple answer; any explanation has to take account of a wide variety of influences including genetic factors, environmental factors, lifestyle preferences and the cultural environment of children (Dehghan et al., 2005).

▶ *Medical/genetic factors*. There are a few conditions that can cause weight gain in children, such as leptin deficiency, hypothyroidism and the side effects of drugs such as steroids (Dehghan et al., 2005).

▶ *Diet*. In recent years, food has become more affordable in the minority world. The emphasis placed on food has shifted from one of survival, to food choices becoming lifestyle choices. Whereas, in previous generations, food was cooked at home from basic ingredients, there is a shift to eating meals out of the home and buying pre-prepared foods that are higher in fat and sugar. In addition, there has been an increase in the consumption of drinks, carbonated or otherwise, that are full of sugar. The evidence that children are consuming more calories per day than they used to remains elusive, with some studies indicating that children are consuming fewer calories than in previous years (Dehghan et al., 2005). There is evidence that, within this, the proportion of saturated fat has risen, with 94 per cent of UK children aged 7–10 consuming more than the recommended amounts of saturated fat (BMA Board of Science, 2005).

▶ *Exercise*. It has been suggested that physical activity levels of children have reduced. There are many factors at work: a rise in the amount of television viewing and the playing of computer games, children being taken to school by car, less time spent on physical activities in school and less opportunity for children to 'play out' after school. Research studies have confirmed that children who have low levels of physical activity are more at risk of becoming obese (Swinburn and Egger, 2002). Dehghan et al. (2005) report positive results for school-based interventions in the USA designed to promote higher activity levels in school children, both in taking more exercise, walking or cycling to school and reducing television viewing. These interventions had a positive effect on the reduction of obesity levels. However a British Medical Association (BMA Board of Science, 2005) review of the literature suggests that increasing the level of activity of children in school had little effect on the overall activity levels of children.

The effects of obesity

The BMA Board of Science (2005: 7) identifies a number of health risks associated with children being obese and inactive.

▸ *Metabolic syndrome.* This is a cluster of conditions such as high blood pressure, high blood sugar and high cholesterol together with abdominal obesity which increases the risk of **cardiovascular disease** and type 2 **diabetes.** Early childhood obesity can lead to the development of this syndrome in later childhood and adulthood.

▸ *Type 2 diabetes.* This used to be a disease only seen in adults, but it is increasingly being seen in children. Once someone is diabetic there is an increasing risk that they may suffer cardiovascular disease, kidney failure, visual impairment and poor circulation leading to limb amputation.

▸ *Coronary heart disease.* Several studies have shown a link between weight gain in childhood and an increase in cardiovascular risk as adults. This connection is especially high in obese adults who were obese children.

▸ *Psychological difficulties.* Obese children are at increased risk of discrimination; and adolescents, girls especially, are less likely to be accepted into university, are less likely to form permanent relationships and are less likely to be 'economically well off' (Viner and Cole, 2005).

Obesity in both adults and children adds a significant burden to the National Health Service (NHS). The House of Commons Public Accounts Committee (HCPAC) calculated that obesity already costs about £1 billion a year with further indirect costs to the economy of £2.3 billion to £2.6 billion (HCPAC, 2007).

Preventative strategies to combat the rise in childhood obesity are discussed in Chapters 7 and 8.

Summary

- Nutrition can be looked at in two ways:

  – the nutrient approach, which aims to quantify the nutrients we need for healthy growth and development
  – the food group approach, which aims to identify the different types of foods we need to supply the nutrients we need.

- Nutrients can be divided into macronutrients, that is, carbohydrates, proteins and fats, and micronutrients, that is, vitamins and minerals. Water and fibre are also needed for healthy growth and development.

- The five main food groups are: bread, cereals and potatoes; fuit and vegetables; milk and dairy products; meat, fish and vegetable alternatives; and foods containing fats and sugars.

- A diet deficient in nutrients can lead to ill health. Conditions related to a poor diet include, under-nutrition, obesity, oral disease, iron deficiency anaemia and vitamin D deficiency. Inadequate nutrition can have negative effects on learning and possibly on behaviour.

- Some children may have a food allergy or food intolerance that may cause illness.

- Obesity in children is rising; children are consuming more energy than they need. Causes may include medical or genetic conditions, a change to foods higher in fat and sugar than in previous generations, and a reduction in the amount of exercise taken.

- Obesity can lead to metabolic syndrome, type 2 diabetes, coronary heart disease and psychological difficulties.

Discussion points

- At the moment there is no conclusive evidence about the effectiveness of nutritional supplements on children's learning. Should we routinely give supplements to well-nourished children just to be on the safe side?

- Obesity in children is rising, and preventative measures have to be taken to protect children from becoming overweight. Should the blame be laid at the feet of parents?

Further reading 📖

Dani, J., Burrill, C. and Demmig-Adams, B.(2005) 'The remarkable role of nutrition on learning and behaviour', *Nutrition and Food Science*, 35(4): 258–63.

James, W. (2006) 'The challenge of childhood obesity', *International Journal of Paediatric Obesity*, 1: 7–10. www.iotf.org/documents/IOTFIJPOpapers.pdf (accessed 25 July 2007).

Useful web sites 🖱

The British Nutrition Foundation www.nutrition.org.uk/ has a good section on the important nutrients in our diet (accessed 25 July 2007).

The Department of Health has a good section on obesity with links to childhood obesity:

www.dh.gov.uk/PolicyAndGuidance/HealthAndSocialCareTopics/Obesity/fs/en (accessed 25 July 2007).

The Food Standards web site has relevant sections on the effects of food on children's health, behaviour and learning, including good resources on allergies and food intolerances: www.food.gov.uk/ (accessed 25 July 2007).

This chapter is taken from:
Albon, D. and Mukherji, P. (2008) *Food and Health in Early Childhood*
978-1-4129-4722-0

Promoting Health: It all depends on what we mean by 'health'

GLENN LAVERACK

Health promotion is about improving people's lives and health. But what do we mean by 'health'? There are many different ways to define health, each of them leading to different health promotion strategies. How we define and interpret health largely determines how we approach health promotion. This chapter discusses three main discourses of health and of health promotion and argues that a socio-environmental model of health is most consistent with health promotion's concern with empowerment. I also provide a simple framework of health determinants, and discuss its implication for an empowering health promotion practice.

Our experiences of health

When you ask people to talk about what is health in the abstract, they often reply 'Oh, not being sick, having no disease, keeping fit, not smoking, eating right'. These are the dominant discourses (defined in Chapter 1), or language-woven ways, of thinking about health. Health is portrayed in our culture as an aspect of physical breakdown or invasion (a medical problem) or the result of not heeding the proper lifestyle advice (a behavioural problem). But if you ask people to talk about the last time they felt healthy, when you personalize the question, quite different dimensions arise. They are more likely to talk about a sense of purpose in their lives, some control over their fate, doing enjoyable activities, feeling energetic and vital and, most of all, being loved, enjoying good relationships with friends, being connected to a 'community'.

Labonte (1993) asked participants of several workshops to 'Think of the last time you experienced yourself as "healthy", and jot down a few phrases that describe the feeling, and the context.' Few of the respondents were concerned with disease or ill health and instead identified feelings of 'energy', 'love', 'control', 'happy relationships', 'wholeness' and 'playfulness'. Box 2.1 collects a number of these phrases. Noticeably absent from this list is any reference to disease, and minimal attention is given to physical evaluations such as fitness levels.

Box 2.1 Experiences of health

energized
being loved, loving
being in control
fitting in, doing

(Continued)

relaxed, stress-free
giving/receiving, sharing
outdoors, nature
friends, belonging, meaning in life
able to do things I enjoy
peak physical shape
happiness, wholeness
spiritual contentment

(Labonte, 1993)

Health, the positive expression of our wellbeing, resides in the quality of sharing and caring in our relationships. The word 'health' derives from an old English word, hael, which brings us two other contemporary terms: whole and hello. The folk wisdom of our language posits health as intrinsically holistic. Our health systems may fragment hospitals into departments of particular body parts, or try to differentiate between diseases that are somatic (physical) and those which are psychological (mental). Our public systems may divide into services about health, education, environment or welfare. Our political and economic systems more generally may attempt to separate what is 'public' (government) from what is 'private' (market). But we do not experience our lives as discrete, disconnected events. Whether with friends, or physicians, we usually try to context whatever we experience physically with how we are feeling mentally, with self-judgements about our own behaviours and with some understanding of the role played by our broader living and working conditions.

The different definitions of health and their relation to health promotion practice is discussed in detail elsewhere (Downie et al., 1996; Dines and Cribb, 1993; Ewles and Simnett, 1999; Adams et al., 2002). Here I focus on the relevance of these definitions to the aspects of power and empowerment, the two central themes of this book.

Health, health promotion and social capital

In a fundamental way, our health is a reflection of the quality of our relationships with one another. Social support and network density reflect the language of social psychologists. Community psychologists might refer to the same phenomenon as 'community capacity', 'community competence' or 'community empowerment'. Political economists have recently coined the term 'social capital' to capture this caring and sharing dimension of our communal living. Putnam et al. (1993) have written widely and were early commentators on social capital and define it as the features of social organization such as networks, trust, facilitated coordination and collaboration. These are elements that are important to the process of community empowerment, discussed later in Chapter 4, by linking individuals to the groups and organizations that allow collective (community) action. Active participation within these social networks builds the trust and cohesiveness between individuals that are important to mobilize and create the resources necessary to support collective action.

Lee Adams, Mary Amos and James Munro (2002), three British health promoters, discuss the role of social capital in improving and sustaining health in three ways:

- by emphasizing the importance of social approaches to health promotion;
- by suggesting that social capital can act as a buffer against the worst effects of deprivation; and
- by focusing attention on the importance of social relationships and networks to community-based health efforts, for example through community empowerment, to reduce inequalities in health.

The notion of social capital suggests that inequalities in health are in part influenced by power imbalances in society and the ability of communities to empower themselves in redressing a lack of equity. By building community empowerment we can also build social capital. The risk is that the idea of building social capital may divert our attention away from the causes of inequality onto its effects, thus obscuring our analysis. Adams et al. (2002) also caution that our expectations of social capital in health promotion practice should be modest as many of the assumptions underpinning this concept, including its sustainability in a community context, need to be further examined. However, this does not invalidate the importance of community empowerment as an approach in health promotion practice.

The World Health Organisation's definition of health

The subjective or lay meanings people give to health does not imply that the term loses all precision in meaning. Cross-cultural studies indicate that people's experiences of health, such as those in Box 2.1, can usefully be organized under the following six broad categories:

1 Feeling vital, full of energy.
2 Having a sense of purpose in life.
3 Experiencing a connectedness to 'community'.
4 Being able to do things one enjoys.
5 Having good social relationships.
6 Experiencing a sense of control over one's life and one's living conditions.

(Blaxter, 1990; Labonte, 1993; 1998)

These six categories make sense of the World Health Organisation's classic definition of health as 'a state of complete physical, mental and social wellbeing, and not merely the absence of disease or infirmity.' Physical wellbeing is concerned with concepts such as the well functioning of the body, biological normality, physical fitness and capacity to perform tasks. Social wellbeing includes interpersonal relationships as well as wider social issues such as marital satisfaction, employability and community involvement. The role of relations, the family and status at work are important to a person's social wellbeing. Mental wellbeing involves concepts such as self-efficacy, subjective wellbeing, social competence and psychological hardiness.

Terri Jackson, Sally Mitchell and Maria Wright (1989), three Australian commentators on community development, recount the story of how and by whom the WHO definition was written. It was written soon after the Second World War by a WHO official who had spent the War working in the Resistance. He had come to this definition from this experience and explained that he had never felt healthier than during that terrible period: for he daily worked for goals about which he cared passionately; he was certain that should he be killed in his dangerous work his family would be cared for by the network of Resistance workers. It was under these circumstances that he felt most healthy, most alive. The definition of health was originally developed by a person who was passionately involved with others to change social and political structures. In other words, they are involved in taking control over those things which affect their lives and by doing so empower themselves and improve their own health and wellbeing as well as that of others with whom they associate. Rootman and Raeburn (1994) provide a later account in which the definition seems to have arisen originally as a medical solution to the ills of the world, as seen immediately post-War, the irony being that the definition is now so often seen as liberating health from the thrall of the medical model and definition.

Whatever its origins, the WHO conceptualization of health as an ideal state of physical, social and mental wellbeing that enables people to fulfil their health has been thoroughly cross-examined and criticized for not taking other dimensions of health into account, namely the emotional, spiritual and societal aspects of health. The definition has also been criticized for viewing health as a state or product rather than as a dynamic relationship, a capacity, a potential or a process. But mostly the definition has been criticized for specifying an idealistic state that is impossible to attain (Aggleton, 1991).

People are not concerned if their health is perfect but instead are concerned with the trade-offs they have to make in order to gain their optimum health. Cohen and Henderson (1991: 3) cite examples of people who are diseased or ill and yet still perceive themselves as being healthy and willing to bear the discomfort and pain of an illness because it does not outweigh the inconvenience, loss of control or financial cost of having the condition treated. These individuals undertake a cost-benefit analysis in regard to achieving optimum health 'where the cost of any further improvement outweighs the value attached to that improvement'. At an individual level, these are the 'positive' health outcomes to which health promotion programmes can contribute and have varying degrees of importance to people at different times in their lives. They are the 'trade-offs' people make in deciding what they need, or want to do, to experience being healthy.

Contemporary health approaches in health promotion

There are at least five established approaches to health promotion that are discussed in the literature: the medical approach; the behavioural approach; the educational approach; the client centred approach; and the socio-environmental approach. These are discussed elsewhere (Ewles and Simnett, 1999; Downie et al., 1996) and here I focus on three of the main contemporary approaches in health promotion – the medical, the behavioural and the socio-environmental – as being especially relevant to shaping the way in which we design, implement and evaluate programmes. For example, the medical approach views health as an absence of disease or disease-producing physiological conditions. The behavioural approach views health in terms of the behaviour and lifestyle of individuals, and the socio-environmental approach views health as being influenced by social and environmental conditions. These differing views largely determine the strategies programme planners select, and the outcomes or criteria they use to evaluate success. The development of these approaches in recent decades has resulted not only from the changes in our scientific understanding of health determinants artd risk factors, but also from a growing pressure from individuals, groups and social movements concerned with the health impacts of social and environmental conditions.

The medical approach

Despite the evolution of competing health approaches, it is the medical approach that remains dominant, socially and within health bureaucracies. This approach evolved as a result of scientific discoveries and technological advances in the eighteenth and nineteenth centuries and a greater understanding of the structure and functioning of the human body. As knowledge and understanding increased, the body became viewed as a machine that needed to be fixed. A professional split between the body and mind developed; the body and its physical illness was the responsibility of physicians, while psychologists and psychiatrists looked after the condition of the psyche. The focus remained on the external causes of ill health and was reinforced by the constant threat of disease and death, particularly to children, from epidemics such as polio and scarlet fever. The medical profession established itself in the dominant position, and many other health professions modelled themselves on the medical approach to gain legitimacy. These include the fields of nursing, physiotherapy and, until recently, health promotion (Baum, 1990).

The medical approach is primarily concerned with the absence of disease and the treatment of illness. More recently it has become concerned with disease prevention amongst high-risk individuals, those persons whose genetic pre-disposition, behaviour or family and personal history place them at statistically greater risk of disease. The medical approach historically has assumed that elite 'experts' know best. Disease prevention programmes in the medical approach are usually delivered in a top-down approach based upon the experts' knowledge. However, a growing body of new knowledge and pressure from social movements challenged the dominance of the medical approach. By the 1970s this had led to a broadening of health knowledge to include a variety of behavioural, lifestyle and social factors.

The behavioural/lifestyle approach

Lifestyle and behaviours became increasingly central to health promotion in the 1970s. During this period, health promoters (though many still called themselves health educators) recognized that individuals' behaviours and lifestyle could directly influence their own health and the health of others. Examples of programmes from this era include school education, public education and social marketing campaigns around smoking, alcohol abuse, eating high-fat foods, not wearing a seat belt and physical inactivity. The predominant approach to address these issues was education and awareness campaigns to inform individuals about their high-risk behaviours.

Given the complex social and cultural circumstances associated with lifestyle, it is not surprising that many practitioners and researchers found that health education campaigns alone did not succeed very much in changing behaviour.

The lifestyle approach does not necessarily view behaviour as an isolated action under the autonomous control of the individual, but recognizes how it is influenced and conditioned by a complex interplay of social, political and cultural factors. Much of the health promotion work under the lifestyle approach, however, continues to be on individuals rather than on their context. Meredith Minkler (1989) argues that this is because many health promoters are embedded in both western and uniquely American value systems, which place strong emphasis on the responsibility of the individual and the importance of autonomy and personal achievement.

The socio-environmental approach

The lifestyle approach argued for a more comprehensive view to health promotion than simply health education about specific diseases (the medical approach). It presented health promoters with a complex interplay of social and cultural factors that only the most ambitious, long term and complicated of programmes could hope to achieve (Green and Kreuter, 1991). At the same time, there was a growing professional frustration with health education and lifestyle approaches in health promotion because of the tendency to 'victim-blame' individuals by assuming that they were individually responsible for their own actions. The lifestyle approach failed to recognize the structural issues in which personal behaviours are embedded and which also indirectly but powerfully influence health, such as poverty. Inherent in the design of many of these programmes is a power-struggle between professional and client and between communities and health promotion organizations over who identifies or 'names' the health issue(s) to be addressed.

The critiques of the behavioural approach gained momentum during the late 1970s and early 1980s, stemming in part from the feminist, environmentalist and other social movements of this period. These social movements challenged the notion of the medical and behavioural approaches to health by raising concerns for social justice and environmental sustainability. The critiques argued that health, particularly of marginalized groups, was primarily influenced by structural issues such as poverty, housing, over-population and lack of community control. A new, emancipatory discourse on health promotion began to form, one more concerned with social justice and ecological sustainability than with individual behaviour change (see Box 2.2 for a brief discussion of two different, and important, ways of thinking about social justice).

Box 2.2   Health promotion and social justice: equality of opportunity or equality of outcome?

One of the major criticisms of the health promotion discourse as espoused by the Ottawa Charter is that it does not adequately address issues of social justice (Stevenson and Burke, 1991; Labonte, 1993; Canadian Public Health Association, 1996). Social justice has two different meanings. One is 'equality of opportunities', in which socio-political systems seek to maximize people's equal access to public resources and market opportunities, allowing them to experience satisfaction in their lives. The other meaning stresses 'equality of outcomes', in which socio-political systems seek to minimize serious and preventable inequalities between people. This requires a much more 'activist' state concerned with the equitable, or fair, distribution and re-distribution of resources. Don Nutbeam (1997: 14) defines equity in health as meaning '... that people's needs guide the distribution of opportunities for wellbeing'. This implies that people with greater needs, often because of poverty, discrimination or other forms of social exclusion, require and deserve greater opportunities. This is particularly so in developing countries, which often lack the resources taken for granted in richer countries. To move closer to equality in outcomes, including health outcomes, societies need to allow inequalities in opportunity that favour historically disadvantaged groups. For health promoters, this means taking care that those who benefit from their programmes or resources are not disproportionately the better-off. Instead, health promoters need to continue to give priority to groups whose poorer health is determined in large measure by their historically unequal opportunities.

Table 2.1   Three different health explanatory systems

	Medical	Behavioural	Socio-environmental
Health defined as:	biomedical, absence of disease, disability.	medical, plus functional ability, personal wellness, healthy lifestyles.	medical and behavioural, plus quality of life, social relationships.
Health: explained by:	pathology, physiological risk factors.	medical, plus behavioural risk factors.	medical and behavioural plus psychosocial risk factors and socio-environmental risk conditions.
Target for intervention:	high risk individuals.	high risk groups.	high risk conditions.
Sample success criteria:	decreased morbidity age standardized mortality, prevalence of physiological risk factors;	improved individual lifestyles (behaviour change);	improved social relationships and networks;
	improved individual QALYs.	adoption of healthier lifestyles earlier in 'lifecycle';	improved quality of life;
		decreased population physiological and behavioural risk factors.	movement towards social equity (more equal distribution of wealth/power);
			movement towards environmental sustainability.

Source: Labonte, 1993: 33–5.

The overlap between health promotion approaches

Table 2.1 below provides a summary of the different explanatory systems of the three health approaches. While each of these functions exists as a particular health discourse, shaping how practitioners go about their work, their distinctions often can and should blur. They are more like a Russian doll, one inside the other, than wholly separate ways of thinking. The medical approach, the most precise in definition, occupies the smallest doll. The behavioural approach incorporates the medical approach within a slightly larger doll that includes 'space' for individual behaviours and the social norms that shape them. The socio-environmental approach incorporates both the behavioural and the medical in the largest doll, whose new 'space' is cluttered with all of the social, economic and political structures that shape not only individual lifestyles but also people's risks of disease or opportunities for wellbeing.

Sharon, the nurse educator in Box 1.1, is quite right to be focused on people's ability to recover from a life-threatening, painful and often disabling medical event. But even she recognizes that the quality of social interaction amongst her group members is as important as the compliance lessons she is trying to teach them. She already stretches herself a little into the lifestyle approach by looking at their smoking or nutrition choices. But she needs to think further and deeper: what if the people she discharges return home to a house with inadequate insulation or plumbing? Or are members of a family with insufficient means to afford nutritious food? Or has an unemployed and depressed spouse been unable to offer any healing support? Unless these socio-environmental issues become part of how Sharon thinks and plans her work, chances are her patients will simply continue to return to her care with the same illnesses.

To a lesser extent the same applies to Bob in Box 1.1. He's already trying to create supportive environments to help make healthy choices (such as good food and exercise) the easy choices. But what if some of the diabetic women he's trying to help lack any child support or child care? What if a major fear for new migrants is walking in the evening to go to their local recreation centre because they might be attacked or threatened by people with racist attitudes? These are socio-environmental risk conditions that affect their personal choices, even when they know what to do, and want to do it.

As for Jill, her concern with the 'big health issues', such as equity in housing, risks leaving behind some of the very disadvantaged individuals she wants to help. Not every marginalized person wants to become an activist/advocate. Some are even quite concerned about their diets and their smoking, and wouldn't mind non-patronizing help in becoming personally healthier. People who are individually healthier are also better equipped, both physically and psychically, to take on the challenge of social activism.

The necessity to practice thinking through all three approaches at the same time becomes more obvious when we consider an analytical framework that illustrates how social inequalities become health inequities.

What determines health? An analytical framework of health determinants

David Seedhouse (1997), a former health promoter now health philosopher, has accused health promotion of being a 'magpie' profession. Like the bird's confusion of black and white splotches, health promotion lacks consistency in how it defines what it does, explains why it does it and how it accounts for its accomplishments. Seedhouse's point is that there often is inconsistency in how health promoters, and other public health practitioners, approach their work.

Part of this inconsistency derives from confusion over what health promotion seeks to promote: disease prevention, or positive health? But even if a useful model of positive health begins to supplant the 'death by disease' default model of most health systems, there are still two other questions that need answering. First, how are the more individualized experiences of positive health affected by social and environmental conditions? That is, what are the public health implications of positive health? Second, how do practitioners explain the important 'determinants' of health, those individual and social phenomena that comprise its territory of interest?

Several frameworks and models of health determinants now exist (for example, Evans and Stoddart, 1990; Dahlgren and Whitehead, 1992; Labonte, 1998; Starfield, 2001). The one offered in Figure 2.1 was originally developed for the federal Canadian Heart Health Initiative (Labonte, 1992) and the Toronto Health Department (Toronto Department of Public Health,

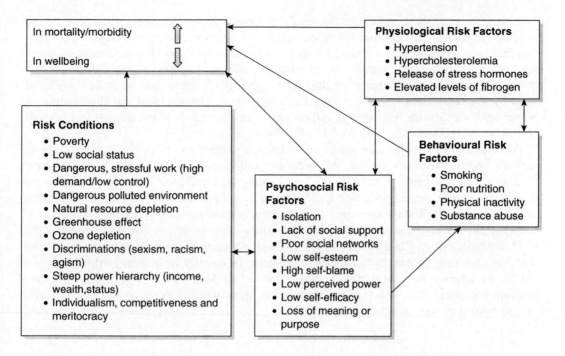

Figure 2.1   An analytical framework for the determinants of health
Source: Labonte 1993; 1998.

I991a) and has subsequently been adopted by the WHO. It is helpful to both the students and practitioners of health promotion and addresses 'risk conditions', surplus powerlessness and learned helplessness, issues that are relevant to one of the core subjects of this book: power.

In summary, the argument this framework advances is that people living in risk conditions independently have more disease and premature death and less wellbeing. Risk conditions describe living and working conditions that are 'deeply structured' by economic and political practices, and by dominant ideologies or discourses. People often internalize the unfairness of their social circumstances as aspects of their own 'badness', thereby increasing their psychosocial risk factors, which are also associated with poorer health outcomes. All of this increases health-threatening physiological risk factors.

The analytical framework describes outcomes as wellbeing or positive health, and as mortality/morbidity. People who experience the risk conditions and risk factors described below are also less likely to report themselves as feeling healthy, or being happy, precisely because they lack the sense of control or capacity and the respectful social relationships that constitute people's experiences of wellbeing.

Risk conditions

The existence of risk conditions, or living and working conditions that, in Giddens's (1984) terms, are 'conditioned and constrained' by economic and political practices, increases disease risk and reduces wellbeing. Some of these conditions are universal and thus (more or less) equitable; for example, everyone suffers with ozone depletion. But most of these conditions are unequally distributed by virtue of being conditions of comparative inequality. One cannot have low status without someone else having high status. One cannot be poor without someone else being wealthy. The higher one's social status (one's power and wealth), the higher one's health status. The more steeply hierarchical this distribution of power and wealth, the greater the difference in health status between top and bottom (Evans et al., 1994; Smith, 1996; Wilkinson, 1996).

There is a huge literature on the effects of risk conditions such as poverty, social hierarchies and inequalities on health, both for individuals and for whole populations (Wilkinson, 1986; 1996). Deaths due to specific diseases and their individual risk factors change over time. Several decades ago, the poor died more frequently than the rich from infectious disease. Today, they die more frequently than the rich from heart disease, or from certain forms of cancer. Similarly, lower social class groups in different countries die from different causes (Smith et al., 1990). In England, they die more frequently from lung diseases and lung cancer. In France, they die more frequently from liver cirrhosis.

I do not attempt to review this literature, but use the framework in Figure 2.1 to demonstrate the effect that 'risk factors' have on health promotion practice and in particular on the role of power and empowerment.

Psychosocial risk factors

The pathways between oppression and unhappiness may be fairly obvious, but the links to disease are harder to identify. Research findings focus more on individuals than on populations, or what Figure 2.1 refers to as 'psychosocial risk factors'. This term describes individual cognitive or emotional states (such as self-esteem or self-blame) that are often reactions to risk conditions, and which also influence our desire and ability to create social networks and support systems. Health can be seen to be determined both by material conditions and relations (risk conditions), and by the meanings one makes of these psychosocial risk factors. Notably, how one comes to understand one's position in human hierarchies (Wilkinson, 1996) and the stress created by economic insecurity (lack of predictability over future employment/income). Occupational stress research finds that those workers with least predictability or control over their work suffer the greatest stress and its associated risks of heart disease. Lower status civil servants suffer disproportionate stress and disease consequent to the employment uncertainty introduced by such business practices as contracting out and down-sizing (Baum, 1990). The process by which structural inequality becomes physical pathology, then, might be described as follows: people living in risk conditions experience distress with the unfairness of their situation (their low status on some hierarchy of power or authority, indicated in part by wealth) and internalize this unfairness as aspects of their own 'badness' or 'failure'. This internalization adds to their distress, if not also to their loss of meaning and purpose, with measurable effects on their bodies such as hypertension and hypercholesterolemia, or what this model calls 'physiological risk factors'. This situation is more likely when the dominant social discourse on success is competitiveness, individualism and meritocracy; where people are presumed to succeed or fail purely on the basis of their own initiative or ability (Lerner, 1986).

This internalization of 'badness' leads to what philosophers describe as false consciousness, 'failing to utilize the power that one has and failing to acquire powers that one can acquire'

(Morriss, 1987 p. 94), what psychologists call 'learned helplessness' (Seligman and Maier, 1967; Seligman, 1975), what political scientists label 'surplus powerlessness' (Lerner, 1986). More cynical commentators sometimes term this as the 'apathy of the poor'. Learned helplessness is a psychological construct that emerged from Martin Seligman's animal research in the 1960s (Seligman and Maier, 1967). Dogs were subjected to inescapable electric shocks. When the barrier preventing their escape from these shocks was removed, the dogs continued to withstand them anyway and did not seek escape. Even if they accidentally avoided the shocks, they did not internalize this learning and continued to endure subsequent shocks. They had resigned themselves to their fate; they had 'learned helplessness'. The dogs, however, did 're-learn' how to escape after repeated 'teachings' by the researchers, in which the dogs were pushed, pulled or prodded away from the area being shocked. Martin Seligman has now coined another term, 'learned optimism', to encompass the dynamic of learning how to develop positive self-images (Seligman, 1990).

Michael Lerner (1986), a political scientist and psychotherapist, argues that a similar phenomenon occurs with persons living in risk conditions. He named this process 'surplus powerlessness', a surplus created by, but distinct from, external or objective conditions of powerlessness. An example of surplus powerlessness is provided in Box 2.3. Individuals internalize their objective or external powerlessness and create a potent psychological barrier to empowering action. They 'do not even engage in activities that meet their real needs. They begin to accept aspects of their world that are self-destructive to their-own health and wellbeing, thinking that these are unalterable features of what they take to be "reality"' (Lerner, 1986). Part of this internalizing process is isolation, removing oneself from active group participation because of low self-esteem and high self-blame. Research affirms this process: poorer people internalize self-blame for their poverty, their self-esteem plummets and they isolate themselves from friends and colleagues (Auslander, 1988; Berkman, 1986; Cohen and Syme, 1985).

Box 2.3   Surplus powerlessness and women living in inner-city housing

Several years ago in a large inner-city housing estate, a community organizing project had formed around food, gardens, housing and welfare. Many of the women involved in this estate complained of having low self-esteem. A principal reason for this was the fact that, by being on welfare, they had ceased being autonomous, self-empowered individuals and had become a form of public property. They had internalized their 'lesser eligibility', a key concept in welfare policy that people on social assistance were only eligible for income that was less than the lowest wage available in the job market. They had become lesser persons. Not only did the women have low self-esteem; they knew they had it, and they pinpointed one of the reasons for it: media stereotypes about welfare recipients. These stereotypes came in two forms: on Saturdays came the story of the super welfare heroine who transforms welfare into a business and, by buying day-old bread and second-hand but functional clothing, manages to virtually 'turn a profit'. On Wednesdays were the 'macaroni and cheese stories' about how horrible it was to barely subsist on welfare. Just as society-at-large externalizes these stereotypes, many of the women had

(Continued)

internalized them. The result was 'surplus powerlessness', a further dis-empowerment. With the first stereotype, they couldn't measure up to the welfare heroine and so experienced themselves as personal failures. With the second stereotype, their reality was consistently portrayed as bleak and uncompromising. A key strategy in their empowerment was to reclaim, and project publicly, positive images of their own lives and experiences. A key role of the health promoter in this project was helping the women to gain the resources, knowledge and access to networks that they needed to accomplish this task. (Labonte, 1998)

There is increasing evidence that factors contributing to chronic anxiety worsen health, especially in the context of grossly unequal societies. For example, the rapid growth of income inequality in the UK from the 1970s to the 1990s and the growth of social exclusion are directly implicated in causing and sustaining health inequalities. Narrowing the gap in equalities means taking action to address social exclusion using strategies that use a range of social, economic and environmental interventions and the empowerment of individuals and communities (Putnam et al., 1993; Kawachi et al., 1997; Macleod et al., 1999).

Michael Lerner (1986) believed that specific group education could overcome self-blame while improving health status and health behaviours. His research involved blue collar workers experiencing occupational stress. Compared to control groups, persons in the experimental occupational 'stress groups' demonstrated statistically significant improvements in such areas as social support, health behaviours, absenteeism and perceived power. The key construct, self-blame, decreased significantly as social support behaviours among stress group participants improved. That 'stress groups' took place under union sponsorship may have been an important factor. Many stressors are embedded in the structure of work, and actions to remedy this problem requires an organized, political effort. Unions, through their collective bargaining, afford individual workers an opportunity to take collective actions on the 'structural' elements of work such as risk conditions, while the stress groups improved social support and coping behaviours. This raises the importance of creating effective political organizations to influence public and private policies that create the risk conditions in the first place.

Behavioural risk factors

People who live in risk conditions, and internalize this as psychosocial risk factors, are also more likely to have unhealthier lifestyles or behavioural risk factors, for example, smoking and consumption of high-fat foods which can serve as stress-coping 'rewards'. Indeed, Meredith Blaxter's UK research (1990) found that if people living in poor conditions did manage to change their health behaviours, but there was no change in their risk conditions, their self-reported health actually worsened! This shouldn't be taken to mean that we must end all forms of oppression before we can focus on the lifestyles of the oppressed. But it calls into question yet again the importance of how we conceptualize the relationship between individual behaviours and social conditions, and where we apportion the focus of our work as health promoters.

Finally, because people caught in this web of risk conditions and risk factors experience less social support and greater isolation, they are often less likely to be active in community groups or processes concerned with improving risk conditions in the first place (Auslander, 1988; Minkler, 1985). This 'feedback loop' reinforces isolation and self-blame, reinforcing the experience of disease or dis-ease. It is also one of the very reasons why an empowerment approach to health promotion has become both more popular and important in recent years. Such an approach, targeting people at greatest social disadvantage, seeks to engage these very people who, on their own, are the least likely to self-organize.

Implications to an empowering health promotion practice

Labonte (1998) identifies four important health promotion practice implications of the risk factors of health determinants, identified in Figure 2.1. First, at the level of national and international public policy, the question for health promotion is only partly one of how much wealth a nation creates. A nation needs sufficient national income or national resources to prevent physically compromising poverty. But once this is achieved, the more basic health promotion concern is how equitably that wealth and the decision-making power it provides is shared within the nation.

Second, working to overcome the learned helplessness or surplus power-lessness of less objectively powerful persons becomes important work, and in three senses:

- it is immediately healthful for the psychosocial wellbeing it creates;
- it is an essential first step in mobilizing community actions in support of those international and national policies that will create more economic and political fairness; and
- it may improve health behaviours over the longer term.

Third, there would be little disagreement among many health promoters that risk conditions are important, but there may be considerable disagreement over how they explain unequal health outcomes. While many health practitioners accept risk conditions as health determinants in their own right, others view them more as 'holding categories', statistically associated with increased rates of smoking, poor diet and indolence. These practitioners become interested in poverty, not for its own sake, but because poor people smoke more. As two researchers put it: that smoking rates are higher in lower-class persons should cause us to ask what is it about social class that causes smoking? (Evans and Stoddart, 1990). However, the really important question to ask, as far as health determinants are concerned, is 'What is it about political and economic practices that causes class?' For a focus on social class as holding categories for health behaviours fails to consider the enormity of health inequalities arising from poverty or social inequality, independent of health behaviour.

Fourth, accepting a social and environmental determinants agenda for health promotion does not mean that practitioners or the health sector have sole responsibility for action. Health professionals may begin their work with an individual or group around a physiological, behavioural or psychosocial risk factor, or around a risk condition. Health promoters must strip the pathways of health determinants back to their 'risk conditions' otherwise they will forever be treating the symptoms and never preventing the cause. The socio-environmental task is to locate these disease and behavioural risks in their psychosocial and socio-environmental contexts (for example, powerlessness, poverty and isolation), to recognize these contexts as independent health risks in their own right, and to recognize the importance of acting around all of the risk conditions. The key to addressing inequalities in health is in reducing the gap between rich and poor and in transforming unequal power relationships which are indicative of our society and working practices. Long term this requires political action on the causes of poverty such as unemployment through policies that influence, for example, welfare services, housing, transport and community health services. Whilst health promoters cannot be expected to change these long term goals by themselves, they do have a crucial role to play in the redistribution of power, the control over decisions and resources that influence people's lives and health. Short term, health promoters can reorientate their professional practice to enable individuals and communities to have greater influence over actions that can bring about social and political change. This is the process of community empowerment and is central to health promotion practice.

This chapter has outlined a simple interpretation of positive health and its implications for health promotion, described three different health promotion approaches, and explained a simple framework of risk conditions for health determinants, and what this means for an 'empowering' health promotion practice. To accept the challenges presented by the political health activist Rudolf Virchow, discussed in Chapter 1, these issues must be connected to how we as practitioners recognize and use power, and is the topic of Chapter 3. Then in Chapter 4 I take the discussion of power further to include the means to attaining power, empowerment, and situate these concepts within the context of health promotion practice.

This chapter is taken from:
Laverack, G. (2004) *Health Promotion Practice*
978-0-7619-4180-4

Overview of Current Research

LYNN PLIMLEY and MAGGIE BOWEN

This chapter will look at some tried and tested approaches, strategies and interventions that have targeted social behaviours, the development of social skills and social understanding.

Over the last 10–15 years, new strategies and approaches have been developed, predominantly for use at school or at home. Quite often the approach will address one area of the triad of impairments – language and communication, for example, is well served by the Picture Exchange Communication System (Bondy and Frost, 1994). Few approaches seem to target the social differences manifest in ASD. Efforts of parents/carers/ practitioners may be on modelling and teaching particular social conventions – hand-shaking, having a ready universal greeting, teaching good manners. However, if the individual with ASD does not understand social situations, or cannot differentiate when to say 'Hello, you look lovely today' (fine for Mum but not for the unknown woman in town) then learnt sayings and rote responses may just highlight individual differences.

Rogers (2000) has called the differences around social interaction as 'perhaps the most defining feature of autism'. The development and improvement of social skills has a correlation with a positive long-term adjustment (Ozonoff and Miller, 1995). Wimpory et al. (2000) highlight the social interaction and communication difficulties of children with ASD who are under 2 years old often have the absence of prerequisites to interaction of pointing, showing, attracting attention. Early difficulties in establishing a means of communication will have an impact upon the development of social behaviours and widen the gap between children with ASD and their peers.

Social stories

Social stories (Gray, 1994, & 2000; **www.thegraycenter.org**) can help the individual with ASD learn how to handle certain situations. The strategy helps to explain the social situation and tries to give both the perspective of other 'players' and their expectations of the individual. The target situation or response is woven into a story with the individual with ASD at the centre and is told either in first or third person. With the individual central in the story, the load on comprehension is lightened because the story is explicit. Gray suggests that certain types of sentences should be used in the story:

- Descriptive: To define what happens – 'where', 'why' and 'what' statements. Occasionally use the word 'sometimes' to give flexibility.
- Directive: To state the desired response in a given situation and phrased in positive terms. Better to use terms like 'will try' rather than 'will do'.
- Perspective: To describe the behaviours, e.g. feelings, reactions, responses of others involved in the situation.

Ideally the story should include between two and five descriptive and perspective statements for every directive statement, so that it does not become a list of dos and don'ts.

Social stories involve interaction with and reinforcement by others. Usage must be consistent, so that if an inappropriate behaviour does occur, the story can be used to cue appropriate behaviour. Involve older individuals and more able children in the writing process. A joint decision can be made to target something that is causing problems and where it is most likely to occur. It may be necessary to involve other people in order to give consistency of usage or approach. Chalk (2003) highlights how social stories have been used well in an adult care setting.

Extra information may be given by illustrating the story with drawings and photographs. The story needs to be used regularly and monitored carefully to gauge whether it has brought about a change in understanding or behaviour.

Example

Shutting the door in the toilet

When I go to the toilet at home I keep the door open

My family knows that it is me

When I go to the toilet in a public place, like McDonald's, I keep the door open

This means that other people can see what I am doing

Other people like to be private when they use the toilet, so they shut the door

They do not want anybody to see what they are doing

Going to the toilet is a private thing to do

I will try to shut the door every time I use the toilet.

Social sentences

Social sentences can be used to help those with ASD to make sense of situations. Short information bites, reminders or prompts are delivered quickly and effectively.

Example

Sometimes people don't answer when you talk to them

Possible reasons:

Maybe they…

did not hear you

weren't paying attention

were busy

Decision/outcome:

I can forget about it, maybe they will answer later.

Social skills groups

Nita Jackson (2002) discusses the valuable social skills group she attended, set up by Essex Social Services with seven young people with Asperger syndrome and four teachers. Nita describes the teachers as friendly and open-minded, who encouraged the group to express themselves. Some social groups, like Nita's, are highly structured and follow a specific issue, e.g. personal space, interrupting, bullying and avoiding danger. Other groups are discussed in Chapter 5. Some schools are now establishing after-school clubs and Saturday clubs for pupils with ASD. When organising leisure activities, a risk assessment may be needed.

CASE STUDY

Social group

A local voluntary sector organisation created opportunities for young adults with Asperger syndrome to develop their social skills. Five individuals had been identified who wanted to improve their skills. The typical profile was of socially interested individuals who became anxious in social situations.

1. Regular social activities were established: group activities with one or two support staff, in natural local settings, such as pubs, restaurants, cinemas, etc.
2. Activities were selected by group members to reflect their own interests.
3. Targets were not set; enjoyment and a relaxed atmosphere were important. Basic ground rules covered behaviour and support for one other; to encourage consideration of the way they inter-acted. As the group became established and members devel-oped confidence, they were encouraged to take responsibility for arranging their activity.
4. As different members preferred different types of activities, and were encouraged to try out new things from time to time, there were opportunities for practice in real situations.
5. Informal feedback was offered during each activity. Group mem-bers were encouraged to support and praise one another. The group was encouraged to reflect on both their individual and shared achievements in occasional meetings. Any incidental outcomes were explicitly stated. For instance, a man with an interest in cinema became confident enough to join a local film group – an outcome of his experiences.

Circle of friends

A circle of friends (CoF) is a social support mechanism that helps the person with ASD to feel less isolated at break times and lunch times, and during group or team work tasks. CoF has the purpose of assisting young people to adapt to settings (Whitaker et al., 1998). A circle usually consists of six to eight volunteers who meet on a regular basis with the 'focus person' and an adult/practitioner. The circle has three main functions:

- offering encouragement and recognising success
- identifying difficulties, setting targets and devising strategies for achieving targets
- helping to put these ideas into practice.

In setting up a CoF in school, it will be necessary to gain support and agreement from the 'focus person' and parents; meet with the whole class to recruit volunteers; gain agreement from the parents of the volunteers; and organise weekly meetings. When an adult is the focus, practitioners need to ensure that their wishes and feelings are respected and that parents/carers are consulted. Permission may not be needed if the focus person agrees and is over the age of majority.

An individual with ASD may choose to make their own CoF with 'like-minded' others. Research by Frederickson, Warren and Turner (2005) found that any changes were in the attitudes of the peers of the target child, rather than any change in the target child's behaviours. While this may make the peers more accepting of the child, the long-term benefits of an attitude change could be negligible. They believe that running concurrent programmes to focus on social behaviours and problem-solving may improve social acceptance and inclusion.

Social Use of Language Programme (SULP)

SULP (Rinaldi, 1993) aims to increase functional language by focusing on pragmatics, which deal with the meaning of words. Learning about pragmatics helps people with ASD to:

- understand the meaning in conversation
- use features of interaction such as facial and non-verbal communication

- develop conversational structures
- examine the wider influence of communication – social situations, back-grounds, attitudes.

The SULP programme makes use of strong visual and graphic stimuli, and deals with age-appropriate issues and everyday situations. It provides opportunities to practise new skills and concepts via motivating activities or tasks. Versions of SULP cover skills for the very young – eye contact, awareness of personal space – through to story packs for teenagers and adults, dealing with examples of appropriate social skills like paying attention to your listener when they are speaking. The programme is often something that speech and language therapists (SALTs) have been trained in.

Behavioural programmes

Work by Davis et al. (1994), Belchic and Harris (1994), Koegel et al. (1992) and LaLonde and Chandler (1995) has used behavioural methods to teach interactional and conversational skills. Davis et al. used a series of rapid requests of child-favoured activities followed by a request to interact. They reported an increase in unprompted initiations and extended interactions which were transferred to other settings.

Belchic and Harris worked with children aged between 4 and 5 and taught them how to initiate and maintain social interaction with their peers, resulting in more time in interactions. Koegel et al. used a reinforcement strategy to encourage interactions but once the reinforcement was removed, the interactions decreased. Many people with ASD do not find social interaction worthwhile for its own value. LaLonde and Chandler used a five-point framework to teach conversational skills with criteria for mastery of each skill area. Increases were in the amount of time spent in interactions and the amount of spoken language for some.

The use of behavioural techniques and their efficacy has been the subject of long and intense debate (see critiques of the Lovaas approach). Their limitations lie in the motivation of the person with ASD in skills that do not come easily. Where extrinsic reinforcement is used (often food), progress can be rapid but maintenance can fail once the reinforcement is removed. Social skills which require discernment and interpretation, and are socially governed often cannot be taught in a universal, rote fashion because every taught response needs a judgement on when and whether to use it.

Using adult-assisted learning

These approaches use significant adults in the lives of people with ASD, such as parents and carers, as opposed to professionals. Work by Dawson and Galpert (1990) trained parents in specific interaction approaches with their young child, and reported an increase in social initiations and tolerance. Krantz and McClannahan (1993) used play scripts to teach play skills and found that as the scripting content diminished, the unscripted initiations increased. Older children had similar results (Stevenson et al., 2000).

Using peer child training

Children with ASD may make and receive fewer social interactions, and make fewer responses in a shorter length of time than their peers, but work by Potter and Whittaker (2001) shows that we often do not pay attention to the times and different ways in which they try to initiate. For example, inappropriate or unwanted behaviours (see Chapter 4) are often a means of communicating something that urgently needs to be brought to our attention. CoF (Whitaker et al., 1998) is one way of using peer child training in social interactions, and work by Mundschenk and Sasso (1995) and Lord and Hopkins (1986) used similar peer priming approaches to CoF. One of the advantages of using peers to train the child with ASD is that they are 'on the spot' and have consistent and continuous access to the child. Laushey and Heflin (2000) used a peer buddy system to increase social interactions with young pre-school children.

Strain and Danko (1995) suggest that the gains apparent in using peer child training could be generalised to the home environment, with parents/carers teaching siblings and relations how to interact effectively with the child.

Social play record

The social play record (White, 2006) is a tool that helps practitioners to assess and develop social play. A comprehensive data collection builds up a holistic social picture of the child and their current skills in a variety of contexts. It gives a range of ideas and opportunities by using worked examples of how to understand the individual and take their present skills forward, by assessing the situation, alongside suggested interventions. The use of self-assessment sheets helps the child to have a voice in outlining their own social preferences, instead of a prescriptive, practitioner-led interaction.

Social skills groups for children and adolescents with Asperger syndrome

The book by Kiker Painter (2006) includes practical sessions to enable the young person with Asperger syndrome to work through social skill essentials, such as understanding tone of voice, the range of emotions, phone conversational skills. The aims and rationale for each taught session are given as well as the equipment needed. Notes for the parents as well as the teacher are included, aiming to make generalisation of skills learnt in each session straightforward.

Computer-assisted learning (CAL)

There has been considerable interest in the area of computer programs using emotion recognition or virtual situations. Some have focused on the development of social skills (Silver and Oakes, 2001; Beardon, Parsons and Neale, 2001) and others have looked at developing areas such as problem-solving (Bernard-Opitz, Sriram and Nakhoda-Sapuan, 2001). This work has capitalised on the common aptitude that people with ASD have for information technology. CAL may remove unpredictability and the need for social interpretation with peers. Smith (2003) reports that CAL research has demonstrated skill-gains in:

- reading and communication skills
- vocabulary acquisition
- fundamental learning.

Baron-Cohen (2003) has also produced a computer-based programme to help people with ASD to study emotion and learn how to interpret facial expressions and vocal tone.

There is a number of websites organised by and for people with Asperger syndrome which offer peer support through Internet chat rooms, and the value of peer support can be immense for this potentially isolated group (Sainsbury, 2000).

Video-assisted learning

Most homes and schools now own a video and/or digital camera to capture instant and spontaneous images. Lewis (1999) had a permanently mounted video camera in her classroom to record events during the day. Using video footage, streamed through computer or played back on a recorder, helped one boy with ASD analyse his interactions with others and make a hypothesis on how and why others reacted as they did. Charlop and Milstein (1989) used a recording of simple and appropriate conversational exchanges with three children as a way of teaching models of acceptable interactions. Using footage from TV 'soaps' with individuals with ASD can help to analyse social events and accompanying behaviours, modes of speech, etc. There is some support for use of these techniques as they focus on visual learning, which many with ASD are said to favour (see Plimley and Bowen, 2006a, for further discussion).

Points to remember

- A number of strategies has been developed to help individuals with ASD with social communication and interaction.
- It is useful to consider strategies such as social stories, social sentences, social skills groups, circle of friends and the Social Use of Language Programme.
- Social Play Record is a tool used by practitioners to assess and develop social play.
- Other strategies that help may involve adults, peers, computers or videos.

This chapter is taken from:
Plimley, L. and Bowen, M. (2007) *Social Skills and Autistic Spectrum Disorders*
978-0-4129-2313-2

Definitions of Special Needs and Relevant Legislation

KATE WALL

Introduction

The term 'special needs' is frequently used in a generic manner and has become indicative of a separate and discrete area of education and wider society, yet we are currently undergoing societal changes that promote inclusion in all aspects of our lives. It could be suggested that all people have needs and that these needs will vary as their lives develop and change, some having severely traumatising effects demanding very specific short- and/or long-term support, but at other times causing less impact. At times we all require very specific, individual support and provision but this does not necessarily imply that we are different, or have special needs, more that we are human. We should therefore strive to provide effectively for the individual needs of *all* children at *all* times, enabling each child to achieve his/her full potential. Provision should ensure that each child is offered a range of appropriate, challenging experiences to support development at his/her own pace and ensure success. High-quality early years provision would then respond to the needs of all children, whether or not they have identified special needs.

This chapter discusses definitions of special needs and special educational needs, clarifying commonalities and differences. The changes within early years and special needs are also chronicled to clarify understanding and to place later discussions in perspective. The knowledge of where we have come from should help to make sense of how best we can provide for children's individual needs and where we may be heading in the future.

Current provision in the UK

Within the UK there is a well-documented diverse range of early years provision that has undergone periods of growth and expansion, mostly on a needs-led basis (for example, Abbott and Langston, 2005; Baldock et al. 2005; Maynard and Thomas, 2004; Oberhuemer and Ulich, 1997; Pugh, 2001). This chapter identifies significant developments during the twentieth century and to date, reflecting on research, government initiatives and legislation. Combined with an examination of the range of provision available to today's youngest children and their families, this leads to the clarification of definitions for the purposes of this book.

Development of nursery provision in the UK

Late 1800s–early 1900s

At the beginning of the twentieth century there was no statutory pre-school provision in the UK, although in Europe the importance and value of pre-school provision had been identified and early years settings were encouraged. As far back as 1869, the French government supported the development of crèches and continued to support further expansion and development. Van der Eyken commented on early European developments, concluding that:

> What we see throughout the nineteenth century in Europe therefore, is a ferment of ideas, of quick development and of official recognition for the world of the young child, and by 1908 it was possible to say that half the children between two and five in Belgium, a quarter of those in France and between 2 and 10 per cent in Germany were regularly attending institutions of some kind. (Van der Eyken, 1967: 60)

In the UK at this time there was no such perceived need for early years provision. Few women worked, with most remaining at home to fulfil their duties as wives and mothers. However, some 3- and 4-year-old children were placed in elementary classes alongside their older peers, remaining seated for the majority of the school day and following inappropriate curricula set for older children. Learning, sometimes in classes of 60 children, was by rote and severe punishments were administered for misdemeanours. Today, at the beginning of the twenty-first century, we would express grave concern at this scenario and the resulting effects of inappropriate curricula and early formalisation on very young children, yet these very issues are still debated. Discussions regarding the age of school entry in the UK compared with other European countries are frequently highlighted in the media, as are discussions about the formalisation of early learning.

In 1908 the Education Act gave local education authorities (LEAs) the power to offer free nursery education in nursery classes housed within elementary schools. This followed the 1905 Board of Education's report highlighting the inappropriateness of these elementary classes for under 5s. However, without legislation to enforce such provision this did not secure nursery education for all 3- to 5-year-olds, simply those living near to schools which offered the service. By allowing, rather than compelling, LEAs to provide nursery education, the government of the day missed an opportunity to create a coherent and comprehensive nursery education service for all children. Subsequent governments have followed a similar pattern, although the current government, at the beginning of the twenty-first century, is working towards a free nursery place for every 3- and 4-year-old whose parents desire it.

Some early pioneers

In the early 1900s, and even in previous centuries, despite the lack of government support there were early years pioneers who recognised, very clearly, the value of early years education. There was an increasing need to provide for the growing population of children requiring daycare, owing to a continuing increase of the female workforce, but also for children with special needs. These special needs could be the effects of poverty and war, major factors of the time, resulting in 'over-crowding, malnutrition, poor hygiene, disease and the ravages of poverty' (Van der Eyken, 1967: 65).

Robert Owen (1771–1858) was one of the earliest and most influential early years pioneers. A cotton-mill manager in New Lanark, Scotland, Owen reduced the working hours of young children in his mill and set up a school for the children of mill workers. Owen, according to David (1990: 18), 'believed that environmental factors, particularly during the earliest years of life, shaped the future citizen, and what he worked for was the education of an engaged future citizenry, not a subjugated and underachieving one'. Although we may question Owen's motives, his school encouraged children to explore play activities within a philosophy similar to Froebel. Friedrich Froebel, a German educator, was responsible for opening Germany's first kindergarten in the mid-1800s. He acknowledged the importance of play for young children and advocated kindergartens that encouraged exploratory play using appropriate resources to stimulate and extend children's knowledge. This philosophy still exists today but is, in the eyes of some, compromised by the introduction of the Foundation Stage, which they view as too formal and structured for 3- and 4-year-old children in the UK. The issue surrounding the importance of play in the early years remains as contentious today as ever.

Sisters Rachel and Margaret McMillan devoted their lives to the plight of young, poor children. Margaret's main interests lay in children's education while Rachel's energies were related to children's health, perhaps an early example of health and education working together. In 1906 the sisters were instrumental in the introduction of the school meals system and in 1913 opened their first nursery school in Deptford with its own outdoor play space, which prospered rapidly. Owing to the poor general state of the nation's children at the time, the McMillan sisters were providing for many children with special needs and at the same time campaigned for nursery education for all, as Bradburn summarised:

> She (Margaret) realized that poverty, ignorance and disease were not only harming an adult population but mortgaging the growth of the next generation also.
>
> She yearned to change the system which created the conditions she abhorred. At the same time she realized that sick children could not wait for political reform. She fought to cure the dirt and disease that she saw everyday in the mothers and children around her, and kept up the fight for political reform as well. (Bradburn, 1976: 45–6)

The McMillan sisters continued throughout their lives to work for a nationwide nursery education system for all children.

Maria Montessori, founder of the Montessori Education system, first published her work 'the Montessori Method' in 1912, based on observations of her own young children and placing the child at the heart of their own learning process. Within a Montessori classroom the adult is a guide to the child, supporting the child's exploration and discovery but not intervening or imposing. A range of Montessori materials (didactic teaching materials) enable the child to explore, develop skills and self-check. These central materials are part of a broader range of stimulating experiences offered to the child. Beaver et al. (2000) summarise the method:

> The child is at the centre of the Montessori method. She (Montessori) believed that children learn best through their own spontaneous activity and that they have a natural inquisitiveness and eagerness to learn. The role of the adult is to provide a planned environment that will allow the child the opportunity to develop skills and concepts. (Beaver et al., 2000: 81)

Early–mid-1900s

In 1907, and again in 1916, a case for separate and discrete early years provision was raised, as was the suggestion that children should not be compelled to commence formal education at the age of 5, but without positive results. It was, however, the beginning of an understanding that a different form of education was required for our youngest children.

In 1918 the Maternal and Child Welfare Act separated daycare and education, placing responsibility for daycare provision within the remit of the Department of Health (DoH), with education remaining under the Board of Education. At the same time, the 1918 Education Act gave local authorities the power to support nursery education for children aged 2 to 5 years, but specifically to promote healthy physical and mental development.

By the late 1920s the UK government appeared to view nursery education from a more positive perspective with an education enquiry committee report in 1929 recognising the different needs of under 5s and identifying a need for separate nursery education.

Grace Owen (1928: 15), the honorary secretary to the Nursery Schools Association, concluded at the time that: 'It cannot be long before nursery schools for children between two and five years of age are the accepted instrument for securing adequate nurture for very young children.' This is an ideal yet to be achieved in the twenty-first century.

1940s

Until the start of the Second World War there was little change in the range of provision available. Benefits to children, short and long term, were still not well researched and children's developmental needs and the importance of appropriate early years provision not recognised by all. Robson (1989: 4) highlighted: 'The developmental needs of the child seemed secondary to political, economic and social factors and the pamphlet (Nursery Schools and Nursery Classes 1936) described the under-fives "problem" as being due to modern housing conditions, the growth of traffic and all kinds of pressing social, industrial and financial considerations'.

In 1943, the Board of Education White Paper again highlighted a need for nursery provision, concluding that nursery schools were needed nationwide to offer appropriate educational experiences to the very young. The 1944 Education Act that followed continued to support the notion of nursery education, stating that: '(the 1944 Education Act) placed the duty to provide nursery education in the hands of LEAs' (David, 1990: 21). Sadly the country then experienced economic difficulties and the hoped for expansion of nursery provision was severely compromised before it had started.

During the Second World War the government supported pre-school provision by way of grants, predominantly to release women to war-related workplaces as the majority of the male workforce was fighting for their country. In addition, the women needed to supplement the poor wages sent home by their husbands. Once the grants were removed after the war, many of the nurseries closed, thus returning the nation to a diversity of pre-school provision and most parents to a lack of useful provision, dependent on where they lived and their financial status.

1950s–1970s

After the end of the Second World War, growth in pre-school provision continued in an ad hoc manner but availability varied geographically. Throughout the 1950s and 1960s, when the population was fast overtaking available housing, the sheer lack of available space for housing development resulted in the building of many high-rise flats. This produced additional concerns for young children and families as the basic design of such accommodation limited socialisation for adults and children alike, and left many families isolated from friends, family and their local community. Over the years many of these tower blocks became run-down, and high-rise estates were often known (and in some cases still are known) for their problems of vandalism, crime, drug and alcohol abuse, anti social behaviour and social deprivation. Young children housed in such tower blocks were often 'prisoners' in their own homes as parents experienced tremendous difficulties in simple tasks such as taking small children down to ground level to meet with friends and playmates. As many parents chose to have their children within two or three years of each other, even the most basic trip to the supermarket was problematic if you had two or three under 5s to cater for. At a time when nursery provision was still not available to all, the quality of opportunities and experiences offered to these children could be described as minimal and lacking challenge, a view supported by Willis:

> One aspect of designing flats which has not hitherto been given sufficient attention is that of providing adequately and imaginatively for children's play. Very many comments have been made as to the undesirability of bringing up children in flats and general regrets are expressed that this should occur at all; nevertheless, with the present density standards for inner and middle rings of London, large numbers of children will inevitably be spending their formative years on flatted estates. It is therefore of urgent importance that a suitable environment should be planned for them. (Willis, 1953: 19–20)

The Plowden Report (CACE, 1967) highlighted the value of early years provision that led to some expansion of nursery provision, but these developments were predominantly in inner-city areas deemed to have exceptional needs (educational priority areas). Additional expansion at this time came mainly from the private sector and voluntary agencies, with an increase in campaigning for more provision for the under 5s.

The playgroup movement

Throughout the 1960s the playgroup movement expanded nationally, responding directly to local need and the lack of state provision. Van der Eyken concluded:

> The efforts of these groups have done a great deal to stimulate concern about the under-fives. No one, however, would suggest that these self-help solutions are in any way an alternative to the provision of proper facilities and trained supervision for young children. They have arisen out of a

growing recognition by parents of the needs of their children. At considerable personal sacrifice these parents are doing what they can to fill a void that they recognise exists. Inevitably their efforts can only alleviate the need. To satisfy that need is the responsibility of society as a whole. (Van der Eyken, 1967: 83)

Often being held, and still being held, in church halls or community centres, playgroups were predominantly run by mothers who maintained a rota to attend and supervise 3- to 4-year-olds at play, charging a nominal fee to cover expenses. Few of these mothers had formal training, qualifications or experience of such work. Since the first playgroups were introduced the Pre-School Playgroups Association (now the Pre-School Learning Alliance – PLA) has been instrumental in providing guidance, training and support to all playgroups as well as continuously campaigning for the early years.

1970s–1990s

In 1972, the Conservative government boldly pledged to provide free nursery education for every 3- and 4-year-old within ten years, another government commitment to early years education that was to remain unfulfilled. By the mid-1980s, little progress had been made, as highlighted within the Policy Analysis Unit report which concluded that:

> In Britain there is hardly any provision at all for two year olds and part-time care only for 20 per cent of three year olds. Low priority has been given by successive Governments to child-care for under-fives, and there   is no longer any statutory responsibility on local authorities to provide facilities for pre-school children, except those 'at risk'. (Policy Analysis Unit, 1986: 2)

The Children Act (1989) brought together preceding public and private law relating to children and identified a core value of the welfare of the child being 'paramount'. The Act also reinforced the importance of the family and of those who have 'parental responsibility' for children, trying to redress the balance between 'the needs and rights of children and the responsibilities and rights of parents' (Beaver et al., 2000: 196).

The Children Act defined 'children in need' and made clear how local authorities should provide for them, enabling children to remain at home with their families whenever appropriate. In addition, regulations were set for daycare providers covering such issues as space available, staffing ratios and qualifications of staff, all of which were monitored via the annual inspection process.

The terminology within the Children Act (children in need) should not be confused with educational terminology (special needs or educational needs). Refer to the 'definitions' section at end of this chapter for clarification.

1990–1997

From this point in time there was little change in early years provision offered to 3- to 4-year-old children until the 1990s when the Conservative government introduced nursery vouchers as part of a renewed drive to expand nursery provision.

The Nursery Education and Grant Maintained Schools Act (1996) formalised the Nursery Voucher Scheme and offered parents of children in their pre-school year vouchers to exchange for sessions with local providers.

Instead of the anticipated expansion of available provision offering greater choice to parents, many playgroups were forced to close. The incentive of monetary gain encouraged schools to open empty classrooms as nursery classes and some parents, perhaps misguidedly, perceived pre-school provision in schools as more 'educational' and thus 'better than' playgroups. Some schools added to parents' dilemmas by guaranteeing reception class places to nursery class attendees only. Playgroups were also subject to inspection by the social services department (SSD), whereas nursery classes on school premises were not.

For voluntary sector providers, registering with the scheme meant increased income, without which they were no longer financially viable, but also brought about the introduction of Office for Standards in Education (OFSTED) inspections demanding changes in methods of assessment, monitoring, recording and policy production. Groups registered on the scheme were expected to follow the Desirable Learning Outcomes (SCAA, 1996), outlining six areas of learning to be addressed with the children.

At this changeable time, training for playgroups and other voluntary providers was instigated around the country, as was support for groups to cope with the extra administrative tasks. As from 2000, Desirable Learning Outcomes were replaced by *Early Learning Goals* (QCA, 1999) as part of the Foundation Stage of learning designed to prepare children for the National Curriculum following school entry. The Foundation Stage applied to children from the age of 3 years until the end of the reception year in primary school, so more changes and expectations were placed on early years providers.

1997–2006

In 1997 a new Labour government, with their commitment to progression in the early years, was elected.

At this point initial guidance emerged regarding the evolution of *Early Years Development and Childcare Partnerships* (EYDCPs) and a requirement for authorities to produce Early Years Development and Childcare Plans, from April 1998. McKenna (1999: n.p.) outlined the role of EYDCPs as having: 'an initial remit for ensuring that all four year olds have access to a free, good quality nursery education place if their parents wish it. This partnership had to include representatives from statutory, voluntary and private sectors, the health authority, parents and other interested parties.'

Also in 1998 the government issued its *National Childcare Strategy* aiming to 'ensure that all families have access to the childcare which meets their needs' and continuing: 'We want to ensure that good quality, affordable childcare is available to meet the needs of all neighbourhoods' (Internet 3). At the time it was considered that the strategy 'was more ambitious in scope than anything produced by the previous government' (Baldock et al., 2005: 22), who continued to identify the five key areas of focus within the strategy:

- tackling child poverty in the UK
- supporting increased partnerships in the early years
- encouraging further expansion and innovative practice
- breaking down the division between 'care' and 'education' and placing responsibility within the Department for Education and Employment (DfEE)
- improvements in the regulation of provision nationwide.

This National Childcare Strategy was seen as a positive step to improved services for all young children and their families, and in 1999 the *Working Tax Credit* was introduced to encourage parents to return to work if they wished to, although parents faced a small mountain in trying to complete the forms and gain access to the money. It was felt that the government's commitment to an increase in childcare places would enable some parents to resume working and thus support the agenda to reduce poverty, but the commitment still fell short of full nursery entitlement for all young children. SureStart was a key element of the revised programme of change which offered interagency provision in areas designated as socially deprived, as 'services needed to be developed to support young children and families in their earliest years of life to combat multiple disadvantages that had a significant negative influence on children's life chances' (Baldock et al., 2005: 43). Parents were involved from the start in the planning and implementation of the local community setting to ensure the needs of the community were heard, respected and included. Following the initial setting up of the SureStart pilot settings the government has continued to roll out the programme nationwide over subsequent years. Integrated settings, with interagency philosophies, became a futher area for government expansion with the intention of providing interagency and integrated settings in every community in England. This was combined with the establishment of the *National Professional Qualification in Integrated Centre Leadership*, to ensure effective leadership of such centres.

Following the re-election of the Labour government in 2001 the speed of change in early years, which some felt had already been considerable, seemed to take on renewed vigour. Building on their previous term's raft of changes, the commitment to continue with their policies was clear.

The *Education Act 2002* implemented the recommendations from the White Paper, 'Schools: Achieving Success'. This act 'is a substantial and important piece of legislation intended to raise standards, promote innovation in schools and reform education law' (Internet 4). Relating to early years the key areas of change lay in:

- introduction of the Foundation Stage profile to replace baseline assessment
- the role of the LEA in childcare and early education
- changes to the inspection process for childminders, daycare and nursery education
- renewed focus in promoting and safeguarding the welfare of children.

While emphasis had been placed on pre-school children (generally aged 3–5 years) up until this point, the government's next major initiative was the *Birth to Three Matters Framework* (DfES/SureStart Unit, 2002), offering structure to working with the very youngest children for the first time. The overarching aims were:

- to value and celebrate children, their individuality, efforts and achievements
- to value and support the adults who live and work with children
- to provide opportunities for reflection
- to inform and develop practice
- to acknowledge there are no easy answers (Abbott and Langston, 2005: 6).

That practitioners view the child holistically is fundamental to this framework, within which four aspects of early childhood are identified: a strong child, a skilful communicator, a competent learner and a healthy child. The framework further divides the child developmentally, with each section of activities being age appropriate:

1 Heads up, lookers and communicators (0–8 months).
2 Sitters, standers and explorers (8–18 months).
3 Movers, shakers and players (18–24 months).
4 Walkers, talkers and pretenders (24–36 months).

The accompanying guidance 'alerts practitioners to the ways children may be expected to develop in relation to each component "Look, Listen, Note" which suggests what to observe of children's behaviour and responses' (Abbott and

Langston, 2005: 11). Information is also offered regarding effective planning and practice. All this is contained within a clear philosophy of exploratory play and learning.

In 2003 the Children's *National Service Framework* (NSF) evolved – 'a 10-year programme intended to stimulate long-term and sustained improvement in children's health ... the NSF aims to ensure fair, high quality and integrated health and social care from pregnancy right through to adulthood' (Internet 5). Offering a set of standards to be achieved, standard 8 refers specifically to disabled children and children with complex needs, so is particularly relevant to this text.

Arguably the most significant document to reach our desks has been *Every Child Matters* (ECM) (DfES, 2003). Reviewing the situation and research at that time the government revealed the following facts relating to young children (Internet 6):

- There had been a fall in the number of children living in relative low income (from 34 per cent in 1996/97 to 28 per cent in 2002/03).

- This has been matched by a fall in the number of children living in absolute poverty (from 34 per cent in 1996/97 to 17 per cent in 2002/03).

- Three million of the 12 million children in this country have experienced the separation of their parents.

- As of January 2004, 1.4 million (17 per cent) school children had special educational needs (SEN), of whom almost 250,000 (3 per cent) have a statement.

- There are at least 500,000 disabled children in England.

- As of 31 March 2004 there were 61,000 looked after children in England.

- As of 31 March 2004 there were 26,300 children on Child Protection Registers.

Such findings encouraged the government to maintain their drive to improve outcomes for all children, and in 2004 a barrage of supplementary guidance documents emerged outlining the changes planned for the future of al children and young people in an attempt to improve their outcomes through the ECM framework:

- *Every Child Matters: Change for Children* (DfES, 2004a)
- *Every Child Matters: Change for Children in Schools* (DfES, 2004b)
- *Every Child Matters: Change for Children in Social Care* (DfES, 2004c)
- *Every Child Matters: Change for Children in Health Services* (DfES, 2004d)
- *Every Child Matters: Working with Voluntary and Community Organisations to Deliver Change for Children and Young People* (DfES, 2004e)
- *Every Child Matters: Next Steps* (DfES, 2004f).

The ECM framework sets out the national framework for change from central government through local authorities to practitioners and parents, with the NSF being integral to the developments. Following ECM's considerable consultation process, the Children Bill was 'the first step in a long-term programme of change, It creates the legislative spine for developing more effective and accessible services focused around the needs of children, young people and their families' (DfES, 2004f: s. 2.2). The central aims were to:

- establish the five outcomes across the full range of services for all children – to be healthy, stay safe, enjoy and achieve, make a positive contribution and achieve economic well-being
- appoint a Children's Commissioner for England to lead on and monitor developments
- ensure that at local level partnerships between all relevant parties exist to inform planning and provision
- ensure the safety of all children at all times
- establish Children's Trusts which will 'secure integrated commissioning leading to more integrated service delivery and better outcomes for children, young people and their families' (DfES, 2004f: s. 2.20). EYDCPs are likely to be incorporated within the new Children's Trusts
- establish a Director of Children's Services in each authority, 'to ensure clear accountability across the children's services functions of the local authority' (DfES, 2004f: s. 2.28).

The ECM framework supports the view that while many children are successful and achieve their potential there are many who do not, so at a more local level the overarching aims are to be addressed through supporting families, giving children a positive start in life, early intervention and effective provision, integrated inspections, combined with reforms of the children's workforce to ensure higher-qualified staff who are able to provide effectively for all children. The ECM framework of change is further supported by the *Children Act* (DfES, 2004g) which legislated for some of the key changes eg: Directors of Children's Services, improved interagency working systems and practices, integrated inspections and the Children's Commissioner. The Act also reviewed child protection procedures and identified strategies to reduce the number of children 'slipping through the net'. Another indication of the government's commitment to change in early years came in the form of *Choice for Parents, the Best Start for Children: A Ten Year Strategy for Childcare* (HM Treasury, 2004). In recognition of the growing wealth of research highlighting the vital importance of the earliest years in a child's life, the strategy addresses family issues surrounding work and family life. The four areas addressed within this strategy are:

- choice and flexibility – parents to have a greater choice about balancing work and family life
- availability – affordable, flexible, high-quality childcare places that meet their circumstances
- quality – high-quality provision with a highly skilled childcare and early years workforce
- affordability – families to be able to afford flexible, high-quality childcare (HM Treasury, 2004: 1).

The *Children's Workforce Strategy* consultation document (DfES, 2005a) emerged from within the ECM framework and builds on the ten-year strategy. It will, hopefully, clarify the expectations for the workforce providing for our youngest children and claims that: 'Success depends in a large part on the capacity and quality of those people who plan, manage and deliver services at the front line. We need a skilled and more stable workforce in sufficient numbers, led and deployed around the needs of children and young people' (DfES, 2005a: 3). This ambitious and long-awaited reform will address issues such as qualifications, pay and conditions, retention and recruitment, and strong leadership. The reform documentation was then followed by the *Common Core of Skills and Knowledge for the Children's Workforce* documentation (DfES, 2005b) which sets out the levels of required knowledge in each of six key areas:

- effective communication and engagement
- child and young person development
- safeguarding and promoting the welfare of the child
- supporting transitions
- multi-agency working
- sharing information (DfES, 2005b: 4).

When considering the expanse of documentation published since 2001 the reader can begin to understand how and where many of these initiatives begin to dovetail and build on the anticipated success of each other. Through a comprehensive review and a clear vision, the government is hoping to enable greater choice and flexibility for families and their children as well as ensuring high-quality and effective provision for all children, within frameworks specifically designed to address the needs of each child, at each stage of their formative years. At all times the safety and protection of children is seen as of paramount importance. However, while this array of change may appear to be highly desirable and of great value to all, there are many criticisms that could be raised, such as who is to ensure that the Children's Trust do not simply become a new name for local authorities? How are early years practitioners expected to find time to access, read and assimilate the complex information contained within the vast array of publications? How will the changes be implemented at local level and will there be equity nationwide regarding funding? Time will tell, but I am sure that, despite the innovations that have emerged, each with commendable justification, problems and difficulties are also likely to emerge.

Range of early years settings

As can be deduced from the preceding section the range of early years settings has grown considerably and continues to grow. While under the umbrella of making more choice available for parents, the considerable array could present as a confusing range which will still not ensure equality of access for all parents and their children as all communities may not be able to offer the 'full range' of services.

Historically, providers could be divided into three broad categories and have been well documented (for example, Maynard and Thomas, 2004; Pugh, 2001). The range of provision includes:

1 Statutory services:
   (a)   primary schools – providing for children from 4 to 11 years
   (b)   nursery schools and classes
   (c)   day nurseries and family centres
   (d)   home-based support.

2 Private services:
   (a)   childminders
   (b)   private nursery schools
   (c)   private day nurseries
   (d)   workplace nurseries
   (e)   nannies/au pairs
   (f)   out-of school clubs.

3 Voluntary services:
   (a)   playgroups (pre-schools)
   (b)   groups affiliated to charitable organisations.

Now, early in the twenty-first century, we need to add SureStart settings, early excellence centres (EECs), children's centres and wrap-around care in schools. SureStart summarise the aims of the government: 'By 2010 there will be a SureStart children's centre in every community, offering access to integrated early years activities, childcare and family services. We expect children's centres to be developed from existing SureStart programmes, early excellence centres and the mini SureStart Local Programme in many areas' (Internet 1). When this is combined with the increase in schools offering breakfast clubs and after-school clubs we can see the beginnings of more flexibility for families, which many would view as positive. However, there are some issues:

- If you live in a rural location without transport, how accessible will your nearest integrated setting be in reality?
- How can we ensure parents have sufficient information to make informed decisions and choices when the rate of change is so rapid and the range of settings is considerable?

In conclusion, early years provision has developed according to need and at varying rates, owing to a lack of consistent government funding. The current range of provision is only now becoming more unified following very recent legislation, guidance and increased funding.

Historical development of special needs provision and legislation in the UK

Readers are referred to Farrell (2004: 10–15) for a useful table of milestones offering more detail than is possible within this section.

An exploration of the development of special needs provision will highlight key chronological events, indicating a progression from eighteenth-century perspectives to the present day.

An early example of special needs practice occurred in Paris at the turn of the nineteenth century when Itard began working with a 'wild child' discovered in Aveyron, France, who had reputedly been brought up by animals in the wild. Itard's work identified the boy's apparent deafness. Sèguin, a pupil of Itard's, who later worked in the USA, identified that people with significant difficulties could have communication difficulties that impaired their development and ability levels, and therefore they were not necessarily imbeciles or ineducable.

During the eighteenth century the first public schools for the deaf and the blind, respectively, were opened, followed in the early nineteenth century by the development of asylums for 'idiots'. Throughout this historical period children with special educational needs were, for the most part, unacceptable to society. For religious, societal and/or cultural reasons parents often experienced great shame and tremendous guilt, and in some cases either abandoned their children or kept them hidden from society.

In 1870, *Forster's Education Act* provided education for all children – a significant move forwards – including those who had previously been considered young adults as opposed to children, and whose needs, special or otherwise, were clearly misunderstood.

In the 1890s, LEAs were required to make special provision for all blind and deaf children, and were given the option to provide for 'mentally defective' children.

Following the Boer War it became apparent in the UK that the standards of health and fitness of the armed forces were of an unacceptably low standard, creating national concern. School meals and medical inspections were introduced under the 1909 Education Act in an attempt to alleviate future problems. During this period Binet's intelligence tests were introduced to assess the intelligence of the young.

Throughout the 1920s and 1930s Freud's work was becoming established, offering explanations for adult behaviours and feelings, and linking them back to early childhood experiences. This highlighted implications for the importance of those early experiences. At this time the first child guidance clinic was founded to respond to the prevalent problems of poverty and lack of work, and their impact on the young children of the time.

The *Education Act 1944* instigated the appointment of a Minister for Education and the formation of the Ministry of Education, and stated that LEAs 'should have regard to the need for securing that provision is made for pupils who suffer from any disability of mind or body by providing special educational treatment' (Ministry of Education, 1944: 5). *The Handicapped Pupils and School Health Regulations* of 1945 identified 11 categories of disability: blind, partially blind, deaf, partially deaf, delicate, diabetic, educationally subnormal, epileptic, maladjusted, physically handicapped and with speech defects. At this stage medical practitioners undertook diagnoses and children were placed in the most appropriate facilities, resulting in many children being sent away from their homes to boarding schools. Within the 1950s many parents rebelled against this 'medical model' of diagnosis as their children, often very vulnerable, were transported considerable distances from their families and local communities resulting in the children becoming even more vulnerable.

The 1970 *Education (Handicapped Children) Act* (DES, 1970) placed the responsibility of special needs provision within the remit of LEAs and, as a result, special schools were created for children with:

- moderate learning difficulties (MLD)
- severe learning difficulties (SLD)
- severely subnormal difficulties (SSD).

Perhaps one of the earliest references specifically regarding special needs within the early years was the *Court Report* of 1976 which highlighted the need for focus on the screening of health and development in the early years to identify difficulties early within a developmental framework.

In 1978, the *Warnock Report* (DES, 1978) was published having examined in great detail the provision available at the time for all 'handicapped children and young people'. This report, innovative at the time, was to inform subsequent legislation and significantly change the face of special needs provision. One of the key issues raised was that all children have the right to an education and, as society was now more accepting of 'difference', that for children experiencing difficulties we should be committed to 'educating them, as a matter of right and to developing their full potential' (ibid.: 1.11). The fact that this basic principle needed stating reflects somewhat negatively on the education system and societal perspectives prior to 1978. The report continued to suggest a continuum of special needs as opposed to children fitting into one or more categories. The report clarified that children can experience short- and/or longer-term needs, and that provision must be flexible to accommodate change.

Within the report were clear recommendations for LEAs (not health authorities) to assume responsibility for assessing and identifying young children with possible special needs. Furthermore, methods of assessment were detailed to move forwards from the sole use of intelligence quotient (IQ) tests. The report made clear that a variety of methods should be employed to ensure the most effective provision according to need and that within child factors should be considered in conjunction with additional possible causal factors, including those within the school/setting.

Parental partnerships were seen as crucial for effective provision if all children with special needs were to achieve their full potential. The child should be assessed as an individual with a differentiated curriculum reflecting this, if appropriate.

The Warnock Report also debated the notion of integration through a reflection of existing practice in special schools, concluding that there were, at that time, three main forms of integration:

1 Locational – where special provision is available as a separate entity on the same site, but the children are not a part of the mainstream classroom.

2 Social – where children remain in their special unit/class for core subject teaching but attend mainstream classes for some subjects such as art, music and physical education (PE).

3 Functional – where children with special needs are full members of the mainstream classes and class teachers take full responsibility for their education.

The ensuing *Education Act 1981* echoed the key principles of the Warnock Report and placed special educational needs provision firmly on the legislative agenda. Key points included:

- LEAs were given the responsibility of identification and assessment of special educational needs.
- Multidisciplinary assessments could lead to a formal assessment of special educational needs, culminating in a statement of special educational needs, which would be reviewed annually.
- Focus to be placed on individual needs rather than categories of need.
- Provision for children with special educational needs to become the responsibility of the LEA.
- All categories of handicap were removed.
- Effective parental partnerships should be established.
- Integration should occur wherever practicable.

In addition, definitions of special educational needs were consolidated (DES, 1981, s. 1.1):

> Children have a learning difficulty if:
> They have significantly greater difficulty in learning than the majority of children of their age, or
> They have a disability which prevents or hinders them from making use of the educational facilities generally provided in schools, for children of their age. It continued, that a child has a learning difficulty if he/she:
> Has a learning disability which requires educational provision that is additional to, or otherwise different from, the educational provision made generally available within the school, or:
> If he/she has a physical disability.

The *Children Act (1989)* consolidated previous public and private laws regarding the welfare of children. Additional definitions and revised terminology were clarified:

> A child shall be taken as 'in need' if:
> He is unlikely to achieve or maintain, or to have the opportunity of achieving or maintaining, a reasonable standard of health or development without the provision for him by services by a local authority under this Part;
> His health or development is likely to be significantly impaired, or further impaired, without the provision for him of such services;
> Or,
> He is disabled. (DoH, 1991: s. 2.3).

Further definitions include:

> a child is disabled if he is blind, deaf or dumb or suffers from mental disorders of any kind or is substantially and permanently handicapped by illness, injury or congenital deformity or such other disability as may be described ... (Ibid.)

'development' means physical, intellectual, emotional, social or behavioural development; and 'health' means physical or mental health. (Ibid.)
family, in relation to such a child, includes any person who has parental responsibility for the child and any other person with whom he has been living. (Ibid.)

The Children Act also clearly identified a need for effective multidisciplinary working systems, as summarised by Anderson-Ford (1994: 20): 'The Children Act, like the 1981 Act, clearly defines the need for communication between teachers, the school health service and social services departments (SSDs) as well as between the LEA and SSDs at a senior management level.'

The *Education Reform Act 1988* (DfEE, 1988) introduced the National Curriculum, outlining core and foundation subjects, with flexibility for modification to accommodate the learning needs of children with special educational needs. A key focus of the Act was to ensure that all children had equal access to a broad and balanced curriculum.

The *Disability Discrimination Act*, in 1990, demanded that all schools should have admission statements for children with special educational needs, but specifically for those with physical disabilities. Schools needed to ensure that all pupils had equal access to facilities, resources and curriculum, and that an anti-discriminatory philosophy existed. One may have argued, however, that the limitations, general conditions and planning of some school and pre-school buildings rendered this Act difficult to adhere to, despite the best of intentions of staff and governors alike.

Part three of the *1993 Education Act* (DfEE, 1993) addressed problems and issues that had arisen since the implementation of the 1981 Act. Major reviews of the 1981 Act highlighted key areas for change, as outlined by Lindsay (1997: 20): 'The Act was inconsistent, inefficient and clearly did not meet the objective of ensuring each child with SEN received a quality assessment, and provision to meet the needs identified.'

As a result, the 1993 Act offered guidance on both identification and assessment and created special educational needs tribunals to offer parents opportunities to debate decisions with LEAs. Interestingly, several voluntary agencies (for example, Network 81) had been established over the previous decade to address the issues of children with special educational needs and their families, in many instances working with parents on individual cases, offering advice and support, but at the same time campaigning for the rights of children with special educational needs. Further examples of supporting agencies can be found at the end of this chapter.

In summary, the 1993 Education Act revised the 1981 Act and introduced the following amendments/additions:

- School SEN policies must reflect the new approach.
- Greater responsibility should be given to parents within positive, effective working partnerships.
- Independent tribunal system should be established.

The *Code of Practice* (DfEE, 1994) guidance document (as opposed to legislative) was introduced in 1994, detailing the responsibilities previously laid down within the 1993 Act. It offered LEAs and practitioners very clear and specific guidelines on all aspects of special educational needs provision, including:

- identification of SEN
- assessment of SEN
- a new five-staged assessment process, culminating in a statement of SEN
- regular reviews of progress, provision and statements
- the introduction of the special educational needs coordinator (SENCO).

One of the key issues for all early years practitioners was that provision for children below the age of 5 years was included within section 5 of the Code of Practice, giving support to the philosophy of early identification and intervention within a multidisciplinary framework. All maintained schools and registered early years providers were expected to adhere to the guidance given within the Code of Practice, which was intended to be a working document, within which changes could be accommodated, depending on the child's responses to the intervention given.

Early years providers were to establish policy documentation for special educational needs and ensure:

- all parents were familiar with such documents
- all members of staff were knowledgeable in special educational needs provision
- familiarity with a range of agencies who work with children with special educational needs and their families.

At that particular time, with playgroups dominating pre-school provision, these requirements were considerable as, although very skilled and knowledgeable adults staffed such groups, they often lacked formal qualifications and, more specifically, special needs training. Training programmes were introduced nationwide, mainly through either LEAs or the Pre-School Playgroup Association to ensure that all children's needs could be addressed.

The newly created role of SENCO (DfEE, 1994: para. 2.14) brought with it considerable requirements and responsibilities, as summarised by Smith (1996: 9):

- Taking responsibility for the day-to-day operation of the school's SEN policy;
- Liaising with and advising fellow teachers;
- Coordinating provision for pupils with SEN;
- Maintaining the school's SEN register and overseeing the records of all pupils with SEN;
- Liaising with parents;
- Contributing to staff in-service training;
- Liaising with external agencies.

In reality, many SENCOs were already full-time practitioners and these responsibilities were therefore additional, although in some instances new appointments were created. However, pre-school providers also had to maintain a SENCO and, with many playgroup employees remaining in post for relatively short terms, this created ongoing difficulties for many groups.

The five stages of assessment detailed within the Code applied to children from birth, although the Code did not expect special educational needs to arise during the first two years of a child's life, unless the child had a specific condition from birth and/or major health and development difficulties. The Code stated that for children under 5 years of age and not yet attending school, the five-stage approach should still be applied but it was not anticipated that many formal statements of need would result. In summary the stages of assessment were:

> Stage 1: Class or subject teachers identify or register a child's special educational needs and, consulting the school's SEN coordinator, take initial action.
> Stage 2: School's SEN coordinator takes lead responsibility for gathering information and for coordinating the child's special educational provision, working with the child's teachers.
> Stage 3: Teachers and the SEN coordinator are supported by specialists from outside the school.
> Stage 4: The LEA consider the need for a statutory assessment and, if appropriate, make a multi-disciplinary assessment.
> Stage 5: LEA consider the need for a statement of special educational needs and, if appropriate, make a statement and arrange, monitor and review provision. (DfEE, 1994: s. 1.4)

The final statement of need was to be the result of a multidisciplinary assessment, gathering information from all practitioners involved with the child, plus the parents.

The Code outlined the requirements for effective planning of provision for individual children on the special needs register (Individual Education Plans – IEPs), which could include such information as a summary of the difficulties, steps taken to accommodate those needs, details of parental views, resources (materials and human) required, detailed targets for future working, and information on assessments, monitoring and reviewing the provision.

The Code of Practice has now been revised, with the National Association for Special Educational Needs (NASEN) being instrumental throughout. A consultative document was sent to all members and the resulting recommendations and comments passed to the Department for Education and Skills (DfES) (NASEN, 2000).

One important change within the Revised Code of Practice (DfES, 2001d) is a whole chapter relating to identification, assessment and provision in the early years. Consecutive governments have begun to acknowledge the value and place of early years provision and are working towards places for all 3- and 4-year-old children that require it. In addition, the importance of early intervention for special educational provision is now well documented, as referred to by the DfEE (1997: 13) within their Green Paper outlining government intentions and future pathways for meeting special educational needs: 'early diagnosis and appropriate intervention improve the prospects for children with special educational needs, and reduce the need for expensive intervention later on. For some children, giving more attention to early signs of difficulty can prevent the development of SEN'.

The *Nursery Education and Grant Maintained Schools Act* (DfEE, 1996) was a major advancement and acknowledgement of early years provision which introduced the Nursery Voucher Scheme with concise requirements for providers who wished to become a part of the scheme and receive vouchers redeemable for funding. Although previously discussed within this chapter, a reminder at this juncture is appropriate when reflecting on special educational needs provision within a historical perspective. All providers needed to have 'due regard' to the SEN Code of Practice, again requiring additional training and resources for many pre-school providers.

The *Special Educational Needs and Disability Discrimination Act 2001* incorporated further changes for education and as a result the *Special Educational Needs Code of Practice 2001* was published followed by the Disability Discrimination Code of Practice.

The *Special Educational Needs Code of Practice* (DfES, 2001d), as previously mentioned, included a section on identification, assessment and provision of special educational needs in early education settings. The five-staged approach from the 1994 Code was now replaced by a 'graduated response' incorporating Early Years Action and Early Years Action Plus:

Once practitioners have identified that a child has special educational needs, the setting should intervene through *Early Years Action*. If the intervention does not enable the child to make satisfactory progress the SENCO may need to seek advice and support from external agencies. These forms of intervention are referred to (below) as *Early Years Action Plus*. (DfES, 2001d: s. 4.11)

The new Code of Practice (DfES, 2001d) identified key changes from the original Code of Practice (DfEE, 1994) as:

• A stronger right for children with SEN to be educated at a mainstream school

• New duties on LEAs to arrange for parents of children with SEN to be provided with services offering advice and information and a means of resolving disputes

• A new duty on schools and relevant nursery education providers to tell parents when special educational provision is being provided for their child

• A new right for schools and relevant nursery education providers to request a statutory assessment of a child. (DfES, 2001d: iv)

Another area emphasised within the new Code of Practice was the value of and need for effective multidisciplinary working systems, providing for the needs of children within a 'seamless' service that addressed the needs of children as well as their parents. However, practitioners and organisations such as NASEN have identified possible shortcomings within the guidance, including the lack of provision for non-teaching time for SENCOs to allow for planning, preparation and record-keeping (although the guidance suggests that this should be reviewed within settings), plus the recurring issue of training and funding. Considerable importance is placed on parental partnerships and multidisciplinary working, but these place additional demands on SENCOs' time to create, monitor, review and maintain systems and processes. It could be that without the allocation of specified time to undertake such activities the outcomes may be limited, although working practices inform us that many SENCOs achieve this despite the time implications.

In a similar vein practitioners working with early years children needed additional training to ensure up-to-date knowledge and understanding of the new guidance documents and the necessary skills to implement them. There is a need for specific and extensive special educational needs training for early years practitioners, and new guidelines and legislation will intensify this need. A comprehensive nationwide training system would accommodate this, but government funding would be needed.

The Disability Discrimination Act *Draft Code of Practice (Schools)* (Disability Rights Commission 2001: 7) offered guidance to educational establishments on 'preventing discrimination against disabled people in their access to education'.

A person with a disability was defined as one 'who has a physical or mental disability which has an effect on his or her ability to carry out normal day-to-day activities' (ibid.: 14) and the Code of Practice identified two key duties relating to educational settings to ensure that pupils with disabilities are not discriminated against:

- Not to treat disabled pupils less favourably; and
- To make reasonable adjustments to avoid putting disabled pupils at a substantial disadvantage. (ibid.: 15)

The Disability Discrimination final Code of Practice has now been published (Internet 7). With the array of human rights legislation that now exists (United Nations Convention on the Rights of the Child, 1989; Human Rights Act, 1998; Special Educational Needs and Disability Discrimination Act, 2001) early years practitioners must ensure that the special needs provision reflects the rights of the children and their families. While we may, as a society, be moving towards inclusive education for all children, we must not ignore those children and/or parents who request a separate form of specialised education for their children.

From 2002 Parent Partnership Services were to be in place in every authority to ensure that all parents of children with special needs had access to up-to-date information and advice regarding their child's education. This was to support them in making informed decisions about their choice of early years setting and school for their child.

The SEN tribunal service (from the 1993 Education Act) was renamed the *Special Educational Needs and Disability Tribunal* (SENDIST) to ensure issues of disability discrimination could be addressed, if appropriate, during parental appeals regarding the authority's decisions about their child's needs and provision.

The Audit Commission published their findings of a review of SEN provision in 2002. *Special Educational Needs: A Mainstream Issue* explored the progress of authorities and settings in managing and providing quality services for children with SEN and concluded that: 'Whether and how children's needs are identified appears to be influenced by a range of factors, including their gender, ethnicity and family circumstances, where they live and which school they attend. ... Some continue to face considerable barriers to learning' (Audit Commission, 2002: 51). The report made ten recommendations for improvement.

Together from the Start: Practical Guidance for Professionals Working with Disabled Children (Birth to 2) and their Families was published by the DfES and DoH in 2002 and explored the delivery of services for the very youngest children with disabilities. While the common themes appeared – early identification and provison, partnerships with parents and interagency working – it also highlighted the need for strategic direction for this particular age group. Noticeably three key barriers to existing provision were highlighted: lack of sensitivity at the time of diagnosis, inconsistent patterns of provision and the lack of coordination between multiple service providers which it addressed in more detail (DfES and DoH, 2002: 3). Within an inclusive climate the guidance suggests that as most birth to two year olds will spend most of their time within the family home priority must be given to authorities ensuring effective and responsive intervention within an effective partnership system with parents and other agencies.

The same year saw the publication of *Supporting Families Who Have Children with Special Needs and Disabilities* (SureStart, 2002) which used the Together from the Start definition of special needs (SureStart, 2002: 5):

A child under four years of age has a disability or special needs if she or he:

• Is experiencing significant developmental delays, in one or more of the areas of cognitive development, physical development, communication development, social or emotional development and adaptive development; or

• Has a condition which has a high probability of resulting in developmental delay.

The purpose of the guidance was to ensure 'access to a good quality service from SureStart programmes; ensure issues of access and quality; help develop awareness of the needs of families and how to respond appropiately; build on and share knowledge and information about special needs services' (ibid.: 3). The document continues to outline current procedures and effective provision taking into account interagency working, parent partnerships, early assessment and intervention. The need to respect and value contributions of parents, other professionals as well as the whole community emerge as ongoing themes.

SureStart then issued their guidance entitled: *Area Special Educational Needs Coordinators (SENCOs) – Supporting Early Identification and Intervention for Children with Special Educational Needs* (Sure Start, 2003). This guidance 'sets out the envisaged role and practices of Area SENCOs as they empower all those working with children in the early years to create inclusive and effective early learning environments' (ibid.: 2). Aiming at a target of one Area SENCO to every 20 non-maintained early years settings by 2004 (ibid.: 2), the guidance continues to identify the roles he/she will adopt and what knowledge and skills are necessary to undertake the job. Interestingly, the original intention of ensuring Area SENCOs were qualified teachers was later removed from the draft document and senior managers have the right to set their own qualifying criteria.

In 2004 this was followed through within the *Early Support Pilot Programme* (Internet 8) which adopted the main principles from Together from the Start.

The *National Service Framework* (2003) referred to earlier contained eleven standards to be met, with standard 8 specifically relating to children with disabilities and/or complex health needs. This standard states that: 'Children and young people who are disabled or who have complex health needs receive coordinated, high quality child and family centred services which are based on assessed needs, which promote social inclusion and, where possible, which enable them and their families to live ordinary lives.' (Internet 4 – SEN updates). The standard then identifies key themes to support the standard:

* Services which promote social inclusion
* Access to hospital and primary health care services
* Early identification
* Early intervention and support
* Palliative care
* Safeguarding young children
* Multi-agency transition planning. (Internet 4)

Also in 2004, *Removing Barriers to Achievement: The Government's Strategy for SEN* (RBA) was published (DfES, 2004h) and took into account many of the recommendations of the Audit Commission's report. Dovetailing with the government's array of early years and children's strategies at that time, but most specifically the ECM, the RBA strategy outlined the government's vision for continued improvements in SEN provision. Chapters focused on early identification, removing barriers to learning, raising expectations and achievements, delivering improved partnerships and interagency working. The strategy 'sets out the government's vision for enabling children with special educational needs to realize their potential and a programme of sustained action and review over a number of years to support early years settings, schools and local authorities in improving provision for children' (Internet 4). We also saw the establishment of a team of *National SEN Advisers* in 2004 to work with local authorities in an advisory capacity.

It should be noted that many of the changes in early years already discussed in this chapter also make references to special needs provision. For example, the National Service Framework, Every Child Matters and the Code of Practice all share common aims of improving early identification and intervention, family support, inclusive services, working with parents, skilled early years workforce and interagency working. Early in 2005 the government produced their report entitled, *Improving the Life Chances of Disabled People*, with the ambitious aim that: 'By 2025, disabled people in Britain should have full opportunities and choices to improve their quality of life and will be respected and included as equal members of society' (Internet 9). Of the four key areas identified, one relates specifically to families with young disabled children ensuring that provision is tailor made to respond to individual child and family needs and that parents should have access to their own individualised budgets offering them greater choice and control over their provision. This links directly to the government's *Direct Payments Scheme* (DoH, 2004) which offers parents of disabled children (aged 0–17 years) the option of receiving direct payments from the government to arrange their own package of services to respond to their child's needs. Currently social services and/or LEAs provide funding and set up and pay for the services offered.

Baroness Warnock, the original leader of the Warnock committee in the 1970s, also contributed to the inclusion debate in 2005 by producing a leaflet which appeared to suggest a U-turn in her original views from the 1970s. She concluded that: 'pressure to include pupils with problems in mainstream schools causes "confusion of which children are the casualties"' (Internet 10). Special schools, she claims, still have a place, as inappropriate placement in mainstream does not guarantee inclusion. She continues to suggest that it would be more financially viable to retain some special schools as opposed to closing them all and attempting to replicate their provision in every mainstream school. Attracting much media attention at the time, her views received considerable criticism. The *Independent Panel for Special Education Advice* (IPSEA) suggested that: 'Mary Warnock's 2005 attack on statements needs to be commented on because she is accorded the status of special educational needs guru by politicians and the media, and this risks her recent contribution to the debate being accorded a significance which it does not merit' (2005: 9).

The Disability Rights Commission published the *Special Schools Debate* in July 2005 (Internet 7) which examined 'educational opportunities for disabled children'. Highlighting that significant improvements had been made, the report concluded that children with disabilities 'continue to experience inequality in the education system' (Internet 7). Schools are seen as critical to future progress in three specific areas:

- Providing children and young people with the opportunity for self-development, reaching their individual potential and successful transition to independent adult life and contributory citizens.
- Transmitting society's values to children and young people.
- Offering a place and a reason for interaction between different children and communities. (Internet 7)

The report supports the government's progress and recommendations in documentation such as RBA and clearly defines a need for society, government and practitioners to end discussion relating to where children should be educated (special or mainstream) and begin developing our thinking and practices to support an education system 'which fosters and promotes disabled people's belonging and inclusion' (Internet 7).

This report was closely followed in October 2005 by an *Inquiry into Special Education Needs* by IPSEA. While summarising the current situation relating to SEN assessment and provision, the report highlighted some areas for improvement, such as improved DfES responses to complaints about LEAs, possible changes to the SENDIST service and an improved role for government itself in leading future changes.

Summary

Early years provision has changed considerably over the past century to offer a diverse range of opportunities to young children and their families, and all registered early years providers must now have due regard to the Special Educational Needs and Disability Discrimination Act 2001 (DfES, 2001c), hopefully ensuring appropriate special educational provision for all children within an interagency framework. However, issues such as funding, training, resources and accommodation can impact on the levels of provision available and the range offered in different areas of the country and in different settings, so we are still a long way from a system that is truly equitable to all children at all times. Huge strides have been made, but further progress is still needed to ensure optimum achievement for all very young children.

As the field of early years has been incorporated within special needs legislation and guidance comparatively recently, monitoring and reviewing provision must continue to address any current and future issues. Continued evaluation and research in the field will support this process.

Special educational needs provision, both generally and in the early years, has received more national attention over the past 20 years than ever before and, while we can acknowledge that the central aim is to strive continuously to improve systems and provision, the current situation (and relevant legislation and guidance) is not necessarily the answer to ensure equal and appropriate provision for all. As Farrell concludes, we are currently in a situation balancing both positive and negative aspects:

> On the positive side parents now have a much louder voice, there are more mechanisms to support them and they have far greater rights of appeal ...
>
> Perhaps more important are the continued problems associated with the bureaucratic and cumbersome statutory assessment procedures which, despite the proposed changes in the new Draft Code, still seem to be a millstone round the necks of all those involved in striving to provide the best quality education to pupils with SEN and their families. (Farrell, 2001: 8)

The reader is recommended to access directly documents referred to in this chapter for more detailed information, as only the briefest of overviews has been possible.

Definitions

The following terminology is used throughout this book:

Early years/young children are those aged 0–8 years, but this book will focus predominantly on the under 5s or pre-school children as there is a plethora of information available on children of statutory school age.

Early years provider/provision/setting refers to any practitioner or establishment providing opportunities and/or support to 0–5-year-old children. This will include pre-school groups, nurseries, nursery classes, childminders, daycare, special needs units/classes/schools, early excellence centres, children's centres, wrap around care, SureStart centres and educare groups.

Parents refers to any person, parent or otherwise, assuming 'parental responsibility' for the child.

Professionals/practitioners refers to any person working with children in any setting, whether or not they hold professional qualifications.

Special educational needs (SEN) are any difficulties experienced by a child requiring additional or different educational provision to be made.

Special needs (SN) are those difficulties experienced by a child that do not necessarily result in a special educational need.

Special needs or individual needs?

Despite legalistic, educational and societal definitions I would suggest from personal experiences that all children, like all adults, have individual needs that will change in type, severity or nature during different phases of their lives. It should be our aim as early years practitioners to enable all children to achieve their optimum potential whether they are identified as having 'special needs', 'special educational needs', or not.

Key issues

❖ Early years special needs provision is now placed on the legislative agenda placing considerable expectations on early years practitioners.
❖ Legislation and guidance now incorporates special educational provision, disability discrimination and human rights.
❖ The speed of change has been considerable.
❖ While we can continue to work towards inclusion, with the individual needs of all young children and their families being met, there are still key issues to address.
❖ Monitoring and research should be encouraged to ensure progression.

Some suggestions for discussion

Item 1

Assess the training needs of all practitioners in your setting with regard to special educational needs. Examine in particular:

* knowledge of recent legislation and guidance
* knowledge and skills to provide for the special needs of all attending children

Item 2

In the light of your responses to item 1, identify any training needs and how you might address them.

Item 3

Examine the special needs policy for your setting.

* Does it need updating in the light of recent guidance and legislation?
* Does it offer clarity of understanding for practitioners and parents?

Item 4

Assess the special needs recording systems you have in place.

* Are they up to date, reflecting recent legislation and guidance?
* Is the documentation system practical to manage?
* Is documentation accessible to parents and, if so, is it written in an appropriate language and presented in an appropriate format?

Suggested further reading

Department of Education and Science (DES) (1978) *The Report of the Committee of Enquiry into the Education of Handicapped Children and Young People* (Warnock Report). London: HMSO. (Chapter 2, 'The historical background'.)

Department for Education and Skills (DfES) (2001d) *Special Educational Needs Code of Practice*. Nottingham: DfES.

Department for Education and Skills (DfES)/SureStart Unit (2002) *Birth to Three Matters: A Framework to Support Children in their Earliest Years*. London: DfES.

Department for Education and Skills (2003) *Every Child Matters*. London: DfES.

Farrell, M. (2004) *Special Educational Needs: A Resource for Practitioners*. London: Paul Chapman Publishing.

Maynard, T. and Thomas, N. (eds) (2004) *An Introduction to Early Childhood Studies*. London: Sage.

Useful websites

Advisory Centre for Education (ACE) www.ace-ed.org.uk

British Association for Early Childhood Education (BAECE)
www.early-education .org.uk

Department for Education and Skills www.dfes.gov.uk

Department of Health www.doh.gov.uk

Disability Rights Commission (DRC) www.drc.org.uk

Early Support Pilot Programme www.espp.org.uk

Every Child Matters www.everychildmatters.gov.uk

Independent Panel for Special Educational Advice (IPSEA) www.ipsea.org.uk

National Association for Special Educational Needs (NASEN) www.nasen.org.uk

National Children's Bureau, Early Childhood Unit www.ncb.org.uk

National Early Years Network www.neyn.org.uk

Network 81 (for parents of children with special educational needs)
www.network 81.co.uk

SureStart Unit www.surestart.gov.

This chapter is taken from:
Wall, K. (2006) *Special Needs in the Early Years*, Second Edition
978-1-4129-2949-3

Origins of Abuse and Neglect

CHRIS BECKETT

- Risk factors
- Patterns of maltreatment
- Premeditated abuse
- Absence of love
- Stress-related abuse and neglect
- Competence-related abuse and neglect
- Abuse by children

Having considered the signs and consequences of abuse and neglect in Part II, I will now consider the question of when and why abuse and neglect occurs. In this chapter I will consider the range of external factors that are associated with abuse and neglect. I will then consider the different ways in which, in particular cases, parents and others may end up abusing or neglecting children and consider what the best response is in each case. In the following four chapters I will look more closely at some specific contexts.

Risk factors

Just as we must have some understanding of how maltreatment affects a child's development if we are to know how to intervene and change things for the better, so we need some understanding of what factors may make it more likely that people will maltreat children so as to be able to make the right decisions about how to respond to particular situations.

One way of approaching these sorts of questions is to look at families where abuse or neglect has occurred and to compare the characteristics of these families with those of other families where there has been no concern about maltreatment. It is then possible to identify 'risk factors', characteristics that occur more frequently in situations where maltreatment occurs than they do in other situations.

Fatal abuse

Cyril Greenland (1987) produced a list of risk indicators based on studies of 107 actual child deaths in the UK and Canada. The risk factors which Greenland came up with are listed in Table 8.1. Exercise 8.1, below, invites you to consider their implications.

Exercise 8.1

In the inquiry report into the death of Jasmine Beckford (London Borough of Brent, 1985) it is suggested that such tragedies might be avoided by using findings such as those of Greenland as an assessment tool to identify high-risk families. Look through the list in Table 8.1. What difficulties can you see in using it in such a way?

Table 8.1 Indicators associated with increased likelihood of child death through non-accidental injury

Characteristics of parent
Themselves abused or neglected as a child
Aged 20 or less at the birth of their first child
Single parent/separated; partner not biological parent of child
History of abuse/neglect or deprivation
Socially isolated; frequent moves; poor housing
Poverty; unemployed/unskilled worker; inadequate education
Abuses alcohol and/or drugs
History of violent behaviour and/or suicide attempts
Pregnant, or post partum (i.e. has recently given birth); or chronic illness

Characteristics of child
Previously abused/neglected
Under five years old at the time of abuse or neglect
Premature or low birth weight
Birth defect; chronic illness; developmental lag
Prolonged separation from mother
Cries frequently; difficult to comfort
Difficulties in feeding/elimination
Adopted, foster or step-child

Source: Greenland (1987).

Comments on Exercise 8.1

What probably struck you is the broadness of the categories. For example, being a single parent is one of the nine characteristics of parents, but obviously most single parents do not abuse or neglect their children. Their presence on this list merely reflects the fact that there were a higher proportion of single parents among the parents of the 107 children in Greenland's sample of child death cases than there are in the general population. Likewise, not all premature or adoptive babies are abused, and their presence in the list simply reflects the fact there were higher proportions of premature babies and of adoptive babies among the 107 than there are in the population in general.

Lists like Greenland's may tell us something, in a general sense, about the different characteristics of abusive families, but they are very little use in predicting abuse in any given individual instance, since clearly it would not make any sense to treat every lone parent, or every parent who was under 20 when her first child was born, or every parent of a premature child, as a high-risk case. It *is* true that if a number of these factors were present in a single case the situation would certainly look more risky than the average family. For instance, if a mother of 17, who had been physically abused herself as a child, was a heroin user and had convictions for violent offences, was caring on her own for a premature baby who was ill and cried a lot, then this would certainly be a situation in which there was a well-above-average risk of abuse or neglect of some kind occurring, but then again, you might have guessed this even if you hadn't seen Greenland's list or read this book.

The type of methodology used in studies such as Greenland's is known as *actuarial,* because it is essentially the same as that used by actuaries, the people employed by insurance companies to calculate the statistical likelihood of different kinds of accidents for different groups of the population. Actuaries, for example, have worked out that young men are more likely to have car accidents than older men or women, and as a result young men have to pay higher car insurance premiums. In this sense, being a young man is a 'predictor' of traffic accidents – or a risk factor – but this does not mean (a) that most young men will have traffic accidents, or (b) that other people will not have traffic accidents, or (c) that being a young man is, of itself, a *cause* of traffic accidents.

In relation to child protection work, there is a lot of muddled thinking about this sort of thing, which leads to many people having quite unrealistic ideas about the ability of professional agencies to predict abuse. I will return to this in Chapter 14. For the moment I simply make the point that there is no assessment tool that will tell you for certain which situations are dangerous and which are not and that, while risk factors or predictors such as those listed by Greenland do help to suggest in a general way what kinds of situations *may* result in abuse, none of them should be seen as an inevitable (or even necessarily a probable) *cause* of abuse.

Sexual abuse

Child sexual abuse does not have the same link with socioeconomic status as exists in the case of physical abuse and neglect. 'A growing number of studies have reported weak or no association between measures of family socioeconomic status and risks of CSA' (Fergusson and Mullen, 1999: 37–8). There are, however, statistical links between sexual abuse and marital dysfunction, the presence of step-parents in the family, parental alcoholism and parental criminality, though once again I emphasize that this does not mean that most step-parents or alcoholics are sexual abusers. The victims of sexual abuse are more likely to be female than male – the risk for girls being 'two to three times higher than the risk for males' according to Fergusson and Mullen (1999: 36) who, by combining the findings of a variety of studies, also arrive at the following 'weighted average' figures:

- Abusers of girls are 97.5 per cent male, while abusers of boys are 78.7 per cent male.
- Some 10.4 per cent of child sexual abuse involved close family members, including parents, step-parents and siblings.

- 'The most frequently reported perpetrators were acquaintances of the victim.' On average 47.8 per cent of perpetrators were described as acquaintances.
- 'CSA perpetrated by parent figures is relatively uncommon … with the weighted average estimate suggesting 3.3 per cent of CSA incidents were perpetrated by natural fathers.'
- The weighted average for step-parents was 2.7 per cent, but 'the fact that rates of perpetration by stepparents are similar to rates of perpetration by natural parents, suggests that stepparents are more likely to commit CSA, since there are far fewer stepparents in the population than natural parents.' Anderson et al. (1993) suggested that step-parents were roughly ten times more likely to sexually abuse than parents.

(List compiled from Fergusson and Mullen, 1999: 45, 47. These weighted average figures should be treated with some caution, since the studies they are compiled from often came up with widely divergent findings.)

Statistical associations and causality

As I have already warned, the fact that a certain factor is associated in a statistical sense with abuse, does not mean that abuse is inevitable, or even necessarily likely, when that factor is present.

Another important point to note is that an association between abuse and a given factor does not necessarily mean that this factor is or can be a *cause* of abuse. A statistical association between A and B, whatever A and B might be, tells you only that A is more common when B is present. This could mean that A is caused by B, or that B is caused by A, or that both are caused by another factor. Very commonly in complex human systems there is 'circular causality': A and B *cause each other*. (Imagine A is a thermostatic switch and B is the temperature of a room: each one controls the other.) These points may seem rather academic at this point but I will come back to them in a more concrete and specific way in later chapters. For the moment I am simply cautioning you against coming to simplistic conclusions about causation on the basis of statistical associations.

Patterns of maltreatment

Another way of approaching the question of what causes some parents to abuse or neglect their children is one that, in a medical context, would be described as 'clinical'. A clinical approach is based, not on actuarial calculations, but on observation of actual cases and of patterns that recur, and on a process of learning what helps and what does not, which allows tentative models to be developed as to what is going on. Adopting more of a 'clinical' than an 'actuarial' approach, I would suggest that, as an alternative to dividing up child maltreatment into physical abuse, sexual abuse and so on we could instead classify it according to the kinds of context in which it occurs, on the lines of the following:

1 *Premeditated abuse* in which the abuser is drawn towards some sort of abusive behaviour in order to meet some need or desire of his or her own, and in which the abuse is deliberate, planned – and fantasized about – in advance. The main instance of this sort of abuse is sexual abuse, but it could also be said to apply to some cases of feigned or induced illness as discussed

in Chapter 5, in which parents deliberately make their children ill, or get them diagnosed as ill, in order to meet psychological needs of their own. These kinds of behaviour are difficult to understand for those who are outside of it. Most adults probably cannot imagine *wanting* to sexually abuse a child, let alone acting on it. As a result, these premeditated abusive patterns are probably the least amenable to a 'commonsense' approach.

2   *Absence of love.* Even very abusive parents often love and are loved by their children but it can happen that emotional abuse or neglect is linked to the fact that a child is simply not loved, wanted or valued by the parent. This may be a temporary phase (many people have times when they just can't *feel* love for another person) but it can happen that there simply *is* no love.

3   *Stress-related abuse and neglect.* A good deal of abuse and neglect is linked to stresses of one kind or another, to which different individuals are more or less vulnerable. This kind of maltreatment is probably the easiest for most people to understand. Any parent who has ever snapped at her children after a difficult day at work has, in a small way, 'been there'. Under stress-related abuse and neglect we might also include abuse and neglect that occurs in situations where parents have drug and alcohol or mental health problems, but I will leave discussion of these situations to the next chapter.

4   *Competence-related abuse and neglect.* Some maltreatment of children is related to ignorance about children's needs. In most cases this sort of problem should not come under the umbrella of child protection at all, but it sometimes does, especially when issues of competence overlap with other issues.

Reality is always more complicated than any attempt to classify it. These categories do in fact overlap and shade one into another, but I hope that by using them in the following discussion I will highlight the fact that child abuse and neglect is not a simple unitary phenomenon, but something that can occur in many different ways for many different reasons.

Premeditated abuse

What makes an adult set out to deliberately abuse a child? Why do some adults become sexually preoccupied with children? One factor that is common to a significant proportion of sex abusers is that they themselves were sexually abused as children: 'estimates of the percentage of CSA perpetrators who report being sexually abused in childhood typically range from 20% to 30%', according to Fergusson and Mullen (1999: 49). But these figures still mean that the majority of sexual abuse perpetrators are not themselves victims of sexual abuse. Similarly, and it is important to note this in order to avoid unfairly stigmatizing abuse survivors, most victims of abuse do not become perpetrators.

However, if you look back at the discussion on the psychological effects of sexual abuse in the last chapter, you can see how some of these effects – such as 'traumatic sexualization' and the habit of 'dissociation' – could result in some individuals:

(a)   learning to view children and childhood as 'sexual',
(b)   coming to view closeness, intimacy and power in extremely sexual terms,
(c)   being able to 'dissociate' from normal inhibitions and taboos,
(d)   developing difficulties with forming normal relationships and finding closeness and intimacy in that way, and
(e)   developing a sense of powerlessness and a need to compensate for this by obtaining power over others (see, for example, Finkelhor and Browne, 1986; Erooga and Masson, 1999).

But sexual abuse in childhood is not the only developmental route through which an individual can grow to have children as his primary objects of sexual interest. Emotional immaturity, fear of adult relationships, a preoccupation with power and control and fear of rejection are all overlapping factors which may lead an individual down this pathway. Being sexually abused is just one of a number of experiences that may predispose him to have these particular characteristics.

As well as trying to understand sexual abuse in terms of its historical origin in a person's life, we can also look at it as a behaviour that sustains itself in the present, asking ourself the question as to what is it about this behaviour that is so powerfully self-reinforcing. Wolf (1984) proposed that offenders are typically individuals with low self-esteem who get into a cycle in which they retreat into isolation, using sexual fantasy and masturbation to make themselves feel better and to obtain an illusion of being in control. Fantasy then leads on to planning and carrying out actual abusive acts. Dawn Fisher summarizes the rest of Wolf's cycle as follows:

> Once they have committed the offence, itself a highly reinforcing event, the diminished sexual excitement following ejaculation (either as part of the abuse or subsequently through masturbation), is followed by a period of transitory guilt … In seeking to reconstitute his self-image the offender typically uses further distorted thinking to alleviate his guilt and anxiety, by minimising or justifying the abuse and promising himself that he will not do the same again. However, underlying this he is left with the knowledge that he has committed a sexual offence, resulting in further damage to his self-esteem, bringing him back to the feelings he had at the start of the cycle. (Fisher, 1994: 19–20)

Once a person is on the pathway of sexual abuse it is very difficult to get off it and there are many striking parallels between the behaviour and thinking of sexual offenders with that of people addicted to drugs. Distorted thinking is characteristic of addictions of all kinds. This allows the addict to carry on doing something which he knows to be wrong – and harmful even to himself – by somehow denying to himself what he is doing. Interestingly these mental contortions closely resemble some of the defence mechanisms by which *victims* of abuse cope psychologically, by telling themselves 'this isn't happening to me', and it is worth noting that a significant proportion not only of sex offenders, but also of alcoholics and drug addicts, are themselves victims of childhood abuse.

Sexual abusers of children, like other addicts, become extremely skilled at minimizing and rationalizing their conduct. They get very good at concealing from themselves and others the extent of their problem and at releasing themselves from responsibility for their own behaviour by (a) blaming others and (b) mental compartmentalization, or 'splitting'. And, as the lives of other kinds of addict can become increasingly organized by their habit, so also can the lives of sexual abusers of children become organized around finding opportunities for more abusive behaviour. Interactions with others can then become essentially manipulative, not pursued for their own sake, but aimed at making new opportunities for abuse. Sexual abusers become highly skilled at manipulation, at identifying vulnerable children (typically children who are short of adult attention, and are perhaps already the victims of neglect or abuse), and 'grooming' them for abuse. They may also become adept at identifying vulnerable adults who will give them access to children (as in the novel *Lolita*, by Vladimir Nabokov).

These skills of manipulation, deception and self-deception, built up by constant practice, can make sexual abusers highly plausible. *It is not safe or sensible to make judgements about the dangers posed by such people, or their responsiveness to treatment, unless you have specialist training and have a sufficiently specialized role to allow you to accumulate a lot of experience in this area.*

Although the parallels between the behaviour of sexual abusers and other kinds of addict is, I think, striking (and I will return to them in the next chapter) there are of course also differences. There is, for one thing, a moral difference, in that drug addiction does not involve making another human being into an object of gratification in the way that sexual offenders do, even though it can often result in the needs of others being unnoticed or disregarded. Another factor found in sexual abusive behaviour but for which there is no exact parallel in the case of other addictions, is the way in which fantasy and masturbation (and often pornography) become part of the cycle, fuelling the sexual obsession and allowing the offender to not only 'groom' his victim for abuse but also, as it were, to *groom himself* for further offending.

Implications for assessment and intervention

Protecting children who have been sexually abused is generally a matter of ensuring that they have carers who are capable of preventing the abuser (or abusers) from being given further opportunities to abuse them. This often entails assessing, and trying to support and strengthen, the ability of other adults around the child to stand up to the abuser, and to recognize and resist his attempts at manipulation.

Of course, where the abuser is an important figure to the child, the ideal intervention entails helping the abuser to give up abusive behaviour, but the treatment of sexual offenders – and assessment of the risks that they continue to pose – is a difficult and complex area, and is not something that should be undertaken by professionals who do not have specialist knowledge and experience. In the absence of clear and compelling evidence to the contrary from an authoritative source, child protection plans need to be based on the assumption that a sexual abuser continues to present a high risk indefinitely if he is allowed unsupervised contact with a child.

Absence of love

> Not feeling loved by your parent is deeply painful. Your attachment figure is the person to whom you instinctively turn at times of need, but all you find is indifference, or in more extreme cases, loathing… But of course it is not just hurtful to feel that your well-being and safety are not uppermost in the mind of your carer, it is also frightening. If a parent rejects you, particularly when you are in a state of need or distress, then where might you find comfort or understanding? (Howe, 2005: 90)

It is important to acknowledge that some parents simply do not care about their children and deeply resent that child's existence and all the inconvenience that this causes. Some too feel this way about a specific one of their children, perhaps because of the circumstances of the child's birth or conception, or because the child is a disappointment in some way, or a reminder of someone or something that the parent would rather forget, or because of some aspect of their own childhood experience. It is a mistake to simply assume that, at some level, deep down, parents – and perhaps particularly mothers – *always* love their children. But a huge amount of shame and guilt is attached to admitting, even to yourself, that you do not love your own child. Indeed the idea is so shocking – remember the discussion on child protection and deep taboos in Chapter 4 – that it can be hard for professionals to hear such an admission even when it is made. ('You don't really mean that, surely!' is the sort of response that professionals may be tempted to make.) It is important to listen to what parents say about this and to help them say it because a great deal of courage is required on the parent's part.

Step-parents sometimes find it impossible to care for children who are not their own. Another situation in which love sometimes fails to happen is in adoption. Like the grafts which gardeners attempt between one plant and another, adoptions sometimes just do not 'take'. Adoptions of older children, in fact, may break down in as many as 40 or 50 per cent of cases (PIU, 2000) though of course most do so without becoming child protection cases, and I do not wish to suggest that in every case, the problem is a failure to learn to love the child.

Stress-related abuse and neglect

In order to think about the ways in which different kinds of stress may push adults towards physical abuse, emotional abuse or neglect, I find it helpful to draw upon the notion of *horizontal stressors, vertical stressors* and *system levels,* which I take from Betty Carter and Monica McGoldrick (1989). *Horizontal stressors* refer to challenging events that occur as we move through life, some of which are predictable, some of which are not. An illness, for example, would be a horizontal stressor, as would a car accident, or the birth of a child, or a school examination. *Vertical stressors,* on the other hand, are areas of difficulty that we carry from the past. Life becomes particularly stressful when horizontal and vertical stressors intersect. For example, a difficult exam is moderately stressful for most people, but may be far more stressful for a person from a family background in which a person's worth is measured by academic achievement. *System levels* are the different levels at which both horizontal and vertical stressors operate. Each individual encounters her own unique challenges and carries her own unique legacy from the past, but so does each family, community, or even nation.

Taking this simple model back into the arena of child abuse and neglect, you will see that some of the risk factors identified by Greenland (1987) could be seen as horizontal stressors – a child who is sick or cries a lot, for instance, or a parent's own illness. A parent's history of having been abused or neglected herself as a child, on the other hand, would be a vertical stressor. As in the example I gave in the previous paragraph, danger points are likely to arise when horizontal and vertical stressors interact. Thus a screaming child is a stressor for any parent, but if the parent was himself habitually ignored or shouted at when he was in distress as a child, he may well find a screaming child much more difficult to cope with than would a parent whose own parents consistently responded to his distress. For a parent whose own screams of distress were ignored, the sound of a screaming child may bring up powerful – even overwhelming – feelings of loneliness, impotence and rage. It is not difficult to see how such feelings may sometimes translate themselves into physical abuse. Sometimes they result in children being battered to death.

The risk factors in Greenland's list also describe stressors that operate at several different system levels. Each individual carries her own unique history. But stressors such as poverty, poor housing and unemployment may affect whole communities. And whole communities, too, may carry vertical stressors (such as, for instance, an awareness that the area where they live is seen by the rest of the town as a 'sink estate'). It is a very serious limitation of the inter-professional child protection system that it is largely powerless to address factors such as poverty, poor housing and unemployment, even though these clearly and demonstrably have a very direct impact on the ability of parents to cope. (I will return to this topic in Chapter 12.)

But one system level, other than the individual one, that it *is* possible to address at the casework level, is that of the family. It is important to remember that vertical stressors can be carried and reproduced by families over many generations, and that changing the way an individual operates may require changes to be made by those around her too, and for the whole family to operate in a different way.

Exercise 8.2

The following case is an instance of neglect, though I suspect that the British professional system would deal with the case as a 'child in need' rather than a 'child protection' case. What vertical and horizontal stressors are present in this situation?

Robert, aged 14, is picked up by the police at 2 a.m. with some friends in a disused lock-up garage, where they have been drinking and inhaling solvents and seem to intend to spend the rest of the night. It transpires that Robert has been away from home for two days, although his mother, Janice, a single parent, has not reported him missing.

Janice says he does what he likes and when she tries to stop him going out he shouts abuse at her and pushes her out of the way. He is taller and heavier than she is. He regularly stays out all night, and misses school nearly 50 per cent of the time. He also helps himself to money from his mother's purse. Janice is resigned and seemingly indifferent to this. Asked why she does not report him missing, she shrugs and says 'What's the point? Even if the police do find him he'll only go out again the next night.' She says he should be in care, because she can't do anything with him.

Janice is 42. Her own father walked out of the family home when Janice was six and did not maintain contact. Her mother remarried and Janice was abused by her step-father, sexually and physically, until her mother and her step-father separated when she was 12. Her mother could not cope with her, and at the age of 13 she entered the care system, after which her mother only had intermittent contact with her. She had several moves within the care system and suffered further abuse there at the hands of a male residential social worker.

The family live on state benefits. She has a younger son, John, aged ten, by a different father. John attends school and is presenting no difficult behaviour problems for Janice, or his school, as yet, though she says he is starting to copy Robert.

(Continued)

(Continued)

Comments on Exercise 8.2

The most obvious current – 'horizontal' – stressor in this situation is surely adolescence and the challenging behaviour associated with adolescence. Most parents find this difficult to cope with at times: it typically involves having to insist on certain boundaries against constant pressure to drop them. Janice seems to have abandoned any attempt to hold this line, and as a result her son is putting himself in some danger, apart from creating problems for himself in the future. Coping with this task alone as a single parent is probably harder than doing so with the support and reassurance of another parent, so being alone is another horizontal pressure. Another is poverty and its practical consequences.

Among the vertical (historic) stressors are, I suggest, the following:

- *Janice's history of abuse by men, and therefore her experience of powerlessness in relation to men. This must make it harder to stand up to a son who is now, physically, a young man.*
- *The fact that Janice's own mother felt unable to parent her after the age of 13. This must make it feel harder to parent a child who is older than that age.*
- *Janice's rejection by her own parents. This will make her vulnerable to feelings of rejection and prone to employ various psychological defences to ward off the anxiety and pain that rejection evokes. I suggest that Robert's angry defiance of her will feel like rejection and that a common defensive strategy would be to (a) give way to him to avoid his anger, and (b) shut down her own positive feelings for him so as to make his rejection of her less hurtful.*

You will see that the three examples of vertical stressors that I have suggested are, in the current situation, interacting with the horizontal stressor of Robert's adolescent transition, making it far harder to cope with than it would be for another parent who was not carrying the same baggage from the past.

I would suggest that an approach to this case that is based simply on demanding that Janice takes more responsibility for her son, is not likely to work, because she already has her answer: 'Take him away. I can't cope.' But taking Robert into care is unlikely to work either. To really address the difficulty would require addressing the patterns of behaviour and emotional response which they have got into as a result of their particular family history.

Parenting children is a stressful activity at times for all parents, but most parents manage to get through it without lapsing into seriously abusive behaviour. (I do not think that many parents could claim *never* to have behaved in an abusive or neglectful way.) My suggestion is that abusive or neglectful behaviour becomes more likely when the stresses of parenting are combined with other horizontal stressors from other sources, and/or with vertical stressors that are the legacy of the past.

Implications for assessment

Looking at the problem in this way, assessment becomes a matter of trying to identify the horizontal and vertical stressors, at various levels, that are contributing to the abusive or neglectful behaviour. The more difficult part of this is identifying the vertical stressors, which are of course invisible, and which individuals and families may not themselves be consciously aware of. But some of the patterns which might suggest the presence of powerful vertical stressors might include:

- Extreme distress/anger caused by a child crying or making demands.
- A preoccupation with order, tidiness or control, within which childish behaviour becomes a nuisance and a threat.
- A preoccupation with academic achievement. In my experience this is a not uncommon cause of abusive behaviour when children fail to meet parents' expectations. It may be more common in middle-class families, and more common in some cultures than others.
- An inability to say no to a child, or to set boundaries, resulting in a child becoming more and more demanding. This may result from feelings of powerlessness on the part of the parent which may well date back to childhood experience.
- Very negative and rejecting messages directed towards a child. Sometimes these simply reflect the fact that the child was never wanted.
- Particular children being singled out either for positive or negative attention as against other children in the family.
- Children being strongly identified with a particular parent, or with particular grandparents or other family members, suggesting that feelings about that family member are also being projected onto the child.

Implications for intervention

In a minority of cases, the conclusion of such an assessment may be that a parent simply does not have the emotional resources to cope adequately and safely with the demands of a child on top of the other things – both in the present, and from the past – that she has to deal with. More commonly though, such an assessment will identify stressors in the present and from the past which have contributed to abusive or neglectful behaviour. Sometimes a child protection plan may be able to actually reduce or remove some of the present (horizontal) stressors. If part of the problem is that child and parent never get a break from each other, for instance, it may be possible to arrange for the child to have some day care. If part of the problem is overcrowded housing, then it may be possible to negotiate a move to a bigger place. Some horizontal stressors – lack of money for instance – may not be within the scope of child protection professionals to tackle, though, and a child protection plan may be able to offer no more than opportunities for parents to discuss different strategies for dealing with their situation.

In the case of vertical stressors, the best approach varies from individual to individual and family to family. Some people find it helpful to develop a clearer understanding of 'where they are coming from' and why they are distressed by particular things. Some may need help to move on from painful events in the past, which they have never acknowledged or grieved, and which therefore have become volcano-like sources of unpredictable distress. Some may respond better to a more pragmatic approach, aimed less at understanding the past and more at finding different ways of behaving in the future, which will allow them to leave past patterns behind them. Opportunities to talk, reflect and be listened to are important for any of these approaches.

Work on such matters does begin to cross over into the realm of what would be called 'therapy', and child protection professionals need to consider, in consultation with family members, whether they are the best placed people to do it. Do they possess the necessary skills and experience, or the time? Would family members prefer to work on these difficult issues with someone who was not also involved in the policing and administrative aspects of child protection work? It is difficult in a child protection climate that is much preoccupied with information gathering and information sharing, but I would suggest that one issue that needs to be considered when entering this sort of area of work is how people's privacy is going to be protected.

Professional intervention as a stressor

For most families intervention by child protection agencies is a considerable source of stress in its own right. In many cases it will interact with, and activate, vertical stressors. For poor families, social work intervention may be yet one more instance of humiliation at the hands of the state. A parent who was herself in the care of social services as a child, and who was unhappy there – or even abused there, as in the example given in Exercise 8.2 – might find the intervention of a social worker into her family life particularly difficult. If an intervention has the effect simply of adding to the stressors on a family, then it is likely to actually *increase* rather than decrease the risk of child maltreatment.

The implications of this are that, first, as I discussed in Chapter 2, it is sensible as far as possible not to use the 'child protection' route as a way of helping children, if there are other, less intimidating ways of providing help. Secondly, if the child protection route must be followed, it is essential that something is actually offered to the family, and that their difficulties and their efforts to cope are acknowledged.

Competence-related abuse and neglect

It sometimes happens that behaviour appears at first sight to be neglectful or abusive but seems in fact to be the result of genuine ignorance about the needs of a child or the role of a parent. Some adults may have lacked appropriate role models while growing up; some are very isolated and have little access to sources of advice. Some parents have wildly unrealistic expectations of what a child should be capable of at a given stage of development, or simply do not know what children need in terms of diet, or physical care, or stimulation. Some have no idea as to how to set boundaries to keep them safe. Occasionally even cases of sexual abuse may have a competence component, if the perpetrator is a child or has a learning disability and seems to have a genuine lack of understanding about appropriate sexual behaviour.

When there seems to be a lack of knowledge or of parenting skills, an appropriate form of intervention is education: the provision of advice, information, instruction or role models. In my experience, however, it is seldom the case that apparent abuse or neglect is *purely* competence based. If a parent was consistently dressing a child in ways which were inappropriate to the weather, for instance, I would be hesitant to conclude that this was the result of simple ignorance, since observation alone would indicate that a child was too cold or too hot. Failure to notice the child's discomfort would therefore seem to me to indicate that the parent was not very 'switched onto' their child's needs, perhaps because of the existence of other stressors which were taking away a great deal of the parent's attention.

Another reason why a parent might not pick up on a child's needs is lack not of competence but of *confidence*. Some people have learnt not to trust their own judgement or commonsense, perhaps as the result of consistently receiving negative messages. A purely educational approach, aimed at imparting factual information about child-rearing, may sometimes be counterproductive in such cases, since it may have the effect of further 'de-skilling' the parent: confirming that they do not know what to do and cannot trust their own judgement. As Tucker and Johnson (1989) put it, support offered to parents should be 'competence promoting' rather than 'competence inhibiting'.

Tucker and Johnson's comments were addressed in particular to those working with mothers with learning difficulties. In families where parents have learning difficulties, issues of competence are particularly relevant, and often contentious, and I will separately discuss this area of work in Chapter 10.

Abuse by children

I will conclude this chapter by noting that child abuse can be perpetrated by other children and teenagers as well as adults. In fact, in the case of sexual abuse, abuse by children and young people constitutes a very substantial proportion of all detected abuse. Looking at criminal statistics for England and Wales, Erooga and Masson (1999: 1–2) found that 'children and young people aged between 10 and 21 years accounted for 47 per cent of all cautions for sexual offence; and 13.5 per cent of findings of guilt as a result of a court process'.

Adolescence is the time when a large proportion of adult offenders report having started out on their abusive careers: as many as 50 per cent, according to Abel et al. (1985). This means that identifying cases of abuse by children is important not only for the sake of the current victims but also as a means of 'nipping in the bud' abusive careers in which perhaps hundreds of children might subsequently be abused by a single, persistent offender. As with other kinds of abuse, however, no infallible checklist exists that would allow us to recognize in advance those individuals who will go on to become abusers, but among the factors associated with sexually abusive behaviour by children and young people, are the following:

- Abnormal sexual environments, including families where sexual boundaries were too rigid or too relaxed.
- Sexualized models of compensation, where sex is seen as a comfort in difficult times.
- A parental history of sexual or physical abuse.
- History of drug or alcohol use in the family.
- Parental loss.
- Social isolation, lack of confidence, lack of social skills and maladaptive coping skills. (Summarized from Calder et al., 1997: 51.)

Chapter summary

This chapter has looked at the reasons that child maltreatment happens – the when and why of child maltreatment – including the psychological origins of abusive behaviour. I have looked at:

- 'risk factors' or 'predictors' of abuse, what they are, and what their limitations are in predicting specific instances of abuse
- different ways in which abuse or neglect can arise – I divided these into 'premeditated abuse', absence of love, 'stress-related abuse and neglect' and 'competence-related abuse and neglect'
- 'premeditated abuse' and sexual abuse in particular; its possible origins, both in terms of the past experience of abusers, and in terms of the ways that abusive behaviour reinforces and maintains itself in the present
- absence of love as a factor in some cases of abuse and neglect
- the ways in which stress, both in the 'here and now' and from the past, can be a factor in abuse
- the extent to which some forms of neglect and abuse may arise from lack of competence
- abuse by children and adolescents.

In the next chapter I will move on to look at two particular contexts in which child protection issues can arise: families where one or more parents abuses alcohol or drugs, and families where one or both parents have mental health problems.

This chapter is taken from:
Beckett, C. (2007) *Child Protection*, Second Edition
978-1-4129-2092-6

Implementing Early Years Policy

20

PETER BALDOCK, DAMIEN FITZGERALD and JANET KAY

This chapter discusses several issues:

- The implementation of policy at national, local and individual setting levels will be discussed.

- As part of this discussion, an extended case study will be considered to illustrate some of the ways in which policy is implemented at the different levels and issues arising from this implementation.

- The chapter begins with a discussion about what is expected of policy makers in terms of approaches to development and implementation of policy, planning and communication of policy developments, and the type of research, monitoring and evaluation activities that best support effective policy making.

The implementation of policy involves a process through which the ideas, intentions, principles and practicalities of specific policy plans and developments are made real. At national level this can be through the enactment of legislation, the development of new organizational structures or changes to existing organizations, and the transfer or alteration of responsibilities within or between local and national government. At local level this can be through the development of new local authority structures or agencies, new ways of working, and new protocols for working arrangements between agencies and other bodies such as voluntary organizations. Policy implementation can also mean new jobs and careers, new conditions of service and qualification structures within the workforce. At setting level, implementing policy may be through new organizational structures, changed or new policies, different ways of working, job descriptions and arrangements with other agencies.

Often legislation is required to pave the way for significant policy changes, but other developments take place under existing law. In the simplest terms, new policy is the result of government activity in planning and delivering implementation strategies (including legislation) for policies developed by departments and agencies. However, implementation of policy is complicated, reflecting interactions between a wide range of stakeholders in the early years including those within and outside government.

Modern policy making

There are certain features of policy making at the beginning of the twenty-first century that are intended to promote effectiveness and value for money. Modern policy is expected to be efficient in terms of achieving planned outcomes in a cost-effective way and not delivering any unexpected side effects that may render it ineffective or costly. Policy making is increasingly influenced by evidence from research into the best way of achieving policy goals, and on evaluations of existing policy to determine its effectiveness. To this extent, modern policy is evidence-informed and draws on lessons learned about the success or otherwise of previous policy (NAO, 2001). The government has promoted improvements in the quality of policy to try to develop long-term strategies and reduce both fragmentation in policy making and the risks of policy either being ineffective in achieving its aims or having unforeseen negative and costly side effects.

The Centre for Management and Policy Studies in the Cabinet Office works with departments and agencies within government to help them develop skills in and approaches to effective policy making. According to the National Audit Office (NAO) there are nine characteristics of modern policy making. It should:

- be forward looking

- be outward looking

- be innovative and creative

- use evidence

- be inclusive

- be joined up

- evaluate

- review

- learn lessons.

(NAO, 2001)

Currently, the central focus is on what policy actually achieves and this is supported by an expectation that there will be an evaluation of policy outcomes to ascertain whether policy goals have been met. This type of approach is now common in early years policy development with evaluations being conducted by academics and/or professional organizations using DfES or other government department or agency funding. For example, the National Evaluation of Children's Trusts (NECT) was commissioned in April 2004 by the DfES and the Department of Health to evaluate the pathfinder Children's Trusts established in 2003. In line with the development of stronger links between government departments, academics and professional organizations in terms of policy development (discussed in the previous chapter), the evaluation was commissioned by the DfES and the Department of Health and conducted by academics at the University of East Anglia in conjunction with the NCB (NECT, 2004). The evaluation of the 35 Children's Trust pathfinder projects was intended to inform policy implementation, giving early messages to practitioners involved in developing integrated service delivery. Such evaluations provide information about best implementation strategies for new or emerging policy developments and also legitimize these in terms of the stakeholders involved.

Modern policy making involves ensuring new policies are considered in terms of cost, impact, risks and priorities. Policy development now requires a consideration of a range of different options for achieving policy goals, and risk and cost analyses of these in order to determine the option most likely to succeed. There are also requirements to consult with stakeholders, pilot new policies and consider their impact before extending policy developments more widely. As such, departments are required to draw up implementation plans for policy developments. These plans can include:

- a timetable for delivering policy

- roles and responsibilities for those involved in delivery

- strategies for tackling barriers to policy development

- strategies for monitoring and reporting performance

■ flexible approaches (listening, monitoring, reviewing).

(NAO, 2001)

The ways in which implementation plans are developed in the field of early years policy is illustrated in the case study of Every Child Matters discussed below.

Activity

Consider policies in your workplace or placement. Choosing one of these policies, and with reference to the list above (implementation plans), discuss the following with a colleague or mentor:

■ How is the policy implemented?

■ Who is responsible for which aspects of implementation?

■ How are barriers to implementation being dealt with and by whom?

■ What are the arrangements for monitoring and reviewing the effectiveness of the policy?

Two other issues have become central to modern policy making. Firstly, using the Internet to communicate information about proposed policies, to publish policy documents, to provide a forum for debate and to conduct consultations on proposed policy. Government departments and agencies and professional organization websites are now major vehicles used to communicate the details of policy implementation plans and, in the case of the latter, to debate and interpret the meaning of new policy on behalf of particular audiences. Research and evaluation study reports are published on government and other websites, providing extensive information about the reasoning behind particular developments and the effectiveness of these when put into practice. Timetables for introducing new policy are published along with the consequences of policy implementation for different stakeholders including parents and children. For example, *Every Child Matters* is explained in a children's version on the DfES website. Practitioners now have unprecedented opportunities to access information about early years policy developments and to view and take part in the critical debate that usually accompanies such developments. However, the opportunity to contribute to a consultation does not necessarily lead to making an impact on the shape that policy will take (see Barnardos, 2003).

The 'Useful Websites' section at the end of the book gives details of the key websites for accessing this type of information in respect of early years policies and the debate around these. Individuals and organizations within the early years can use this information to keep up with policy developments in the field and to consider the impact of policy development at service delivery level within the context of their own role and/or agency.

A second issue concerns the way in which policies have increasingly been developed as 'packages' in line with the New Labour philosophy of 'joined up' policy making as discussed in the previous chapter. Policy making now increasingly focuses on tackling linked issues through a range of interconnected policies. This is exemplified in the sorts of policy 'packages' that have been developed to tackle poverty and social exclusion, to promote 'welfare to work' and to improve the life chances of all children, which were discussed in the previous chapter.

The case study discussed below illustrates how the concept of 'packages' of policies has been developed in the field of early years policy in order to tackle a range of interlinked policy goals. It also demonstrates many of the other features of modern policy making as discussed above and in particular explores the ways in which the relationships and debates between stakeholders have become crucial in determining the shape of early years policy. However, firstly, the stages of policy implementation will be discussed.

Stages of policy implementation

In Chapter 3, we looked at the influences on policy development and how they interact to determine policy goals. Once policy goals are determined the government has the complex job of implementing these by directing and monitoring changes at national, local and individual practice levels. The success of policy depends on the ways in which implementation plans are introduced, communicated, debated and interpreted through practice.

New policy is often introduced through consultation documents, called Green Papers, published by the relevant government department or agency. Originally, these contained ideas and thoughts about how policy could be developed rather than specific proposals, although this is not now always the case (see case study below) as Green Papers tend to contain more concrete and fully-formed policy proposals than previously.

In early years policy making, consultation is usually with local authorities and the broad range of children and families voluntary sector organizations and research institutes in the field. Organizations and individuals will send their written responses to the relevant government department or agency and such responses are usually published on the Internet by the organizations involved. The extent to which consultation responses influence government plans can vary and tends to depend on the confidence the government has in implementing their plans successfully; the extent to which there is general acceptance of those plans; the anticipated difficulties of implementing policy at local level; and whether proposed amendments will change the basic structure of new policy.

Once the consultation process is completed, the government may draw up a more specific report containing concrete proposals for policy developments called a White Paper. White Papers 'signify a clear intention on the part of a government to pass new law' (TheyWorkForYou.com, 2005). A White Paper is not generally a consultation document although it may promote discussion about the detail of new legislation. A White Paper normally leads to the introduction of a Bill, which is a draft new law (Law Society, 2005). Not all policy requires legislation to implement as discussed in the case study below.

Effectively, a Bill travels in a predetermined process through Parliament as outlined in Figure 4.1. The stages of Parliamentary process are designed to ensure that there is time for considered debate about all aspects of the legislation; for amendments to be tabled and discussed, agreed or disagreed; and for scrutiny by relevant bodies and committees to ensure that the legislation is robust and not fatally flawed. In the case of large, complex or very influential Bills progress through Parliament will be scrutinized by the media and concerned organizations. After the final stage, Royal Assent, when a Bill becomes law, there is a gap in time before the Act is implemented. For example, in the case of the Children Act 1989, implementation took place over a two-year period. This time is used to interpret the legislation at local and national levels and to put in place policies and structures, including financial measures, to ensure that the legislation can be successfully implemented.

The process may then involve intense activity on the part of government to issue guidelines and information about how to implement the policy or legislation at local level if this is required. This may include briefings and conferences, written advisory documents and meetings with key local government bodies. Within local authorities information about expected changes will be disseminated through staff briefings, invitations to stakeholders to consult, and workshops to debate and plan with those stakeholders.

Implementing the proposals in *Every Child Matters*: A case study

The implementation of *Every Child Matters* will be discussed as an extended case study of how policy affecting early years is put into practice at different levels. The discussion will include looking at the roles of different national and local organizations in ensuring implementation; how expectations are disseminated to local level; and the role of national and local government officers and professional bodies in developing and establishing implementation plans. Finally, the impact on different sectors of the workforce will be discussed in the light of the range of changes to structures and work practices.

Implementation at national government level

The Green Paper *Every Child Matters* (DfES, 2003) incorporated a raft of policy proposals, which effectively extended and continued the drive towards integrated service planning and delivery for children and families. As discussed in Chapter 3, the impetus for this particular raft of policy developments came from the recommendations of the Laming Report into Victoria Climbié's death, although this single event acted as a catalyst for putting planned government policy into place rather than as the sole reason for policy change. To a large extent, the Green Paper was intended to extend existing policy plans further. However, new policy principles were also introduced with a shift from focusing mainly on areas of disadvantage to include more emphasis on universal services to all children. As with a great deal of policy impacting on the early years, the recommendations of the Green Paper covered a wider range of policy areas including family and youth justice. However, changes to how young children are supported and protected are key elements of the developments.

One of the key influences on the development of the Green Paper was the Inter-Agency Group (IAG). Formed in 2002 in response to issues arising from the Laming Report, the IAG is a group of representatives from key agencies in children's services such as local authority directors' organizations in education and social services, e.g. the Association of Directors of Education and Children's Services, and children's charities, e.g. Barnardos, NSPCC and NCH. Originally convened by the President of the Association of Directors of Social Services (ADSS), the group have met since 2002, becoming influential in their advice to government on issues arising from the Laming Report, including the Green Paper. One of the main outcomes of the group has been to bring together the views of the statutory and voluntary sectors and to convey these views to policy makers in

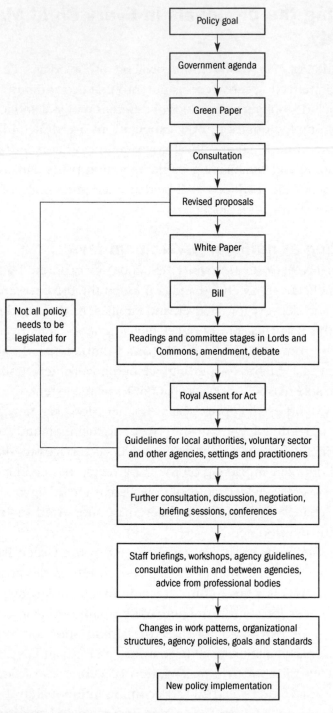

Figure 4.1 Stages of policy implementation for the early years

central government through their contacts with ministers, such as the Children's Minister, and senior civil servants in the DfES.

One of the main issues at national level was the need to 'join up Whitehall' and create much more cohesive planning for children's services between the DfES, Department of Health and Home Office (Waterman and Fowler, 2004). The Children's Minister post was established in mid-2003 along with a new sector within the DfES – the Children, Young People and Families Directorate – providing a focus for integrating children and families services within central government and bringing together responsibility for:

- children's social care

- childcare and pre-school support

- careers advice

- family support

- legal services.

(Waterman and Fowler, 2004)

In addition, the establishment of the Sure Start Unit within the DfES in 2002 was a significant step in establishing an integrated approach to policy development within the government. This is reflected in the confidence with which cross-departmental issues are handled within the proposals.

The Green Paper, published in September 2003, set out a range of recommendations for changes in the way that children's welfare and progress are supported. A Green Paper is basically a consultation document, setting out intended changes and inviting comment on these. One definition of a Green Paper is a 'tentative report of British government proposals without any commitment to action' (TheyWork-ForYou.com, 2005). However, this Green Paper varied from this norm in that there was little that was tentative about the report. This is discussed in more detail below.

Key aims of the Green Paper included:

- linking child protection services to universal services for all children

- tackling chronic problems of poor communication and information sharing between services for children

- strengthening accountability and management of services to children

- developing a better trained children's workforce

- integrating efforts to support children's welfare with those to develop children's potential.

These aims were clearly placed in the context of existing government policy to tackle poverty and social exclusion for children and families.

The Paper also stated that changes were to be focused on four key areas:

- Supporting parents and carers.

- Early intervention and effective protection.

- Accountability and integration of services.

- Workforce reforms.

Key developments proposed were:

- Creating Children's Centres in the 20 per cent most deprived wards.

- Promoting full-service extended schools.

- Funding to increase out-of-school activities.

- Funding to extend Child and Adolescent Mental Health Services (CAMHS).

- Extending speech therapy services.

- Tackling homelessness.

- Reforming the youth justice system.

Within these proposals some specific developments were identified that would bring about changes to early years service provision. One of the key themes within these proposed changes is that of integration of service delivery. In a sense, this concept came out of the perceived failure of different children's services to work effectively together to ensure children's safety and welfare. This message is not new. Although it was a central finding of the Victoria Climbié inquiry, it was also a central finding of many previous child death inquiries including Jasmine Beckford's and Kimberley Carlile's in the 1980s. Some of the specific developments proposed included:

- Removing barriers to information sharing between services.

- Ensuring each child/family had a lead professional responsible for co-ordinating and monitoring service delivery.

- Developing schools and Children's Centres as delivery points for a wide range of services to improve the speed and efficiency of the response to identified need.

In order to achieve new levels of accountability and to integrate services a number of structural changes at local authority level were proposed:

- New Directors of Children's Services for integrated education and children's social services.

- Development of Children's Trusts to include some children's health services and other relevant agencies.

- A lead council member for children.

- Replacing ACPCs with Local Safeguarding Children Boards.

At national level proposals included:

- a Minister for Young People, Children and Families

- a Children's Commissioner

- workforce reform including a common qualifications framework and training routes for those working with children and a Children's Workforce Unit in the DfES.

The Green Paper was the subject of widespread attention among those involved in children's services and within the media, with a large number of organizations commenting on and publishing their responses to the proposals. The breadth of the debate was described as 'unprecedented' in the follow-up document *Every Child Matters: Next Steps* (DfES, 2004a). The debate was supported and promoted through a series of regional conferences to brief stakeholders about the proposals and provide a forum for discussion. In addition to the Green Paper itself, a children and young people's version was disseminated and consultation groups set up to get the views of a sample. Altogether, 1,500 adults and 3,100 young people responded to the consultation exercise. However, Barnardos queried whether their extensive consultation with children and young people actually influenced the outcomes at all (Barnardos, 2003).

In March 2004, the paper *Every Child Matters: Next Steps* was published, summarizing this response to the Green Paper and coinciding with the introduction into Parliament of the Children Bill. *Next Steps* included:

- an explanation of the proposals within the Children Bill

- an explanation of the aspects of change which did not require legislation

- the outcomes of the consultation process.

The consultation endorsed the government's proposals within the Green Paper to a great extent, supporting both the principles underpinning the changes and the practical measures suggested. However, there were a number of areas where the concerns were expressed particularly around the issues of resourcing the proposals; ensuring all stakeholders were fully involved; and ensuring that local flexibility was maintained in delivering integrated services. More specifically, these included:

- the extent to which all stakeholders, especially voluntary and community sector organizations, were involved in the developments

- the lack of clarity about the role of the Director of Children's Services and Children's Trusts and whether this model would be flexible to meet the requirements of all localities

- whether there would be sufficient funding and resources to support the developments in local authorities

- whether the role of the Children's Commissioner would be sufficiently robust.

The agencies expressing most concerns were voluntary sector organizations anxious to clarify their role in the new integrated local structures. Within the Green Paper there was a lack of detail about how these agencies would be included in the new structures and whether they would be adequately represented in planning. Proposals to merge local authority departments clearly signalled the key role of local authorities in planning and service delivery but left some concerned that other agencies such as health and the police may be marginalized.

At local government level the response to the Green Paper demonstrated some concerns about implementation strategies. The Local Government Association

(LGA, 2004) urged that implementation of the Green Paper plans should take place within a framework of flexible options for structural changes within local authorities. The LGA emphasized that local authorities should have the flexibility and freedom to choose how they proceeded with integrating service planning and provision. This was echoed within debates about implementation within some local authorities. In particular the emphasis on Children's Trusts as the only way forward was not accepted by all.

The Children's Commissioner role caused some particular concerns because it seemed to be couched in vague terms that left many questions about what the powers of the Commissioner actually might be. For example, the Commissioner has a role in involving children and gaining their views, but only a very restricted role in reviewing individual children's cases. This is in contrast to the Welsh Commissioner who has more extensive powers, for example to request and get information. The Children's Minister claimed that the vagueness surrounding the role in the Green Paper was because of the need for further consideration of the Children's Commissioner role. What is unclear is why the Commissioner for England's role still needed further consideration when the role of the Welsh Commissioner has been providing a model for several years.

The media focused to a considerable extent on plans to introduce a ban on smacking within the Children Bill. The long-running and periodically heated debate about banning smacking of children in line with many other European countries was resurrected by these proposals and this drew media attention more noticeably than any other aspect of the proposals. The strong pro-smacking lobby campaigned successfully to reduce the impact of the proposals, despite a rebellion by 47 Labour backbenchers who voted for an outright ban.

The outcome was a compromise that satisfied neither the anti-smacking children's rights lobby nor the pro-smacking organizations. While the changes got rid of the contentious provision in previous legislation that some physical abuse of children could be defended on the grounds of 'reasonable chastisement', this does not constitute a total ban on smacking as lobbied for by organizations such as 'Children are Unbeatable!'. Instead a compromise was pushed through that continued to allow mild forms of physical punishment within the law, but outlawed forms of punishment that caused visible bruising or mental harm to the child. The government has long fudged the smacking issue in response to its concerns about the possible electoral losses associated with a firm and outright ban.

The media also tapped into concerns about the ethics of the proposed electronic data sharing between agencies. These concerns focused on the need to review both the Human Rights Act and the Data Protection Act to allow for data sharing to take place. Lack of detail about the safeguards around privacy and confidentiality and concerns about the impact on children's rights were central to this debate.

Normally, the next step after a Green Paper would have been to publish a White Paper, as discussed earlier in this chapter. However, in this case the government took the unusual step of drawing up the Children Bill, missing out the White Paper stage. This decision may have been taken to ensure speed in implementing the policy developments, but in some senses it may have been because the *Every Child Matters* Green Paper was much more detailed and specific in its provisions than Green Papers usually are. There is also speculation from some quarters that the government's haste was due to concerns that further tragedies might occur before new policy was in place to protect children. The decision to miss out on a White Paper caused some unease in that there were fears that certain aspects of the proposals may be legislated on before they were fully developed, for example the role of the Children's Commissioner, as discussed above.

Although ostensibly a consultation document, *Every Child Matters* was largely a finished product, detailing proposed policy changes which have mainly survived the consultation stage with few changes. It was clear that the government was determined to take forward their plans rapidly and with few concessions to those who were involved in the wider consultation. Despite the significant level of response to the Paper, no major changes were made to the original proposals, which raises questions about the purposes of the consultation process.

The provisions of the Children Bill were also outlined in *Every Child Matters: Next Steps* and discussed in relation to the outcomes of the consultation. The Children Bill included areas where policy change needed to be facilitated by legislative change. Not all aspects of policy change require legislation to implement, but where there are existing laws facilitating policy, legislation may be needed to allow change to take place. Some of the areas where legislation was needed to bring about the changes outlined in *Every Child Matters* are:

- introducing a Children's Commissioner for England responsible for promoting the views and interests of children within and outside Parliament

- outlining the functions of Children's Commissioners in Wales, Scotland and Northern Ireland

- requiring local authorities to make arrangements to work in partnership with other agencies, particularly with the voluntary and community sectors

- setting up Local Safeguarding Children Boards to monitor and direct multi-disciplinary child protection work

- establishing the role of Director of Children's Services within every local authority

- an integrated inspection regime covering a wide range of children's services headed by Ofsted

- a lead council member for children in each local authority.

Interestingly, although the Bill contained clauses about encouraging and facilitating the development of Children's Trusts, the development of these was not made statutory. The Children Act 2004 included enabling clauses that laid down the legal basis for establishing Children's Trusts. As such, the role of Children's Trusts was clarified in terms of their key function of pooling budgets, staff, services and other resources to provide more integrated services, but despite the government's expectations that all authorities will eventually establish Trusts they are not specified as such in the Act. This meant that the provision of the Act allowed for more flexibility at local authority level as to how they will organize children's services than was initially anticipated (Ashrof, 2005)

The passage of the Children Bill through Parliament was turbulent, taking nine months, and being characterized by the tabling of amendments and reamendments as a 'tug of war' took place between the Lords and Commons over some of the more controversial parts of the Bill. The main disappointments for children's charities and agencies were the compromises or decisions made about the information databases; smacking ban; and the role of the Children's Commissioner for England (*Community Care*, 2004).

The information database remained an issue after the Act was passed, partly because of lack of clarity about how it would work. Children who receive any mainstream services will be on the database, which effectively means the majority of children, as most will receive services from Primary Care Trusts (PCTs). Concerns included the replacement of the locally based Child Protection Registers with the national database, which could lead to vital information about children who may be abused getting lost in a much bigger pool of information. Some concerns were based on the Civil Service's poor track record in introducing major Information and Communications Technology (ICT) systems.

Activity

Ask several parents about their views on the introduction of the database.

■ Do they feel happy about a range of professionals having access to information about their children?

■ What sort of controls do they think should be in place to protect confidentiality? Do parents know the reasons for having the database?

■ What are the benefits and risks to children associated with the database?

■ Collate your answers and discuss with colleagues or a mentor.

The Education Select Committee's inquiry into the government's child welfare reform strategy has reported that the proposed database is too complicated and much too costly to be feasible. One expert witness, Richard Thomas, pointed out that a database of 11 million children could make it more, not less, difficult to identify problems and issues for individuals. This issue highlights some of the problems created by the volume and range of provisions within the Green Paper and the difficulties of progressing the strategy on a multitude of fronts simultaneously.

As discussed above, the role of the Children's Commissioner, which had been questioned at Green Paper stage particularly by voluntary sector organizations, was the cause of some of the turbulence. Children's rights groups such as the Children's Rights Alliance wanted the Children's Commissioner to have a role in supporting and developing children's rights issues and safeguarding children's rights. They wanted the Children's Commissioner to have a much wider remit to investigate cases, like the Commissioners in Wales, Scotland and Northern Ireland. However, there was strong opposition to this approach from Margaret Hodge, the then Children's Minister, and Baroness Ashton, Minister for Sure Start, and with a few minor concessions their view prevailed, despite an initial defeat in the House of Lords. This opposition to a rights-based role seemed to be based on the view that in such a role the Commissioner would get bogged down in individual cases (*Community Care*, 2004).

The outcome disappointed many children's agencies and children's rights groups with concerns that the Children's Commissioner for England has a weak role with fewer powers than his counterparts elsewhere in the UK and Europe.

There were also concerns about the role of the Commissioner for England for non-devolved matters in Wales and reserved matters in Scotland, which could lead to confusion about responsibilities in some areas.

The Children Bill became law as the Children Act 2004, paving the way for the changes outlined above. The key focus of the Act was enabling rather than prescribing change, allowing local authorities flexibility in how they implemented the proposals. Other changes that have not required legislation have been detailed in *Every Child Matters: Change for Children* (DfES, 2004b) as discussed above.

Implementation at regional and local level

One thing that has been clear from the start of the implementation of the Every Child Matters strategy is that local authorities were in line for the bulk of the structural and cultural change and that this would take place mainly within existing budgets. Although the strategy was influenced by and largely welcome to the TAG, representing key organizations involved in the implementation, this did not detract from the overwhelming scale of the task. Central government has provided a massive amount of guidance and information to support this process.

One of the central features of the implementation of the Green Paper proposals has been the extent of information made available to support the changes. The government website www.everychildmatters.gov.uk has been a central resource for disseminating the ethos and principles of the reforms and detailing what is expected of local authorities and other key agencies to ensure the changes are made. Local authorities and other key agencies have been advised by documents outlining their roles and the deadlines for achieving each phase of change under the general heading of 'Every Child Matters: Change for Children'. This information has been accompanied by a timetable for implementing changes, which includes deadlines for the issue of guidelines and introduction of:

- a duty for agencies to cooperate with each other

- integrated services (Children's Trusts)

- an integrated Children and Young Person's Plan

- a Director of Children's Services in each local authority

- a lead member for Children's Services in each local council

- an integrated inspection framework.

Support at regional level came largely through the appointment of regional change advisers to support local developments with a budget of £20 million. Change is particularly focused on the development of Children's Trusts and co-located teams. Typically, within local authorities there were staff briefings to provide information about the planned new structures, invitations to consult, and workshops on inter-agency aspects of change. Bodies within local government involved in such discussions included ACPCs and strategic planning groups.

It may seem that the implementation of the strategy was well coordinated and informed, leading to smooth transitions. However, there were a number of major concerns about the implementation of the strategy at service provision level. Implementing large, complex policy packages like Every Child Matters, which requires significant structural and cultural change, is a major challenge to local authorities. One issue, which is not uncommon in policy implementation of any sort, is the budget local authorities have had to bring about the changes. Local authorities were advised by Margaret Hodge to be smarter with their money when asking for more. The budget for change at local authority level is £22 million in 2006/07 and £63 million in 2007/08. This was not considered enough by local authorities and there was a view that it may limit the effectiveness of the implementation:

> **Observers feared the limited funds meant that the Act would meet the same fate as the Children Act, 1989, which was regarded as a sound piece of legislation that didn't fulfill its expectations as a result of lack of funding**
> (Ashrof, 2005)

Another issue is the range of problems associated with 'introducing innovative programmes into mainstream services' (Dawson, 2004: 24). Although local authorities had more flexibility to do this than initially anticipated, to achieve these changes required massive cultural and structural change. Local authorities had the responsibility of addressing structural change and how this would be achieved (a significant problem in itself), but there was very little said at central government level about the cultural change required to make integrated services work. It was anticipated that there would be both institutional and personal resistance to change among the workforce in the face of new regimes, new management structures, new ways of working and new cultures.

The emphasis on structural change may mask the need for cultural change as different workforces with their own ways of working, goals and motivations, philosophies and work practices come together. One concern has been that the government simply has failed to recognize the enormity of the transition required within local government to successfully integrate services. Multi-disciplinary teams were hardly a new concept, but evidence shows that many are left to cope with 'complex and unforeseen challenges' including different training, jargon, priorities, world views and working traditions (Rickford, 2005). Frost (2005) and his colleagues researched the work of several multi-agency teams to explore the issues and challenges in successful integration. He determined that the teams faced challenges in the following areas:

- structural

- ideological

- procedural

- inter-professional.

Frost found that teams either worked towards conflict resolution or conflict avoidance and that having another external agency (a common enemy?) to work against was effective in achieving better integration. He concluded that factors for success were:

- appropriate structures and systems, e.g. co-location

- shared professional beliefs and ideologies

- time for professional knowledge sharing

- active learning contexts.

At the time of writing, the Children's Workforce Development Council is about to take up the task of supporting workforce developments to achieve the goals of the Every Child Matters strategy. One of its roles is to ensure a common culture between different sectors is developed. However, it is clear that to achieve cultural change takes time and effort and is not achievable through merely making structural changes. As Dame Denise Platt, Chair of the Commission for Social Care Inspection, said at the 2004 Inter-Agency Group Conference: 'In practice, integration too often means new boundaries around old behaviours' (Platt, 2004).

Reflection

■ Consider the last time you worked with or had contact with practitioners/professionals from another disciplinary background or agency.

■ Were there any areas of difference in your view of the work you were doing, e.g. the needs of a child and family?

■ Did you focus on the same issues or have different ideas about what was important?

■ Where your goals the same?

■ Think about how comfortable you felt working with someone from a different professional background.

Cultural and structural change means different things for different sections of the workforce. Social services workers have been concerned that they will be overwhelmed by education and health as their separate departmental bases disappear. This view may be exacerbated by the continuing lead that education takes in the development of children's services. At the time of writing, 50 per cent of Directors of Children's Services are designated to take up the posts in late 2005 and 90 per cent of these are former Chief Education Officers (CEOs) rather than Directors of Social Services, many of whom retain their role of head of adult social services (Hunter, 2005). It is widely acknowledged that ex-CEOs have a steep learning curve in areas normally firmly within the remit of children's social services, such as providing statutory child protection services. CEOs generally lack understanding or experience of safeguarding children and this lack could be dangerous for children (*Community Care*, 2005). Concerns focused around the possibility that changes that impacted more on social services than education underestimated the cultural differences between them and could result in a loss of senior social services managers. This in turn could lead to the destabilization of ongoing services to children and families during the transition period and jeopardize child protection services in the longer run (ADSS, 2005; Waterman and Fowler, 2004).

Other concerns expressed by the ADSS include the emphasis on co-location of staff and whether this had become a goal in itself rather than a means of delivering effective multi-agency services to children and families. Also, their report highlighted the fact that while other agencies have a duty to cooperate in the delivery of integrated services, Directors of Children's Services had no powers to make them fulfill this duty (ADSS, 2005).

It is clear that local authorities have had to find their own ways to implement the changes within the hard-won boundaries of flexibility agreed by central government and also within the requirements of a rapid implementation timetable. This has meant that the changes have been implemented at different rates between local authorities with some lagging behind and mixed progress (Jackson, 2005). Jackson highlights the different approaches to development of pathfinder Children's Trusts within two authorities to demonstrate the diversity of approaches and argues that the developments are not about 'bricks and mortar' but about finding ways of working in partnership that work within the particular context. There is no single approach to integration that will work in every context. The conclusion is inevitable – overcoming barriers between professionals trained to think their way of working is best will take years to achieve and involve massive cultural and structural change.

The current focus on integration within local authorities may result in the issues that arise from further integration with other agencies such as health and voluntary services for children becoming a secondary consideration. The emphasis on local authority leadership and the role of Children's Trusts may divert efforts from developing the wider partnerships that would more closely involve these agencies.

Implementing Every Child Matters is one of the biggest challenges to local authorities for more than 30 years. Many issues will continue to cause concern and generate discussion for years to come. For example, the role of schools continues to unfold, with concerns that they may not be the best place to deliver services to children and families who may have a poor opinion of, and relationship with, education (*Community Care*, 2005).

Conclusion

- The implementation of the Every Child Matters strategy is part of much broader policy developments that include the National Health Framework and the ten-year strategy for childcare, designed to make widespread changes to the ways that mainstream and specialist services are delivered to children.

- The case study highlights the complex processes by which policy is developed and implemented and the key stages in this process. It also highlights the roles of different bodies and individuals, emphasizing that policy making and implementation is

▶

essentially a human activity with all the unpredictability and flawed nature of human activities. Despite the apparently rational nature of the processes involved, policy plans are put into action by a process of negotiation between bodies of different levels of power and influence. In this case, government plans have survived the process largely unscathed and despite the many ongoing concerns there is a general climate for change and consensus about the broad direction this should take.

Key factors in implementing the strategy within Every Child Matters were:
- the role of key ministers and civil servants within newly integrated central government bodies, which reflected a strong commitment to improving children's welfare services
- the complex and ongoing interactions between these ministers and senior civil servants and representatives of the voluntary sector and local and regional bodies such as IAG
- the media role in highlighting particular issues for attention
- the government's success in defeating or reversing key amendments as the Bill passed through Parliament
- placing local authorities at the centre of implementation of the strategy.

However, the strategy is large and detailed and many issues remain to be resolved in implementing it effectively, including delivering an effective and safe information database; successfully promoting cultural change to support integrated teamwork; and ensuring that partnership is successful with the range of organizations and agencies outside local government Children's Services Authorities.

📖 Further reading

Waterman, C. and Fowler, J. (2004) *Plain Guide to the Children Act*, 2004, Slough: NFER (Contains an annotated copy of the Act with a useful preliminary discussion explaining aspects of the legislation and how it was developed. The annotations explain the meanings of different parts of the Act).

Keeping up to date with new early years policy means reading magazines such as *Nursery World* and *Community Care* and newspapers such as the *Guardian* and *Independent* – all of which can also be found online.

The main government websites for following early years policy developments and key documents are listed at the end of the book.

This chapter is taken from:
Baldock, P., Fitzgerald, D. and Kay, J. (2005) *Understanding Early Years Policy*
978-1-4129-1028-6

Analysing the Impact of Policy

PETER BALDOCK, DAMIEN FITZGERALD and JANET KAY

This chapter explains some key issues:

▨ It sets out a number of approaches that can be taken to analyse policy. It includes examples drawn from current policies to set this in a practice context and to promote an understanding of how drawing on research evidence and comparison with other countries can assist this analysis.

▨ Although some specific policy examples are used, the varied approaches to assist analysis and many of the questions posed would apply equally to the range of policies in early years services.

When analysing the potential impact of any policy it is important to look broadly. It can help to think about this in terms of completing a jigsaw puzzle. At the start you connect the edges. This gives an outline shape and some information about what the finished puzzle will look like, but it does not provide the whole picture. Over time you try different pieces together, move them around and gradually the whole picture starts to fall into place. By the time the puzzle is complete it is likely that you will have handled each of the pieces several times and will have thought carefully about how they fit together, referred frequently to the box to compare the emerging puzzle and complete picture. Analysis is very similar to this. The pieces of the puzzle can be seen as representing policies. To gain a more in-depth understanding of different policies is difficult, but there are a number of approaches that you can take to help achieve this. Analysing policies is about look- ing at how they fit with current policies and practice, looking at how different parts of the policy impact on different stakeholders and how all this fits together in providing appropriate and responsive services for children, families and the wider community.

To analyse policy you can contrast current approaches with historical evidence, consider how policy impacts on varied stakeholders, consider themes running through different policies or contrast the approach in the countries of the UK with other countries. By drawing on one or more of these methods it is likely that you will be able to identify benefits and areas for development within policies and begin to gain a more analytical view of the impact of policy on the lives of children, parents and practitioners.

Why analyse policies?

Policy formation and implementation is a complex process that can take a considerable amount of time. A challenge for all policies is reconciling different priorities between those whom the policy will affect, such as practitioners, parents and children (National Audit Office, 2001). A number of different elements also need to be considered, including the implementation costs, the ability of services and service providers to deliver the policy aims, potential benefits, impact on different stakeholders and sustainability. Many policies aimed at children and families can cover a broad remit. For example, Sure Start local projects may bring together health, social services, education and voluntary services to respond to the requirements of individual families or sections of the community. It is also likely that the broader a policy, which covers many policies in the area of children and family services, the more likely it is to impact not only on other people but also on other policies. A potential risk with this broad approach is that not all those the policy is intended to benefit may do so. Sanderson (2003) contrasts the approach of evidence-based practice and the belief in government departments that 'what counts is what works'. At a simple level this does not seem problematic. In the context of complex policies, though, it is likely that an approach to analysing policy that simply aims to say whether a policy is working or not working will not capture the true impact of the policy, which is likely to include positive and negative elements. Sanderson (2003) highlights other problems with this approach. What is meant by the term 'what works'? Just because a policy is working for a parent does not mean it works for a child or a policy that works in one area will work in another. There is also a heavy government focus on measuring outcomes, usually through targets, but not everything is easily measurable or attributable to one specific policy. To overcome this, it is important to take a systematic and detailed approach to analysing the impact of policies that may provide the means to:

- decide if the information is accurate and how it will impact on practice

- argue why some aspects of policy are preferable to others

- identify aspects of good practice

- identify where there are shortcomings

- ensure high quality services

- identify gaps in policy and service provision

- highlight how policy is meeting the requirements of different stakeholders

- offer a critical appraisal of a new approach to service delivery

- offer a critical appraisal of a local, regional, national or international policy.

Since 1997 a number of policies have been introduced into children and family services. The National Childcare Strategy set out the government's intention to increase provision across the maintained, voluntary and private sectors through a number of initiatives. Quality Protects (part of the government's strategy for tackling social exclusion for looked-after children who are in the care of local authorities) aims to improve the outcomes for the most disadvantaged and vulnerable children in society. Children's Trusts, which will be implemented in most areas by 2006, aim to integrate locally based education, social services and some health services for children and young people (DfES/Department of Health, 2004). More recently the government has produced the Children's National Service Framework, which sets out long-term plans for sustained improvement in health from birth through to adulthood (Department of Health, 2004). These policies may be more accurately seen as a package of several programmes (NAO, 2001), which aim to provide equal opportunities and enhance the outcomes for each child and family. Consequently when analysing the impact of these policies it will be necessary to explore which objectives have been met, which have not and if all those intended to benefit from the policy have done so.

Levels of policy

Policies can be designed and implemented at different levels. National polices, which set out detailed arrangements, are often formulated in response to legislation. For example, the Children Act 2004 will lead to policies being implemented that will impact on the organization of children's services, strategies to improve the well-being of all children, and support to address the diverse needs of looked-after children. In response to this, organizations, local authority service providers and educare settings may amend existing policies or implement new policy to ensure that working practices take account of the new legislation. Analysis can be carried out on policy at each of these levels. This approach can provide valuable information to see how far a policy is meeting the stated aims and objectives and if the statements and philosophies of the policies are evident in practice (Fitzgerald, 2004).

Approaches to analysing the impact of policy

As seen in earlier chapters, policies can impact on different aspects of service provision and take time to become embedded. Policies can also be analysed at different stages – from initial design, at implementation, through to ongoing maintenance of the policy (NAO, 2001). Glass (2001) argues that when analysing what works it is necessary to think broadly. For example, when looking at poverty, policies that link to housing, quality of public services and the urban environment can all contribute to reducing poverty. Sure Start, Health Action Zones and the New Deal are all examples of policies that can contribute to tackling the impact of poverty on children and families in communities with high levels of deprivation and social exclusion. A clear challenge for any analysis of policy is to consider not only the benefits of individual policies but also if different policies complement each other and enhance well-being or potentially if the complexity leads to confusion and a lack of clarity about the overall aims and objectives.

Does policy represent the perspectives of all stakeholders?

Most policies will impact on a range of stakeholders, including children, parents, practitioners and often members of the wider community. Policy can also create difference between stakeholders within the same category. For example, when changes were introduced to childminding, the increased professionalism and impact of regulation caused some childminders to stop working, and led to a significant decline in numbers. This was seen as a problem by some and as an advantage by others. When analysing the impact of policy it is important to consider if policies have succeeded or failed in addressing the diverse issues of the different stakeholders who are affected by the policy. Over the past decade the UNCRC could be seen as a one vehicle that has helped policy to move beyond a welfare perspective. For children this has potentially positive benefits: it sees them as having rights as well as being the recipients of adult protection and places expectations on governments to ensure the rights of children are respected, addressed in policy and the outcome evaluated. The impact of this is that the interests of children should now be paramount in policy design and implementation, they should be able to exercise rights and their views should be consulted and acted upon (Lansdown, 2001). Although this may not happen in all instances, it does provide a basis on which an analysis of policy in respecting and promoting the right of children to be consulted can be assessed.

Activity

Read the following scenario, which describes a typical daily scene for almost every young child in England, and think carefully about the policies that the education provision is based on and how well each of them take account of the perspective of the child.

Sarah is six years old and is in Year 1 with 28 other children. She is with some of her friends from the reception class but her best friend from reception is in the other Year 1 class. She has had some difficulties with reading and has one-to-one support from a teaching assistant three times a week to help her with reading.

She enjoys being at school but misses being able to play with different toys and outside on the bikes and climbing frame. Her favourite lesson is art as she likes to paint the people she has heard about in stories. Sarah likes to write some words on her paintings about the characters in stories and her teacher helps her to do this.

Initially it may seem that there are very few explicit policies here but this may be because so many policies are taken for granted. Each of the following aspects of policy or practice could potentially impact on Sarah:

- School starting age
- The National Curriculum
- Literacy and Numeracy Strategies

- Special Educational Needs Policy

- Ofsted expectations

- School results targets

- National Primary Strategy

- Governing body decisions.

From this list the only clear reference to the need to consult children is contained in the Special Educational Needs Code of Practice (DfES, 2001), which emphasizes, 'the importance of finding out the ascertainable wishes and feelings of children and involving them when decisions are made that affect them' (section 4, p. 3). This would only apply if Sarah had been identified as having a Special Educational Need, which may not be the case. The important point from this, however, is that just because there is an expectation, through the UNCRC, that children will be consulted, it does not automatically mean they will be and this needs to be highlighted in any analysis of policy. Although the National Curriculum and the National Primary, Literacy and Numeracy Strategies may have strengths, it could be argued that the approach they dictate to learning is not the most appropriate for young children and it is likely that if consulted, children in Key Stage 1 would choose an approach to learning that resembles more closely that of the *Curriculum Guidance for the Foundation Stage* (QCA/DfEE, 2000).

Generally speaking one of the areas in the UK where the impact of various policies is felt most by children is education, but it is potentially the area where their views have the least impact or are not considered at all. Even where children are consulted, however, this may not equate with their views being respected and acted upon. Tisdall and Davis (2004) raise questions about the effectiveness and ethical considerations of some approaches to consultation based around school councils and whether they lead to democratic communities. This is not meant to suggest that all attempts to consult children are flawed, but it does highlight the need to look systematically at the strategies that are in place to allow organizations to claim that children are consulted. The following questions clearly show how careful analysis can help to appraise the approaches in place to listen to and act upon the views of children:

- Do all children have the right to participate, or is participation focused on more articulate or older children?

■ Do the approaches provide the basis for children to take on decision-making positions?

■ Is consultation acted on or is it simply tokenistic?

■ Is feedback provided to the representatives to show what progress has been made?

Recently the Scottish Executive took a systematic approach to consult children about Special Educational Needs policy review. The review aimed to involve children at different stages of the process. This was achieved by consulting an initial group of 39 children, further consultation with a group of 46 children and young people and finally questionnaires completed by a group of over 100 children and young people. The strengths of this process were that it included children with disabilities and those with English as an additional language, and the views of the respondents were used to inform policy makers at early stages of policy design. During the process feedback was offered to each group but no regular involvement of children or young people in the policy development group was put in place although this was asked for. Overall, the involvement of the children and young people led to some changes but there were limitations on what was implemented, which shows that limitations of power between children and adults still existed (Tisdall and Davis, 2004). Even though there were still limitations in this approach it does show how children can be involved and provides a basis for analysing whether the perspective of children is in evidence at policy design, implementation and maintenance stages.

Another example of how a major policy can impact on children is the changing role of classroom assistants. Their numbers have increased by over 100 per cent in eight years and this rise looks set to continue (Eyres et al., 2004). Initially, policies which have led to this (such as the Literacy Strategy, increased inclusion of children with additional needs or disabilities in mainstream education, initiatives to cut teacher workload) would seem to be beneficial. But has this increase only brought benefits, and if so, has everybody benefited?

Activity

Think about the increase in the number of support staff in early years and Key Stage 1. List some of the potential benefits and disadvantages of this policy for support staff, teaching staff and children.

Your benefits and disadvantages may have included some of the following:

Potential benefits	Potential disadvantages
Children receive more individual support	Some children become labelled as needing additional support from a young age
Increased employment opportunities for support staff	Reducing the professional status of the teaching role
Increased career opportunities for support staff	Changes driven by need to cut teacher workload rather than to increase career opportunities for support staff
Support for teachers as tasks can be shared among a team (increased work–life balance)	Support staff taking on roles that were previously teaching roles and are not paid at an equivalent level
Often brings opportunities for helpers from the community to take on paid roles	Limited access to appropriate training and a career framework to ensure progression opportunities

The fact that there are potential benefits and disadvantages with increasing the number of support staff in education does not mean that the policies that have led to this are bad. It does illustrate though, that analysis of these points is important as it can highlight the potential advantages and disadvantages from the perspective of the different stakeholders that are affected and help to identify where further developments are necessary. Eyres et al. (2004) support many of these points as their research found that even young children were aware of the many different adults in nurseries or classrooms and found this generally helpful as long as there was a level of stability in staffing. In terms of how children saw these different people, they generally did not perceive significant differences in adults' roles within the classroom. It is difficult to speculate why, but this does raise issues around different pay scales, access to training and career opportunities. If the split between the role of the teacher and support staff is becoming harder to identify, there may be implications for workforce remodelling and the opportunities and challenges this brings in terms of pay and career structure. A response to many of these potential disadvantages could be the introduction of Higher Level Teaching Assistant status, which, to be achieved, requires each person to follow a recognized course of training. It is still far from clear what the policies that have led to these increases will mean in terms of progression and pay for those who have achieved the necessary standards to receive the award (Teacher Training Agency, 2004).

Parents have a pivotal role both within the family and when working in partnership with educare settings and are stakeholders in many policies aimed at early years education and care. When parents and practitioners work together there can be significant benefits for them in terms of self-esteem and for children as they see a unified approach between the home and setting. This can also help practitioners to have a greater understanding and respect for each family (Fitzgerald, 2004). The approach of the government to families is about providing opportunities for them to lift themselves out of poverty and break down barriers that lead to social exclusion. To achieve these aims policies have been implemented to increase childcare provision, offer financial support and ensure a minimum wage level (Roberts, 2001). It is also important to analyse whether there are implicit assumptions within policies based on idealized images or assumptions of the family. In the past the government has championed marriage as the most stable environment for children to be raised in (Home Office, 1998), but many children flourish in non-traditional families (Diamant, 1999). Family relationships, the quality of parenting and levels of support are examples of important variables and show the potential negative impact of conveying certain types of family as second best (Roberts, 2001). Analysing the likelihood of policies to enhance these variables, rather than focusing on promoting one type of family structure above another, is clearly important.

Using past reports and service developments to appraise policy

Activity

■ Read through the overview of the National Childcare Strategy and consider the following questions before reading this section:

■ What are the potential positive impacts of the National Childcare Strategy for children, parents and service providers?

■ What are the potential negative impacts of the National Childcare Strategy for children, parents and service providers?

■ What evidence can be used to assess whether the targets set out in the National Childcare Strategy have been achieved?

■ What barriers may exist to achieving the targets set out in the National Childcare Strategy and how could these be overcome?

■ Are there any difficulties in accessing the overall impact of this national policy?

Why do we need a National Childcare Strategy?

The availability of good childcare is critical today. More women go out to work, there are fewer extended families, divorce and family separation have risen and people tend to move around the country more so parents do not have relatives nearby who could help.

In 1998 when the Prime Minister launched the Strategy, there was a shortage of childcare places, information was scarce on how parents could find them and places were often expensive. The Strategy set out to address that.

Why is good quality childcare important?

The early years are critical to children's development. High quality experiences with trained and committed staff will prepare children most effectively for later learning. Childcare helps children grow up happy and confident and introduces them to the joys of play and books.

Suitable childcare is a great benefit to parents so they can balance their working lives and domestic commitments and is a vital route out of poverty for families enabling parents to work, pursue a career, learn or train, confident that their children are being cared for in a safe and stimulating environment.

And it creates rewarding employment for those helping to establish childcare provision, or work with children.

What did the Strategy propose?

Accessible, affordable and quality childcare for children aged 0 to 14 (and to 16 for those with special educational needs or disabilities) in every neighbourhood.

What has the Strategy achieved?

A major expansion in childcare provision with substantial numbers of new places in the public, private and voluntary sectors and with a wide variety of types of childcare providers. Since 1997, more than 553,000 new childcare places have been created across the country, benefiting over 1,007,000 children.

▶

The Government has invested heavily in training, developing and increasing the size of the childcare workforce (which grew by 21% to 275,000 between 1998 and 2001); introduced National Standards highlighting a series of minimum quality levels for Under 8s childcare; strengthened the regulation and inspection of providers; and improved information about what is available.

Parents have also been given substantial help with the cost of their childcare with the introduction of the Working Families Tax Credit, including a childcare tax credit element. The Government has also encouraged the growth of integrated early years education, childcare and family services on one site through Early Excellence Centres, Day Centres and other providers. Following the Education Act 2002, schools are being encouraged to provide and host a range of services, including childcare, for the local community through the new Extended Schools programme.

(Source: http://www.number-10.gov.uk/output/Page1430.asp)

The principles of the National Childcare Strategy and the emphasis it places on high quality early educare experiences are vitally important for families and can have a significant positive impact on children's development. Evidence to support this analysis can be drawn from research and evaluations of service provision. For example, findings from the EPPE project support the aims of the National Childcare Strategy in terms of providing educare for children and emphasize the need to ensure it is of high quality (Sylva et al., 2004). The *Curriculum Guidance for the Foundation Stage* (QCA/DfEE, 2000) supports many of the principles by emphasizing the need for equal and inclusive access for all children and the need to provide well-structured and appropriate play-based experiences. For families, particularly where there is only one adult in the household, strategies to make childcare more affordable are likely to be beneficial. There are also wider implications for communities in terms of increased employment opportunities within the childcare workforce. A commitment to ensure there is appropriate training and ongoing support to ensure well-qualified and motivated staff is seemingly given. All in all the policy sets out a number of ambitious plans that would seem to be welcome to all families with children.

But the National Childcare Strategy has not resulted in a similar level of provision in all parts of the United Kingdom. Some areas have a number of maintained settings, which often include trained teachers who can have a positive impact on over-all levels of quality (Sylva et al., 2004). Other areas have a number of integrated Children's Centres, where parents are able to access a range of support services for members of the family. The government has recognized the importance of provid-ing joined-up services with the recent announcement of the expansion of Children's Centres, but even with 3,500 centres, the majority of children will not receive edu-care in this type of integrated provision (HM Treasury et al., 2004). A potential difficulty with any national policy, however, is that it may propose similar responses for all families. But children and families are not a homogenous group and policies need to be able to take account of this. Ongoing funds also need to be available to deliver the service and to carry out a systematic evaluation of the benefits it brings (Ghate, 2001). The emphasis on children and families has certainly risen on the political agenda since 1997 and is likely to remain high, whichever party forms the government, but *more* provision does not necessarily equate to *better* provision. To be clear, if there are benefits to increased provision, Ghate (2001) argues the impor-tance of systematic evaluation that includes the views of service users and providers.

Perhaps the most fundamental question that policies need to address is 'what works for children?' The treasury response to this has been to impose a number of public service agreements on departments to ensure there are clear accountability measures in place. For example, Sure Start, which has the aim of improving health and well-being and lifting families out of poverty, has attracted large amounts of funding to help meet the targets set out in the National Childcare Strategy. The Strategy also assumes that all families will prefer to access educare rather than care for their child at home. Some families may decide that caring for their child at home is their preferred option but there is far less support available for this choice. This may result in some families, perhaps because of lower income levels, feeling they have no choice but to return to work, as they are not able to manage financially. The government has given a commitment to extending the maternity leave period and allowing parents to share the leave, but the full impact of this is likely to take several years to achieve (HM Treasury et al., 2004).

To assess whether the targets of the National Childcare Strategy have been achieved a range of evidence can be used. Government statistics about the number of educare places, levels of poverty and the average cost of childcare can help to make an assessment. Reports from the Early Years Directorate of Ofsted can look at quality in specific settings and more generally across the sector. Information from evaluations and early years organizations can also be useful. For example, the Joseph Rowntree Foundation highlighted how educare provision has improved but families still face a range of logistical difficulties in accessing provision because it is often provided in different locations and at times that do not fit easily with work patterns or the needs of different children (Joseph Rowntree Foundation, 2003). The content of provision can also be assessed for quality. It can be argued that a positive development for the educare sector is the introduction of *Birth to Three Matters* (for children from 0 to 3) (Sure Start Unit, 2002) and the *Curriculum Guidance for the Foundation Stage* (for children from 3 to 6) (QCA/DfEE, 2000) as they take account of the developmental needs of young children and promote an appropriate curriculum. In contrast the introduction of these two separate curriculum documents and the formal approach of the Key Stage 1 curriculum could be seen as adding to, rather than reducing, the fragmentation of the sector. An alternative response to this could have been to introduce one curriculum that addressed the developmental needs and well-being of children in the early years, similar to the approach being developed in Wales. This also offers a potential comparison with which to analyse the English system (Welsh Assembly, 2004).

Overall there are likely to be benefits that are the direct result of the National Childcare Strategy although it can be difficult to accurately assess these. For example, since 2000 there has been a reduction in child poverty, less deaths in children due to injury, lower levels of infant and child mortality and an increase in the number of infants being breast fed. Alongside this there has been a rise in childhood obesity, increased levels of asthma and diabetes and a reduction in the number of children being immunized against measles (Bradshaw, 2002). Within different communities there may have been a number of policies operating, such as Sure Start, neighbourhood renewal initiatives, educational projects, New Deal schemes and Health Action Zones (Kurtz, 2003), which can make it difficult to attribute change to one specific policy. This is discussed by Kurtz (2003) in relation to conflicting evidence between policies that aim to reduce social exclusion and the different explanations that can be linked to rises in specific disorders, which 'indicates the complexities in interpreting the relationship between overall national trends in health indicators and policy initiatives' (p. 176). Although health measures do not relate directly to the National Childcare Strategy, it does clearly highlight the need for caution in attributing specific change to one national policy without the evidence to link outcomes with implementation initiatives. Based on this it could also be argued that an analysis of any national policy, especially in terms of assessing whether targets have been achieved, is best undertaken through local evaluations that are more able to identify specific benefits and disadvantages in the context of the range of policy initiatives that are likely to be in place.

Approaches to analyse policy: evaluative themes

A range of questions can be asked to promote the analysis of policy. Dowling (1999) suggests that commitment to educare can be seen in terms of four broad themes: insufficiency, diversity, lack of resources and commitment. To analyse the impact of policy, questions can be asked that relate to the level of commitment in terms of provision and resources to implement policy plans at a regional and local level. They can relate to how likely policies are to lead to integrated, high quality provision for each child and family. This approach to analysing policy can be applied at different levels, for example to evaluate a broad government policy (e.g. the National Child-care Strategy) or the implementation of policy within a setting (e.g. implementing the Special Educational Needs Code of Practice in a nursery setting).

The framework suggests a number of questions in different areas that could be applied to evaluate policy. It is unlikely, and perhaps unnecessary, that all of the questions would be applied to one policy. Decisions will need to be made about what is being evaluated and the purpose of the analysis. If it is for an essay, which is aiming to contrast the approach of central governments pre and post 1997 to educare, it is likely that a number of commitment and resource questions will be raised. If the aim is to evaluate the level of participation of families and children in issues that affect them in their nursery, the focus may be on questions drawn from the diversity section.

The following questions are not meant to be seen as a definitive response to achieving a comprehensive analysis of policy. They could be seen as offering a starting point to promote in-depth analysis, a stimulus to add a critical dimension to analysing policies, or as a vehicle to promote critical discussion of specific issues. If the aim is to offer a broad overview, it may be useful to include discussion of questions from each section. For a more in-depth analysis of an aspect of policy, questions may be drawn mainly from one area. It is also likely that the initial questions asked would do two things: provide answers and raise more questions.

Commitment

- Is there clear leadership at national, regional and local levels?

- Is there a commitment to integrated services and strategies in place to achieve this?

- Is there evidence of commitment across central departments and professions to developing integrated services for children and families?

■ Are messages from research being integrated into policy and practice to raise the quality of educare services?

■ Is there a commitment to increase the level and quality of educare services?

■ Is there commitment to promoting the involvement of children and families in service planning and evaluation?

Insufficiency

■ Does the level of provision match demand in all areas of the UK?

■ Are there sufficient educare places for all children who require them?

■ Are there differences between urban and rural locations?

■ Does the timing of provision match the needs of children and families?

■ Are there an adequate number of practitioners with appropriate qualifications?

■ Are there policies/plans in place to overcome any gaps in insufficiency?

Resources

■ Does the level of resources from central government recognize and allow the development of the educare sector?

■ How are resources being allocated and shared at a local level?

■ Are resources being increased over time to allow the development of educare provision?

■ Are resources sustainable in the long term, particularly outside the maintained sector?

■ Are resources appropriate to the requirements of service users?

Diversity

■ Does the range of provision meet the diverse requirements of children and families?

■ Do all children and families have equal access to provision?

■ What support and training is available to practitioners to ensure they have the skills to respond to all children and families?

■ Do policies value and promote the integration of each child and family?

■ Are providers aware of the diversity of family structures and do they respond to this appropriately?

■ Are the voices of each child and family heard equally?

International evidence

Several countries now have policy initiatives similar to those of the UK, which are aimed at providing services that respond to the requirements of children and families, particularly those with lower income levels. Another similarity of many of these countries with the UK is the emphasis on preventative responses which address all aspects of support that families may need through the provision of joined-up services (Vimpani, 2002). This evidence can provide another approach to analysing the likely impact of UK policy and providing a forum to debate the potential impacts of approaches that are similar to those in other countries.

In the USA there has been an increase in both the number of children using daycare facilities and the duration of time they spend there. In response to this the issue of quality has arisen, but in the absence of a national plan, such as the National Childcare Strategy, individual states have responded in different ways. But evidence of the importance of high quality environments from the United States is very similar to the UK: the higher the quality of the setting the better the cognitive, linguistic and social outcomes for children. High quality indicators include high child/staff ratios, higher levels of qualified staff, knowledge of child development and positive interactions between staff and children. In contrast, research shows that most aspects of provision were of medium to poor quality (Grisham Brown and Hallam, 2004). An important message from this is that just because it is known what contributes to good quality, it cannot be assumed that this will be evident in day-to-day practice. The direction can be set out in policy documents but this will then require substantial effort to embed the principles of the policy into practice. Another important message to come out of the evaluation was the importance of consulting daycare providers to get an accurate reflection of early care and education initiatives (Grisham Brown and Hallam, 2004). Questions can be asked about how this compares with the UK and may suggest that revisions to quality assurance processes and evaluations are needed to take more account of the views of practitioners.

In Australia the development of early childhood services has followed a similar path to the UK. There has been a heavy educational focus in policy and varied initiatives have caused an arbitrary division between caring and teaching. This has led to differences in levels of training, qualifications and philosophies underpinning service provision, which in many respects remain evident. Kindergarten provision, which children usually access the year before school, is seen to be good and has an educational focus. In contrast childcare and day care is seen to be aimed at the socially disadvantaged and about meeting health and safety needs of children (Jillian, 1996). Evidence of this arbitrary division and the unsystematic development of early years services mirrors the historical development of UK services and provides comparisons to analyse the potential impact for current policies to move to less fragmented and more integrated early years services. The levels of early years care and education offered in Australia also have some similarities with the targeted approach of providing Sure Start local projects in England, which may result in less advantaged communities feeling stigmatized and raises questions about the need for a national childcare policy that leads to national levels of provision. What is clear, though, from international evidence is that a long-term policy commitment, backed by appropriate funding, will be necessary to bring about sustainable improvements in educare in the UK and this may not always sit easily alongside the quick-fix approach to societal issues (Vimpani, 2002).

International evidence can be useful for analysing approaches to child and family policy in the UK. Glass (2001) argues that caution needs to be applied if there is an unquestioned assumption that what works in other countries can be directly applied in UK contexts. There are likely to be aspects of policy, such as service design and raising the quality of educare provision, that will work, but others may not. Any analysis of policy should consider this and ask what aspects of policy are transferable and what may be culture dependent. For example, the approach to funding in the USA is very different to the UK and introducing a policy that works well there may not achieve the same outcomes here. When using international evidence to appraise UK policy, as well as asking 'what works?', Glass (2001) suggests there is another fundamental question that needs to be considered: What is worth doing for children?

Conclusion

■ Analysing policy is a complex process, particularly in the area of early years as policies have become increasingly complex.

■ Nonetheless, it is important to be able to make an appraisal of the broad issues and how they are likely to impact on the various stakeholders (including those whom polices are intended to have an impact on and those who may be affected indirectly).

■ To assist readers with this process the chapter has suggested a number of approaches that can be helpful. It is by no means the only way to undertake analysis of policies but it is hoped that it provides a starting point and may generate other ideas. The approaches outlined included:

- Measuring the effectiveness of polices according to outcomes (e.g. how many additional childcare places have been created and how long these have been sustained for).
- Assessing the ability of a policy to represent the perspective of different stakeholders, particularly children who may not be empowered through policy.
- A comparison with past developments and evaluation reports.
- Assessing the approach of policy against research evidence (e.g. examining whether the pedagogical approach of early years curricula is developmentally appropriate for young children).
- Evaluating policy against a range of themes, including the level of commitment from government and policy makers, the level of resources allocated to implementation and sustainability and the ability of the policy to respond to the diversity of stakeholders.
- Comparison with international approaches and evidence, but with attention to the level of transferability within the context of the UK and the policy approach in operation.

📖 Further reading

One of the best ways to feel more confident with evaluating policy is to read widely to gain an understanding of how authors have approached the evaluation of policy. An approach to evaluating early years policy can be informed by reading magazines such as *Community Care* and newspapers such as the *Guardian* and *Independent*, all of which can also be found online.

Roberts, M. (2001) 'Childcare Policy', in P. Foley, J. Roche and S. Tucker (eds) (2001) *Children in Society: Contemporary Theory, Policy and Practice*, Basingstoke: Palgrave. (Provides a useful overview of how the international context, through the UNCRC, has had an increasingly significant impact on policy design and implementation in the UK. Any evaluation of UK policy will need to take account of this.)

Another important consideration is how well the views of children are taken account of in policy design and implementation. There is a general consensus that children are now more involved but this may not always be the case.

Tisdall, E.K.M. and Davis, J. (2004) 'Making a difference? Bringing children's and young people's views into policy making', *Children and Society*, 18(2), 131–42. (Discusses a range of issues around the involvement of children and considers at what stages their views are taken account of and most importantly the impact that this involvement has.)

This chapter is taken from:
Baldock, P., Fitzgerald, D. and Kay, J. (2005) *Understanding Early Years Policy*
978-1-4129-1028-6

An Introduction to Reflective Practice

22

GILLIE BOLTON

We do not 'store' experience as data, like a computer: we 'story' it.

Winter 1988, p. 235

You understand how to act from knowledge, but you have not yet seen how to act from not-knowing.

Chuang Tsu trans. 1974, p. 68

I'm no longer uncertain about being uncertain: uncertainty is now my mantra.

Reflective practice student

Reflective practice is positioned firmly as a dynamic developmental process in this interdisciplinary second edition. The term has lost some credence, becoming a catch-all name for a wide range of activities from deep life, work and organisation-changing critique to rote box-ticking practices seeking to make professionals accountable to and controllable by increasingly beaurocratic and market-led organisations. This second edition offers practical and theorised methods for understanding and grasping authority over actions, thoughts, feelings, beliefs, values and professional identity in professional, cultural and political contexts. It clearly delineates processes for critical reflection upon the forms, values and ethics of institutional organisations and structures in which professionals work. This critique can result in radical movements for change.

Most training and post-experience courses include elements of reflective practice; the danger lies in undertaking it because it is just the thing to do. Such an attitude cannot support reflection and reflexivity.

The paradox is that reflective practice is required by the masters, by the system. Yet its nature is essentially politically and socially disruptive: it lays open to question anything taken for granted. Enquiry-based education, 'education for creativity, innovativeness, adaptability, ease with difference and comfortableness with change . . . [is] education for instabililty' (Reid and O'Donohue 2004, p. 561).

Smooth running social, political and professional systems run on the well-oiled cogs of stories we construct, and connive at being constructed around us.

Welcoming of diversity can be mere window dressing. Effective reflective practice and reflexivity are transgressive of stable and controlling orders; they lead cogs to decide to change shape, change place, even reconfigure whole systems.

The structures in which our professional and personal roles, values and everyday lives are embedded are complex and volatile. Power is subtle and slippery; its location is often different from how it appears. Deep reflection and reflexivity for development involve:

- *authority* and *responsibility* for personal and professional identity, values, action, feelings;

- *contestation*;

- willingness to stay with *uncertainty*, *unpredictability*, *questioning*.

Paradoxically the route is not through angry uncomfortable confrontation: such revolution leads to destructive cycles of action and reaction. The route is through spirited enquiry leading to constructive developmental change and personal and professional integrity based on deep understandings. It is *creative*, *illuminative*, *dynamic*, *self-affirming*, but not a thornless rose bed. People only learn and develop when they enjoy the process, and benefit personally. Serious professionals have cavilled at such creative methods, and use of deeply accessible varied sources of wisdom.

Einstein (1929) was successful partly because he doggedly and constantly asked questions for which everyone thought they knew the answers. Childlike, he asked why?, how?, what?, rather than accepting givens or taken-for-granteds. He 'love[d] the *questions themselves* like locked rooms', and certainly '*live[ed]* the questions' (Rilke [1934] 1993, p. 35).

Stories are the mode we use to make sense of ourselves and our world. This world and our lives within it are complex and chaotic: seemingly governed by forces not only beyond our control, but beyond our understanding. We tell and retell episodes both minor and major to our colleagues, to our loved ones, to therapists and priests, to strangers on the train, to a wedding guest (Coleridge 1834). This can merely be a process of tucking ourselves securely under a quilt patchworked out of safe and self-affirming accounts: our stories can only too easily be essentially uncritical. Or, even worse, they are censoring tools: 'cover stories' (Sharkey 2004). This self-protectiveness can ensure that our stories are not exploring sensitive issues, but are expressions of what we feel comfortable with, or would like to be.

> It was still snowing as [Pooh Bear] stumped over the white forest track, and he expected to find Piglet warming his toes in front of the fire, but to his surprise he found that the door was open, and the more he looked inside the more Piglet wasn't there.
>
> Milne [1928] 1958, p. 163

Effective reflective practice can be like looking for Piglet: the more you look, the more it seems not to be there. It is only when you have the courage to stop looking and trust the reflective and reflexive processes that you will begin to perceive the areas you need to tackle. Discovering what you need to reflect upon and the route to altering things is an exhilarating journey. Afterwards the insights and inevitable changes seem obvious. Although reflective practice has become a standard in initial and continuing professional education and development, it is a state of mind, an attitude, an approach, and therefore elusive to curriculum planners. It is an educational approach which makes the difference between twenty years of experience or one year of experience twenty times.

One way forward is to focus on NON-critical incidents, or perhaps non-'critical' aspects of such events. Insight is gained by respecting the reflective and reflexive processes to light upon and enlighten that which most needs examination. These areas might not sock us in the face as 'critical'; they are probably ones which have been allowed to pass unnoticed because focusing upon them is more problematic, often for unexamined personal or professional reasons. 'Critical' incidents, such as giving the wrong vaccine because they had been stored higgledly-piggledly in the fridge, will inevitably be examined. The events we 'forget' most need reflection, and give rise to the deepest reflexivity: 'we need to attend to the untold' (Sharkey 2004). Joy-Matthews et al. (2004; see also Goldberg 1991) recommend a human resource development exercise: writing what you *do not* remember. Plato, who said 'the life without examination is no life' (Plato trans. 2000, p. 315), reckoned education is finding pathways to what we do not know we know.

Reflective practice and reflexivity are not subjects but a pedagogical approach which should 'pervade the curriculum' (Fanghanel 2004, p. 576): the pearl grit in the oyster of practice and education. To be effective they need dynamic methods. The method of travel affects what happens along the way and the destination. A medical student commented: 'we spend so much time studying medicine that we never have time to study sick people'. Reid and O'Donohue (2004) argue that enquiry-based learning should become the organising logic of entire teacher education programmes, with students learning *through* enquiry rather than being prepared *for* enquiry. Curricula need shaking up, and more enquiry-based methods introduced. *Curriculum* is Latin for race course (Rome's Piazza Navone was one): perhaps we need to lose an association with ancient Romans.

A story is an attempt to create order and security out of a chaotic world. But for our experiences to develop us – socially, psychologically, spiritually – our world must be made to appear strange. We, and our students, must be encouraged to examine our story making processes critically: to create and recreate fresh accounts of our lives from different perspectives, different points of view, and to elicit and listen to the responses of peers. Listening critically to the stories of those peers also enables learning from their experience. It is the exploration of experience, knowledge, values, identity that matters, rather than any attempt to arrive at a 'true' account (Doyle 2004).

important knowledge about reality always comes out of [writing] . . . through a . . . transformation of reality by imagination and the use of words . . . When you succeed in creating something different out of . . . experience, you also achieve the possibility of communicating something that was not evident before . . . But you cannot plan this transmission of knowledge.

Llosa 1991, p. 79

Postulating what other actors might have thought and felt, empathising with them and the situation, as well as imaginatively reconstructing the situation in fresh ways, offers understandings and insights as no other process can. For example, a practitioner can retell a story from the point of view of students or clients, reconstruct it with the genders of the actors reversed, or create a satisfactory ending in place of a horrible one.

Effective reflective practice and reflexivity meet the paradoxical need both to tell and retell our stories in order for us to feel secure enough, and yet critically examine our actions, and those of others, in order dynamically to increase our understanding of ourselves and our practice.

What do we call it?

The term *reflective practice* is not a terribly useful one. The metaphor it embodies is limited: a mirror reflection is merely the image of an object directly in front of it – faithfully reproduced back to front. What is the reflection of shit? Shit. *Reflective practice writing*, however, is a creative adventure right through the glass to the other side of the silvering. Such reflective practice can take us out of our own narrow range of experience and help us to perceive experiences from a range of viewpoints and potential scenarios. It can do this by harnessing a vital human drive – to create stories about our lives, and communicate them.

Perhaps this approach should be called *flexive*. Flexion means 'alteration, change, modification', and 'a bend, curve, and a joint', whereas reflection means 'the action of turning [back] or fixing the thoughts on some subject' (*Shorter Oxford English Dictionary*), with the associated definition of the reversed reproduction of an image. This makes *reflection* sound as dynamic as *rumination*: a sheep chewing smelly cud. I have a cartoon of a sheep nose to nose with the reflection of herself and the surrounding meadow. She's saying: 'I'm sure the grass is greener in the mirror, but whenever I try to reach it, this ugly ewe bars the way and butts me on the nose.'

The mirror image model of reflection suggests there is a me *out there* practising in the big world, and a reflected me *in here* in my head thinking about it. If I think about it constructively enough I will be able to alter my practice and my relation to you out there. This model is located in modernist duality: *this* in dialogue with *that*, *in* and *out*, or *here* and *there*. Here is an ancient Zen text:

You must first forsake the dualities of: self and others, interior and exterior, small and large, good and bad, delusion and enlightenment, life and death, being and nothingness.

Tsai Chi Chung trans. 1994, p. 95

The through-the-looking-glass model involves far wider potential interactions, opens up more developmental reflexive and reflective space than is possible with a Cartesian-based one. 'Reflection is the central dynamic in intentional learning, problem-solving and validity testing through rational discourse' (Mezirow 1981, p. 4). Yes, true, but there is an awful lot more than just the 'rational' for us to explore. Professionals cannot fully crawl through the glass. They can still explore the wide and rather perplexing other side of reflection: turn their world inside out and back to front, not just think about it rationally.

Reflective practice: a political and social responsibility

Reflective practice can fall into the trap of becoming only confession. Confession can be a conforming mechanism, despite sounding liberating, freeing from a burden of doubt, guilt and anxiety (Bleakley 2000b). Confessing has a seductive quality because it passes responsibility to others. Practitioners need to take responsibility for their actions and values, and their share of responsibility for the political and social situations within which they live and work. The desire to hold an audience with a 'glittering eye' (Coleridge 1834) is strong. Jennifer Nias, a researcher into the experience of women teachers (Nias and Aspinwall 1992), noted with surprise that all her potential interviewees were keen to tell their autobiographies at length. People always are: but they do not want their stories questioned; this is the role of reflective practice.

Reflective practice is more than an examination of personal experience; it is located in the political and social structures which are increasingly hemming professionals in (Goodson 2004). Their right to make moral and professional judgements is being eroded; they are being reduced to technicians, their skills to mere technical competencies. In order to retain political and social awarenesses and activity, professional development work needs to be rooted in the public and the political as well as the private and the personal.

To this end, examinations of practice need to be undertaken alongside open discussions with peers on pertinent issues, an examination of texts from the larger field of work and politics, and discussions with colleagues from outside the practitioners' own milieu. Reflective practice work can then become politically, socially as well as psychologically useful, rather than a mere *quietist* navel-gazing exercise. It supports, demands even, practitioners thinking about values:

If we had asked people to talk about their values in abstract terms, we would have received generalised responses. By asking them to tell [write] stories about important experiences, we were able to see something of how values reveal themselves in a complex, varied and shifting way in practice.

Pattison et al. 1999b, p. 6

Values which underpin practice are rarely analysed or questioned. Through reflexive practice professionals realise dissonance, or dissatisfaction with their own values in practice, or those of their organisation, leading them to make dynamic change. This might not be easy, particularly if they realise an action has been against their own ethical code, or that they are in an untenable but unalterable situation (Rowland 2000). Examining such fundamental areas requires a supportive, confidential, carefully facilitated environment.

Goodson creates a distinction between *life stories* and *life history*. The latter is the former plus appropriate and challenging data from a wide range of sources, and evidence of vital discussion with colleagues. 'The life history pushes the question of whether private issues are also public matters. The life story individualises and personalises; the life history contextualises and politicises' (1998, p. 11). Noel Gough (1998) uses a similar method with postgraduate students in education. He says he *plays* with the method, which he calls *currere* – a term coined by Pinar (1975) and Grumet (1981).

Gomez et al. (2000, p. 744) found how education students' reflection was unchallenging and non-risk-taking, because they only wrote personal narratives of their classroom teaching, from their own point of view. 'The nature of personal stories as ones that people actually lived limited the ways in which they could be interrogated. Questioning the viewpoint resulting from an event in someone's life was tantamount to challenging her overall integrity.' Future student narratives will be written from multiple perspectives, enabling challenge and insight.

Cartoons in another study offered a 'playfully ironic dimension for intensifying the process of critical reflexivity' (Cavallaro-Johnson 2004, p. 423). Visual images, which allow subtexts to appear unwittingly, prevented the autobiographical stories from being uncritical and confessional. I would argue that a range of different forms of text, such as from different points of view, can similarly offer layers of unwitting subtext.

Re-view

A film or story is a dynamic fresh look through the eyes of more than one actor. Replaying back what 'actually' happened is impossible: any retelling will inevitably be affected by the view of the person doing the retelling. Effective reflective practice enables the exploration of a range of viewpoints and possibilities:

Stories are a lens through which I view the world to make sense of my experiences and those of my colleagues and patients. In writing some of these stories I am able to focus on complex issues that have previously appeared distorted by time and emotions. Metaphors shed light on subjects that I had been unaware of before, patterns stand out in ways that I had not hitherto understood.

Mark Purvis

Reflective practice is learning and developing through examining what we think happened on any occasion, and how we think others perceived the event and us, opening our practice to scrutiny by others, and studying texts from the wider sphere. Reflexivity is finding strategies for looking at our own thought processes, values, prejudices and habitual actions, as if we were onlookers. It is a focusing closer and closer. In the film *Blow-up* the only evidence for a murder is a small, insignificant-seeming detail in a photograph. This tiny detail is blown up and up until the evidence is clear. No detail is potentially too trivial or insignificant to write, think and talk about. These vital details might have gone unnoticed at the time, as in *Blow-up*.

Many professions facilitate others to understand their lives and themselves better, and hopefully improve things thereby. A practitioner cannot support another in this way if they are not aware and open themselves (Murray 1982). Bringing the personal into the professional can increase empathy between client and professional (Smyth 1996). Aesthetic experience (such as writing) can leap over the seeming gap between the personal and the professional self, and the seemingly impossible gap between the safe and rehearsed story and possibly dangerous new stories. This can only bring greater unity and wholeness of experience to the practitioner or educator, and greater empathy between them and their client. Job satisfaction will increase, and work-related stress decrease:

Perhaps the most accessible form of freedom, the most subjectively enjoyed, and the most useful to human society consists of being good at your job and therefore taking pleasure in doing it – I really believe that to live happily you have to have something to do, but it shouldn't be too easy, or else something to wish for, but not just any old wish; something there's a hope of achieving.

Levi 1988, p. 139

Writing stories and sharing them in a trusted, confidential, facilitated forum of peers, or within supervision, is a way of increasing job satisfaction and effectiveness, and is the process offered by this book. Explorative and expressive writing is pivotal: the writing of a story or poem is a first-order activity. The writing, the essential discussions and the writing of additional stories from different angles with the support of the group, is a creative explorative process in its own right –

not a tool in professional reflection. Course participants do not think and *then* write, the writing is the vehicle for the reflection: reflection *in* writing. Not only does writing enable the most appropriate reflection, but also, as a participant commented, 'one of the values of writing is that you can freeze the film: reflect upon one frame or a short series, then run the film backwards and review a previous scene in the light of reflections upon a later one. This would be difficult to do in talking: it wouldn't make sense; impossible to do during action.'

> I consider writing as a *method of inquiry*, a way of finding out about yourself and your topic. Although we usually think about writing as a mode of 'telling' about the social world, writing is not just a mopping-up activity . . . Writing is also a way of 'knowing' – a method of discovery and analysis. By writing in different ways, we discover new aspects of our topic and our relationship to it. Form and content are inseparable.
>
> Richardson 2000, p. 345

The psychologist Oliver Sacks studied people who were missing, or effectively missing, part of their brain, and the bizarre things this led to. In his essay *The Man who Mistook his Wife for a Hat*, he studies 'Dr P.' who could see, but had lost 'visual perception, visual imagination and memory, the fundamental powers of visual representation . . . insofar as they pertained to the personal, the familiar, the concrete'. Sacks concludes:

> Our mental processes, which constitute our being and life, are not just abstract and mechanical, but personal as well – and as such involve not just classifying and categorising, but continual judging and feeling also. If this is missing, we become computer-like, as Dr P. was. And by the same token, if we delete feeling and judging, the personal, from the cognitive sciences, we reduce *them* to something as defective as Dr P. – and we reduce *our* apprehension of the concrete and real . . . Our cognitive sciences are themselves suffering from an agnosia essentially similar to Dr P.'s. Dr P. may therefore serve as a warning and parable – of what happens to a science which eschews the judgmental, the particular, the personal, and becomes entirely abstract and computational.
>
> Sacks 1985, p. 19

Reflective practice can learn from Sacks's 'warning and parable', and be open to as much of ourselves as is possible. A reflective practice suffering from agnosia will not get us terribly far.

Effective reflective practice encourages the seeking of understanding and interpretation of principles, justifications and meanings (Morrison 1996). It involves interrogating both our *explicit* knowledge, such as known and quantifiable evidence-based knowledge, and *implicit* knowledge – 'a collection of information, intuitions and interpretation' (Epstein 1999, p. 834) based on experience and prior knowledge (for further analysis of types of knowledge, see Eraut 1994; Belenky et al. 1997). Implicit knowledge is tried and tested, gained initially from experience, observation, or study. Intimately known, its appropriate application is intuitive. This does not necessarily mean that it is right, any more than knowledge gained from randomised control trial research (explicit) is.

Such re-viewing of knowledge and experience can lead practitioners to perceive a need for change in their world, their relation and attitude to it, and the attitudes of others. One of my students stated: 'this is not an academic module, but an assertiveness training course'. Asserting yourself inevitably involves challenging social structures.

One of the greatest benefits to a student in a learning situation, or a client with a practitioner, is the sense of their relatedness to the professional: that they are interested, involved, and care. In medicine this has been called the *placebo effect* of the physician as *healer*: 'the attitude of the doctor can make an appreciable difference to the psychological response of the patient who feels the need to be understood and listened to empathically' (Dixon et al. 1999, p. 310). To give the people we work with confidence in us as professionals, we have to be secure and happy enough ourselves in our roles, and not anxious or inhibited.

How can that happen in overworked, overstressed professions, which are getting less appreciated daily? One of the ways of being an empathetic, effective practitioner is to be reflexive as well as reflective.

Reflection is an in-depth consideration of events or situations outside of oneself: solitarily, or with critical support. The reflector attempts to work out what happened, what they thought or felt about it, why, who was involved and when, and what these others might have experienced and thought and felt about it. It is looking at whole scenarios from as many angles as possible: people, relationships, situation, place, timing, chronology, causality, connections, and so on, to make situations and people more comprehensible. This involves reviewing or reliving the experience to bring it into focus. Seemingly innocent details might prove to be key; seemingly vital details may be irrelevant.

Reflection involves reliving and rerendering: who said and did what, how, when, where, and why. Reflection might lead to insight about something not noticed in time, pinpointing perhaps when the detail was missed.

Reflexivity

A reflexive-minded practitioner will then ask themselves, why did this pass me by: where was my attention directed at that time? Reflexivity is: 'what are the mental, emotional and value structures which allowed me to lose attention and make that error?' This deep questioning is missed out if the practitioner merely undertakes reflection as practical problem-solving: what happened, why, what did I think and feel about it, how can I do it better next time?

Reflexivity is making aspects of the self strange: focusing close attention upon *one's own* actions, thoughts, feelings, values, identity, and their effect upon others, situations, and professional and social structures. The reflexive thinker has to stand back from belief and value systems, habitual ways of thinking and relating to others, structures of understanding themselves and their relationship to the world, and their assumptions about the way that the world impinges upon them. This can only be done by somehow becoming separate in order to look at it as if from the outside: not part of habitual experience processing, and not easy. Strategies are required, and the support of others. This critical focus upon beliefs, values, professional identities, and how they affect and are affected by the surrounding cultural structures, is a highly responsible social and political activity.

Reflexivity involves coming as close as possible to an awareness of the way I am experienced and perceived by others. It is being able to stay with personal uncertainty, critically informed curiosity as to how others perceive things as well as how I do, and flexibility to consider changing deeply held ways of being. The role of a trusted other, such as a supervisor or peer-reader of an account, is vital.

Mindfulness is an invaluable approach. A conscious exclusion of other elements of life, apart from that which is being attended to (Johns 2004), is achieved when senses and awarenesses are tuned into present action: the opposite of multitasking (Epstein 1999). Being mindfully aware develops communication, ability to use implicit knowledge in association with explicit knowledge, and insight into others' perceptions. Frank speaks of *practical wisdom*, from Aristotle: '*Phronesis* is the opposite of acting on the basis of scripts and protocols; those are for beginners, and continuing reliance on them can doom actors to remain beginners' (2004, p. 221).

The observation skills and awarenesses required of a reflective writer develop mindfulness, and are developed by it. Both require an acute and aware focusing upon what is happening at any time. Doctor-writer Verghese exhorts: 'We should be ministers for healing [and educating], storytellers, storymakers, and players in the greatest drama of all: the story of our patients' [and students'] lives as well as our own' (2001, p. 1016).

An example: Sam, a midwife, brought a furious account of an angry mother she had attended as an NHS midwife: 'stupid, hostile upper-middle class bitch who felt she had the right to boss me around, tell me what to do'. The birth had been exhausting and disastrous for both mother and midwife: Sam still felt bitter twenty-five years later. The reflective practice group offered insight and comparative cases, and suggested Sam wrote an account from the mother's perspective.

The following week saw a very different Sam: 'I don't know exactly what was wrong, but I do know, having relived it from this mother's point of view, that she was upset and confused. Because I saw her as a stupid, middle-class bitch who thought she could have everything she wanted her way, I never listened to her properly. I think I'll see demanding mothers in a different way in future.'

Telling the truth?

The narratives we tell and write are perspectival. Looking in through a window at experience to reflect on it from outside is impossible. Professionals, however open about themselves and their practice, can only perceive and understand from their own viewpoint, broad and empathic as that might be. To be objective is to be 'not influenced by personal feelings or opinions in considering or representing facts; impartial, detached' (*OED*). Yet, 'We don't see things as they are, we see them as we are' (Nin, quoted in Epstein 1999, p. 834).

Individual perspectives and values can be widened and deepened. One can look on the glass and only see one's self reflected, or through it as in George Herbert's hymn: 'A man that looks on glass, / on it may stay his eye; / or, if he pleaseth, through it pass, / and then the heav'n espy.' Lewis Carroll's Alice does even better: she crawls right through the looking-glass, leaving her stuffy Victorian rule-bound world, entering a world in which everything 'was as different as possible', things are 'all alive', where dynamic connections are made between divergent elements.

A creative leap is required to support widening and deepening of perspective, and the ability to mix tacit knowledge with evidence-based or explicit knowledge effectively. The professional arena can be opened up to observations and reflections through the lens of artistic scrutiny. We are still anchored to our own perspective, but these perspectives will be artistically and critically enhanced. We cannot pass through the mirror's silvering, and can inevitably reflect only upon ourselves, our own thoughts and experiences. Artistic processes such as writing can, however, enable a harnessing of, for example, material such as memories which we do not know we remember, and greater access into the possible thoughts and experiences of others. The perspectival nature of such writing is acknowledged (i.e. they do not purport to be objective or true), and the many skills used are those of literature.

Professional writers are being heard clearly, both students (DasGupta and Charon 2004; Hatem and Ferrara 2001; Gomez et al. 2000) and practitioners (Clough 2002; Loughran 2004; Bolton 1999b; 2003a; see also the *Annals of Internal Medicine: Physician-Writers Reflection* series, e.g. Shem 2002). Samuel Shem says fiction writing has been an essential way for him of humanising medicine (2002).

Writers acutely observe small details and subtle nuances of behaviour and situations. A teacher- or clinician-writer observes details missed by good observant teachers or clinicians (see Charon 2004). Try it. Observe a student or client walking into your practice place. Capture on paper how they hold themselves, breathe, move their limbs, their characteristic gestures and sayings. What do they remind you of – a cat?, a big soft armchair?, a locked filing cabinet?

A writer has the unparalleled privilege also of entering into the life of another. That this person is a character on a page does not make it any less of a privilege. Deep understandings can be gained by entering (virtually) another's feeling, thinking, perception and memories. This is writing beyond what you know, and has to be: if you know where writing is going to take you, start at that known point, and write on into the unknown. Try it. Take the person you have just described. Write the conversation they might have had on returning home that night. Remember this is an artistic exercise: don't think about it, let your hand do the writing, free of the police officer of your mind. If you add in something about how they got home, where they live or drink, you really are allowing your imagination to take you through the glass. You tap into latent understandings which have possibly not been so fully exercised before.

This is fiction; the writing has been invented imaginatively: it removes the straitjacket of *what really happened*. Writers are therefore free to draw deeply upon their imagination and aesthetic sense, and their intuitive knowledge of social and human areas such as relationships, motives, perspective, cause and effect, ethical issues and values.

It matters not a jot that you do not depict what actually happened, or what your student or client really thought. What does matter is that you have brought what you understand and think about this person into the forefront of your mind. Medical students write patients' illness stories in the voice and vernacular of the patient, imaginatively and vicariously entering patients' contexts. They 'become the other' through creative writing (Engel et al. 2002, p. 32). It is not quiddity we seek – the real nature or essence of a thing – but our experience of it.

Sharing this writing with a colleague can offer effective reflection upon understandings. Rewrite with the fresh insight gained. And perhaps a colleague, also present at the encounter with the patient, might write an account. Reading each other's account will offer the different perspectives from which you unwittingly work.

This method of reflection does not jeopardise professional accuracy of perception (Mattingley 2000). Neither does it impose distorted interpretations about patients (Garro and Mattingley 2000) because its purpose is to explore and express what is already there in clinicians' and educators' understanding and perception. It brings this to the fore to be reflected upon critically and effectively. It also brings to the forefront of attention the perspectival nature of our perception. No one can know *what really happened* in any situation. Perhaps it might become clear that the doctor understood the patient very differently from the nurse, or the teacher might think and write one thing today, reflect upon it perhaps with peer(s), and write something different tomorrow, their perception enhanced by the writing and discussions. Such a collection of stories can build up a composite picture, and what was thought and felt – getting as close as possible to *what really happened*.

Kevin Marsden, a special-school teacher, and Masters in Education reflective practice student tells a classroom story:

Malcolm

One morning we were doing number work. Malcolm was struggling to recognise sets of two. He was troubled by the book in front of him and sat slumped on an elbow.

I had one of those 'bright ideas' teachers tend to get. Let's make it more practical. 'Malcolm,' I said. 'Look at Darren. How many eyes has he got?'

Malcolm looked at Darren. Pointing with his finger he slowly counted in his deep voice, 'one . . . two'.

'Good, well done,' I said. 'Now look at Debbie, how many eyes has she got?'

Pointing carefully again Malcolm intoned slowly, 'one . . . two'.

'That's great, Malcolm, now look at Tony, count his eyes.'

'One . . . two.' Let's take this a step further, I said smugly to myself.

'Now Malcolm, look at Matthew. Without counting can you tell me how many eyes he has got?'

Malcolm looked at me as if I had gone mad. 'OK that's fine Malcolm, you just count them like you did the others.'

Relieved he slowly repeated his methodical counting: 'one . . . two'.

There is a magical moment in teaching, when the penny drops, the light goes on, the doors open. Success is achieved. I was starting to worry. We weren't getting there!

'Malcolm, how many eyes has Naheeda got?' Malcolm counted slowly, as if it was the first pair of eyes he had ever seen. 'One . . . two'.

'Good, you're doing really well.'

We carried on round the class. Eager faces looked up to have their eyes counted. I was growing desperate as we ran out of children. Was I leading Malcolm on an educational wild-goose chase? Were we pursuing an idea that was not yet ready to be caught?

The last pair of eyes was counted. 'One . . . two.' The finger carefully went from eye to eye. There was only me left. 'Malcolm,' I said, trying to hide my desperation, 'how many eyes have I got?' Malcolm studied my face carefully. He looked long and hard at my eyes. I waited expectantly in the silence. His brow furrowed. Finally he spoke.

'Take your glasses off.'

Kevin Marsden

Kevin read this to his established sub-group of five teachers. They trusted and felt confidence and respect for each other's professional abilities and views. Kevin was able to share his frustrations and sense of failure; the group learned about the methods, joys and problems of special-school teaching. They were able to explore the probability that Malcolm had had a different understanding of his task than did Kevin. Possibly Malcolm thought he was to count the eyes, rather than 'guess' how many each had. To do this he would have had to ask for spectacles to be removed so he could see clearly. The situation of a mismatch between a teacher's intentions and a child's understanding must happen so often.

Why reflective practice now?

The grand stories of patriarchy/patriotism, religion, family and community no longer bind society. We look to counsellors, psychologists, teachers, clerics, life partners, GPs or social workers for essential support. Marriages founder and professionals increasingly experience stress as they now have the burden previously carried by a nexus of local and family community.

Faith in that great god science has also been shaken: 'Science, in my view, is now at the end of certainty' (Prigogine 1999, p. 26). There has been a powerful frontier (boundary) between science (and scientific professions like medicine) and the arts since the Enlightenment. A blinkered view of what constitutes knowledge and experience cannot be held for much longer.

If any of us are out of touch with any part of ourselves we are in an impoverished state. The dominant culture is scientific, but the scientist who concentrates on this side of themselves exclusively is as impoverished as is the musician or writer who concentrates only on the artistic.

Paul Robertson (Director of Medici String Quartet), 1999

The age of post-Newtonian belief in our ability to order ('master' even) our world is going. It led to a mess: the rise of clinical depression and the spread of the deserts, for example. The assumptions that an objective view of the world (Kantian) is 'grown-up', that we should shed our subjective view along with sand and water play, are being questioned (see also Sacks 1985, pp. 1–21).

An ethnographer can no longer stand on a mountain top from which authoritatively to map human ways of life (Clifford 1986). Practitioners cannot confidently diagnose and dictate from an objective professional or scientific standpoint; teachers do not know answers. The enmeshment of culture and environment is total: no one is objective.

'Since the seventeenth century, Western science has excluded certain expressive modes from its legitimate repertoire: rhetoric (in the name of "plain" transparent signification), fiction (in the name of fact), and subjectivity (in the name of objectivity). The qualities eliminated from science were localised in the category of "literature"' (Clifford 1986, p. 102). These categories have returned from that 300-year marginal position, to be embedded alongside the scientific approach.

Holistic coherent understandings which might support us out of our alienated mess are increasingly entertained. 'We now see the world as *our* world, rather than *the* world' (Reason 1988). Complementary healing considers our wholeness, not just within ourselves, but also within our environment and community. 'We seek a knowing-in-action (and thinking-in-action) which encompasses as much of our experience as possible' (Reason, ibid.).

Ideal professionals, gathering data on which to base their pedagogy, diagnosis or care, are like social anthropologists. Geertz suggested that successful ethnographers create a 'thick description': a web of 'sort of piled-up structures of inference and implication through which the ethnographer is continually trying to pick his way' (Geertz 1973, p. 7). The reflective practice writer who explores and experiments with different writing approaches, using whatever seems appropriate at the time, is like Lévi-Strauss's *bricoleur* (1966). This knotted nexus has then to be understood and interpreted to some degree: 'a good interpretation of anything – a poem, a person, a history, a ritual, an institution, a society – takes us into the heart of that of which it is the interpretation' (Geertz [1973] 1993, p. 7). An effective reflective practitioner attempts to understand the heart of their practice. Understandings gained in this way, however, are always partial; the deeper the enquiry, the enquirer realises the less they know and understand: *the more you know, the more you know you don't know*. Geertz also stresses that it is vital not to generalise across cases but within them. Having got somewhere near the heart of clients' or students' stories and poetry, practitioners can begin to act upon this understanding.

Professionals writing about their work, sharing it with colleagues in order to offer insight, and relating this to a wider field professionally and politically, are together engaged in an activity rather like Reason's *co-operative enquiry method*, in which researcher and subject collaborate in all the stages of research, including reflecting on the experience and making sense of it (Reason 1988). The practitioner takes a full share of responsibility. All too often professionals act in the mould of traditional researcher; acting *on* people: collecting data, and coming to conclusions in camera. There is a similarity with heuristic research (Moustakas 1990; Etherington 2004)

'In this way, it may be possible to avoid providing care which is dry, barren and – perhaps the greatest sin of all – unimaginative' (Smyth 1996, p. 937). Effective reflective practice can enable care or education which is alert and alive to the client's or student's needs and wants, whether professed or not. It can enable the practitioner to use their skill, knowledge and experience creatively and lovingly, and look forward with a greater confidence.

Angela Mohtashemi, a management consultant, shares her experience of reflective writing in organisations:

As I help organisations become more effective through better communication and engagement with their employees, I introduce reflective writing wherever I can as a tool for teamwork, learning and development and coaching. The workplace is a tough, manipulative environment where people are often expected to comply without challenge, to 'live the company's values', to 'display the right behaviours' and even to adopt the corporate language. One's sense of self can become fragile and this limits potential. Whenever I have used writing with groups or individuals they have commented on the sense of liberation and the feeling that they are getting to the heart of things.

Sometimes I have run workshops or team sessions specifically to explore reflective writing, sometimes incorporate it into other situations. A writing activity, such as writing about your name, can be a great icebreaker. I recently ran a session on writing for personal and organisational develop-ment as part of a leadership course my firm runs jointly with a university business school. The session incorporated learning theory, my own experi-ence, principles of reflective writing and practical activities. These activities were typical of the techniques I use and included free writing and using unfamiliar imagery to look at the daily work experience.

Free writing, although very simple, fulfils many purposes and is often a revelation to people. A number of participants went to their action learning sets keen to use free writing to explore organisational issues before dis-cussing them with the group. They were excited about the patterns that emerged and about the honesty of a conversation with one's self. I encour-age people in action learning sets to reflect about the experience afterwards. One wrote to me later:

> I spent almost 2hrs writing up how I felt during our discussion and how I intended to change my behaviour as a result. It was tremendously thera-peutic and enjoyable, which I found surprising, as I have, until now, been avoiding writing down anything about how I feel – so Thank You!

Sue Smith wrote:

> Bringing the issue was like opening a door and seeing a crack of light – and seeing a very small slither [sic] of a room. Once the door was opened fully – which happened when I started to look at the amount of change I'd undergone – I could see the room in its entirety – and appreciate how full and intricate the things in there were.

Sue Smith has a tremendous opportunity to change people's lives. Writing helps her find a way to pause and reflect, to argue with herself until she believes what she says and can then find the voice to persuade others. In that way, writing can be a powerful force for change.

When I first began this work I feared the response would be cynicism and doubts about its relevance. After all, most workplaces are based on rational and 'scientific' management practices: plans, budgets, facts, timelines, blue-prints etc. There is little place for emotion and individual expression. My fears were wrong. Every time the response has been very positive and unleashed the power people can have when they bring their whole selves to work. One team member said the writing was 'one of the most exciting, interesting and engaging things I've done since I've been with the firm'.

Angela Mohtashemi

Reflective practice and reflexivity according to the principles and practice outlined here is a valuable developmental process for any teacher, social worker, clinician or student. It can take its non-judgemental camera down to any aspect of practice, with patients, colleagues, administrative and other staff, the interface of home and work, and the impact of experiences in the past on present actions. No feeling, thought or action is too small or too big for this zoom or wide-angle lens.

This chapter is taken from:
Bolton, G. (2005) *Reflective Practice,* Second Edition
978-1-4129-0812-2

Professional Reflection: Identity, agency and change

CHRISTINE FORDE, MARGERY McMAHON,
ALASTAIR D. McPHEE and FIONA PATRICK

Chapter outline

This chapter challenges the notion that professional reflection is necessarily beneficial to practice. While it argues for its usefulness as a learning tool, it cautions that more sophisticated models of reflective practice need to be used to promote practice change. It looks at the development of one such model within the Scottish Qualification for Headship, and argues that the culture of reflective practice tends to place the onus for change on the individual practitioner, rather than on looking at the political, policy and institutional contexts within which change needs to take place.

Keywords

■ Reflective practice

■ Critical reflection

■ Social dynamics

■ Introduction

Reflective practice is now seen as one of the key ways for teachers to develop understanding of their work at all stages of their career. Given the current tendency to question levels of teacher professionalism, and the tendency for policy and standards to stress performativity, models of reflective practice can offer teachers an opportunity to develop their professional identities and teaching practices within what can be a challenging working environment.

Use of reflective practice is now so widespread across a range of professions that it has almost become clichéd. Yet it has the potential to be a powerful support for professional learning and development. However, not all models of reflective practice are equally valuable, or equally sophisticated, and reflective practice has tended to become subsumed into performance measures, particularly where it is linked to salary enhancement via CPD. Of course, care must be taken not to stereotype the role of the teacher as being either a critical reflective practitioner or a straightforward policy deliverer. The reality is more complex than that, and teachers' roles will most likely fall between these two paradigms. Teachers cannot choose simply to ignore government and local authority policy but, in asserting a claim to professional status, they must deliver this policy in a way that best enhances children's opportunities for learning.

This chapter explores some of the issues involved in using reflection to enhance professional practice, but it also looks at some of the difficulties surrounding the concept of reflection, and asks whether or not we need to look at professional development in a wider context rather than focusing mainly on the individual teacher.

■ What is reflective practice?

It is intended that using critical reflection will allow teachers to identify what they do well and what they need to do to improve in their practice. Using reflective practice is now widespread among many professional groups, both at the initial training stage and during CPD. It is especially prevalent in teaching and nursing where it is believed that modern professionals must think consciously about their practice to move them towards deeper levels of awareness not just about what they do but about why they do it. As Burrows writes: 'If professional practice is about change, development and meaningful conscious action, the art of reflection becomes a pre-requisite' (Burrows, in Maich et al., 2000: 309).

Open-minded and flexible approaches

Reflecting on practice is therefore meant to enable practitioners to be more open-minded and adopt more flexible approaches to their work, so that they are better able to cope with modern working practices which are often characterized by the need to respond to, and initiate, change. It has therefore become popular in those professions where change has become a consistent feature and where it is often imposed: teaching, social work, nursing and general medical practice. With respect to the training of doctors, Mamede and Schmidt state that the 'changing context of health care delivery and the growth of the medical knowledge base are placing high demands on the doctor's expertise. Indeed, clinical practice has become increasingly characterized by change, ambiguity and complexity' (Mamede and Schmidt, 2004: 1302). In any profession that is prey to ambiguity reflective practice is now seen as a means to enable professionals to cope with and respond to imposed change which may leave them struggling to find a definitive purpose for their professional role.

Underlying beliefs and assumptions

In addition, reflective practice is meant to promote analysis of underlying beliefs and assumptions that practitioners might hold without having a full appreciation of why they hold them and what alternative beliefs might have equal credence. Particularly in teaching, our own educational experiences 'create deeply ingrained attitudes and beliefs' that form the personal philosophy which underlies our professional practice (Griffin, 2003: 207). This philosophy can exert a powerful influence to the point that it may override what is presented to us during our professional education (see Griffin, 2003: 208). For example, with beginning teachers (and with some who are more experienced) a common notion is that theory and professional studies tend to be less relevant to them than learning that takes place in schools. The dominant notion is often that

> field experiences – no matter how they are designed – are the best way to acquire professional knowledge and competence as a teacher. This notion can be observed in student teachers' negative attitude towards theory … and their uncritical way of evaluating any kind of field experience as simply the best learning context in teacher education. (Hascher et al., 2004: 626)

Using reflective practice with students may therefore enable them to see a value to their academic studies that they had not seen before because it challenges them to look consciously at what they take for granted in terms of their underlying attitudes.

Empowerment

At its strongest, the reflective practice movement asks us to go beyond the individual level to critique institutional and government policy and practices. And for writers like Sachs, the goal of reflective practice is not just to change the individual but to empower them to move towards activism and a 'questioning of the status quo' (Larrivee, 2000: 296). It may be that reflective practice has become popular precisely because its focus is on individual change while giving opportunities to critique existing institutional and management practices. Many professionals feel disempowered by managerialism and reflective practice seems to give us a way of focusing on ourselves: if we do not have the power to change the system at least we can critique it, and at least we can try to change our own practices in ways that might resist the worst excesses of the managerialist style. As we shall see, this emphasis on changing the self has both positive and negative repercussions.

Reflective practice: the search for a definitive model

It is easier to say what reflective practice is meant to do than to say what it is. Many models exist, and there is confusion over how to define reflective practice conceptually. Courses and texts that advocate reflective practice suggest a variety of methods: narrative storytelling that allows the practitioner to interrogate their versions of events; reflective journals; critical incident technique; reflective group discussions; problem-based learning and so on. McLaughlin (1999: 10) mentions the lack of a coherent philosophy or practice and the fact that reflective practice rests on such a variety of models that it is difficult to say definitively what it actually is. Models of reflective practice do tend to stress, following Schon and Argyris, the concept of reflection in and on action, and of reflection leading to practice change.

However, it is difficult to give a definitive model of reflective practice. Certainly, those models which advocate reflection can help us to make implicit knowledge about our practice more conscious. They can also help us to examine our unexamined beliefs and attitudes and to understand the impact they have on our practice (see Thurlow Long and Stuart, 2004). However there are doubts about the levels of reflection reached by professionals, especially those who are beginning their professional education. Many find difficulty in moving from descriptions of practice to analysis, particularly with a view to placing their experiences within broader contexts and issues for practice (see Admiraal and Wubbels, 2005).

Gould and Masters (2004: 54) highlight the widespread enthusiasm for reflection but note also the criticism that 'centres on the lack of a common definition, its unproven benefits and the absence of a universally acceptable structure for its implementation'. It may be that seeking a definitive model is not strictly necessary. What may be required is for professionals to work with a model that can be used across a range of disciplines, a model of reflection which recognizes the need for change not only at individual level but within wider institutional and policy contexts. We return to this issue later in the chapter when the Scottish Qualification for Headship is discussed.

Certainly, those models of reflection which are most beneficial tend to be those that are based on encouraging practitioners to critique their practice and the assumptions and values that underlie it (see Day, 2000). It is important, too, that reflection focuses on 'personal, social, institutional and broad policy contexts in which practice takes place, and the implications of these for the improvement of that practice' (Day, 2000: 123). In addition, reflection does allow one means for professionals to 'grapple with and understand the complexities of practice and the uncertainty and confusion that they provoke. Rather than looking to external sources for answers individual practitioners are enjoined to look within themselves through a process of reflection' (Taylor, 2003: 245). However, this very stress on individual solutions to complex issues can mean that the onus for change rests less on the institution in which the professional works, and more on each professional her/himself.

Despite the lack of a definite model, there is evidence to suggest that practitioners do feel that reflection is beneficial to them. It is worth looking at research evidence here to try to ascertain in what ways reflection can help professionals to consider their practice.

■ Reflection and learning

Certainly, many professionals do find it difficult to reflect at a critical level. This is especially the case with beginning teachers and with those who are newly qualified. However, as Harrison et al. (2005) note, with support, critical reflection can be achieved and can be helpful in developing practice and can encourage newly qualified teachers towards a sense of agency. It can also help to make explicit tacit knowledge (Sparrow et al., 2005) and can encourage practitioners to link their existing knowledge to research and theory in their field.

In addition, reflection can help practitioners to see themselves as able to make decisions over their work in terms of defining their own practice (see Pedro, 2005: 50). It is also helpful at the stage of initial teacher education in terms of trying to help students to see teaching as being a complex and dynamic activity rather than as a behaviourist enterprise (Pedro, 2005: 51). Of course, this is not as straightforward as it sounds, because each professional needs to develop her or his own understanding of what reflective practice means for them, and the lack of definitive models does not help her or him in this task. Having said this, student teachers can be helped to become more reflective and critical given appropriate levels of support (see Pedro, 2005).

Individual understanding and beyond

Seeing teaching in a broader, less reductivist sense, is important, as is gaining understanding of the elements of the work that rely on artistry and emotion. Reflection can help us to see that we bring a range of personal as well as professional skills to our work. Johansson and Kroksmark (2004: 358) mention the benefits of reflection in helping us to recognize and develop 'intuitive pedagogical action' which might otherwise go unnoticed or be downplayed. There seems to be a wealth of tacit pedagogic knowledge that teachers simply enact without thinking, and yet this knowledge and these intuitive actions can often constitute successful teaching (see Johansson and Kroksmark, 2004).

Reflection can also enable professionals to go beyond their own individual perspectives to see how their work has an impact on others. It should encourage practitioners to challenge their own assumptions about the client group they work with, and to begin to develop new insights into the purposes of their practice not just for themselves but for their clients (see DeMulder and Rigsby, 2003). It can also encourage a sense of expertise and of valuing our own professional ability in a policy culture that may lead to feelings of demoralization. In other words, it can lead to a stronger sense of our professional self (DeMulder and Rigsby, 2003: 278). This may lead to a stronger sense of self-efficacy and a more robust ability to cope with change and with difficult working situations. In addition, reflection may allow us to examine difficult and challenging situations and discuss these with others to form new understandings of where the challenge lies, and how we could approach similar situations in more effective ways. This is particularly the case where the situation arises from particular moral or ethical considerations.

Giving students, at whatever level, the opportunity to reflect with others on their courses offers them the potential to form supportive relationships, to talk about and to reflect on issues that arise within their practice (see Gould and Masters, 2004). This is where the use of what Gould and Masters (2004) call 'facilitated reflective groups' can be helpful. In advocating these, they recognize that students need support in order to make these groups successful. Gould and Masters (2004: 57) note a tendency in the early stages of their work with mental health nursing students for the group discussions to lose focus, and to fail to make best use of opportunities for reflection. Most notably, in the early discussions deeper levels of reflection were not achieved (Gould and Masters, 2004: 58). It was here that the role of the tutor as facilitator was important in moving students towards more sophisticated reflective practice. Gould and Masters (2004: 59) state that students did become more critically aware during their course, and did try to put elements of their learning into practice. So, in encouraging students to become critically reflective it must be remembered that critical reflection is a skill that needs to be learned, and needs the support of tutors to facilitate reflective opportunities.

There are, then, potential benefits to the use of reflective practice. But in advocating its use we should take care not to adopt a simplistic model of reflection and we should be aware of some of the difficulties associated with its use. In particular we should look at what exactly we are asking practitioners to reflect on and change. In asking them to change their practice we may be asking them to change their understandings of how they practice and of what they regard as their professional role. Ultimately we may be asking individuals to alter their identities and we may be placing too much emphasis on individual change without looking carefully enough at the contexts within which they work. These issues are explored more fully in the following sections.

■ Reflection: changing our practice or changing ourselves?

In debating this issue, it is important not to become polarized (see Heath, 1998). Professional education cannot rest upon one model of practice: it is as unhelpful to claim that reflection should be the overriding basis of professional development as it is to place complete faith in research findings to help us to improve our practice. Professional development needs to be based on a more holistic understanding of what constitutes relevant professional knowledge. Heath (1998: 291) argues that what is required is 'a realistic position and use that will enable successful implementation and the full potential of reflection to be reached in diverse practice settings and contexts'.

Undoubtedly, reflecting on our practice can lead us towards a fuller understanding of our professional role and how we fulfil this. But concerns have been raised, most notably in nursing studies, about whether reflection is being used to change practice or to change our professional identity towards a specific model of the 'good' practitioner (however this is conceived). Reflection is 'extolled as being good for nursing and nurses' (Cotton, 2001: 512), just as it is seen as being empowering for teachers. For many professionals this constitutes an underlying assumption to their initial education and their continuing professional development: you will be a better nurse, teacher, doctor or social worker if you reflect on your practice. But to what extent in current policy is the 'good' practitioner one who follows policy rather than challenges it? Again, there is polarization evident: the 'good' practitioner is a more complex being than either the policy compliant or the 'activist professional' models suggest.

Reflection may well lead to better practice but, as McLaughlin (1999: 11) asks, is a 'reflective teacher *ipso facto* a good teacher? How, for example, is a weak reflective teacher different from a strong unreflective teacher?' He makes two further points that are important. First, it is not straightforward to define 'what counts' as good professional practice (McLaughlin, 1999: 17). Secondly he notes that '[f]lawed reflections, (of whatever kind) can inhibit good practice' (McLaughlin, 1999: 18). Even when carried out diligently and critically, reflection can become an end in itself and so need not affect practice at all. Any claims that reflection leads to improved practice must be examined in terms of whether practitioners can demonstrate lasting positive change for themselves and their clients, and this type of evidence is difficult to find.

Pressure to reflect or willingness to develop?

Reflective practice has now become so much a mainstay of professional education that a culture has been set up where 'not to reflect on ... practice, or to refuse to participate in reflective strategies ... may be seen as unacceptable, unprofessional and unnatural alternatives' (Cotton, 2001: 514). To question reflective practice could lead to being labelled *unprofessional*, or to be seen as not caring about improving professional practice. Newell (1992: 1326) comments that reflective practice is 'regarded by many authors as of particular importance to continuing professional excellence'. Once again, this is an assumption rather than a demonstrable outcome, but it has become an almost unquestioned element in professional education: the root to excellence is through reflection.

Certainly there is evidence that practitioners believe that reflection helps them to improve practice. Burnard's study of nurse educators points to their beliefs about the benefits of reflection (see Burnard, 1995: 1171):

- improved confidence
- increased thoughtfulness
- improved possibility of getting practice 'right'
- realizing that there is 'no right answer'
- taking a more systematic approach to practice.

However, since these beliefs are all based upon practitioners' perceptions of improvements, it is difficult to ascertain whether or not objective improvement took place. Moreover, Greenwood (1993: 1183) considers the discrepancies that can arise between what practitioners believe is good practice and what they actually do. Knowledge of 'good' practice may arise through reflection, but within stressful working environments we may not always act in accordance with our beliefs about best professional practice.

This leads into the question of the extent to which we can stand back from our practice and assess it unemotionally, rationally and objectively? In one sense, it is positive that practitioners can form their own meanings of what it is to be a nurse or a teacher. But, in another sense, it can lead to a view of practice which is based on 'common-sense' understandings of professional practice, where theory and research are seen as less valid and less practical than professionals' own view of their work. Of course, reflective exercises should ask professionals to reflect not just on their own experiences, but to underpin those reflections with reading and research. However, in looking at the reflective writing of beginning and experienced professionals, the writing is too often characterized by 'merely thinking about what you're doing' rather than by critique and evaluation that leads to improved practice and service to clients (Burnard, 1995: 1169).

Valid reflection or just another story?

These issues also lead to the question of how meaningful our reflections are especially when they are based on our memory of events, sometimes events that are far removed in time? Newell writes that the

> nature of memory is such that forgetting information takes place all the time … However, much forgetting is often subject to considerable individual bias. Equally, attention at the time of acquisition is selective …

> The issues of bias in forgetting and selection at acquisition suggest that accurate reflection may be either impossible or so fundamentally flawed as to be of little value. (Newell, 1992: 1327)

We tend not to remember accurately or fully, nor do we take in the full extent of events at the time, especially where these professional events are stressful (see Newell, 1992: 1327). If we cannot reflect objectively, and we remember events selectively, what value is there to reflection – are we not simply constructing one story of our practice to replace one that already exists? And if we are, does this matter? It may be the case that the difficulties Newell associates with memory are only partially problematic, in that reflection may help us to try to uncover how we remember things and what alternative perspectives we might take when analysing our practice. However, it is also the case that, in advocating the use of story writing and analysis, we guard against what Taylor (2003: 249) calls 'romantic realism' in which practitioners' reflective stories move away from the 'naive realism' that the events they describe have objective truth, but instead 'take on a therapeutic or emancipatory aspect' (Taylor, 2003: 249).

It may be that reflective practice places too much confidence in the 'power of language' (Atkinson, 2004: 379) to effect change. Atkinson (2004: 380) writes that reflective practice assumes that any professional is 'a self-conscious, reflective and hardworking individual whose practice is consciously planned and initiated', which we may well be. But Atkinson questions the role of emotion and subjectivity in how we understand our professional roles, and questions the extent to which reflective practice can give us an adequate platform for exploring our subjective understandings of what we do.

While Atkinson's point is valid, what are the repercussions of asking us to question our emotional and subjective constructs? It may be that in asking us to interrogate our professional values, assumptions and beliefs, reflective practice actually risks undermining our core identity as professionals. At what point can we trust our professional identity and the values and beliefs it rests upon? At what stage in our professional development can we stop interrogating and reinventing our professional selves? We are meant to become empowered, but this implies a shift of power from the institutions and policy towards the individual practitioner (see Gilbert, 1995).

In reality, the strictures placed on professionals by managerialism and by government and institutional policy can make empowerment a tenuous notion. It is also an ambiguous notion: even as authors write of the reflective practitioner or the activist professional, the reality for many is that they develop any autonomy and agency they have within professional cultures that are often based on performance management. The concept of the activist professional takes the notion of the reflective practitioner to new moral heights: not only must the professional reflect, but act to change systems. It is questionable whether this is a helpful premise.

Does reflection empower?

There are, then, issues about whether or not deep reflection on our professional practice and identity constitute a reinventing of the professional self that actually empowers or disempowers. Gilbert (1995) sees empowerment as resting on the question of where power actually lies, and mentions the work of Foucault in looking at disciplinary power (see Gilbert, 1995: 867). For Foucault, power can be both a positive and a negative force: it can be used to dominate and control, or it can act as a potential for agency. Important to this last sense is a critical attitude, or 'the art of not being governed or of not being governed like this and at this price' (Foucault, in Barratt, 2004: 195). Here lies the potential strength of reflection, not as it is often presented in a naive sense of discussing individual practice, but seen as a critical endeavour that takes account of the individual's place in their professional context. For teachers, reflective practice undoubtedly has the potential to enable them to understand the richness and complexity of classroom and school life, and to develop a sense of agency and ownership of their work.

However, it is important to distinguish reflection that is enabling, complex and difficult, from that which has been simplified and used as a tool of managerialism, in particular where it has become a normative expectation of those working towards promotion or undertaking initial education. Reflective practice should not be a further stage in our induction into the normative expectations of what a teacher is or should be. Nor should it be about creating a specific professional type. The danger of this conceptualization of reflective practice is that it can become what Foucault might describe as a technology of the self, where it is used to 'define the individual and control their conduct' (Besley, 2005a: 313). There is a danger within the culture of reflective practice that professional identity becomes something to be continually worked on, 'transformed and improved' as Foucault puts it (1977: 136). Of course, we should not make the mistake of denying the individual agency we have to shape our own professionalism, but it can be difficult to resist and to fully recognize norms of professional practice, especially when building our professional identity and practice at an early stage.

It is also important to recognize forms of reflective practice which become confessional and which focus too much on individual change, rather than on individual development within a professional context. One of the concerns with the dominance of the reflective practice culture is the potential for reflection to be confused with confession (see Gilbert, 2001). As Besley notes (2005b: 369), we live in a 'confessional age' where we should ask, '[w]hat is the effect on us of confessing our selves either publicly or privately?' This last question is relevant to any professional who is expected to engage in reflective practice. We should take care in seeking to understand our professional practice, and as teacher educators in asking others to critically reflect, that we do not become focused on an 'obligation to endlessly reinvent' ourselves as professionals (McNay, 1996: 146).

We have no doubt about the potential of reflective practice, when well used, and when well designed, to allow professionals to renew their ideas about practice and refresh their enthusiasm for their work. Critical reflection can provide us with a powerful learning tool, but it needs to be constructed in a way that recognizes the students' cognitive development, the social dynamics of the workplace, development of professional identity and the multiple factors involved in the specific contexts that professionals find themselves in. The next section looks at an example of the complexities and benefits of reflective practice when used in the professional development of head teachers.

■ The social dynamics of reflective learning

All aspiring head teachers in Scotland now have to undertake the Scottish Qualification for Headship (see Reeves et al., 2005). It is a two-year course of professional development that has at its heart a model of reflective practice that tries to recognize the complexities of meaningful workplace learning and the usefulness of reflection as a focus for learning. It tries to bridge three key theoretical models of CPD:

1 that which focuses on knowledge and skills within the attainment of competences
2 that which sees learning as constructivist with meaning being made by individuals in the context of the institutions they work in (see Reeves et al., 2005: 254)

3 following Lave and Wenger, that which sees professional learning as taking place within the social practices of the workplace (see Reeves et al., 2005: 255).

To this end, participants in the programme undertake taught elements, but there is a strong emphasis on collaborative working and discussion, on reflection, on workplace learning and on understanding that changing individual practice has repercussions beyond the individual practitioner (see Reeves et al., 2001). But the SQH model recognizes that, in and of themselves, each of these three models has its own difficulties. It therefore tries to take elements of each and redevelop them within a new framework for professional development that can take account of situational factors, micro-political issues in the workplace, collegiality and the need for CPD to engage the learner to work towards not just behavioural but conceptual change (see Reeves et al., 2005). Ultimately it aims at 'supported action' within the workplace where professional knowledge is acquired, developed and used (Reeves et al., 2003: 7).

Importantly, Reeves et al. (2005) note the impact of change on professional identity and emotion. They write that

> Changing practice is situated in interaction between the individual and others in the context of the work setting and appears to be characterized by contestation. It is not a purely rational process. The conceptual development of SQH candidates encompassed their professional persona and their relationship to others, it was not simply a matter of developing ideas or acquiring knowledge from self and emotion. The whole person was engaged since at stake was maintaining a respectable professional identity ... (Reeves et al., 2005: 269)

This idea of engaging the whole person is a powerful one, but not without challenge for the individual professional and for the teacher educator, because it uncovers not just the micro-politics of the workplace but the micro-politics and power relations of the learning environment in which the CPD takes place. It also takes on board the recognition that it can be difficult for practitioners to change their practice because institutional practices militate against the transfer of new understandings of practice into reality (see Sparrow et al., 2005).

Leadership

Day's research (2000) with school principals in England, also illustrates the need for effective leadership to be based on reflective practice to some extent. It highlights the fact that these principals engaged in reflection that critiqued their practice and that 'reflection was integral to their success' (Day, 2000: 124). Essential to their efficacy as managers were also a set of core values which promoted not just their own agency but the agency of their staff: fairness, equity and equality of opportunity (Day, 2000: 124). Importantly, in trying to implement these values in the face of the strictures of government policy and the challenges of raising standards, reflection was seen as being crucial to coping with difficulties and complexities of school leadership (Day, 2000: 124).

Power

Reflection can therefore be an important means of identifying core leadership values. Centring CPD for teachers and potential school managers on reflection therefore gives opportunities to think about these issues. But basing CPD on reflective practice also raises questions of power, in particular, concerning the relationship between the professional and the CPD provider/tutor. How do we encourage participants to reflect and engage in change to professional practice within a relationship of equal power (something that can be difficult within the role of CPD provider)? To what extent should the provider be a mentor, a supporter or a 'critical friend' in encouraging critical reflection, particularly when the provider is in the dual role of teacher and assessor? And, when encouraging critical reflection, to what extent does the provider of CPD encourage the student towards professional agency in an ethical manner?

As McNay highlights (1996: 159) issues of power link into moral and ethical concerns: 'To decide whether an individual is being manipulated rather than persuaded involves issues of responsibility and moral considerations about the extent to which it is legitimate to limit or impair the choices of others.' Those who encourage professionals to engage in meaningful reflection have a responsibility to develop an understanding in the practitioner that individual reflection should not lead to change which might limit or impair the choices of others with whom the professional is involved. It is important to recognize the perspectives of those we work with when we reflect, and to try to listen to what they say and what they want as we strive to become better practitioners. It is important to ask ourselves as we reflect or as we encourage reflection in others, do we listen, or do we overpower the perspectives of those we work with and work for? (See Miehls and Moffat, 2000.)

The development of the Scottish Qualification for Headship, and the work of Day with school leaders, serve as a reminder that reflective practice can enable participants to renew their conceptual understanding of their professional roles at what can be a challenging time: the move into, or the further development of, a leadership role. It also serves to show the multiple levels involved in changing practice. The work of Reeves et al. (2005: 270)

> raises doubts about the whole idea that 'changing' individuals is an adequate basis for seeking to change practice. It shows that there is a complex dynamic involved where one individual cannot change what she does without the acquiescence, compliance and participation of others ... Concentrating on developing practitioner competence as solely an individual characteristic needs to be challenged ...

Changing the individual is not enough: if we are to improve learning for pupils in our schools then we must focus on change at school level, and this is a complex process. Any process of individual reflection, change and development needs to take account of the cultural factors at work in institutions such as schools and hospitals, and to take account of how the individual's professional identity meshes with that culture or otherwise (see Reeves et al., 2003: 20).

■ Conclusion

It is important, then, to look at wider contexts for professional development: how to implement policy but retain ownership of teaching work; how to improve individual practice within the school as an organization; how to ensure that reflection leads to sustained efforts to improve learning for all pupils. It may be that to focus on individual teacher development is to miss the opportunity to think about what the school can do to further pupil learning and to encourage the professional development of its teachers.

In the next chapter we focus on this issue: teachers do not work in isolation, and if they are to develop professionally they need to have support within their schools to do so. And in looking at how children's learning experiences can be improved, the school policy and forms of management need to be the focus as much as what teachers do in their classrooms. It may be that current policy initiatives that stress instrumental approaches to learning as a means to raise standards miss the point of the school as a learning organization and so place too much emphasis on individual teacher change rather than on how teaching takes place within the social dynamics of schools.

This chapter is taken from:
Forde, C., McMahon, M., McPhee, A.D. and Patrick, F. (2006) *Professional Development, Reflection and Enquiry*
978-1-4129-1937-1

Partnerships with Parents

24

KATE WALL

Introduction

As the government continues to legislate for partnerships with parents, this chapter explores the purposes, benefits and characteristics of partnerships with parents and discusses ways we can establish systems and processes to ensure that partnerships work effectively. Parental and professional perspectives are explored and examples of good practice discussed to tease out the factors we should all be addressing to ensure that partnerships are enabling for all parties. In addition, we explore barriers to partnership, perceived or otherwise. David (1994: 10) echoed the need for effective partnerships and suggested ways forward: 'How workers are enabled to empower families, to work in partnership with them, to cater flexibly for what the families themselves identify as their needs seems to be the challenge for professional and voluntary agency managers for the 1990s' – a view that still applies today.

Partnerships with parents do not naturally evolve, and early years workers should never presume to have empathy with, or understand, all parents. At best we can respect, listen and use the systems in place to support parents, ensuring they have total understanding of everything that occurs, are aware of their rights and feel able to contribute positively at all stages. If appropriate systems are not currently in place then they should be planned and established.

Partnerships should ideally comprise an equal balance between practitioners and parents, with both parties working towards the most appropriate outcomes to support children with special needs in achieving their full potential. Robson (1989: 126) explored equality within partnerships, highlighting the possible imbalance: 'A successful partnership is based on equality, whereby each partner recognises and benefits from the talents, skills, expertise and knowledge of the other. At times one partner may adopt a relatively passive role, in other situations a more active role.'

Parental involvement or partnership?

It may be suggested that in early years settings, parents are generally welcome to visit, discuss their children's progress and participate in a range of activities within the group. This can be beneficial for all parties involved, particularly children, as the skills and expertise of parents can be used within the group to enhance existing practice. However, on school entry the involvement of parents often diminishes to invitations to assemblies, listening to children read and helping with fund-raising activities. As children then progress to the junior and secondary phases parental involvement diminishes yet further, creating a distance. Thus parental involvement and participation are susceptible to change as children progress through the educational phases. Rennie (1996: 197) identifies five distinct stages as a developmental progression of parental involvement within a setting that could be reflected on as planning and policy-making processes progress:

1 Confidence-building for all involved.

2 Awareness-raising and starting participation.

3 Real involvement.

4 Parent–teacher partnership.

5 Parents as co-educators.

As parents approach early years settings for the first time there already exists a common ground between them. They all have children of similar ages, are about to embark on attendance, have spent the previous few years nurturing and developing their children to the best of their ability and wish for their children to succeed. This common ground presents a bond between parents that can be positively used by the setting to the benefit of all, sharing experiences, discussing common problems and capitalising on personal skills. It is a starting point from which outstanding achievements can be realised if fostered within an ethos of positive partnership.

For most children the preceding years will have been spent at home with a parent/carer so the introduction to an early years setting can be traumatic. This is not only for the children but also the parents and, if the youngest child in the family is embarking on attendance, then it may be even harder for the parent/carer to accept. The feelings of no longer being needed to support the child in the same way can have severe effects and, while all parents want to see their child settle in happily and confidently, there can be a sense of ironic disappointment if the child does just that. For the child with special needs the transfer to an early years setting may be more problematic and requires sensitive handling as the parent/carer may feel even more protective and find it much harder to transfer their child's care to others. It is therefore important that practitioners plan the induction process thoroughly in an attempt to eliminate, or at least diminish, possible anxieties. Familiarity with the child and his/her family can ease this process considerably, particularly if it is achieved via a combination of home visits and visits to the setting. Issues of concern, procedures, policies and information-sharing can all be explored in a more informal manner prior to admission, and this will, hopefully, be seen as a two-way process.

The parent/carer has the most concise knowledge about the child, including his/her likes and dislikes, progress to date, appointments attended, referrals made, reports written and friends. This can all be used to support the child's transition through the induction process and in future planning.

Practitioners should recognise and respect the depth and breadth of learning that parents have already undertaken with their children, which can be under-estimated and undervalued. Parents have a tendency to see the early education of their children as 'nothing special' or describe it as 'what parents do', but parents are responsible for supporting their child's development and skill-learning such as walking, talking, toilet training, social skills, self-help skills, behaviour and playing. This prior learning, albeit unstructured and unplanned, has never-theless taken place within the home and the parents should accept full credit for this. A key issue to be considered is involvement versus partnership. Involvement infers that parents would participate in some activities within the setting, whereas partnership implies equality, respect and involvement in every aspect of the setting's work from the management group, through planning and delivering the curriculum to working alongside and with practitioners on an equal footing. Langston (2003: 55) considers that:

> true partnership demands as much of one partner as the other and implies that each partner has equal rights and responsibilities. To work in partnership then, is both time consuming and demanding, and can only really emerge over time, when parents and practitioners understand each other's roles, respect one another's rights and individuality, trust one another, and feel confident.

Parental issues affecting partnership

Many issues, such as low self-esteem, hours of employment, social deprivation and poverty, and feelings of inadequacy, can affect the level and quality of parental involvement, and any of the issues may present one or more barriers to meaningful participation.

Time can also be a critical factor, even for those parents who do not work during the day, as they may wish to support partnerships with several settings attended by their children or they may experience childcare difficulties for younger children. Any parents who do not appear to be very involved with our settings should not, therefore, be assumed to lack interest or desire to participate. It will be our responsibility to respond to their needs and to remove barriers.

Quality of partnership

If, as practitioners, we strive to accommodate all parents in a meaningful way, we will also share the rewards, but true partnership will very much depend on the quality of the relationships and the perceived benefits to all parties. Inviting parents into the staffroom of a setting to repair damaged equipment may be of little benefit and cannot be described as an effective partnership. Parental and professional roles should support each other in a 'complementary' manner as Beveridge comments:

> The concept of partnership is based on the recognition that parents and teachers have complementary contributions to make to children's education. Accordingly, it is central to the notion of partnership that schools should demonstrate that they not only listen to, but also value, parents' perspectives. Many teachers aim to do this, but it must be acknowledged that the parental experience of contact with the school can be far removed from the partnership ideal. (Beveridge, 1997: 56)

Dale (1996: 2) also raises the issue of the quality of partnership: 'the term "partnership" does not tell us a great deal about the extent of the cooperation and reciprocity between two or more partners, except to suggest that there is some form of mutual cooperation and influence'. As a simple example, a bilingual child may enter an early years setting. Although a non-English speaker, his/her mother can be encouraged to attend sessions to watch and participate, as she feels able. Initially she may choose to stay in the background, helping with the setting up of activities, making drinks and washing up but, hopefully, over a period of time, she can be encouraged to participate further. Eventually her English should begin to develop and her confidence enhanced. In time she may feel more able to support the learning of staff and children alike by introducing new activities related to cooking, traditional stories, dress and religious festivals from her own country and culture, as well as adding to more general topic-based work. Opportunities could arise for the mother to participate in adult education classes, help in a crèche and have regular contact with a range of outside professionals. With increased involvement and understanding of how the setting works she could be elected to the management group and become a full working partner of the setting. From this scenario everyone benefits, but only if the setting is committed to working with parents. Draper and Duffy support this view concluding that:

For many staff the opportunity to work in partnership adds a new dimension to their work. Practitioners can assume their experience of family life is the way it is and working with parents from diverse communities widens their views on families and family life. Differences can be shared, respected and explored. Home life provides many opportunities for learning the setting can build on. (Draper and Duffy, 2001: 149)

Partnerships with the parents of children with special needs may be compromised by the existence of special schools and units that prohibit or limit regular face-to-face contact with parents. At their most basic level partnerships begin with the establishing of relationships, but these take time and effort to plan and develop. In a mainstream setting parents will arrive on a more frequent and regular basis where meaningful interaction can develop naturally. If, however, your child is transported several or many miles away to attend a special facility, then this interaction is immediately compromised. If parents do not have transport then regular contact is further compromised. Thus it may be suggested that for special schools and units parental partnerships may need considerably more effort in planning and maintaining. However, the fact that parents are not in regular contact with a setting does not mean that practitioners should not make the effort to establish effective partnerships, as supported by Hurst:

This does not prevent them from taking seriously parents' need to be kept informed and to have regular contact with the practitioner responsible for their children. It is the awareness of parents' needs and the willingness to be adaptable in developing ways of meeting these needs which are the most important. (Hurst, 1997: 108)

Home–school liaison teachers and family centres

During the 1960s and 1970s there emerged an increased understanding of the influences of a range of factors on children's social development and, as a result, a greater awareness of social deprivation. In several counties new roles emerged to address these needs, such as home–school liaison teachers. More family centres were established, some funded by education departments and some by social services departments, to address the effects of social deprivation in specific localities and/or 'educational priority areas'.

Home–school liaison teachers were generally assigned to an infant/primary school and/or a family centre. Their roles included the breaking down of barriers between schools and families, encouraging attendance at early years settings, supporting local pre-school providers, responding directly to the needs of the families and working closely with other agencies. Owing to the localities in which they worked, generally areas of poor housing, high unemployment and with very young parents, much of their work involved children and families with special needs, in the broadest sense. Therefore, special needs input, educational or otherwise, became a key feature of their work. In many instances the home–school liaison teacher acted as a mediator or enabler between the families and the systems and processes in place to help them, but invariably non-educational issues such as claiming appropriate child benefits would emerge. If, as in Chapter 2, we acknowledge the effects of the family on the child, then to enable a parent to resolve financial difficulties would reduce stress and pressure, and ultimately benefit the child. At such times the practitioner could advise and support, introducing the family to the appropriate department or agency that could best respond to their difficulties. Owing to budgetary restraints many of these roles were discontinued during the late 1980s or practitioners were absorbed within family centres. While many would reflect positively on the successes of these roles, an alternative viewpoint is offered by Edwards and Knight:

> It could be said that the attempts of the 1970s at encouraging parental involvement because of perceived deficits in the home environment rested on a set of assumptions about the supremacy of middle-class attitudes and values. An unkinder view would be the suggestion that early years practitioners as a group were struggling to be recognised as professionals and were therefore willing to take on parental involvement schemes ... (Edwards and Knight, 1994: 113)

However, having experienced at first hand such work in the 1970s and 1980s, I would raise several issues to establish debate. First, I would agree that early years professionals were, and still are to a degree, fighting a battle to gain respect for the value and importance of their work, along with an acknowledgement of their expertise, knowledge and skills. This battle has been long-standing and will probably continue into the future, although it is hoped that recent government initiatives will help raise the profile of practitioners, as early years work is not the 'easy option' that some may suggest. Secondly, I consider that some excellent home–school partnerships were established at that time which still thrive today. As the direct result of the work of one such practitioner, the following are indicative of some of the initiatives established within a family centre, which have continued to grow and develop since the 1980s:

- parental support groups – led by parents, including representation on governing bodies and LEA committees
- regular visits from representatives of outside agencies within the family centre to respond to parental and family needs
- a parents' newsletter, written, produced and distributed by parents
- parenting classes on a range of subjects from 'Understanding the curriculum' to 'Cooking on a budget'

- increased and positive use of a wide range of parental skills within the school
- increased attendance at parents' evenings and open events
- twice weekly, parent-run crèche
- increased input of local community within the school.

Positive change or enforced change?

Practitioners are unlikely to sustain a philosophy that does not support individual families. An ethical question emerges, however, as to whether our particular knowledge and skills should empower us to enforce change on families, especially if this is in direct conflict with our commitment to respecting all cultural backgrounds. If a child is at risk in any way then practitioners have a clear duty to intervene, but when we consider issues such as poor parenting skills, we must first debate what defines good, bad or inadequate parenting and justify our right to encourage change.

If we consider that a particular parenting style is unsatisfactory, then we should reflect carefully before encouraging change. There are families who are bringing up their children in the same way that they were brought up, so are repeating a learned parenting style. If this style does not harm the child in such a way as to demand action, then should we suggest that improvements could be made? This action could be perceived as an insult to family members from previous generations and would possibly not support continued partnership. Similarly, when undertaking home visits we may be surprised by some of the home environments we attend. However we should not assume, using our own standards and expectations, that any home is inappropriate, or any parent is disinterested in their children. We are not there to judge, simply to support the needs of the family and children and this support can be informed by our home visits.

SureStart

The current government initiative to fund SureStart projects nationwide is a direct attempt to alleviate the effects of poverty and deprivation, and provide young children and their families with the means to improve the opportunities available to them.

This was intended to enable the creation of local SureStart groups, comprising parents and professionals from a variety of agencies working together to identify areas of provision that could be improved. SureStart's philosophy relies on effective and collaborative partnership between local families and local professionals without which their aims cannot be achieved. The level of that partnership will very much depend on the individuals involved, the balance of power and the levels of input, respect and shared perspectives.

Practitioners have sometimes pinpointed parents as responsible or partly responsible for their child's difficulties. For example, practitioners may take the view that a child's behaviour difficulties are the direct result of home circumstances and/or parenting style. From this negative standpoint, to work on the behaviour difficulties in the isolation of the setting could have limited success. Unless meaningful interaction can be entered into with the parents in a supportive ethos, then progress may be limited. Only through a process of parents and practitioners working together will this situation be likely to improve, having identified joint difficulties/goals. In line with the government's planned workforce reforms, SureStart workers can now access qualifications at higher education level to enhance provision as well as their own career opportunities. Many such qualifications will include elements relating to parental partnerships.

Characteristics of positive partnerships

So what are the key features and characteristics of positive partnerships? When defining principles of nursery education Goodall suggests that quality provision should include:

A partnership which:

- Acknowledges, celebrates and capitalises on parent or carer involvement, as the child's first educator;
- Is flexible, negotiated and responsive to the needs of individual parents and their families;
- Provides opportunities whereby nursery colleagues offer parents or carers a range of options;
- Is centred upon their own child, themselves, their families and their community;
- Allows them to become active partners in their child's education. (Goodall, 1997: 163)

These principles, while aimed at general nursery education, can equally be applied as a basis for good practice in any early years setting to the benefit of every child, whether he/she has special needs or not.

The National Association of Special Educational Needs (Internet 11) offers eight key principles of effective practice for children with special needs in the early years, including one that focuses on partnerships: 'The fundamental rights and responsibilities of parents should be recognised and respected. They should be full partners in all aspects of assessment, provision and intervention. They should have access to all relevant information regarding their children and participate in all decisions affecting them.'

If we want partnerships with parents to be effective, supportive and of benefit to all parties, it is clear that we must view our work with parents as complementary. We should welcome parents into our settings and ensure that our working practices respect the knowledge, skills and expertise that parents can share with us. A child is known best to his/her parents, and their first-hand knowledge can benefit our work and, thus, the child. If a child is interested and motivated, he/she will be more likely to achieve success.

There is a wealth of research available highlighting the positive outcomes of effective parental partnerships. One such example is the study of Mortimore et al. (1988) identifying factors affecting school effectiveness. Although the study is now quite dated, the principles are still relevant today. Improved educational outcomes were used as a marker of school effectiveness, with the research concluding that increased parental links and interaction within the school helped to increase academic achievements and thus enhance overall school effectiveness. More up-to-date texts upholding the importance and need for effective partnerships with parents include Jones (2004), Miller et al. (2005), Tassoni (2003), Weinberger et al. (2005) and Whalley (2001).

Throughout identification, assessment and reviewing of special needs provision, parents have a right and a duty to participate fully. If the early years setting promotes positive partnerships from the outset, then parents and practitioners will be familiar with the stages of assessment and monitoring systems in place. Relevant information will have been shared with parents, their views considered and valued, and they would be fully aware of any action that was to be taken. Within a supportive environment parents would be aware of their rights and share in planning and provision.

Characteristics of effective partnerships could be:

- approachability, care and concern
- channels for two-way communication
- clarity and style of communication
- helping parents see what they may contribute
- providing opportunities for those contributions
- providing encouragement and support (adapted from Wolfendale, 1997: 64–7).

In addition I would suggest:

- providing accessible information about special provision
- keeping parents informed and updated
- equality, trust and respect.

Positive outcomes for practitioners

A feeling of mutual trust and respect should enhance practitioner confidence. Knowing that with input from parents we are maximising the learning opportunities for the child, and thus improving learning outcomes, should support staff motivational levels. When practitioners work alongside parents in a setting, they will be confident that parents understand the way in which they work and the pressures they may be under. This greater understanding could help when practitioners are discussing issues with the wider parental audience, as parents who have supported the work of the setting will have a greater awareness of the day-to-day reality.

Shared responsibilities in the setting can also help to alleviate practitioner workload, as long as each role is carefully planned and parents are well prepared. Parents are not replacement practitioners but can support and enhance the work of the practitioner, and the selection of tasks undertaken by the parents will reflect the practitioner's views on control, balance of power and the parent's capabilities.

Practitioners should gain increased knowledge about the children from the parents, which will inform planning. A child's likes and dislikes, fears and worries, strengths and weaknesses may be viewed differently by parents and practitioners, so the sharing of information can only be beneficial.

Positive outcomes for parents

Through observing practitioners, parents may gain an improved understanding of the importance of providing appropriate activities, positive role models and supporting children's learning, which could lead to improved support within the home and, thus, improved learning outcomes for the children. Playing a greater part in their child's learning and development should also increase parental confidence.

If we believe that all parents are eager to see their children progress and develop, then it follows that to have played a greater part in that progress will be incredibly motivating. Parents can feel proud of their input in the setting and the direct help and support they are giving both practitioners and children. As a result, self-confidence should be raised, and parental development and learning will have taken place.

Positive outcomes for children

Arguably, the children will benefit most from effective partnerships, as they will feel part of a supportive network free of tensions between home and setting. Miller et al. (2005: 48) consider that: 'The central question that should be asked of any partnership arrangement is – to what extent is it directly or indirectly benefiting the children?' Children are sensitive to conflict around them which can place them in a compromising position and indirectly affect their learning. In a simple example, a child who is naturally very fond of the practitioner could be upset overhearing his/her parents in conflict with the practitioner. The child may be uncomfortable within the setting or even refuse to attend or conversely be uncomfortable at home. The child's security could be severely compromised and, as young children need consistency and security, this will have a negative effect.

Enhanced learning opportunities may emerge within the home situation, reinforcing the learning within the setting and, in some cases, parents will be enabled to participate more actively at home because of their enhanced confidence and their observations of setting activities. An effective parental partnership system should therefore lead to improved educational outcomes and achievement, and all parties will reap the benefits and rewards.

When focusing on children with special needs parental partnerships may present more obstacles but the benefits, especially to the children, cannot be stressed more, as suggested by Drifte (2001: 24): 'it is for the benefit of all concerned, but most particularly the children, that a sound and positive working relationship between home and educational setting is established and maintained'.

Levels of partnership

Hopefully, the days are gone when practitioners were viewed as the 'expert professionals' that made all the decisions. Historically, there followed a period when parents were encouraged to play a greater part in their child's education and care, and we are continuing to move towards more empowering partnerships, in fact all the government guidance and legislation place great emphasis on effective parental partnerships.

However, there are still some parents who feel intimidated or uncomfortable interacting with professionals, for a wide variety of reasons. It may be that their own negative school experiences compromise their ability to work with professionals or that they still view practitioners as 'the experts', with whom they could not enter into purposeful discussions. Wolfendale (1989: 17) concluded: 'One of the most common reasons given by parents for not being involved in their child's pre-school centre is lack of confidence in the face of professional expertise.'

As previously mentioned, parental involvement within early years settings can be tremendously varied, ranging from attending concerts to full and total participation in the daily working life of the setting. As required by current legislation and guidance, all settings must identify the ways in which they involve parents. In addition, practitioners should ensure this is a process which supports real partnership and is not just a policy response to government requirements. For a full and meaningful partnership to exist there should be equality between the parties, with the balance of power being equal.

Both parties must therefore feel that their input is valued. At the stage of initial diagnosis of special needs, parents may need time to adjust and be unable to be effective partners, but with support and encouragement it should be anticipated that parents will be enabled and empowered to take a more active and equal part as time progresses.

While the philosophy and nature of early years settings often lend themselves more readily to parental involvement, settings invariably *expect* a level of participation from parents, which is clearly stated within the policy documents and information given to parents. This is possibly linked to the equality between parents and professionals in this phase, where many groups will have parental input on committees and the daily workings of the group will be open to all for scrutiny and discussion. As a rule, pre-school settings are less formal and have greater flexibility to accommodate visitors and parents. However, in some settings there still exists a certain level of professional control over the domain and, thus, power is reluctantly shared. In addition, planning, recording and delivering the Foundation Stage and/or the National Curriculum places considerable pressures on practitioners, who may argue that there simply is not enough time to become involved in parental partnership schemes requiring additional time, organisation and planning. So perhaps the level of parental participation is directly linked to the equality or inequality of power within the setting.

Hopefully, the days when schools had signs barring entrance to parents are gone, but as Rennie (1996) concluded, while many schools have disposed of such prohibitive notices, they maintain the philosophy.

Legislation and guidance

With specific relation to children with special needs the legislation and guidance that has evolved over the years has continued to emphasise parental rights, children's rights and the need for effective parental partnerships, although Paige-Smith (1997: 41) sees: 'education policy and practice restricting the rights of parents to participate in decision-making'.

The Warnock Report (DES, 1978) offered a complete chapter on parental partnerships and parental rights, with regard to children with special needs, emphasising the need for positive and equal partnerships with schools.

The subsequent Education Act 1981 and circular 1/83 encouraged parental input in assessment processes and gave significant legal rights to parents. While the formal assessment process was introduced, it did not offer parents the right of redress if dissatisfied with any decisions or statements made relating to their child, unless there were factual errors. This was later addressed when SEN tribunals were introduced.

Although the 1981 Education Act reformulated special needs provision, the limitations of the Act were soon realised. As a result, a range of parental voluntary support groups emerged to campaign for continued improvements and to support parents in the short term. One such organisation, Network 81, was established by two parents following the difficulties they had experienced with their own child's education. They were aware of their right to be involved in decision-making but found it hard to fight against a system that presented continuous bureaucratic obstacles to their input in the processes.

The Code of Practice (DfEE, 1994) outlined the key responsibilities of the role of SENCO and offered a basic principle relating to parental partnerships: 'Partnership between parents, pupils, schools, LEAs and other agencies is important' (ibid.: 1.2). The Code continued (ss 2:28–2:33) to outline requirements of providers, including registered early years providers, relating to parental partnership covering the areas of:

- SEN information needed for parents
- arrangements needed to ensure effective partnerships
- means of ensuring accessibility to information.

The Code of Practice introduced Individual Education Plans as a detailed working record of provision made to date and planned for the future. This was a result of significant parental lobbying following the 1981 Act as it was felt that such a record could be a shared document between practitioners and parents, giving parents the opportunity to see the targets that were being set for their child and to give them a say in the planning of those targets.

Within the revised Code of Practice (DfES, 2001d) came a requirement for LEAs to have in place Parent Partnership Schemes and to extend the remit of partnerships, as Emad (2000: 49) confirms: 'An important shift in the revised code of practice is the proposal to offer partnership services to all parents of children with SEN, not just those who have a statement or who are undergoing statutory assessment.'

The Children Act 1989 (DoH, 1991) also made reference to parental participation and partnerships by highlighting the rights and responsibilities of parents, and emphasising the need to take into account the child's wishes and feelings in any decision-making processes. The area of pupil participation in decision-making is further highlighted within the Code of Practice (DfES, 2001d). The revised Children Act (DfES, 2004g) has an underlying principle of 'the importance of parent and carers in improving the well-being of children' (ACE, 2005a: 15)

The fact that a whole chapter in the SEN Code of Practice (DfES, 2001d) is devoted to this area highlights the importance that is now placed on partnerships, which are seen as enabling and 'empowering' parents. The ethos of a shared responsibility is made clear:

The work of the professionals can be more effective when parents are involved and account taken of their wishes, feelings and perspectives on their children's development. This is particularly so when a child has special educational needs. All parents of children with special educational needs should be treated as partners. (Ibid.: s. 2.2)

The Code continues to identify the responsibilities of LEAs and settings, plus the need for settings to involve parents fully from the initial identification of a child's difficulties, through Early Years Action and Early Years Action Plus. However, if all settings have effective parental partnerships in place, then the transition to discussing a child's specific difficulties should be made easier, as mutual respect, understanding and the sharing of information would already occur. Communication should therefore be seen as a key feature of effective partnerships.

The Every Child Matters framework (DfES, 2003) aims to secure improved outcomes for all children, young people and their families, and considers everyone's 'voice' must be heard in planning and delivering the considerable changes that are currently taking place. This includes the voice of parents.

Inspection requirements

Within the new combined inspection framework, under which all registered providers are inspected, there is an expectation that all providers should be able to demonstrate their commitment to effective, working parental partnerships and SEN provision. Thus providers will need to have in place effective partnerships and policies to ensure all parents are informed of the desire for a positive parent–setting partnership.

Foundation Stage requirements

The Foundation Stage guidance (QCA, 2000: 9) offers a clear acknowledgement of the need for effective parental partnerships in early years settings, which will be assessed as part of the inspection process: 'When parents and practitioners work together in early years settings, the results have a positive impact on the child's development and learning. Therefore, each setting should seek to develop an effective partnership with parents. A successful partnership needs a two-way flow of information, knowledge and expertise.'

The guidance offers nine features of good practice clearly highlighting the benefits to all parties, such as the sharing of information, expertise and the child's learning experiences.

Parental involvement in observation, assessment and reviewing progress

When practitioners are observing children owing to initial concerns over possible difficulties the child may be experiencing, it is important that parents are fully informed. It may be that once the concern has been discussed parents can offer explanations, such as bereavement in the family or family tensions. If observations follow, then parents should be informed and involved at every stage. If mutual understanding exists at this point then, hopefully, any further action needed will be entered into in a framework of respect, with both parents and practitioners sharing the same goal.

If the child makes only limited or no progress, then Early Years Action (DfES, 2001d: s. 4.24) would be entered into and, again, parents should be full participants in any discussions and decision-making that emerge: 'Settings should make sure that parents are as fully involved as possible with their child's education and should always be fully informed about how the setting is seeking to meet their child's needs.'

Parents can support the work of the practitioner by working at home with the child to ensure consistency of approach between home and setting, and to support their child's progress. If further intervention is required through Early Years Action Plus and statutory assessment, then parents should remain as partners throughout.

Factors supporting positive partnerships

Having effective policies in place to support our work with parents and children with special needs is a key element of our work. So how can we ensure that policies respond to the needs of all parties and satisfy legislative requirements?

Policies

All registered providers, that is, all maintained schools and all registered early years providers, must have in place SEN policies and written policies regarding existing parental partnerships. In addition, there are expectations in place for all LEAs (QCA, 2000). Some LEAs may have outline policy documents available that can be accessed and adapted for individual settings. The LEA parent partnership officer, early years officers and/or early years forums would also be useful contacts for support and advice when drafting policies. There seems little benefit in reinventing the wheel when a host of documentation already exists that can readily be adapted.

Settings should include parents in the planning and reviewing of partnership policies to ensure that parental perspectives are considered fully. Practitioners should strive to create policies that empower parents and practitioners alike, to support the work of the setting, the parents and the child. If parents are not asked to contribute to the creation of our policies, how can we ensure we are responding directly to their needs, having taken into account their views?

Creating or evaluating policies

When formulating or reformulating policies, all participating personnel should be involved to ensure every perspective is explored and to avoid making presumptions on behalf of unrepresented parties. The SENCO would take the lead, with his/her role ensuring: 'there is effective communication with parents, a shared dialogue in all matters impacting on their child and to involve them generally in their child's holistic development' (SureStart, 2003: 13). Regarding policy creation, Smith (1996: 52) recommends the following questions as a basic guideline for planning SEN policies which ensure parental partnership:

- How can we ensure that information relating to special needs reaches the parents who need it?
- Do parents feel that they can approach the school at any time if they have a concern?
- Do parents know who to contact about special needs?
- What channels do we use for communicating between home and school?
- How do we communicate with parents if we have a concern about their child?
- Do we have effective methods of gathering information from parents?
- Are parents actively involved in IEPs?
- Are review meetings organised in a way which supports parental contribution?

The responses to these questions should give clear indications of existing gaps and ensure all relevant areas for consideration have been explored purposefully. At this point policies can be developed and planning for partnerships set up. All relevant parties should be totally committed to partnership and be motivated to employ their utmost to ensure success, as any resistance or concern about issues may compromise success before any partnership is established.

If policies are already in place then regular reviews are pertinent, again ensuring all parties are involved. Views regarding current policies can be invited and used as a basis for discussion to identify problems, concerns and ways forward. If possible or practical a worthwhile exercise could be to create a simple questionnaire for completion by staff and parents alike. This gives everyone the opportunity to reflect individually or with colleagues or friends and offer constructive comments in an anonymous manner which may encourage improved outcomes. The results or findings could then be circulated to all who participated and used as a basis for further discussions. If we do not seek parental views and respond to them, we are presuming we know their views and are excluding them from the process.

Reviewing existing policies

As a setting it would be worth exploring precisely what information, support and participation is needed for parents and, conversely, what information, support and participation is needed from parents. Discussions could include areas such as information, mutual support, participation opportunities, skill-sharing and teaching.

Information
Information will pass between the two parties for mutual benefit, and obviously in the interests of the children. Settings should reflect on how information is shared regarding:

- the curriculum
- record-keeping systems
- planning
- identification of special needs
- monitoring progress
- the graduated response
- other local providers
- interagency working.

It may be useful for a member of staff or parent to collate such information as it emerges into a resource file that is readily accessible to all interested parties for reference and to support discussions. Conversely, staff can benefit from parental information about their children, the locality and the availability of resources that could prove useful to other parents. A noticeboard for open use by parents and staff alike can be a useful method of sharing information that encourages parents into the setting. Newsletters which encourage parental input are also a useful tool, especially if parents do not visit the setting regularly.

Mutual support
Simply offering parents a meeting place can encourage beneficial supportive discussions and the sharing of ideas. Parents of children with special needs may feel more comfortable talking to another parent who may share an understanding of the issues causing concern. Sharing common ground can be tremendously supportive and may help alleviate feelings of isolation and difference. Ideas, suggestions and sources of support could be shared and strong bonds formed that can enhance self-confidence for all parties, ultimately benefiting the children. Staff could also be involved in these meetings, if invited.

Participation opportunities
All parties need to be aware of existing participation opportunities and the readiness to welcome any new initiatives that may be suggested. Practitioners

must also be ready to justify the existing range, or limitations, of participation as there may be parents who have experiences in other settings or new ideas that they wish to have considered. An open, encouraging environment will ensure that parents will be listened to and that their ideas will be welcomed. Parents will often come prepared to suggest an initiative having clearly thought it through in advance and having some or many of the required resources in hand. With minor effort on behalf of the setting, a very positive, parent-led initiative could emerge.

Skill-sharing

Parents, staff and practitioners can all benefit from the sharing of knowledge, expertise and skills. Parents, staff and combined training sessions can be established, with all parties being encouraged to share skills. A whole range of sessions could be arranged on such aspects as behaviour management, immunisations, safety in the home, cooking with children, cooking from around the world, dealing with bureaucracy and purposeful play.

Skill-sharing could also extend to parents' skills being used within the setting, from gardening expertise to fluency in a foreign language. Parent-to-parent skill-sharing could evolve with parents establishing babysitting circles, social visits and so on. A vast range of opportunities exists.

Teaching

Parents can become real partners in the learning that takes place within the setting or within the home if they are involved in the planning as well as the delivery. Through a two-way interchange of ideas, practitioners and parents can support the child's progress together. Problems can arise when there is clearly a lack of interaction between home and school, which can result in a child's needs being compromised.

Issues compromising partnership

It would be pertinent to initiate discussion relating to the issues that compromise or inhibit any expansion of parent partnership, to make all parties aware of issues from inside and outside the setting that may compromise or prohibit partnerships. This may lead to the resolution of some issues, or at least to the planning of resolution, and an enhanced awareness of those that do not appear amenable to resolution. Debating these issues and any others that may emerge should enable a clarification of possible ways forward and would certainly benefit all as an awareness-raising exercise. Policy documents could then be pulled together, including existing practices and an action plan for the future.

Practitioners should accept that not all parents will be keen and enthusiastic to enter a partnership but may feel nervous, lacking in confidence or even being antagonistic, but all will have a strong emotional commitment to their child. Reports exist to suggest two distinct types of parents of children with special needs, those who are involved and those who are reluctant (Blamires et al., 1997). The initial and early contacts with parents are therefore vital to the future of the partnership, and practitioners should attempt to support all parents in becoming active and involved partners.

Legislation and bureaucracy can also create tensions for parents, so the LEA as well as the individual setting should strive to ease the situation through giving support and information. Guides to LEA special needs provision should be readily accessible to all parents and practitioners, and it would be helpful to involve parents in the design and format of such information as it needs to be constructive, easy to understand and in the parents' home language.

Local education authorities and individual settings must have clear policies and guidelines available to parents, as well as having policies for resolving conflict situations.

In working practice

If we are committed to working with parents, we must acknowledge the benefits, examine our own working practices and recognise that this area of work does not simply happen but that we need to plan, establish and monitor partnerships to ensure positive outcomes are experienced by parents, children and practitioners.

When preparing to welcome new children into our settings, parents should be given information regarding:

- the setting and the policies of the setting
- how practitioners will plan for, monitor and review their child
- which professionals will be involved
- which professionals may be involved in the future
- the roles and responsibilities of professionals
- the requirements of the SEN Code of Practice (DfES, 2001d)
- how parents can support the work of the setting.

Once children are established within the setting, we should continue to ensure that parents are active participants in their child's progress through informing them regularly of the child's activities, successes, concerns, any changes that may be occurring in the planning and implementing of provision, and how they can help within the home situation. Equally, parents should feel able to inform the setting of activities, successes, concerns and changes. Parents should feel that they are not only involved with their child's setting but are real and active partners, taking a shared responsibility.

Summary

If the children we work with are to be given the best opportunities to reach their full potential, then practitioners need to work together with parents and other professionals to ensure that this becomes a reality. We cannot do this without parental support, nor should we wish to. If we accept the benefits of effective parental partnerships, then it follows that we should establish, monitor and review our working practices to reflect this philosophy. As a starting point we should assess:

- how welcoming our setting is to *all* parents and children (including fathers)
- how involved we want parents to become
- our induction and settling-in procedures
- the parental partnership policy
- our information-sharing processes
- if parents understand the roles and responsibilities of all those involved with their child
- how involved parents are in decision-making
- the information that we expect parents to share with us
- the information we expect to share with parents
- the record-keeping systems
- how well staff members deal with parents
- if staff members are always available to discuss issues with parents
- whether there is somewhere for such discussions to take place
- how we expect parents to work with their child in the home
- how aware parents are of supporting agencies
- how well parents are prepared for and supported in review meetings.

While not an exhaustive list, an exploration of the issues would be a useful starting point for reflection on current practices and moving towards improved practices. Dale concludes:

> What makes it so hard to evaluate is that the real cost can only be assessed through establishing the cost of its absence: of families who are frustrated and dissatisfied and fail to be helped by the services on offer and therefore perceive themselves as unsupported. Partnership practice has a price – but can we as a society afford or justify the alternative? (Dale, 1996: 307)

Similarly, Wall (2005: 44) emphasises the importance of this work:

> Every new guidance document or law that emerges is sure to make reference to our having effective partnerships with parents and our work in this area will be scrutinized in our inspections. We could pay lip service to these requirements but if we appreciate the benefits to all parties, and especially the children, then we should be prepared to examine our practices and address any areas that fall short of our ideal.

Key issues

❖ Parents should be respected and their feelings and contributions valued.
❖ Practitioners should acknowledge the benefits of effective, meaningful partnerships.
❖ Practitioners should work towards empowering parents.
❖ Practitioners should review existing partnership policies and ensure that practices reflect policies.
❖ Partnerships cannot be assumed; they need to be planned, established and reviewed regularly.
❖ The success or failure of partnerships will depend on the quality of the relationships and the equality within those relationships.

Some suggestions for discussion

Item 1

Brainstorm the benefits of parental partnerships to parents, children with special needs and practitioners, as perceived by the staff.

Item 2

Discuss what is expected of parents and the setting within a partnership. Discuss how parents are informed of setting expectations. Discuss how staff can evaluate parental expectations.

Item 3

Examine the setting's existing parental partnership policy and discuss:

• Are all parents given equal opportunities to participate?
• Are we using every opportunity to welcome parents before their child begins attendance?
• How do we encourage reluctant parents?
• What information is shared with parents?
• Are we simply involving parents in some aspects of our work or embarking on real partnerships?
• How appropriate is the format of information shared?
• How and where do we discuss issues of concern with parents?
• How do we prepare parents for review meetings?
• What opportunities exist for parents to be a part of the decision-making processes within the setting?

- If parents do not attend meetings and open days, what steps are taken to follow up?
- Does the setting listen to and support parental initiatives?
- How do staff deal with parental conflict/disagreement?

Item 4

Consider the usefulness of surveying parents to assess parental perspectives on the effectiveness of your partnership systems. What questions might you ask parents? Make a list and sample it on a small number of parents.

📖 Suggested further reading

Draper, L. and Duffy, B. (2001) 'Working with parents', in G. Pugh (ed.), *Contemporary Issues in the Early Years*, 3rd edn. London: Paul Chapman Publishing.

Jones, C. (2004) *Supporting Inclusion in the Early Years*. Maidenhead: Open University Press.

Whalley, M. (2001) *Involving Parents in their Children's Learning*. London: Paul Chapman Publishing.

This chapter is taken from:
Wall, K. (2006) *Special Needs in the Early Years*, Second Edition
978-1-4129-2949-3

25 The Challenge of Leading Multi-agency Teams

CAROL AUBREY

> This chapter takes a detailed look at models of multi-agency working, facilitating factors and barriers, and the challenges in practice as experienced by a large group of professionals. Case studies of particular professional groups (speech and language therapists, a special educational needs team and a social worker) are presented in order to tease out both the strengths and challenges of such work.

7.1 Introduction

As noted earlier in the book, since 1997 the English government has invested heavily in early childhood services with the introduction of Early Excellence Centres, Sure Start and Neighbourhood Nursery programmes. This has led to a dramatic increase in the number of integrated centres offering education and care, family support, adult training, health and welfare services. With the introduction of children's centres as central to the delivery of services to families, this work has increased rapidly (see the government's strategy for *Special Educational Needs, Removing Barriers to Achievement*, DfES, 2002; Green Paper, DfES, 2003a; the ten-year childcare strategy, *Choice for Parents, the Best Start for Children*, HMT, 2004; *National Service Framework for Children*, DoH, 2004 setting standards for health and social services and the interface of those services with education; and the *Children Act*, DfES, 2004). Children's centres, originally conceived as serving the poorest wards, have been projected as a universal service to support all children and families through early years education, high-quality and flexible childcare, involving parents in their children's learning, adult learning, family support and outreach services, child and family health services, support for parents and children with special needs, and forging links with Job Centre Plus as well as other local training providers, further and higher education institutions.

Not only do leaders of children's centres come from different disciplines and have different training but, in their role as providers of 'service hubs' within the community, they are recruiting and employing staff themselves from a range of disciplines related to health, social care and welfare, and education. This means that children's centres have a significant role to play in developing the childcare workforce and offering new staff training opportunities at a time when the leaders themselves may have had limited leadership training opportunities. Given the stress in government policy on working across professional and organizational boundaries, it is important to consider that despite the potential to help solve complex societal problems, multi-agency working may require more resources of time, effort, creative thinking and money than single agencies and, as such, additional resources may be justified. Since there may be a range of models, methods and motives for engaging in interprofessional or multi-agency practice, as well as interdisciplinary research and development, it is important to be clear about what is involved.

7.2 Challenges to collaboration

A range of factors may challenge collaboration between different agencies and professional groups such as:

- poor communication between professionals and the range of professional languages and discourses that they use (Pietroni, 1992);
- the sheer complexity of the social problems that practitioners may encounter (real and perceived);
- the changing nature of family structure and hence the loss of support networks of the extended family;
- the increased population migration and mobility within and between countries that also serves to weaken kinship ties;
- the nature and variety of existing professional 'partnerships' that include different sectors of early childhood services (statutory, voluntary and private);
- the number and type of professional or agency groups involved, primarily from education, social care and welfare, and health-related fields, but including financial support and income maintenance;
- professionals working from a range of practice settings and not necessarily, or even probably, co-located;
- the value differences within and between professions that arise from professional traditions and customs acquired before, during and after training;

- a professional knowledge base or discipline that may have origins in the natural sciences, for health-related fields or social sciences for education and social work;
- differences in relative status, income and career progression that may create professional rivalry;
- the different but related policies and priorities for practice and staff professional development and improvement across the field;
- the nature of the professional 'teamwork' involved, its structure and function, the mix of professionals and their formal relationships (Øvretveit et al., 1997);
- workforce reform with national standards for under-8s daycare and child-minding (DfES, 2003c), the ten-year childcare strategy (HMT, 2004) and the rationalization of qualifications, the single Early Years Foundation Stage from birth to 5 years, and the continuous quality service improvement and inspection framework (DfES, 2006).

Given the many factors that influence relations within and between agencies and professional groups, it is essential to identify the challenges and benefits that working in multi-disciplinary teams can raise in considering the designing and leading of harmonious integrated services for children and families. It serves to highlight the complexity of working towards a shared philosophy, vision and principles with parents, children, community and all partners as well as developing shared identity, purposes and common working practices with all. It is a challenge for integrated centre leaders and it is a challenge for local authorities with the primary duty and responsibility for delivery of integrated services.

7.3 Questions to ask

Given the importance to early childhood leadership of multi-agency work, the key challenge is developing accessible, integrated services through partnership that are experienced as coherent and continuous by children, families and communities. Two key questions are raised for consideration:

- How much do we really know about effective multi-agency working?
- What are the key factors for their success and what kinds of challenges are raised?

7.4 What do we know about effective multi-agency working?

Sloper (2004) in a review of the literature on multi-agency working concluded that there was little evidence on the effectiveness of multi-agency working itself or of different models of such working in gaining improved outcomes for children and families. That said, consistent findings on facilitators for and barriers to joint working have been uncovered. At the organizational level, facilitative factors have been identified in the areas of planning, implementation and ongoing management. Planning, for instance, is found to be supported by clear aims and objectives, defined roles and responsibilities, staff commitment, strong leadership and a multi-agency steering management group, an agreed timetable for implementation of changes, linkages into other planning and decision-making processes and good systems of communication, information-sharing and adequate IT systems. Meanwhile, ongoing management and implementation demands shared and adequate resources, recruitment of the right staff, with the right experience, knowledge and approach, joint training and team-building, appropriate staff support and supervision, monitoring, evaluation of the service and reviewing policies and procedures in the light of changed circumstances. Existing professional and agency cultures as well as previous experience of multi-agency working have also been found to help. A corresponding *lack* of such facilitating factors was inevitably found to create barriers. Other factors such as constant reorganization, frequent staff turnover, lack of qualified staff, financial uncertainty, different professional ideologies and agency cultures were also found to hinder joint working. It was noted in the review that there was a clear need for methodologically sound local evaluations of multi-agency services, as well as multi-site studies that investigated the effects of different facilitating factors and models of working on outcomes for parents and children and included exploration of costs on effectiveness (Atkinson et al., 2002; Cameron et al., 2000; Liabo et al., 2001). As Milbourne (2005: 677) has noted, the idea of inter-agency work is not new but 'current policy approaches neglect to consider the diverse models of collaboration that practitioners may need to develop in practice'.

7.5 Models of multi-agency working

Atkinson et al. (2005: 8) identified five models of multi-agency activity based on their purpose:

Decision-making group   – providing a forum for professionals from different agencies to meet, discuss ideas and make decisions.

Consultation and training– for professionals from one agency to enhance the expertise of those of another by providing consultation and/or training for them.

Centre-based delivery   – gathering a range of expertise together in one place in order to deliver a more co-ordinated and cohesive response to need.

Co-ordinated delivery – to draw together a number of agencies involved in the delivery of services so that a more coordinated and cohesive response to need could be adopted.

Operational-team delivery – for professionals from different agencies to work together on a day-to-day basis and to form a cohesive multi-agency team that delivered services directly to clients.

Interestingly, decision-making groups and co-ordinated delivery were the most frequent types of multi-agency activity encountered within their sample, while operational-team delivery was the least frequently encountered. It was found by Atkinson et al. that many initiatives, in practice, were a conglomerate of these models and it would appear that this would also be the case for integrated centre provision. It should also be noted that the majority of models were focused on organization of professionals and that did not ensure families received a co-ordinated service. Moreover, as Watson et al. (2000; 2002) stressed, there was little evidence to show the extent to which models are implemented or what effects they have in practice. Where members of different agencies worked together, a more holistic approach could be achieved when a 'primary provider' or key worker took responsibility for delivering a direct and unified programme and the family were seen as equal partners. This finding is consistent with Robinson's (2006) call to focus on strategies that work directly on strengthening the conditions that enable effective practice and weaken the effects that hinder it.

7.6 Organization of professional groups

Sanders (2004) went further to question the very term 'multi-agency', noting distinctions among *groups* of professionals, occupations, sectors, agencies and disciplines as well as a differing focus of *operations* of work, teamwork, collaboration, co-operation and integration. Furthermore, he noted the disadvantages and barriers of working together such as costs in terms of time taken away from contact with clients to liaise, consult, co-ordinate as well as administrative and communication costs. In respect of primary health care teams, Øvretveit (1990) noted barriers to efficiency associated not only with lack of time but with understanding the purpose of interprofessional practice, understanding the roles of others, professional rivalry, exclusion of significant others (non-professionals), ownership of resources, discrimination and racism, and ways of ensuring that assessment is effective.

Øvretveit et al. (1997) identified significant dimensions of teamworking: degree of integration, membership of a permanent work group; processing pathways of clients; and management (how the team is led and how practitioners are managed). Indeed, a very important aspect of team functioning is the creation of management structures and the corresponding exercise of professional autonomy. There is also a need to establish responsibility for managing the total resources of the team that relates to job descriptions, reviewing of work and performance appraisal/supervision. In the case of the latter, where supervision may be undertaken by a senior staff member, this may be clinical advice where the supervisee remains accountable for the quality of work undertaken, clinical supervision where the senior staff member is accountable for the quality of supervisee's work, management monitoring to ensure adherence to agency procedures and full management, where the manager assumes responsibility for both clinical and organizational components of the role. Øvretveit et al. then proceeded to describe five types of management and supervision structure for teams: *profession-managed; single manager; joint manager*, a mixture of the previous two; *team manager-contracted*, who contracts in services of other professionals; and *hybrid*, based on the other four models.

As noted by Glass (2006), given the lack of experience of multi-agency early years services, the challenges to creating multi-agency management structures should not be underestimated. In terms of effectiveness, a recent report by the National Evaluation of Sure Start (NESS), Melhuish et al. (2005) set out to consider links between aspects of Sure Start local integrated centre programme implementation and levels of effectiveness judged in terms of child and parental outcomes for 150 programmes included in their impact study. The 18 dimensions related to:

- *what was implemented* (service quality, service delivery, identification of users, 'reach', reach strategies, service innovation and service flexibility);
- *the processes underpinning proficient implementation of services* (partnership composition, partnership functioning, leadership, multi-agency working, access to services, evaluation use and staff turnover); and
- *holistic aspects of implementation* (vision, communications, empowerment and ethos).

Their results indicated that links between the processes of programme implementation and impact on children and families living in programme areas could be detected, with better-rated programme implementation (what they did and how they were doing it) linked to beneficial outcomes, especially for parents. The fact that the effects of programme implementation were found to be slight might have been associated with the time it takes for programmes to reach full capacity in programme delivery. Furthermore, although effective leadership and multi-agency teams were categories included in the evaluation and data were collected from a national survey, interviews, delivery plans, organizational charts and annual reports, no further light was shed on these dimensions. In this context, the difficulty of demonstrating the indirect effect of leadership should not be underestimated as noted by Robinson (2006).

7.7 Views on multi-agency working from four integrated centres

In order to capture changing perspectives on multi-agency working in local Sure Start integrated centre programmes, we worked in more depth with two of our integrated centre leaders as well as two of their colleagues who together led four local integrated centre programmes in the same location as our over-all leadership project.

We used multiple ways to gather information over a three-year period in the lives of the four local Sure Start integrated centre programmes between 2003 and 2006 as they shifted towards children's centre status. The centres had been established over periods of time from one to five years, yet all served very distinct social, cultural and ethnic inner-city communities. An initial survey of 79 staff and partnership board members and 34 follow-up interviews with rep-resentatives of particular agencies, their lead professionals and parents explored facilitating factors and barriers to multi-agency working. We then followed up this work with case studies of three single- and joint-agency working: with the speech and language therapy team representing health, an early years worker, educational psychologist and outreach worker representing special education, and a social worker representing social care and welfare, using interviews, doc-ument analysis and, in one case, observation of professional training being delivered.

Those who took part included team members from the integrated centre programmes, representatives from the accountable body – in this case the pri-mary care trust (PCT) – and the lead agency or local council, members of the programme partnership boards, including parents, as well as representatives of specific agencies and their professional leaders.

The survey questions were focused on multi-agency activity, key challenges and the key challenges for their success, drawing upon a study of multi-agency working of Atkinson et al. (2000; 2001) and Tomlinson (2003) from the National Foundation for Educational Research (NFER). These were piloted with professionals from a range of backgrounds, for example health, education and psychology. The in-depth interviews then probed areas highlighted from the survey, in particular, topics that had generated mixed and ambivalent responses. For the case studies, interviews explored views of the professionals concerned, their professional leaders and integrated centre leaders themselves on the distinctiveness of their role, facilitating factors and barriers, targets and effectiveness. Documents gathered included person specifications and service-level agreements where available and information related to professional activ-ities, such as leaflets for parents and other professionals, data related to targets and outcomes as well as records of work carried out. The quality of evidence available varied from service to service, reflecting in part differing contracts and therefore relationships to the management structure of the integrated centre programme of the agency concerned as well as the leading agency.

7.8 What we found out

It was noted above that a real challenge was posed for local authorities with the primary duty and responsibility for delivering integrated services to children and families. Our survey confirmed this.

Local authority structures and boundaries

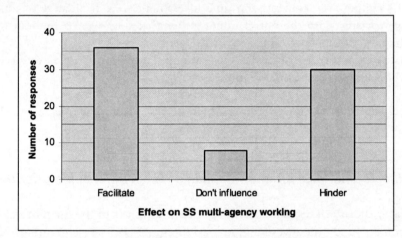

Figure 7.1 *Local authority structures and boundaries*

As Figure 7.1 shows, views about the influence of local authority structures and boundaries on multi-agency working were mixed with a half of our respondents feeling they facilitated, slightly less thinking they hindered multi-agency working and with a sizeable minority (11 per cent) reporting that they had no particular influence. The factors thought to facilitate multi-agency working within the integrated centre programmes were related to being able to use systems and people already in place in order to advise or to promote this type of work.

Working relationships within the teams and with the parent agencies of team members, as well as with other voluntary and statutory agencies, were seen as both facilitating and as a force for development of multi-agency working, thus enabling integrated centre programmes to deliver services that were needed.

Working closely with other organizations enables our integrated centre to 'fill the gaps'.

Practical factors thought to hinder multi-agency working related to geographical boundaries, where these were different for the various agencies involved with the integrated centre programme. Different terms and conditions of work, holiday allowance, pay scales and policies and procedures, as well as staff employment matters were also highlighted.

Staffing arrangements and time investment of integrated centre programmes

The majority of respondents (three-quarters) thought that resources in the form of staffing arrangements and time investment were facilitative of multi-agency working, with the rest claiming either that they were a hindrance or that they did not to know one way or the other.

Qualitative responses suggested that time given to setting up new services was seen as essential to establish joint working.

Being able to work closely with the multi-agency team influences our work together.

Individuals' and local programme teams' expectations and priorities

The vast majority of respondents thought that resources in the form of staffing arrangements and time investment in local integrated centre programmes facilitated multi-agency working, while a few thought them a hindrance or claimed not to know.

It was felt that staff had a high expectation of working as a multi-agency team. The development towards a fully integrated team, however, appeared to be slower than desired. This was felt to be due to several factors. Staff not being clear about their roles within the team was considered a concern. Concern was also expressed regarding management of staff who, in many cases, remained line-managed and supervised by the parent organization and the tensions or problems this could cause were emphasized.

The development of multi-agency working has been slow. 'Baggage' brought by the local programme members and in some cases, the professional management being maintained within the statutory agencies needed to be overcome.

Aims and objectives of local integrated centre programmes

Aims and objectives of the local programmes were regarded by the vast majority as facilitative of multi-agency working, with just a few stating that they did not know. It was emphasized that the aim of the integrated centres was to empower and provide a service for the communities they served, reflecting their needs.

> The aim of the programme is to deliver services in a different way, responding to community needs to work with families at most risk, to ensure their children have the best possible access and start in life.

It was generally agreed that the integrated centre aimed to work in a multi-agency manner. The centre also acted as a conduit, bringing together, and helping other agencies in adapting to a multi-agency style of working.

> A number of agencies in the area would not get together formally if it were not for the local integrated programme.

> Planning ensures complementary working to clear aims and objectives.

Confidentiality and information-sharing strategies between the various agencies

Views about confidentiality and information-sharing strategies between the various agencies involved were mixed (Figure 7.2).

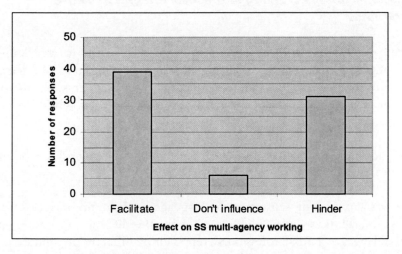

Figure 7.2 *Confidentiality and information-sharing strategies between agencies*

Rather more respondents thought that these strategies facilitated rather than hindered such work, with a minority feeling that they had no influence.

Several had a positive experience of this process. It was acknowledged, however, that this was a problem for all four integrated centres and that systems and protocols needed to be developed to reduce the amount of time wasted by staff and, indirectly, families on this matter.

> Strategies need to be in place to facilitate multi-agency working. Organizationally, different agencies have different strategies that are not mutually understood.

These difficulties appeared to occur both across organizations that worked with the local integrated centre programmes and across the multi-agency team itself, due to the nature of local team members' employment conditions.

The accountable body for its part was highlighted by several respondents as a hindrance.

> The lack of information-sharing has ground to a halt several very positive programmes we have tried to put into place. Mostly on behalf of the accountable body!

The need for sharing information was seen by many as essential in order for the services to provide successful services.

The need for development of a common language across professional groups working in the local integrated centre programmes

As emphasized earlier in this chapter, respondents felt a need for development of a common language across professional groups working in local integrated centre programmes. The overwhelming majority of respondents felt that there was a need for a common language across professional groups, while 7 per cent did not and 6 per cent did not know one way or the other.

> Common language reduces isolation and increases partnership working which is essential in order to be effective.

There was also a strong sense that the language used should be accessible for parents. Overall, issues were highlighted about the difficulty in developing a universal language across professionals, representing different disciplines. It was also suggested that 'effective communication channels [could] overcome issues of different "languages"'.

Budgets and finance arrangements

As to whether budgets and financial arrangements created a conflict within and between agencies, a general lack of programme funding, a raised concern about sustainability and a recognition of the need to create more effective use of resources, views were very mixed. Given that the local integrated centre programmes have now become designated as children's centres with control and funding handed over to local authorities and 'ring-fencing' of Sure Start money abolished by 2008, without regard for their commitment or capacity to provide adequately resourced centres, these findings are challenging (Figures 7.3 to 7.6).

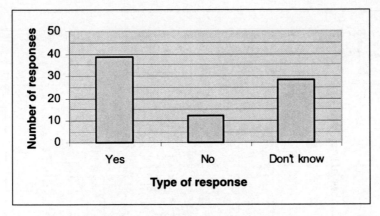

Figure 7.3 *Concern about conflicts within or between agencies that provided staff*

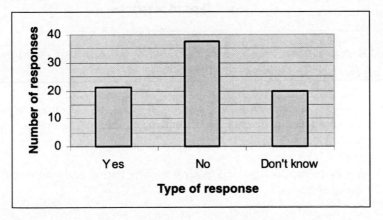

Figure 7.4 *Concern about general lack of programme funding*

Tensions specifically between the lead agency and accountable body were highlighted by qualitative responses. There was believed to be a need to establish good agreements between the two in order to reduce possible conflicts of interest.

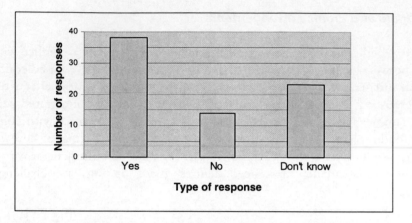

Figure 7.5 *Concern about sustainability of the services and, thus, uncertainty of funding*

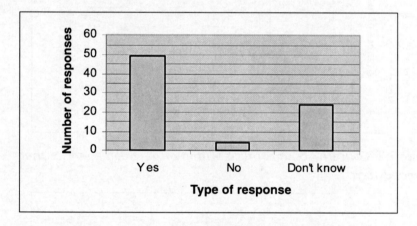

Figure 7.6 *A need to create more effective use of resources (human and material) by reducing repetition and overlap*

There is always concern about conflicts when partnership working is in place, however, a good agreement reduces the prospect. Duplicate services to parents means a waste of resources.

We need a more radical approach to reduce competition and ensure collaboration across agencies.

It was noted by more than one local programme that services were started up when the programmes did not have their own buildings from which to operate. This was felt to be unacceptable.

To start programmes with no buildings or venues is ludicrous.

Roles and responsibilities adopted by individuals working within local integrated centre programmes

The majority of respondents felt that issues around roles and responsibilities adopted by individuals working within the integrated centre concerned the need to understand better the roles of others, and half reported conflicts over areas of responsibility. The vast majority recognized the need to go beyond existing roles to work in new ways.

It was felt by some that in the past understanding others' roles and responsibilities, as well as the need to work in new ways had proved difficult.

> These have all been challenges to most of the individuals and agencies involved.

This was felt to be an area in which most felt the need for continued improvement.

> It is vital that all team members understand the role of others in order to effectively offer service.

Several respondents with different roles within the integrated centres understood the initiative to be about 'blurring the edges of your role to take new responsibilities and to work in a new way'.

Aims of specific agencies competing with local integrated centre programme aims

Respondents were mixed in view and less certain of whether or not aims of specific agencies competed with local programme aims as a result of different government targets, differences in target groups and different emphases on preventative versus crisis intervention (see Figures 7.7 to 7.9).

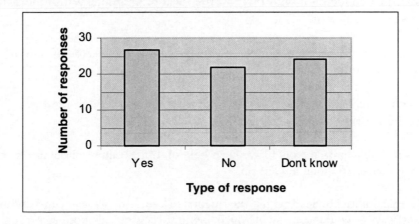

Figure 7.7 *Differences in the target group/s*

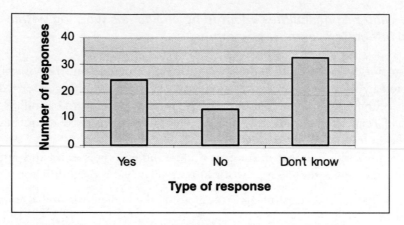

Figure 7.8 *Different government targets*

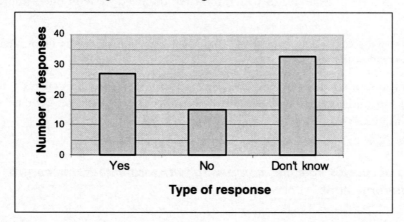

Figure 7.9 *A focus on preventative work versus crisis intervention*

It would appear from the responses that the aims of some agencies were regarded to be identical with those of the local programme. With others they were seen as different.

> Targets are different from [agencies] which need not be a cause of 'competition' but complementary.

Still others recognized that complementary working, although ideal, was hindered by existing working cultures.

> A strategic approach would have been helpful. But a culture of competition for initiatives/funding hinders this.

> The flexibility provided within the integrated centre to achieve targets with new ways of working, many of which, being successful have not been recognized by mainstream services.

Several respondents expressed the view that the ethos of all agencies was changing and becoming much more prevention focused.

> There is a general move towards preventative work that places integrated centre work at the heart of the government's agenda – which all agencies are beginning to recognize.

Non-financial resources creating challenges

The majority of respondents felt that non-financial resources created a challenge to multi-agency working. Areas highlighted were allocation of time, provision of staff and physical space in which to work together effectively.

Responses also revealed that availability of non-financial resources were thought to create a challenge, resulting in a less effective delivery of services than might otherwise be the case. Buildings and venues from which to work were slow to become available and recruitment of staff to carry out such work was also slow.

Physical space in which to work was perhaps the largest problem across all local integrated centre programmes. Programmes became operational without their own or adequate facilities. Even when facilities were open there might not be enough space for all staff.

> New offices, but no storage and teams too large for premises.

> We barely have enough room to work now. Building work due now is intended to reduce our space further. There is insufficient room to meet with parents/groups at the present site. It is against safe working practices to leave anyone working in the office on their own.

These observations provide further interesting insights into staff's own perspectives on the change and development taking place in the field, that complement those expressed in Chapters 2, 3 and 4.

Communication within and between agencies working with the local integrated centre programmes

The majority of respondents felt that poor communication within and between agencies created problems between those working at different levels within agencies, with half reporting that this could create different availability of professionals from different agencies and undermine successful multi-agency work through poor communication between different local government departments.

A clear understanding of each other's roles and the cultures of the agencies from which they originated was felt to be important to alleviate some of the problems, or potential problems that might occur within the teams. In some cases this was felt to be due to a lack of communication between the agencies involved.

Because protocols have still not been agreed.

It was also highlighted by several respondents that, despite these problems at the strategic level, the local programme teams were delivering services in a multi-agency manner.

Although we are made up of different agencies we all work very well as a team.

The effect of professional and agency culture on integrated centre practice

Respondents' views on the effect of professional and agency culture on professional practice were mixed. A quarter felt that multi-agency working did disrupt existing agency cultures values and ways of working; one half claimed it did not and the rest did not know one way or the other. Nearly two-thirds, however, felt that specific policy and practice differences hindered shared practice. The majority felt that different data management systems affected information sharing and did impact upon shared practice (see Figures 7.10 to 7.12). (Appendix 7 examines in more depth the multiple sources of values and potential value conflict underpinning multi-agency working.)

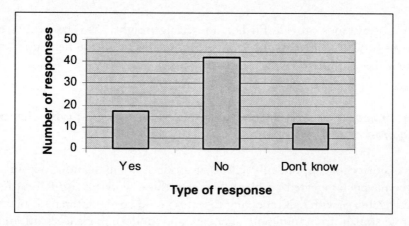

Figure 7.10 *Multi-agency working disrupts existing agency cultures (values and ways of working)*

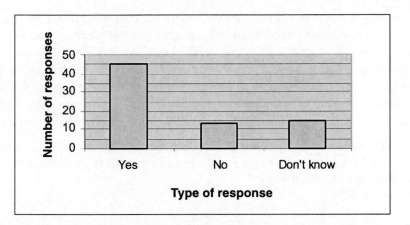

Figure 7.11 *Specific policy and practice differences hinder shared practice*

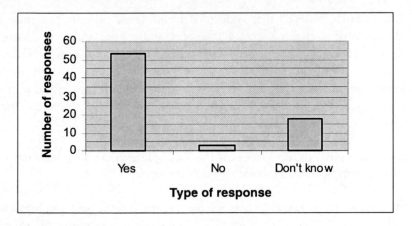

Figure 7.12 *Different data management systems which affect information sharing impact upon shared practice*

Sharing information between professionals working for the local programmes as well as within agencies involved with them was regarded as problematic, with comments suggesting that staff were 'still awaiting some baseline information'. It was noted, however, that attempts were being made to eliminate such problems.

The strategy of the management in the local integrated centre programmes

In terms of management strategy, the vast majority felt that multi-agency working was strongly supported and promoted at management level in order to remain credible at delivery level but were less sure whether management strategy drive was organized carefully to carry along the various participants from each agency. A majority did feel that the integrated centre management strategy encouraged like-minded individuals who sought new ways of working in order to meet shared goals and work across existing management structures.

Overall qualitative responses indicated that the management strategy of local programmes supported multi-agency working and these new ways of working were imperative to success. There were felt to be problems at the level of leading agencies, whereby the work at local programme level was being hindered.

> I don't believe that there is enough discussion and agreement at senior management level. However, there is a willingness to make it work lower down – at programme manager level.

Training opportunities for team members

The vast majority believed that additional multi-agency training to meet the extended role of agencies would be helpful and shared an active desire to engage with other agencies at the delivery level. Views were more mixed as to whether there should also be 'single agency' development.

Additional responses indicated that it was generally felt training in a multi-agency manner was necessary in order for team members to develop understanding of each other's roles:

> Knowledge is vital to the success of the local programme; this can only be gained by sharing of information through training.

The vast majority of respondents believed commitment and willingness of team members to be involved in multi-agency work was sustained by an active desire to engage with other agencies at the management level, at the delivery level and by a 'bottom up' as well as a 'top down' management approach. This finding is consistent with the findings reported in Chapter 3.

Specific responses indicated strongly that there was willingness to be involved in multi-agency work at both the strategic and operational level and that both helped to sustain this work.

> 'Bottom-up' allows practitioners to feed back voices of the local community and to identify gaps in provision. 'Top down' allows for clear protocols and clear line management in areas of emerging practice to be clarified.

Leadership or drive of individual integrated centre programme managers

The majority felt that leadership or drive of individual integrated centre leaders demonstrated clear strategic direction, showed tenacity to overcome obstacles to progress, and could bring together the team in order to bring about change and overcome obstacles.

Overall, respondents were very positive about the leadership of the local integrated centre programmes. Some of the problems that had been dealt with were highlighted as examples of the strength of the programme leaders.

> Delivered services even without having buildings. Operated without adequate, or no base – homeless.

These findings are illuminating in their insight into both facilitating factors and barriers at the local level and assessment of the role of integrated centre leadership. Views on leadership were very positive in terms of providing strategic direction, having tenacity and bringing the team together to overcome obstacles. Commitment of staff teams to sustaining multi-agency teamwork was also stressed. Aims of the integrated centre were seen to facilitate multi-agency working. Barriers were also identified in the form of local authority structures and boundaries, uncertainty concerning budgets, and non-financial resources of staffing, time and space, hence, sustainability. It was acknowledged that knowledge and understanding of roles and responsibilities within and between agencies was important and that the aims and culture of individual agencies could conflict with or disrupt multi-agency working. The need for additional training was identified. (Appendix 8 provides an exemplar framework for planning, implementing and reviewing a team exercise.)

Interprofessional training needs

The implications are that further interprofessional development is needed in order to develop collaborative teamwork that addresses tensions in working relations within and between agencies in a context of instability and change. But this is training that needs to go beyond information exchange towards a fundamental reconception of a workforce that is flexible in approach and in career progression, that takes place over time through learning both in the workplace as described in earlier chapters and also through more sustained professional development that addresses values, culture, roles and expertise. Championing integrated working throughout the integrated centre and within the local community is one thing but, significantly, this is a new challenge for local authority personnel themselves who may be 'line managing' integrated centres with less experience and expertise than the leaders themselves. One response to this situation, as noted by Glass (2006), where commitment to excellent provision is uncertain, is an increase in control and prescription at a time when resources are almost certain to be reduced.

7.9 A closer look at the challenges of multi-agency working

Despite real enthusiasm of the local integrated centre programme members concerned, the survey respondents suggested that effective multi-agency working had not always been easy to achieve. Multi-agency work by its very nature could disrupt existing professional and agency culture, and conflicts over areas of responsibility could arise. Establishment of common aims within and across agencies was regarded as essential but, in practice, was less straight-forward to establish, with new roles and responsibilities needing to be made explicit at all levels and effective communication developed to increase under-standing of these. Practices established to protect confidentiality were still cre-ating tensions and information-sharing strategies could still be improved. Allocation of budgets and financial organization, as well as non-financial resources, had created a major challenge to multi-agency working. That said the vast majority believed that integrated centres facilitated multi-agency working in terms of staffing arrangements, teams' expectations and priorities. Staff training was seen to have an important function in developing new ways of working. It was generally highlighted throughout that multi-agency team-working was strongly promoted and supported by integrated centre leaders.

The next step was to look more forensically at the views and interpretations of challenges as experienced by talking in greater depth to professionals at a number of levels within the organizations concerned, partnership and team members of varying levels of seniority as well as a representative of the lead agency and accountable body. Four areas were examined: knowledge of struc-tures; roles and responsibilities; data protection and information-sharing; and communication.

Knowledge of structures

Discussing the role of leading agencies in ensuring that the financial details outlined in local plans were executed, representatives of the agencies acknowl-edged a lack of capacity and hence a delay in prioritizing support for inte-grated centre work. This resulted in members of the finance team being employed on temporary contracts as well as becoming involved in areas out-side their remit, such as legal and estate management issues. Partnership board members varied in their level of understanding of the roles and functions of the leading agencies. Team members for their part identified the strategic com-mitment and financial role and were aware of the absence of permanent staff in the finance department. There was an awareness that as the leading agencies developed, more effective ways of working in partnership, 'things could be achieved more quickly and efficiently', though this was not always apparent at operational level.

Roles and responsibilities

The representatives of the leading agencies emphasized their priorities at a strategic and operational level and recognized that having two leading agencies (representing education and health) added complexity and thus challenge to multi-agency working. This could have a less than positive effect on local integrated centre programmes in terms of time taken to make decisions. Both agreed that integrated centre goals complemented those of their parent agencies. Partnership board members were more mixed in response. Some partnership board members agreed that local programme aims complemented the goals of their parent agency in meeting government targets and this impacted positively on client groups. Others emphasized that working clearly within the terms of reference facilitated local centre leaders, supporting, establishing and developing relationships between families and the local programme. Others were less certain and wondered whether services might be duplicated. Team members of the local programmes expressed a variety of views about the nature of aims of partner agencies and integrated centre work. It was highlighted that the programme offered an innovative approach. One felt that her parent agency was 'very mistrusting of any new initiative' and another declared that her parent agency had little to do with the local integrated centre programmes. Another stressed the impact of external influences such as changing priorities at government level. Yet another indicated the possible tensions between relative emphasis on prevention and intervention that could impact on the parent agency. Some felt confident in managing staff and working at the same time alongside existing programmes and engaging with 'hard to reach' families.

Staffing, resources and work-space

Challenges related to staffing were emphasized by all groups of participants. The leading agencies referred to the challenges posed to staff being employed on temporary contracts and acknowledged lack of office space as a challenge, Partnership board representatives noted the length of time taken to recruit a new programme leader when the previous incumbent had left. Others mentioned problems with recruiting health-related professionals. Yet another mentioned the challenges associated with changing professional practice and integrating professionals from diverse disciplines. With respect to space, reservations were expressed about the desirability of co-locating with another statutory agency. Team members acknowledged the challenge of managing a professionally diverse team, a sense of isolation and a lack of training. Notwithstanding this, staffing arrangements were viewed positively and, despite short-term discomfort and frustration, construction of a new building was generally viewed positively.

Data protection and information-sharing

Representatives of the leading agencies both acknowledged challenges regarding information-sharing between team members and the PCT. Some partnership board members also mentioned ongoing challenges regarding lack of information-sharing of the PCT. It was recognized that different organizations had different arrangements and it was also recognized that the issue was being addressed. Team members also described the PCT as 'taking a controlling role in respect of data protection and information-sharing'. Reluctance of agencies to share information was highlighted. Identifying and accessing client information was regarded as a major challenge by some participants. The need for shared procedures and protocols with a strategy for placing confidential information on shared computer drives was indicated.

Communication

Challenges posed at the strategic level in the authority were identified by representatives of the leading agencies and the impact of constantly changing national policies was also mentioned. It was agreed that centrally held information could be a hindrance to communication and that improved IT networks were needed. At the operational level, it was noted that team members were used to working in different ways. At the level of individual integrated centre programmes, regular meetings of the programme leader with the partnership board and team members were part of an effective communication strategy. In terms of leadership style of the programme managers, it was reported that there was a real willingness and a strong personal commitment to learn, share and 'take the lead'. Partnership board members advocated the use of multiple communication channels, acknowledging the challenge in the face of multiple locations and a sizeable team. Jargon was acknowledged by one member as a barrier to parental engagement, though others indicated that formal partnership board meetings and informal face-to-face communication were successful. Team members felt that formal methods of communications through meetings, telephone contacts, daily transfer of internal post, information chats and social events were successful but that the number of locations, underuse of IT, availability of part-time staff and different ways of working were regarded as a challenge by some.

What emerged strongly from the in-depth discussions with staff from four integrated programmes was a sense of staff from different backgrounds and skills striving towards common goals and shared values, despite barriers to effectiveness and efficiency in the form of shifting national policy. Local authority structures inevitably were too slow in response to financial arrangements and 'contracting in' of services from different professionals. A lack of space, split-site accommodation, challenges to data-storing, information access and sharing, and communication were also barriers. It should be noted at this point that the emphasis has been placed on processes underpinning proficient implementation of multi-agency services, such as partnership functioning, leadership and holistic aspects of implementation such as communications. Rather less emerged that related to what was implemented, service quality and delivery, identification of users and strategies to reach, improve and sustain services over time.

In order to obtain a stronger sense of targets set, preventative strategies employed, perceived effectiveness as well as facilitating factors and barriers from the perspective of specialist services themselves, brief case studies of agency work in the field of social work, speech and language therapy services and special education support were carried out.

7.10 Case studies

Speech and language therapy

All four integrated centre programmes had a speech and language therapist as part of their team, two working at 0.5 of a week, one at 0.7 of a week and one full-time. A detailed personal specification encompassing duties in three key areas was provided: their clinical role, their training role and their team/service role. The speech and language therapists met with their professional leader every three months as a group, and with one another more often to share ideas, new practice and to make visits to other local programmes. There was also collaboration at the strategic level with the whole mainstream speech and language therapy service. All members of the local programme speech and language therapy team worked to achieve agreed targets to increase the proportion of children having normal levels of communication, language and literacy at the end of the foundation stage (at age 5 and at the end of the reception year in school) and to increase the proportion of young children with satisfactory speech and language development at age 2. To achieve these targets, therapists worked in local nurseries providing advice for staff on communication levels of individual children and working with identified children to help them develop communication skills, both individually and in a group. They provided training for nurseries, parents and professionals, took part in local programme activities with other members of the team, carried out joint assessment sessions to ascertain children's communication skills and followed up requests for contact from other personnel such as the health visitor, nursery staff or parents, making home visits and working with individual parents. Therapists did not have a defined caseload, although some children in the local programme areas received input from mainstream and programme therapists or solely from the local programme therapist.

An initial audit was carried out of speech and language skills of 3-year-old children entering local programme nurseries in 2003 and repeated in 2006.

Moreover, annual data from Sure Start Speech and Language Measures (Harris, 2002) were collected on 60 children across projects per year. In terms of achievements, the projects were now experiencing more referrals from both service users and outside agencies such as social services, indicating an increased awareness of the importance of early speech and language communication. Identified facilitating factors were the supportive integrated centre leader and team, the opportunity to work in new and flexible ways and the availability of increased resources. Identified barriers were difficulties in recruiting suitably trained speech and language therapy assistants in the local programme areas and the lack of suitable premises in which to carry out training. In terms of effectiveness, the speech and language therapy team had been keen throughout to secure evidence for the benefits of an indirect service delivery including the collection of case study data over a three-year period as examples of early intervention, resulting in children not needing a referral to the mainstream speech and language therapy service. What stood out from the investigation was the clear articulation by therapists of an identified professional knowledge base. This comprised a range of core clinical activities and training responsibilities that distributed this knowledge base as widely as possible to other professionals such as health visitors, midwives, community nurses and parents and that took best account of early intervention in the preventative sense for the majority, as well as recognizing the need for more specialized intervention for a smaller number of children with longer-term additional needs.

Special educational needs service

In respect of a target to increase the number of children who had their special educational needs identified in line with 'early years action' and 'early years action plus' of the *Special Educational Needs Code of Practice* (DfES, 2001) and to have an individual action plan in place, the speech and language therapists had also been involved in city-wide training for parents and new special educational needs (SEN) co-ordinators. Moreover, the original steering committee of one of the local programmes had made a proposal to have a multi-disciplinary SEN team attached to the programme in order to address at a very early stage, children's special or additional needs. Accordingly, the programme leader secured the input of an educational psychologist for two days a week, a pre-school SEN teacher's input for two and a half days and a parent partnership outreach worker's input for two and a half days. While the *Code of Practice* assigned a statutory role to each of these team members in the statutory assessment of SEN, in the context of their local integrated centre programme role, the team felt that judging their work in terms of caseload might be inappropriate and thus their reported 'case' numbers were quite low. Over one exemplar year, for instance, the pre-school SEN teacher supported a small number of parents and children; the outreach worker made some home visits and provided caseload co-ordination for a few parents and a larger number of children; the educational psychologist provided consultation for a relatively small number of parents and children. They felt however, that their effectiveness should be judged in terms of 'quality not quantity'. The opportunity to work more indirectly through family, community and other professionals was relished though it was less clear how this aspect of the work was monitored and evaluated or its impact judged. The criteria in the pre-school teacher's service level agreement did however specify the amount of time to be dedicated to working directly with individual children or indirectly by contributing to the development of local integrated centre services and supporting other staff. Terms such as 'prevention' and 'intervention' did not appear to be interpreted in the same manner by all professionals and it was not always clear where work carried out with children and families referred to the traditional 'acute' client group and when, where or how access to different groups with milder difficulties and delays was secured.

In common with the speech and language therapists, the SEN team felt that working with the local multi-agency team was a facilitating factor in their work and 'everything was so much quicker while they were more approachable and accessible'. Identified barriers to SEN work by the team included differences in professional cultures, values and working practices that generated different agendas and resulted in different modes of performance management.

The perceived ethos of the local programme with its emphasis on self-referral could create potential barriers for 'hard to reach' groups, who would then become progressively harder to reach. Their professional leaders noted that in the long term the support services they represented were neither staffed nor resourced to provide an indirect service delivery at the preschool stage. In any case, as a review of Ramey and Ramey (1998) suggested, in order to be effective, early intervention needs to be direct, intensive and sustained. For her part, the local integrated centre programme leader expressed concern that the annual expenditure on the SEN team amounted to nearly 7 per cent of the annual budget, while staff absences totalling 220 days in one year had had some considerable impact of professional contact.

Social work intervention

Meanwhile, another local integrated centre programme with the high rates of child protection cases proposed to employ a social worker to develop preventative strategies. Clear targets were set for local integrated centre programmes at the time to reduce re-registration on the child protection register within the space of 12 months by 20 per cent. In fact, there was no evidence of increase or decrease in child protection rates over the period that the local integrated centre programmes had been in operation. A social work post was thus created in this local programme, specifying 0.5 of the week to develop preventative strategies in the local integrated centre programme area and 0.5 of the week in the local social services office to deal with statutory child protection work for under-5s. Within six months, this post broke down and the social worker left. The continuing and developing pressures from the statutory role were perceived by the social worker to 'take precedence' and this she felt hindered what could be achieved in the preventative role. There did seem to be grounds for participants' views that this part-time preventative post, in practice, was not satisfactory but it was also acknowledged that the professional concerned should have been more 'proactive'. The social worker herself felt that 'having a job without a well-defined role was really hard … very much like a spare part' and that she had really to be given guidance of an agreed and realistic job specification, service level agreement with appropriate supervision and, hence, accountability for work carried out. While joint supervision was reported to be taking place, it appeared that there was some mismatch in expectations with respect to preventative working practices with families between the two managers concerned, as well as perceived lines of accountability for the statutory element of the post. It was acknowledged in this case, as by participants in the other case studies, that having no caseload and the support of a multi-agency team with time and resources should have been regarded as facilitative. Barriers to preventative social work, it was reported by the social worker, included the negative image of social workers and general mistrust of them. She explained that this was a 'big barrier' as people wanted to be 'left alone to get on with their lives'. The role of local integrated centre programmes was 'more voluntary' on the family's side – about wanting services and wanting to join groups as well as wanting help. In this respect, the social worker noted that one had to intervene with a family in order for prevention to occur. This was 'not befriending but somehow more voluntary, less statutory and less punitive'.

In the longer-term, as with the SEN case study, questions were raised by the professional leader about the feasibility of resourcing social work posts that carried no caseload. 'Prevention' was defined here as the promotion of well-being of child, family and community, and thus *all* services had a role and responsibility with a focus on preventing the need for more targeted and specialist services (level 1 or universal services). It was acknowledged, however, that 'too many resources were focused on meeting those needs at level 4 (with a high risk of harm) and level 3 (medium risk requiring a complex multi-agency response), with insufficient resources being available when needs first become apparent (at level 2 or low risk). The result was that 'as though in a vortex children were drawn into expensive interventionist services too quickly'.

7.11 Leadership by the many

The views of participants and the case studies highlighted the complexity of the challenge facing multi-agency integrated centre workers. Co-locating staff from partner organizations to work together when they were still employed by that parent agency with different terms and conditions, working hours, pay scales, holiday allowances and information-sharing strategies, created particular tensions. Though staff clearly had an appetite for the new and 'hybrid' professional that was being thrown up, many of the tensions described here relate to the particular model of multi-agency working in operation. Staff from a particular agency were co-located to work together but were still employed by their own agency, hence, conforming to Øvretveit's (1996) notion of joint management (or leadership). Moreover the challenge of local authority structural constraints, on one hand, and of the shifting and developing internal organization of a children's centre team, on the other, as they 'formed and reformed' multi-agency teams in response to changing requirements both within the organization and outside in a corresponding shifting outside environment may be aptly described as 'knot-working' (Engeström et al., 1999). Within the new children's centre agenda where professionals from different services will continue to work with a hybrid management system, it can be envisaged that existing tensions will not be eradicated. The findings serve to remind us of the investment needed in terms of finance, time and staff resources in order to develop new multi-agency ways of working. It is essential in such a climate that hasty judgements are not made about the impact of local integrated centre programmes, as they seek to acquire new knowledge and skills that are neither stable nor well-defined, and professionals within them learn to work in new ways with corresponding lack of definition and stability.

This chapter has attempted to provide an account of integrated centre programmes as they have moved towards children's centre status. At the level of practice, there is much to be learned by a leader about the challenging process of setting up and establishing a new range of multi-agency services. There was general agreement among the professionals involved that the programmes encouraged and resourced more flexible ways of working, though in the case of the individual social worker this faced her with the additional challenge of defining and developing a new repertoire of skills in terms of service innovation and flexibility, identification of families and 'reach' strategies that from her point of view were insufficiently supported and guided. By contrast, the speech and language therapists, both individually and collectively, with the support of their mainstream service and professional leader were able to develop new and flexible ways of working in order to provide accessible services for other professionals, clear pathways for individual families to follow to access them and strategies for identification of children and families, and shared staff training that were monitored, assessed and fed back into the planning process. The SEN case is a reminder that a large outlay of resource (staff and money) will not compensate for a service that is less well defined overall in terms of service vision, planning, implementation and evaluation of the impact on children and families living in the area and where staff morale, if sickness rates provide any sort of indication, is not high. Moreover, the case studies suggest a relationship between the processes of direct service implementation, impact on children and families, and overall quality (albeit indirect) of leadership provided

Everything points towards the view that success is highly dependent upon the energy, imagination and expertise of individual professionals or professional groups and their leaders who, despite structural barriers and constraints of performance frameworks are able to make a difference, whatever the circumstances. This chapter leaves unexamined in any very direct way the effects on and experiences of the families and communities themselves.

Despite the real enthusiasm of the local integrated centre programme members concerned, the survey respondents suggested that effective multi-agency working had not always been easy to achieve. Multi-agency work by its very nature could disrupt existing professional and agency cultures, and conflicts over areas of responsibility could arise. Establishment of common aims within and across agencies was regarded as essential but, in practice, was not always easy to achieve, with new roles and responsibilities needing to be made explicit at all levels and effective communication developed to increase understanding of these. Practices established to protect confidentiality were still creating tensions and information-sharing strategies could still be improved. Allocation of budgets and financial organization, as well as non-financial resources, had created a major challenge to local multi-agency working. That said, the vast majority believed that their local integrated centre programme facilitated multi-agency working in terms of staffing arrangements, teams' expectations and priorities. Staff training was seen to have an important function in developing new ways of working.

It was generally highlighted throughout that multi-agency team working was strongly promoted and supported by local programme leaders. Despite this, what emerged most strongly from the interviews was the impact on the work of integrated centre leaders of line management by the leading agencies who had overall control of financial arrangements and 'contracting-in' of the services of different professionals. Given that control and funding for children's centres is now being handed over gradually to local authorities, these findings underline the growing importance of effectiveness and cost-effectiveness. In fact, staff with different backgrounds and skills strove towards common goals and shared values despite barriers to effectiveness and efficiency, in the form of constantly shifting social, cultural and educational policies, local authority structures, lack of space and split-site challenges to data storing, information-sharing and communication.

This chapter attests to the power of leadership in context by 'the many'. The presence of the local integrated centre leaders is unmistakable but there is a strong sense of the 'many professionals' taking responsibility for creating and sharing knowledge and an unchallenged assumption that it is their task to remove the barriers that hinder this process. It is a reminder that it is the cultivation of leaders at many levels in the local programmes that together must collectively shape the future of their organization in a time of change.

▶ Models of effective multi-agency working are still to be identified, although facilitating factors have been identified.

Practitioner's views 7.1

The strategic leader of our leaders was keen to review the effectiveness of multi-agency working and, in particular, the influence of different models of such working in improving outcomes for children and families. While the evidence on effective multi-agency practice is scant, we can be more certain about facilitating factors and barriers, where consistent findings emerge.
Facilitators include:

- *clear aims;*
- *roles and responsibilities and timetables that are agreed between partners;*
- *a multi-agency steering group;*
- *commitment at all levels of the organizations involved;*
- *good systems of communication and information sharing, including IT systems; and*
- *support and training for staff in new ways of working (there is some evidence that interprofessional programmes of continuing education can remove barriers to joint working).*

We now need to find out more about:

- *the relationship of different models of multi-agency working in services for children to outcomes;*
- *the relationship of facilitating factors to outcomes; and*
- *assessment of cost-effectiveness.*

This chapter is taken from:
Aubrey, C. (2007) *Leading and Managing in the Early Years*
978-1-4129-3497-8

10% off discount vouchers for SAGE Early Years Books

10% off voucher
Exclusive to John Smith's bookshop

Developing Learning in Early Childhood

Tina Bruce
978-0-7619-4176-7 • £21.99

 campus John Smith's Bookshop, University of East London, Stratford Campus, University House, Stratford E15 4LZ

10% off voucher
Exclusive to John Smith's bookshop

Food and Health in Early Childhood

Deborah Albon and Penny Mukherji
978-1-4129-4722-0 • £17.99

campus John Smith's Bookshop, University of East London, Stratford Campus, University House, Stratford E15 4LZ

10% off voucher
Exclusive to John Smith's bookshop

Early Childhood

Tina Bruce
978-1-4129-2076-6 • £20.99

campus John Smith's Bookshop, University of East London, Stratford Campus, University House, Stratford E15 4LZ

10% off voucher
Exclusive to John Smith's bookshop

Leading and Managing in the Early Years

Carol Aubrey
978-1-4129-3497-8 • £23.99

campus John Smith's Bookshop, University of East London, Stratford Campus, University House, Stratford E15 4LZ

10% off voucher
Exclusive to John Smith's bookshop

Professional Development, Reflection and Enquiry

Christine Forde, Margery McMahon, Alastair D. McPhee and Fiona Patrick
978-1-4129-1937-1 • £21.99

campus John Smith's Bookshop, University of East London, Stratford Campus, University House, Stratford E15 4LZ

10% off voucher
Exclusive to John Smith's bookshop

Understanding Early Years Policy, Second Edition

Peter Baldock, Damien Fitzgerald and Janet Kay 978-1-84787-447-4 • £21.99

campus John Smith's Bookshop, University of East London, Stratford Campus, University House, Stratford E15 4LZ

10% off voucher
Exclusive to John Smith's bookshop

Researching Children's Experiences

Sheila Greene and Diane Hogan
978-0-7619-7103-0 • £22.99

campus John Smith's Bookshop, University of East London, Stratford Campus, University House, Stratford E15 4LZ

10% off voucher
Exclusive to John Smith's bookshop

Child Protection, Second Edition

Chris Beckett
978-1-4129-2092-6 • £20.99

campus John Smith's Bookshop, University of East London, Stratford Campus, University House, Stratford E15 4LZ

10% off voucher
Exclusive to John Smith's bookshop

An Introduction to Child Development, Second Edition

Thomas Keenan and Subhadra Evans
978-1-4129-1115-3 • £22.99

campus John Smith's Bookshop, University of East London, Stratford Campus, University House, Stratford E15 4LZ

10% off voucher
Exclusive to John Smith's bookshop

Reflective Practice, Second Edition

Gillie Bolton
978-1-4129-0812-2 • £21.99

campus John Smith's Bookshop, University of East London, Stratford Campus, University House, Stratford E15 4LZ

10% off voucher
Exclusive to John Smith's bookshop

Health Promotion Practice

Glenn Laverack
978-0-7619-4180-4 • £22.99

campus John Smith's Bookshop, University of East London, Stratford Campus, University House, Stratford E15 4LZ